LIUWE H. WESTRA

# THE APOSTLES' CREED

## ORIGIN, HISTORY, AND SOME EARLY COMMENTARIES

BREPOLS

2002

# INSTRVMENTA PATRISTICA ET MEDIAEVALIA

## Research on the Inheritance of Early and Medieval Christianity

Founded by Dom Eligius Dekkers († 1998)

© 2002 BREPOLS ✹ PUBLISHERS (Turnhout – Belgium)
Printed in Belgium
D/2002/0095/78
ISBN 2-503-51395-6

# THE APOSTLES' CREED

# INSTRVMENTA PATRISTICA ET MEDIAEVALIA

Research on the Inheritance of Early and Medieval Christianity

43

THEODORO KORTEWEG
MAGISTRO

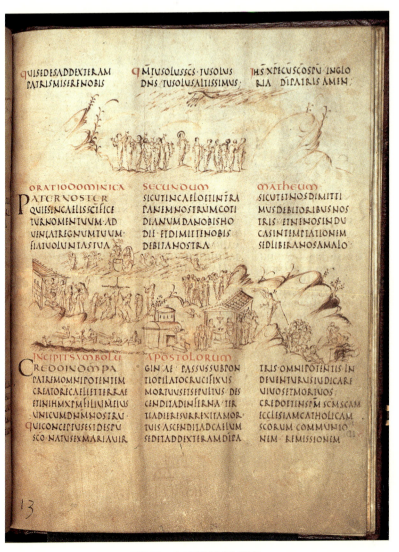

QUISEDESADDEXTERAM        QMIUSOLUSSCS TUSOLUS        IHS XPECUSCOSPU INGLO
PATRISMISERENOBIS         DNS TUSOLUALTISSIMUS         RIA DIPATRIS AMEN

ORATIODOMINICA            SECUNDUM                    MATHEUM
PATERNOSTER               SICUTINCAELOETINTRA         SICUTETNOSDIMITTI
QUIESINCAELISSCIFICE      PANEMNOSTRUMCOTI            MUSDEBITORIBUSNOS
TURNOMENTUUM AD           DIANUMDANOBISHO             TRIS ETNENOSINDU
UENIATREGNUMTUUM          DIE ETDIMITTENOBIS          CASINTEMPTATIONEM
FIAIUOLUNTASTUA           DEBITANOSTRA                SEDLIBERANOSAMALO

INCIPITSUMBOLU            APOSTOLORUM                 TRIS OMNIPOTENTIS IN
CREDOINDMPA               GIN AE PASSUSSUBPON         DEUENTURUSIUDICARE
PATREMOMNIPOTENTEM        TIOPILATOCRUCIFIXUS         UIUOSETMORTUOS
CREATORICAELIETTERRAE     MORTUUSETSEPULTUS DES       CREDOETINSPM SCMSCAM
ETINIHMXPMFILIUMEIUS      CENDITADINFERNA TER         ECCLESIAMCATHOLICAM
UNICUMDNMNOSTRU           TIADIERESURREXITAMOR        SCORUM COMMUNIO
QUICONCEPTUSESTDESPU      TUIS ASCENDITADCAELUM       NEM REMISSIONEM
SCO NATUSEXMARIAUIR       SEDETADDEXTERAMDIPA

13

UB Utrecht MS. 32 fol. 90 R

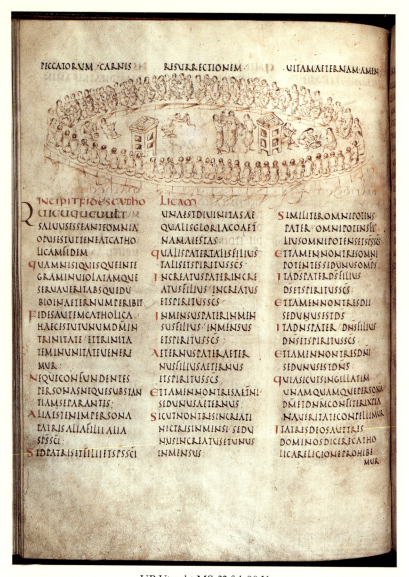

INCIPIT FIDES CATHO LICAM

Quicuquevult · saluus esse ante omnia opus est ut teneat catho licam fidem ·

Quam nisi quisque inte gram inuiolatam que seruauerit absque du bio in aeternum peribit ·

Fides autem catholica · haec est ut unum dm in trinitate · et trinita tem in unitate ueneri mur ·

Neque confundentes personas neque substan tiam separantes ·

Alia est enim persona patris alia filii alia sps sci ·

Sed patris et filii et sps sci

una est diuinitas ae qualis gloria coaeter na maiestas ·

Qualis pater talis et filius talis et spiritus scs ·

Increatus pater increa tus filius · increatus et spiritus scs ·

Inmensus pater in men sus filius · inmensus et spiritus scs ·

Aeternus pater aeter nus filius aeternus et spiritus scs ·

Et tamen non tres aeterni sed unus aeternus ·

Sicut non tres increati nec tres inmensi · sed unus inmensus et unus inmensus ·

Similiter omnipotens pater · omnipotens fi lius omnipotens et spssc̄s ·

Et tamen non tres omni potentes sed unus omps ·

Ita ds pater ds filius ds et spiritus scs ·

Et tamen non tres dii sed unus est ds ·

Ita dns pater · dns filius dns et spiritus scs ·

Et tamen non tres dni sed unus est idns ·

Quia sicut singillatim unam quamque persona dm et dnm confiteri xpiana ueritate conpellimur ·

Ita tres deos aut tres dominos dicere catho lica religione prohibe mur ·

UB Utrecht MS. 32 fol. 90 V

# PREFACE

When entering upon the project of which the present book is the outcome, I could not imagine what lay ahead of me. My original commission was to write a commentary on a number of anonymous credal texts. This commentary was intended to be a companion volume to a more encompassing text edition, to be prepared for the *Corpus Christianorum* series by Martien Parmentier. My task would be to assess the date and place of origin of those texts that were connected with the Apostles' Creed. Within this project, the several formulations of the Apostles' Creed were expected to become the main tools for such an assessment.

Soon, however, as seems to be the fate of all such well-defined four-year study programmes, it turned out that things were not so straightforward. In fact, the present book has been written completely back to front. First, I had to prepare the appendix of text editions because, as will be argued more than once, a sound critical edition is a primary prerequisite for reconstructing a form of the Creed from any given text.

Next, I reconstructed as precise a form of the Apostles' Creed as possible from these newly established texts, and tried to connect such a reconstruction with what was known of the history of that Creed in chapter 4. Here, I encountered the next difficulty, viz. that most if not all students of the Apostles' Creed had assumed some sort of a regional development of that venerable formula, but none of them had taken the trouble to describe this process in sufficient detail. Thus, I was forced to study not only my own small number of anonymous witnesses but basically any source text for the form of the Apostles' Creed from earliest times down to around 800, which resulted in the writing of chapter 3. My findings about the way that a fixed liturgical text such as the Apostles' Creed could change over the course of the centuries were collected separately in chapter 2.

Naturally, one cannot write about the development of a text without paying attention to its origin, so adding chapter 1 proved necessary in the end as well. Here, I experienced the curious sensation of having to rethink all my premises at the last moment because of the publication of a new and rather revolutionary account of the birth of the Apostles' Creed. It is up to the reader to decide to what degree this rethinking has been successful.

Arriving at the preface at last, I feel pleasurably obliged to thank many people. The first of these are my parents, *heit en mem*, who enabled me to study in my own way and according to my own wishes. Next, but by no means second to them, I want to thank my wife Baukje for her constant encouragement during a project which constantly turned out to be taking more time than the latest estimate. Our two children are happily unaware of what it has meant to have someone writing a dissertation in the vicarage. The same does not hold true for the members of my congregations in Lollum, Waaksens, Burchwert, Hartwert, and Hichtum. They always stimulated me to finish the work and were very encouraging when the moment of its completion drew nigh. In addition, the directors and staff members of *Bouwbedrijf Burggraaff* always courteously allowed me to use their fax when quick contact with the outside world was of the essence.

Although aware of the risk that readers might connect any flaws in this book with them instead of with the author, I feel nevertheless obliged to express my indebtedness to thòse who added considerably to the possible merits of this book. Of those who taught me during my studies, I would like to mention three by name. Prof. H. Roldanus introduced me to the world of church history and patristics. Prof. S. Radt allowed me to benefit from his ever thoughtful criticism even after I finished my classical studies, and will always remain an inspiring example of philological devotion to me. Prof. H. Hofmann curtly wrote "no creeds in a thesis" in the margin of the first draft of my 1990 thesis on Ovid, in which I had cautiously expressed myself as 'believing' a certain opinion to be preferable to another. I am glad that he was nevertheless willing to take a seat in the *leescommissie* all the same.

I wish to thank both the Katholieke Theologische Universiteit Amsterdam (*piae memoriae*) and the Katholieke Theologische Universiteit te Utrecht for the generous way they allowed me to conduct my studies during the years 1992-1995. Martien, later Profesor, Parmentier proved an ideal supervisor, allowing me true academic freedom without losing sight of the long-distance goal. Moreover, much of my work would have been impossible without his thorough investigations and preparations. Prof. Gerard Rouwhorst turned out to be the *promotor* in the original sense of the word who was needed to round off the project. Several scholarly conferences gave me the opportunity to present my work, for which I also wish to express my gratitude here.

Next, the various staff members of the University Libraries in Utrecht, Groningen, and Ljouwert (Leeuwarden) deserve mention. The combination of expertise, helpfulness, and ready service of the latter two should, alas, be standard in more places. Abroad, many libraries answered my questions or received me in the kindest of ways. Sometimes, I succesfully requested the intervention of a person *in situ*, for which I would like to thank Bianca van der Aa, Hanneke de Vries, Gianni Nazzi, Prof. G. Bartelink, and my compatriot Wytse Keulen. Alco Meesters and Wytse Keulen also willingly provided me with data or photocopies from the Groningen University Library in the final stages of the work. The latter, now I come to think of it, drew my attention to the present project by leaving an advertisement on our doormat, so those who appreciate the result should honour him as the man with whom it all began.

Alco Meesters, Wytse Keulen, and Hans van Rijsen kindly read earlier drafts of this book and offered useful comments. Père Leroy let me use the unpublished work of his deceased assistant M. Ntshiniti on two pseudo-Chrysostomic sermons, and Profs. Kinzig and Vinzent most kindly sent me copies of their work on the Creed. I owe an interesting reference to Hilary of Poitiers entirely to Prof. D.H. Williams. Mark and Elena Stuijt-Cavagnaro and Jantsje Sikma patiently turned my drafts into intelligible Italian and French letters respectively. My friend Rommert Tjeerdsma was helpful in coping with some problems of a bibliographical nature. Julia Harvey was a patient and capable corrector of English for a stubborn Frisian. Of course, all those who have ever met me in the flesh know that my English is in reality much worser.

In the last months, much has been asked of Roland Demeulenaere and the other staff members of *Corpus Christianorum* as well as the printers of *Cultura* and *Universitas*. I hope that they are as satisfied with the results of their efforts as I am.

Finally, I regard it in the same light as paying a long-standing debt to dedicate this book to my teacher and now colleague Theo Korteweg. Under the pretext of teaching me some Hebrew in his free hours (*sic*), he exposed me to the world of learning and Humanism and conveyed to me the difference between having an opinion and thinking for oneself.

# INTRODUCTION

I believe that no other single text, with the exception of the Bible, has provoked so much Christian literature as the Apostles' Creed. This is rather striking because the Apostles' Creed does not figure in the Eastern churches, and many Roman Catholic Christians only come across it in the context of baptism. In both of these traditions, the only Creed to be used in the weekly services is the Creed of Nicea-Constantinople, the *Credo* that has been put to music by innumerable composers almost since the beginning of liturgical song. The Apostles' Creed, on the other hand, has only a few musical settings. As far as compositions in prose are concerned, however, the stream of popular theological works on the Apostles' Creed shows no signs of drying up, whereas the Nicaeno-Constantinopolitan and so-called Athanasian Creeds apparently have to content themselves with an occasional scientific work. This stream not only springs from authors within the realm of the Protestant, Anglican, and Evangelical churches, some of which require a weekly or even daily recital of the Apostles' Creed, but also from Roman Catholic theologians, who clearly keep the remembrance alive that the Apostles' Creed is one of the 'three great Western Creeds'[1].

As is only to be expected, all of these writings differ widely in their interpretation of the Apostles' Creed. Nobody will be surprised to hear that a Roman Catholic author has other things to say about the words of the tenth article *Sanctam ecclesiam catholicam* than a Protestant one. But differences go deeper than just the interpretation of one or a number of articles. One also meets considerably, sometimes even fantastically divergent accounts concerning the meaning or intention of the complete text. Thus, the Apostles' Creed is credited by one author with being a distinctly anti-Gnostic text, whereas another derives its contents directly from the religion of the ancient Egyptians. The articles of the Creed may be linked with scriptural quotations or with problems of modern life. They

---

[1] The use of the name 'ecumenical Creeds', which one may also encounter, should be discouraged for the double reason that the Apostles' Creed has never been used in the Eastern Church (although comparable texts have) and, more importantly, that the so-called Athanasian Creed is a purely Latin text with no Greek or Eastern counterpart.

may be described as meant to incite the faithful to contemplation, to good works, or to writing their own creed.

Nevertheless, all these widely differing interpretations of the Apostles' Creed have many things in common as well. First of all, they almost invariably assume that the Apostles' Creed has one single all-important purpose - whatever that purpose may be. In combination with this, they tend to connect all the articles of the Apostles' Creed, sometimes down to minute details of formulation, with that same unifying purpose, which thus takes on the features of an underlying programme. Again, this same purpose is connected with the origin of the Apostles' Creed, at which point most authors make one or two references to historical studies. In contrast to this avowed importance of the history of the origin of the Apostles' Creed for its interpretation, however, the majority of modern publications tend to treat the results of scholarship on this point in a rather cursory way. With a few exceptions, not only do they leave it to their readers to consult the relevant secondary literature, but the conclusions that they do acknowledge are usually sadly behind the times or even blatantly wrong.

In the present book, I do not intend to replace or even to invalidate any of the current interpretations of the Apostles' Creed in popular theological literature. What is more, I intend to say hardly anything about its contents or its meaning, let alone its message. As anyone who is familiar with modern literature on the Apostles' Creed knows, this message, in any interpretation, can without too much difficulty be retraced to the New Testament. What I do intend to do is to study anew the origin and earliest history of the Apostles' Creed as a Christian formula, a combination, that is, not of thoughts but of words. It is my purpose here to join the scholarly discussion concerning the questions of where and when this formula originated and how it developed, and perhaps to bring it one or two steps further. In other words, I leave it to the readers to interpret the Apostles' Creed for themselves, and to do this in the way they think best. But if anyone consults this book wanting to learn more about what we can and cannot know about the oldest environment both of the complete Creed and of its constituent articles, I hope that he or she will not lay it aside disappointed.

In my study of this historical Christian formula, following basic logic, I start with an investigation of the origin of the Apostles'

Creed. Thus, the first chapter is devoted to two main questions. The first is when and where should we postulate the first use of the Apostles' Creed. The second, perhaps surprisingly, is how was it exactly formulated. Both were hotly debated topics in the first half of the twentieth century, and the results of this debate were brilliantly summarized in 1950 by Kelly's *Early Christian Creeds*. Later contributions to the discussion, however, received markedly less attention, and the need for an up-to-date summary has made itself increasingly felt since the nineteen-seventies. In the process of trying to write such a summary, I was forced to think anew about the basic assumptions of credal research by the appearance of, to all intents and purposes, a completely novel theory on the birth of the Apostles' Creed that was launched by the joint efforts of the German scholars Kinzig and Vinzent. The resulting argument has become rather more tortuous than was originally intended, so that, for the benefit of readers who are not thoroughly acquainted with twentieth-century scholarship on this point, I felt forced to the perhaps somewhat unusual device of prefixing some pages of preliminary notes to the first chapter. Nevertheless, the chief purpose of this chapter remains answering two basic questions, viz. when and where the Apostles' Creed was born and what was its original formulation. An answer to the second question can, of course, only be gained by means of reconstruction.

It has already been hinted that the question of the original wording of the Apostles' Creed may appear a startling one to anyone who is accustomed to its use in modern times as a single, well-defined formula that is not subject to change or innovation. Such, however, was not the situation in the first four or five centuries of its history. From the very first, no two witnesses to its existence yield an identical version of the text of the Apostles' Creed. Nevertheless, these formulae are sufficiently similar that it is safe to infer that they all testify to what is essentially one and the same text, viz. the Apostles' Creed, and some patristic authors even expressly say so. Thus, the conclusion is inevitable that the wording of the Apostles' Creed could change and did change over the course of time. Therefore, in the second chapter of my study I try to detect the factors that made it possible for fresh formulations or even complete additions to enter the Creed. After all, the belief that the wording of a creed should remain stable is only natural and will be seen to be almost as old as the Apostles' Creed itself. Nevertheless, changes occurred, as the sources leave us no room to doubt, and the question therefore is how they could. To answer this question, I have endeavoured to find statements in the source texts themselves on the subject of credal change. In addition, I have tried to reconstruct the process of some of the concrete changes in the wording of the Creed, again to the extent that the sources allow of such a reconstruction. Despite the sparse data, it appears possible to formulate at least some possible factors that can be expected to have played a role in the process of credal change, and to assess the way in which this change was in all probability received.

Given the process of change in the form of the Apostles' Creed, its students have tried to detect some hidden system in the resulting variations. For more than a century, the existence of such a system has indeed been claimed by the theory of the so-called regional types. According to this theory, the Apostles' Creed knew distinct developments in the main regions of the Western Church. Some authors venture the reconstruction of one or more of these regional types, but practically all agree that two, say, Spanish variants of the Apostles' Creed should resemble each other more than a variant from, say, Gaul, Italy, or Northern Africa. As a matter of fact, what is found in chapter 2 of the present study of the causes as well as the process of change in the Apostles' Creed does indeed support this theory. Nevertheless, a fresh investigation of the theory of credal types seemed to be justified for a number of reasons. Thus, the third chapter of my study is entirely devoted to this investigation. To that purpose, I have endeavoured to collect all hitherto known quotations of the Apostles' Creed (as well as a few new ones) from the period between the origin of the Creed and the rise of a common standard, which can be dated to about 800. The idea of such a collection is not new, but earlier works of this kind are either based on editions of the source texts that have been replaced by better ones since or suffer from an insufficiently critical use of them. Thus, each alleged witness to the Apostles' Creed has been studied anew, a study that either resulted in putting a text aside or in a further analysis. As a result, I present 38 complete or fragmentary formulations of the Creed, all of which can with a fair amount of certainty be dated and located. Next, I endeavour to reconstruct how all these different formulations could originate.

This reconstruction is done separately for each region, resulting in six different regional histories of the Apostles' Creed. Finally, I turn to the question of whether these regional histories yield certain features which all variants of the Creed in a given region should have in common. It turns out that such features do indeed exist for each region, but that not all of the different features of the Creed can be connected to a single region. Thus, I am able to close the third chapter with the reconstruction of five different regional types, a reconstruction that has not been attempted on this scale before.

The important place that the Apostles' Creed has held both in the early and the medieval Western Church has resulted in a considerable number of more or less popular sermons or treatises on the Creed - a situation, actually, not too unlike the modern one. Some of these texts could be studied in the context of chapter 3, but a good number of them are either anonymous or pseudonymous and consequently of completely unknown origin. Since the moment of birth of the theory of regional credal types, the possibility that an anonymous text could be connected with a certain region on the basis of its particular quotations from the Apostles' Creed has been envisaged, but a systematic investigation along these lines had, as far as I could ascertain, never been tried. Such an investigation is therefore ventured upon in chapter 4 of my study. Again, I have tried to assemble as many texts referring to the Apostles' Creed and roughly earlier than 800 as possible, but this time all of more or less unknown origin. Here, completeness was much more difficult to achieve than in chapter 3. Not only is there the suspicion that many texts remain hidden and unedited in some of the great European manuscript libraries (at least one such hitherto unknown text is presented in this book), but the increasing stereotypy of credal interpretation towards the end of the period under investigation (again, a modern parallel suggests itself) is also a complicating factor. Because of the latter, it is often difficult to decide whether two similar *expositiones symboli* should be considered as variants of one and the same text or as distinct sermons that make use of highly traditional material, and I am well aware that a number of my decisions in this respect may be questioned. As a matter of principle, all anonymous sermons on the Apostles' Creed that have received a separate entry in either the *Clauis Patrum Latinorum* by *Corpus Christianorum* or the *Kirchenschriftsteller* by the Beuron

*Vetus Latina* team, the two authoritative reference works on early Christian Latin literature of our time, have been included. All texts that are included in chapter 4 are fully analyzed as to their credal quotations, and in each case as detailed a reconstruction as possible of their underlying form of the Creed is offered. As was to be expected, these 'new' variants of the Apostles' Creed only add to the variety that already emerged in the course of chapter 3. Nevertheless, practically all variants of the Apostles' Creed that are found in chapter 4 can without difficulty be connected with the regional types from chapter 3. In a few cases, the 'new' variants have forced me to make a small adaptation in the reconstruction of these types, and one source resists being assigned a place and date of origin on this basis.

All in all, in this study I hope to offer an up-to-date and complete discussion of the currently available sources for the form of the Apostles' Creed in the period during which it had not yet attained a fixed formulation. Moreover, I endeavour to reconstruct how this formulation developed over this period, a span of 400 or 500 years. This reconstruction is by its very nature fragmentary, as only a fraction of the relevant Christian literature on the Creed has come down to us. In all probability, every single bishop of the Latin Church in this period held at least two sermons on the Apostles' Creed a year. The total number of different variants of the Creed that have ever been in use should therefore be considered for ever beyond our reach. Nevertheless, it has proved possible to write a history of the Apostles' Creed that comprises its origin, its first manifestation, the factors that caused it to change, as well as its extant variants, linked up as much as possible with concrete times and places. Anyone who objects that such a history is incomplete without an account of the theology of the Creed over the same period is undoubtedly right in a general way. But before embarking upon a project to fulfill this demand, such a person should first take a look at the work of Ferdinand Kattenbusch. His volume on the form of the Apostles' Creed, in many respects an important precursor of the present work, consists of some 400 pages. For the volume on the meaning of the Creed, he needed more than a thousand.

This study closes with a number of, I hope, useful appendixes and indexes. In the first of these, all texts that are discussed in the fourth chapter can be found. Two of these are copied from an existing edition, but most are presented in a new and critical one. These texts are intended for inclusion in one of the future volumes of *Corpus Christianorum*, but it seemed pointless to publish a number of detailed studies on texts that would be available to no one else for a number of years to come. Next, all the variants of the Apostles' Creed that play a role in this book are enumerated again in the second appendix. Thirdly, the reader is able to see at a glance which texts that figure in the totally outdated but still oft-consulted *Bibliothek der Symbole* by Hahn are discussed in my study, and where. The usual indexes (*locorum, auctorum, rerum*) conclude the work.

Finally, a number of remarks on terminology and spelling seem to be in order. First of all, I use 'Apostles' Creed' as an umbrella term for any of its historical manifestations, which are indicated with phrases like 'form of the Creed', 'variant of the Creed', or occasionally 'credal variant'. Two such variants have been assigned specific names by earlier scholarship: the so-called *textus receptus* and the so-called Old Roman Creed. I have retained these two names, but not taken over other ones that may occasionally be found in secondary literature, such as 'Old African Creed' or *uetus Gallicanum*. The term 'Creed' (capitalized) will only be used, as it is in this introduction, as a synonym for 'Apostles' Creed'. All other creeds are designated by the term 'creed' (not capitalized), with the exception of the combinations 'Nicene (Nicaeno-Constantinopolitan) Creed' or 'Creed of Nicea (Nicea-Constantinople)', and 'Athanasian Creed'.

Further, the Creed is divided into twelve articles. This is more or less common practice, though German scholars sometimes divide it into three. It should be observed, however, that the traditional division into twelve articles antedates the more elaborate variants of the Creed, one of which was to become the standard text that is still used today. As a result of this, many authors from the fifth and sixth centuries onwards have felt some difficulty in assessing which exactly are the twelve articles of the Creed. For the sake of clarity, I have adopted the device of treating the three major additions of the Descent to Hell, the Communion of Saints, and Eternal Life as separate articles, and giving them, where necessary, the numbers 4a, 10a, and 12a. Thus, the following division will be used:

article contents

All quotations from the Apostles' Creed will start with a capital letter, regardless of whether it is a cluster of articles, an article, or just a single word. Capitals will also be used, as they are in the list above, to indicate the contents of the several articles. Within credal quotations, the only punctuation marks used are commas. They are placed either between two articles (including the three major additions mentioned above) in longer quotations or within an article in shorter ones. Thus, I quote *Passus, crucifixus, mortuus et sepultus* but *Passus crucifixus mortuus et sepultus, descendit ad infernum*. Commas are only used within an article where no alternative position is possible, otherwise they are omitted. Thus, I quote *Et in Iesum Christum, filium eius unicum dominum nostrum*, as *Vnicum* can be taken not only to belong to *Filium* but also to *Dominum*.

Unless indicated otherwise, in all Latin quotations I follow the text (but not always the punctuation) of the latest critical edition, where necessary adapted to the spelling of the *Oxford Latin Dictionary* as well as standard Latin grammar. A similar procedure has been adopted in the case of quotations from the Creed. This implies that *Credo in* will always be constructed with an accusative, even if an edition has, for example, *Credo in deo patre*. I am well aware that a phrase like *Credo in deo patre* occurs time and again in manuscripts but, in my opinion, it should rather be explained as

a writing variant for *Credo in deum patrem*, caused by the circumstance that the distinction between the accusative and ablative
cases became obliterated in colloquial speech, than as a distinct variant in the wording of the first article. Similarly, the form *Sedit* in
the sixth article will be treated as a deviate spelling of *Sedet*, not as
a perfect in opposition to the more usual present. Again, we know
that both grammatical forms tended to be pronounced in the same
way, so that an author wanting to express that the Creed states
that Christ 'sat down' instead of 'is sitting' at the Right Hand of
the Father would have adopted any device rather than writing
*Sedit*, which would probably not have been perceived as being different from *Sedet* in the period under discussion.

## PRELIMINARY NOTE TO CHAPTER ONE

Initially, the first chapter of this book was conceived as a history of the study of the origin of the Apostles' Creed. When I embarked upon writing it, scholarship was more or less unanimous that the Creed had originated as a third or fourth-century Roman liturgical text. As the main subject of my study was to be the history of the form of the Creed in subsequent centuries, it did not seem necessary to investigate all the sources which had been adduced for assessing the time, place, and circumstances of its origin anew. Nor did it seem fruitful to undertake an evaluation of the available studies of that problem. Instead, my first chapter was intended to be a short introduction to the question of the origin of the Creed, summarizing the main conclusions of scholarship, exercising mild criticism on certain details, and contributing an occasional original thought of my own.

Alas, it was not to be. This scholarly idyll was disturbed by the irruption onto the scene of the Germans Vinzent and Kinzig, who challenged the very first results of credal studies in 1995, the one in his Heidelberg *Habilitationsschrift*, the other in a well-attended lecture for the Patristic Conference at Oxford. Thus, their respective studies offer a completely alternative theory on the origin of the Creed, which does not develop the existing scholarly tradition but rather stands alongside it. Since the origin of any text constitutes the logical starting point of its further history, and Kinzig and Vinzent considerably shifted the origin of the Creed both in place and in time, I could not avoid a critical study of their thoughts.

Nevertheless, a systematic investigation of all the problems that are connected with the birth of the Apostles' Creed still remained well outside the scope of this book. Thus, the first chapter has received a rather mixed character. On the one hand, it still constitutes a chronological account of credal scholarship, at the same time, however, it contains my discussion and, as I endeavour to show, refutation of the ideas of Kinzig and Vinzent.

For that reason, it seems useful to present a summary of the argument of the first chapter. This summary is intended to state beforehand which questions are discussed there and which are not. Moreover, it will bring out more clearly the overall structure of the chapter, which is at times rather obscured by the switches between historical account and polemical argument. Thus, I hope it will serve those who propose, for whatever reason, to work through the complete chapter as well as students who only want to consult it for some specific point.

In chapter 1.1, then, I present the current Latin form of the Apostles' Creed (or *textus receptus*). Kelly's argument that this form should be dated to the seventh century is accepted but not separately investigated. One of the main questions of this book is posed - where do the numerous different forms of the Creed come from, and how should their variety be explained?

In chapter 1.2, the first answer to this question in the history of scholarship is described - the several existing variants all go back to a so-called Old Roman Creed, which is testified to by a number of manuscripts as well as Marcellus of Ancyra (Usher and Vossius, seventeenth century).

In chapter 1.3, I summarize the results of nineteenth-century scholarship - the theory of an Old Roman Creed is generally accepted, its wording is reconstructed, and it receives the designation $R$ (Caspari and Kattenbusch). Questions that remain are what is the relationship between $R$ and more or less similar creeds in the East, and what is the ultimate origin of $R$.

In chapter 1.4, I recapitulate the arguments for the existence of $R$; three isolated manuscripts as well as Marcellus of Ancyra testify to its wording, Rufinus of Aquileia informs us that this wording (or a closely resembling one) was in fourth-century Roman use. The question remains why $R$ was included in Marcellus of Ancyra's *epistula ad Iulium papam*.

In chapter 1.5, I present Vinzent's opinion on this last question. According to him, $R$ as it occurs in Marcellus's letter forms an integral part of the text, so that Marcellus should be considered its author. Thus, $R$ should be reckoned among the many Eastern (doctrinal) creeds of the period, that all have a place in a (doctrinal) debate. The acceptance of $R$ in Rome should, according to Vinzent's argument, be explained as due to the success of Marcellus's formulation.

In chapter 1.6, I develop two arguments against Vinzent's explanation. First, the fact that $R$ fits in well with Marcellus's theological position does not automatically imply that it could not have been taken over from Rome. As a matter of fact, Vinzent does not spare any effort to show that Marcellus continually uses and reformulates older credal texts. Secondly, an impressive number of sources suggest that *R* was in Roman use well before 340, the date of Marcellus's letter. There is a third argument against Vinzent, but to apply this, it is necessary to anticipate my chronological account of credal scholarship.

In chapter 1.7, I therefore present one of the results of twentieth-century scholarship, viz. the distinction between creeds and *regulae fidei*. This distinction, which has become generally accepted since the work of Kelly, entails that creeds originally are summaries of faith with a fixed wording which belong to a liturgical context, whereas *regulae fidei* were formulated according to the needs of the moment in a doctrinal or a polemical context. From the fourth century onwards, *regulae fidei* are supplanted by doctrinal creeds (like those of Nicea), combining a fixed wording with a polemical scope.

In chapter 1.8, then, I develop my third argument against Vinzent. First, I contend that Vinzent blurs the distinction between liturgical creeds and *regulae fidei* (or between liturgical creeds and doctrinal ones, which amounts to the same thing). Next, I argue that precisely the fact that Marcellus is writing a doctrinal creed makes it improbable that part of it would be taken over for liturgical use (whereas conversely, nothing prohibits the use of liturgical text in a doctrinal creed). Thus, I consider Vinzent's attempt to present an alternative account of the origin of *R* as a failure.

In chapter 1.9, therefore, I return to my history of credal scholarship to present three major twentieth-century contributions. Firstly, it was discovered that *R* probably originated as the result of a fusion between two older formulae, viz. a Trinitarian and a Christological one (Holl). Secondly, it was established that *R* is a Western text, and that it must have originated independently of its Eastern counterparts (Lietzmann). Thirdly, a text was discovered that bears a close resemblance with *R*, viz. the baptismal questions of the allegedly Hippolytan '*traditio apostolica*' (Schwartz and Connolly). The first two of these discoveries have found almost general acceptance. The third, however, needs a systematic discussion again.

In chapter 1.10, I present Kinzig's account of the birth of *R*. According to him, *R* originated as a new, declaratory, creed that was formulated by elaborating the baptismal questions of the *Sacramentarium Gelasianum Vetus*.

In chapter 1.11, I argue that Kinzig's theory rests upon the assumption that baptismal questions as well as liturgical creeds as summaries of faith should be as precise and complete as possible. Both the sources and the nature of these formulae, however, testify to the opposite so that Kinzig's theory loses its main buttress. On the other hand, Holl's theory is supported by the fact that the Christological part of the Creed occurs separately as early as the second century. Therefore, I dismiss Kinzig's account of the birth of *R* as well.

In chapter 1.12, I discuss the importance of Schwartz's and Connolly's discovery for the origin of the Creed. The reconstruction of an Hippolytan *traditio apostolica*, which has been attempted several times in the twentieth century, should be considered impossible by now. Nevertheless, one of the alleged source texts, the so-called *collectio Veronensis*, still contains a set of Latin baptismal questions which probably stems from fourth or fifth-century Italy, perhaps even from Rome. It seems certain, therefore, that there is a connection between these questions (stamped *H* by Kelly) and the very similar formula of *R*.

In chapter 1.13, I discuss the relationship between baptismal questions and declaratory variants of the Apostles' Creed in general. Kinzig claims that there is a fundamental difference, but this is not borne out by the sources, which treat the two as more or less interchangeable. I conclude, therefore, that the traditional opinion, according to which *H* and *R* are two variants of the Apostles' Creed, is basically valid.

In chapter 1.14, I return to my history of credal scholarship again which, in the second half of the twentieth century, mainly centred around the question of the relationship between *H* and *R*. According to Kelly, *H* and *R* were in Roman use simultaneously. According to Holland, who criticizes Kelly's theory, *H* constitutes the official third-century Roman baptismal creed, whereas *R* is its fourth-century successor. Neither Kelly's nor Holland's position is completely satisfactory.

In chapter 1.15, the contribution of Smulders is discussed. He demonstrates convincingly that $H$ represents an earlier stage in the development of the Creed than $R$, so that $R$ cannot be the first form of the Apostles' Creed (an opinion that may still be found). Moreover, Smulders introduces a new element to the discussion, viz. certain conservative traits in a number of later variants that are found elsewhere in the Western Church. Thus, he reconstructs 'pre-R', a mid-third-century ancestor of $R$, from which, in his opinion, all variants of the Apostles' Creed descend. Relative unfamiliarity with Smulders's ideas has resulted in $R$ being still usually taken to be the ancestor of the other Latin variants. In his opinion, $H$ descends from a still earlier form but has not exerted any influence on the later development of the Creed.

In chapter 1.16, I criticize Smulders's evaluation of $H$ but applaud his main conclusions. Thus, I take $H$ and $R$ as sister forms, both descending from a more original form of the Apostles' Creed, which was also the ancestor of the other variants. I offer a tentative reconstruction of this form, and baptize it 'proto- $R$'. In my opinion, proto- $R$ may well be the result of the fusion that was postulated by Holl. In all probability, it should be dated prior to 250.

In chapter 1.17, finally, I summarize the main argument which leads to my reconstruction of the protohistory of the Apostles' Creed, and offer some thoughts on its prehistory as well.

# CHAPTER ONE

## The Origin of the Apostles' Creed

### 1.1 Introduction

The Apostles' Creed has been in use in the whole of the Western Church for more than a thousand years. In the Roman Catholic tradition, its use is mainly confined to the baptismal rite. In the Protestant and Anglican Churches, it may also figure in the weekly or even daily services, although the baptismal use can also be found there [1]. Nowadays, the Apostles' Creed is usually heard in the vernacular but all its translations are considered to represent one and the same 'official' Latin text [2]. In order to distinguish this text from other variants of the Creed, it bears the name *textus receptus* or *T* [3]. The use of *T* (or some very similar variant) seems to have become general thanks to the efforts of Charlemagne, who strove for a common liturgical practice in the Western Church [4]. *T*, then, runs as follows:

*Credo in deum patrem omnipotentem, creatorem caeli et terrae*
*et in Iesum Christum, filium eius unicum dominum nostrum*
*qui conceptus est de spiritu sancto, natus ex Maria uirgine*
*passus sub Pontio Pilato, crucifixus, mortuus et sepultus*
*descendit ad inferna*

---

[1] See for example Kelly 1976, 368. More details and literature about the use of the Apostles' Creed may be found in Vokes 1978, 544-545 (its place in the monastical tradition), Barth 1978, and Schröer 1978.

[2] Luther, however, added the word *Christianam* to the tenth article, which accounts for a number of exceptions to this rule in the Protestant tradition.

[3] This designation seems to have been introduced by Kattenbusch: see Kattenbusch 1894, 189. It seems best, therefore, to use the name *T* for the variant to which Kattenbusch attached it and for that one only. Nevertheless, that this variant and no other constitutes **the** official text of the Apostles' Creed is still more a matter of tacit scholarly agreement than of fact (see for example Denzinger 1991, 33-34 for differences in the text of the Creed between various official Roman Catholic printed documents; compare Kattenbusch 1900, 867: "Ob es jemals zu einer eigentlichen "Einführung" von T als derjenigen Form des "Symbols der Apostel" gekommen ist, die allgemeingültig sei, steht dahin ..."). It should be noted that this circumstance has influenced and rather obscured the scholarly discussion about the origin of *T*: see below, footnote 7.

[4] See below, chapter 2.1, pp. 73-74.

*tertia die resurrexit a mortuis*
*ascendit ad caelos*
*sedet ad dexteram dei patris omnipotentis*
*inde uenturus est iudicare uiuos et mortuos*
*credo in spiritum sanctum*
*sanctam ecclesiam catholicam*
*sanctorum communionem*
*remissionem peccatorum*
*carnis resurrectionem*
*et uitam aeternam* [5] .

Despite the traditional designation 'Apostles' Creed' or '*symbolum apostolorum*', no serious theologian any longer holds that the Creed was composed by the Apostles themselves, which was the current view in the Middle Ages [6]. As a matter of fact, it seems impossible to find a copy of *T* before the end of the eight century [7]. This does

---

[5] Text according to Kelly 1976, 369 and Kattenbusch 1900, 761.

[6] See Kelly 1976, 1-4 for additional colourful details.

[7] It seems to occur first in the so-called *ordo Romanus antiquus*: see Kattenbusch 1900, 760, Kelly 1976, 368-369, and Denzinger 1991, 33-34. Quite similar formulations, however, can be found in late eighth-century sources like Pirminius's *scarapsus* (see below, chapter 3.2, pp. 136-137) and *sacramentarium Gellonense* 2282 and 2320 (CPL 1905c; CCSL 159, 327 and 335-336; see for the date CCSL 159A, XVIII; see for facsimiles Burn 1909, plates VIII-IX). Nevertheless, the commonly found statement that *T* is first found in Pirminius's *scarapsus* is not true, as the *scarapsus* offers a form of the Creed with *Surrexit* instead of *Resurrexit*, without *Est* after *Venturus*, and without *Et* before *Vitam aeternam* (see below, chapter 3.2, pp. 136-137 again for more details). This inaccuracy, which I reproduced myself in Westra 1995, 370n6, seems to go back to Kelly who claims: "The creed which results from piecing together the twelve clauses which he cited coincides exactly with T, except that it reads SAT (*sedit*) instead of SITS (*sedet*) ..." (Kelly 1976, 399). This enabled Vokes, who clearly uses the name *T* for the same form of the Creed as Kelly and Kattenbusch, to state that this formulation is first found in Pirminius, and then go on to discuss the **differences** between *T* and the text in the *scarapsus* (Vokes 1978, 528 and 538). Surprisingly, Kattenbusch himself makes the identical mistake when discussing the credal variant of the anonymous *symbolum apostolorum* CPL 1758: see below, chapter 4.11, footnote 43. Similarly Smulders, though he does not quote *T*, says that Pirminius "brought it from his native country in the south-west of Gaul or northern Spain. There T originated sometime in the sixth century" (Smulders 1970, 236). To make things even more complicated, Denzinger gives a slightly different form of the Creed as "T" (with *Est* after *Venturus*, but without *Et* before *Vitam aeter-*

not mean, however, that the Apostles' Creed did not exist before 800. In the four or five preceding centuries, there are a good number of texts which are designated *symbolum* or *symbolum apostolorum*. Although none of these is identical to *T*, they resemble it rather closely. As far as one can tell, they all mention belief in the Father, the Son, and the Holy Spirit (in that order), all contain phrases like *deum patrem omnipotentem, filium eius unicum*, all dwell on Christ's Birth, Passion, Resurrection, and so on. In short, all these texts may safely be branded variants of the Apostles' Creed. The examination of a good number of these variants will constitute the main portion of the present book [8]. But before we can study these different variants of the Apostles' Creed and their mutual relationships more closely, it will be a good idea to devote a few words to the origin of this text first [9].

## 1.2 First Investigations

The question of the origin of the Apostles' Creed is a comparatively recent one. Although the discovery that neither the New Testament nor the patristic literature of the first three centuries supports the idea of a literally Apostolic origin of the Creed, which discovery soon grew into a *communis opinio* in Protestant and Anglican circles, the questions of the date and place of its origin or even of its authorship were hardly treated until the late nineteenth century. There are two notable seventeenth-century exceptions,

---

*nam*) and treats Pirminius's text as a distinct variant, although he states that this "bietet schon alle Elemente des allgemein angenommenen Textes ("T")". In addition, Denzinger presents an "anfängliche" and an "abgewandelte" form of "T" (Denzinger 1991, 31-34). Similarly, Kelly's claim that it is *T* which we find in several ninth-century psalters (see Kelly 1976, 425-426) is probably too positive. In the Utrecht Psalter (ff. 90R-90V), the form of the Creed differs from *T* in four, albeit minor, points: it reads *Caelum* instead of *Caelos*, omits *Est* after *Venturus*, adds *Et* in the ninth article, and omits it again before *Vitam aeternam*.

[8] We shall not touch upon the question of the origin of *T*. Kelly's conclusion that this form of the Creed, or at least a very similar one (see previous footnote), probably stems from seventh-century South-West Gaul (Kelly 1976, 411-420) seems to be generally accepted: see Barbian 1964, 13-15 and Vokes 1978, 538-541. But compare Angenendt 1972, 69-70. Kattenbusch's discussion of this problem is still very valuable: see Kattenbusch 1900, 778-794.

[9] In our discussion of this knotty problem, we shall mainly rely on secondary literature.

however: Gerardus Joannes Vossius's *Dissertationes tres de tribus symbolis* ... (Amsterdam, 1642) and James Usher's [10] *De Romanae ecclesiae symbolo apostolico vetere* ... (London, 1647).

Vossius was the first to draw attention to a text that would later turn out to be a corner-stone for credal research: Rufinus of Aquileia, *expositio symboli* (CPL 196; *c.* 404). In this work, Rufinus explicitly mentions the fact that his own form of the Creed is different both from the Roman form and from the creeds that are in use in the Eastern part of the Church [11]. This, Vossius argues, coupled with the fact that the first Christians did not need anything like a creed, shatters the case of those who still defend the Apostolic origin of the Creed. In his opinion, the Apostles' Creed was probably not composed by a single person, but by various members of the Roman clergy, not at one moment, but in the course of the first centuries of the Church [12].

Vossius's conclusions coincide in a remarkable way with those of Usher, who discovered two practically identical variants of the Creed which were significantly shorter than $T$ in the manuscripts *Bodl. Laud. Gr.* 35 and *BM Cott.* Galba A XVIII (or Psalter of Aethelstan) [13]. Usher concluded that these testified to the existence of an older and more original form of the Creed and, like Vossius, assigned this shorter form of the Creed to Rome. Usher also found a number of similar shorter variants of the Creed in several patristic writers [14]. Although Vossius's and Usher's insights are nowadays considered fundamental [15], their main theses, viz. that the Apostles' Creed knew different forms in the patristic period, and that one of these was considerably shorter than $T$ and of Roman origin, did not meet with much approval or even attention in the first two hundred years after the publication of their studies [16].

---

[10] Their names are sometimes written Voss or Vos, and Ussher or Usserius.

[11] See below, chapter 2.3, pp. 79-80 with footnotes 32 and 33 for full quotations and discussions of the relevant passages.

[12] See Kattenbusch 1894, 6-8, De Ghellinck 1949, 27-28, and Wickenden 1993, 116-120.

[13] For the exact wording of these variants, see Kattenbusch 1894, 64 and Kelly 1976, 102 and 104.

[14] See Kattenbusch 1894, 8 and De Ghellinck 1949, 28-29.

[15] See for example Kelly 1976, 5: "... G.J. Voss (1642) and Archbishop Ussher (1647) inaugurated the modern era of credal studies". Differently Kinzig 1999b, 536 and 554.

## 1.3 The Nineteenth Century: Caspari, Kattenbusch, and the Hypothesis of R

The nineteenth century again saw some progress in the field of credal research. Here, the name of Carl Paul Caspari is of prime importance. His contribution mainly consists of an indefatigable search for "Quellen", a word that recurs in the titles of many of his publications that contain pieces concerning the Apostles' Creed [17]. Caspari's influence can be said to be threefold. First of all, he inaugurated an era of more systematic study of the origin and history of the Apostles' Creed by his implicit claim that neither one can be described without a close scrutiny of all the material that is available [18]. In the second place, his search for source texts brought to light numerous new documents [19] and inspired other scholars to do similar work [20]. In the third place, he formulated a thesis about the origin of the Creed which was to give direction to subsequent scholarship for more than half a century.

According to this thesis, then, the modern form of the Creed (*T*) and its numerous Latin variants all descend from one and the same Roman formula (1), which is identical to the shorter variant that was discovered by Usher (2). Again, this Roman formula constitutes only one among many descendants, Eastern and Western, of the 'original Creed' (3), which in its turn is supposed to have originated, somewhere in the East, in or shortly after the Apostolic age (4) [21].

---

[16] See Kattenbusch 1894, 8-15 and De Ghellinck 1949, 29-35.

[17] These are the three volumes of his *Ungedruckte, unbeachtete und wenig beachtete Quellen zur Geschichte des Taufsymbols und der Glaubensregel* ... (Caspari 1866, 1869, and 1875), his *Alte und neue Quellen* ... (Caspari 1879), the first volume of his *Kirchenhistorische Anecdota* (Caspari 1883a; the second volume never appeared), and his edition of Martin of Braga's *de correctione rusticorum* (Caspari 1883b). See Kattenbusch 1894, 18-19 and De Ghellinck 1949, 44.

[18] See Kattenbusch 1894, 18-20 and De Ghellinck 1949, 43-44.

[19] See for example Frede 1995, 125-126.

[20] Caspari's most important successors in this respect were Andrew Ewbank Burn and Germain Morin: see Burn 1898 and 1900, and Morin 1894, 1904, 1905, 1923, and 1927. The third edition of Hahn's *Bibliothek der Symbole* (1897), which constitutes a rather uncritical collection of all kinds of credal texts, can also be seen as stimulated by Caspari's work: see Hahn 1897, IV.

[21] See Kattenbusch 1894, 18-22 and De Ghellinck 1949, 43-49 for an extensive survey of Caspari's work; Caspari gives a summary of his argument on the origin of the shorter, Roman, variant of the Creed in Caspari 1875, III-VI.

Quite soon, Caspari's two first conclusions came to be considered solidly established, whereas a lively discussion ensued about the relationship between Usher's short Roman form of the Creed and its Eastern counterparts and about the question of when and where the 'original Creed' had seen the light. The exact date and place of origin of $T$ also became objects of study [22].

What Caspari did not get round to was achieved by Ferdinand Kattenbusch. His truly monumental monograph *Das apostolische Symbol* ... (1894 and 1900) was recognized from the date of its publication as the first really scientific study of the origin and history of the Apostles' Creed [23]. It is neither possible nor necessary to mention all the views and discussions that are presented in this two-volume study. In one respect, however, Kattenbusch's work deserves our closer attention. This is his discussion of Usher's shorter, Roman, form of the Creed.

First of all, Kattenbusch connected the term 'altrömisches Symbol' [24] with Usher's shorter, Roman, formula for good, and introduced the abbreviation $R$ as its most practical designation. Moreover, he seems to have been the first to lay down the wording of $R$. As in the case of $T$ [25], everyone had hitherto agreed that there was an Old Roman Creed, to be reconstructed from a number of source texts, but Kattenbusch was the first to work out such a reconstruction. Finally, Kattenbusch presented the grounds for assuming the existence of $R$, and provided it with a date. As these last points are of fundamental importance for the rest of our study, it will be convenient to dwell upon them at some length.

It seems best, however, first to present the wording of $R$ in Greek and Latin, the two languages in which its sources present themselves. $R$, then, runs thus:

Πιστεύω εἰς θεὸν πατέρα παντοκράτορα
καὶ εἰς Χριστὸν Ἰησοῦν, τὸν υἱὸν αὐτοῦ τὸν μονογενῆ, τὸν κύριον ἡμῶν
τὸν γεννηθέντα ἐκ πνεύματος ἁγίου καὶ Μαρίας τῆς παρθένου

---

[22] See De Ghellinck 1949, 111-116. Good examples of the discussion in this period are Harnack 1896 and Hahn 1897, 127-128n344.

[23] See De Ghellinck 1949, 63-64.

[24] Or '*Vetus Romanum*', or 'Old Roman Creed'. The term goes back, of course, to Usher, and was already in use before Kattenbusch.

[25] See above, chapter 1.1, footnote 7.

τὸν ἐπὶ Ποντίου Πιλάτου σταυρωθέντα καὶ ταφέντα
τῇ τρίτῃ ἡμέρᾳ ἀναστάντα ἐκ νεκρῶν
ἀναβάντα εἰς τοὺς οὐρανούς
καθήμενον ἐν δεξιᾷ τοῦ πατρός
ὅθεν ἔρχεται κρῖναι ζῶντας καὶ νεκρούς        *no Descent*
καὶ εἰς πνεῦμα ἅγιον
ἁγίαν ἐκκλησίαν
ἄφεσιν ἁμαρτιῶν
σαρκὸς ἀνάστασιν,

or:

*Credo in deum patrem omnipotentem*
*et in Christum Iesum, filium eius unicum dominum nostrum*
*qui natus est de spiritu sancto et Maria uirgine*
*qui sub Pontio Pilato crucifixus est et sepultus*
*tertia die resurrexit a mortuis*
*ascendit in caelos*        *no Descat*
*sedet ad dexteram patris*
*unde uenturus est iudicare uiuos et mortuos*
*et in spiritum sanctum*
*sanctam ecclesiam*
*remissionem peccatorum*
*carnis resurrectionem* [26].

## 1.4 The Evidence for R

That these two formulae were in use in the fourth-century Roman church is one of the central hypotheses of modern credal studies [27]. But it remains a hypothesis, and although as such it has been commonly accepted, it nevertheless has not always passed

[26] Text according to Kattenbusch 1894, 64-76. The Greek formula is identical to Kattenbusch's reconstruction from *BM Cott.* Galba A XVIII; the Latin one cannot be found in this form in Kattenbusch's work but can safely be deduced from his evaluation of the three Latin source texts. Kelly (1976, 102) presents the Latin version of *R* in exactly the same words.

[27] It is commonly accepted that the Greek variant is the original and the Latin one the translation: see for example Kattenbusch 1894, 69-71 and Kelly 1976, 111-113. The only exception to this consensus that I could find is Kraft (1980, 29), who reveals to us that *R* was originally written in Latin and translated into Greek by Marcellus of Ancyra.

unchallenged. It will be necessary, therefore, to spend some time on
the arguments upon which it has been founded as well as on those
of its adversaries.

First of all, then, it should be recognized that there are only four
direct witnesses to the text of *R*: the three manuscripts *Bodl. Laud.
Gr.* 35 (sixth or seventh century; Latin), *BM Cott.* Galba A XVIII,
also known as the Psalter of Aethelstan (eighth century; Greek),
and *BM Cott.* 2 A XX (eighth century; Latin), together with Marcellus of Ancyra's *epistula ad Iulium papam* (CPG 2801; *c.* 340 [28]).
As is only natural, none of the sources exhibits a text that is
exactly identical to that of one of the others. In particular, the differences between Marcellus's letter and the other three are considerable. One of the first difficulties, therefore, is the question of
whether these four sources may be used to reconstruct one and the
same text at all.

A second difficulty is due to the fact that none of these four
sources seems to be aware of a connection between the creed it contains and Rome. This is not so, however, with a fifth source, Rufinus's *expositio symboli*. In this work, Rufinus quotes and comments
upon the variant of the Creed that was in use in the Aquileian
church of his day, but indicates the places where this variant deviates from the one of the Roman church. This seems to be the only
place in the extant patristic literature that provides explicit clues to
both the existence and the outline of a form of the Apostles' Creed
in Rome [29].

The case for positing *R* as a form of the Creed that was in use in
fourth-century Rome rests on the following considerations. First of
all, Rufinus states in so many words that the Creed had already
been used there for some considerable time: *Verum priusquam inci-
piam de ipsis sermonum uirtutibus disputare, illud non importune
commonendum puto, quod in diuersis ecclesiis aliqua in his uerbis
inueniuntur adiecta. In ecclesia tamen urbis Romae hoc non deprehenditur factum* and *Sciendum quod duo isti sermones in ecclesiae Roma-*

---

[28] Marcellus of Ancyra, *epistula ad Iulium papa*; GCS 37, 256-259.

[29] For places which testify to its existence and use there only, see below,
chapter 1.5, footnotes 44-46. Later quotations of one or two articles of the Creed
are found in the work of Leo the Great and Arnobius the Younger: see below,
chapter 3.6, p. 211.

*nae symbolo non habentur* [30]. Moreover, though quoting the Aquileian form of the Creed, Rufinus indicates where this variant and the Roman one part ways [31], so that his *expositio* enables us to gain information concerning this Roman form of the Creed. It is of vital importance, however, to recognize that Rufinus's indications can only be used to reconstruct the contents, not the wording of this Roman formula [32].

This general outline of the fourth-century Roman form of the Creed as yielded by Rufinus's *expositio* corresponds exactly with the formulae in the manuscripts *Bodl. Laud. Gr.* 35 and *BM Cott. Galba A XVIII* and, apart from one point of difference, with that in *BM Cott.* 2 A XX as well [33]. In other words, Rufinus's *expositio* proves the existence of an Old Roman Creed and lists its contents, whereas the wording of a creed with the same contents is preserved by the three manuscripts that have just been enumerated. The conclusion seems safe, therefore, that these three manuscripts are direct witnesses to R.

Finally, Marcellus's letter is also usually taken to support the hypothesis of R. In this letter, Marcellus is not concerned with commenting upon any creed, Roman or otherwise, but rather is making a statement of his own doctrinal position to demonstrate his orthodoxy [34]. Nevertheless, the second part of this statement is strikingly similar to the Greek version of R, although there are, apart from points of wording, some real differences between the two formu-

[30] Rufinus of Aquileia, *expositio symboli* 3 and 5; CCSL 20, 135-136 and 140; see also *ibid.* 16 (CCSL 20, 152). See below, chapter 1.6, footnote 53 for more extensive quotations.

[31] This seems to be a safe conclusion: see Kelly 1976, 105-106. It should be borne in mind, however, that Rufinus does not explicitly state that such is his procedure. See for more details below, chapter 2.3, pp. 78-80.

[32] See Kelly 1976, 105 and 106-107. For the important distinction between texts that testify to the wording of a form of the Creed and those that testify to the contents of one, see below, chapter 3.1, pp. 101-106.

[33] The difference is the addition of *Catholicam* to the tenth article in *BM Cott.* 2 A XX. That this manuscript nevertheless testifies to R and not to some other form of the Creed is convincingly argued by Kattenbusch: see Kattenbusch 1894, 65 and 74-75.

[34] See Kattenbusch 1894, 73, Kelly 1976, 108-109, and Vinzent 1995, 404-405 and 1999, 218-219.

lae [35]. It is the combination of this close resemblance and the fact
that Marcellus wrote his letter to the bishop of Rome which has
led scholars since the time of Usher to the assumption that Marcellus must be tacitly quoting an official Roman formula in order to
win Julius to his cause [36].

## 1.5 An Alternative Theory: Vinzent

These, in a nutshell, are the traditional arguments for the existence and reconstruction of a fourth-century Roman creed. The
hypothesis of R, however, also has its adversaries. The most important of them is Markus Vinzent who, in a lengthy excursus to his
1995 Habilitationsschrift on pseudo-Athanasius, *contra Arianos* IV
(CPG 2230; *c.* 340 [37]), endeavours to show that the complete credal
section in Marcellus's letter, the central paragraph of which so closely resembles R, springs entirely from the author's pen. A more
elaborate version of this excursus ('Die Entstehung des "Römischen
Glaubensbekenntnisses"') has been published in the volume *Tauffragen und Bekenntnis* (1999), in which Vinzent's thoughts on the Creed
have been clustered with those of Wolfram Kinzig and Christoph
Markschies [38], whose contributions will receive attention below [39].

Vinzent begins his argument with the statement that, prior to
Marcellus's letter, no single indication for the existence of a Roman
creed can be pointed out, and that the first echoes of his credal

[35] Marcellus's letter omits Πατέρα in the first article and adds Ζωὴν αἰώνιον
to the twelfth.

[36] See Kattenbusch 1894, 73-74 and Kelly 1976, 109-110.

[37] For the date, see Vinzent 1995, 595-596.

[38] In this later work, Vinzent has considerably extended his argument. Its
publication came too late, however, to enable me to base my discussion of his
views entirely on it. I shall, therefore, mainly refer to Vinzent's 1995 publication,
adding, where possible, the relevant references to the more recent work. As far
as I can tell, the latter does not offer fundamentally different opinions from the
former. Also in 1999, Kinzig and Vinzent offered a kind of synthesis of their
theories in an article in the *Journal of Theological Studies* (Kinzig 1999b). This
publication will be referred to in the same way.

[39] We shall not discuss the positions of Francis John Badcock and Heinrich
Kraft. Badcock wrote a number of articles to show that R is basically an Antiochene text. His views have not found many adherents: see De Ghellinck 1949,
228-231 for a brief analysis. The best exposition of this theory is offered by Badcock 1933b. Kraft gives a most fantastic account of the origin of the Apostles'
Creed, without adducing a single piece of evidence: see Kraft 1980.

formulation are already found in the 'Eastern' creed of Serdica (342 or 343) [40], a credal text of Auxentius of Milan (d. 374) [41], and one of Apollinaris of Laodicea [42]. None of these witnesses betray any awareness of a similarity between their texts and a Roman creed [43].

On the other hand, that such a thing as a Roman creed existed at all is for the first time suggested by a number of late fourth-century sources: Augustine of Hippo [44], Ambrose of Milan [45], and two of the source texts for the *traditio apostolica* [46] that is ascribed to

[40] See Hilary of Poitiers's *collectanea antiarriana Parisina* A IV 2 (CPL 441; CSEL 65, 69-73). For the date, see Kelly 1976, 274.

[41] Quoted by Hilary of Poitiers in his *contra Arrianos* 14 (CPL 462; PL 10, 617-618). Vinzent's (1995, 395n123) characterization of this text as "weitgehendes Zitat des heilsökonomischen Teils", however, is erroneous: see below, chapter 3.5, footnote 299. Later on, Vinzent is more cautious: see Vinzent 1999, 404.

[42] Apollinaris of Laodicea, κατὰ μέρος πίστις (CPG 3645; Lietzmann 1904, 167-185). Vinzent (1995, 395n125) dates this creed to about 360.

[43] Vinzent 1995, 394-395. This point was already made by Badcock, too: see Badcock 1933b, 297-302. The same thought appears in Vinzent 1999, 398-406, but now following instead of preceding his argument for a Marcellan authorship of *R*. Compare also Vinzent 1999, 394: "Erst gegen Ende des vierten und dann im fünften Jahrhundert beginnt sich die Meinung durchzusetzen, daß es ein römisches Bekenntnis gibt, welches apostolische Autorität besitzt. Kein einziger Zeuge allerdings behauptet, daß dieses Bekenntnis in der römischen Gemeinde entstanden ist". This last observation would only make sense if Rome had been the Apostles' main working domain. The thought is absent from Kinzig 1999b.

[44] Augustine of Hippo, *confessiones* VIII ii 5 (CPL 251; CCSL 27, 116). This text was written around 400.

[45] Ambrose of Milan, *epistula extr. coll. 15* (*Maur. 42*) 5 (CPL 160; CSEL 82, 3, 305) and *explanatio symboli* 4 (CPL 153; CSEL 73, 6). The exact date of the letter is unknown but it must have been written between 384, the beginning of Siricius's papacy, and 397, the year of Ambrose's death. In his later publication, Vinzent is silent about both sources and only claims that "In Mailand trifft man es vermutlich erst nach Ambrosius an" (Vinzent 1999, 398n1232). His reference to Kattenbusch 1900, 393 (*ibid.*) does not justify such a conclusion, which is, moreover, entirely incongruent with the latter's views; see for example Kattenbusch 1900, 394: "Man kann vielleicht sagen, dass Ambr. *aus* dem Symbol nicht viel zu machen gewusst habe, *mit* ihm hat er nach den Umstanden doch etwas zu machen gewusst".

[46] The so-called *collectio Veronensis* and the *canones Hippolyti*. Vinzent (1995, 396-400) dates them to the second half of the fourth century. The implications of the *traditio apostolica* for the early history of the Apostles' Creed will be discussed further below: see chapters 1.12-1.15.

Hippolytus (CPG 1737) [47]. On the basis of this evidence, Vinzent disputes the general opinion that Marcellus testifies to a creed that was already in use in the Roman church of his days and suggests that the borrowing may well have been the other way round: could not the so-called Old Roman Creed be an original Marcellan formulation that was so successful that it established itself as the creed of Rome, in which new role it started to exert its influence over the Western Church [48]?

Having posed this question, Vinzent embarks upon a lengthy and detailed comparison of Marcellus's doctrinal passage with several other Eastern creeds [49]. If anything, this analysis makes crystal clear that the whole credal passage in Marcellus's letter fits his theological thought exactly [50]. This brings Vinzent to the conclusion that Marcellus must have composed his creed himself in the way other creeds were written in those days as well, viz. "im Blick auf

---

[47] Vinzent 1995, 395-401. Rufinus of Aquileia (see above, chapter 1.4, pp. 28-29) should of course be added to the number of first witnesses. Vinzent's (1995, 402n150) remark that Rufinus does not indicate all places where the Roman and Aquileian form of the Creed part ways is pointless: see Kelly 1976, 105-107 and below, chapter 2.3, 78-80. In his later publication, Vinzent is even more severe: "... alle Bekenntnisse, die im Wesentlichen den Text des *Romanum* (oder *Apostolicum*) bieten, gehören dem vierten Jahrhundert (einziger Zeuge: Markell von Ankyra) bzw. späteren Jahrhunderten an ..." (Vinzent 1999, 190). Vinzent's (1999, 186) later discussion of Rufinus's testimony hardly deserves the qualification 'scientific'; see below, chapter 3.5, footnote 355 for the details. The entire argument is reduced to the phrase "A careful comparison of all *regulae fidei*, baptismal interrogations and confessions of faith suggests the following conclusion: The observation by H. von Campenhausen and A. M. Ritter according to which declaratory confessions do not emerge until the fourth century, is borne out by the evidence available to us" in Kinzig 1999b, 554.

[48] Vinzent 1995, 402-403; compare Vinzent 1999, 196-197.

[49] Vinzent 1995, 403-492 (1999, 197-382); the relevant texts are quoted in full on pp. 406-408, 416-421, 442-444, and 460-463 (Vinzent 1999, 247-249, 271-276, 309-310, and 331-336). Somewhat surprisingly, the baptismal questions of the *Sacramentarium Gelasianum Vetus* (CPL 1899) have been added to these Eastern credal texts in Vinzent's later work (see also below, chapter 1.8, footnote 80).

[50] This implies that both the absence of Πατέρα and the presence of Ζωὴν αἰώνιον (see above, chapter 1.4, footnote 35) are deliberately meant by the author, and cannot be explained as due to scribal errors or additions, as has hitherto been done too easily by credal scholars: see for example Kattenbusch 1894, 71-72 and Kelly 1976, 110-111.

aktuelle Fragestellungen und Diskussionen" and "unter Einbezug und Berücksichtigung der gegnerischen Ansätze und Positionen" [51].

## 1.6 Evaluation of Vinzent's Arguments

Despite Vinzent's valuable study of the Marcellan text, his conclusion that R (or rather: its immediate source) is in fact a product of Marcellus of Ancyra is unconvincing. There are at least three reasons for arriving at this judgement.

First of all, Vinzent's conclusion seems to rest too much upon the assumption that in 340, the probable date of Marcellus's letter, no such thing as a Roman creed existed. Statements like "Der erste und der zweite Bekenntnisteil sind, wie sich zeigt, eng miteinander verbundene Abschnitte. Sie lassen sich in ihrer Formulierung am ehesten als Antilogie zu Asterius lesen. Den zweiten Teil als nicht von Markell persönlich formuliertes Stück aus dem Gesamttext herauszulösen und im Ganzen als Zitat einer älteren Pistis auszuweisen, läßt sich mit dem bisherigen Ergebnis nicht vereinbaren" [52] occur time and again in his work, but boil in fact down to an argument which runs as follows: Marcellus knew what he wrote, *ergo* he did not use a Roman form of the Creed. If there were no indications for the existence of such a form in Marcellus's time, nothing could indeed be said against such a statement. Although it is true that neither Rufinus nor any other witness explicitly testifies to its existence in the year 340, their claim that there was an Old Roman Creed is unambiguous. Moreover, Ambrose, Augustine, and Rufinus all strongly suggest that the use of the Creed in Rome was an old and venerable tradition [53]. In this light, it seems rather short-sighted

---

[51] Vinzent 1995, 489-491 (Vinzent 1999, 377-382); see also *ibid.* 415-416, 439, and 449 (Vinzent 1999, 270-271, 303, and 319; Kinzig 1999b, 550-558).

[52] Vinzent 1995, 439; practically the same words in Vinzent 1999, 303.

[53] See Ambrose of Milan, *epistula extr. coll. 15* (*Maur. 42*) 5: ... *credatur symbolo apostolorum, quod ecclesia Romana intemeratum semper custodit et seruat* (CSEL 82, 3, 305); Augustine of Hippo, *confessiones* VIII ii 5 (writing of events in the year 356 or 357: see Hadot 1971, 250): *Denique ut uentum est ad horam profitendae fidei, quae uerbis certis conceptis retentisque memoriter de loco eminentiore in conspectu populi fidelis Romae reddi solet ab eis qui accessuri sunt ad gratiam tuam, oblatum esse dicebat Victorino a presbyteris ut secretius redderet, sicut nonnullis qui uerecundia trepidaturi uidebantur offerri mos erat* (CPL 251; CCSL 27, 116); Rufinus of Aquileia, *expositio symboli* 3: *In ecclesia tamen urbis Romae hoc non deprehenditur factum, pro eo arbitror quod neque haeresis ulla illic sumpsit*

to accept the existence of a Roman creed in, say, 360 but to deny it
in 340. In other words, why is it so improbable that Marcellus made
use of this Roman creed when he also "sich dennoch nicht scheut,
zum Teil wörtlich Wendungen und Theologumena des Asterius zu
übernehmen ..." [54]?

It would be unfair to suggest that Vinzent completely denies the
use of a creed in Rome in the fourth century. Up to that point, he
accepts the testimonies of Ambrose, Augustine, and Rufinus. However, according to his theory, the use of a creed like R in Rome
only started under the influence of Marcellus's letter [55]. That such
a procedure must be deemed highly improbable is our second argument against Vinzent's conclusion.

What Vinzent seems to see as a circumstance in favour of a
Roman borrowing from Marcellus, viz. the fact that texts resembling R crop up in the East earlier than in the West [56], is only half
of the truth. What he fails to mention is that the Western echoes,
though later, resemble R much more closely than their Eastern,
though earlier, counterparts. The echoes of R that are found in
Auxentius of Milan (a native of Cappadocia), Apollinaris of Laodicea, and the 'Eastern' Creed of Serdica concern the wording of only
a small number of articles, whereas Western creeds as offered by
Ambrose, Nicetas of Remesiana, Augustine, and Priscillian of Avi-

---

*exordium, et mos inibi seruatur antiquus eos qui gratiam baptismi suscepturi sunt
publice, id est fidelium populo audiente, symbolum reddere, et utique adiectionem
unius saltim sermonis eorum qui praecesserunt in fide non admittit auditus* (CCSL
20, 136). See also footnote 59 below.

[54] Vinzent 1995, 456 (1999, 327); see also Vinzent 1995, 459 (the same words
in Vinzent 1999, 330): "... daß Markell wie auch die Synodalen in Antiochien aus
dem Credo des Asterius diejenigen Passagen, die ihnen als unanstößig galten,
aufgriffen oder, wenn sie nicht der eigenen theologischen Meinung entsprachen,
sie im eigenen Sinne erweiterten, umformulierten, kürzten oder durch passendere
Wendungen ersetzten". Compare the opinion of another Marcellan scholar, Martin Tetz: "Liegt uns nun die altrömische Bekenntnistradition bei Marcellus in der
Form einer Glaubensregel vor, ist von vornherein an freie Handhabung der über-
kommenen Bekenntniselemente zu denken" (Tetz 1989, 118-119). In other words:
a Marcellan borrowing of a Roman creed could fit in with Vinzent's other conclusions equally well.

[55] See above, chapter 1.5, footnote 48 and Vinzent 1995, 491 (1999, 382).

[56] See Vinzent 1995, 395-396. This argument seems to be absent from Vinzent
1999 and Kinzig 1999b.

la [57], to name only the earliest [58], not only stay closer to its wording but also reproduce the general outline of R, i.e. they echo only the middle part of Marcellus's credal text and ignore the opening and closing sections. If we really are to assume that R originated as only a paragraph in Marcellus's doctrinal exposition, we shall need an explanation for the fact that it was used in a number of variants as a creed in Avila, Milan, Aquileia, Remesiana, and Hippo, and that in less than three quarters of a century [59], whereas such a development did not take place in the East. Vinzent fails to

---

[57] See below, chapter 3, for a full discussion of these variants of the Creed.

[58] An even earlier possible witness is Cyprian of Carthage, who in two of his letters quotes baptismal questions which he designates *symbolum*: see below, chapter 3.4, pp. 160-163 for the relevant passages and an elaborate discussion. It cannot be taken for granted, however, that Cyprian really has a form of the Apostles' Creed in mind, because he only quotes three phrases. Moreover, his testimony is at least one hundred years older than our first witness to the use of the Creed in Rome (see above, footnote 53). On the other hand, Cyprian himself uses the term *symbolum* to refer to the formula he is quoting, the same term that is used for the Apostles' Creed in later texts, and the wording of his quotations does not contradict the identification. Thus, until the opposite has been proved, it seems best to consider Cyprian as the first direct witness to the Apostles' Creed. Anyhow, to exclude Cyprian as such only for the reason that he quotes his *symbolum* in the form of baptismal questions, as is done in Kinzig 1999b, 542-546, is too artificial a solution: see below, chapter 1.13.

[59] Similarly, it is difficult to see how the Roman clergy, less than a century later, could claim that this allegedly Marcellan formula was composed by the Apostles or even by Peter himself. See Pope Caelestinus I, *epistula 13* (430; CPL 1624) 7-8 (*Quis umquam non dignus est anathemate iudicatus uel adiciens uel retrahens fidei? ... Inter multa quae a te impie praedicata uniuersalis recusat ecclesia, symbolo ab apostolis tradito plangimus haec uerba fuisse sublata quae nobis totius spem uitae salutisque promittunt*; Schwartz 1925, 9) and Pope Sixtus III (*sedit 423-440), epistula 5: Iuuit animorum uota nostrorum qui uideret symbolo a se primo inter apostolos tradito derogari* (CPL 1624; *ibid.* 107). Compare also Vigilius of Thapsus, *contra Eutychetem* (CPL 806; late fifth century) IV 1: *Illa primitus uno diluens uolumine quae Leonis obiciuntur epistolae, cuius hoc sibi primo capitulum iste nescio quis proposuit: Fidelium uniuersitas profitetur credere se in deum patrem omnipotentem, et in Iesum Christum filium eius unicum dominum nostrum. Huic capitulo ob id iste calumniatur, cur non dixerit: In unum deum patrem, et in unum Iesum Christum filium eius, iuxta Nicaeni decretum concilii. Sed Romae, et antequam Nicaena synodus conueniret a temporibus apostolorum usque ad nunc, et sub beatae memoriae Caelestino cui iste rectae fidei testimonium reddidit, ita fidelibus symbolum traditur, nec praeiudicatur uerbo ubi sensus incolumis permanet* (PL 62, 119).

give such an explanation [60]. On the other hand, the fact that there are some more general parallels between R and a number of Eastern creeds shortly after 340 does not necessarily imply that these creeds directly derive from R, since all creeds by definition cover more or less the same ground [61]. Again, if R is of Marcellan origin, we shall also need an explanation of why Πατέρα was added to it and Ζωὴν αἰώνιον was removed. Vinzent does not offer such an explanation either. But in the alternative case, the omission of Πατέρα and the addition of Ζωὴν αἰώνιον are perfectly accounted

[60] Or: what is the difference between a 'Herauslösung' of part of the text by credal scholars as a substantial quotation and a 'Herauslösung' by the Roman clergy of the same part for use as a distinct creed? Vinzent's remark that "Auch wenn die gesamte Pistis von Markells Brief eine auf die aktuellen Widerstände und Kämpfe zugeschnittene Neuformulierung des Nizänums ist und als markellische Glaubensäußerung, wie "Antiochenum IV" zeigt, offensichtlich von den Gegnern sogleich aufgenommen und kritisiert wurde, so ist vor allem der mittlere Teil mit seinem konzisen, auf die untrennbare Verbindung von Vater, Inkarniertem und Geist angelegten Zuschnitt ein bündiges, den nizänischen Glauben neu ausdrük-kendes die Ökonomie umreißendes Kurzbekenntnis. Da es im nachnizänischen Kampf nicht mehr so sehr um die Fragen der Präexistenz, sondern immer mehr um die der Ökonomie und des Geistes geht, ist verständlich, daß gerade dieser zweite Teil von Markells Pistis eine außerordentliche Wirkungsgeschichte be-sitzt" (Vinzent 1995, 491; compare Vinzent 1999, 381) can hardly serve as such, as the contexts of the fourth and fifth-century occurrences of the Creed have nothing to do with a 'nachnizänischen Kampf um die Fragen der Ökonomie und des Geistes' (see below, chapter 3). A remark like "Gerade der zweite Teil von Markells Pistis, der jeglicher für Nizäner anstößiger Theologumena entbehrte, war damit eine außerordentliche Wirkungsgeschichte bereitet. Als an der Ökono-mie ausgerichtetes Bekenntnis konnte Markells isolierter zweiter Bekenntnisteil gerade in derjenigen Liturgie Eingang finden, der (sic; LHW) der Eröffnung der Heilsökonomie für den Menschen diente, nämlich der Tauffeier" (Vinzent 1999, 381) betrays an increased awareness of the problem, but still fails to offer an ex-planation of how part of Marcellus's 'Pistis' came to be 'isoliert'. Similarly Vinzent 1999, 391-392: "Nicht das nizänische Bekenntnis und auch nicht das ... Serdicense erlangten allgemeine Anerkennung im Westen, sondern man begnügte sich mit dem von Markell in seinem Brief dargelegten Symbol ... Daß man hieraus offen-kundig vor allem den ökonomisch-trinitarischen Teil schätzen und isolieren konnte, dürfte mit der klugen Gliederung des markellischen Bekenntnisses zusam-menhängen, welches im mittleren Teil ein ganz und gar ökonomisch orientiertes Bekenntnisganzes (!; LHW) bot ...". Compare also our third argument against Vinzent's conclusion: see below, chapter 1.8.

[61] Moreover, there is good reason to assume that both the Old Roman Creed and the creeds of the Eastern Church share certain older material: see below, chapter 1.11, footnote 114 and chapter 1.17, pp. 70-72.

for by Marcellus's theological interests, as is pointed out by Vinzent's analysis.

Thus, the assumption that the Roman clergy took over a part of Marcellus's doctrinal section to use it as a creed leads to considerable difficulties, whereas no real arguments can be offered against the alternative possibility that it was Marcellus who did the borrowing. Viewed in this light, Vinzent's thesis of a Marcellan origin for *R* becomes less and less probable. But there is a third and, to all appearances, conclusive argument against his reconstruction of the early history of the Old Roman Creed, which is bound up with the contribution to credal studies of John Norman Davidson Kelly. It is to his work, therefore, that we shall now turn.

### 1.7 The Contribution of Kelly

The appearance of Kelly's monograph *Early Christian Creeds* in 1950 marked a new phase in credal research. This work has seen numerous imprints [62], and seems to have settled a number of questions for good. One of its main contributions towards the understanding of the early history of the Apostles' Creed consists of a better and more exact terminology than what was usual in the first half of the twentieth century and before.

According to Kelly, then, the word 'creed' primarily denotes a declaratory statement of faith with a fixed wording [63], and creeds in this sense are not found in sources prior to the fourth century [64]. Kelly observes that the earliest extant variants of the Apostles' Creed which meet his criterion are connected with a specific liturgical context: the rites of the so-called *traditio* and *redditio symboli*. These two rites constituted the conclusion of the catechumenate, and as such the preparation for baptism. During the *traditio*, the bishop recited the Creed for the catechumens, the catechumens were expected to recite it in their turn during the *redditio*. On both occasions, a sermon on the Creed and on the meaning of its several articles could be delivered [65].

---

[62] We shall refer to the second impression (1976) of the third edition (1972) throughout. In the parts that concern us here, this edition does not show any significant deviations from the first edition.

[63] Kelly 1976, 30.

[64] Kelly 1976, 38.

[65] See Kelly 1976, 31-39.

Of course, before the use of creeds in the strict sense of the word came into vogue, Christians already confessed their belief. As far as we can tell, more or less fixed formulae to that purpose came into being soon after the Apostolic age. Kelly argues that the triple questions and responses with which people were baptized constituted one such formula. Although these questions may have strongly resembled the wordings of later declaratory creeds, it is important to recognize that it was not the reciting of a formula, but the answer to a question that essentially made up the confession of the baptizand [66]. Somewhat confusingly, Kelly in places nevertheless designates the baptismal questions as 'interrogatory creeds' [67].

Another kind of confession that was in current use before the rise of declaratory creeds is the so-called *regula fidei* [68]. Although it has taken some time for this insight to break through [69], it is nowadays usually accepted that the *regula fidei* was not only a different kind of text from either the declaratory creed or the baptismal questions [70], but also had distinctly different contents [71]. Kelly stresses that,

---

[66] Kelly 1976, 40-48.

[67] Compare for example Kelly 1976, 50: "... the only creed, if creed is the right designation for it, directly connected with baptism was the baptizand's **assent** to the minister's questions regarding his beliefs" (my stress) and 107 (referring to the baptismal **questions**): "... St Hippolytus's interrogatory baptismal creed". The question whether Kelly's designation is justified will be discussed below: see chapter 1.13.

[68] The term is first found in Irenaeus's *demonstratio* 3 (CPG 1307; SChr 62, 31), probably written between 185 and 203: see PO 12, 752. Smulders (1971, 360-361a) finds the first *regula fidei* in the martyr acts of Justin (*c.* 165). Perhaps the best characterization of the *regula fidei* can be found in a separate study by Louis William Countryman, who defines the *regula fidei* as "an oral composition preserved and handed on by "composition in performance"" (Countryman 1982, 226), probably with an antiheretical purpose (*ibid.*, 223), in which the basic contents of Christian faith were formulated (*ibid.*, 216). See also Hanson 1962, 75-129 for a general discussion and 124-125 for a definition ("... an account of the teaching of the Church as it is known to the writer who uses the concept of the rule, believed to be continuous and virtually identical with the teaching ... from the time of the apostles").

[69] See Von Campenhausen 1972, 211n5.

[70] See Van den Eynde 1933, 281-313, Vokes 1978, 532, Smulders 1980, 7-8, and Ritter 1993, 94.

[71] See Hanson 1962, 64 and especially Smulders 1971, 357-364. In a later study by Hanson (1975, 170) the distinction is blurred again. Smulders 1971 is

although both present a concise summary of Christian belief, there
is one fundamental difference between a *regula fidei* and a creed:
whereas the latter knows a fixed wording by definition, the former
always remained free in its formulation [72]. Although this insight was
not new [73], Kelly seems to be the first to draw the important lesson
from it that, for that reason, an author who presents a *regula fidei*
cannot at the same time be claimed as a witness to a creed [74]. It is
ironical to note again that, however right Kelly is in giving this
warning, he does not hesitate to designate *regulae fidei* as "creeds,
in the looser, less exact sense of the word" [75]. This probably facilitated his conclusion that the *regula fidei* can be seen as the forerun-
ner of the baptismal questions ('interrogatory creeds') and thus also
of the Creed [76].

the only study I know of the development of the contents of the *regula fidei*.
Some of Smulders's conclusions are slightly modified by Westra 1997, 142-145.

[72] See Kelly 1976, 95-96: "Admittedly great stress is laid on orthodox belief
by many of the writers we have consulted, and they are all convinced that there
is one, universally accepted system of dogma, or rule of faith, in the Catholic
Church. But this is never unambiguously connected, even by theologians like St
Irenaeus and Tertullian, with any set form of words. Though they frequently cite
the rule of faith, it is plain that their citations are neither formulae themselves
nor presuppose some underlying formula." See also Hanson 1962, 60-65 and
Vinzent 1999, 198-199. As a matter of fact, any time a writer claims to present
**the** *regula fidei*, we should be aware that we can only see **a** *regula fidei*.

[73] See De Ghellinck 1949, 218-219.

[74] Kelly 1976, 96.

[75] Kelly 1976, 94. Compare also the titles of subchapters like "The Creeds of
St Justin" (p. 70) and "Tertullian's Creeds" (p. 82). It should be mentioned here
that the patristic sources sometimes also closely link the two. See for example
Augustine of Hippo, *sermo de symbolo ad catechumenos* I 1: *Accipite regulam fidei
quod symbolum dicitur* (CCSL 46, 185), *sermo 213* 2: *symbolum est ergo breuiter
complexa regula fidei ...* (Morin 1930, 442), and *sermo 186* 2: *Nam quomodo in
regula fidei confiteremur credere nos in filium dei, qui natus est ex uirgine Maria
...* (PL 38, 1000). As Rodomonti (1995, 128) rightly remarks, these places do not
imply that Augustine equates *symbolum* and *regula fidei*, but express that he
considers the Apostles' Creed as normative for Christian faith. Eichenseer does
not discuss this point in so many words, but seems to reason along similar lines:
see Eichenseer 1960, 348. A non-Augustinian place is Rufinus of Aquileia, *expositio symboli* 2: see below, chapter 2.3, footnote 20. Compare also the statement
by Kattenbusch, quoted below, chapter 1.9, footnote 95 and Barbian 1964, 9-11.

[76] See Kelly 1976, 94-99, where a continuous development is assumed from
the earliest New Testament formulae of faith via similar material in the writings
of the Apostolic Fathers and the *regula fidei* to the baptismal questions. Similar

## 1.8 Evaluation of Vinzent's Arguments (continued)

Although these inconsistencies in Kelly's terminology have sometimes obscured the fact, one could state that he has created a 'new
consensus' that comprises the following points: the first unambiguous testimonies to the existence of declaratory creeds only crop up
in the fourth century (1), these are connected with the *traditio* and
*redditio symboli*, not directly with baptism (2), and creeds are different from *regulae fidei* (3) [77]. The third element of this consensus in
particular is extremely important as too many students of the
Creed, even after the appearance of Kelly's monograph, have, either
tacitly or openly, assumed that the *regula fidei*, being older than the
Creed, must therefore be its direct ancestor [78]. Nevertheless, though

ideas can be found in Barbian 1964, 9, Vokes 1978, 531-532, Stead 1987, 2-3,
and Young 1991, 7-9. See also footnote 78 below.

[77] The term 'new consensus' in this context goes back to Ritter, who formu-
lates the same three points in a slightly different way: see Andresen 1993, 152;
see for the same thought already Ritter 1984, 402-406 and Vokes 1978, 531-532:
"Die ersten klaren Belege für das altrömische Bekenntnis in deklaratorischer
Form stammen aus dem 4. Jh.", "Wie vielmehr J.N.D. Kelly gezeigt hat, war
der Kontext ihrer Entstehung nicht die Taufe an sich, sondern das entwickelte
System des Katechumenenunterrichts", and "Es wäre ein Irrtum, das fixierte
Glaubensbekenntnis oder Symbol mit der *regula fidei* gleichzusetzen". Although
Vinzent (1995, 393-394) seems to think otherwise, Vokes's conclusion that "Wenn
r also im Westen für die Zeit vor dem 4. Jh. keine Zeugnisse für deklaratorische
Bekenntnisse finden, kann das nur bedeuten, daß es sie vorher tatsächlich nicht
gab" does not belong to a consensus of any sort: see Kelly 1976, 49 and Ritter
1984, 407. The rendering of the 'consensus' in Kinzig 1999b, 538-539, preceded
by the statement "In his seminal article 'Glaubensbekenntnisse' in the *Theologische Realenzyklopädie* Ritter described this 'new consensus' ...", is downright
misleading. Of course, Vinzent's claim is true when one confines the meaning of
the word 'creed' to private and synodal creeds (see below, pp. 42-43 with footnote 85 for this kind of text). Thus, it is not surprising to read in Kinzig 1999b,
538: "They (viz. Von Campenhausen and Ritter; LHW) claimed that before the
fourth century there were no declaratory creeds but that these creeds were developed by synods using the *regulae fidei*". But that is only possible if one
ignores all the early references to the Apostles' Creed enumerated above (see
chapter 1.6, footnote 53 and pp. 34-35). Thus, Vinzent actually fails to meet
the standard that is formulated in Kinzig 1999b, 554: "The confession in Marcellus' epistle ... has ... to be set within the wider context of the emergence of
creeds and has to be interpreted in connection with this wider context".

[78] Thus, Hanson (1962, 60-65) first argues that baptismal questions and *regulae fidei* belong to two, quite independent, traditions and corrects Kelly's way of

Vinzent mentions this 'new consensus' with approval [79], the fundamental error in his reconstruction consists precisely in the blurring
of the distinction between *regulae fidei* and creeds [80].

That Vinzent indeed does so is evident, to give two concrete
examples, from two statements which occur in central passages of
his study. When commenting upon the structure of Marcellus's doctrinal exposition, he writes: "Daß dreigliedrige Glaubenssymbole bis
zum ersten drittel (sic; LHW) des vierten Jahrhunderts die Ausnah-
men sind, zeigt eine ganze Reihe älterer Regulae fidei" [81]. Now,
according to the 'new consensus' as Vinzents presents it, creeds,

talking about *regulae fidei* as creeds, but continues to state that declaratory
creeds were born from baptismal questions under the influence of the *regula fidei*: see Hanson 1962, 66-74 and 124-127, 1975, 170-171, and 1992, 207. Even
more confusing is Hanson 1976, 26: "... rules of faith, i.e. longer, ampler, looser
statements than creeds, but historically related to them. Creeds were first regarded as bare, skeletonic summaries of the rule of faith, but later, in the fourth
century, creeds began to be enlarged so much as to become in the end indistin-
guishable from the rule of faith, and gradually came to take its place". Similarly,
Eichenseer (1960, 75-76) explains the Creed as a "Zusammenfassung ... des Glau-
bens- oder Wahrheitsregel". Compare also Rordorf 1995, 51 (writing about the
Church's struggle with Gnosticism in the second century): "Zu allgemeiner Anerkennung als "Glaubensregel" gelangte damals das altrömische Taufsymbol ...".

[79] Vinzent 1995, 393-394+n114; compare Vinzent 1999, 331n1035 and Kinzig
1999b, 537-540.

[80] This ignoring of genre distinctions is probably also the reason why Vinzent
can, without any difficulty, treat the baptismal questions of the *Sacramentarium
Gelasianum Vetus* in the same way as a number of Eastern synodal and private
creeds: see above, chapter 1.5, footnote 49 and Vinzent 1999, 199 and 236. An
even more positive statement is found in Kinzig 1999b, 555: "There is, however,
some reason to suppose that the synodal members (viz., of the synod of Antioch
in 324; LHW) when formulating their creed drew not only on the opponents'
rules, but also on the baptismal formula of Matt. 28:19 and on baptismal interrogations. The use of the baptismal formula and older interrogations can be seen
from the threefold structure of the creed, something that is absent from both
Arius' and Alexander's creeds. In addition, there are some striking literal parallels to the baptismal interrogations preserved in the *OGS*. The synods used these
existing *Vorlagen*, because they were aware of the novel character of what they
were doing, i.e. creating a 'synodal creed'". This explanation seems more novel to
me than the procedure of the synod. To mention only one flaw in this reasoning:
both the threefold structure of the synodal creed and its supposedly novel formulations can be sufficiently explained as inherited from the *regula fidei*: see below,
pp. 42-43. Compare also below, footnote 85.

[81] Vinzent 1995, 466; similarly Vinzent 1999, 339 and Kinzig 1999b, 554.

i.e. 'Glaubenssymbole', do not occur at all before the fourth century, let alone tripartite ones, so that he could have dispensed with his lengthy list of *regulae fidei* to prove his point. On the other hand, even if his observation were right that real Trinitarian *regulae fidei* only seem to occur by way of exception [82], this does not say anything about the wording or content of **creeds**. In theory, a Trinitarian creed could have been in use for a century or more in a church which only knew monarchical or dyadic [83] *regulae fidei* (and the same holds true for the opposite situation), as creeds and *regulae fidei* are two distinctly different kinds of texts.

Next, in his final evaluation of the evidence, Vinzent states: "Diese Erklärung der vorliegenden, zwischen 318 und 341 entstandenen Bekenntnisse läßt kaum zu, daß Markell anders als alle Verfasser von Bekenntnissen vor und nach ihm auf ein bereits geprägtes "Romanum" zurückgegriffen hat. Keiner der an der Auseinandersetzung beteiligten Theologen oder Synodalen kommt auf ein solches Bekenntnis oder auch nur auf eine ähnliche römische Glaubensregel zu sprechen" [84]. That Marcellus used a Roman 'Glaubensregel' or *regula fidei* has, as far as I can tell, never been claimed. In all probability, such a text never existed, either before or after the arrival of Marcellus's letter in Rome. If Marcellus had made use of a Roman *regula*, he would indeed probably have said so. Similarly, one would have expected to meet some mention of the fact if the opposite process had occurred. But in all probability, neither a Roman borrowing of a Marcellan *regula* nor a Marcellan borrowing of a Roman *regula* ever happened. What did, then?

At this point, it is important to realize that the proper designation for that section of Marcellus's letter that we have hitherto indicated with 'doctrinal passage' or some such term, is in fact not '*regula fidei*' or simply 'creed' (or, according to Vinzent, 'Bekenntnis'), but 'private creed' ('Privatbekenntnis'). Private creeds comprise a distinct kind of doctrinal text that came particularly to the fore in the fourth century, when the Trinitarian and Christological battles were being fought. In this period, it sometimes was vital to pronounce a statement of one's orthodoxy, and this was precisely

[82] But compare Smulders 1971, 362-363.
[83] See Smulders 1971, 359 on this distinction.
[84] Vinzent 1995, 490; similarly Vinzent 1999, 378 and Kinzig 1999b, 557.

the purpose of private creeds [85]. In common with the *regula fidei*, these creeds offered a concise summary of faith, whose contents and wording were to a considerable extent dictated by the needs of the moment [86]. Thus, Vinzent is right in connecting Marcellus's private creed with second and third-century *regulae fidei* as well as with contemporary private and synodal creeds [87]. The Apostles' Creed as we meet it in Rome and the rest of the Western church, however, does not bear the character of a doctrinal but rather of a liturgical text [88]. In other words, the question of the relationship between Marcellus's letter and the Old Roman Creed is not one of the relationship between two closely resembling '*regulae*', one Roman, one Marcellan, but one of the relationship between a doctrinal and a liturgical creed which happen to share a significant number of phrases. Viewed in this light, Vinzent's claim that one section of such a private creed could without any problem be taken over for liturgical use becomes less and less probable [89]. It is incon-

---

[85] See for example Kelly 1976, 205-211 and Ritter 1984, 408-410. The well-known synodal creeds like those of Nicea and Nicea-Constantinople are, of course, a subgroup of this category, which could perhaps be better designated 'doctrinal creeds'. Vinzent offers a fascinating analysis of the way in which such doctrinal creeds, both private and synodal, were composed: see Vinzent 1995, 403-532 (1999, 235-382). In this light, it is all the more surprising to read the statement about the novel character of writing **synodal** creeds as opposed to **private** creeds in Kinzig 1999b, 555 (see above, footnote 80).

[86] This is worked out on a more theoretical level in Vinzent 1999, 235-240 and Kinzig 1999b, 552-557.

[87] Thus also Hanson 1962, 69, Hanson 1975, 171, and Ritter 1993, 96-97. On the other hand, the claim that "To distinguish between the 'rule' and 'private creeds' only adds to the confusion with which research on the creeds already abounds" (Kinzig 1999b, 541) seems to be a step too far. The fact that the *regula fidei* is by definition free in its wording (see above, chapter 1.7, pp. 38-39 with footnote 68), whereas the opposite holds true for a doctrinal creed, remains a real difference.

[88] This fact is too often ignored in discussions about the origin of the Creed. For a favourable exception, see Young 1991, 3: "Creeds did not originate, then, as 'tests of orthodoxy', but as summaries of faith ... that were traditional to each local church ...". See also Harmless 1995, 274-285, in particular 279: "Just to hear these words meant the *competentes* were passing an important threshold".

[89] That we find the Apostles' Creed first used in the context of the catechumenate (see above, chapter 1.7, p. 37) does not make any difference. When attending the *traditio symboli* after being a catechumen for a period of three years or more, the baptizands were supposed to know what was sound doctrine and

ceivable in the light of what we know of the fourth-century use of private creeds that a certain part of one such creed would suddenly be endowed with the honour of crowning the Roman catechumens' learning period and opening, as it were, the door of the baptistery for them [90]. Nothing in Marcellus's letter suggests such a use, nothing in the Roman source texts such an origin.

what was not. In other words, they did not need to **learn** anything about **doctrine** any more, but they received a **liturgical formula** with which to give a **symbolic** proclamation of their faith. See for this important point, which is too often ignored by adherents of the 'new consensus', Smulders 1970, 238-240 and Harmless 1995, in particular 54-55, 85-86, 126-128, 276-277 ("Thus [Augustine] distinguished belief from understanding ..." and "Thus one finds Augustine making few points in these catecheses [viz., the *sermones in traditione symboli*; LHW] that do not appear elsewhere in his public sermons. In other words, the Creed's wording may have been secret, but both its tenets and his explanation of them were very much part of the public domain"), and above, previous footnote. Compare also Augustine of Hippo, *sermo 212* 2: *Quicquid enim in symbolo audituri estis, iam diuinis sanctarum scripturarum litteris continetur et omnia carptim ubi opus erat soletis audire ... Hoc est ergo symbolum quod uobis per scripturas et sermones ecclesiasticos iam catechumenis insinuatum est, sed sub hac breui forma fidelibus confitendum et proficiendum est* (SChr 116, 182-184) and *sermo 214* 1 and 12: *Et ea quidem quae breuiter accepturi estis, mandanda memoriae et ore proferenda, non noua uel inaudita sunt uobis. Nam in sanctis scripturis et in sermonibus ecclesiasticis ea multis modis posita soletis audire ... Quod ideo symbolum dicitur quia ibi nostrae societatis fides placita continetur, et eius confessione tamquam signo dato Christianus fidelis agnoscitur* (Verbraken 1962, 14 and 21). From this point of view, it would be better to omit the several variants of the Apostles' Creed from the next edition of Denzinger's *Encheiridion*.

[90] When Vinzent (1999, 395) claims: "Hinweise hingegen, die es nachvolziehbar machen, wie Markells Bekenntnis sich allmählich in den westlichen Städten und Gemeinden hatte durchzusetzen können (sic; LHW), lassen sich anführen. Ich kann diesen Weg hier nur skizzieren", he ignores this difficulty. Compare Vinzent 1999, 397: "Offenkundig wurde das markellische Bekenntnis in seinem ökonomischen Triasteil spätestens seit der Mitte des vierten und vermutlich häufiger noch zu Beginn des fünften Jahrhunderts als antiarianisches Bekenntnis in Taufliturgien übernommen und diente als Grundlage für Taufkatechesen, in denen die Abgrenzung von Häresien ein wichtiger integrierter Bestandteil war". But the **Apostles'** Creed has, at least in patristic times, never been the **basis** for the teaching of the catechumens, as is pointed out in Smulders 1970, 238-239. Similarly Vinzent 1999, 240 and Kinzig 1999b, 557: "Gradually some creeds lost their original character. Creeds ... became points of reference within liturgy and catechesis and were handed down as such. However, to describe this later development in all its complexity would by far exceed the limited scope of this article"; compare also Kinzig 1999b, 558-559. Nevertheless, in the absence of any

On the other hand, precisely the difference between the Apostles' Creed in Rome as a liturgical text and Marcellus's private creed as a doctrinal one may account for two difficulties which are felt by Vinzent in connection with the traditional explanation. We shall now pay attention to these two objections before continuing our own analysis.

The first of these difficulties is that Vinzent would expect the fact that Marcellus makes use of a Roman formula to be mentioned in the sources, whereas not even an allusion to such a borrowing can be found in either Marcellus's own writings or those of his contemporaries [91]. But it should not be forgotten that Marcellus, his opponents, and his supporters were all involved in a doctrinal debate. Thus, they were concerned with doctrinal arguments which were continually being compared, tested, and sharpened in order to find a doctrinal formulation that best met the requirements of the times. In such a situation, it is not strange that Marcellus himself is silent about the source of the middle part of his creed, as the borrowing of a liturgical text could hardly serve to strengthen his doctrinal position [92]. Nor is it surprising that his procedure did not rouse any comment from his contemporaries, as the quotation of a liturgical text hardly contributed to the doctrinal debate. As a matter of fact, one wonders whether Marcellus's opponents, being Greeks, would have been sufficiently acquainted with Roman liturgical usage to recognize R when they saw it.

positive indications that this 'later development' is indeed what happened with the middle portion of Marcellus's doctrinal creed (and that within less than twenty years: see above, chapter 1.6, footnote 53), such a possibility seems extremely improbable. A comparison with the long-term process of the establishment of the Nicaeno-Constantinopolitan Creed in liturgies where it did not, generically speaking, belong is instructive here: see Kelly 1976, 345-357.

[91] Compare Vinzent 1995, 490: "Keiner der an der Auseinandersetzung beteiligten Theologen oder Synodalen kommt auf ein solches Bekenntnis oder auch nur auf eine ähnliche römische Glaubensregel zu sprechen. Auch Markell selbst erwähnt nichts, was entsprechend zu deuten wäre" (similarly Vinzent 1999, 378-379 and Kinzig 1999b, 557).

[92] This does not automatically mean, however, that Marcellus's quotation was "an ingenious move designed to provide an absolutely unimpeachable proof of his orthodoxy by the innuendo that he considered the Pope's own baptismal confession the best expression of his faith" (Kelly 1976, 103). Other grounds are also conceivable. In any case, no serious explanation can afford to neglect Vinzent's conclusion that Marcellus's private creed as a whole excellently fits his theological position (see above, chapter 1.5, p. 32).

In the second place, Vinzent feels that a lengthy and literal quotation is inappropriate in an otherwise private creed [93]. Here, however, it should be pointed out that only a fairly accurate quotation,
which left the structure of the Roman formula unimpaired and only
incidently deviated from its wording, would be recognized by the
Roman addressees. As we shall see below, the most distinctive features of the Old Roman Creed were not its ideas, which belonged to
common Christian teaching, but its structure and more or less fixed
wording. Thus, we are back again at Usher's conclusion that Marcellus must have wanted to include these elements in his personal
formulation of faith. From the point of view of a student of the
Creed, to figure out the reasons for this procedure would constitute
one of the more desirable projects for Marcellan scholarship.

## 1.9 Twentieth-century Developments

We assume, therefore, following the mainstream of credal scholarship, that the Apostles' Creed can be traced back to early
fourth-century Rome at least, where, in a wording that is nowadays
designated *R*, it played a role as a declaratory creed in the rites of
*traditio* and *redditio symboli*. The next question is, of course,
whether this is all one can say about its early history. Is *R* really
the earliest glimpse we get of the Apostles' Creed, or are there
sources that point to even older versions? Similarly, one would like
to know how and when the Creed was born, either in the form of *R*
or in some other wording. From what date on can we really speak
of the 'Apostles' Creed'?

As we have seen, Caspari postulated the existence of some original creed as early as shortly after the Apostolic age, which would

---

[93] See Vinzent 1995, 439 (1999, 303): "Den zweiten Teil als nicht von Markell
persönlich formuliertes Stück aus dem Gesamttext herauszulösen und im Ganzen
als Zitat einer älteren Pistis auszuweisen, läßt sich mit dem bisherigen Ergebnis
nicht vereinbaren" and 459: "... daß Markell wie auch die Synodalen in Antiochien aus dem Credo des Asterius diejenigen Passagen, die ihnen als unanstößig
galten, aufgriffen oder, wenn sie nicht der eigenen theologischen Meinung entsprachen, sie im eigenen Sinne erweiterten, umformulierten, kürzten oder durch
passendere Wendungen ersetzten. Daß dies grundsätzlich die Methode im Um-
gang mit älteren Glaubensbekenntnissen bei Theologen und Synoden zumindest
der ersten Hälfte des vierten Jahrhunderts charakterisiert, belegen die angestell-
ten und die nachfolgenden Vergleiche" (similarly Vinzent 1999, 330).

have given birth again to a number of different creeds, of which $R$ was only one among many [94]. Kattenbusch had a different view: according to him, $R$ constitutes the first Christian creed, its origin is Roman, and several daughter forms found their way to the East and to the West [95]. He is able to do so by treating references to the *regula fidei* as references to $R$ [96] and assuming a date as early as 100 AD for its birth [97].

For a considerable time, as has already been mentioned above, neither Caspari's nor Kattenbusch's nor any other view on the earliest history of the Creed managed to establish itself [98]. This situation suddenly changed, however, in the period between the two World Wars, when three major contributions were made to investigations into the origin of the Apostles' Creed. First, Karl Holl made the discovery that $R$ can be seen as consisting of a short Trinitarian formula, comprising the first, second, and final four articles [99], and a Christological one, comprising articles three to eight [100]. Since the separate existence of both threefold baptismal questions and Christological formulae like the one occurring in $R$ could be shown to have an early date, the conclusion that the Apostles' Creed was

[94] See above, chapter 1.3, p. 25.

[95] This does not mean, however, that Kattenbusch makes each and every credal formulation descend from $R$. He considers $R$ to be the ancestor of every **similar** form, but leaves room for independent ones as far as they exhibit a different 'Gepräge'. But these, he states, do not really deserve the name 'creed': "Man sollte davon absehen, diese Formeln als "Symbol" zu bezeichnen, da ihrer keine zu ihrer Zeit, soweit wir sehen, diesen Namen getragen hat, keine auch diejenige Bedeutung gehabt hat, die das wirkliche Symbol charakterisiert: jene besondere liturgisch-katechetische Stellung (die R überall, auch im Orient, bekam) und jene theologisch-polemische als regula fidei, (die ihm im Abendland überwiesen wurde)" (Kattenbusch 1900, 278).

[96] See for example Kattenbusch 1900, 326: "Wenn R um die Zeit, wo Marcion und Valentin auftraten, schon in der Geltung als regula stand ...". Compare also the quotation in the previous footnote.

[97] See Kattenbusch 1900, 329-330 for a cautious formulation of this conclusion. The central parts of his argument comprise Kattenbusch 1894, 368-392 and 1900, 277-335.

[98] See De Ghellinck 1949, 111-116 for an instructive overview of the different opinions by 1914.

[99] This means that the term 'Trinitarian formula' is not quite adequate. We shall continue to use it, however, as this usage has become current in this context.

[100] Holl 1928, 115-121.

the product of the fusion of these two elements soon established
itself as a *communis opinio* [101]. In other words, the birth of the
Apostles' Creed was equated with the moment of fusion of its two
main constituents. Thus, the question of its origin was reduced to
that of the date and place of this fusion. The question of the exact
wording of the first variant of the Creed, however, even after this
discovery, was still an open one.

    Next, Hans Lietzmann in an impressive number of publications
established the conclusion that $R$ cannot have been the ancestor of
any Eastern creed [102]. The important implication of this conclusion
is that $R$ must have originated as a Roman text. In other words,
since Lietzmann, it is as useless to look for the origin of $R$ in the
East as it is to look for that of the Eastern liturgical creeds in
Rome. The Apostles' Creed and its Eastern counterparts belong to
two distinct traditions [103]. Although Holl's and Lietzmann's results
soon became part of a new consensus of some sort, other questions,
especially those of the relationship between the Eastern and Western
credal traditions and of the origins of the two short formulae that
make up $R$, continued to be highly controversial [104].

    In fact, the third contribution that was hinted at above was
already made before the Great War, although it took some time
before its importance for the study of the origin of $R$ was generally
recognized - the discovery that a set of baptismal questions that

---

[101] See Kelly 1976, 122 and 126. Refinements and more elaborate theories (for
example, claiming theological significance for details of construction: see Lietzmann 1962, 272-281) did not find general acceptance: see De Ghellinck 1949,
144-152 and Kelly 1976, 119-126.

[102] Lietzmann 1962 (originally 1922), 194-213, summarized in Kelly 1976, 197-
204. See for a detailed discussion of Lietzmann's work De Ghellinck 1949, 157-
178.

[103] The statement in Kinzig 1999b, 552 ("... we have to bear in mind that,
contrary to claims by earlier scholars, the credal developments in East and West
must not be separated from one another. Rather, both the Eastern and Western
confessions of faith were initially developed in one single and coherent historical
process") should be understood as again referring to doctrinal creeds only again
(see above, chapter 1.8, footnote 77), and thus does not really contradict this
result. As a matter of fact, Kelly's reproduction of Lietzmann's argument (see
previous footnote) is warmly applauded by Kinzig 1999b, 535-536.

[104] See De Ghellinck 1949, 239-248. A good impression of this state of affairs
is provided by Michel 1941 and Leclercq 1953. The account of this chapter of the
history of credal research in Kinzig 1999b, 536-537 is rather unbalanced.

closely resembled the wording of R could be connected with the name of the Roman presbyter and antipope Hippolytus (exiled in 235). This discovery was independently presented in 1910 and 1916 by two scholars (Eduard Schwartz and Richard Hugh Connolly), who claimed that a number of canonical texts could be proved to descend directly from Hippolytus's *traditio apostolica*, which had been considered lost until then [105]. In other words, in a period when Kattenbusch's early date for the birth of R had definitively been discarded but its Roman origin been vindicated, a very similar Roman formula cropped up that was considered to hark back to at least the first half of the third century. It is only natural that the problem of the exact relationship between R and Hippolytus's *traditio apostolica* became an object of lively debate [106].

These three discoveries - the origin of the Apostles' Creed as a fusion of two older elements, its distinctness from Eastern creeds, the connection with Hippolytus of Rome - may safely be said to have marked credal research for more than half a century. Before we can discuss the further development of this research, however, it is necessary once more to anticipate more recent contributions. First, we should discuss a theory which offers an alternative to Holl's account of the birth of R. Moreover, some developments in Hippolytan scholarship deserve our attention.

## 1.10 Another Modern Alternative: Kinzig

Wolfram Kinzig in his study "'... *natum et passum* etc.'" Zur geschichte der Tauffragen in der lateinischen Kirche bis zu Luther' [107] offers a new theory on the origin of R. He takes as his starting point a type of the baptismal questions which we first find

---

[105] Schwartz 1910 and Connolly 1916. See Botte 1963, IX-XI for a concise summary of their argument. These texts are the *constitutiones Apostolorum* (preserved in four different versions; CPG 1730), the *collectio Veronensis LV (53)* or Verona palimpsest (Latin; CPG 1731), the *sinodos Alexandrina* (preserved in three or four different versions again; CPG 1732), the *epitoma seu constitutiones per Hippolytum* (Greek; CPG 1741), the *canones Hippolyti* (Arabic; CPG 1742), and the *testamentum domini* (preserved in no less than six different versions; CPG 1743). Of these, the *collectio Veronensis*, the *sinodos*, and the *canones Hippolyti* seem to preserve the oldest material. See now Markschies 1999, 3-13.

[106] See De Ghellinck 1949, 148-185.

[107] Kinzig 1999a.

in the *Sacramentarium Gelasianum Vetus* (CPL 1899). The distinctive feature of this type is the use of a short second question, which refers to Christ's saving work with the words *natum et passum* only. Thus the *Sacramentarium Gelasianum Vetus* has: *Credis in deum patrem omnipotentem? Credis et in Iesum Christum filium eius unicum dominum nostrum, natum et passum? Credis et in spiritum sanctum, sanctam ecclesiam, remissionem peccatorum, carnis resurrectionem?* [108]

Kinzig then presents an overview of the baptismal questions as found in a great number of medieval liturgical sources. This reveals that the majority are of the shorter type found in the *Sacramentarium Gelasianum Vetus*, whereas only a minority represent the longer type of the baptismal questions in the *collectio Veronensis*. Moreover, Kinzig detects an echo of the shorter version of the second question in Arnobius the Younger's *commentarii in psalmos* (CPL 242), a Roman work of the first half of the fifth century. Kinzig finds that the first and third questions of the *Sacramentarium Gelasianum Vetus* agree exactly with the first and final four articles of *R*, but that the second question differs markedly from the Christological part of *R* [109].

Kinzig does not accept the more or less common explanation that this shorter second question is a deliberate abbreviation of the Christological section in *R* [110]. His main argument for this position is that the second 'Gelasian' baptismal question cannot be an abbreviation of a longer form because the baptismal questions, as sum-

---

[108] *Sacramentarium Gelasianum Vetus* 449 and 608; Mohlberg 1968, 74 and 95-96.

[109] Kinzig 1999a, 78-85.

[110] Thus already Kattenbusch 1894, 51 and 76n31; similarly Kelly 1976, 347 and 427. That this interpretation is not a new one appears from Charlemagne's *epistula ad Odilbertum* (written at some point in the years 809-812), where we read: *Nosse itaque per tua scripta aut per te ipsum uolumus ... de credulitate quomodo credendum sit in deum patrem omnipotentem, et in Iesum Christum filium eius natum et passum, et in spiritum sanctum, sanctam ecclesiam catholicam, et cetera quae sequuntur in eodem symbolo* (MGH, legg. II 1, 847). As the words *in eodem symbolo* clearly refer to the Apostles' Creed, and Charlemagne knew the Creed in a wording approximating to or identical with *T*, the conclusion seems safe that he understood the phrase *Natum et passum* as an abbreviation for the complete Christological sequence of articles three to eight.

maries of the faith to which the baptizand was about to pledge himself, would have to be as precise and complete as possible [111].

All this leads him to four conclusions: (1) the baptismal questions of the *Sacramentarium Gelasianum Vetus* are the immediate model for *R*; (2) in later times, different variants of the Apostles' Creed influenced the formulation of the baptismal questions; (3) the baptismal questions of the *Sacramentarium Gelasianum Vetus* are older than *R* (this follows from (1)); (4) they should probably be dated to the third century (because *R* appears in the fourth century) [112].

In other words: Kinzig dates *R* to the fourth century, considers it the first exponent of the Creed, and claims that it was formulated by analogy with the Roman baptismal questions which have been preserved for us in the *Sacramentarium Gelasianum Vetus* [113].

---

[111] Kinzig 1999a, 77: "Wäre es denn tatsächlich vorstellbar, daß ausgerechnet dann, wenn der Täufling durch seine(n) Paten seinen christlichen Glauben bekennen soll, die hierzu verwendete Formel abgekürzt ist? Muß diese Formel nicht schon deshalb vollständig sein, um Mißverständnisse auszuschließen und den geforderten Glauben so präzise wie möglich auszudrücken?" When formulating his conclusions, Kinzig gives a different argument ("Da nicht einzusehen ist, warum die Tauffragen (kurze Fassung) im ersten und dritten Artikel im Sinne von R hätten formuliert oder überarbeitet werden sollen, im zweiten aber nicht, ist anzunehmen, daß R auf der Basis der Tauffragen formuliert oder überarbeitet wurde und nicht umgekehrt"; Kinzig 1999a, 85-86 [similarly Kinzig 1999b, 544-545]), but this only makes sense if one accepts his earlier assumption. One could also formulate: "Da nicht einzusehen ist, warum R im ersten und dritten Artikel im Sinne der Tauffragen (kurze Fassung) hätte formuliert oder überarbeitet werden sollen, im zweiten aber nicht, ist anzunehmen, daß die Tauffragen auf der Basis von R formuliert oder überarbeitet wurden und nicht umgekehrt".

[112] Kinzig 1999a, 85-87. See also previous footnote.

[113] In Kinzig 1999b (557-558), this theory is combined in such a way with Vinzent's, that Marcellus of Ancyra becomes responsible for the composition of *R* by taking over the first and third Roman baptismal questions as they stood, replacing the second with a formulation of his own, and making this new product declaratory in form. Although this is not mentioned in Kinzig 1999b, this implies that Marcellus also adapted the wording of the first and third questions by omitting Πατέρα and adding Ζωὴν αἰώνιον: see above, chapter 1.4, footnote 35 and chapter 1.5, footnote 50. Kinzig and Vinzent do not seem to be aware that this again implies that, according to their theory, the Roman clergy, when taking over the middle section of Marcellus's doctrinal creed, must again have readapted the first and final four articles to the traditional Roman baptismal questions, but failed to do so with the third and fourth articles.

Although Kinzig does not mention Holl's theory, his own view seems to be incompatible with it. The question whether or not we should accept Kinzig's theory thus now arises.

## 1.11 Evaluation of Kinzig's Arguments

The mere fact that Holl and his contemporaries could point to the existence of the Christological sequence as a set formula as early as the second century [114] already speaks against Kinzig's theory. But there is is a more important argument rejecting Kinzig's account of the birth of *R*.

Kinzig claims that a formula with which people pledged themselves to Christian faith must bear a complete character and could not stand any abbreviations [115]. But this is only an assumption and as such it is probably false. As a matter of fact, all our available evidence points in the opposite direction. It has long been established that the Old Roman Creed (or, for that matter, its immediate predecessors) was indeed **a** summary of faith, but by no means **the** summary of faith of a certain group in a certain period. It was never intended to be complete in any way or to draw a line against heresies, which functions were covered by the *regula fidei*, not by creeds or baptismal questions [116]. This is confirmed by a fact to which Kinzig justly draws attention, namely that the shorter 'Gela-

---

[114] See above, chapter 1.9, footnote 101. See for the history of the Christological sequence in both the Eastern and the Western Church Smulders 1971, 360-363, Smulders 1975, 417-421, and Westra 1998, 142-145. Some of Kinzig's authorities for the early use of the phrase *natum et passum* (Kinzig 1999a, 89-91+nn316, 320, 321) also betray themselves as references to the more complete Christological sequence under closer scrutiny. Thus Tertullian *aduersus Praxean* I 1: ... *omnipotentem mundi conditorem* ... *ipsum dicit patrem descendisse in uirginem, ipsum ex ea natum, ipsum passum* ... (CPL 26; CCSL 2, 1159); Clement of Alexandria *excerpta ex Theodoto* 23, 3: διὸ καὶ καθ' ἑκάτερον ἐκήρυξε τὸν σωτῆρα, γεννητὸν καὶ παθητὸν διὰ τοὺς ἀριστερούς ... καὶ κατὰ τὸ πνευματικὸν ἐξ ἁγίου πνεύματος καὶ παρθένου (CPG 1139; GCS 17, 114); Hippolytus's *contra Noetum* 1, 2: καὶ αὐτὸν τὸν πατέρα γεγεννῆσθαι καὶ πεπονθέναι καὶ ἀποτεθνηκέναι (CPG 1902; Butterworth 1977, 43); Damasus *epigramma 39* 1-3: *Qui natum passumque deum repetisse paternas/ sedes atque iterum uenturum ex aethere credit,/ iudicet ut uiuos rediens pariterque sepultos* ... (CPL 1635; Ferrua 1942, 179). See for the last also Vinzent 1999, 187-188. A formula that is quoted in Kattenbusch 1900, 378n40 can be added to these.

[115] See above, chapter 1.10, footnote 111.

sian' questions remained in use all through the Middle Ages along-side their longer counterparts [117]. If his own hypothesis were right, however, we probably would not find a single trace of a shorter second baptismal question [118]. In other words, just as we see both longer and shorter sets of baptismal questions during the Middle Ages and later, nothing prohibits a similar cohabitation of two sets of baptismal questions in an earlier period - one combining a short Trinitarian formula with the Christological sequence, and one com-

---

[116] See Smulders 1971, 357-366 and 1975, 409-410. Compare also Hanson 1962, 64-68 and 1975, 170-171. In this latter reference, Hanson calls the Apostles' Creed "a curious and rather useless, though venerable relic". According to him, it "rather resembles a doctrinal washing line, and as a summary of the Christian faith it has as much consistency, coherence and logic as a washing line." It may be appropriate to point at least to one deliberate abbreviation of the Creed in the so-called Book of Dimma: see below, chapter 3.6, p. 221. Compare also the important observation by Smulders (1971, 363) concerning the Christological sequence in the *regula fidei*: "The sequence may be abridged, but not added to". Similarly Kattenbusch 1900, 486n15: "Die Verkürzung des christologischen Teils war leicht und einfach, die des dritten kaum möglich; dass er als Einheit so behandelt wird, dass alle Stücke wie auf derselben Linie stehend vorgebracht werden, entspricht zweifellos der eigentlich authentischen Idee des Symbols".

[117] Moreover, the *Sacramentarium Gelasianum Vetus* itself also clearly presupposes R or a very similar formula in the piece *Haec summa est fidei nostra ...*, where we read: *Hic unigenitus dei de Maria uirgine et spiritu sancto secundum carnem natus ostenditur. Hic eiusdem crucifixio et sepultura ac die tertia resurrectio praedicatur. Hic ascensio ipsius super caelos et consessio in dextera paternae maiestatis agnoscitur, uenturusque ad iudicandos uiuos et mortuos declaratur* (*Sacramentarium Gelasianum Vetus* 315; Mohlberg 1968, 50). The fact that this piece follows the *traditio* of the **Nicaeno-Constantinopolitan** Creed seems to guarantee the antiquity of its use in the Roman rite, and therefore of R or some similar form of the Apostles' Creed. Compare also Kattenbusch 1900, 436-437 and De Ghellinck 1949, 174.

[118] Similarly, a number of sets of baptismal questions that are stamped 'sonstige' by Kinzig (1999a, 172-183) clearly illustrate that the wording of the baptismal questions was far from sacrosanct. For example: *Credis patrem et filium et spiritum sanctum unius esse uirtutis? Credis patrem et filium et spiritum sanctum eiusdem esse potestatis? Credis patrem et filium et spiritum sanctum trinae ueritatis una manente substantia deum esse perfectum?* (*Missale Gallicanum Vetus* [CPL 1922] 172; Mohlberg 1958, 42). As far as I can tell, Kinzig does not comment upon these and other deviating formulations. It seems clear, however, that the wording of the baptismal questions continued to develop freely after that of the Apostles' Creed had already become more or less fixed. See also Kattenbusch 1900, 485-486n15 and 775n25. The question of the relationship between the many different sets of baptismal questions that are found in various martyr acts with R (see for example Kinzig 1999a, 128-132; compare also below, chapter 3.6, p. 210) deserves a separate study.

bining it with the phrase *natum et passum* [119]. It seems best, therefore, not to abandon the more traditional theory on the origin of *R*
as yet.

### 1.12 Hippolytus, the *traditio apostolica*, and the *collectio Veronensis*

When we thus regard the Apostles' Creed as a Roman text which
saw the light when the so-called Christological sequence (articles
three to eight) was combined with a set of Trinitarian baptismal
questions (articles one, two, and nine to twelve), the question to
which period this fusion should be dated arises. Here, the relationship between *R* and the set of baptismal questions that were first
discussed by Schwartz and Connolly definitely deserves our attention. Kelly, who still assumed that these questions hark back to
Hippolytus of Rome, who, according to the sources, must have been
active in the first third of the third century, tentatively dated the

---

[119] The question of which set first saw the light of day is difficult to answer.
Perhaps the fact that the longer set received the name *symbolum* may be taken
to favour its priority. In that case, the shorter set, using *natum et passum*, could
be explained either as the product of a parallel development or as a simple abbreviation. A similar parallel development is assumed by Kinzig (1999a, 105) to
explain the Milanese formula *Credis in dominum nostrum Iesum Christum et in
crucem eius?* (Ambrose of Milan, *de sacramentis* II 7 20; CPL 154, CSEL 73, 34).
The formula *natum et passum* is clearly very old, going back at least to Irenaeus
of Lyons, *aduersus haereses* III 16 6 (*c.* 200): *alterum quidem passum et natum, et
hunc esse Iesum, alterum autem qui in eum descendit, qui et ascendit iterum, et hunc
esse Christum adnuntiant* (CPG 1306; SChr 211, 310): see Kinzig 1999a 88-89 and
1999b, 547n50. An interesting place is also *acta Petri* 23: *Viri Romani, deus nascitur, crucifigitur?* (Lipsius 1891, 71). For the date and place of origin of the *acta
Petri*, see Bremmer 1998, 14-20, Westra 1998, 147, and Poupon 1998. It should
be observed, however, that all these places focus on the human side of Christ's
work, and that this circumstance would hardly favour the mentioning of one of
the other predicates from the Christological sequence. This has the important
implication again that the frequent use of *natum et passum* or some such phrase
in a **polemical** context is not sufficient grounds to legitimate the assumption
that the same phrase also figured in **liturgical** texts of the same period. Kinzig
does not pay any attention to this aspect in his study. The possibility that baptismal questions with *natum et passum* originated considerably later than Kinzig's
first authority for the phrase itself, and as a deliberate abbreviation in which the
complete formula was presupposed, should therefore not be abandoned too soon.
Compare also the cases where *et reliqua* or similar words are added to short baptismal questions: see for example Kinzig 1999a, 177; compare also chapter 1.10,
footnote 110 above.

birth of $R$ to the end of the second century [120]. Nevertheless, this theory appears to stand in need of revision for a number of reasons. First of all, it is necessary to say at least something about the extremely difficult and complicated problem of the date and origin of the *traditio apostolica*.

The fact is, that if a Hippolytan work called *traditio apostolica* (or rather: ἀποστολικὴ παράδοσις) ever existed, it should now be considered lost. Earlier scholarship, following Schwartz and Connolly, endeavoured to reconstruct its wording from a number of clearly related witnesses [121]. Nowadays, however, students of these sources are much more cautious and refrain from making any reconstructions, treating the 'sources' as separate texts [122]. Many of these texts seem to contain material of different provenance themselves, so that one should not connect them too quickly with a certain place and period [123]. Finally, many 'traditional' Hippolytan works are nowadays considered to belong to several, not necessarily Roman, traditions [124].

In the light of these trends in Hippolytan scholarship, it seems best to abstain from referring any longer directly to a third-century *traditio apostolica* [125]. The fact remains, however, that in the so-called *collectio Veronensis*, one of the traditional sources for the 'Hippolytan' *traditio*, we find a set of baptismal questions, the wording of which comes very close to $R$. This fragmentary liturgical text was written at the end of the fifth century but may well represent material from the last quarter of the fourth [126]. It would therefore

[120] See Kelly 1976, 126-130. I reproduced this date in Westra 1996b, 527.

[121] See above, chapter 1.9, footnote 105 and for example Dix 1937, lii-liii, Botte 1963, XI-XVII and XLIII-XLIV, and Geerard 1983, 226. An excellent evaluation of this project is now offered by Markschies 1999.

[122] See for example Metzger 1988 and 1991, Bradshaw 1989, Brent 1995, 184-195, 306, and 465, and, especially for the baptismal questions, Markschies 1999, 57-74.

[123] See Metzger 1991, 293 for this particular point.

[124] See Simonetti 1977, Geerard 1983, 256-257, and, for a more conservative opinion, Marcovich 1986. Brent 1995, 365-367 tries to offer a solution by assuming different traditions in a "multicultural Rome" (367). Compare also Simonetti 1996.

[125] Similarly Markschies 1999, 56: "Die sogenannte *Traditio Apostolica* scheidet als selbständige Quelle für historische und theologische Argumentationen aus."

[126] See Botte 1963, XVII-XX and Markschies 1999, 58.

be very improbable for there to be no relationship at all between
the baptismal questions of the *collectio Veronensis* and the Old
Roman Creed [127].

It now seems to be the place to present the text of the baptismal
questions of the *collectio Veronensis* in full:

> ... [128]
>
> *Credis in Christum Iesum, filium dei*
> *qui natus est de spiritu sancto ex Maria uirgine*
> *et crucifixus sub Pontio Pilato et mortuus est et sepultus*
> *et resurrexit die tertia uiuus a mortuis*
> *et ascendit in caelis*
> *et sedet ad dexteram patris*
> *uenturus iudicare uiuos et mortuos?*
> *Credis in spiritum sanctum*
> *et sanctam ecclesiam*
> *et carnis resurrectionem?* [129]

## 1.13 Baptismal Questions and Declaratory Formulae

The differences between this text and *R* are of two types. First of
all, the form of *R* is declaratory, using *Credo*, whereas the *collectio
Veronensis* has the interrogatory form, with *Credis*. Moreover, the
questions deviate from *R* in points of formulation and content.
The most important of these are the use of *Filium dei* (*R*: *Filium
eius unicum dominum nostrum*), of *Ex Maria* (*R*: *Et Maria*), of
*Viuus a mortuis* (*R*: *A mortuis*), and the absence of the Remission
of Sins (*R*: *Remissionem peccatorum*) [130].

As we have seen, Kelly considers baptismal questions
("interrogatory creeds") and declaratory summaries of faith ("creeds
in the strict sense of the term") as more or less interchangeable
manifestations of the same phenomenon, of which the baptismal
questions came first [131]. This enabled him to treat the formula of

---

[127] Moreover, there seems to be a distinct connection with Roman liturgical
usage: see Ysebaert 1962, 5 and 355n1.

[128] The first question has not been preserved in the Verona palimpsest.

[129] Text according to Botte 1963, 46 and 48 and Markschies 1999, 58.

[130] The other differences, which mainly concern construction and style, need
not concern us here. See below, chapters 2.2 and 2.3, pp. 79-80.

[131] See above, chapter 1.7, p. 38 and Kelly 1976, 40-49.

the *collectio Veronensis* as a variant of $R$ [132]. This point of view has been adopted by most subsequent scholars [133]. A different opinion is held by Kinzig, who clearly treats the Creed and the baptismal questions as two distinct kinds of text [134].

Two things should be distinguished here - Kinzig's contention that the baptismal questions are older than declaratory creeds, and his rigid distinction between the two. To begin with the first, his observation that we find baptismal questions much earlier than declaratory creeds [135] is, generally speaking, true. Nor is this surprising, as the rite of baptism, in which questions are asked and answered [136], is as old as the first century, whereas declaratory creeds are connected either with the *traditio* and *redditio symboli* (probably third-century rites) or with the doctrinal debates that start in the fourth century.

But among the various witnesses to the Apostles' Creed, this distinction does not seem to play a role any more. As Kinzig points out himself, both longer and shorter sets of baptismal questions follow the fluctuations in wording of the (declaratory) Creed by adding, for example, *Creatorem caeli et terrae, Sanctorum communionem*, and *Vitam aeternam*. As a matter of fact, it is difficult to see why a change in the wording of the baptismal questions could only come

---

[132] See below, chapter 1.14, pp. 60-61.

[133] See Hanson 1962, 62, Holland 1965, 262-263, Smulders 1970, 245-246 and 1975, 410, and Vokes 1978, 532. Differently Markschies 1999, 56 and 57-74 and Vinzent 1999, 189.

[134] See above, chapter 1.10, p. 51. See also Kinzig, 1999b, 550: "It follows ... first that we do possess a baptismal creed dating from pre-Constantinian times and secondly that the Roman Creed is indeed based on this baptismal creed which was, however, not in declaratory but in interrogatory form. This does not mean, however, that the *declaratory* (stress by Kinzig; LHW) creed itself had originally a liturgical Sitz im Leben. Rather, for reasons which we will explain below it had initially no place in the liturgy of baptism at all, but served to 'safeguard the Christian truth against heresy' and was, therefore, apologetic in character. The declaratory creed, therefore, has to be seen in the tradition of the rules of faith of the second and third centuries". Similarly Eichenseer 1960, 76, where, with a reference to Kelly (!), it is claimed that only from the sixth century on "kam es zur allmählichen unorganischen Verbindung und Vermischung von Frage- und Aussage-Credo".

[135] Also Kinzig 1999a, 87-88.

[136] See above, chapter 1.7, pp. 37-38. Irenaeus of Lyons seems to be the first direct witness to the use of baptismal questions: see Kinzig 1999a, 127.

about **after** a change in a declaratory form of the Creed had occurred [137]. One may well wonder whether Kelly's point of view, according to which the baptismal questions are nothing more than the Creed in interrogatory form, may not come near the truth after all [138].

This hypothesis is strengthened by a number of sources. Thus, in Pirminius's *scarapsus* we indeed find a declaratory as well as an interrogatory form of the same version of the Apostles' Creed [139]. Similarly, Martin of Braga in his *de correctione rusticorum* (CPL 1086; shortly after 572) refers to the Creed as *symbolum quod in* **baptismo** *accepistis, quod est:* **Credo** *in deum patrem omnipotentem*, but shows in the same work that he did not use a declaratory form of the Creed for baptism but rather three questions [140]. Compare also the formulation of the baptismal questions in pseudo-Maximus's *tractatus de baptismo 2* (= Anonymus Veronensis, *sermo 6*; CPL 222) 3: *In hoc ergo fonte antequam uos toto corpore tingueremus interrogauimus:* **Creditis** *in deum patrem omnipotentem?* ... [141], whereas (probably) the same author in another sermon states: *Postquam enim dixerimus in symbolo:* **Credo** *in deum patrem omnipotentem* ... [142]. In fact, the variety of manifestations of the Creed does not seem

---

[137] Thus Kinzig 1999a, 86: "Gleichzeitig läßt sich aber erkennen, daß das *Apostolicum* (bzw. seine Vorformen) zu unterschiedlichen Zeiten und in unterschiedlichen Regionen auf die Tauffragen zurückgewirkt hat". For a curious longer declaratory variant of the Creed that has clearly been influenced by the shorter baptismal questions, see Kattenbusch 1900, 748n36.

[138] Nevertheless, we again meet sets of baptismal questions without any direct resemblance to the Apostles' Creed in a later phase: see above, chapter 1.11, footnote 118. A possible explanation is that the Apostles' Creed spread over Western Europe alongside the rites of the *traditio* and *redditio symboli*, that is to say, in declaratory form. Thus, it is possible that churches adopted the (declaratory) Creed in these rites but remained faithful to older usage in their baptismal rites (or considered themselves freer to coin new formulations there).

[139] Pirminius, *scarapsus* 10 and 12; Jeckers 1927, 41 and 43. See below, chapter 3.2, pp. 136-137 for quotations and more details.

[140] See below, chapter 3.3, pp. 146-148.

[141] Sobrero 1992, 119.

[142] Pseudo-Augustine, *sermo 238* (= Anonymus Veronensis, *sermo 2*; CPL 368) 1; Sobrero 1992, 91. See below, chapter 4.1, footnote 3 for more details on this source. The reverse procedure also occurs: in the anonymous *tractatus symboli* CPL 1751, the Creed is first quoted as *Credo in deum patrem omnipotentem* ..., and immediately below referred to as ... *in symbolo quia dictum est: Credis in deum patrem omnipotentem?* (*tractatus symboli* 7-8; below, p. 470).

to limit itself to the declaratory and interrogatory forms only. Thus, Pirminius presents his own variant of the Creed for a third time at the end of the *scarapsus*, but now in exhortatory form [143]. Again, Priscillian of Avila makes his version of the Creed dependent on the repeated participle *credentes* [144]. Similarly, the use of the plural *Creditis* in the quotation above seems to be caused by the fact that a plural audience is addressed, rather than representing some collective rite of baptism. On the other hand, the existence of shorter or deviating sets of baptismal questions [145] also makes Kelly's simple equation a little bit too straightforward. It seems best, all in all, to maintain that the Apostles' Creed may be found both as a declaratory creed and in the guise of baptismal questions (not to mention other possibilities), but that each set of baptismal questions need not reflect the wording of the Creed.

To return to the '*traditio apostolica*', when we encounter such a situation in the fourth century and later, when at least some measure of liturgical fixity had been attained, it is difficult to imagine a rigid distinction between declaratory predecessors of $R$ (if there were any) and baptismal questions like those of the *collectio Veronensis* at an even earlier date [146]. In other words, the question of the priority of the declaratory or the interrogatory form seems to vanish. It just depends on whether the fusion between the Trinitarian and Christological formulae which gave birth to the Apostles' Creed [147] took place before or after the introduction of the *traditio* and *redditio symboli* [148]. In either case, the wording of the baptismal

---

[143] *Fratres, credite in deum patrem omnipotentem* ... (Pirminius, *scarapsus* 28a; Jeckers 1927, 64-65).

[144] See below, chapter 3.3, pp. 145-146.

[145] See above, chapter 1.11, footnote 118.

[146] Thus Eichenseer, who distinguishes strictly between the declaratory Creed and the baptismal questions (see above, footnote 134), nevertheless admits "die formale und inhaltliche Ähnlichkeit, ja nahezu Gleichheit von Symbolum und Tauffragen" and explains it as "nur zu verständlich, ... das die Vorbereitung abschließende Glaubensbekenntnis den schon vorhandenen sakramentalen Fragen nachzugestalten" (Eichenseer 1960, 96). This seems rather forced.

[147] See above, chapter 1.9, pp. 47-48.

[148] The occurrence of the second and ninth articles of the Creed with *Et* instead of *Credo* (in the declaratory form), together with the fact that the former seem to represent a more original formulation than the latter (see below, chapter 3.7, pp. 229 and 247) seems to favour the second possibility. But see Smulders 1970, 247-250 for the difficulties connected with this question.

questions of the *collectio Veronensis* clearly reveals that these questions on the one hand and *R* on the other may safely be taken as two variants of the Apostles' Creed.

## 1.14 The Relationship between the Baptismal Questions of the *collectio Veronensis* and *R*: Kelly and Holland

The question now, of course, is how these variants can be so different in their formulation and what is their exact relationship. Can one of the two be said to be more original than the other (or even be its parent), or are they sister forms, descending from some common ancestor? And, most importantly, does their combined evidence enable us to say something more about the early history and origin of the Apostles' Creed?

Perhaps surprisingly, the discovery of Hippolytus's '*traditio apostolica*' did not at first have much impact on the discussion of the origin of the Creed [149]. Most scholars in the first half of the twentieth century were ready to date the Apostles' Creed in the form of *R* to the end of the second century or to an even earlier period. The general trend seems to have been that the baptismal questions of the '*traditio apostolica*' were a more or less contemporaneous variant of *R*. In other words, Hippolytus was a witness to *R*, and *R* was a witness to the authenticity of the *traditio* [150].

But how should one regard the relationship between the two formulae now? Kelly, who sums up the results of his predecessors, of course still assumes an early third-century origin for the *traditio apostolica* [151]. He thinks that "several formulae were in current use" in Rome at this date and that *R* and the *traditio* testify to one of these each. According to him, no fixed formula existed at this time, and he speaks of the two creeds as "close relatives" that "jostled

---

[149] The 'dissolution' of the *traditio apostolica* has not made all earlier discussions worthless as most investigators have taken the *collectio Veronensis* as the most reliable witness to the wording of the 'real' *traditio apostolica*.

[150] See for example De Ghellinck 1949, 183-185. For more sophisticated positions, see *ibid.*, 152-157 and 257-258.

[151] He also uses Botte's reconstruction of the 'original' *traditio apostolica* rather than the text of the *collectio Veronensis*, but this does not make any difference for our discussion of his position.

against each other like the members of a family"[152]. Kelly's hypothesis about the flexibility of liturgical texts in the early third century may well be true but that does not relieve us of the task of explaining the differences between them. If both texts are really members of one family, what then is their exact family relationship? Moreover, even if liturgical formulae in general were not yet fixed in this period, the formulae that we possess have been written down so that they must at least have been fixed at that moment. So the question remains, did R derive from the questions of the *collectio Veronensis*, or did the questions derive from R, or did both formulae derive from a common source, or should we think of some other solution?

This question was only tackled some fifteen years after the publication of Kelly's monograph by David Larrimore Holland in an article that appeared in *Church History*[153]. Holland criticizes Kelly for the concept of credal families, which he considers unnecessary. If, he claims, there really were no fixed liturgical formulae at the beginning of the third century, that fact alone would account for most of the differences between the baptismal questions in the *traditio apostolica* and R. Moreover, he continues, we do not have a single proof that different Roman creed forms existed in the third century, nor do we have a trace of R at such an early date. Consequently, he proposes the theory that the baptismal questions in the *traditio apostolica* constitute the official third-century baptismal creed of Rome, and that R represents a later form of this same creed[154].

Holland's criticism of Kelly's position hits the mark in one respect - Kelly's concept of credal families is indeed unclear and it does not explain the relationship between what we find in the *collectio Veronensis* and R[155]. His own theory, however, is not fully

[152] Kelly 1976, 114-119.

[153] Holland 1965. A lucid summary of the argument in this article can be found in Holland 1970, 140n51.

[154] Holland 1965, 262-272.

[155] One remark of Kelly's is significant in this respect. He states (Kelly 1976, 118): "The other variations of language between H (Kelly's abbreviation for the baptismal questions of the '*traditio apostolica*'; LHW) and R ... serve to emphasize the difference between the two creeds. It is difficult to believe, for example, that anything was gained by altering the precise BY THE HOLY SPIRIT FROM THE VIRGIN MARY ... to R's simpler FROM THE HOLY SPIRIT AND THE VIRGIN MARY,

satisfactory either. First of all, his claim that the baptismal questions of the *traditio apostolica* represent an official Roman formula
from the beginning of the third century remains improbable in the
light of the evidence that has been brought into the field by
Kelly [156]. In the second place, his explanation of how *R* derives from
the baptismal questions in the *traditio* [157] is only partly convincing.
Of course, shifts in construction and formulation like those mentioned by Kelly [158], the change of *Mortuus* to *Sepultus*, or rather
the deletion of *Mortuus est et*, and the presence in *R* of *Vnicum*,
*Dominum nostrum*, and *Remissionem peccatorum*, can easily be
explained on the basis of Holland's assumption, but things are different with *R*'s use of *Eius* instead of *Dei* and the absence of *Viuus*.
Holland dismisses the first difference as a matter of stylistic variation [159], but this seems to be rather too easy. Of course, replacing
*Eius* with *Dei* is not a very radical change, but it is highly questionable whether the opposite could be done without comment. Besides,
the replacement of *Eius* by the more explicit *Dei* seems quite natural, but what reason could there be to insert *Eius* instead of *Dei*?
Similarly, it seems very improbable that the redactor(s) of *R* would
have ventured to delete the meaningful *Viuus*. Apparently, Holland
indeed felt some difficulties of this kind because he dwells for some
length on the reasons why Hippolytus might have inserted *Viuus*.
But according to his own theory, he should have explained its deletion by the redactor(s) of *R* [160]!

any more than by changing WILL COME TO JUDGE ... to WHENCE HE WILL COME
TO JUDGE". Although Kelly does not say so explicitly, he seems to suggest here
that, despite the then prevalent liturgical freedom, both texts were fixed in their
wording and that they did **not** influence each other's formulations. (Holland
[1965, 264-265] wrongly concludes from this passage that Kelly assumes the existence of **several** credal families in early third-century Rome.)

[156] In addition, it should be considered refuted by modern Hippolytan scholarship: see above, chapter 1.12, footnote 122.

[157] Holland 1965, 272-274.

[158] See footnote 155 above.

[159] Holland 1965, 273.

[160] Holland 1965, 273.

## 1.15 The Contribution of Smulders

A new solution to these problems was proposed in 1970 by Pieter Smulders in an article in *Bijdragen* [161]. Smulders partially accepts Holland's criticism of Kelly and starts a fresh investigation into the question of the relationship between $R$ and the baptismal questions of the *'traditio apostolica'* [162]. A new and fundamental element in his discussion is the consideration that the words *Vnicum* and *Dominum nostrum*, which are present in $R$, are not only absent from the baptismal questions of the *collectio Veronensis*, but also from a number of later variants of the Creed [163]. Smulders dismisses the explanation that churches, either deliberately or by accident, would have dropped these meaningful elements from their form of the Creed. According to him, therefore, the only possibility is that *Vnicum* and *Dominum nostrum* were not yet present in the Creed when other Western churches began to borrow this text from Rome for their own use. As the baptismal questions of the *'traditio apostolica'* do not exhibit these words either, he argues that these represent an earlier stage in the development of the Apostles' Creed in this respect than $R$ [164].

Smulders's ideas seem not to have received the attention they deserve [165]. Nevertheless, his point may well be fundamental. If his

[161] Smulders 1970. Three sequels to this article were published in 1971, 1975, and 1980.

[162] Smulders 1970, 245-246.

[163] *Vnicum* is absent from the forms of Faustus of Riez, the pseudo-Augustinian *liber testimoniorum fidei*, Augustine of Hippo (African form), Nicetas of Remesiana; *Dominum nostrum* from three variants that have been transmitted in different copies of a sermon by Caesarius of Arles as well as one of the credal variants in the Bobbio Missal; both are missing in the variants of Salvian of Marseilles, a certain Arian fragment from Illyria, and the Book of Dimma. These texts, not all of which were known to Smulders, will be presented and discussed in chapter 3 below. See for an overview of their different formulations of the second article chapter 3.7, pp. 225-227.

[164] Smulders 1970, 244 and 246-249.

[165] His name cannot be found in the bibliographies of Kelly 1976, Vokes 1978, or Ritter 1984. The two references to his work in Vinzent 1999 (246n835 and 353n1109) both seem to be unfair to me. In the first, the fact that Vinzent discards Smulders's (1970, 250-254) overview of credal variants because it contains sources "die in ihrer Zuschreibung und Datierung unsicher waren und sind" is rather arbitrary. In the second, Vinzent claims that Smulders says exactly the opposite of what he does say: compare Vinzent 1999, 353 ("Ältere *Regulae fidei*

contention that creeds tend to grow but never shrink is true - and
the evidence definitely points in that direction [166] - the absence of
certain usual formulations in variants of the Creed will have to be
taken as indicative of either age or conservatism. In particular,
Smulders's connection of the baptismal questions of the *collectio
Veronensis*, which are generally considered to be both Roman and
comparatively old, with later formulations from other parts of the
Western Church is convincing. When we find a number of variants
of the Creed without *Vnicum* or *Dominum nostrum*, and these words
are absent from an early Roman formulation as well, the conclusion
seems to be inevitable that these later Western forms derive from
precisely such a Roman form [167]. The presence of *Vnicum* and *Dominum nostrum* (or similar words) in the majority of the Western
forms [168] should thus be explained as due to the influence of the
later Roman variant *R*.

Smulders works out this hypothesis in such a way that he arrives
at the concept of 'pre-R', a form of the Apostles' Creed identical to
*R* except for the absence of *Vnicum* and *Dominum nostrum* and parent of all known variants of the Apostles' Creed [169]. But what is the
relationship between 'pre-R' and the baptismal questions of the *collectio Veronensis*? Smulders tentatively dates 'pre-R' [170] towards the

---

sind zum Teil reich, zum Teil arm in der Aufzählung der Daten vom irdischen
Dasein des Herrn bis zu seiner Himmelfahrt, auf jeden Fall variieren sie erhe-
blich und zeugen davon, daß diesbezüglich kein normatives Modell eines Sum-
mariums existierte") with Smulders 1971, 363: "But most Rules have a fully developed six or seven member Christological profession, running from the Virgin
birth to the second coming. As in the Creeds ..., this sequence shows a remarkable stability".

[166] See below, chapters 2.5 and 2.6, pp. 93-94.

[167] This conclusion seems to be supported by the striking fact that precisely
the words *Vnicum* and *Dominum nostrum* (or their counterparts), even when they
are present in a certain form of the Creed, hardly receive any attention in most
*expositiones symboli*: see Westra 1997, 419-420. This aspect might well be worth
closer investigation.

[168] See below, chapter 3.7 pp. 225-227.

[169] Smulders 1970, 246-247 and 1971, 350. Kattenbusch had already considered, but rejected, a similar theory: see Kattenbusch 1900, 594-595n189. Compare also Kelly 1976, 141-142 and Eichenseer 1960, 200-201. In Westra 1996b,
527, I did not yet fully appreciate the force of Smulders's arguments.

[170] That is, 'pre-R' as the parent form of all Western variants of the Creed.
Smulders's reasoning is obscured here by his ambiguous use of the term. Some-

middle of the third century [171]. According to him, therefore, it is later than the 'Hippolytan' baptismal questions which he considers to represent a "side branch" within the development of credal formulations in Rome [172]. Smulders adduces two arguments for this position. First of all, the model of the baptismal questions must have lacked the Remission of Sins, whereas this article "is present in R and is found in all Western Creeds" [173]. Secondly, Smulders considers the additions of *Mortuus* (or in his opinion: the replacement of *Sepultus* with *Mortuus*) and *Viuus* to be "hardly of any importance" [174] and thus denies them a place in the early history of the Apostles' Creed. To sum up: according to Smulders, the history of the Apostles' Creed begins with a formula which was the parent of all later variants, R included, whereas the baptismal questions of the *collectio Veronensis* are the result of the modification by Hippolytus of a still earlier form, but did not exert any direct influence upon the development of the Apostles' Creed.

## 1.16 A New Hypothesis: Proto-R

As has already been suggested above, Smulders's theory seems to hit the mark in two respects. First of all, it offers a plausible explanation for the circumstance that a number of formulations that we already meet in R are nevertheless absent from later forms of the Creed. Secondly, it explains the differences between R and the baptismal questions of the *collectio Veronensis* as differences between two forms that derive from a common ancestor. Nevertheless, this theory cannot be maintained in the form Smulders presented it in 1970.

times it seems to denote one and only one formulation ("Pre-R lacked the qualification ONE with God and with SON, and also the profession OUR LORD": Smulders 1970, 260), and sometimes any form of the Creed prior to R ("a pre-R Roman form", "a pre-R Creed": Smulders 1970, 245 and 260).

[171] Smulders 1970, 245.

[172] Smulders 1971, 350. Compare Smulders 1970, 247: "We may therefore conclude that Hippolytus took over an existing Roman Creed of good standing, in which he made a few smallish modifications ...".

[173] Smulders 1970, 244.

[174] Smulders 1970, 246. In addition, Smulders (*ibid.*) pays particular attention to the formulation of the tenth article. But this discussion relies too much on the assumption that the wording of the 'real' Hippolytan *traditio apostolica* can be recovered from the several source texts.

First, a modification is necessary which is connected with the formula of the *collectio Veronensis*. Smulders still ascribes this to Hippolytus of Rome and thus dates it to the beginning of the third century [175]. But we have seen that, in the light of modern Hippolytan scholarship, a late fourth-century date is much more probable [176]. Thus Smulders's special treatment of the baptismal questions of the '*traditio apostolica*' becomes unnecessary. *R* and these baptismal questions can simply be considered sisters, both being early forms of the Apostles' Creed.

Next, Smulders' evaluation of the presence of *Mortuus* and *Viuus* as well as the absence of *Remissionem peccatorum* in the baptismal questions of the *collectio Veronensis* seems to stand in need of correction. With regard to the latter, his remark that all Western forms of the Creed mention the Remission of Sins is not true - it is missing in two different versions of a sermon on the Creed that was composed by Caesarius of Arles [177]. Similarly, the additions of *Mortuus* and *Viuus* in the fourth and fifth articles also correspond to later Western developments [178]. Thus, the baptismal questions of the *collectio Veronensis* look more like a normal Western variant of the Creed which shares some of its features with *R*, some with later forms, and has some unique features as well, than the outcome of an isolated 'side branch' of the development of the Creed.

This is also suggested by a deviation from *R* in the 'Hippolytan' baptismal questions which Smulders does not mention, viz. the omission of the words *A mortuis* in the fifth article. This does not seem to be an idiosyncrasy or a scribal error but rather a variant which may be found in later forms of the Creed as well [179]. Thus, the combined evidence of *R*, the baptismal questions of the *collectio Veronensis*, and later Western forms of the Creed, points in the

---

[175] Smulders 1970, 241.

[176] See above, chapter 1.12, pp. 55-56.

[177] See below, chapter 3.2, footnote 75 with p. 124 and pp. 127-128.

[178] *Mortuus* is added in the variants represented by the same sermon of Caesarius of Arles, in Pirminius's *scarapsus*, in the *Missale Galicanum Vetus*, and in two variants in the Bobbio missal; *Viuus* may be found in the forms of the Creed that are offered by Martin of Braga, the Mozarabic *Missale Mixtum* and *Liber Ordinum Episcopalis*, Ildefonsus of Toledo, Etherius of Osma and Beatus of Liébana, and Nicetas of Remesiana: see below, chapter 3.7, pp. 234 and 238.

[179] Thus several Gallican, Spanish, and North Italian formulations: see below, chapter 3.7, p. 238.

direction of an original form of the Creed to which all known forms hark back, and which may therefore best be designated proto-R.

In the light of the foregoing, it seems possible to offer a reconstruction of proto-R. We shall indeed do so presently, but a number of considerations should perhaps be offered beforehand. First of all, it is important to remember that the reconstruction of the common parent of all known variants of the Creed does not necessarily represent the very first form of the Creed, viz. the product of the fusion between a Trinitarian formula [180] and the Christological sequence. Secondly, there is a certain degree of difference between two of our oldest variants of the Creed, R and the 'Hippolytan' baptismal questions, with respect to their construction. The baptismal questions make frequent use of Et to connect the several articles, whereas R usually prefers an asyndeton. It seems impossible to ascertain which should be considered original. When we follow the construction of R, therefore, this is an arbitrary choice inspired by the fact that later forms of the Creed strongly tend to do the same. Similarly, we choose to offer a reconstruction in Latin and in the declaratory form, although the original formulation of the Creed may well have been Greek and interrogatory in form. Here, we are again just following the majority of later variants [181].

As far as the date of proto-R is concerned, hardly anything definite can be said. We do not know whether it was born immediately before it spread over the Western church, or in a more remote past. Moreover, although it seems certain that the "great borrowing process" [182] has taken place, no single source seems to testify to the process itself. But if Cyprian of Carthage really testifies to the situation after the spread [183], Smulders's date of c. 250 [184] will be a safe *terminus ante quem* for the birth of proto-R.

---

[180] That is to say, a formula mentioning belief in the Father, the Son, the Holy Spirit, the Church, and the Resurrection of the Flesh.

[181] For the second and ninth articles, we choose the formulation with *Et*, not with *Credo*, as the former seem to be the more original of the two: see above, chapter 1.13, footnote 148. Also, in some other points of wording (the use of *Et* in the third article, the word order in the fourth and the fifth articles, the use of *Est* in the eighth) we shall follow R rather than the testimony of the *collectio Veronensis*. These cases will receive due discussion below: see chapter 3.7, pp. 233-235, 236, 239, and 245.

[182] Smulders 1970, 246.

[183] See above, chapter 1.6, footnote 58.

[184] See Smulders 1970, 244-245.

Proto-*R*, then, the hypothetical parent of all extant variants of
the Apostles' Creed, may be reconstituted in the following way:

> *Credo in deum patrem omnipotentem*
> *et in Christum Iesum, filium eius*
> *qui natus est de spiritu sancto et Maria uirgine*
> *qui sub Pontio Pilato crucifixus est et sepultus*
> *tertia die resurrexit*
> *ascendit in caelos*
> *sedet ad dexteram patris*
> *unde uenturus est iudicare uiuos et mortuos*
> *et in spiritum sanctum*
> *sanctam ecclesiam*
> *carnis resurrectionem.*

## 1.17 Summary and Closing Remarks

This is the point at which one should stop the investigation of
the origin of the Apostles' Creed. Despite the great number of publications, only a small number of conclusions seem to rest upon
positive evidence. The first of these is that the use of one uniform
formulation is only an eighth-century or younger phenomenon. This is
proved by the great number of different forms of the Creed which we
find between the fourth century and the eighth. These different forms
will be duly discussed in the third and fourth chapters of our study.

Next, the testimonies of Augustine, Ambrose, and Rufinus reveal
that the ancestor of all these variants must be sought in Rome.
These authors do not yield an exact date for this hypothetical
ancestor but, together with Cyprian of Carthage, they strongly suggest a third-century origin.

In the third place, the wording of the (or perhaps a) fourth-century Roman variant of the Creed is provided by Rufinus, a number
of anonymous manuscript witnesses, and to a lesser extent Marcellus of Ancyra.

In the fourth place, the wording of a number of later variants of
the Creed (among which the baptismal questions of the *collectio
Veronensis* hold an important place) leads to the conclusion that it
is not this fourth-century Roman formulation (*R*), but rather a
shorter and therefore older one (proto-*R*) that should be considered
the common parent of all extant variants of the Apostles' Creed. As

$R$ is considerably longer than proto-$R$, and $R$ belongs to the fourth century, it seems safe to date proto-$R$ prior to the second half of the third century. It is important to realize that one cannot say whether the declaratory formulation (connected with the rites of *traditio* and *redditio symboli*) or the interrogatory one (connected with baptism) should be considered original.

In the fifth place, the separate existence both of formulae to pledge belief in the Father, the Son, the Holy Spirit, the Church, and the Resurrection and of some commemorating Jesus Christ's Birth, Crucifixion and Death, Resurrection, Ascension, and Session at the Right Hand of God makes it extremely probable that the first variant of the Creed, be it proto-$R$ or an even earlier form, originated as the result of the fusion of precisely two such formulae. The date of this fusion is unknown.

It seems impossible, and is anyhow for our purposes unnecessary, to go beyond this. There are simply no sources to trace the formulations with which Roman Christians pledged themselves to the triune God further back [185]. Every statement about declaratory creeds or baptismal questions before the fusion of the Trinitarian and Christological formulae belongs to the realm of speculation. Nevertheless, since we have paid attention in the course of this chapter not only to various formulations of the Apostles' Creed but also to the Christological sequence, the *regulae fidei*, short baptismal questions, and private and synodal creeds, it seems appropriate to conclude with an account in which something is said about the mutual relationships of all these phenomena. It will be clear that this

---

[185] Sometimes Justin Martyr's Apology I 61, 3 (*c.* 150; CPG 1073) is used to reconstruct a set of earlier baptismal questions that antedate the questions of the *collectio Veronensis* (see for example Kelly 1976 72-73 and Hanson 1962, 60). Referring to baptism, Justin indeed writes: ἐπ᾽ ὀνόματος γὰρ τοῦ πατρὸς τῶν ὅλων καὶ δεσπότου θεοῦ καὶ τοῦ σωτῆρος ἡμῶν Ἰησοῦ Χριστοῦ καὶ πνεύματος ἁγίου τὸ ἐν τῷ ὕδατι τότε λουτρὸν ποιοῦνται (Goodspeed 1914, 70). But any reconstruction of a baptismal formula is uncertain. Moreover, the text does not provide any clue that Justin is referring to a formula either, so that it is better to leave Justin's Apology out of account here. Thus, Holland (1965, 280n52) and Smulders (1971, 359-360; compare also Vokes 1978, 532) take this passage as witnessing not baptismal questions, but the *regula fidei*. Similarly, Kinzig 1999a does not mention Justin in his overview of patristic sources for the baptismal questions either. Vinzent (1999, 196n703 and 341) is slightly more positive. Compare also above, chapter 1.13, footnote 136.

account does not claim to be anything more than at best a well-founded guess.

In a stimulating and much-quoted paper, Hans Freiherr von Campenhausen has argued that in the first two generations of the Church, three very short 'confessions' were in vogue - "Jesus is the Christ", "Jesus is God's Son" and "Jesus is Lord" [186]. According to Von Campenhausen, these formulae were not confined to certain liturgical contexts but could best be characterized as tags or slogans that were used time and again by members of the small Christian community [187]. Their principal function was the individual or communal expression of the acceptance of Jesus as the Lord of one's life [188]. Quite soon, however, a different kind of 'confession' was formulated to emphasize within the context of the docetist controversy that Jesus had really been man. This was the statement "Jesus has come in the flesh" [189]. This could be stamped the first Christian doctrinal formula and it soon grew into complex statements that closely resemble the Christological sequence of the later *regula fidei* and Apostles' Creed [190].

As far as this antidocetist type of confession is concerned, Von Campenhausen suggests that it is the direct ancestor of the antignostic *regula fidei* that crops up in the second century [191], and this seems quite plausible. But what happened to the first type of confession? Von Campenhausen seems to think that it just faded away when the second type arose [192], but this is hardly convincing. It may be true that acclamations and private confessions were at a certain

---

[186] Von Campenhausen 1972, 215-224.

[187] Von Campenhausen 1972, 231-235. Nevertheless, if such a tag really was a **formula**, it must have originated in **one** specific context. Von Campenhausen seems to be blind to this implication of his theory.

[188] Von Campenhausen 1972, 225-226. A similar set of 'first confessions' with the same function was reconstructed by Ferdinand Hahn in 1980 (Hahn 1980, 3-7). I cannot see why Hahn (1980, 14n7) regards Von Campenhausen's picture as "eine wesentlich andere Beurteilung der Frühgeschichte des christlichen Bekenntnisses".

[189] Von Campenhausen 1972, 235-238. Hahn (1980, 8-10) assumes an even older more or less doctrinal confession which probably ran "God raised him from the dead". He points out that the 'original' three confessions are associated with the verb ὁμολογέω, whereas πιστεύω is used for this second type.

[190] Von Campenhausen 1972, 238-247.

[191] Von Campenhausen 1972, 253.

[192] Von Campenhausen 1972, 235.

moment no longer felt to be fit for general use, but that does not imply that such confessions completely disappeared. The testimony of Justin clearly suggests that in second-century Rome, in some way or another, the baptizand's faith in the triune God was mentioned [193]. It could be surmised, then, that an original Trinitarian [194] baptismal 'creed', either declaratory or interrogatory, is the second-century successor of the first-century 'general' acclamations and confessions [195].

The picture that arises from all this is the following. In the first century, short, purely Christological acclamations and confessions were used in various Christian contexts. By the turn of the century, a slightly longer but still purely Christological confession arose for antidocetist purposes which gave birth to the so-called Christological sequence before 150 [196]. In the meantime, the older private confessions remained in use in the baptismal context. Maybe for antignostic reasons, *regulae fidei*, taking up the older Christological sequence, as well as Trinitarian baptismal formulae, were born. At some point between 150 and 250 the Christological sequence was fused with just such a Trinitarian baptismal formula in Rome [197]. The hypothetical Roman creed proto-*R* which, probably from the third century onwards, spread all over the Latin Church and was expanded in different ways in different places, was the (or a) fruit

---

[193] See above, footnote 185.

[194] It is important to bear in mind, however, that a Trinitarian structure, however natural to us, only gradually imposed itself upon both baptismal formulae and *regulae fidei*: see for example Stenzel 1958, 83-93, Smulders 1971, 362-363, Kelly 1976, 40-42, Kleinheyer 1989, 30 and 47, and now Vinzent 1999, 339-343. Thus also Von Campenhausen, though denying the existence of baptism in Jesus's name alone: see Von Campenhausen 1971, 5-7 and 16. Differently Rordorf 1995, 53.

[195] Compare Smulders's theory that the wording of the first article of the Creed goes back to an acclamation: see Smulders 1980, 11-14. Similarly Young 1991, 13: "Creeds have their genesis in doxology ...".

[196] See for a more sophisticated account of the origin of the Christological sequence Smulders 1975, 417-420.

[197] Hahn (1980, 13) considers this to be a fusion between his original two types of confession. In his view, the second type not only accounts for the Christological sequence, but also for the fact that this new creed began with the word πιστεύω. For a similar but much less detailed account of this process, see Rordorf 1995, 53-54.

of this process [198]. In the fourth century, synodal and private creeds took over the function of the *regula fidei*.

From this moment on, creeds came to be regarded as inviolable summaries of faith, and the era of credal studies, which still continues, can be said to have begun. Despite this view, however, the free development of the Apostles' Creed continued for three or four centuries more. It is to the study of this development that we shall now turn.

[198] For the question whether proto-*R* was born as a declaratory or as an interrogatory formula, see above, chapter 1.13, p. 59 with footnote 148.

# CHAPTER TWO

## Changes in the Form of the Apostles' Creed

### 2.1 The Traditional Explanation: Regional Types

At some point between the birth of proto-$R$ and the end of the fourth century, the Apostles' Creed spread throughout the Western Church [1]. It figured most prominently in the rites of the *traditio* and *redditio symboli*, but was also used during baptism, as the existence of the interrogatory form demonstrates [2].

The most striking feature of the form of the Apostles' Creed during this period is its diversity. As far as we can tell, no two forms of the Creed from this period are exactly identical [3]. This situation continued until the days of Charlemagne, who in 811-813 decreed the use of one and the same form of the Creed for all clergy in his realm. We do not have any direct knowledge of the form he favoured, but it was in all probability the so-called *textus receptus* or $T$, which attained a monopoly in the Frankish countries from the ninth century onwards [4]. Since Rome followed suit at some date in the ninth, tenth, or eleventh century [5] and the deviant forms of the Creed in Africa and Spain had already disappeared due to the Arab invasions, it is indeed only $T$ or some practically identical

---

[1] See Smulders 1970, 237-238 and 244, Kelly 1976, 30-33 and 179-181, and Vokes 1978, 536-537.

[2] See above, chapter 1.7, p. 37 and 1.13.

[3] Thirty-eight different witnesses to the form of the Creed will be presented in chapter 3 below, and fifteen more in chapter 4. Of these, only the two Roman ones (LEO and ARN) seem to refer to the same variant: see below, chapter 3.6, pp. 210-211.

[4] See Kelly 1976, 423-426 and Vokes 1978, 541-542. The words of Kattenbusch (1894, 196-199) on the selection of $T$ still deserve attention. Nerney (1952, 374) gives a different account, according to which $T$ was already in general Gallican use before Charlemagne ascended the throne.

[5] See Kelly 1976, 426-434 and Vokes 1978, 542-543. At an earlier date, the Roman church had already shifted from $R$ (or a similar form) to the Nicaeno-Constantinopolitan Creed for the use in the rites of *traditio symboli*, *redditio symboli*, and baptism. Something similar seems to hold true for the Spanish churches: see Kelly 1976, 346-348. For a different opinion, see Burn 1909, 8-9.

form that we find when we encounter the Apostles' Creed after 800 [6].

The credal variety in the period from the fourth down to at least the eighth century has led scholars to compare the several variants. Since Kattenbusch, the first to claim the existence of "Typen von provinzialem Charakter" [7], students of the Creed have been convinced that certain regional peculiarities can be detected in the various forms of the Creed during the period under discussion. Thus, Hahn clearly presupposes the same idea when he speaks about "die allmähliche Entwickelung ..., welche in den einzelnen Ländern das Symbol durchgemacht hat" [8]. Smulders also mentions "a neat tendency toward regional forms" [9], whereas Kelly speaks of "a number of regional sub-groups with their own local idiosyncrasies" [10] and Vokes of "Provinzialsymbole" [11]. Most of these authors, probably bearing in mind natural boundaries like mountains and seas, mention the regions of Gaul, Spain, Africa, and Northern Italy (with the exception of Rome, we do not have any witnesses from Southern Italy), to which sometimes those of the British Isles and the Latin Balkans are added [12].

Unfortunately, this is the point where most scholars stop. Not much thought has hitherto been paid to the question of how these

---

[6] Of course, the use of older, shorter variants of the Apostles' Creed may have continued in a number of churches. The paucity of the sources hardly allows any detailed statements here. But though the process itself remains for the most part obscure, its outcome is clear enough - at a certain moment, $T$ came to be considered the one and only official form of the Apostles' Creed. Nevertheless, even the official acceptance of $T$ did not banish all variety in the wording of the Creed. See above, chapter 1.1, footnotes 3 and 7. Similarly, Kelly (1976, 425-427) speaks of "trivial variations" (p. 427) that continue to occur. Kattenbusch (1900, 973n18) even claims: "Immerhin ist auch T in den Kleinigkeiten seines Wortlauts offenbar einer gewissen Verwilderung ausgesetzt gewesen".

[7] Kattenbusch 1894, 193-195 and 1900, 778-779.

[8] Hahn 1897, V-VI.

[9] Smulders 1970, 244.

[10] Kelly 1976, 179-180.

[11] Vokes 1978, 535.

[12] Such a division is supported by the different types of Latin liturgy as well as the frontiers between the various Romance languages. See, for example, Gamber 1958, 8-9 and Elcock 1975, 13-15.

regional credal types came into existence [13]. Not even a reliable overview of the most important variants of the Creed is available [14]. Nor has a fundamental question yet been answered, viz., what are the concrete features of these regional types? Do we know what it is exactly that distinguishes a Gallican form of the Creed from a Spanish or an Italian one? [15] As there are still some fifteen anonymous credal commentaries which have not yet been ascribed to a specific region and period, this last question is not without relevance [16].

Therefore, it seems worthwhile to conduct a fresh investigation of the various witnesses to those regional types of the Apostles' Creed. We intend to do two things here. In the present chapter, we shall try to gain a better picture of the processes that played a role in the divergence of forms of the Creed in the period under discussion, and to find out whether these processes favoured the birth of regional credal types. In other words, what was it that made proto-$R$ and its descendants change, and could it bring about regional diversity? In chapter 3, we shall examine as many extant variants of the Creed as possible to see whether they really testify to the existence of regional types of the Apostles' Creed, and if so, what are their features. In chapter 4, then, we shall discuss a number of credal variants of unknown origin and try to assess their dates and provenances.

---

[13] Smulders, who claims that "the remodeling on the Roman example" (suggesting that all Western churches already had some kind of creed and remodelled this on the basis of proto-$R$) "could hardly be achieved without the active collaboration of the bishops of Rome and the major sees in the provinces" (Smulders 1971, 355) seems to be the only exception, but even then, his remark is more concerned with a process of spread than with a process of change.

[14] August and Georg Ludwig Hahn's *Bibliothek der Symbole und Glaubensregeln der alten Kirche* (originally 1842, third edition 1897, reprinted 1962) is still useful for purposes of orientation, but is of course hopelessly out of date. The same holds true for Kelly's much shorter overview with discussion (Kelly 1976, 172-181). Kelly presents only a small part of the available witnesses, sometimes even from editions that were already outdated when he wrote his book.

[15] Only Kattenbusch (1894, 194-199) reflects on the features of his three regional types, but he arrives at distinctions of a rather general nature. He is slightly more positive in Kattenbusch 1900, 778-779.

[16] See below, chapter 4.

2.2 Two Types of Credal Variety

First of all, it is essential to reflect on the nature of the differences between the various local forms as they have come down to us. For this purpose, it will be convenient to re-examine the three variants of the Creed that were introduced in the previous chapter: the Old Roman Creed (R), the baptismal questions of the *collectio Veronensis* (for which Kelly introduced the designation *H*), and the *textus receptus* (T) [17]. Moreover, we have postulated a common parent for all three variants which we have baptized proto-R [18].

When we compare R, H, and T with each other and with proto-R, there seem to be two ways in which one form can differ from another. Sometimes the difference concerns points of wording and construction, and sometimes it affects the contents of the Creed. Examples of the first type are *Ex Maria uirgine* (H, T) versus *Et Maria uirgine* (R), *Crucifixus sub Pontio Pilato* (H) versus *Qui sub Pontio Pilato crucifixus est* (R), and the three formulations *Ascendit ad caelum* (T), *Ascendit in caelos* (R), and *Et ascendit in caelis* (H). Examples of the second type are: *Creatorem caeli et terrae* (present in T, absent from R and proto-R), *Descendit ad inferna, Sanctorum communionem,* and *Et in uitam aeternam* (present in T, absent from H, R, and proto-R), *Vnicum, Dominum nostrum,* and *Remissionem peccatorum* (present in T and R, absent from H and proto-R), and *Filium dei* (H) versus *Filium eius* (T, R, and proto-R). How did these two types of difference come about in the history of the Apostles' Creed?

2.3 Awareness and Appreciation of Credal Variety in the Sources

At this point, it is important to examine the way in which the local churches regarded the Apostles' Creed in the period under discussion. That the Creed really stemmed from the Apostles themselves is claimed for the first time towards the end of the fourth century by Ambrose (340-397): *Sancti ergo apostoli in unum conuenientes breuiarium fidei fecerunt ... Ergo apostoli sancti conuenientes*

---

[17] See above, chapter 1.3, pp. 26-27 and chapter 1.4, chapter 1.12, and chapter 1.1, pp. 21-22.

[18] See above, chapter 1.16.

*fecerunt symbolum breuiter* [19] and can be found in various later Latin commentaries on the Creed [20]. Kattenbusch is probably right when he says that the idea of the Apostolic origin of the Creed was generally accepted in the West and had spread with the text itself [21].

This widespread idea of the Apostolic origin of the Creed would not of course facilitate the making of deliberate changes in its text. This is supported in an indirect way by texts that stress the importance of the faithfulness of the Roman church to the original text [22] or urge the catechumens to learn the Creed by heart and never to forget or to change it [23]. Ambrose is even more explicit in his *explanatio symboli*: *Si unius apostoli scripturis nihil est detrahendum, nihil addendum, quemadmodum nos symbolum quod accepimus ab apostolis traditum atque compositum commaculabimus? Nihil debemus detrahere, nihil adiungere* [24].

[19] Ambrose of Milan, *explanatio symboli* (CPL 153) 2-3; CSEL 73, 3-4). See also Ambrose's *epistula extr. coll. 15 (Maur. 42)* 5: *Sed si doctrinis non creditur sacerdotum ... credatur symbolo apostolorum* (CPL 160; CSEL 82, 3, 305).

[20] See Quodvultdeus of Carthage, *de symbolo 2* I 1: *Sacramentum symboli quod accepistis ... noueritis hoc esse fidei catholicae fundamentum, super quod aedificium surrexit ecclesiae, constructum manibus apostolorum et prophetarum* (CPL 402; CCSL 60, 335), Eusebius 'Gallicanus', *sermo 2 de symbolo* 1: *Ita apostoli et ecclesiarum patres ... elegerunt uerba breuia et certa ... et hoc symbolum nominauerunt* (CPL 977; CCSL 101B, 829), and Rufinus of Aquileia, *expositio symboli* 2: *Omnes igitur* (viz. the Apostles) *... breue ... praedicationis indicium ... componunt atque hanc credentibus dandam esse regulam statuunt. Symbolum autem hoc multis et iustissimis ex causis appellari uoluerunt* (CPL 196; CCSL 20, 134).

[21] Kattenbusch 1900, 18-20.

[22] Ambrose of Milan, *epistula extr. coll. 15 (Maur. 42)* 5: *... symbolo apostolorum, quod ecclesia Romana intemeratum semper custodit et seruat* (CSEL 82, 3, 305); Rufinus of Aquileia, *expositio symboli* 3: *... in diuersis ecclesiis aliqua in his uerbis inueniuntur adiecta. In ecclesia tamen urbis Romae hoc non deprehenditur factum ...* (CCSL 20, 136).

[23] For example Augustine of Hippo, *sermo 215 de symbolo* 1: *Accepistis ergo et reddidistis quod animo et corde semper retinere debetis, quod in stratis uestris dicatis, quod in plateis cogitetis, et quod inter cibos non obliuiscamini, in quo etiam dormientes corpore corde uigiletis* (CPL 284; Verbraken 1958, 18) and 'Eusebius Gallicanus' *homilia 9 de symbolo* 1: *Superest, carissimi, ut hoc paucorum uerborum salubre compendium et numquam delendum ex nostro corde ita teneamus, ita intimis sensibus recordemur, ita incessabiliter meditemur, siue in secreto siue in publico, siue in domo sedentes siue in itinere gradientes, ut prius anima a corpore quam munimen istud ab anima separetur* (CPL 966; CCSL 101, 99).

[24] Ambrose of Milan, *explanatio symboli* 7 (CSEL 73, 10).

On the other hand, the several different formulations of the Creed yielded by the sources prove undeniably that variety in the wording of the Creed was a general phenomenon in the early Western Church. Moreover, there are at least two authors of whom it is certain that they were conscious of this variety.

The first of these is Rufinus of Aquileia, who clearly claims acquaintance with several different forms of the Creed: *In ceteris autem locis ... propter nonnullos haereticos addita quaedam uidentur* and *Orientales ecclesiae omnes paene ita tradunt ...* [25]. Fortunately for our purpose, Rufinus enables us to identify two of these forms more exactly. First of all, he starts most if not all sections of his exposition with a quotation of the relevant article. Since Rufinus states that in expounding the Creed he will follow the form of the Aquileian church with which he was baptized himself [26], we are in a position to reconstruct a form of the Creed that must have been in use in late fourth-century Aquileia [27]. Secondly, Rufinus also mentions a form of the Creed which he calls *ecclesiae Romanae symbolum* [28]. This form may safely be equated with *R*, the fourth-century Roman form of the Creed. Rufinus indicates where these two forms of the Creed differ [29].

The fact that Rufinus draws attention several times to differences between his own Aquileian form of the Creed and that of the Roman church of his day enables us to say something more about his appreciation of these differences. For that purpose, it will be convenient to present the text of our reconstruction of the Aquileian form of the Creed as it is yielded by Rufinus's *expositio*. This reconstruction runs as follows:

> *Credo in deum patrem omnipotentem, inuisibilem et impassibilem*
> *et in Iesum Christum, unicum filium eius, dominum nostrum*
> *qui natus est de spiritu sancto ex Maria uirgine*
> *crucifixus sub Pontio Pilato et sepultus*
> *descendit in inferna*

[25] Rufinus of Aquileia, *expositio symboli* 3 and 4; CCSL 20, 136 and 137. For a similar statement, see above, footnote 22.

[26] Rufinus of Aquileia, *expositio symboli* 3: *Nos autem illum ordinem sequemur, quem in Aquileiensi ecclesia per lauacri gratiam suscepimus* (CCSL 20, 136).

[27] See below, chapter 3.5, pp. 196-199 for the relevant quotations and details.

[28] See below, footnote 32.

[29] This has, despite various criticisms, been sufficiently demonstrated by Kelly: see Kelly 1976, 102 and 104-107. See also above, chapter 1.4, pp. 28-29.

*tertia die resurrexit*
*ascendit in caelos*
*sedet ad dexteram patris*
*inde uenturus iudicare uiuos et mortuos*
*et in spiritum sanctum*
*sanctam ecclesiam*
*remissionem peccatorum*
*huius carnis resurrectionem* [30].

The points in which this form of the Creed deviates from $R$ [31] are the following: the addition of the words *Inuisibilem et impassibilem* to the first article, the formulation of the second article with *Iesum Christum* ($R$: *Christum Iesum*) , *unicum filium eius* ($R$: *filium eius unicum*), the use of the preposition *Ex* in the third article ($R$: *Et*), the absence of *Qui* in the fourth article and the position of *Crucifixus* ($R$: *Crucifixus est*) before instead of after *Sub Pontio Pilato*, the addition of the Descent to Hell, the absence of *A mortuis* from the fifth article, the formulation of the eighth article with *Inde* ($R$: *Vnde*) and without *Est*, and the addition of *Huius* to the twelfth article.

All in all, however, Rufinus mentions only three of these differences in his commentary. These comprise the Aquileian addition of the words *Inuisibilem et impassibilem* to the first article, the presence of the Descent to Hell, and the formulation of the last article as *Huius carnis resurrectionem* [32]. All the other differences are passed over in silence. Since Rufinus makes it abundantly clear that he considers the Roman form of the Creed to be the original one, and it is the Creed rather than its Aquileian variant that he wants to comment upon, the inevitable conclusion is that Rufinus does not

---

[30] For an extensive discussion of this reconstruction, see below, chapter 3.5, pp. 196-199 again.

[31] For the text of $R$, see above, chapter 1.3, pp. 26-27.

[32] Rufinus of Aquileia, *expositio symboli* 5: *His additur: Inuisibilem et impassibilem. Sciendum quod duo isti sermones in ecclesiae Romanae symbolo non habentur* (CCSL 20, 140), *expositio symboli* 16: *Sciendum sane est quod in ecclesiae Romanae symbolo non habet additum: Descendit in inferna* (CCSL 20, 152), and *expositio symboli* 41: *Et ideo satis cauta et prouida adiectione ecclesia nostra symboli docet, quae in eo quod a ceteris traditur: Carnis resurrectionem, uno addito pronomine tradit: Huius carnis resurrectionem* (CCSL 20, 177). See for more details below, chapter 3.5, footnotes 357, 358, and 365.

fail to mention such a substantial number of differences out of neglect or carelessness, but rather because he does not regard them as differences at all.

The three deviations which Rufinus mentions explicitly all have some real theological significance (at least in the eyes of Rufinus) [33], and most if not all of the differences that are passed over by him are of a linguistic or stylistic nature [34]. Thus, we may formulate the following rule: for Rufinus, the only real differences between two forms of the Creed are differences which affect its content, and differences between two forms of the Creed with respect to wording and style are not differences at all. In other words, although, in Rufinus's opinion, the original variant of the Creed has a second article which runs *Et in Christum Iesum, filium eius unicum dominum nostrum*, he may freely present the same article in the wording *Et in Iesum Christum, unicum filium eius, dominum nostrum* without, in his opinion, changing the Creed. On the other hand, when the Creed originally begins with the article *Credo in deum patrem omnipotentem*, and Rufinus adds the words *Inuisibilem et impassibilem* to it, he considers this to be a deviation from the Creed, and feels obliged to explain and defend it.

[33] See Rufinus, *expositio symboli* 5: *His additur: Inuisibilem et impassibilem. Sciendum quod duo isti sermones in ecclesiae Romanae symbolo non habentur. Constat autem apud nos additos haereseos causa Sabellii* ... (CCSL 20, 140), *expositio symboli* 16 and 26: *Sciendum sane est quod in ecclesiae Romanae symbolo non habet additum: Descendit in inferna. Sed neque orientis ecclesiis habetur hic sermo. Vis tamen uerbi eadem uidetur esse et in eo quod sepultus dicitur. Sed quoniam erga scripturas tibi diuinas amor et studium subiacet, sine dubio dices mihi oportere haec magis euidentibus scripturae diuinae testimoniis approbari* ... *Sed et quod in infernum descendit euidenter praenuntiatur in Psalmis, ubi dicit: Et in puluerem mortis deduxisti me. Et iterum* ... (CCSL 20, 152-153 and 160-161), and *expositio symboli* 43: *Quod enim adiunctum est: Huius, uide quam consonum sit omnibus his quae de exemplis diuinorum uoluminum memorauimus. Quid enim aliud indicatur in dictis Iob, quae superius exposuimus, cum dicit quia: Resuscitabit pellem meam, quae haec nunc haurit, id est, quae ista tormenta perpetitur? Nonne aperte dicit huius carnis resurrectionem futuram, huius inquam quae tribulationum et temptationum cruciamenta nunc sustinet? Sed et apostolus* ... (CCSL 20, 179).

[34] The use of *Ex* instead of *Et* may have originated in a desire for more theological precision (see below, chapter 3.7, pp. 232-233), but as Rufinus does not draw attention to the use of the preposition here, it seems safe to assume that he did not assign it any special importance. The absence of *A mortuis* after *Resurrexit* (present in *R*) should perhaps not be stamped as a purely stylistic matter, but on the other hand does not seem to have any bearing on the meaning of the article.

The other author of whom it is certain that he knew of at least two different forms of the Apostles' Creed is Augustine of Hippo. In several of his writings he provides us with clear quotations of the Creed. What is important for us here, is that these quotations as a group do not testify to one and the same form of the Creed, but rather to two distinct variants. The first of these may be found in *sermo 213* (CPL 284; before 410) and *sermo de symbolo ad catechumenos* (CPL 309; after 418), the second in *sermo 215* (CPL 284; date unknown) [35]. The first two texts are sermons that were held on the occasion of the *traditio symboli*, the third on that of the *redditio symboli*. Perhaps surprisingly, Augustine never so much as mentions this unique procedure, let alone offers a reason for it. Less surprisingly, scholarship has been searching for an explanation for this situation since it became aware of it. The commonly accepted explanation is that Augustine, having been baptized in Milan, first learnt the text of the form of the Creed that was in use in the Milanese church and kept using it throughout his life as his own 'personal' form but, working in Hippo, did not break with local liturgical tradition there and thus did not abolish the use of the local credal variant of his North African bishopric [36].

It will be convenient to present the text of the two forms of the Creed to which Augustine testifies here. First of all, the variant that may be reconstructed from his *sermo 213* and *sermo de symbolo ad catechumenos* is the following:

*Credo in deum patrem omnipotentem*
*et in Iesum Christum, filium eius unicum dominum nostrum*
*qui natus est de spiritu sancto et uirgine Maria*
*sub Pontio Pilato crucifixus et sepultus*
*tertia die resurrexit a mortuis*
*ascendit in caelum*
*sedet ad dexteram patris*

[35] For the dates, see below, chapter 3.5, footnote 324 and chapter 3.4, footnote 210.

[36] Thus already, following Caspari, Kattenbusch 1894, 91-92 and 1900, 13n8. See also Eichenseer 1960, 105-107, Smulders 1970, 237n10, Kelly 1976, 172-173 and 175, Vokes 1978, 535-536. Of these authors, Kattenbusch and Smulders consider *sermo de symbolo ad catechumenos* as a spurious work, but they have not been able to convince the majority of Augustinian scholarship. See below, chapter 3.5, footnote 325.

*inde uenturus iudicaturus uiuos et mortuos*
*et in spiritum sanctum*
*sanctam ecclesiam*
*remissionem peccatorum*
*carnis resurrectionem* [37].

Next, the form of the Creed that is presented by Augustine's *sermo 215* runs thus:

*Credo in deum patrem omnipotentem, uniuersorum creatorem, regem*
  *saeculorum, immortalem et inuisibilem*
*(credo?) et in filium eius Iesum Christum, dominum nostrum*
*natum de spiritu sancto et uirgine Maria*
*crucifixum sub Pontio Pilato et sepultum*
*tertia die a mortuis resurrexit*
*ascendit in caelum*
*sedet ad dexteram patris*
*inde uenturus est iudicare uiuos et mortuos*
*(credo?) (et?) in spiritum sanctum*
*[remissionem peccatorum*
*resurrectionem carnis]*
*in uitam aeternam*
*per sanctam ecclesiam* [38].

[37] It should perhaps be pointed out again that Augustine himself does not link this form of the Creed with Milan in any way. Nevertheless, the fact that he was baptized there at the hands of Ambrose, as well as the close resemblance between this form and that of Ambrose's *explanatio symboli* (see below, chapter 2.4, pp. 87-88), seem to be sufficient grounds for the traditional explanation. For more details and a full discussion of our reconstruction, see below, chapter 3.5, pp. 185-189.

[38] For the use of brackets, square brackets, and questions marks, see below, chapter 3.1, p. 107. For details and and a full discussion of the reconstruction, see below, chapter 3.4, pp. 163-168. It is important to note again that Augustine does not say in so many words that he is quoting the Creed in the form that has just been recited by his catechumens, nor that this was the traditional form of the church of Hippo. It is nevertheless certain that this was not the form which Augustine knew when he came to Hippo. Thus, if Augustine began to use a formulation of the Creed that was new to him, the explanation that he was motivated to do so by local liturgical practice presents itself as a logical one. An additional argument for this hypothesis is the close resemblance of this form of the Creed with that of Quodvultdeus of Carthage (see below, chapter 3.4, pp. 168-178).

It appears that the differences between Augustine's two forms of the Creed are certainly no less numerous or striking than those between the two variants mentioned by Rufinus. Compared with the Milanese form, the Hipponic one presents an addition to the first article (*Vniuersorum creatorem, regem saeculorum, immortalem et inuisibilem*), a different word order (*Filium eius* before *Iesum Christum*) and the absence of *Vnicum* in the second article, differences of construction (*participium coniunctum* instead of relative clause) and word order (*Virgine Maria*) in the third article, similar differences in the fourth and fifth articles, the use of *Iudicare* instead of *Iudicaturus* in the eighth article, the addition of *In uitam aeternam* to the twelfth article, and the position of the Holy Church at the end of the Creed.

Striking as some of them may be, Augustine hardly ever mentions these differences [39]. This seems to be all the more strange as both forms must have been used during one and the same sermon. From *sermo 214*, another sermon for the occasion of the *traditio symboli*, we learn that Augustine first made some general remarks on the nature of the Creed, then the complete text of the Creed was recited (either by Augustine himself or by some other member of the clergy), and finally each article of the Creed was expounded [40]. The catechumens were supposed to learn the Creed by heart as it was presented to them during the *traditio symboli*. Thus, if the common hypothesis that Augustine, when becoming bishop of Hippo, both met with and continued to use a local variant of the

[39] There is one possible exception: the words *Quomodo carnis resurrectionem? Ne forte putet aliquis quomodo Lazari, ut scias non sic esse additum est: In uitam aeternam* (*de symbolo ad catechumenos* IX 17; CCSL 46, 199) seem to refer to the fact that the words *In uitam aeternam*, which did not occur in the Milanese variant of the Creed which Augustine is expounding in this work, must at some time have been added to the Hipponic form of the Creed. But see also below, chapter 3.5, p. 195 with footnote 353.

[40] Augustine of Hippo, *sermo 214* 1-2: *Sed collecta breuiter et in ordinem certum redacta atque constricta tradenda sunt uobis, ut fides uestra aedificetur et confessio praeparetur et memoria non grauetur. Haec sunt quae fideliter rententuri estis et memoriter reddituri. Post hanc praelocutionem pronuntiandum est totum symbolum sine aliqua interposita disputatione: Credo in deum patrem omnipotentem, et cetera quae sequuntur in eo. Quod symbolum nostis quia scribi non solet. Quo dicto adiungenda est haec disputatio. Ista quae breuiter audistis, non solum credere sed etiam totidem uerbis memoriae commendare et ore proferre debetis ...* (Verbraken 1962, 14-15).

Creed is right, it is this Hipponic form that must have been recited
before Augustine started his exposition, though the credal quotations with which he interlarded this exposition were taken from his
'personal' Milanese variant.

Thus, Augustine seems to go even further than Rufinus in his
obliviousness to the variety in the wording of the Creed in his day.
Although Rufinus is silent about variety in formulation, word order,
and construction, he at least mentions differences which affect the
content of the Creed; Augustine shows hardly any awareness of
such differences. The conclusion thus seems to be justified that, for
Augustine, even differences with respect to content between two
forms of the Creed were not really differences at all. In other words,
for Augustine there was no real difference between a form of the
Creed with the addition *Vniuersorum creatorem, regem saeculorum,
inuisibilem et impassibilem* and one without, or between a form of
the Creed which mentioned the Church immediately after the Holy
Spirit and one in which the article on the Church concluded the
whole Creed.

As far as we can tell, this attitude towards credal change and
credal variation was probably general in the early Church. Although
Augustine and Rufinus are the only two authors who testify to different forms of the Creed themselves, most members of the church
and at least its bishops must have known that different forms of the
Creed were used in different places. None of our sources, however,
betray any signs of discontent with this situation or condemn a certain variant as deviating from the 'original' Apostles' Creed [41].

---

[41] The only two exceptions I know of are Ambrose of Milan and Faustus of
Riez. See Ambrose's *explanatio symboli* 2-4: *Scio in partibus maxime orientis quod
ad ea, quae primo tradita sunt a maioribus nostris, dum quasi fraude alii, alii diligentia, fraude haeretici, diligentia catholici, dum ergo illi fraudulenter conantur irre-
pere, addiderunt quod non opus est, dum isti fraudem praecauere contendunt, fines
maiorum uelut pietate quadam et incuria uidentur esse progressi ... Hoc habet scriptura diuina. Numquid supra apostolorum fines progredi audaci mente debemus?
Numquid nos sumus apostolis cautiores? Sed dicis mihi: Postea emerserunt haereses! Nam et dicit apostolus: Oportet haereses esse, ut boni probentur. Quid ergo?
Vide simplicitatem, uide puritatem! Patripassiani cum emersissent, putauerunt
etiam catholici in hac parte addendum: Inuisibilem et impassibilem, quasi filius
dei uisibilis et passibilis fuit! ... Fides integra aduersus Sabellianos, exclusi sunt
Sabelliani, maxime de partibus occidentis. Ex illo remedio Arriani inuenerunt sibi
genus calumniae, et quoniam symbolum Romanae ecclesiae nos tenemus, ideo inuisi-*

Therefore, the general assumption that in the early Church, the Apostles' Creed was considered essentially one seems to be correct and what we call differences between two forms of the Creed were considered variations and nothing more [42]. Even additions like *Creatorem caeli et terrae*, *Descendit in inferna*, *Sanctorum communionem*, and *Vitam aeternam* were probably not always regarded as changes in the text of the Creed, so that there was no difficulty in the fact that, for example, two variants, one of which contained these additions while the other lacked them, both could claim to be the one and only 'Apostles' Creed' [43].

*bilem et impassibilem patrem omnipotentem illi aestimarent et dicerent: Vides, quia symbolum sic habet? Vt uisibilem filium et passibilem designarent!* (CPL 153; CSEL 73, 4-6) and Faustus of Riez, *de spiritu sancto* I 2: *Sed opponis mihi et dicis non statim in hoc uerbo deum posse monstrari* (viz. the Holy Spirit) *quo dicimus: Credo et in spiritum sanctum, quia sequitur: Credo in sanctam ecclesiam catholicam. Primo nescio quomodo ecclesiam catholicam nominare audeat Macedonius, qui extra catholicam exul salutis exclusus est, ex illorum factus numero de quibus dicitur: In circuitu impii ambulabunt. Ergo dicis: Credo in sanctam ecclesiam catholicam. Quid supponendo exiguam, id est 'in' syllabam, ingentem caliginem subtexere conaris? Credimus ecclesiam quasi regenerationis matrem, non in ecclesiam credimus quasi in salutem auctorem* (CPL 962; CSEL 21, 104).

[42] Thus also Kattenbusch 1900, 13 and Kelly 1976, 106-107 and 110.

[43] Similarly Kattenbusch 1894, 193-194 and 195-196. This conclusion is supported by the fact that we have several *expositiones symboli* which first quote one form of the Creed in full, and then proceed to comment upon a different variant: see below, chapter 3.2, pp. 121-127 and 138-141. An even more extreme example is provided by Facundus of Hermiane's (sixth century) *epistula fidei catholicae in defensione trium capitulorum* (CPL 868), where the Nicene Creed (*N*), the Nicaeno-Constantinopolitan Creed (*C*), and the Apostles' Creed are simply designated as "the creed". See chapter 14: (with reference to the article on the Last Judgement) ... *quod contra nullam aliquando haeresem, ut illud de aequalitate patris et filii in Nicaeno concilio contra Arium, uel de omnipotentia spiritus sancti in Constantinopolitano contra Macedonium* **in symbolo** *est additum* (CCSL 90A, 422), and chapter 20: ... *credere se in deum patrem omnipotentem et in Iesum Christum filium eius et in spiritum sanctum, quod* **symboli** *tenet auctoritas* ... (CCSL 90A, 423). In the first quotation, *symbolum* designates at the same time *N* and *C*, in the second, it indicates the Apostles' Creed. In a similar way, Faustus of Riez blurs the distinction between *N*, *C*, and the Apostles' Creed when he states: *In quibus uerbis etiam trecentorum decem et octo sacer numerus sacerdotum emergentem Arrii ac Macedonii damnauit errorem: Credo in deum patrem, credo in filium eius unicum dominum nostrum, credo et in spiritum sanctum* (Faustus of Riez, *de spiritu sancto* I 1; CSEL 21, 102). Although the introductory sentence states that *C* will be quoted, what we find tallies more with the Apostles' Creed. Rufinus also, when discussing the differences in the first two articles between his

2.4 Testimonies for Changes of Wording in the Creed

Nevertheless, the question of how both kinds of change, minor deviations in wording as well as theologically more significant additions, originated remains. Although the source material for changes in the form of the Creed is very meagre indeed, we do have some witnesses for this process [44].

To start with the category of changes of wording, we can first point to the situation in Rome. We have seen that at least two variants of the Apostles' Creed must have been in use in the church of Rome: *R* and proto-*R*. Quite probably, the baptismal questions of the *collectio Veronensis* (*H*) represent a third Roman variant of the Creed [45]. Although the exact formulation of proto-*R* is beyond reconstruction, it is clear that either 'Hippolytus' changed (to give only two examples) *Et Maria uirgine* to *Ex Maria uirgine* and *Qui sub Pontio Pilato crucifixus est et sepultus* to *Et crucifixus sub Pontio Pilato et mortuus est*, or some later Roman did the opposite. Unfortunately, however, we can hardly say anything about the time of

form of the Apostles' Creed and other, Eastern, creeds, seems to view the former and the latter only as variants of one and the same text: *Credo, inquit, in deum patrem omnipotentem. Orientales ecclesiae omnes paene ita tradunt: Credo in unum deum patrem omnipotentem. Et rursum in sequenti sermone, ubi nos dicimus: Et in Iesum Christum, unicum filium eius, dominum nostrum, ita illi tradunt: Et in unum dominum nostrum Iesum Christum, unicum filium eius, unum scilicet deum et unum dominum secundum auctoritatem Pauli apostoli profitentes* (Rufinus of Aquileia, *expositio symboli* 4; CCSL 20, 137). More awareness of the fact that the Apostles' Creed on the one hand and the Nicene or Nicaeno-Constantinopolitan one on the other are two different creeds is shown in Vigilius of Thapsus, *contra Eutychetem* IV 1: see above, chapter 1.6, footnote 59. Nevertheless, Vigilius is convinced that both creeds refer to the same truth. See also John Cassian's statement about the creed of Antiochia: *Symbolus ergo, haeretice, cuius textum superius diximus, licet omnium ecclesiarum sit quia una omnium fides, peculiariter tamen Antiochenae urbis atque ecclesiae est, id est illius in qua tu editus, in qua institutus, in qua renatus es* (John Cassian, *contra Nestorium* [CPL 514; c. 430] VI vi 1; CSEL 17, 331). Compare Kattenbusch 1894, 92 for this place.

[44] Of course, the numerous different variants of the Creed are all witnesses to the **fact** that the formulation of the Creed has changed many times. But although we have a fair number of different variants, there are very few witnesses indeed for the **process** of change, i.e. two distinct wordings of the Creed which, with a reasonable amount of certainty, were used in the same place at different times.

[45] See above, chapter 2.2, footnotes 17 and 18.

these changes. If, for example, *Et Maria* was changed to *Ex Maria*, the change could be dated to some time in the fourth century, as *R* (using *Et*) was probably in use at the beginning of that century, whereas the formula of the *collectio Veronensis* (using *Ex*) should probably be dated to its end, and it seems natural to date the change to some time between their respective birth hours. But there are still many uncertain factors connected with this reasoning.

In the case of the Milanese form of the Creed, however, we are treading on surer ground. It has already been mentioned that Augustine, in all probability, testifies to the form of the Creed with which he was baptized at the hands of the Milanese bishop Ambrose in 387 in his *sermo 213* and *sermo de symbolo ad catechumenos* [46]. Fortunately, we also possess a testimony that goes back to Ambrose himself in his *explanatio symboli*. It seems safe to accept this little sermon as genuinely Ambrosian [47], although the text as we have it is not based upon a written version by Ambrose himself but rather on the notes of someone who was present when the *explanatio* was delivered [48]. We do not find a complete version of the Creed in the *explanatio*, since the anonymous member of the audience only wrote down in full the shorter quotations that occurred within the explanatory part of the sermon and limited himself to simply giving the beginnings and ends of the longer quotations which presented the complete wording of the Creed [49]. As yielded by Ambrose's *explanatio symboli*, the text of the Milanese form of the Creed runs as follows:

*Credo ...*
*et in ... filium eius unicum dominum nostrum*
*qui natus ... spiritu sancto ex Maria uirgine*
*sub ... et sepultus*
*tertia die ... a mortuis*
*ascendit ...*
*sedet ad dexteram patris*
*unde ... et mortuos*
*et in spiritum sanctum*

[46] See above, chapter 2.3, p. 81 with footnote 36.
[47] See below, chapter 3.5, footnote 311.
[48] See CSEL 73, 8*.
[49] See below, chapter 3.5, pp. 186-187 with footnotes 312-314.

*... ecclesiam (...?)*
*remissionem [peccatorum*
*carnis] resurrectionem* [50].

Despite the fragmentary character of the credal quotations in
Ambrose's *explanatio symboli*, we can nevertheless detect certain
small differences with the testimony to the Milanese form of the
Creed in *sermo 213* and *sermo de symbolo ad catechumenos* of Augustine [51]. These are Ambrose's *Ex Maria uirgine* as opposed to Augustine's *Et uirgine Maria* and Ambrose's *Vnde uenturus* as opposed to
Augustine's *Inde uenturus*. Here we have two minor changes that
must have occurred within quite a short period, either between the
beginning of Ambrose's episcopate in 373 and Augustine's baptism
in 387, or between Augustine's baptism in 387 and Ambrose's death
in 397 [52]. But how did they come about?

Two possibilities seem to present themselves at this point. As one
particular change is always made by one particular person, either
Ambrose or Augustine must be responsible for the difference
between the two forms of the Creed. In other words: either Augustine offers a faithful quotation of the formula with which he was
baptized in 387 and Ambrose changed the wording of this variant
afterwards, the reflection of which is then found in the *explanatio
symboli*, or the *explanatio* presents the form of the Creed which
Ambrose always used, and Augustine made some changes to it [53].

Of these two possibilities, the latter is more probable than the
former. We can hardly imagine why Ambrose should change *Vnde*
into *Inde* and *Ex Maria uirgine* into *Et uirgine Maria* or vice versa
during his episcopate. First of all, we have to reckon with a bishop's
natural conservatism concerning the liturgical formulae he uses. If

---

[50] For the use of ellipsis and other features of punctuation, see below, chapter
3.1, p. 107. See for a detailed discussion of this reconstruction below, chapter 3.5,
pp. 185-189.

[51] See above, chapter 2.3, pp. 81-82, for a reconstruction of the Milanese form
of the Creed from these works.

[52] Here, the uncertain date of Ambrose's *explanatio* is a complicating factor.
See below, chapter 3.5, footnote 311.

[53] There is a third possibility, viz. that the *explanatio* represents an earlier
Ambrosian form of the Creed and that Augustine testifies to a change that was
made by Ambrose before 387. For our present purposes, this possibility can be
ignored.

there is no reason to change, for example, *Vnde* into *Inde*, a bishop who is accustomed to using *Vnde* will not suddenly start using *Inde*. Moreover, a bishop's clergy or, if the *traditio* and *redditio symboli* were public rites, even his flock of lay believers would certainly protest if the wording of the Apostles' Creed, which they probably all knew by heart, was changed from one day to the next [54]. That the *traditio* and *redditio symboli* were public rites in Milan as they were in Rome [55] is at least suggested by the fact that Ambrose's *explanatio symboli* was written down by someone who was present at the ceremony. That this cannot have been one of the catechumens is borne out by the text itself: *Illud sane monitos uos uolo esse, quoniam symbolum non debet scribi, quia reddere illud habetis. Sed nemo scribat. Qua ratione? Sic accepimus, ut non debeat scribi. Sed quid? Teneri. Sed dicis mihi: Quomodo potest teneri si non scribitur? Magis potest teneri si non scribatur. Qua ratione? Accipite. Quod enim scribis, securus quasi relegas, non cottidiana meditatione incipis recensere. Quod autem non scribis, timens ne amittas cottidie incipis recensere* [56]. The possible corrective role of the community of believers is explicitly mentioned by Rufinus for Rome: ... *mos inibi seruatur antiquus eos qui gratiam baptismi sucepturi sunt publice, id est fidelium populo audiente, symbolum reddere, et utique adiectionem unius saltim sermonis eorum qui praecesserunt in fide non admittit auditus* [57]. That the local clergy could also have a certain influence on the form of the Creed is proved by the case of Augustine, whom we know to have used the Hipponic form for the *traditio* and *redditio symboli* in his African bishopric, though he was previously wont to use the Milanese form [58].

---

[54] This is not necessarily in contradiction with the conclusion of the previous section that people hardly appreciated different forms of the Creed as such. It is not the fact that the Creed appeared in a slightly deviating form but rather the fact that a set formula which they knew well was suddenly being replaced by a different one that would annoy the believers.

[55] See above, chapter 1.6, footnote 53. Compare also, for the middle of the fifth century, Leo the Great's *epistula 124 (ad Palaestinos)* 8: ... *obliti symboli salutaris et confessionis quam pronuntiantes coram multis testibus sacramentum baptismi suscepistis* ... (CPL 1656; Schwartz 1932b, 163).

[56] Ambrose of Milan, *explanatio symboli* 9; CSEL 73, 11-12.

[57] Rufinus of Aquileia, *expositio symboli* 3; CCSL 20, 136.

[58] See above, chapter 2.3, footnote 38.

In the light of all this, it is difficult to imagine why Ambrose
would take the trouble to make such tiny changes as *Inde* for *Vnde*
or *Et uirgine Maria* for *Ex Maria uirgine* during his episcopate [59].
The other possibility, however, is much easier to imagine. When
Augustine received the Creed from Ambrose, the text (as opposed
to the content) must have been more or less new to him, and to a
certain extent he was free to make minor changes in the wording if
this better fitted his personal taste or Latin usage. Such a process
may be envisaged between his attending the rites of the *traditio* and
*redditio* in 387 [60] but also at a later moment; as far as we know,
when reciting the Creed in private, no one checked whether Augustine was remaining faithful to the wording he used during his *redditio symboli*. Even linguistic or stylistic assimilation to African usage
during his Hipponic period should be considered a real possibility.

## 2.5 Testimonies for Change in the Content of the Creed

For the other type of change, the insertion of certain theologically important words and phrases into the Creed, the sources are
equally parsimonious. Although we know of a good number of additions of this kind, the process of insertion is usually intangible.

If we first take a look at proto-*R*, *R*, and the baptismal questions
of the *collectio Veronensis* again, we can state that at some date
between the birth of proto-*R* and that of *R*, some member of the
Roman clergy must have added the word *Vnicum* to the second
article. The same can be said with respect to the phrases *Dominum
nostrum* and *Remissionem peccatorum*, but we know nothing about
the reasons for and circumstances of these additions. The same
observation holds true for the replacement of *Eius* with *Dei* in the

---

[59] Another possibility, viz. that Ambrose did not know a fixed wording of the
Creed by heart but only had some general idea of its content, is very improbable.
The Creed was learnt by heart by all Christians who were about to be baptized,
and general ideas are not learnt by heart whereas fixed formulae are.

[60] When addressing his own catechumens, Augustine stresses the fact that a
faultless and literal repetition of the form that will be presented to them is not
a necessary condition for baptism: see his *sermo 213* 11: ... *nemo trepidet, nemo
trepidando non reddat. Securi estote, patres uestri sumus, non habemus ferulas et
uirgas grammaticorum. Si quis in uerbo errauerit, in fide non erret* (Morin 1930,
449-450).

second article and the addition of *Viuus* to the fifth, two changes for which an even wider temporal margin should be allowed.

There is only one example from later credal texts of a similar change that can be assigned to a certain place and period. Here, Rufinus and Chromatius of Aquileia are our informants. Rufinus, who wrote his *expositio symboli* at the beginning of the fifth century [61] but comments upon the form of the Creed with which he was baptized [62], quotes the final article of the Creed as *Huius carnis resurrectionem* [63]. However, in one of Chromatius's *tractatus in Mathaeum*, which were written between 397 and 407 [64], we find the more extended formulation *Huius carnis resurrectionem, in uitam aeternam* [65]. Since Chromatius delivered these sermons in his capacity of bishop of Aquileia, it seems reasonable to infer that he is quoting from the form of the Creed that he used himself in the baptismal rite. Moreover, we know that Rufinus was baptized, probably in 370, by the same Chromatius when the latter was still a priest [66]. It seems safe to infer, therefore, that at some point between 370 and 407 the clause *In uitam aeternam* was added to the Aquileian form of the Creed, quite possibly by Chromatius himself.

Chromatius is silent about the reasons that induced him (or one of his predecessors, or the clergy of the Aquileian church) to make this addition to the Creed. We are more fortunate, however, with two other additions in the Aquileian form of the Creed: the phrase *Inuisibilem et impassibilem* in the first article and the particle *Huius* in the twelfth. Although the sources do not allow us to attach an exact date to these additions, they do inform us concerning the reasons for their insertion. As far as the former is concerned, Rufinus states explicitly that the words *Inuisibilem et impassibilem* were added to the Creed in the church of Aquileia to counter Sabellianism: *Constat autem apud nos additos* (viz. *duo istos sermones*) *haereseos causa Sabellii, illius profecto quae a nostris Patripassiana*

---

[61] See below, chapter 3.5, footnote 355.
[62] See above, chapter 2.3, footnote 26.
[63] See above, chapter 2.3, pp. 78-79.
[64] See Frede 1995, 365; but compare CCSL 9A, VI-VII.
[65] See below, chapter 3.5, pp. 206-207.
[66] See Kelly 1955, 3.

*appellatur* [67]. Rufinus refers to the second addition when explaining his belief in the Resurrection of the Flesh in his *apologia contra Hieronymum* (CPL 197, written 401): *Verum ad maiorem rei fidem addo amplius aliquid, et calumniosorum necessitate compulsus singulare et praecipuum ecclesiae nostrae mysterium pando. Etenim cum omnes ecclesiae ita sacramentum symboli tradant ut, postquam dixerint: Remissionem peccatorum, addant: Carnis resurrectionem, sancta Aquileiensis ecclesia, dei spiritu futuras aduersum nos calumnias praeuidente, ubi tradit carnis resurrectionem addit unius pronominis syllabam, et pro eo quod ceteri dicunt: Carnis resurrectionem, nos dicimus: Huius carnis resurrectionem. Quo scilicet frontem ut mos est in fine symboli signaculo contingentes, et ore carnis huius, uidelicet quam contigimus, resurrectionem fatentes, omnem uenenatae aduersum nos linguae calumniandi aditum praestruamus ... Sed nihil ut uideo profuit nobis tanta haec cautela spiritus sancti. Inueniunt adhuc male loquaces linguae calumniandi locum: Membra, inquit, singula nominatim nisi dixeris ... resurrectionem carnis negasti* [68]. It is perhaps difficult to accept that the Holy Spirit guided the Aquileian church in order to vindicate Rufinus's orthodoxy, but it seems equally improbable that Rufinus could make such a statement if the purpose of adding *Huius* to the final article of the Creed had been any other than stressing, against those who explained the article otherwise, that **this** flesh will rise again.

## 2.6 A Theory of Credal Change

If our analysis of the available material is correct, we can say that there are two ways in which the text of the Creed could change. First of all, people could change details of wording in the form that they have received. Thus we have seen that Augustine's reproduction of the form of the Creed with which he had been baptized in Milan contained certain grammatical and stylistic deviations. For this aspect, it is important to realize that most if not all believers first came into contact with the Creed by oral transmission

---

[67] Rufinus of Aquileia, *expositio symboli* 5; CCSL 20, 140. Compare also Ambrose of Milan, *explanatio symboli* 4: *Patripassiani cum emersissent, putauerunt etiam catholici in hac parte addendum: Inuisibilem et impassibilem ...* (CSEL 73, 5).

[68] Rufinus of Aquileia, *apologia contra Hieronymum* I 5; CCSL 20, 40. For the date, see Frede 1995, 732.

- the Creed was recited to them in the *traditio symboli*, but they did not receive any written text [69]. Therefore, a minor change that did not affect the content of the Creed could easily, perhaps even unconsciously, occur. Should someone not remember the precise wording of the Creed exactly, he (or she) would be inclined to change it in such a way as to make it fit his (or her) personal Latin usage. This is probably the explanation for the difference between the Milanese form of the Creed as recorded by Ambrose on the one hand, and by Augustine on the other.

Secondly, people could add certain elements to the Creed that did affect its content, as for example either Chromatius or some other member of the Aquileian clergy must have added *In uitam aeternam* to his form of the Creed at a certain moment. Of course, such a change can hardly occur unconsciously, and it seems natural to look for theological reasons here and in similar cases. This is indeed supported by Rufinus's explanation for two other credal additions. In doctrinal questions, the general formulation of the Apostles' Creed has always been capable of different and even rival explanations [70]. It is not strange, therefore, to consider the possibility that a bishop who wanted to exclude certain, in his eyes heretical, interpretations of the Creed adapted its text to meet this end. This may well be what the bishop of Aquileia did at a certain moment between 370 and 407, and in any case it is what Rufinus's

---

[69] As far as I can tell, the only modern study that pays attention to this point is Benvin 1989. But the author confines his discussion to points of pronunciation and spelling: see Benvin 1989, 204-205 and above, introduction, pp. 12-13, for some critical notes.

[70] See above, chapters 1.8 and 1.11, in particular footnotes 89 and 116 for the limited doctrinal importance of the Creed. One can also point to the anonymous complaint: *Huius symboli forma multis etiam haereticis in specie confessionis uidetur esse communis* (pseudo-Ambrose, *exhortatio de symbolo ad neophytos* [CPL 178] 4; p. 415); see below, chapter 4.2 for this text and a discussion of its origin). With *haeretici*, the anonymous author means the Arians in particular. In this context, it is illuminating to hear an Arian voice as well: *Item nullo modo praeponunt in scriptis suis patrem filio, insuper et damnant omnes qui praeponunt patrem filio, et tamen ipsi praeponunt patrem filio in symbolo dum dicunt: Credis in deum patrem omnipotentem creatorem caeli et terrae? Credis et in Christum Iesum filium eius?* (*fragmenta theologica Arriana* [CPL 705] 10; CCSL 87, 244). This source will be discussed more fully below, chapter 3.6, pp. 216-217. For more modern times, we could of course point to the different explanations of the word *Catholicam* in the tenth article of *T* by Protestant and Roman Catholic authors.

words about the additions *Inuisibilem et impassibilem* and *Huius*
suggest [71]. The circumstance that there were probably no written
versions of the Creed for a considerable part of the period under
discussion [72] can only have facilitated such a procedure [73].

Both ways of changing the text of the Creed seem to favour the
traditional theory of regional diversity. As far as the first is concerned, people's Latin usage must have been largely dependent on
their linguistic environment. Although Latin as a written medium
was a highly unified language, there were of course numerous regional features by which speakers could be identified as belonging to
certain parts of the Empire [74]. This will not only have pertained to
pronunciation, but also to peculiarities of word order and grammar.
Therefore, it is probable that deviations from the wording of proto-*R*
like *Virgine Maria*, *A mortuis resurrexit*, and *Ad caelum* will be
concentrated in certain areas rather than scattered all over the
Western Church. Orally, their spread was limited by the fact that
each region had its own usage, and in written form they were probably not even recognized as differences at all.

---

[71] This suggestion is strengthened by the Augustinian exhortation: *Quomodo
carnis resurrectionem? Ne forte putet aliquis quomodo Lazari, ut scias non sic esse,
additum est: In uitam aeternam* (Augustine of Hippo, *sermo de symbolo ad catechumenos* IX 17; CCSL 46, 199). But it is not certain whether Augustine refers here
to the historical motives of the clergy of Hippo for making this addition or to its
function for the catechumens he is presently addressing. Compare Ehrman's discussion of intentional changes in Bible manuscripts: "Scribes altered their sacred
texts to make them "say" what they were already known to "mean."" (Ehrman
1993, 276).

[72] The so-called *disciplina arcani* even prohibited the writing down of the
Creed during the fourth and fifth centuries; see Powell 1979, 6-7.

[73] Compare the description by Dieudonné Dufrasne of the probable process of
redaction of the so-called *Euchologion* of Serapion of Thmuis (CPG 2495), quoted
in Metzger 1992, 31: "Dans l'aire de la liturgie, des formules et des prières circu-
lent qu'un évêque peut apprécier et adopter pour constituer l'euchologe de son
église. Il se peut cependant que l'évêque devienne rédacteur partiel, en modifiant
les prières pour y introduire des formules théologiques, des accentuations pasto-
rales, des tournures stylistiques auxquelles il tient particulièrement ...".

[74] To give a well-known example, Augustine states that his and the Italian
pronunciation of Latin were clearly different. See his *de ordine* II xvii 45: *Me
enim ipsum, cui magna necessitas fuit ista perdiscere, adhuc in multis uerborum
sonis Itali exagitant et a me uicissim, quod ad ipsum sonum attinet, reprehenduntur.
Aliud est enim esse arte, aliud gente securum* (CPL 255; CCSL 29, 131).

As far as substantial additions to the Creed like *Creatorem caeli et terrae* and *In uitam aeternam* are concerned, things are of course different. They can hardly have made their entrance unnoticed, and people who read or heard such an addition for the first time must have asked questions about it [75]. In such a way, discussion could ensue both in the region where the addition had originated (when people became acquainted with an innovation during a *traditio* or *redditio symboli* in their own church) and farther away (when someone read, for example, an Augustinian *sermo de symbolo* which used a different form of the Creed from his own). Such a discussion could of course result in other churches, both nearby and far away, adopting the phrase in question as well. This, however, would be more natural for churches that had close links with the one that had first made the addition than for others. First of all, if an addition had been added somewhere for doctrinal reasons, these can hardly have been purely local but must have had some weight also in neighbouring places. For example, if a certain bishop, together with his clergy or even all his church members, decided to add *In uitam aeternam* to the Creed because some of his believers felt uneasy about their fate after the resurrection of the flesh, it is improbable that this fear would be limited to his church only. If his remedy were felt to meet the requirements, it would be only too natural for churches that had to cope with the same problem to adopt the same policy as well. Thus, such an addition could easily spread within a certain region. On the other hand, churches which were farther away that became acquainted with an addition in written form would have to defend their decision to all their neighbours if they decided to adopt a similar course. This would not, of course, make it impossible for an addition to travel, for example, from Aquileia to Carthage, but it would certainly make such a process much more difficult than a 'simple' spread over Northern Italy [76].

[75] Nevertheless, as most if not all of these additions can be interpreted as explanations or specifications of the immediately preceding words (compare below, chapter 2.7, p. 97), the possibility cannot be excluded that perhaps some of them entered the Creed as glosses that were no longer recognized as such. But to investigate this possibility would involve a study of the patristic and early Medieval interpretation of the Creed.

[76] Compare Eichenseer 1960, 198. A parallel suggests itself with the description of the spread of New Testament manuscripts in Aland 1989, 65: "Wir müs-

## 2.7 Summary and Further Hypotheses

The Apostles' Creed was an important Roman liturgical text which began its triumphal spread all over the Western Church in the third century and was considered, at least from the fourth century onwards, to stem from the Apostles themselves. Nevertheless, when we encounter the first non-Roman formulations of the same, a fundamental diversity is what first leaps to the eye. In this chapter, we have investigated how this diversity could have come about. In other words, how could a liturgical formula develop into so many different variants?

When we take a closer look at the way in which the several variants of the Apostles' Creed differ from each other, two kinds of difference soon present themselves, differences with respect to wording and differences with respect to content. The first comprises points of syntax (relative clause or participle construction), word order (*Ex Maria uirgine* or *Ex uirgine Maria*), formulation and style (*In caelum* or *Ad caelos*), and also a gloss-like addition like *A mortuis* after *Resurrexit*. Under the second heading, we should place additions like *Vnicum, Dominum nostrum, Descendit in inferna, Remissionem peccatorum*, and *In uitam aeternam*.

The writings of Ambrose of Milan, Rufinus of Aquileia, Augustine of Hippo, and Faustus of Riez enable us to draw some conclusions about the appreciation of both kinds of difference, and about the way that they could have come about. Here, the combined testimony of Ambrose and Augustine shows that differences of wording could easily occur when one person learnt the Creed from another. It seems quite possible that the changes that led to these differences occurred more or less unconsciously, and even if not so, neither the change itself nor the resulting difference was appreciated as such.

As far as differences that affect the contents of the Creed are concerned, we have found three positions. For Rufinus, these differ-

sen uns die Ausbreitung einer Schrift kreisförmig vorstellen, einem Stein vergleichbar, der in einen Teich geworfen wird: ringförmig breiten sich die Wellen nach allen Seiten aus. Sobald eine Schrift sich durch immer neue Abschriften in einer Kirchenprovinz oder deren Metropole durchgesetzt hat, kann sie infolge der engen Verbindung der Kirchenprovinzen untereinander sehr schnell in andere Bezirke vordringen, wo dann die beschriebene Entwicklung von neuem beginnt ... Aber lediglich in Kirchen mit alter eigener Tradition oder in Kirchengebieten, die relativ isoliert ... leben, kann man ... an einer eigenen Textform festhalten".

ences are real but legitimate as long as they contribute to maintaining orthodox belief. In his eyes, they constitute a specification of, not an innovation in the meaning of the Creed. For Augustine, these additions do not even seem worth mentioning. His liturgical practice reveals that he considered formulations of the Creed that differ in this, more fundamental, respect as equipollent representatives of one and the same text. Nevertheless, these changes that (in our eyes) affect the content of the Creed must of course go back to a concrete cause. From Rufinus, we learn that such a cause was probably connected with the concern to make a dogmatic point or to clarify a part of the Creed that could be interpreted in more than one way. Thus, these changes were probably made deliberately and with a distinct purpose. However, the way in which both Rufinus and Augustine (of whom the latter's attitude towards credal variety seems to have been more or less general in the pre-Carolingian period) treat these differences has the important implication that what we stamp an addition to the content of the Creed was not really seen as an addition in the period that we are studying, but rather more as a specification of a truth that was already implicitly present in the Creed. Finally, Ambrose and Faustus testify to a more critical attitude towards credal additions and changes. According to Ambrose, even the purpose of combatting heresies may never legitimate any tampering with the work of the Apostles. Faustus takes an adversary to task who, in his opinion, purposely contorts the meaning of the Creed by adding a preposition. Nevertheless, Faustus does not comment upon the use of a substantial addition by the same adversary, which implies that he probably did not conceive of it as such.

Both ways of change revealed by the sources seem to favour the traditional opinion that, before credal uniformity became the rule, several regional types of the Creed were in existence. Changes in wording were probably triggered by people's personal Latin usage, grammatical developments, and more or less fashionable ways of expression, phenomena that in all probability bore a regional character and, together with other factors, constituted the later Romance languages. Thus, we should be willing to accept different developments in the wording of the Creed in the regions of Italy, Gaul, Spain, Africa, and the Latin Balkans. As far as changes with respect to content are concerned, they were probably caused by theological problems or controversies. These, of course, were not necessarily limited to one particular region, but the ensuing changes in the form of the Creed would, especially in the light of the high esteem in which the Creed was held and the occasional resistance which such changes could meet, more easily spread within their region of origin than travel across the whole Western Church.

Thus, we can conclude that, at least from a more theoretical point of view, the existence of regional types of the Apostles' Creed in the pre-Carolingian period does seem probable. It will be well, then, to take a closer look at the various witnesses to the form of the Creed. For the sake of argument, we shall take as a working hypothesis that the form of the Creed indeed developed along the lines that we have drawn in this chapter. If this hypothesis is correct, it will be possible to divide the various deviations from the original form of the Creed into changes of wording and changes of content. Of these, we should, generally speaking, expect changes of wording to remain limited to one region only. A change of content, on the other hand, should not only have a firm regional base, but may also be found in more than one part of the Latin West. The following chapter will reveal whether or not these hypotheses are supported by the source material.

# CHAPTER THREE

## In Search of Regional Types of the Creed

### 3.1 Introduction and Methodological Points

In the present chapter, we shall endeavour to marshall as many witnesses as possible for the form of the Creed in order to test the hypotheses that were formulated at the close of the previous chapter. For that purpose, it seems best to gather together the source material for each region separately. Much work in this respect has already been done by earlier scholars. The works of Hahn and Kattenbusch constitute a mine of information that already yields most of the available texts. Some more sources were discovered by later students of the Creed, and one or two witnesses that are adduced in this study have not previously been noticed by credal scholars. It is our hope, therefore, that we can present an overview of sources for the text of the Creed that is the most complete one that has hitherto been published.

An important question is of course which regions should be distinguished. Kattenbusch divides the sources for the form of the Creed into the following groups: 'italische Symbole', 'afrikanische Symbole', and 'westeuropäische Symbole'. The latter group is subdivided into 'Symbole aus Spanien' and 'Symbole aus Gallien resp. dem fränkischen Reiche'[1]. Thus, he distinguishes the regions of Italy, Africa, Spain, and Gaul (including neighbouring territories). Hahn, in his turn, considers no fewer than seven regions: Italy, Africa, Spain, Gaul, the British Isles, Germany, and the Nordic countries (Norwegia and Iceland)[2]. More recently, Kelly mentions the regions of Italy, Upper Moesia (the Latin Balkans), Africa, Spain, and Gaul[3]. Smulders gives the same regions, albeit not

---

[1] Kattenbusch 1894, VI-VIII. Kattenbusch is sceptical, however, about the possibilities of distinguishing between Gallican and Spanish variants of the Creed: see Kattenbusch 1894, 189-199. Kattenbusch 1900, 778-779 is slightly more positive.

[2] Hahn 1962, IX-XII.

[3] Kelly 1976, 172-178. A similar presentation to that of Kelly is already found in Badcock 1930, 73-77 and 1938, 89-116. Badcock's analysis is rendered less useful by the fact that he draws indiscretely from *regulae fidei*, credal quotations, and references to the contents of the Creed for his reconstructions. Moreover,

always with the same names, in a slightly different order [4]. Finally, O'Callaghan mentions the regions of Gaul, Africa, Italy, Germany, Scotland, Ireland, and Spain [5].

It has already been mentioned that most of these authors probably take natural boundaries like mountains and seas into account, and that this seems to be justified by the different types of Latin liturgy and the later emerging Romance languages [6]. Nevertheless, not all the regions that have been enumerated above are equally fruitful for the purposes of our study. Some of them yield a fair number of sources for the form of the Creed, but others only one or two or even none. Thus, the region of Gaul is quite well represented with no less than fifteen witnesses. Spain is next with seven, Africa yields four, Northern Italy five [7], the Latin Balkans three, and Ireland only two. The witnesses that have been adduced for the form of the Creed in other regions turn out to lose much of their value [8].

The same observation can be made for many of the other alleged sources. To give an illustration, we shall presently discuss more than thirty witnesses, whereas Hahn draws the evidence for his seven regions from no less than 105. This restriction on our part is caused by the circumstance that, in order to test our hypotheses, it is essential to know the ways in which the several variants of the Apostle's Creed differ **precisely** from another and from their hypothetical common parent. If we want to know how deviations in wording and differences with respect to the content of the Creed spread through the Western Church, we need reliable sources which

Badcock presents and interprets his material in the light of his main thesis, which, *pace* Kinzig and Vinzent, is considered superseded by more recent studies: see above, chapter 1.5, footnote 39.

[4] Smulders 1970, 237-238n10.

[5] O'Callaghan 1992, 285-287. A considerable number of the texts that are enumerated by all these authors are also presented in Kinzig 1999a, 116-183. Kinzig, however, strictly limits himself to baptismal questions, and does not operate with a regional classification.

[6] See above, chapter 2.1, p. 74 and footnote 12.

[7] With the exception of Rome, we do not have any certain sources for the form of the Creed in Italy South of the Apennines. It seems prudent, therefore, not to apply the conclusions that are yielded by a limited number of North Italian sources to the whole of the peninsula.

[8] See below, chapter 3.6, footnote 413 for more details.

contain exact formulations of the Apostles' Creed as it was used at a certain date in a certain place. This demand implies that, for our purposes, a source for the form of the Creed should meet a number of concrete requirements.

First of all, it is essential to realize that not all credal texts say something about the author's form of the **Apostles'** Creed. In particular synodal creeds and creeds that have been written to prove the author's orthodoxy make use of structures and concepts that are present in the Apostles' Creed but cannot be taken to say anything about a particular form of that formula. Secondly, we shall investigate only credal variants in Latin, as it is in this language that the Apostles' Creed was used in the liturgy of the early Western Church. Thus, we shall not pay attention to any of the (mostly rather late) translations of the Creed into one of the vernacular languages. In the third place, a source for the form of the Creed must be available in a critical edition. That this requirement is an essential one has been sufficiently borne out by the history of the study of, for example, Rufinus's *expositio symboli* [9]. In the fourth place, texts that are later than the beginning of the ninth century will be excluded from our analysis, as the *textus receptus* had ousted most if not all regional forms of the Creed by then [10]. In the fifth place, since we are investigating the development of the Creed in relation to a number of distinct regions, only those sources with a more or less certain date and place of origin will be used. In the sixth place, the circumstance that we are studying the form of the Creed (as opposed to, for example, its ideas, liturgical use, or interpretation) compels us not to look for allusions to the Creed or descriptions of its content, but rather for quotations [11].

This last requirement deserves some more elaborate discussion. As is the case with most historical documents, the authors whose

[9] See below, chapter 3.5, pp. 196-198 and footnotes 356, 359, 361, and 362.

[10] See above, chapter 1.1, p. 21 and chapter 2.1, pp. 73-74 with footnote 6.

[11] Van den Hoek 1996 studies the way that earlier authors are quoted in Clement of Alexandria. Many of her observations apply to quotations of the Creed as well (see below). The main difference between credal quotations and literary ones like those in Clement seems to be that the latter "without exception ... are heavily abbreviated and condensed" (Van den Hoek 1996, 235), because Clement, like many other ancient authors, made use of notes and excerpts from other works when composing his own: see *ibid.* 225-227.

work we are investigating did not write them to satisfy our curiosity. For our purposes, we would ideally like to have a text of the entire Creed in all our sources, with all the articles quoted from the first to the last, in such a way that it is certain that we not only have the content, but also the exact formulation of the variant in question. Unfortunately, this is only rarely the case. Nevertheless, we do have a number of liturgical texts that meet these criteria [12]. Inscriptions of the Creed would of course be equally reliable, but only two such inscriptions seem to have been found thus far, and both are rather fragmentary [13].

Texts that only refer to isolated parts of the Creed - words, articles, or clusters of articles - are encountered more often than quotations of a complete credal variant. Although there are exceptions, most of these texts require some solid philological spadework to ascertain how much they really say about the exact wording of the author's form of the Creed. Here, we meet the problem that an author may quote one article and only indicate or allude to another in the same text. Sometimes, it is hard or even impossible to decide whether one has to do with a credal quotation, or rather with an allusion to the Creed or an indication of its content [14]. Nevertheless, a number of helpful indications can be mentioned here.

Thus, quotations that are explicitly marked as such are particularly valuable [15]. Quotations of this kind are usually introduced by phrases such as *symbolum habet* or *dicitur in symbolo*. In the case of sermons or treatises that were written with the explicit intention of commenting upon the Creed, one often finds *sequitur* as a quotation marker. But even in these cases, three things should be borne in mind. First of all, one should realize that an author who marks the beginning of a credal quotation does not necessarily do the

---

[12] See Hen 1995, 44, for the particular value of liturgical texts as historical sources.

[13] De Waal 1896, with its promising title *Il Simbolo Apostolico illustrato dalle iscrizioni dei primi secoli*, is only concerned with collecting epigraphical evidence for early Christian belief in the content of the Creed. See De Waal 1896, 3: "... vorrei ... dirigere la vostra attenzione alle *iscrizioni* dei primi secoli, le quali dànno testimonianze alle dottrine contenute nel sacro Simbolo".

[14] Thus, Van den Hoek (1996, 228-229) distinguishes between quotations, paraphrases, and reminiscences.

[15] See Van den Hoek 1996, 229: "Quotations are, of course, most identifiable when the ancient authors themselves inform us that they are quoting".

same at its end. In other words, it is not always immediately clear
where the quotation ends and the commentary begins. Sometimes,
the beginning of the commentary is consistently indicated by means
of the tag *id est* or a similar phrase. In other cases, a syntactic
break may be taken as a certain indication that the quotation has
ended and the commentary begun [16]. Sometimes, however, the line
is not so easy or even impossible to draw [17]. Secondly, writers of
*expositiones symboli* or similar texts are not always concerned with
quoting every single word or even every single article of the Creed.
This implies that when a text does not contain references to phrases
that do occur in other forms of the Creed, we should not automatically conclude that these phrases were really absent from the
author's variant of the Creed [18]. Thirdly, authors may add certain

---

[16] A good example is provided by Caesarius of Arles, *sermo 9*: ... *ut nulla haeresis Christum alium esse diceret, cum unum utique esse constaret quem sub Pilato
passum symbolum tradidisset. Crucifixus mortuus et sepultus, tertia die resurrexit.
De manifesta et re probata a multis domini resurrectione licet euidentissime Euange-
lia testata sint, tamen etiam apostolus praedicauit* ... (CPL 1008; CCSL 103, 49).
Here, the phrase *Crucifixus mortuus et sepultus, tertia die resurrexit* can neither
be directly connected with the foregoing nor with the following sentence. Thus,
the two syntactic breaks mark this phrase as a literal quotation from the Creed.
Compare the section on the Resurrection of Christ in Quodvultdeus of Carthage,
*sermo de symbolo 3* VI 1 and 10: *Tertia die. Triduana mors domini per prophetas
et praedicta est et promissa et impleta* ... *Tertio die propheta litori incolumis est red-
ditus, die tertia Christus de sepulcro surgens super caelos est exaltatus* (CPL 403;
CCSL 60, 358-359). In this section, only the opening words *Tertia die* can lay
reasonable claim to constituting a quotation.

[17] Thus, in Augustine, *sermo 215* 3, we read: *Credimus in filium eius Iesum
Christum, dominum nostrum, deum uerum de deo uero, dei patris filium deum, sed
non duos deos, ipse enim et pater unum sunt, et per Moysen populo insinuat dicens*
... (CPL 284; Verbraken 1958, 19). It seems clear that the words *Credimus et in
filium eius Iesum Christum* refer to the Creed, and that with the words *et per
Moysen* ... we have reached the commentary, but the question where the line
between the two should be drawn cannot be answered with absolute certainty
in the absence of additional information (see below, chapter 3.4, pp. 163-165 for
more details). Compare also Eusebius 'Gallicanus', *homilia 10 de symbolo 9*: *Sequitur: Inde uenturus, iudicaturus de uiuis et mortuis* (CPL 966; CCSL 101, 119),
where the words *iudicaturus de uiuis et mortuis* look like an integral part of the
quotation but are exposed as part of the commentary by a later quotation (see
below, chapter 3.2, p. 135.

[18] Thus, Faustus of Riez, bishop in the second half of the fifth century, quotes
the third article of the Creed as follows in his *de spiritu sancto* (CPL 962) I 3:
*Cum autem catholica confiteatur ecclesia: Conceptus de spiritu sancto, interrogandi*

small particles like *et*, *ergo*, *enim*, *credo*, or *in* to introduce their credal quotations. This is particularly frequent in the final articles, but
it occurs in other parts of the Creed as well [19]. Similarly, part of the
Creed may be presented in an abbreviated form [20].

*sunt hoc loco Macedoniani ...* (CSEL 21, 105). Here, we have an explicit quotation where it is clear where it begins and ends. But in Faustus's *epistula 7* (CPL
963) we find another explicit quotation, now of the second and third articles: ...
*iuxta symboli auctoritatem, ut alia praetermittam, qua dicimus: Credo et in filium
dei Iesum Christum, qui conceptus est de spiritu sancto, natus ex Maria uirgine.
Qui si talis error ...* (CSEL 21, 205). This second quotation reveals that the first
one is both incomplete (omitting the second part of the article) and abbreviated
(skipping the words *Qui* and *Est*). Similarly, Augustine fails to quote or even to
mention the fifth article in his *de symbolo ad catechumenos*, although all the other
articles are quoted or at least unambiguously indicated. See for these cases below, chapter 3.2, p. 116 with footnote 55 and chapter 3.5, p. 192 with footnote
339.

[19] Thus, Peter Chrysologus in his *sermones de symbolo* (CPL 227) quotes the
tenth article of the Creed as *Sanctam ecclesiam*, but also as *Et sanctam ecclesiam,
Credimus sanctam ecclesiam, Credo in sanctam ecclesiam*, and *In sanctam ecclesiam*:
see below, chapter 3.5, pp. 203-204 with footnotes 391-396 for more details and
exact references. A good example of the same phenomenon is offered by John
Cassian's *contra Nestorium* (CPL 514; *c.* 430). Cassian first offers a clearly literal
quotation of a substantial portion of what he calls the Antiochene creed: *Textus
ergo ac fides Antiocheni symboli haec est: Credo in unum et solum uerum deum
patrem omnipotentem, creatorem omnium uisibilium et inuisibilium creaturarum, et
in dominum nostrum Iesum Christum filium eius unigenitum et primogenitum totius
creaturae ... qui propter nos uenit et natus est ex Maria uirgine, et crucifixus sub
Pontio Pilato et sepultus, et tertia die resurrexit secundum scripturas, et ascendit in
caelos, et iterum ueniet iudicare uiuos et mortuos, et reliqua* (*contra Nestorium* VI iii
2; CSEL 17, 327). Of course, the Antiochene creed to which Cassian refers was in
Greek (see Kelly 1976, 184-186), but it is clear from what follows that Cassian
consistently uses one and the same translation of that formula (in *contra Nestorium* VI iv 2, we meet the identical quotation, but now with *Et in caelos ascendit*: CSEL 17, 329). Further on, however, we find explicit and apparently literal
quotations that nevertheless show small additions. Thus, in *contra Nestorium* VI
vi 4, we read: *Credo enim dixisti in dominum nostrum Iesum Christum filium eius
unigenitum et primogenitum totius creatu*rae (CSEL 17, 332). Similarly, *contra
Nestorium* VI ix 2 repeats the article about the Crucifixion with a twofold *Est*
added: *Propter nos ergo, inquit symbolus, dominus noster Iesum Christus uenit et
natus est ex Maria uirgine, et crucifixus est sub Pontio Pilato et sepultus est ...*
(CSEL 17, 335-336). See also Kattenbusch 1894, 222n6 for these instances.
Nevertheless, the difference between these, albeit slightly adapted, quotations
and a real paraphrase of the Creed remains clear. See *contra Nestorium* VI xvii
2-3: *Non credens ergo in carne editum necesse est etiam passum esse non credas.
Non credens autem illius passionem quid reliquum est nisi etiam resurrectionem*

More frequently, however, quotations from the Creed are neither explicitly nor implicitly marked as such. In these cases, it becomes less easy to distinguish between literal quotations, modified quotations, and allusions to the content of the Creed. Here, we have adopted the following policy. In *expositiones symboli* and other texts that are explicitly concerned with saying something about the Creed, we shall treat phrases that could give the wording of the Creed as it was known to the author as quotations, except when other parts of the text make this assumption unlikely. Thus, when we read the words ... *ut qui erat unigenitus natus ex deo solus esset primogenitus ex mortuis inter homines multos et dignaretur seruos uocare fratres dicens: Ite, dicite fratribus meis ut eant in Galilaem. Ibi me uidebunt. Ascendit in caelum, sedet ad dexteram dei patris omnipotentis. Vbi et quomodo sit in caelo dominicum corpus* ... [21] in Ildefonsus of Toledo's *de cognitione baptismi* 50-51 (*c.* 660; CPL 1248), we take the phrase *Ascendit in caelum, sedet ad dexteram dei patris omnipotentis* as a credal quotation [22]. This seems to be a legitimate procedure for the double reason that these or strongly similar words also occur in other credal variants of the Creed, and that quotations of the Creed are precisely what one expects in such a text. On the other hand, a statement like *Hi etiam resurrectionem carnis nos credere reprehendunt* in Augustine's *de trinitate* (early fifth century; CPL

---

neges ... *negans ergo passum et mortuum, negans quoque ab inferis resurgentem, consequens utique est ut neges etiam ascendentem* ... *ergo, quantum in te est, dominus Iesus Christus neque ab inferis resurrexit neque caelum ascendit nec ad dei patris dexteram sedit neque ad illum qui expectatur examinationis ultimae diem ueniet nec uiuos ac mortuos iudicabit* (CSEL 17, 344).

[20] Thus, we meet an abbreviated and adapted quotation of the beginning of the Christological part of the Antiochene creed that is quoted by John Cassian (see previous footnote) in his *contra Nestorium* VI x 4: *Dixisti in symbolo: Credo in Iesum Christum filium dei, credo in deum uerum ex deo uero, homousion patri, qui descendit et sepultus est* ... (CSEL 17, 338). See for another useful example Kattenbusch 1894, 140.

[21] Campos Ruiz 1971, 289.

[22] Although the words *Ascendit in caelum, sedet ad dexteram dei patris omnipotentis* are clearly a distinct syntactic unit, they can nevertheless be read as part of Ildefonsus's argument, as Christ is the subject of the preceding passage and his body in the one that follows. Here, only the fact that Ildefonsus is writing about the Creed justifies the interpretation as a quotation. See also the case of Augustine's *sermo 215* below, chapter 3.4, pp. 163-164. Compare for the difference with the criterion of the 'syntactic break' footnote 16 above.

329) [23] seems better left out of our analysis, as there is nothing here to suggest that Augustine is quoting the Creed, even though there are forms of the Creed which exhibit the formulation *Resurrectionem carnis*. Such, then, will be our common procedure with all possible or adduced credal quotations in texts that are not directly concerned with the Creed. Even if the author had the Creed in mind in such a place, that would not automatically mean that he offers a quotation of the Creed as well, but a reference or even allusion to its contents would be equally possible [24].

[23] Augustine, *de trinitate* IV xvi 21; CCSL 50, 188. See also below, chapter 3.5, p. 190.

[24] For an ideal example of the cautiousness necessary in the study of possible credal quotations, see Kattenbusch 1900, 809-810n78. In other contexts, too, scholars have raised the question of quotations that do not agree exactly with the source text. Besides Van den Hoek (see above, footnote 11), we have found others who should at least be mentioned here. First of all, it should be observed that practically the same problems occur in the case of possible New Testament quotations in the work of patristic authors: see Aland 1989, 179-180: "Denn von Fall zu Fall ... muß entschieden werden, ob es sich um ein Zitat aus einer neutestamentlichen Schrift handelt ... oder nur um eine Anspielung. Handelt es sich um ein Zitat, ist zu entscheiden, ob der Schriftsteller hier bewußt umformt oder aus dem Gedächtnis zitiert oder ob man davon ausgehen kann, daß er es aus dem ihm vorliegenden Neuen Testament abgeschrieben hat". Similarly Valkenberg, when discussing scriptural quotations in Thomas of Aquino, distinguishes a group of misquotations, that is, quotations in which the wording of the Bible has been changed by contamination with similar or related texts: see Valkenberg 1990, 53. We do not deny that patristic authors may unintentionally change the wording of some or more articles when quoting the Creed, but because there was no official version of the Creed yet, we shall never be able to spot such instances. In fact, in the period that we are investigating, we must consider such misquotations as changes in the wording of the Creed: see above, chapter 2.6, pp. 92-93. This is exactly what is claimed for manuscript copies of biblical texts by Ehrman 1993, in particular 29-31, 46n121, and 279-280: "Reproducing a text is in some ways analogous to interpreting it" (29), "understanding a text ... involves putting it "in other words."", and "Whereas all readers change a text when they construe it in their minds, the scribes actually changed the text on the page. As a result, they created a new text, a new concatenation of words ..." (280). In the last quotation, one could read 'bishops' for 'scribes' and 'in the rite' for 'on the page'. Finally, Whittaker makes the point that as a rule classical and post-classical philosophical commentaries change the wording of the text they are commenting upon when quoting it: see Whittaker 1989, in particular 69-70 and 94-95. The reason for this procedure was of a more or less literary character - the source text was probably so familiar to his public that the commentator could add a touch of originality to his work by using modified instead of literal quotations:

With these criteria in mind, we shall proceed with a close investigation of the available witnesses in order to find out whether we can indeed detect the regional types that have been postulated since the days of Kattenbusch. In this investigation, each source text will receive an abbreviation in order to facilitate reference and comparison. Also, the necessary details concerning date and place of origin of each source text will be presented. Next, the text itself will be subjected to a longer or shorter analysis in order to assess as exactly as possible the wording of the credal variant to which it testifies [25]. The treatment of each source text will close with a presentation of this variant or at least our (partial) reconstruction of it. This reconstruction will be, for the sake of convenience, in the declaratory form. Here, we shall make use of ellipsis to indicate that a reconstruction is incomplete but that the source text does not provide any information on either wording or contents of the missing parts, of ellipsis between brackets and with a question mark added to indicate that the reconstruction may be incomplete at the relevant point but that there is no way of finding out whether it really is or not, of question marks between brackets to indicate that a part of the reconstruction is uncertain, and of square brackets to indicate words in the source text that give the content, but not necessarily the wording of parts of the Creed.

## 3.2 Gallican Forms of the Creed

There are quite a number of credal texts which stem certainly, or at least very probably, from Gaul. Overviews can be found in Kattenbusch, Hahn, Kelly, Smulders, and, more recently, O'Callaghan [26]. Not all these texts serve our purposes equally well, however.

see Whittaker 1989, 66-68. Again, such a procedure may or may not have been followed by the authors of the *expositiones* that we shall presently study, but we lack the means to prove such a possibility. But compare Kattenbusch 1900, 741: "Caes. scheint überall nur zu rethorisieren".

[25] In this analysis, the opinions of the credal scholars on whose work we draw here will be mentioned where we reach different conclusions from theirs. Also, the work of scholars who have made special study of a certain source will be examined.

[26] Kattenbusch 1894, 158-184 ("Symbole aus Gallien resp. dem fränkischen Reiche"); Hahn 1897, 69-85 ("Symbolformeln der Gallischen Kirche"); Smulders 1970, 237n10; Kelly 1976, 178-179; O'Callaghan 1992, 285-287. See also Burn

First of all, we have to exclude a good number of texts that offer a summary of Christian faith but do not refer to the Apostles' Creed. Texts of this kind include the creed of Victricius of Rouen (c. 400) [27], the creed of Leporius of Marseilles (written in 418 or 419) [28], the creed of Gregory of Tours (d. 594) [29], the anonymous *fides Romanorum* (CPL 552) [30], the so-called Jacobi's Creed (CPL

1909, 1-12 for a short but interesting study of a "Gallican type of the Creed" (p. 12).

[27] This text appears as a personal formulation of faith which contains several traditional elements. See Victricius of Rouen, *de laude sanctorum* 4: *Miseremini igitur, miseremini. Habetis quod ignoscatis. Confitemur deum patrem, confitemur deum filium, confitemur sanctum spiritum deum* ... (CPL 481; CCSL 64, 74-75). For the date of this work, see Frede 1995, 788. Compare Kattenbusch 1894, 174-175, Hahn 1897, 70 and 285-286, and Mulders 1957, 284-286 for this creed.

[28] This lengthy doctrinal piece (beginning *Ergo confitemur dominum ac deum nostrum Iesum Christum, unicum filium dei* ...; reprinted in Hahn 1897, 299-301) occurs in Leporius's *libellus emendationis* (CPL 515), a letter in which the author recants certain Christological views that were contained in an earlier work. Leporius seems to refer to the Apostles' Creed in the introductory part with the words ... *atque iuxta symboli ueritatem id quod secundum priorem definitionem nostram, ubi non impietate aliqua sed seducebamur errore, dicere uerebamur de Maria deum natum, nunc constantissime confitemur* (Leporius of Marseilles, *libellus emendationis* 2; CCSL 64, 113). Nevertheless, the ensuing positive formulation of the author's new position hardly shares any formulations with the Apostles' Creed (thus also Kattenbusch 1894, 174). See Leporius of Marseilles, *libellus emendationis* 3-7 (CCSL 64, 114-119). For the date of this work, see Frede 1995, 606.

[29] Gregory presents this creed in the introduction of his *historia Francorum* (CPL 1023) as an assertion of his orthodoxy: *Scripturus bella regum cum gentibus aduersis, martyrum cum paganis, ecclesiarum cum haereticis, prius fidem meam proferre cupio ut qui legerit me non dubitet esse catholicum ... Credo ergo in deum patrem omnipotentem. Credo in Iesum Christum, filium eius unicum dominum nostrum, natum a patre, non factum* ... (Gregory of Tours, *historia Francorum* I; MGH mer. I.1 [ed. alt.], 3-5). Here, we have a personal formulation of faith which uses several liturgical, doctrinal, and scriptural phrases. Compare for this creed Kattenbusch 1894, 175-176 and Hahn 1897, 73 and 336-337.

[30] This text was ascribed to the fourth-century Gallican writer Phoebadius of Agen by Kattenbusch (1894, 171-173) and subsequently by Hahn (1897, 69-70 and 258-260), but its origin is nowadays considered uncertain. Matters are considerably complicated by the fact that the text exists in two recensions (the shorter one beginning with the words *Credo in deum patrem omnipotentem et unigenitum Iesum Christum* ..., the longer one with *Credimus in unum deum omnipotentem et in unum unigenitum filium eius* ...), which have been transmitted under several different names: see CCSL 69, 266. A critical edition of both recensions may be found in CCSL 9, 129-131; a slightly different text of the longer recen-

1752) [31], and the alleged creed of Adalbertus Morinensis (second half of the ninth century) [32].

Next, there are a number of texts which clearly refer to the Apostles' Creed but do not allow us to draw any conclusions about

sion alone is presented in CCSL 69, 267-268. To make things even more difficult, three other anonymous texts exist which are unmistakably related with the so-called *fides Romanorum*, viz.: the *dicta de fide catholica* (pseudo-Augustine, *sermo 235*), beginning *Credimus in unum deum patrem omnipotentem et unigenitum filium eius* ... (CPL 201; Simonetti 1960, 307-308), the *fides sancti Hieronymi*, beginning *Credo in unum deum patrem omnipotentem, uisibilium et inuisibilium factorem* ... (CPL 553; CCSL 69, 275), and the *de fide catholica* or *de fide apud Bethlehem*, beginning *Credimus in unum deum patrem omnipotentem et in unum dominum nostrum* ... (CPL 554; CCSL 69, 271-272). See for the various opinions on these four texts Dekkers 1995, 68 and 193 and Frede 1995, 430. The discussion of these texts in earlier literature is extremely hard to follow as different scholars frequently use different names for the same text and sometimes even confuse the several texts. Illuminating contributions may nevertheless be found in Morin 1904, Wilmart 1906 (especially 297-298n1), De Aldama 1934, and Simonetti 1960. All these texts clearly presuppose acquaintance with the structure and the content of the Apostles' Creed, but belong to the distinctly different tradition of the 'doctrinal' creeds (see above, chapter 1.8, pp. 42-43).

[31] This text, beginning *Credo in unum deum sanctam trinitatem, id est patrem omnipotentem, factorem caelestium omnium* ..., is edited and commented upon by Parmentier 1991. Of earlier credal scholars, only Kattenbusch (1894, 182-183) seems to have paid any attention to it. Kattenbusch makes the cautious suggestion that the text may have a Gallican origin, but such a thing is by no means certain: see Parmentier 1991, 354 and 377-378. This text again belongs to the sub-genre of the 'doctrinal' creeds.

[32] Hahn (1897, 363) presents a "Glaubensbekenntnis des Bischofs Adalbertus Morinensis": *Confiteor sanctam atque ineffabilem trinitatem, patrem et filium et spiritum sanctum, unum deum naturaliter esse, unius substantiae* ..., with a reference to Labbeus 1671, 1884. This is a short formulation of faith which only vaguely reminds one of the Apostles' Creed (see Hahn 1897, 80-81n97 and Kattenbusch 1900, 839 for a brief discussion). This formula, however, occurs in Labbeus (1671, 1884-1885) as part of a *professio altera generalis ordinandi archiepiscopi*. Hahn seems to have made a mistake here as the real *professio Adalberti* is found some pages earlier: *Ego, huius sedis ordinandus archiepiscopus et sacro ministerio uestro, sancti patres, praedicationis officium suscepturus, confiteor sanctam atque ineffabilem trinitatem* ...; Labbeus 1671, 1881-1884). Ironically, the text that was thus overlooked by Hahn explicitly refers to the Apostles' Creed: *Qui secundum apostolicum symbolum de semper uirgine Maria, quae ueraciter dei est genitrix, secundum carnem natus, passus, mortuus, resurrexit et in caelos ascendit, sedet quoque ad dexteram dei patris omnipotentis, inde uenturus iudicare uiuos et mortuos* ... (Labbeus 1671, 1884). As far as I can see, this interesting reference to the Creed has not been noticed before, and would certainly deserve closer study.

their authors' formulation of the same. Thus, we have to leave aside the early eighth-century *uita sancti Eligii episcopi Nouiomagensis* (CPL 2094) [33], the *liber de sacramento baptismi* by Leidrad of Lyons (written 812) [34], the *libellus de mysterio baptismatis* that has been claimed for Magnus of Sens (*sedit* 801-818) [35], the *liber de ordine baptismi* by Theodulph of Orléans (d. 821) [36], and a formula in the commentary on Hebrews by pseudo-Haimo of Halberstadt [37].

[33] This *uita* contains a sermon of Eligius (*sedit* 640-660; one may also meet the indication *Nouiomensis* instead of *Nouiomagensis*), in which we find a not necessarily complete paraphrase of the Creed: *Promisistis e contra credere uos in deum patrem omnipotentem, et in Iesum Christum filium eius unicum dominum nostrum, conceptum de spiritu sancto ...* (*uita Eligii episcopi Nouiomagensis* II 15; PL 87, 525 [according to the edition in MGH mer. 4, 705, this is chapter II 16; the portion that contains the credal piece has been omitted by the editor there, but crops up again as part of the *praedicatio sancti Eligii episcopi* in an appendix, *ibid.* 751-752; the relevant section also in Hahn 1897, 79]). A short discussion (together with a reproduction) of this paraphrase is offered in Kattenbusch 1894, 176. See for date and sources of this *uita* Dekkers 1995, 689 and Frede 1995, 61.

[34] This work contains an explanation of the word *symbolum* as well as an elaborate description of the content and meaning of the Creed: *Symbolum Graece, Latine uero interpretatur indicum uel collatio, hoc est ... Post apostolicum symbolum certissima fides, quam magistri ecclesiarum tradiderunt, haec est scilicet ut profiteatur patrem et filium et spiritum sanctum unum deum inuisibilem ...* (Leidrad of Lyons, *liber de sacramento baptismi* 4-5; PL 99, 859-561). Compare Kattenbusch 1894, 181-182 and Hahn 1897, 80n196 and 356-357 for this text. This text and those that are mentioned in the next two footnotes all seem to combine thoughts and phrases from anonymous *expositiones* like CPL 1758-1762 (see below, pp. 474-535) with features of more doctrinal creeds.

[35] In this short work, the meaning of the word *symbolum* and the content of the Creed are briefly discussed again: *Symbolum Graece, Latine indicium et signum uel collatio interpretatur ... Qualiter itaque credere in deum patrem omnipotentem et in filium eius Iesum Christum et in spiritum sanctum et cetera qui baptizandi sunt profitentur ...* (Magnus of Sens, *libellus de mysterio baptismatis*; PL 102, 981-982). From *Qualiter itaque ...* onwards, this section is reproduced in Kattenbusch 1894, 181 and Hahn 1897, 355. For a discussion of this text and its authorship, see Kattenbusch (*ibidem*) and Hahn 1897, 80n196 and 355n763.

[36] In this work, the author describes and explains the different rites that are connected with baptism in an elaborate way. When coming to the *traditio symboli*, he dwells on the meaning of the word *symbolum* and briefly indicates the content of the Creed: *... quia post exorcizationem et exsufflationem symboli sequitur traditio. Quod symbolum Latine indicium uel signum uel collatio interpretatur. Indicium ... Haec de symbolo et nomine eius dicta sint. Ceterum fides quae in hoc symbolo continetur ita ab his qui baptizandi sunt intellegi debet, ut credant in deum*

Again, the following texts can safely be omitted because they either were not written in Latin or too late for our purposes: a twelfth-century Franco-Norman translation of the Creed [38], the creed of Honorius of Autun (also from the twelfth century) [39], and the *abbreuiati symboli apostolorum expositio* of Theobald of Tours (thirteenth century) [40]. Similarly, we shall not discuss the *sermo seu confessio de sanctissima trinitate* which has been transmitted under the name of the fifth or sixth-century bishop Eleutherius of Tournai as this text is generally considered to be a forgery from the eleventh or twelfth century [41]. Again, three anonymous credal texts from the

*patrem omnipotentem* ... (Theodulph of Orléans, *liber de ordine baptismi* 5-7; PL 105, 227-228, partly reproduced in Kattenbusch 1894, 180 and Hahn 1897, 355-356). Compare for this text Kattenbusch 1894, 180-181 and Hahn 1897, 79.

[37] The relevant passage runs thus: *Fundamentum paenitentiae uocat unde primum instrui debet qui baptizandus est. Si tamen ad aetatem intellegibilem peruenit, hoc est ut credat dominum Iesum Christum genitum ex deo patre ante omnia saecula, natum de Maria uirgine in fine temporum pro salute generis humani sine semine uiri, passum, mortuum, resurrexisse tertia die, ascendisse ad caelos, uenturum ad iudicium ut reddat unicuique secundum opera sua, resurrectionem corporum et immutabilitatem animarum, bonos in gloriam, malos in poenis manere, omnipotentem deum trinitatem habere in personis, unitatem in substantia* ... (pseudo-Haimo of Halberstadt, *expositio in Epistulam ad Hebraeos* 6; PL 117, 858. Kattenbusch (1894, 214-215) and Hahn (1897, 81n197) rightly classify this passage as an "Anspielung an das Taufbekenntnis". The work in which this reference occurs seems to stem from an unknown author from the ninth century or later: see Kottje 1995.

[38] Heurtley 1858, 91-93; for a reproduction and short discussion of this variant see Hahn 1897, 82-83+n203.

[39] Honorius of Autun, *speculum ecclesiae, de natiuitate domini, fides catholica*: *Credo in deum patrem omnipotentem, creatorem caeli et terrae et totius creaturae. Et credo in suum unigenitum filium* ... (PL 172, 823-824). See Kattenbusch 1894, 183-184 and Hahn 1897, 113-114+n284 for a reproduction and discussion of this text. According to Hahn (1897, 113n284), this creed does not stem from Autun in Gaul but from Augst in the neighbourhood of Basel, but compare Kattenbusch 1900, 865-866. Hahn's only follower in this respect seems to be O'Callaghan: see O'Callaghan 1992, 286.

[40] This text is a minute commentary on the Creed in which, following the introduction, a complete variant of the Creed is quoted (*Vsitata tamen et fidei catholicae formula haec est. Credo in deum patrem omnipotentem* ...; Caspari 1883a, 294-295). See Hahn 1897, 83+n204 for a reproduction and short discussion of this credal variant; Kattenbusch (1900, 761) wrongly identifies it with *T*.

[41] Moreover, this sermon perhaps alludes to but certainly does not quote from the Apostles' Creed when speaking about Christ: *Incarnatus est, homo factus est, passus est, deinde factus oboediens usque ad mortem ... Idem etiam Christus die tertia a mortuis resurrexit, deinde in caelos unde descenderat ascendit ... Omnes credant*

ninth century and later that were edited by Caspari [42] and two passages from the work of (probably) pseudo-Alcuin [43] are mentioned
here, but will receive no attention in our analysis below.

Moreover, a number of texts will be excluded from our analysis
for the reason that they are not available in a critical edition. This
applies to Amalarius of Trier's (*sedit* 810-814; also known as Ama-

---

*illum inde uenturum et mortuos et uiuos iudicaturum* (PL 65, 84-85). Kattenbusch
(1894, 175 and 1900, 756n51) rightly points out that the Nicene Creed also plays
a role here. One can find similar credal allusions in the *sermo de trinitate* in the
same collection: *Credite in unum deum patrem omnipotentem, et in filium eius,
dominum nostrum Iesum Christum ... Credite dominum nostrum Iesum Christum
propter salutem hominum et saeculi liberationem de caelis descendisse, incarnatum
...* (PL 65, 87-88). For the origin of the sermons of pseudo-Eleutherius, see Dekkers 1995, 326-327 and Frede 1995, 441.

[42] The first of these is a short treatise in which the Creed is quoted and expounded article by article: *Credo in deum patrem omnipotentem, qui deus et pater
est, deus potestate, pater bonitate ...* (Caspari 1879, 283-285). For the form of the
Creed that emerges when one puts together all the relevant quotations, see Hahn
1897, 80-81+n197. In the other two texts, the anonymous authors, who are both
heavily indebted to Martin of Braga's *de corructione rusticorum* (CPL 1086; see
below, chapter 3.3, pp. 146-148), at a certain point remind their audience of the
moment of their baptism and thus quote the Creed in interrogatory form: *Iterum
interrogati a sacerdote fuistis: Creditis in deum patrem omnipotentem, creatorem caeli et terrae? Respondistis: Credo. Et in Iesum Christum ...* (Caspari 1883a, 198-199)
and *Post istam abrenuntiationem diaboli iterum interrogati estis a sacerdote credere
uos in deum patrem omnipotentem. Et tunc respondistis: Credimus. Et in Iesum
Christum ...* (Caspari 1883a, 203-204). Hahn (1897, 81-82) presents both credal
variants in declaratory form and discusses some of their peculiarities. Although
Hahn presents all three texts as witnesses for the form of the Creed in Gaul,
their origin could just as easily be different: see Caspari 1879, 285-286, Caspari
1883a, LVI-LVIII, LXXI-LXXII, and CVII-CIX, Kattenbusch 1894, 209-210
and 212, Kattenbusch 1900, 464n46, and Frede 1995, 125.

[43] These are *de diuinis officiis* 41, a concise commentary on each article of the
Creed (*Symbolum Graece, Latine collatio siue signum uel indicium ... Credo in
deum. Aliud credo deo, aliud deum, et aliud in deum ...*; PL 101, 1271-1273) and
*disputatio puerorum* 11, an extensive treatment of the Creed in question and answer form (*Sed quoniam sicut nosti omnes per fidem saluari credimus, rogo ut dicas
mihi quomodo fidem tuam intellegis uel etiam in quem credis? - Ego credo in deum
patrem omnipotentem, creatorem caeli et terrae. - Quare dicitur omnipotens ...*; PL
101, 1136-1143). Both texts are just mentioned in Hahn 1897, 80n197; Kattenbusch (1900, 866-867 and 869) offers a short discussion. The Migne edition ranks
the first under the *dubia* and the second under the *spuria* of Alcuin's works; see
also Kattenbusch 1900, 867 and Kelly 1976, 425.

larius of Metz) *epistula ad Carolum Magnum de caeremoniis baptis-mi* [44] and the pseudo-Augustinian *sermones 240-242* (CPL 368) [45].

Lastly, Hahn mentions the pseudo-Augustinian *expositio super symbolum* CPL 365 and the anonymous *expositio fidei* CPL 1763 as sources for the form of the Creed in Gaul [46]. These texts will receive due attention in the next chapter [47] so they will not play a role in the present one [48].

[44] This work contains a short exposition in which the Creed is quoted and ex-pounded article by article: *Symbolum autem sic: Credo in deum patrem omnipo-tentem. In dominum uiuum et uerum* ... (Amalarius of Trier, *epistula ad Carolum Magnum de caeremoniis baptismi*; PL 99, 896). The discussions by Kattenbusch (1894, 178-179 and 1900, 744-745) and Hahn (1897, 100-101+n260) clearly reveal that a critical edition of Amalarius's *epistula* is a necessary preliminary for the study of the underlying form of the Creed. The edition of Amalarius's exposition in Haußleiter 1898 constitutes a substantial improvement compared with the Migne text but still does not use all available manuscripts and, moreover, is not based on an autopsy of the codices but on the several older editions. It should be noted that a similar letter connected with Amalarius in the manuscript tradition is probably to be ascribed to Hildebold of Cologne (d. 818): see Morin 1896, Kattenbusch 1900, 826n22a, and Kruse 1976, 89-132. This letter contains a set of short baptismal questions (reproduced in Kinzig 1999a, 148) and the Nicene Creed, but no direct reference to the Apostles' Creed. See Morin 1896, 290-291 for the text.

[45] These three sermons all offer an explicit quotation of the complete Creed, either article by article or in one piece: ... *omniumque linguarum peritia repleti symbolum composuerunt. Petrus dixit: Credo in deum patrem omnipotentem. Vbi dicit patrem* ... (pseudo-Augustine, *sermo 240* 1; PL 39, 2189), ... *cuius textum uobis modo deo annuente dicemus. Petrus dixit: Credo in deum patrem omnipoten-tem. Iohannes dixit* ... (pseudo-Augustine, *sermo 241* 1; PL 39, 2190), and ... *iam ad istius symboli professionis sacramentum textumque ueniamus, quod in hunc mo-dum incipit: Credo in deum patrem omnipotentem* ... (pseudo-Augustine, *sermo 242* 1-2; PL 39, 2192). All three texts certainly seem to stem from Gaul: see Machiel-sen 1990, 208-209 and Frede 1995, 272-273, compare also below, p. 127. In view of the attention these texts have received from credal scholars (see Kattenbusch 1894, 190-193 and 210-211n16, Hahn 1897, 50-52nn86-87, Kattenbusch 1900, 461-463, 769-777, 868-869n120, 945-946, Morin 1930, 755, and Madoz 1938a, 44n1), it is remarkable that they have not yet received a critical edition. For the pseudo-Augustinian *sermo 243 de symbolo*, which is sometimes connected with the three preceding ones, see below, chapter 4.1, footnote 4.

[46] Hahn 1897, 73-75.

[47] See below, chapters 4.4 and 4.16.

[48] In addition, Smulders (1970, 237n10) mentions the *confessio* of Saint Patrick (CPL 1100) as a text that may bear Gallican features. See for this text below, chapter 3.6, p. 208 and footnote 415. Again, O'Callaghan (1992, 285) lists the

The source texts that remain, then, are the following.

Ambrosian *explanatio symboli ad initiandos* (CPL 153) as it is preserved in its Sankt Gallen manuscript among the Gallican sources for the form of the Creed; for the variant in question, see Caspari 1879, 220-221. O'Callaghan (1992, 286), without offering any arguments, also takes Nicetas of Remesiana's form of the Creed as a Gallican credal variant. See below, chapter 3.6, pp. 212-216, for this source. Next, Hen (1995, 63n25) gives a number of sources for the *traditio symboli* in Merovingian Gaul. Apart from Caesarius of Arles, the *Missale Gallicanum Vetus*, and the Bobbio Missal, which will be discussed in the present section (see below, pp. 121-127, 137-142 and footnote 141), these do not testify to the wording of the Creed. The remaining texts that are mentioned by Hen are Avitus of Vienne's *sermo 12 de symbolo* (CPL 994; two fragments only: see MGH AA VI 2, 122), the acts of the Synod of Agde of 506 (CPL 1784; despite Hen's hint, I could not find any reference to the *traditio symboli* in these), the anonymous *expositio antiquae liturgiae Gallicanae* (CPL 1925; the *traditio* is just mentioned), the *Missale Gothicum* (CPL 1919; does not offer the wording of the Creed), the *Sacramentarium Gelasianum Vetus* (CPL 1899; *traditio* of the Nicaeno-Constantinopolitan Creed), and the Luxeuil Lectionary (CPL 1948; contains lectures only). Finally, there is a possible quotation of the third article of the Creed in Hilary of Poitiers, *commentarius in Matthaeum* (c. 353; CPL 430) I 3: *Nam conceptum ex spiritu sancto, natum ex Maria uirgine omnium opus prophetarum est* (SChr 254, 94). In particular, the absence of a subject and the asyndeton strongly suggest that we have a literal quotation here. On the other hand, Hilary likes to omit the subject in similar constructions: see SChr 254, 83. Kattenbusch, who did not know of this passage, enumerates many instances where Hilary seems to betray his knowledge of the Creed (Kattenbusch 1900, 382-384n46 and 898n56). See for example Hilary of Poitiers, *de trinitate* IX 51: *Oblitus es mediatoris dispensationem et in ea partum cunas aetatem passionem crucem mortem? Et renascens non confessus es ex Maria filium dei natum?* and X 65: *Alius enim nobis est Christus crucifixus alius dei sapientia, alius sepultus alius descendens, et alius filius hominis alius filius dei ... Vel qui in dextera dei est non ipse est qui resurrexit? Vel qui resurrexit non idem mortuus est? Vel qui mortuus est non idem condemnat? ... Si itaque haec omnia Christus unus est, neque alius est Christus mortuus alius sepultus, aut alius desendens ad inferna et alius ascendens in caelos ... Numquid ambigitur quin Iesus Christus homo ex mortuis resurgens super omnes caelos uscendens a dextris dei sit? Numquid descendisse ad inferos corpus quod in sepulcro iacuit dicetur? Si itaque qui descendit ipse et ascendit et neque corpus descendisse ad inferos creditur, et resurgens de mortuis corpus ascendisse in caelos non ambigetur, quae hic praeter occulti sacramenti et incogniti mundo ac principibus saeculi fides relicta est? Vt cum idem atque unus sit descendens et ascendens, unus quoque nobis Iesus Christus sit et dei filius et hominis filius et uerbum deus et homo caro, et passus et mortuus et sepultus et resurgens et in caelos receptus et sedens a dextris dei ...* (CPL 433; CCSL 62a, 429 and 519-520).

SAL    Salvian of Marseilles's *de gubernatione dei* (middle of the
       fifth century; CPL 485) [49].

This text, our earliest witness for the form of the Creed in Gaul,
gives an explicit quotation, though of the first two articles only:
*Credo, inquis, in deum patrem omnipotentem, et in Iesum Christum
filium eius. Ergo primum ...* [50]. The word *inquis* is a clear quotation
marker, and with *Ergo primum* the author resumes his argument
again. Salvian refers to these words as belonging to the *symbolum* [51], but unfortunately does not quote it up to the third article.
This means that Salvian's form of the second article may well have
ended with the words *Filium eius*, but that we cannot be sure that
something like *Vnicum* or *Dominum nostrum* did not follow.

Thus, SAL testifies to a Massilian form of the Creed as follows:

*Credo in deum patrem omnipotentem
et in Iesum Christum, filium eius (...?)*
...
...

FAU-R   Faustus of Riez's (bishop from *c.* 457 to *c.* 490) *de spi-
        ritu sancto* (CPL 962) contains some quotations from
        and allusions to the Creed, which can be supplied with
        quotations from his *epistula 7* (CPL 963).

The two texts that contain the testimony for Faustus of Riez's
variant of the Creed [52] are a bit problematic. The first quotation from

---

[49] For earlier scholarship, compare Kattenbusch 1894, 174n1 and Hahn 1897,
72n166; for the date see SChr 220, 11-15, Dekkers 1995, 173, and Frede 1995,
747.

[50] Salvian of Marseilles, *de gubernatione dei* VI vi 32-33; SChr 220, 384.

[51] *In spectaculis enim apostatatio quaedam fidei est et a symboli ipsius et caelestibus sacramentis letalis praeuaricatio* (Salvian of Marseilles, *de gubernatione dei* VI
vi 31; SChr 220, 382). See also *ibid.* VI vi 33-34 (SChr 220, 384).

[52] Kattenbusch, Hahn, Kelly, and O'Callaghan not only take Faustus's *de spiritu sancto*, but also the texts FAU, EUSh9, and EUSh10 (see below, pp. 119-121
and 130-136) to testify to Faustus's form of the Creed: see Kattenbusch 1894,
158-164, Hahn 1897, 70-71n154, Kelly 1976, 178, and O'Callaghan 1992, 285.
But there are some real differences between all four sources (as was already seen
by Bergmann 1898, 83-84), and FAU, EUSh9, and EUSh10 are nowadays generally denied to Faustus (see below, footnotes 64 and 95). Glorie, the latest editor of FAU, EUSh9, and EUSH10, though he does not assume a common
authorship for these three texts either, nevertheless tries to reconstruct one "*sym-*

the Creed is found in the opening chapter of Faustus's *de spiritu
sancto*: *In quibus uerbis etiam trecentorum decem et octo sacer numerus
sacerdotum emergentem Arrii ac Macedonii damnauit errorem: Credo
in deum patrem, credo in filium eius unicum dominum nostrum, credo
et in spiritum sanctum* [53]. Brief reflection suffices to show that this
must be an incomplete quotation. We not only miss articles three to
eight, but the words *Omnipotentem* and *Iesum Christum*, which were
probably already present in proto-*R*, are lacking as well. Only the
ninth article seems to be quoted completely. These impressions are
reinforced by a number of other instances in the work of Faustus.

For the first article, we indeed find the more familiar *Credo in
deum patrem omnipotentem* [54]. The second article, together with the
third, is quoted again in Faustus's *epistula 7*: *Credo et in filium dei
Iesum Christum, qui conceptus est de spiritu sancto natus ex Maria
uirgine* [55]. The difference between the form of the second article in
*de spiritu sancto* on the one hand (*Credo in filium eius unicum dominum nostrum*) and that in *epistula 7* on the other (*Credo et in filium
dei Iesum Christum*) is not easily explained [56]. The best solution is
perhaps to assume that Faustus used a second article in the form
*Credo et in filium dei Iesum Christum, unicum dominum nostrum,*

bolum '*Gallicanum*" from them: see CCSL 101B, 898-899. Similarly, Denzinger
(1991, 30-31) combines the testimony of FAU-R with that of CY-T (see below,
pp. 128-129) to reconstruct one form of the Creed. Burn (1909, 2-3) does the same
on the basis of FAU-R, CY-T, and pseudo-Augustine, *sermo* 244 (CPL 368), which
he connects with Caesarius of Arles (see below, chapter 4.8).

[53] Faustus of Riez, *de spiritu sancto* I 1; CSEL 21, 102. Although Faustus alludes to the Nicene and Nicaeno-Constantinopolitan Creeds here, the quotation
clearly comes from the Apostles' Creed (see also above, chapter 2.3, footnote 43).

[54] ... *cum iam in principio symboli dixerint: Credo in deum patrem omnipotentem, duos eum habere patres* ... (Faustus of Riez, *de spiritu sancto* I 3, CSEL 21,
105). It should be noted that this need not be a complete quotation either -
nothing prevents the presence of *Creatorem caeli et terrae* or some such phrase in
Faustus's form of the Creed.

[55] ... *iuxta symboli auctoritatem, ut alia praetermittam, qua dicimus: Credo et* ...
*uirgine. Qui si talis* ... (Faustus of Riez, *epistula 7*; CSEL 21, 205). The quotation
in *de spiritu sancto* I 3 of the third article (*Cum autem catholica confiteatur ecclesia: Conceptus de spiritu sancto* ...; CSEL 21, 105) is thus exposed by this same
passage as incomplete and abbreviated. See also above, chapter 3.1, footnote 18.

[56] In Westra 1996a, 70, I did not yet fully appreciate the importance of the
first quotation for the wording of the second article of Faustus's form of the
Creed.

and that he adapted the wording of the article to the needs of the moment in both quotations. In the opening passage of *de spiritu sancto*, he is concerned with bringing out the universal belief in the coequality of the Holy Spirit with the Father and the Son [57] and therefore quotes the first, second, and ninth articles of the Creed as concisely as possible. Thus, he shortens *Filium dei Iesum Christum* to *Filium eius*, but retains *Vnicum dominum nostrum*, because this predicate stresses the Son's coequality with the Father. In his *epistula 7*, on the other hand, his aim is to show that in Christ, God is the father of mankind and a human being the mother of God at the same time [58], and therefore omits *Vnicum dominum nostrum* in his quotation of the second article [59]. As far as the the ninth article is concerned, this is quoted twice afterwards in *de spiritu sancto* I with the same formulation as in the initial chapter, and thus poses few problems [60].

Faustus then quotes the tenth article of the Creed in the second chapter of his *de spiritu sancto*. For a good evaluation of this quotation, it will be convenient to reproduce a larger portion of the text here. Faustus addresses his opponent as follows: *Sed opponis mihi et dicis non statim in hoc uerbo deum posse monstrari* (viz. the Holy Spirit) *quo dicimus: Credo et in spiritum sanctum, quia sequitur: Credo in sanctam ecclesiam catholicam. Primo nescio quomodo ecclesiam catholicam nominare audeat Macedonius, qui extra catholicam*

---

[57] *Et quia oportet ut errantibus quasi paruulis et ignaris prima Christianae traditionis elementa repetamus, in hac symboli perfectione et unitas euidenter aperitur et trinitas, dum ter repetita confessio patri et filio et spiritui sancto unum credulitatis reddit obsequium. In quibus uerbis* ... (Faustus of Riez, *de spiritu sancto* I 1; CSEL 21, 102).

[58] *Tu autem quod gemino errore praeuentus scribendum putasti sub duarum naturarum conuentu suscipi non debere ut deus pater hominis sit, ut homo mater dei sit, nos unam dei hominisque personam fiducialiter et salubriter asserentes in eo, qui erat in principio et qui sub redemptionis nostrae tempore factus est in similitudine carnis peccati, id est in ueritate hominis et similitudine peccatoris, nos, inquam, ita deum patrem hominis sub personae unitate testamur, sicut sub eiusdem unitatis amplexu matrem dei hominem confitemur iuxta symboli auctoritatem* ... (Faustus of Riez, *epistula 7*; CSEL 21, 204-205).

[59] Kattenbusch (1900, 977) seems to claim that neither *Dei* nor *Vnicum* were part of the second article of Faustus's form of the Creed.

[60] ... *ante quem omnis homo diabolo renuntians confitetur: Credo et in spiritum sanctum* and ... *quo dicimus: Credo et in spiritum sanctum* (Faustus of Riez, *de spiritu sancto* I 1 and 2; CSEL 21, 103).

*exul salutis exclusus est, ex illorum factus numero de quibus dicitur:*
*In circuitu impii ambulabunt. Ergo dicis: Credo in sanctam ecclesiam*
*catholicam. Quid supponendo exiguam, id est 'in' syllabam, ingentem*
*caliginem subtexere conaris? Credimus ecclesiam quasi regenerationis*
*matrem, non in ecclesiam credimus quasi in salutem auctorem* [61]. From
Faustus's words, it appears that his adversary quoted the tenth article as *Credo in sanctam ecclesiam catholicam*, and that Faustus considers the preposition *In* an insertion here. Since he does not object
to his adversary's use of *Credo* (though the quotation of his incen-
tive above could be extended to twice its length), but only dwells
on the abuse of the preposition *In*, it seems safe to assume that
Faustus read *Credo* in the tenth article of the Creed himself and
that for the rest of the article as well, he used the same formulation
as his adversary. Thus, we reconstruct Faustus's form of this article
as *Credo sanctam ecclesiam catholicam*.

This implies again that a third instance in *de spiritu sancto*, which
mentions the three final articles of the Creed, can only be taken as
an indication of the content and not of the wording of Faustus's
form of the Creed: ... *ut sanctam ecclesiam, sanctorum communionem,*
*abremissa peccatorum, carnis resurrectionem, uitam aeternam credamus*
*in deum ...* [62].

FAU-R, then, testifies as follows to the form of the Creed in
Riez:

*Credo in deum patrem omnipotentem (...?)*
*credo et in filium dei Iesum Christum, unicum dominum nostrum*
*qui conceptus est de spiritu sancto, natus ex Maria uirgine*
...

...

*credo et in spiritum sanctum*
*credo sanctam ecclesiam catholicam*
*[sanctorum communionem*
*abremissa peccatorum*
*carnis resurrectionem*
*uitam aeternam].*

---

[61] Faustus of Riez, *de spiritu sancto* I 2; CSEL 21, 104.
[62] Faustus of Riez, *de spiritu sancto* I 2; CSEL 21, 104.

FAU   A *tractatus de symbolo* (CPL 977) that has been trans-
      mitted under the name of one Faustinus (sometimes iden-
      tified with Faustus of Riez). According to Caspari, the
      first editor of this text, it was put together from various
      homilies of Faustus of Riez by some later author at some
      date between 500 and 700. Bergmann considers the con-
      nection with Faustus even looser. Glorie, its latest editor,
      agrees with Caspari and Bergmann in denying this text to
      Faustus, and connects it with the so-called *collectio Euse-
      biana* [63]. Both Dekkers and Frede classify it among the
      *spuria* of Faustus of Riez [64].

FAU cannot be used to reconstruct a complete variant of the
Creed. Although some articles are quoted in a quite accurate way,
others are only indicated. It will be convenient, therefore, to take a
closer look at this text. After the introduction, difficulties start
immediately with the first article: *Nunc ergo ipsa symboli uerba
uideamus. Credo in deum patrem. Aliud est credere in deum, aliud in
deum patrem ...* [65]. After explaining this difference, the author moves
on to the second article. As the author is not always concerned with
providing literal and complete quotations of each article (see
below), one should bear in mind the possibility that he only wanted
to comment upon the words *Credo in deum patrem* and simply
stopped his quotation of the first article there, but that *Omnipotentem* or some such term was nonetheless present in his form of the
Creed. This has the important implication, however, that we cannot
know whether or not additions like *Creatorem caeli et terrae* figured
in the variant of the Creed that is expounded here either.

The second and third articles, on the other hand, seem to be
quoted not only literally but also completely [66]. Here, the commen-

---

[63] See Dekkers 1995, 312-314, Frede 1995, 456-460, and in particular Kasper
1991, 373-385 for information and literature on this sermon collection.

[64] Caspari 1879, 257-281, Bergmann 1898, 86-91, CCSL 101, xxi, Dekkers
1995, 316, and Frede 1995, 460.

[65] Eusebius 'Gallicanus', *sermo 2 de symbolo* 2; CCSL 101B, 829.

[66] *Sequitur: Credo et in filium eius Iesum Christum, dominum nostrum. Si filius deus non esset ...* and *Ordo autem symboli ... ita humilitatem susceptae carnis
asseruit dum dicit: Conceptus de spiritu sancto, natus ex Maria uirgine. Ergo ...*
(Eusebius 'Gallicanus', *sermo 2 de symbolo* 2 and 3; CCSL 101B, 830 and 831).

tary covers only a small part of the quotations, so that it seems probable that these are complete.

Next, the fourth article is clearly presupposed, but nothing can be distilled from the text concerning its formulation: *Et sicut uere natus, ita et uere mortuus et sepultus* ... *In cuius passione Pilati praesidis signata sunt tempora, ne forte aliquem alium crucifixum haeretica mentiretur impietas* [67]. Similarly, we cannot be certain whether the Descent to Hell figured in the author's form of the Creed or not.

Next, articles five to ten are all introduced by *sequitur*, so that we may safely assume that they are quoted in a literal way. For articles five and seven, however, we should reckon with the possibility of truncated quotations as in the case of the first [68]. Especially in the case of the seventh article, it is not easy to reach a conclusion. In the quotation (see previous footnote) we miss the word *Patris* (present in *H*, *R*, and proto-*R*). We have to choose, therefore, between either the insertion of *Dei*, in which case *Patris* or even *Patris omnipotentis* has been passed over in the same way as *Omnipotentem* (or *Omnipotentem, creatorem caeli et terrae*) in the first article, or a change from *Patris* to *Dei*. The latter possibility becomes more attractive in the light of the commentary on the seventh article: *Sedet ergo ad dexteram dei, id est, sedem in patris dextera, hoc est, in eius gloria et beatitudine collocauit* [69]. Here, the words *id est* seem to stamp *Sedet ergo ad dexteram dei* as a repeated quotation. Moreover, the explanation *in patris dextera* would be superfluous if the word *Patris* was already present in the underlying form of the Creed.

When we turn to the final articles, it should be noted that the Communion of Saints and the eleventh article are only indicated,

---

[67] Eusebius 'Gallicanus', *sermo 2 de symbolo* 4; CCSL 101B, 831. Glorie marks the words *mortuus et sepultus* as a quotation, though they are absent from the reconstruction of his *"symbolum 'Gallicanum'"* (see CCSL 101B, 898).

[68] *Sequitur: Tertia die resurrexit. Hunc itaque* ... *Sequitur: Ascendit in caelum, sedet ad dexteram dei. Numquid* ... *Sequitur: Inde uenturus iudicare uiuos et mortuos. Quem tanti* ... *Sequitur: Credo in spiritum sanctum. Ita est* ... *Sequitur: Sanctam ecclesiam catholicam. Quae est* ... (Eusebius 'Gallicanus', *sermo 2 de symbolo* 5-9; CCSL 101B, 831-833).

[69] Eusebius 'Gallicanus', *sermo 2 de symbolo* 6; CCSL 101B, 831.

whereas the twelfth article and the addition of Eternal Life are again quoted literally [70].

All in all, we can state that FAU is a reliable witness for articles 2, 3, 6, 7 (probably), 8, 9, 10, and 12; that article 1 and perhaps article 5 as well are not quoted in a complete way; that neither the presence nor the absence of the Descent to Hell can be proved; and that nothing can be said about the formulation of articles 4 and 11 and the Communion of Saints in the variant of the Creed the author expounds.

This leads to the following reconstruction of the underlying form of the Creed in FAU:

*Credo in deum ...*
*credo et in filium eius Iesum Christum, dominum nostrum*
*conceptus de spiritu sancto, natus ex Maria uirgine*
*...*
*tertia die resurrexit (...?)*
*ascendit in caelum*
*sedet ad dexteram dei (?)*
*inde uenturus iudicare uiuos et mortuos*
*credo in spiritum sanctum*
*sanctam ecclesiam catholicam*
*[sanctorum communionem*
*abremissio peccatorum]*
*carnis resurrectionem*
*uitam aeternam.*

CAE-A   The introductory part of the *expositio uel traditio symboli* in part C of the *Missale Gallicanum Vetus* (CPL 1922), which is nowadays better known as *sermo 9* of Caesarius of Arles (bishop from 503 to 542; CPL 1008) [71].

---

[70] *Sequitur ut transeamus ad sanctorum communionem. Illos hic ... ubi secundum symbolum donatur abremissio peccatorum. Ibi enim ... Sequitur: Carnis resurrectionem. Multi etiam ... Sequitur: Vitam aeternam. Credamus ideo* (Eusebius 'Gallicaus', *sermo 2 de symbolo* 10-13; CCSL 101B, 833-834).

[71] *Missale Gallicanum Vetus* 62-63; Mohlberg 1958, 17-18 = Caesarius of Arles, *sermo 9*; CCSL 103, 46-47. For the identification of Caesarius as the author, see Morin 1934a. See for earlier scholarship Kattenbusch 1894, 54, Hahn 1897, 77-78, Kattenbusch 1900, 461-462 and 775-776, and Kelly 1976, 178-179. Hahn and

Here we meet for the first time the ideal case of a variant of the Creed that is quoted both explicitly and in its entirety after a short introduction: *Totum ergo credulitatis pectoris sinum ad uitalis carminis expandamus oraculum. Quod ita incipit: Credo in deum patrem ... uitam aeternam. Amen*[72]. It is important to remember, however, that the sermon in which this form of the Creed occurs has come to us by way of its inclusion in a missal, and that we cannot know, therefore, whether it stems from the author of the sermon, Caesarius, or from the compiler of the *Missale Gallicanum Vetus*, who worked at least a century and a half later in Eastern Gaul[73].

The form of the Creed to which CAE-A testifies runs as follows:

*Credo in deum patrem omnipotentem, creatorem caeli et terrae*
*credo et in Iesum Christum, filium eius unigenitum sempiternum*
*qui conceptus est de spiritu sancto, natus est de Maria uirgine*

Kattenbusch were of course still unaware of the Caesarian authorship of this sermon. Gamber (1958, 39-40) seems to ignore it when he connects this part of the *Missale Gallicanum Vetus* with Northern Italy (see below, footnote 73). It should be noted that what is part C in Mohlberg's edition is designated the 'first part' of the missal by Hahn and Kattenbusch. Gamber uses the label 'Fragment III'. Part B, which also contains a variant of the Creed (see below, pp. 137-138) is designated as the 'second part' and 'Fragment II' by the same authors. For the discussion whether this sermon yields two different variants of the Creed or only one, see below, pp. 124-125. It should be observed that in Morin's edition of the sermons of Caesarius, *sermo 9* is followed by another sermon on the Creed. This sermon, also known as *excarpsum de fide catholica*, has been handed down as a work of Augustine (pseudo-Augustine, *sermo 244* [CPL 368]), but was also considered to stem from Caesarius by Morin (see below, chapter 4.8, p. 347) and thus included in his edition as *sermo 10*. Nevertheless, there are several reasons for doubting the Caesarian authorship of this piece: see below, chapter 4.8, footnote 228 and pp. 346-347. On the other hand, as nothing seems to speak against Caesarius's authorship of *sermo 9*, we have chosen to discuss *sermo 9* here as a firm witness for the form of the Creed in Gaul, and *sermo 10* as one of the texts of unknown origin in chapter 4.8.

[72] Caesarius of Arles, *sermo 9*; CCSL 103, 47.

[73] See below, footnote 125. Gamber (1958, 39-40) claims that this form of the Creed, like that of Bobbio A, "... ist eine Weiterbildung des Textes, wie ihn *Rufin von Aquileia* ... überliefert" (Gamber 1958, 40), but this is hardly justified by the facts. Notwithstanding his own claim, Gamber stamps the liturgy of both the Bobbio Missal and the *Missale Gallicanum Vetus* as 'Gallican'. In his opinion, this 'Gallican' liturgy travelled from Northern Italy to Eastern Gaul at some point in the eighth century: see Gamber 1958, 40-41. This theory does not seem to have found acceptance: see Hen 1995, 47.

*passus est sub Pontio Pilato, crucifixus, mortuus et sepultus*
*descendit ad inferna*
*tertia die resurrexit a mortuis*
*ascendit ad caelos*
*sedet ad dexteram dei patris omnipotentis*
*inde uenturus iudicare uiuos et mortuos*
*credo in sanctum spiritum*
*sanctam ecclesiam catholicam*
*sanctorum communionem*
*remissionem peccatorum*
*carnis resurrectionem*
*uitam aeternam.*

CAE-B    The expository part of the same sermon, which allows us to reconstruct another form of the Creed [74].

The reconstruction of this second form is fairly easy, as practically all quotations are introduced by means of *sequitur, inquit,* or a similar phrase [75]. The only difficulty occurs in connection with the third and fourth articles. It will be convenient to give the text in full here: *Natus, inquit, de Maria uirgine, conceptus est de spiritu sancto, passus sub Pontio Pilato. Requiramus, dilectissimi, cur symboli conditores necessarium iudicarunt ut ipsius etiam Pilati nomen insererent. Ideo utique, quia antichristi multi futuri erant: ut nulla haeresis Christum alium esse diceret, cum unum utique esse constaret quem sub Pilato passum symbolum tradidisset. Crucifixus mortuus et sepultus, tertia die resurrexit. De manifesta ...* [76]. Morin has shown that the

---

[74] *Missale Gallicanum Vetus* 64-65; Mohlberg 1958, 18-21 = Caesarius of Arles, *sermo 9*; CCSL 103, 47-50.

[75] *Et ideo iuuat iterare quod numquam conuenit obliuisci: Credo in deum patrem omnipotentem. Sicut ... ut ipse numerus repetitionis in signo conueniat trinitatis: Credo in deum patrem omnipotentem. Symbolum ... Sic ergo habet exordium symboli: Credo in deum patrem omnipotentem. Deum cum audis ... Sequitur: Credo et in Iesum Christum, filium eius unigenitum sempiternum. Iesus Hebraice ... Vnigenitum, inquit ... Conceptus, inquit, de spiritu sancto. Spiritus ergo ... Natus, inquit, de Maria uirgine ... Sequitur autem in symbolo: Ascendit ad caelos, sedet ad dexteram dei patris omnipotentis. Non corporaliter ... Inde, inquit, uenturus iudicare uiuos et mortuos, credo in sanctum spiritum. Ad excludenda ... Credo, inquit, sanctam ecclesiam catholicam, sanctorum communionem, carnis resurrectionem, uitam aeternam. Amen* (Caesarius of Arles, *sermo 9*; CCSL 103; 47-50).

[76] Caesarius of Arles, *sermo 9*; CCSL 103, 48-49.

words *Natus, inquit* ... constitute the beginning of the second part of
the sermon, which was held one day later than the first part, a
usage that seems to be typical for Caesarius[77]. Now it is clear that
*Natus de Maria uirgine* is a direct quotation. Caesarius probably
started the second part of his sermon in the middle of the third
article because he had given only the first half of this article the
day before. Then follow the words *Conceptus est de spiritu sancto*. These
cannot be a literal quotation, though Morin prints them as such,
since the first part of the third article is quoted in an unambiguous
way without *Est* in the first half[78]. Moreover, it would be very
strange to quote this article in such a back-to-front way. The best
solution, therefore, seems to be that Caesarius inserted the words
*Conceptus est de spiritu sancto*, not as a quotation, but as a reminder
for his audience of the first part of the third article which he had
expounded to them the day before. The next phrase, *Passus sub
Pontio Pilato*, is again best explained as a literal quotation for two
reasons. First of all, Caesarius goes on with *Requiramus, dilectissimi*
... to explain the meaning of these words, and in the second place
they fit exactly together with *Crucifixus, mortuus et sepultus* ...,
which seems to be a certain quotation because of the syntactical
break between *tradidisset* and *Crucifixus* (see above).

When one lists all quotations from CAE-B, the resulting variant
of the Creed is not the same as the one that is given in CAE-A. The
differences are: the phrases *Creatorem caeli et terrae, A mortuis, Descendit ad inferna*, and *Remissionem peccatorum* are present in CAE-A
but absent in CAE-B, CAE-B has a participle construction without
*Est* in the third article whereas CAE-A uses *Qui* with a twofold *Est*,
and CAE-B omits *Est* after *Passus*, and adds *Credo* before *Sanctam
ecclesiam catholicam*[79]. The question is, of course, does CAE-B, the
expository part of the Caesarian sermon, represent the same variant
of the Creed as the one we find in CAE-A, the introductory part, or
is it witness to some different variant?

Kattenbusch seems to have been the first to pay attention to this
problem. He notices some of the differences that are enumerated
above but, mainly because of the identical formulations in the sec-

---

[77] Morin 1934a, 182-183.

[78] See above, footnote 75.

[79] It is possible, however, that Caesarius only repeats *Credo* here to make a
smoother transition from the ninth to the tenth article.

ond and ninth articles, concludes that the exposition in this form had nevertheless been written to comment upon the variant of the Creed that is given in the first part of the sermon. The observation that expositions in general are often "summarisch" and "lax" is probably meant to support this conclusion [80]. Similarly, Morin explains the differences between the credal quotations (in CAE-B) and the entire variant (in CAE-A) by assuming that Caesarius, in the exposition, omitted those portions of the Creed that he did not want to comment upon [81].

This explanation is rather weak, however. As far as Morin's argument is concerned, it should be observed that omitting a quotation hardly spares any time at all. Moreover, we meet many phrases of the Creed (like *Sempiternum, Natus de Maria uirgine, Crucifixus, mortuus et sepultus, Ascendit ad caelos, Sanctam ecclesiam catholicam*) that are quoted but not commented upon in CAE-B. In fact, and this clinches the case against both Kattenbusch and Morin, the author rather seems to take pains to ensure that no part of the Creed is forgotten in CAE-B, even if he does not intend to say something about each.

If CAE-A and CAE-B really testify to two different forms of the Creed, how can we explain their presence in one and the same sermon? A very plausible solution is suggested by Morin himself, who ranks this exposition among the sermons that were not written by Caesarius but by some predecessor of his, and only slightly adapted by Caesarius for his own use [82]. If Caesarius really took over an existing *expositio symboli* here, it would not be strictly necessary for him to adapt every single credal quotation, since he would give the

---

[80] Kattenbusch 1900, 776n27.

[81] "Que le second se ramène au premier ... c'est ce que tout le monde admettra, au moins d'une façon générale ..." and "Césaire, visiblement, se croyait obligé d'être court, et aura retranché de son modèle ..." (Morin 1934a, 184). Kelly (1976, 178+n3) seems to follow Morin in this respect, though he does not mention the problem. In fact, Morin (1934a, 184-186) mentions only some of the differences between CAE-A and CAE-B in his discussion.

[82] This can be deduced from the remarks in CCSL 103, cxxii in combination with the printing of the sermon in Morin's edition of Caesarius. See also his remark about Caesarius's "modèle" that is quoted in the previous footnote. Barbet (1965, 337) mentions Faustus of Riez as a possibility.

actual Arelatan form during the *traditio* all the same. In that case, CAE-A can be taken to contain Caesarius's own variant of the Creed, while CAE-B yields some earlier form [83]. The absence of clauses like *Creatorem caeli et terrae* and *Descendit ad inferna* in CAE-B supports this hypothesis [84].

CAE-B, then, testifies to the following form of the Creed:

*Credo in deum patrem omnipotentem*
*credo et in Iesum Christum, filium eius unigenitum sempiternum*
*conceptus de spiritu sancto, natus de Maria uirgine*
*passus sub Pontio Pilato, crucifixus, mortuus et sepultus*
*tertia die resurrexit*

---

[83] Similarly Burn 1909, 7: "... in these cases we can always extract an earlier Creed from the exposition than that which we find quoted at the beginning, and which probably in each case represents the form familiar to the copyist. Certainly the tendency would always be to assimilate a form". Compare also Aland 1989, 179 for the parallel case of differences between scriptural quotations in a lemma and in the running text of a commentary: "Der Lemma-Text war von Anfang der Überlieferung an in Gefahr, denn der Abschreiber war bei dessen relativer Länge stets in der Versuchung, ihn einfach durch den ihm vertrauten zu ersetzen". In the present case, things are complicated by the fact that this *expositio uel traditio symboli* has not been transmitted among the other sermons of Caesarius, but as part of the *Missale Gallicanum Vetus*. If Morin is right that the sermon was adapted rather than written by Caesarius, there are at least three possibilities. The first is that Caesarius did not change the credal quotations in his model but rather prefixed his own form of the Creed to it, and that the whole *expositio uel traditio* was taken up in the missal. A second possibility is that Caesarius did not change the credal quotations in his model, that one of the compilers of the missal took up the sermon as it stood and prefixed his own credal variant to it. This opens up a third possibility, viz. that Caesarius changed the quotations in the sermon in such a way as to make them fit his variant of the Creed, that the compiler of the missal then took up the sermon as it stood, but prefixed his own variant to it. In the first case, CAE-A represents Caesarius's form of the Creed and CAE-B is some pre-Caesarian form, in the second, CAE-A is a seventh-century form of the Creed and CAE-B is pre-Caesarian, in the third case, CAE-A stems from the seventh century and CAE-B represents Caesarius's form of the Creed. For a further discussion of this question, see below, chapter 4.8, p. 350.

[84] It is only fair to remark that the possibility that the introductory and expository parts of this sermon were first combined by a compiler was at least envisaged by Kattenbusch (see above, footnote 80).

*ascendit ad caelos*
*sedet ad dexteram dei patris omnipotentis*
*inde uenturus iudicare uiuos et mortuos*
*credo in sanctum spiritum*
*credo sanctam ecclesiam catholicam*
*sanctorum communionem*
*carnis resurrectionem*
*uitam aeternam.*

CAE-C   The same sermon, accompanied by some liturgical injunctions and two fragments from the pseudo-Augustinian *sermones 241* and *242*, crops up in a literary manuscript from the first quarter of the ninth century, into which it has apparently been copied from an eighth-century or earlier Gallican sacramentary [85].

As in the case of the form of this sermon that is found in the *Missale Gallicanum Vetus*, the text gives a complete form of the Creed in the introduction (corresponding to CAE-A), but also allows us to reconstruct one from the sermon itself (corresponding to CAE-B). Once again, these two forms of the Creed are not identical [86], nor do they coincide with the forms of CAE-A and CAE-B. Their mutual differences are probably due to a scribe who adapted the first variant to his personal form of the Creed. Since we cannot know whether we should blame the scribe of the original liturgical manuscript or the one of the extant literary manuscript for this, it seems best to exclude this variant from our analysis. The several quotations in the sermon, however, seem to stem directly from a Gallican liturgical source prior to 800 AD so that we can safely use it for our study of the wording of the Creed in Gaul.

CAE-C, then, offers the following variant of the Creed:

*Credo in deum patrem omnipotentem, creatorem caeli et terrae*

---

[85] See Barbet 1965, 335-338. Barbet (1965, 339-345) also offers the text of the 'new' Caesarian sermon in an extremely accurate transcription. As far as one can tell, this text has not previously been noticed by other students of the Creed. When writing Westra 1996a, I was not yet acquainted with it myself.

[86] See Barbet 1965, 338. Barbet (1965, 338-339) continues to discuss the peculiarities of this first form of the Creed.

*credo et (?)* [87] *in Iesum Christum, filium eius unigenitum sempiter-*
*num*
*conceptus de spiritu sancto, natus de Maria uirgine*
*passus sub Pontio Pilato, crucifixus, mortuus et sepultus*
*tertia die resurrexit*
*ascendit ad caelum*
*sedet ad dexteram dei patris omnipotentis*
*inde uenturus iudicare uiuos ac mortuos*
*credo in spiritum sanctum*
*credo sanctam ecclesiam catholicam*
*sanctorum communionem*
*carnis resurrectionem*
*in uitam aeternam.*

CY-T    Cyprian of Toulon's *epistula ad Maximum* (*sedit* 524-546;
CPL 1020) [88].

This letter is again an unproblematic source as Cyprian gives literal quotations of the articles one to eight. Both the quotations and
the concise commentary are either introduced in an explicit way or
marked by the repeated use of *qui* [89].

---

[87] The presence of *Et* is uncertain. In CAE-C, the second article is given twice.
In the first quotation (lacking in CAE-B), *Et* is absent, whereas it is present in
the second: *Ideo iuuat* (*partit* ms.) *iterare quod numquam conuenit obliuisci: Credo*
*in deum patrem omnipotentem creatorem caeli et terrae, credo in Iesum Christum*
*filium eius unigenitum sempiternum, et praedicis totum ... Sequitur: Credo et in*
*Iesum Christum, filium eius unigenitum sempiternum. Iesus Hebraice uocabuli ...*
(Barbet 1965, 340-341, corresponding to CCSL 103, 47-48; compare footnote 75
above).

[88] There are two editions of this text, both of which claim to be the first:
MGH, Epp. III, 434-436 (Gundlach, 1892) and Wawra 1903, 589-594. Both editions intend to provide an exact copy of the manuscript text (Wawra even takes
over the punctuation), but there are nevertheless some thirty differences between
the two editions. One of these occurs in a credal quotation (see below, footnote
90). Generally, Gundlach's edition seems to be more reliable than Wawra's. See
for earlier credal scholarship concerning this text Kattenbusch 1900, 741 and
Kelly 1976, 178-179. See for Denzinger's use of this source above, footnote 52.

[89] *Certe symbolum quod et tenemus et credimus hoc continit: Credo in deum pa-*
*trem omnipotentem, credo et in Iesum Christum filium eius unigenitum dominum*
*nostrum. Ecce, explicitae sunt personae patris et filii secundum deitatem. Quid uero*
*pro redemptione nostra filius unigenitus deus egerit, audi quod sequitur: Qui concep-*
*tus de spiritu sancto, natus ex Maria uirgine. Vtique subaudis: unigenitus deus,*
*quia non alium nominasti personam. Passus, inquit, sub Pontio Pilato. Qui utique*

The credal variant of CY-T runs thus:

*Credo in deum patrem omnipotentem*
*credo et in Iesum Christum, filium eius unigenitum, dominum nos-*
  *trum*
*qui conceptus de spiritu sancto, natus ex Maria uirgine*
*passus sub Pontio Pilato, crucifixus et sepultus,*
*tertia die resurrexit a mortuis*
*ascendit in caelos*
*sedet ad dexteram patris*
*inde uenturus* [90] *iudicaturus uiuos ac mortuos*

...

...

PS-AU    The pseudo-Augustinian *liber testimoniorum fidei* (CPL 976) [91]. This text was once attributed to Faustus of Riez, and definitely seems to stem from early sixth-century Gaul [92].

In chapter XII of the portion of this work that is entitled *de operis unitate*, we find direct quotations of the second, third, and fourth articles of the Creed [93]. The quotations seem to offer the complete text of these articles. The words *Da terrenam in pedibus humilitatem* in particular, introducing the third and fourth articles, seem to confirm that the Descent to Hell was absent from the author's form of the Creed, as otherwise this addition would support his point that the Creed mentions the humility of Christ far too well

---

*filius unigenitus deus. Crucifixus et sepultus. Qui nihilominus unigenitus deus. Ter-*
*tia die resurrexit a mortuis, ascendit in caelos, sedet ad dexteram patris, inde uen-*
*turus iudicaturus uiuos ac mortuos. Qui utique quem superius es confessus, filius*
*unigenitus est* (Cyprian of Toulon, *epistula ad Maximum*; MGH, Epp. III, 435).

[90] Wawra (1903, 591) gives *Inuenturus* as the reading of CY-T here, but the manuscript (*Coloniensis*, Erzbischöfliche Diözesan- und Dombibliothek 212, f. 114R) has *Inde uenturus*: see Burn 1909, plate III.

[91] As far as I can tell, Bergmann (1898, 100) and Kattenbusch (1900, 976-977) are the only other credal scholars who have paid attention to this source.

[92] See Dekkers 1995, 316 and Frede 1995, 303.

[93] *Da in symbolo primi tui capitis eminentiam: Credo, inquit, in filium eius Ie-*
*sum Christum, dominum nostrum. Da terrenam in pedibus humilitatem: Qui con-*
*ceptus, inquit, de spiritu sancto natus ex Maria uirgine, passus sub Pontio Pilato*
*crucifixus et sepultus. De quibus absque dubio pedibus* ... (pseudo-Augustine, *liber*
*testimoniorum fidei, de operis unitate* XII; Pitra 1888, 156 [= PLS 3, 515]).

to omit it from his quotation, either intentionally or unintentionally.

According to PS-AU, these articles have the following wording:

...

*credo in filium eius Iesum Christum, dominum nostrum*
*qui conceptus de spiritu sancto, natus ex Maria uirgine*
*passus sub Pontio Pilato, crucifixus et sepultus*

...

...

EUSh9   *Homilia 9* of the so-called *collectio Eusebiana* (CPL
966)[94]. This homily and the next (EUSh10) have been
ascribed to Faustus of Riez by various scholars since
the eighteenth century, but his authorship has been
denied by Bergmann and their latest editor, Glorie; this
denial has been accepted by Kelly and Frede, but the
question seems not yet to have come to a conclusion[95].
It seems safest, therefore, to treat the homilies as two
separate sources for the form of the Creed[96].

Several difficulties are connected with this sermon. Only a small
number of articles is quoted in such a way that no discussion about

---

[94] See above, footnote 63.

[95] For earlier scholarship see Caspari 1869, 183-184 and 199-213, Bergmann
1898, 71-86, Van Buchem 1967, 49-57, and Griffe 1973, 187-188. For Glorie's
position see Dekkers 1961, 213, CCSL 101, vii-xvii, Kelly 1976, 178n1, and Frede
1995, 455-456. Faustus's authorship has been revindicated by Griffe (1973, 188-
190), Raymond Étaix (see Frede 1999, 74), and Kasper 1991, 382-384. The latter
makes a small but thorough study of the two sermons on the Creed, and also
pays attention to the form of the Creed to which they testify. Nevertheless,
apart from their frequent concordance, a number of differences remain - unless
one wants to explain these away by assuming scribal errors. For the opinion of
earlier students of the Creed, see above, footnote 52.

[96] To make things more complicated, the fragmentary *homilia 76* of the *collectio Eusebiana* also contains some possible credal quotations: *Conceptus ergo est de
spiritu sancto. Vides ...* and *Credo et in sanctum spiritum. Vides ...* (Eusebius 'Gallicanus', *homila 76* 6 and 12; CCSL 101A, 812 and 814). Glorie treats both as
extended quotations in which the words *ergo* and *et* have been inserted by the
author: see CCSL 101B, 898-899. The second decision seems particularly doubt-
ful. As far as the first quotation is concerned, the possibility cannot be excluded
that the author not only added *ergo* but also suppressed *Qui*.

their exact wording is possible. In the majority of cases, however, there is room for a smaller or greater amount of disagreement. We therefore have to take a closer look at this source text.

As in FAU, the expository part of EUSh9 starts with a straight-forward quotation: *Sed iam ipsa symboli uerba uideamus: Credo in deum patrem omnipotentem. Per dei appellationem* ... [97]. It is difficult to say whether the author's variant of the Creed did or did not contain a phrase like *Creatorem caeli et terrae*. As will appear below, the author of this sermon is certainly not concerned with giving quotations of every single article, so that the fact that the text is silent about it is virtually irrelevant. Since the exposition of the word *Omnipotentem* explicitly refers to God's creating activity [98], however, it seems best to assume that this activity was also not explicitly mentioned in the author's form of the Creed.

As far as the second article is concerned, we have two literal, though only partial, quotations: *Sequitur: Et in filium eius. Ex patre ergo filius ... Quod autem dicit: In Iesum Christum, Iesus in nostra lingua* ... [99]. The preposition *in* in the second quotation can best be explained as being deliberately repeated to introduce the accusative *Iesum Christum*, which would otherwise be pending. Whether the second article of the author of EUSh9 exhibited the words *Dominum nostrum* or an equivalent of *Vnicum*, either before or after *Iesum Christum*, is unclear. The sequence *dominus noster Iesus Christus* occurs once in the commentary [100], whereas nothing corresponds to *Vnicum*, but neither fact can be used as hard and fast evidence for the wording of the credal variant under discussion.

---

[97] Eusebius 'Gallicanus', *homilia 9 de symbolo* 2; CCSL 101, 99. The quotation is repeated at a later point in the sermon: see below, footnote 101.

[98] *Hoc ergo ordine credimus in deum patrem omnipotentem. Merito itaque omni-potens creditur qui, cum solum filium de se et de substantia sua genuerit quomodo genuerit lucem de luce, splendorem de splendore protulerit, sic ea omnia ex nihilo in praecepti celeritate perfecit. Cuncta enim quae antea non erant, tamquam subito aliunde producta, ante nutum eius uelociter astiterunt, nulla apparente materia. Origo fuit rerum efficax creatoris imperium ... Intellege illius esse totum, cuius caelo tegeris, cuius terrae gremio sustineris, cuius aere pasceris* ... (Eusebius 'Gal-licanus', *homilia 9 de symbolo* 3; CCSL 101, 101-102).

[99] Eusebius 'Gallicanus', *homilia 9 de symbolo* 4-5; CCSL 101, 102-104.

[100] *Quomodo si cereus illuminetur ex alio ... ita et dominus noster Iesus Christus ... cum patre alius est in persona, sed non alius in substantia uel natura* (Eusebius 'Gallicanus', *homilia 9 de symbolo* 4; CCSL 101, 102-103).

The second article is quoted once more in abbreviated form when the author turns to the ninth article, but this takes us no further [101].

When we turn to the third article, we find a more or less certain quotation of the second part only, whereas the reference to the first part of this article could just as well be an indication of the contents as a quotation: *Iesus Christus filius hominis ipse est qui conceptus est de spiritu sancto, sicut et angelus ista ad beatam Mariam dicit ... Quid mirum si non est uiolata partu quae magis est sanctificata conceptu? Aut quid incredibile si Christus ex uirgine, id est integritas de integritate processit? Natus ex Maria uirgine: non enim nasci debebat ex corruptione uirtus* [102]. The most one can say is that the two parts would fit together to form the complete article, so that the fact that the end of the article is quoted literally could just be an argument to treat the reference to the first part as a literal quotation too [103], but that would all be very hypothetical. It is better, therefore, to use only the second reference for reconstructing the author's form of the Creed here. Nevertheless, the author's discussion clearly reveals that a phrase with *conceptus* was, in his credal variant, also part of the article.

Next, the fourth and fifth articles are only indicated: *Sicut ergo uere natus, ita uere mortuus est propter peccata nostra et resurrexit in spem et iustificationem nostram* [104]. Articles six and seven, on the other hand, are again clearly quoted in their entirety: *Sequitur:*

---

[101] *Dixit primo: Credo in deum patrem omnipotentem. Sequitur: Credo in filium. Et iterum dixit: Credo in spiritum sanctum* (Eusebius 'Gallicanus', *homilia 9 de symbolo* 10; CCSL 101, 107). The repetition of *Credo* is probably due to the author's concern to bring out the coequality of the three divine persons.

[102] Eusebius 'Gallicanus', *homilia 9 de symbolo* 6; CCSL 101, 104.

[103] Glorie indeed considers the first reference as a quotation: see CCSL 101B, 898. Compare also the possible quotation in *homilia 76* 6: see above, footnote 96.

[104] Eusebius 'Gallicanus', *homilia 9 de symbolo* 7; CCSL 101, 104. Glorie considers the words *mortuus est* and *et resurrexit* as partial quotations (see CCSL 101B, 898), but this seems unconvincing. Another possible indication of the fifth article can be seen in the commentary on the word *Omnipotentem*: *Vel quod diuinitas carnem susceperit, uel quod per inuiolatam uirginem ianuam uitae huius intrauerit, uel quod die tertia a mortuis resurrexerit non cogites nec intra te dicas: Quomodo aut quo ordine hoc fieri potuit? Diuina opera non discutienda sunt sed credenda* (Eusebius 'Gallicanus', *homilia 9 de symbolo* 3; CCSL 101, 101).

*Ascendit ad caelos, sedet ad dexteram dei patris omnipotentis. Ascendit itaque ...* [105].

The exposition of the eighth article then opens thus: *Inde ergo uenturus est iudicare uiuos et mortuos. Hic uideamus ...* [106]. This sounds familiar enough, but we should be cautious - it seems certain that *ergo* has been added by the author, which means that we cannot be sure that the rest of the sentence constitutes a literal quotation. For example, in the form of the Creed as it was known to the author, *Est* may well have been absent, or the article may have read *Iudicaturus* instead of *Iudicare*.

With the ninth article we are again on surer ground. The text reads: *Post haec habemus: Credo in sanctum spiritum. Dixit primo ...* [107]. The same holds true for the tenth article: *Sequitur: Credo sanctam ecclesiam catholicam. Secundum ueritatem ...* [108]. After the treatment of the article on the Church, the sermon stops, so that we do not learn anything about either the form or the content of the final articles in the author's form of the Creed [109].

We must conclude, therefore, that EUSh9 can be taken as a reliable witness for the wording of articles 6, 7, 9, and 10, that articles 1 and 2 are perhaps only partially quoted, that this is certainly the case for article 3, that article 8 may not be quoted accurately, and that EUSh9 does not yield any information about the wording of articles 4, 5, 11, and 12.

EUSh9, then, can be taken to witness to the following variant of the Creed:

*Credo in deum patrem omnipotentem*
*et in filium eius (...?) Iesum Christum (...?)*
*[qui conceptus est de spiritu sancto,] natus ex Maria uirgine*

---

[105] Eusebius 'Gallicanus', *homilia 9 de symbolo* 8; CCSL 101, 105.

[106] Eusebius 'Gallicanus', *homilia 9 de symbolo* 9; CCSL 101, 105.

[107] Eusebius 'Gallicanus', *homilia 9 de symbolo* 10; CCSL 101, 107.

[108] Eusebius 'Gallicanus', *homilia 9 de symbolo* 11; CCSL 101, 107.

[109] Glorie takes two phrases from the exposition of the fifth and tenth articles (*Resurrexit ergo ad consecrandam spem nostram ut, si ei forte aliquis carnis resurrectionem dubitauerit, crederet resurgenti* and *Secundum ueritatem caelestium promissorum dat quidem deus in hac uita sine dubio peccatorum remissionem ...* [Eusebius 'Gallicanus', *homilia 9 de symbolo* 7 and 11; CCSL 101, 105 and 107-108]) as quotations of the final articles of the Creed: see CCSL 101B, 899. That might of course be true, but it can be neither proved nor disproved.

...

...

*ascendit ad caelos*
*sedet ad dexteram dei patris omnipotentis*
*inde uenturus est iudicare uiuos et mortuos (?)*
*credo in sanctum spiritum*
*credo sanctam ecclesiam catholicam*

...

...

EUSh10    *Homilia 10* of the same collection. As far as its authorship is concerned, the same applies as in the case of
EUSh9 [110].

Of the three texts FAU, EUSh9, and EUSh10, the last meets our
demands best. All articles except the first and fourth are introduced
by means of *sequitur* [111]. Moreover, the fact that the credal quotations contain many elements that are not treated in the commentary [112] is a safe indication that we may take these quotations to
be complete.

As far as the first article is concerned, this is quoted several
times but probably always in an abbreviated form: *Credo, inquit,*

---

[110] See above, footnote 52.

[111] *Sequitur: Credo et in filium eius unicum dominum nostrum Iesum Christum.
Hic fidem ... Sequitur: Qui conceptus est de spiritu sancto, natus ex Maria uirgine.
Quando audis ... Sequitur: Tertia die rexurrexit. Si ea die ... Quid est autem quod
dicit: Tertia die resurrexit, cum sexta sabbati die ... Sequitur: Ascendit ad caelos.
Docuit omnem animam ... Sequitur: Sedet ad dexteram dei patris omnipotentis. Nihil hoc loco ... Sequitur: Inde uenturus ... Inde uenturus. Ipsa necessitas ... iudicare
uiuos et mortuos* (see text) *... Sequitur: Credo in spiritum sanctum. Sicut ergo pater
... Quod uero sequitur: Sanctam ecclesiam catholicam, sanctorum communionem,
abremissa peccatorum, carnis resurrectionem, uitam aeternam, in deum haec ... Ecclesiam catholicam, id est ... Sequitur: Abremissa peccatorum, carnis resurrectionem.
Peccatorum abremissio ... Sequitur: Credo carnis resurrectionem* (see text) *...* (Eusebius 'Gallicanus', *homilia 10 de symbolo* 3-4 and 6-13; CCSL 101, 115 and 117-
124.

[112] See for example the section on the second article: *Sequitur: Credo et in
filium eius unicum dominum nostrum Iesum Christum. Hic fidem nostram non de
deo et in deum alium declinamus, sed de persona in personam sub una diuinitate
transferimus* (Eusebius 'Gallicanus', *homilia 10 de symbolo* 3; CCSL 101, 115). In
fact, only the words *Credo et* are commented upon here.

*in deum. Ecce ... Credo in deum. Hinc dixit ... Credo ergo in deum. Aliud est ...* [113].

Next, the fourth article is indicated with the words *Crucifixus et sepultus*, after which the commentary continues [114]. In particular the absence of *sequitur*, which is found as an introduction to all the other articles (except, of course, the first), is a strong indication that we do not have a literal quotation here, but rather only a paraphrase or at best a partial quotation.

The evidence for the wording of the eighth article may at first sight seem to be contradictory. The article is introduced thus: *Sequitur: Inde uenturus iudicaturus de uiuis et mortuis.* The first two words of the article are repeated in a second quotation some lines further on (*Inde uenturus. Ipsa necessitas ueniendi ...*), whereas a third quotation reads *Iudicare uiuos et mortuos, iustos et iniustos. Omnes ergo ...* [115]. There is no contradiction, however, if one takes the words *iudicaturus de uiuis et mortuis* not as part of the first quotation but rather as a paraphrase of the second part of the article or even as the first words of the commentary [116].

Finally, the twelfth article of the Creed is quoted in two different forms. First, it is given as *Carnis resurrectionem, uitam aeternam* in a longer quotation which covers the three final articles of the Creed, then it is given as *Carnis resurrectionem* in the introduction to the section on the eleventh article, and when the author comes to the Resurrection of the Flesh, he starts with the quotation *Credo carnis resurrectionem* [117]. The absence of *Vitam aeternam* in the two latter quotations is explained easily enough by the fact that the author does not need to quote the complete twelfth article there because it is apparently not his intention to comment upon Eternal Life. But what should one say of the added *Credo*? Since all three quotations claim in an equal way to be literal ones, and *Credo* is found in only one of them, it seems best to side with the majority here, espe-

---

[113] Eusebius 'Gallicanus', *homilia 10 de symbolo* 2; CCSL 101, 114.

[114] Eusebius 'Gallicanus', *homilia 10 de symbolo* 5; CCSL 101, 115.

[115] Eusebius 'Gallicanus', *homilia 10 de symbolo* 9; CCSL 101, 119-120.

[116] Glorie, who puts a colon before *Iudicaturus*, seems to opt for this solution as well.

[117] Eusebius 'Gallicanus', *homilia 10 de symbolo* 11-13; CCSL 101, 122-124. See above, footnote 111.

cially as its presence in the twelfth article would be stylistically rather awkward [118].

All in all, EUSh10 can be taken to testify to the following variant of the Creed:

> *Credo in deum ...*
> *credo et in filium eius unicum dominum nostrum, Iesum Christum*
> *qui conceptus est de spiritu sancto, natus ex Maria uirgine*
> *[crucifixus et sepultus]*
> *tertia die resurrexit*
> *ascendit ad caelos*
> *sedet ad dexteram dei patris omnipotentis*
> *inde uenturus iudicare uiuos et mortuos*
> *credo in spiritum sanctum*
> *sanctam ecclesiam catholicam*
> *sanctorum communionem*
> *abremissa peccatorum*
> *carnis resurrectionem*
> *uitam aeternam.*

PIRM   The so-called *scarapsus* of Pirminius. This work is generally dated to the first quarter of the eighth century [119].

In this work, a variant of the Creed is offered no less than three times. The first time, each article is explicitly quoted in connection with the name of one of the Apostles: ... *et composuerunt symbolum. Petrus: Credo in deum patrem omnipotentem, creatorem caeli et terrae. Iohannes: Et in Iesum Christum ... Item Thomas dixit: Carnis resurrectionem, uitam aeternam. Amen* [120]. Some pages further, Pirminius describes the baptismal rite and quotes the several formulae that occur in it. In that way, he also offers a set of baptismal questions

---

[118] The use of *Credo* here resembles the cases where a similar verb form is used to make a smoother introduction to a new article: see above, chapter 3.1, pp. 103-104. It is to be observed, however, that in this case the need for a smooth transition is already met by the tag *sequitur*.

[119] The author's name may also be found as Priminius. For the date of this text, see Jecker 1927, 87-88 and 182-183, Kelly 1976, 398, and Kinzig 1999a, 169; but compare Angenendt 1972, 61 and 74. For earlier scholarship, see Hahn 1897, 96-97, Kattenbusch 1900, 766-769, and Kelly 1976, 399-400. It should be pointed out again that Kelly, rather confusingly, identifies the credal variant of the *scarapsus* with *T*: see above, chapter 1.1, footnote 7.

[120] Pirminius, *scarapsus* 10; Jecker 1927, 41.

which make up a complete form of the Creed: ... *et interrogatus es a sacerdote: Credis in deum patrem omnipotentem, creatorem caeli et terrae? Et respondisti: Credo. Et iterum: Credis et in Iesum Christum* ... [121]. Finally, we encounter the Creed in a third place, where it is given in the second person plural: *Fratres, credite in deum patrem omnipotentem, creatorem caeli et terrae. Credite et in Iesum Christum* ... [122]. Apart from certain small differences, which will be given in the footnotes below where necessary, these three variants of the Creed are exactly identical.

Thus, PIRM yields the following form of the Creed:

*Credo in deum patrem omnipotentem, creatorem caeli et terrae*
*et in Iesum Christum, filium eius unicum dominum nostrum*
*qui conceptus est de spiritu sancto, natus ex Maria uirgine*
*passus sub Pontio Pilato, crucifixus, mortuus et sepultus*
*descendit ad inferna*
*tertia die surrexit* [123] *a mortuis*
*ascendit ad caelos*
*sedet ad dexteram dei patris omnipotentis*
*inde uenturus iudicare uiuos et* [124] *mortuos*
*credo in spiritum sanctum*
*sanctam ecclesiam catholicam*
*sanctorum communionem*
*remissionem peccatorum*
*carnis resurrectionem*
*uitam aeternam.*

MGV    The fragmentary *expositio symboli* in part B of the *Missale Gallicanum Vetus* (CPL 1922), which originated most probably around 700 in the neighbourhood of Luxueil [125].

---

[121] Pirminius, *scarapsus* 12; Jecker 1927, 43, reproduced in Kinzig 1999a, 168-169.

[122] Pirminius *scarapsus* 28a; Jecker 1927, 64-65. I cannot see why Kelly (1976, 399) states that Pirminius "reproduces the creed in a loose, inexact fashion" here.

[123] *Scarapsus* 28a (Jeckers 1927, 65) has *Resurrexit*.

[124] *Scarapsus* 28a (Jeckers 1927, 65) has *Ac*.

[125] *Missale Gallicanum Vetus* 25-28; Mohlberg 1958, 9-10. For date and place of composition, see Mohlberg 1958, XXI-XXIII and Dekkers 1995, 632-636. See for earlier credal scholarship Hahn 1897, 77-78 with notes, Kelly 1976, 403, and especially Kattenbusch 1900, 772-775 (but compare footnote 71 above).

Like the Caesarian sermon that is contained in part C of the *Missale* [126], this *expositio* quotes a complete form of the Creed after a short introduction: *Sed iam ad istius sacramenti plenitudinem textumque ueniamus. Quod in hoc modo incipit: Credo in deum patrem ... uitam aeternam* [127]. The ensuing commentary breaks off soon after the treatment of the first article. The commentary exhibits one difference with the form of the Creed that is given in its entirety [128].

The form of the Creed of MGV, then, runs as follows:

*Credo in deum patrem omnipotentem, creatorem caeli et terrae*
*et in Iesum Christum, filium eius unicum dominum nostrum* [129]
*qui conceptus est de spiritu sancto, natus ex Maria uirgine*
*passus sub Pontio Pilato, crucifixus, mortuus et sepultus*
*tertia die resurrexit a mortuis*
*ascendit uictor ad caelos*
*sedet ad dexteram dei patris omnipotentis*
*inde uenturus iudicare uiuos et mortuos*
*credo in sanctum spiritum*
*sanctam ecclesiam catholicam*
*sanctorum communionem*
*abremissionem peccatorum*
*carnis resurrectionem*
*uitam aeternam.*

Bobbio A    The introductory part of the *expositio symboli* in the
Bobbio Missal (or *Sacramentarium Gallicanum*, CPL

---

[126] See above, pp. 121-127 and footnote 71.

[127] *Missale Gallicanum Vetus* 25-26; Mohlberg 1958, 10.

[128] Kelly makes the tantalizing remark that "The complete text of the defective sermon ... is to be found in Cod. Lat. Monacensis (Munich) 6298 of *Sermo pseudo-August.* 242 ..." (Kelly 1976, 403). Kelly does not say how he knows this. The Migne text of this sermon (PL 39, 2191-2193) shows indeed that this exposition and the pseudo-Augustinian *sermo 242* appear as one and the same sermon, but their credal quotations differ. Kelly's subsequent discussion of these credal quotations seems to fit neither Mohlberg's fragmentary nor Migne's complete text exactly. In all probability, Kelly's source here is Burn 1909, 7-8. Burn (*ibid.*, plates V-VII) also offers a facsimile of the form of the Creed in MGV.

[129] The commentary begins its treatment of the second article with the partial quotation *Credo in filium eius* (*Missale Gallicanum Vetus* 28; Mohlberg 1958, 10).

1924), which originated most probably in the same period somewhere in Eastern Gaul [130].

As in the previous case, a variant of the Creed is explicitly announced and quoted in its entirety: *Audite symbolum quod uobis hodie materno ore sancta catholica tradidit ecclesia: Credo in deum ... uitam aeternam. Amen* [131].

Thus, Bobbio A yields the following form of the Creed:

*Credo in deum patrem omnipotentem, creatorem caeli et terrae*
*credo in Iesum Christum, filium eius unigenitum sempiternum*
*conceptum de spiritu sancto, natum ex Maria uirgine*
*passum* [132] *sub Pontio Pilato, crucifixum, mortuum et sepultum*
—*descendit ad inferna*
*tertia die resurrexit a mortuis*
*ascendit ad caelos*
*sedet ad dexteram dei patris omnipotentis*
*inde uenturus iudicare uiuos et mortuos*
*credo in sanctum spiritum*
*sanctam ecclesiam catholicam*
*sanctorum communionem*
*remissionem peccatorum*
*carnis resurrectionem*
*uitam aeternam.*

Bobbio B    The ensuing commentary of the same *expositio* [133].

Here it is possible again to put a number of quotations together to form a complete credal variant. There are only some minor difficulties. First of all, the section on the first article runs thus: *Credo in deum. Ecce addidisti omnipotentem et ueraciter addidisti. Nihil de promissione diffidas sed securus expecta si credis quia omnipotens est*

---

[130] *Missale Bobiense* 183-184; Lowe 1920, 56. See for date and place of origin Wilmart 1924, 38-39 and 99-106 (but compare *ibid*. 51-58). Kinzig (1999a, 168) connects the Bobbio Missal with Northern Italy. According to Vogel (1986, 323-325), who also claims the Missal for Northern Italy, it nevertheless contains Gallican liturgies, albeit with a "mixed character". Compare the opinion of Gamber, quoted above, footnote 73. See below, footnotes 140-141 for earlier scholarship.

[131] *Missale Bobiense* 183-184; Lowe 1920, 56. See for a facsimile Burn 1909, plate IV.

[132] The manuscript reads *Passus*, but this must be a mistake.

[133] *Missale Bobiense* 185; Lowe 1920, 56-58.

*qui promittit* [134]. Although the quotation is limited to *Credo in deum*, it appears from the commentary that the word *Omnipotentem* also belonged to the author's form of the Creed [135]. Thus, it appears that the author is not concerned with quoting every single word of the Creed, which implies again that it is possible that an addition like *Creatorem caeli et terrae* was part of his form of the first article as well.

Similarly, the second article is quoted as *Et in Iesum Christum, unicum dominum nostrum* [136]. Here, the absence of *Filium* is suspect, and a later passage suggests that perhaps the words *Filium eius* have been omitted from the quotation: *Si credidisti deum patrem omnipotentem et in filium eius unigenitum ...* [137].

Finally, the ninth article is quoted as *Credis in spiritum sanctum*. Here, *Credis* is probably best explained as a miswriting for *Credo*, caused by the consistent use of the second person in the immediate neighbourhood of the quotation: *Si iudicatum despicis, iudicem pertimesce. Credis ... Si credidisti deum patrem ...* [138].

For the rest, each article is quoted in an unambiguous way [139]. It is to be observed that the two forms of the Creed that can be found

[134] *Missale Bobiense* 185; Lowe 1920, 57.

[135] This conclusion is supported by the commentary on the ninth article, which begins *Si credidisti deum patrem omnipotentem et in filium eius unigenitum per fidem et spiritum sanctum deum te necesse est confiteri* (*Missale Bobiense* 185; Lowe 1920, 57).

[136] *Missale Bobiense* 185; Lowe 1920, 57.

[137] See above, footnote 135. Compare also the following place from the commentary on the second article: *Hoc est illud sacramentum fidei. Nisi enim filium dei tota mente credideris patrem non potest confiteri. Crede ergo filium dei unigenitum ab unigenito, uiuentem a uiuente, uerum de uero* (*Missale Bobiense* 185; Lowe 1920, 57). Here, the combination of a form of *credo* with the words *filium dei* seems to be used as an indication of the complete second article. As far as the predicate *unigenitum* is concerned, its presence in the underlying form of the Creed seems improbable in the light of the quotation *Et in Iesum Christum, unicum dominum nostrum* (see previous footnote).

[138] *Missale Bobiense* 185; Lowe 1920, 57.

[139] *Qui conceptus est de spiritu sancto, natus ex Maria uirgine. Spiritum sanctum audis ... Passum sub Pontio Pilato, crucifixum, mortuum et sepultum. Nulla trepidatio ... Descendit ad inferna, tertia die resurrexit a mortuis, ascendit in caelis, sedet ad dexteram patris omnipotentis. Si te triduum ... Inde uenturus iudicare uiuos et mortuos. Ecce ille ... Sanctam ecclesiam catholicam, remissionem peccatorum, carnis resurrectionem, uitam aeternam. Nisi credideris ecclesiam dei sanctam ...* (*Missale Bobiense* 185; Lowe 1920, 57).

in the two parts of this *expositio* are not identical. The explanation
for this difference is probably a similar one as in the case of CAE-A
and CAE-B: a compiler took over an older *expositio* in which he
changed the full form of the Creed but not the stray quotations [140].

Bobbio B, then, testifies to the following variant of the Creed:

*Credo in deum ... omnipotentem (...?)*
*et in Iesum Christum, [filium eius] unicum dominum nostrum*
*qui conceptus est de spiritu sancto, natus ex Maria uirgine*
*passum sub Pontio Pilato, crucifixum, mortuum et sepultum*
—*descendit ad inferna*
*tertia die resurrexit a mortuis*
*ascendit in caelis*
*sedet ad dexteram patris omnipotentis*
*inde uenturus iudicare uiuos et mortuos*
*credo in spiritum sanctum*
*sanctam ecclesiam catholicam*
*remissionem peccatorum*
*carnis resurrectionem*
*uitam aeternam.*

Bobbio C    The baptismal questions in the same missal [141].

These three baptismal questions, which are couched in the third
person singular, can be put together without any problems to form
a complete variant of the Creed. We only have to bear in mind that

---

[140] Thus already Kattenbusch 1894, 187n2. This surmise is repeated in Kattenbusch 1900, 776n27, 789n42, and 928n107. Nevertheless, most scholars have
hitherto treated the variants of Bobbio A and Bobbio B as one and the same:
see Hahn 1897, 75-76 (though some of the differences are touched upon in his
notes), Nerney 1953a, 284, Gamber 1958, 40, Angenendt 1972, 70, Vokes 1978,
539, and O'Callaghan 1992, 285. Burn (1909, 5) and Kelly (1976, 400) are the
exceptions.

[141] *Missale Bobiense* 245-247; Lowe 1920, 74-75. See for earlier scholarship
Kattenbusch 1894, 187n2, Hahn 1897, 176, Kattenbusch 1900, 747n32, 776n27,
and 789n42, Burn 1909, 6, and Kelly 1976, 401. In a kind of appendix to the
Bobbio Missal, a fourth (declaratory) variant of the Creed is found: *Symbolum
... fidei a duodecinario numero apostolorum est cum magna cautela collectum et credentibus assignatum. Petrus dixit: Credo in deum patrem omnipotentem ... (Missale
Bobiense* 591; Lowe 1920, 181). This variant, however, lacks a liturgical context,
and its date and place of origin have not yet been determined (see Kelly 1976,
401). We therefore exclude it from our analysis.

the interrogatory form necessitates the use of *Credis* (*Credit*) at the start of each question [142], and that we cannot know, therefore, whether a declaratory variant to which these questions could correspond would begin its second and ninth articles with *Credo* or with *Et*.

That the baptismal questions represent a different credal variant from the two in the *expositio symboli* in the same Missal has been recognized since the days of Kattenbusch [143].

Bobbio C, therefore, can be taken to witness our last Gallican variant of the Apostles' Creed, which runs thus:

*Credo in deum patrem omnipotentem, creatorem caeli et terrae*
*(credo?) et in Iesum Christum, filium eius unicum dominum nos-*
   *trum*
*conceptum de spiritu sancto, natum ex Maria uirgine*
*passum sub Pontio Pilato, crucifixum et sepultum*
*descendit ad inferna*
*tertia die resurrexit a mortuis*
*ascendit in caelis*
*sedet ad dexteram dei patris omnipotentis*
*inde uenturus iudicare uiuos ac mortuos*
*(credo? et?) in sanctum spiritum*
*sanctam ecclesiam catholicam*
*sanctorum communionem*
*remissionem peccatorum*
*carnis resurrectionem*
*uitam habere post mortem, in gloriam Christi resurgere.*

## 3.3 Spanish Forms of the Creed

As in the case of Gaul, it seems useful to compare all versions of the Apostles' Creed which stem from Spain. Although the material is not so abundant as north of the Pyrenees, there is enough to make the investigation a promising one. Overviews of credal texts that stem from Spain are given by Kattenbusch, Hahn, Kelly, and,

---

[142] *Credis in deum patrem ... Credit et in Iesum Christum ... Credit in sanctum spiritum ... (Missale Bobiense* 245-247; Lowe 1920, 74-75, reproduced in Kinzig 1999a, 168).

[143] See above, footnote 140.

most recently, O'Callaghan [144]. Most of these texts yield a variant of
the Apostles' Creed and can be used without any problems for our
study. There are, however, also some credal texts that have to be
excluded from our analysis.

The first of these is the *libellus de fide* by the early fifth-century
author Bachiarius (CPL 568). The author wrote this work in order
to vindicate his orthodoxy and presents an elaborate creed in it,
which, however, hardly bears any resemblance to the wording of
the Apostles' Creed [145]. Secondly, O'Callaghan mentions a creed of
Gregory of Elvira. Whichever text is meant by this, it cannot be
used as a witness for the wording of the Apostles' Creed [146]. Thirdly,

---

[144] Kattenbusch 1894, 152-158 ("Symbole aus Spanien"), Hahn 1897, 64-69
("Symbolformeln der Spanischen Kirche"), Smulders 1970, 238n10, Kelly 1976,
177-178, and O'Callaghan 1992, 285-287.

[145] Bachiarius, *libellus de fide* 4-8: *Verumtamen si magnopere quaeritur ubi
natus sum, accipiatur confessio mea quam in baptismi natiuitate respondi ... Credimus in deum, quod fuit et erat, est et erit, numquam aliud, semper idem ... Hic est
nostrae fidei thesaurus quem signatum ecclesiastico symbolo in baptismo accepimus et
custodimus* (Madoz 1940, 466-468; the same passage, although based on a rather
different text, also in Hahn 1897, 286-288+n242). The references to his baptism
and the *symbolum ecclesiasticum* probably only mean that Bachiarius deems his
formulation of faith essentially identical with the intention of the Apostles'
Creed. Compare Kattenbusch 1894, 157n1 and 1900, 402n73.

[146] O'Callaghan's (1992, 286) reference to Morin 1902, 229-237 (erroneously indicated as Morin **1907**) seems to imply that he has Gregory's *de fide* (c. 360; CPL
551) in mind. The only creed in this work occurs in the introduction, where we
find a slightly deviating Latin translation of the Nicene Creed: *Credimus in
unum deum patrem omnipotentem ...* (Simonetti 1975, 56 [CCSL 69, 221]; compare
Simonetti 1975, 126-127). But O'Callaghan's (1992, 204n44) claim that Gregory
testifies to a form of the Creed which contains the phrase *Deum et dominum nostrum* seems to point in another direction, as such a phrase seems to occur within
Gregory's *de fide* only at the end of chapter 6: *Est ergo deus pater immensus,
aeternus, incomprehensibilis, inaestimabilis, est et filius deus et dominus noster, tan-
tus quantus et pater, sed non aliunde quam pater ...* (Simonetti 1975, 98 [CCSL 69,
238]), a passage that hardly justifies O'Callaghan's claim. Apparently, O'Callaghan has just taken over the wording of a creed that is ascribed to Gregory by
Badcock (*Credimus in unum deum patrem omnipotentem, et in unigenitum filium
eius Iesum Christum deum et dominum saluatorem nostrum, natum ...*: see Badcock
1938, 90). This creed, however, is not taken from Gregory's *de fide* (as is suggested by Badcock 1938, 90n1), but rather from one of the versions of the anonymous *fides Romanorum* CPL 552 (see above, chapter 3.2, footnote 30), as appears from Badcock 1930, 73. See for the date and complicated tradition of Gregory's *de fide* Dekkers 1995, 192-193 and Frede 1995, 498.

there are a number of creeds that were promulgated by church councils held at Toledo (CPL 1790). Like the creed of Bachiarius, these are newly formulated creeds that differ from the Apostles' Creed both in structure and in wording [147].

A direct quotation of the first three articles of the Apostles' Creed occurs in *actio XIII* of the second council of Sevilla (619; CPL 1790). This quotation, however, cannot be used for the reason that the text is not yet available in a critical edition [148]. Finally, there is a creed in the *prologus* to the second book of Beatus of Liébana's *in Apocalypsin*, written in 786. This creed exhibits the general struc-

---

[147] These are: the creed of the first council of Toledo of 400 (= pseudo-Augustine *sermo 233* [CPL 368] 1-2: *Credimus in unum uerum deum, patrem et filium et spiritum sanctum, uisibilium et inuisibilium factorem* ...; De Aldama 1934, 29-37), the creed of the fourth council of Toledo of 633 (*Secundum diuinas enim scripturas et doctrinam quam a sanctis patribus accepimus, patrem et filium et spiritum sanctum unius deitatis atque substantiae confitemur* ...; Martinez Diez 1992, 1992, 181-183), the creed of the sixth of 638 (*Itaque credimus et profitemur sacratissimam et omnipotentissimam trinitatem, patrem et filium et spiritum sanctum, unum deum* ...; *ibid.*, 298-303), that of the eleventh of 675 (*Confitemur et credimus sanctam atque ineffabilem trinitatem, patrem et filium et spiritum sanctum, unum deum naturaliter esse unius substantiae* ...; Madoz 1938a, 16-26), and that of the sixteenth of 693 (*Credimus et confitemur omnium creaturarum quae trinis rerum machinis continentur auctricem atque conseruatricem indiuiduam trinitatem* ...; Madoz 1946, 22-29). Of these, the creed of the eleventh council has not yet received a critical edition, as Madoz was not able to inspect the most important manuscripts: see Madoz 1938a, 11-13. An extended version of the creed of the first council of Toledo was written by the Gallician bishop Pastor in the middle of the fifth century (CPL 559). See for a discussion of all these texts De Aldama 1934 and Madoz 1938a, 1938b, and 1938c; compare also Hahn 1897, 209-213, 235-238, and 242-248 and Aguirre 1980. Kattenbusch makes a number of isolated remarks on some of these creeds, but hardly discusses their contents.

[148] *Item in ipso initio apostolici symboli geminae sic ostenditur in uno eodemque Christo naturae distinctio, deitatis ex patre, dum dicit: Credo in deum patrem omnipotentem, et in Iesum Christum filium eius unicum dominum nostrum, humanitatis ex matre, dum dicit: Natum de spiritu sancto ex utero Mariae uirginis. Ecce ...* (Mansi 1764, 563). That a critical edition is necessary appears from the discussion of these words by Kattenbusch (1894, 156), who uses an edition in which the credal quotations are not identical with those in Mansi's (similarly Hahn 1897, 65n131). Another section of the same *actio* alludes to articles four to eight: *Sola enim caro crucis exitium sensit, sola caro lanceam pertulit, sola caro sanguine et aqua manauit, ipsa sola mortua, ipsa sola in sepulcro posita, ipsa sola tertia die resuscitata, quae etiam glorificata caelos adiit, in qua et uenturus est iudicare in gloria patris, iudicaturus de uiuis ac mortuis* (Mansi 1764, 565).

ture of the Apostles' Creed, but seems to be free in its wording [149]. Now that these credal texts have been excluded from our analysis, it is time to turn to the sources that are more promising for our study of the form of the Creed in Spain [150].

The following seven texts thus remain.

PRIS     The first paragraph of Priscillian of Avila's second *tractatus* (CPL 785), which was probably written as a petition to Pope Damasus shortly after 381 [151].

Priscillian seems to give a complete quotation of each article and each time marks the change from quotation to commentary with the formula *sicut scriptum est*, but cannot be trusted for the grammatical construction of the Creed because he makes each separate article dependent on a participle *credentes* [152]. The repetition of this

---

[149] Beatus of Liébana, *in Apocalypsin* II, *prologus* 9-10: *Ecce caput iunctum cum membra, quod est Christus et apostolica ecclesia, in quem credimus et quem semper cum omnibus Christianis communiter una uoce in symbolo dicimus. Credimus in unum deum patrem omnipotentem, et in Iesum Christum filium eius, qui propter nostram salutem incarnatus est de Maria uirgine, passus mortuus et sepultus est, et resurrexit tertia die a mortuis uiuus* ... (Sanders 1930, 151 [= Camón Aznar 1975, 409]). This creed is reproduced and briefly discussed in Kattenbusch 1894, 398-399 and 1900, 587 and Hahn 1897, 67-68+nn140-150. See for this text also Frede 1999, 53-54.

[150] Smulders (1970, 238n10) still mentions Isidore of Sevilla's *de cognitione baptismi* as a witness to the form of the Creed in Spain, but we do not possess a work of that title by Isidore. The bibliographical reference makes clear that Smulders must have in mind a work by one of Isidore's successors, Ildefonsus of Toledo, which will receive due attention below (pp. 150-152). Isidore does include a short section *de symbolo* in his *de ecclesiasticis officiis* II xxiii (xxii) (CPL 1207; CCSL 113, 97-99), but this tells us nothing about the wording of the Creed.

[151] For date and authorship of this text, see Chadwick 1976, 38 and 64 and Burrus 1995, 2-3 and 50. For the form of the Creed, compare Kattenbusch 1894, 157-158 and 198, Hahn 1897, 64-65+n219, Kattenbusch 1900, 953n154, and Kelly 1976, 177. The observations on the form of the Creed to which the editor refers (CSEL 18, 36 app.) are hardly of interest: see Schepss 1886, 20n1.

[152] *Fidem uero sicut accepimus, ita et tenemus et tradimus, credentes unum deum patrem omnipotentem, sicut scriptum est ... et unum dominum Iesum Christum, sicut scriptum est ... natum ex Maria uirgine ex spiritu sancto, sicut scriptum est ... passum sub Pontio Pilato, crucifixum, sicut scriptum est ... sepultum, tertia die resurrexisse, sicut ... ascendisse in caelos, sedere ad dexteram dei patris omnipotentis, sicut ... inde uenturum et iudicaturum de uiuis et mortuis, sicut ... credentes in sanctam ecclesiam, sanctum spiritum, baptismum salutare, sicut ... credentes remissionem peccatorum, sicut ... credentes in resurrectionem carnis, sicut ... Cuius symboli iter custodientes* ... (Priscillian of Avila, *tractatus II*; CSEL 18, 36-37).

participle, either with or without *in*, in the third part of the Creed is probably only a matter of style and need not imply that Priscillian's form of the Creed really read a threefold *Credo* here. This again implies that the absence of the preposition *in* in the references to the first two articles does not necessitate the conclusion that Priscillian really used a form of the Creed that began with *Credo* instead of *Credo in*. On the other hand, the absence of *credentes in* in Priscillian's quotation of the second article seems to exclude the possibility that he used a declaratory form with a repeated *Credo* here. Next, it should be noted that Priscillian cuts the fourth article in two, and that this is the most probable reason for the fact that a copula is missing in his quotation of that article.

More important is the fact that certain peculiarities seem to be explained best by the assumption that Priscillian deliberately suited his form of the Creed to his personal theology [153].

The form of the Creed to which PRIS testifies, then, is the following:

*Credo (in?) unum deum patrem omnipotentem*
*et (in?) unum dominum Iesum Christum*
*natum (?) ex Maria uirgine ex spiritu sancto*
*passum (?) sub Pontio Pilato, crucifixum (?) et sepultum (?)*
*tertia die resurrexit*
*ascendit in caelos*
*sedet ad dexteram dei patris omnipotentis*
*inde uenturus (?) et iudicaturus (?) de uiuis et mortuis*
*credo in sanctam ecclesiam*
*sanctum spiritum*
*baptismum salutare*
*remissionem peccatorum*
*resurrectionem carnis.*

MART    Martin of Braga's *de correctione rusticorum* (CPL 1086), a sermon which, according to its latest editor, was held in 573 or 574 [154].

[153] See Kelly 1976, 178 and the analysis below, chapter 3.7, p. 223, footnotes 472 and 486, pp. 246-247, and p. 249.

[154] The three modern editions (Barlow 1950, Clols 1981, and Naldini 1991) part ways at a number of points in their text of Martin's baptismal questions: see below. For the date, see Naldini 1991, 19-20 and Barlow 1950, 159. For ear-

In MART, we find the Creed once again in the form of baptismal questions which do not pose any problems: *Post istam abrenuntiationem diaboli iterum interrogatus es a sacerdote: Credis in deum patrem omnipotentem? Respondisti: Credo. Et in Iesum Christum filium eius unicum deum et dominum nostrum ... credis? Et respondisti: Credo. Et iterum interrogatus es: Credis in spiritum sanctum ... Et respondisti: Credo* [155]. We find the first article also in declaratory form in the next chapter: *Similiter dimisistis incantationem sanctam, id est symbolum quod in baptismum accepistis, quod est: Credo in deum patrem omnipotentem, et orationem dominicam ...* [156].

MART yields the following variant of the Creed:

*Credo in deum patrem omnipotentem*
*et in Iesum Christum, filium eius unicum, deum et dominum nostrum* [157]
*qui natus est de spiritu sancto ex Maria uirgine*
*passus sub Pontio Pilato, crucifixus et sepultus* [158]
*tertia die resurrexit uiuus a mortuis*
*ascendit in caelos*
*sedet ad dexteram patris*

lier credal scholarship, compare Caspari 1883b, CI-CVI and 26-28, Kattenbusch 1894, 153-154, and Hahn 1897, 65-66+nn130-137. Kelly (1976, 177+n3) uses MART, ILD, and EB (see below) to reconstruct one sixth-century Spanish variant of the Creed.

[155] Martin of Braga, *de correctione rusticorum* 15; Naldini 1991, 64-66 (Barlow 1950, 196-197; Clols's text [Clols 1981, 40] has largely been spoilt by a serious misprint). The postponement of *Credis* in the second question seems to indicate that Martin's declaratory variant of the Creed began with *Et*. As Martin takes such pains to preserve the formulation of his declaratory form of the Creed, the absence of *Et* in the third question can safely be taken as witness to a ninth article that begins with *Credo*, not with *Credo et* or *Et*.

[156] Martin of Braga, *de correctione rusticorum* 16; Naldini 1991, 68 (Barlow 1950, 199, Clols 1981, 44).

[157] Clols (1981, 40) presents the second article as *Et in Iesu Christo, filio eius unico, domino nostro*. The words *Deum et* (or, for that matter, *Deo et*) are found in only five out of twelve manuscripts, but they could be expected to be omitted rather than to be added in the transmission of the text because they are lacking in *T*.

[158] Barlow (1950, 197) and Naldini (1991, 64) add *Descendit ad inferna* here, but six manuscripts, among them the two oldest, omit it (see Barlow 1950, 175). It seems much more probable that a scribe added the Descent to Hell to a text that lacked it rather than that it was omitted. Compare Kattenbusch 1894, 153-154 and 1900, 899.

*inde uenturus iudicare uiuos et mortuos*
*credo in spiritum sanctum*
*sanctam ecclesiam catholicam*
*remissionem omnium* [159] *peccatorum*
*carnis resurrectionem*
*et uitam aeternam.*

MM    The *traditio symboli* in the Mozarabic *Missale Mixtum*
      (CPL 1929) which was first edited in the fifteenth century
      by Alfonso Ortiz on the authority of Cardinal Ximénès. A
      critical edition by José Janini has only been available since
      1980. According to Janini, the texts of this Spanish missal
      were composed in the sixth and seventh centuries, and
      underwent a certain amount of revision towards the end
      of the seventh century [160].

Here, we find an explicit quotation of the Creed in its entirety:
*Signate ergo uos et respondete: Credo in deum patrem omnipotentem ...*
*et uitam aeternam. Amen* [161].

Thus, the form of the Creed that can be seen in MM is the following:

*Credo in deum patrem omnipotentem*
*et in Iesum Christum, filium eius unicum dominum nostrum*
*natum de spiritu sancto ex utero Mariae uirginis*
*passus sub Pontio Pilato, crucifixus et sepultus*
*tertia die resurrexit uiuus a mortuis*
*ascendit in caelum*
*sedet ad dexteram dei patris omnipotentis*
*inde uenturus iudicaturus uiuos et mortuos*
*credo in sanctum spiritum*
*sanctam ecclesiam catholicam*
*sanctorum communionem*

[159] Clols (1981, 40) reads *Omnem*.

[160] Janini 1983, XXVI-XXXIX. Férotin (1912, XIV-XVII) is prepared to assume an earlier date for their composition, but compare De Bruyne 1913, 421-
428. For the credal variant of MM, compare Kattenbusch 1894, 156 and 195n10,
Hahn 1897, 69+n151, and Kelly 1976, 177-178.

[161] *Missale Mixtum* 517; Janini 1980, 70-71. See for the text of this variant
according to Ximénès's edition PL 85, 395-396; there are no substantial differences between this text and Janini's.

*remissionem omnium peccatorum*
*carnis huius resurrectionem*
*et uitam aeternam.*

LO    The Mozarabic *Liber Ordinum Episcopalis* (CPL 1930). This
text is mainly preserved in one eleventh-century manuscript, but the editors believe that it had already reached
its present form by the seventh or early eighth century at
the latest and that it was composed in Toledo [162].

As in the case of MM, we find a complete declaratory variant of
the Creed here: *Signate ergo uos et respondete: Credo in deum patrem*
*omnipotentem ... et uitam aeternam. Amen* [163].

This form of the Creed runs thus:

*Credo in deum patrem omnipotentem*
*et in Iesum Christum, filium eius unicum, deum et dominum nos-*
*trum*
*qui natus est de spiritu sancto et Maria uirgine*
*passus sub Pontio Pilato, crucifixus et sepultus*
— *descendit ad inferna*
*tertia die resurrexit uiuus a mortuis*
*ascendit in caelos*
*sedet ad dexteram dei patris omnipotentis*
*inde uenturus* [164] *iudicare uiuos et mortuos*
*credo in sanctum spiritum*
*sanctam ecclesiam catholicam*
*remissionem omnium peccatorum*
*carnis huius resurrectionem*
*et uitam aeternam.*

---

[162] The only two editions are Férotin 1904 and Janini 1991. See for date and
origin Janini 1991, 44-45 and Férotin 1904, XII+n1. According to Férotin (1904,
XXI), the rite of the *traditio symboli* might well hark back to the period before
the Gothic invasions of Spain, but Janini (1983, XXXIX) is sceptical about this
theory.

[163] *Liber Ordinum Episcopalis* 350; Janini 1991, 170-171 (Férotin 1904, 184-
186).

[164] Férotin reads *Est* after *Venturus*.

ILD   The *expositio symboli* within Ildefonsus of Toledo's *de cognitione baptismi* (CPL 1248), which was probably written
during the author's episcopate between 657 and 667 [165].

Chapters 31 to 95 of this text comprise an elaborate *expositio
symboli*, in which practically every article is quoted in an unequivo-
cal way [166]. There are nonetheless a few points that need some closer
investigation.

First of all, the second article is quoted as *Credimus et in Iesum
Christum, filium dei unicum, deum et dominum nostrum* (see previous
footnote) [167]. Since both the first and the ninth articles begin with
*Credo* [168], it is extremely improbable that Ildefonsus really began
his second article with *Credimus*. This verb is therefore best
explained as flowing directly from Ildefonsus's pen to introduce the
second article, which in his form of the Creed may then have
started either with *Et* or with *Credo* [169]. Again, it should be observed
that it is slightly ambiguous where the quotation of this article
ends. The text continues: ... *non separatum a deo patre sed et in se
deum et cum patre unum deum. Itaque deus* ... The editor takes the
words *non separatum* as the beginning of the commentary but, at

---

[165] For the date of this work, see Braegelmann 1942, 61 and Campos Ruiz
1971, 226-227. For the credal variant, compare Kattenbusch 1894, 154-156 and
Hahn 1897, 66+nn137-138.

[166] *Est ergo tenor symboli iste, et hic causarum ordo quae continentur in illo: Credo in deum patrem omnipotentem. Quid est credo? ... Hinc sequitur: Credimus et in
Iesum Christum, filium dei unicum, deum et dominum nostrum: non separatum ...
Qui natus est de spiritu sancto et Maria uirgine. Bene confitemur ... Descendit ad
inferna. Cum Christus ... Tertia die resurrexit uiuus a mortuis, iuxta quod dictum
est ... Ascendit in caelum, sedet ad dexteram dei patris omnipotentis. Vbi et quomodo
sit ... Inde uenturus iudicare uiuos et mortuos. Istis nominibus ... Credo in sanctum
spiritum. Haec quae ... Sanctam ecclesiam catholicam. Haec fides ... Remissionem
peccatorum. Bene post commemorationem ... Carnis resurrectionem, et uitam aeternam. Haec uisibilis ...* (Ildefonsus of Toledo, *de cognitione baptismi* 36-83; Campos
Ruiz 1971, 275-311). Nevertheless, Braegelmann (1942, 78) states: "It is difficult
... to obtain the exact wording of the creed."

[167] Ildefonsus of Toledo, *de cognitione baptismi* 39; Campos Ruiz 1971, 278.

[168] See above, footnote 166.

[169] Compare the introduction to the commentary on the seventh article, which
has been quoted together with the sixth (see above, footnote 166): *Credimus
etiam quod sedet ad dexteram patris* (Ildefonsus of Toledo, *de cognitione baptismi*
52; Campos Ruiz 1971, 290).

least in principle, it can also be taken to start with *deum et dominum nostrum* or even with *filium dei unicum*.

Next, the fourth article (apart from the addition *Descendit ad inferna*) is not quoted but only expounded. Kattenbusch assumes that the fourth article ran *Sub Pontio Pilato crucifixus et sepultus*, as Ildefonsus only seems to comment upon the name of Pilatus and Christ's Crucifixion and Sepulture [170]. Attractive though this hypothesis may seem, it cannot be accepted, since Ildefonsus does not always expound every single word of the Creed. For example, in the exposition of the second article, which he (probably) quotes as *Credimus et in Iesum Christum, filium dei unicum, deum et dominum nostrum*, he seems to explain Christ's Son-ship only, and does not explicitly comment upon the name *Iesum Christum* or the apposition *Deum et dominum nostrum* [171].

A final difficulty seems to present itself in the exposition of the ninth article, where the first and second articles are quoted again, but the second article in a different form from the quotation that preceeds the commentary to that article. Moreover, the ninth article itself is quoted in two different forms [172]. The problem, however, is not a real one, as the deviating quotations occur in a passage that Ildefonsus has borrowed from Rufinus's *expositio symboli* [173].

The credal variant that can be extracted from ILD, then, runs as follows:

*Credo in deum patrem omnipotentem*

---

[170] Ildefonsus of Toledo, *de cognitione baptismi* 45-48; Campos Ruiz 1971, 285-287. These four chapters begin as follows: *Pilatus, os malleatoris* ..., *Hic Iesus ... ut ... humiliaret se factus oboediens usque ad mortem, mortem autem crucis* ..., *Sacramentum autem crucis* ..., *Sepultura illa cum creditur* ... See Kattenbusch 1894, 155 and 1900, 889n32; Hahn (1897, 66+n138) shares Kattenbusch's opinion.

[171] See above, text and footnote 166.

[172] *Credo in sanctum spiritum. Haec quae ... Ceterum si solius diuinitatis ratio habeatur, eo modo quo in principio dicitur: Credo in deum patrem omnipotentem, et in Iesum Christum filium eius unicum dominum nostrum, ita iungitur: Et spiritum sanctum* (Idefonsus of Toledo, *de cognitione baptismi* 54; Campos Ruiz 1971, 292).

[173] See Rufinus of Aquileia, *expositio symboli* 33; CCSL 20, 169. This parallel seems hitherto not to have been noticed by the editors of Ildefonsus. Braegelmann (1942, 78) says that Ildefonsus drew on Rufinus by way of Isidore of Sevilla's *de ecclesiasticis officiis*, but that does not apply to this passage.

*(credo?) et in Iesum Christum, filium dei unicum, deum et domi-*
*num nostrum (?)*
*qui natus est de spiritu sancto et Maria uirgine*
*...*
~ *descendit ad inferna*
*tertia die resurrexit uiuus a mortuis*
*ascendit in caelum*
*sedet ad dexteram dei patris omnipotentis*
*inde uenturus iudicare uiuos et mortuos*
*credo in sanctum spiritum*
*sanctam ecclesiam catholicam*
*remissionem peccatorum*
*carnis resurrectionem*
*et uitam aeternam.*

EB   The two books *aduersus Elipandum* by Etherius of Osma
and Beatus of Liébana, which were written after 785 [174].

In this work, we find a complete variant of the Creed being explicitly quoted: *Surgamus ergo cum ipsis apostolis et fidei nostrae sym-*
*bolum quem nobis tradiderunt breui compendio recitemus, quicumque*
*unum dominum, unam fidem, unum baptisma habemus, et fidem* (thus
correctly Stevenson instead of *fide* that is offered by the manuscript) *in qua baptizati sumus in hac peruersitate et duplicitate haere-*
*ticorum non negemus, sed sicut corde credimus ore proprio proferamus*
*publice et dicamus: Credo in deum patrem omnipotentem ... et uitam*
*aeternam. Amen* [175]. In two later chapters, however, phrases from the
Creed are quoted that do not exactly fit into this variant. The first
of these places reads: *In cuius fide iam supra confessi sumus doctri-*
*nam quam ab apostolis accepimus: Credo in deum patrem omnipoten-*
*tem, et in Iesum Christum filium eius unicum deum et dominum*
*nostrum, qui natus de spiritu sancto et Maria uirgine. Quibus tribus*
*sententiis ...* [176]. The difference with the earlier quotation of the
Creed is that the third article lacks *Est* here. Because the authors

---

[174] For the date, see Frede 1995, 314. For earlier credal scholarship on this
text, compare Kattenbusch 1894, 152-154 and Hahn 1897 66-67+n139.

[175] Etherius of Osma and Beatus of Liébana, *aduersus Elipandum* I 21-22;
CCCM 59, 15.

[176] Etherius of Osma and Beatus of Liébana, *aduersus Elipandum* I 35-36;
CCCM 59, 24.

explicitly say that the *tres sententiae* that make up the second credal quotation are taken from the complete form of the Creed that has been quoted before, we are forced to assume that one of the two places is slightly corrupted. The variant with *Est*, however, is supported by a third credal quotation (*ita ut ore proprio profiteantur apostolicum fidei symbolum: Credere se in deum patrem omnipotentem, et in Iesum Christum filium eius unicum deum et dominum nostrum, qui natus est de spiritu sancto et Maria uirgine, et in spiritum sanctum. In qua fide baptizati sunt* [177]), so that it seems best to choose this one for our reconstruction.

In the second place, articles 2 and 3 are given later on in a quite different form from their appearance in the initial quotation. The problem is not a real one, however, since they occur there in a quotation from the pseudo-Augustinian *liber de testimoniorum fidei* [178].

Thus, the wording of the form of the Creed in EB is the following:

*Credo in deum patrem omnipotentem*
*et in Iesum Christum, filium eius unicum, deum et dominum nostrum*
*qui natus est de spiritu sancto et Maria uirgine*
*passus sub Pontio Pilato, crucifixus et sepultus*
*descendit ad inferna*
*tertia die resurrexit uiuus a mortuis*
*ascendit in caelos*
*sedet ad dexteram dei patris omnipotentis*
*inde uenturus iudicare uiuos et mortuos*
*credo in spiritum sanctum*
*sanctam ecclesiam catholicam*

---

[177] Etherius of Osma and Beatus of Liébana, *aduersus Elipandum* II 24; CCCM 59, 128-129. The words *Et in spiritum sanctum* are best understood as an abbreviation for the full *Credo in spiritum sanctum* that we find in I 22 (see above, footnote 175); the entire passage also constitutes an abbreviated quotation (thus already Kattenbusch 1894, 152-153n1).

[178] *Da in symbolo capitis eminentiam: Credo, inquit, in filium eius Iesum Christum, dominum nostrum. Da terrenam in pedibus humilitatem: Qui conceptus est de spiritu sancto natus ex Maria uirgine, passus sub Pontio Pilato crucifixus et sepultus* ... (Etherius of Osma and Beatus of Liébana, *aduersus Elipandum* I 124; CCCM 59, 96). See above, chapter 3.2, footnote 193, for the slightly different source text.

*remissionem omnium peccatorum*
*carnis resurrectionem*
*et uitam aeternam.*

TOL    An inscription from Toledo, which is dated by the editor
to the second half of the seventh century [179].

It is clear from the remains of this inscription that it contains a
variant of the Apostles' Creed [180]. Fragments from the fourth article
onwards are legible, but do not always give equally useful information.

TOL, then, yields the following information concerning the wording of the Apostles' Creed in Spain [181]:

...

...

*(...?) sub Pontio PILATO CRVcifixus (crucifixum?)*
*... descendit AD INFERNa*
*(...?) resVRREXIT (surrexit?) Viuus (...?)*
*... caeLOS*
*SEDET AD ...*
*... IVDICARE (...?)*
*... sanCTVM ...*

...

... [182]

*(...?) carnIS RESVRREctionem (...?).*

## 3.4 African Forms of the Creed

Now that we have studied the Gallican and Spanish variants of
the Apostles' Creed, it seems useful to make a study of the texts
that may contain information about the form of the Creed in Africa

[179] An edition and study of the inscription is offered by Aragoneses 1957. For
its date, see pp. 299-300. This source has not previously been noticed by credal
scholars.

[180] See Aragoneses 1957, 298 and 300-301. Aragoneses offers a somewhat arbitrary reconstruction of the complete credal variant on p. 301.

[181] Letters that have actually been preserved are printed in capitals.

[182] Of the tenth article, only the two letters LI have been preserved. These
could be part of *Catholicam*, but it is also possible that they are the remnants
of an abbreviation for *Ecclesiam*. Between the tenth and twelfth articles, only
one letter has survived, either a V or an O.

as well. Although even fewer traces of early forms of the Apostles' Creed remain from this region of the Western Church than from Spain or Gaul, a separate study of the original form of the Creed in Africa already appeared in 1933 [183]. It seems worthwhile, therefore, to make a fresh investigation of the peculiarities of the African witnesses to the Apostles' Creed.

Various authors have already enumerated witnesses to the form of the Apostles' Creed in Africa [184]. Not all of these adduced witnesses, however, really say something about the African form of the Creed. First of all, the early third-century author Tertullian should be excluded from our analysis [185]. Most texts that are adduced to reconstruct his form of the Creed testify to the *regula fidei*, not to the Creed [186]. In only two or three places does Tertul-

---

[183] Badcock 1933a. This study, however, does not make a reconstruction on the basis of African credal testimonies only, but rather makes abundant use of various Eastern formulae, based on the assumption that an Old African Creed probably came from Asia Minor (see Badcock 1933a, 6-7). Moreover, Badcock does not first reconstruct a number of local or personal variants of the Creed, but immediately tries to assess the form of some 'general' African creed. Rodomonti (1995, 135n61) is one of the few followers of Badcock and claims that this 'Credo africano' is encountered in a more developed form in the sources AU-H, QU, and FU (see below, pp. 163-181).

[184] See Kattenbusch 1894, 134-152 ("Afrikanische Symbole"), Hahn 1897, 54-64 ("Symbolformeln der Carthaginiensisch-afrikanischen Kirche"), Morin 1923, 242-245, Badcock 1933a, Eichenseer 1960, 474n7, Smulders 1970, 237n10, Kelly 1976, 175-176, and O'Callaghan 1992, 285-287.

[185] Hahn (1897, 54-56) reconstructs a complete variant from a number of different places; Kattenbusch (1894, 141-144) is more cautious.

[186] See Tertullian, *aduersus Praxean* II 1-2: *Nos uero ... unicum quidem deum credimus, sub hac tamen dispensatione quam oikonomiam dicimus ut unici dei sit et filius, sermo ipsius qui ex ipso processerit, per quem omnia facta sunt et sine quo factum est nihil. Hunc missum a patre in uirginem et ex ea natum, hominem et deum, filium hominis et filium dei, et cognominatum Iesum Christum. Hunc passum, hunc mortuum et sepultum secundum scripturas et resuscitatum a patre et in caelo resumptum sedere ad dexteram patris, uenturum iudicare uiuos et mortuos. Qui exinde miserit secundum promissionem suam a patre spiritum sanctum, Paracletum, sanctificatorem fidei eorum qui credunt in patrem et filium et spiritum sanctum. Hanc regulam ab initio euangelii decucurrisse* ... (CPL 26; CCSL 2, 1160); similarly *de uirginibus uelandis* I 3: *Regula quidem fidei una omnino est, sola immobilis et irreformabilis, credendi scilicet in unicum deum omnipotentem, mundi conditorem, et filium eius Iesum Christum, natum ex uirgine Maria* ... (CPL 27; CCSL 2, 1209), *de praescriptione haereticorum* XIII: *Regula est autem fidei ut iam hinc quid defendamus profiteamur, illa scilicet qua creditur. Vnum omnino deum esse nec*

lian seem to allude to the contents of his baptismal questions, but these do not even admit a partial reconstruction of any concrete formula [187]. Similarly, the creed of Julian of Eclanum (CPL 775b), which is adduced as an African witness in O'Callaghan's list of "Credal Redactions" [188], is of equally little use, as this text clearly belongs to the genre of the doctrinal creeds [189].

*alium praeter mundi conditorem qui uniuersa de nihilo produxerit per uerbum suum primo omnium emissum. Id uerbum filium eius appellatum in nomine dei uarie uisum a patriarchis, in prophetis semper auditum, postremo delatum ex spiritu patris dei et uirtute in uirginem Mariam* ... (CPL 5; CCSL 1, 197-198), *de praescriptione haereticorum* XXXVI 5: ... *unum deum dominum nouit creatorem uniuersitatis, et Christum Iesum ex uirgine Maria filium dei creatoris* ... (*ibid.* 217); *de carne Christi* V 4: *Crucifixus est dei filius: non pudet quia pudendum est. Et mortuus est dei filius: credibile est quia ineptum est. Et sepultus resurrexit: certum est quia impossibile* (CPL 18; CCSL 2, 881). That these texts have nothing to do with the Apostles' Creed was already demonstrated by Restrepo-Jaramillo 1934 (especially pp. 39-51); compare also Kelly 1976, 85-88 (where the distinction between *regula* and Creed is nevertheless blurred again in the final sentence but one) and Smulders 1971, 363-364.

[187] See Tertullian *de baptismo* VI: *Non quod in aqua spiritum sanctum consequimur, sed in aqua emendati sub angelo spiritui sancto praeparamur. Hic quoque figura praecessit: sicut enim Iohannes antecursor domini fuit praeparans uias eius, ita et angelus baptismi arbiter superuenturo spiritui sancto uias dirigit abolitione delictorum quam fides impetrat obsignata in patre et filio et spiritu sancto. Nam si in tribus testibus stabit omne uerbum dei, quanto magis donum? Habebimus de benedictione eosdem arbitros fidei quos et sponsores salutis, sufficit ad fiduciam spei nostrae etiam numerus nominum diuinorum. Cum autem sub tribus et testatio fidei et sponsio salutis pigneretur necessario adicitur ecclesiae mentio, quoniam ubi tres, id est pater et filius et spiritus sanctus, ibi ecclesia quae trium corpus est* (CPL 8; CCSL 1, 282), *de baptismo* XI 3: *Sed nec moueat quod non ipse* (viz. Christ) *tinguebat: in quem enim tingueret? In paenitentiam? Quo ergo illi praecursorem? In peccatorum remissionem, quam uerbo dabat? In semet ipsum, quem in humilitate celabat? In spiritum sanctum, qui nondum ad patrem ascenderat? In ecclesiam, quam nondum apostolis struxerat?* (*ibid.* 286), *de corona* III 3: *Dehinc ter mergitamur, amplius aliquid respondentes quam dominus in Euangelio determinauit* (CPL 21; CCSL 2, 1042). Compare for these passages Restrepo-Jaramillo 1934, 14-17 and Kelly 1976, 83-85. Other places that are sometimes quoted as testifying to the wording of Tertullian's baptismal questions are even less informative.

[188] O'Callaghan 1992, 286. On the same page, O'Callaghan also mentions the creed of Pelagius (written 417; CPL 731), albeit without connecting it with any region. This doctrinal creed is closely related to the creed of Julian of Eclanum. See Pelagius, *libellus fidei: Credimus in deum patrem omnipotentem cunctorum uisibilium et inuisibilium conditorem, credimus et in dominum nostrum Iesum Christum* ... (PL 48, 488-491 = PL 45, 1716-1718; reproduced in Hahn 1897, 288-292).

Next, there is Facundus of Hermiane's *epistula fidei catholicae in defensione trium capitulorum* (CPL 868; *c.* 568). In the work of this sixth-century African bishop, we read: *Principium itaque symboli hoc est: Credimus in unum deum patrem omnipotentem, et in unum dominum Iesum Christum filium eius, natum ex spiritu sancto et Maria uirgine, qui sub Pontio Pilato crucifixus est et sepultus, tertia die resurrexit a mortuis, ascendit in caelos, sedet ad dexteram patris, unde uenturus est iudicare uiuos et mortuos, et reliqua* [190]. Although this looks like an explicit and complete quotation of the first eight articles of Facundus's own form of the Creed, certain considerations speak against this assumption. Earlier scholars have already pointed out the resemblance between the first two articles of the quotation and those of the Nicaeno-Constantinopolitan Creed (*C*). Thus, the theory emerged that Facundus does not quote his own local variant of the Creed but rather deliberately composed a form that was intended to persuade his adversaries, both in Rome and in Constantinople, of his orthodoxy [191]. This explanation, however, is on the one hand difficult to prove, and, on the other, does not fit the facts. What Facundus tries to do is not prove his own orthodoxy, but rather refute those who condemn the so-called three chapters of Theodorus of Mopsuestia, Theodoretus of Cyrus, and Ibas of Edessa. To achieve this end, he makes particular use of the eighth article of the Apostles' Creed. When speaking about the Creed, however, Facundus seems to mean both the Nicaeno-Constantinopolitan Creed and the Apostles' Creed, treating these texts as if they were

For earlier credal scholarship, see Kattenbusch 1894, 188n6, Hahn 1897, 288-293nn244-284, and Kattenbusch 1900, 433n107. See for the date and further details Dekkers 1995, 252 and Frede 1995, 671.

[189] See Julian of Eclanum, *libellus fidei*: *Credimus in deum patrem omnipotentem omnium uisibilium et inuisibilium conditorem, et in dominum nostrum Iesum Christum, filium dei uiui, per quem creata sunt omnia, non extrinsecus natum aut factum* ... (PL 48, 509-526 = PL 45, 1732-1736; also in Hahn 1897, 293-294). In fact, Julian's authorship of this fifth-century text is far from certain: see Dekkers 1995, 264 and Frede 1995, 585. See Kattenbusch 1894, 209n13 and Hahn 1897, 293n292 for earlier credal scholarhip on this creed.

[190] Facundus of Hermiane, *epistula fidei catholicae* 13, 104-109; CCSL 90A, 421-422. See for the date of this work Frede 1995, 465.

[191] Thus Caspari 1875, 51 and Kattenbusch 1894, 150-152; Hahn (1897, 63n127) explains the quotation as an unconscious mixing of *R* and *C*.

one and the same [192], though Facundus must have known, even though he does not explicitly say so, that these two creeds are not identical in wording and that even the Apostles' Creed existed in different versions. This implies that when Facundus claims to quote the Apostles' Creed, he does not consider himself bound to one specific text and may choose which formulation he uses. Moreover, Facundus expressly states himself that he is not going to give a complete form of the Creed, but only parts of it [193]. This means that Facundus not only feels free to choose between different forms of the Creed, by which he means the various forms of the Apostles' Creed as well as the Nicaeno-Constantinopolitan Creed, but also to adapt the formulation to his own purposes [194]. This is precisely what we find when Facundus gives 'the Creed': the first words of the first and second articles are from *C*, the third article is more free, and the fourth to eighth articles are more or less according to *R*. Therefore, it seems better not to use Facundus's *epistula fidei catholicae* as a witness for the form of the Apostles' Creed in Africa.

Then there is a direct quotation of three articles of the Creed in one of the letters of Ferrandus of Carthage, who lived in the first half of the sixth century. As this letter has not yet received a critical edition, we have to leave aside this source as well [195].

---

[192] Actually, matters are even more complicated: see above, chapter 2.3, footnote 43.

[193] *Cum ipsius symboli uerba non quidem in ordinem prolixitatis uitandae gratia, sed admodum delibando posuerimus* (Facundus of Hermiane, *epistula fidei catholicae* 12; CCSL 90A, 421).

[194] This is probably the explanation for a unique quotation like: *Quod illic* (viz.: *in symbolo*) *subsequitur ... specialiter dictum: Qui uenturus est iudicare uiuos et mortuos* (Facundus of Hermiane, *epistula fidei catholicae* 28; CCSL 90A, 425).

[195] Ferrandus of Carthage, *epistula 5* 8: *Mouet adhuc quoniam, si una est natura Christi, aut ubique diffusa est aut localis. Si ubique diffusa, quare uerba symboli sic recitamus: Tertia die a mortuis resurrexit, ascendit in caelos, sedet ad dexteram patris? Qui respondebit mihi, si ubique diffusa est, quomodo ascendit in caelos? Si ubique diffusa est, quomodo specialiter de ea dicitur: Sedet ad dexteram patris?* (CPL 848; PL 67, 918); compare Kattenbusch 1894, 152n2. Ferrandus's *epistula 3* 7, which is additionally mentioned by Hahn (1897, 62n125), only refers to the contents of the Creed: *... per hanc unius in Christo substantiae praedicationem patrem quoque natum de Maria uirgine, crucifixum sub Pontio Pilato et sepultum uideri* (PL 67, 896); compare Kattenbusch 1894, 152n2. The author's name is also given as Fulgentius Ferrandus.

Again, Kattenbusch refers to the words of bishop Theogenes of Hippo in the *sententiae LXXXVII episcoporum* (CPL 56) in the acts of the synod of Carthage of 256 as testifying to the presence of the phrase *Per sanctam ecclesiam* in Theogenes's form of the Creed. Here, Kattenbusch seems to be reading too much into his source [196]. Kattenbusch only mentions in passing Optatus of Mileve's *contra Parmenianum Donatistam* (CPL 244; *c.* 365), which only alludes to the contents of the Creed [197].

Finally, a number of texts are considered African by Hahn or others, the origin of which is still by no means certain. One of these

[196] Pseudo-Cyprian, *sententiae LXXXVII episcoporum* 14: *Secundum sacramentum dei gratiae caelestis quod accepimus unum baptisma quod est in sancta ecclesia credimus* (Von Soden 1909, 257); compare Kattenbusch 1900, 377n40. Kinzig (1999a, 118-119) reproduces the words of Caecilius of Biltha from the same collection (1), but these are even less informative.

[197] Optatus of Mileve, *contra Parmenianum Donatistam* I 1: *Cunctos nos Christianos, carissimi fratres, omnipotenti deo fides una commendat, cuius fidei pars est credere filium dei dominum iudicem saeculi esse uenturum, eum qui iam pridem uenerit et secundum hominem suum per Mariam uirginem natus sit, passus et mortuus et sepultus resurrexerit, et antequam in caelum ascenderet unde descenderat Christianis nobis omnibus storiam per apostolos pacem dereliquit* (CSEL 26, 3). Two more possible allusions to the Creed are *contra Parmenianum* IV 8 (*Hoc de haereticis dictum est, apud quos sunt sacramentorum falsa connubia et in quorum toris iniquitas inuenitur ... natiuitatis eorum semen exterminatum est qui non crediderunt filium dei in carne natum de uirgine Maria et passum in carne*; CSEL 26, 114) and V 10 (*Nam quicumque a uobis se rebaptizari consenserit, huiusmodi homini non denegatur resurrectio, quia credidit resurrectionem carnis, resurget quidem, sed nudus*; CSEL 26, 140). Compare Kattenbusch 1894, 152n2 and 1900, 389-390n52. See for the date Frede 1995, 652. A similar allusion is found in the probably late fifth-century work *contra Eutychetem* by Vigilius of Thapsus (CPL 806), where we read: *... unde et in symbolo carnis resurrectionem, non animae confitemur* (Vigilius of Thapsus, *contra Eutycheten* IV 17; PL 62, 128). An even less informative reference to the Creed occurs in II 8 of the same work: *Nam dominum passum symboli tenet auctoritas ...* (PL 62, 108). Compare Kattenbusch 1894, 149 for these passages. Allusions to the contents of the Creed can be seen in *contra Eutychetem* I 3 and II 9 (PL 62, 96 and 109). Most of these places were already noticed in the eighteenth century: see Blanchinus 1732, 15 and 21. Blanchinus moreover mentions (*ibidem*, 13) a possible quotation in Vigilius's *contra Arrianos, Sabellianos, Photinianos dialogus* II 17: *Quomodo ait: Vado ad patrem, cum quo et semper erat et a quo numquam recesserat ... nisi quia utique de illo quem assumpserat homine loquebatur, quod ipse erat iturus ad patrem a quo et uenturus est iudicare uiuos et mortuos?* (CPL 807; PL 62, 209). See Dekkers 1995, 272 and Frede 1995, 790-791 for the date of Vigilius and of his work.

is an anonymous adaptation of Fulgentius of Ruspe's *fragmentum 36
contra Fabianum* [198]; two others are the pseudo-Ambrosian *exhortatio
ad neophytos de symbolo* (CPL 178) [199] and the pseudo-Athanasian
*enarratio in symbolum apostolorum* (CPL 1744a) [200], which will
receive due attention in the next chapter [201].

The following four sources thus remain.

CY-C    Cyprian of Carthage's (*c.* 210-258) *epistulae 69* and *70*
        (CPL 50) [202].

[198] This text, as far as I can ascertain, has not yet been edited, but is mentioned by Caspari, who claims: "Der Bearbeiter hat der Auslegung des Fulgentius einen anderen ... Symboltext untergelegt und dieselbe ... nicht unbedeutend verkürzt" (Caspari 1879, 260-261n21; similary Hahn 1897, 62n126). The 'pseudo-Fulgentian' quotations of the Creed are presented in Caspari 1879, 317 and Hahn 1897, 62-63. The testimony of the genuine Fulgentian work will be discussed in the present chapter: see below, pp. 178-181.

[199] See Hahn 1897, 56-57; Kattenbusch (1894, 202-207) files this text as one of his "unbestimmbare Symbole".

[200] See Hahn 1897, 57-58; Kattenbusch (1894, 145-148 and 202n1) is very cautious again.

[201] See below, chapters 4.2 and 4.9. For the so-called Jacobi's Creed (CPL 1752), which is ranked among the African forms of the Creed by Hahn (1897, 64+n128), see above, chapter 3.2, footnote 31.

[202] For the difficulties that are connected with the early date of these two letters as possible witnesses to the Apostles' Creed, see above, chapter 1.6, footnote 58. Probably because of this early date, in combination with the fact that Cyprian does not quote a **declaratory** form of the Creed, most earlier scholars have not included CY-C in their discussions of the history of the form of the Creed: see Kattenbusch 1894, 135-136, Kelly 1976, 46-47, Kinzig 1999a, 127-128 (CY-C as a source for the baptismal questions), and Hahn 1897, 16-17 (CY-C as a source for the *regula fidei* [ *sic!*]). See above, chapter 1.13, for the relationship between baptismal questions and declaratory formulae. Kattenbusch also draws attention to a number of other places in Cyprian's works, but these refer to the content of the Creed at the most. See Cyprian of Carthage, *de mortalitate* (CPL 44) 20: *Qui autem spe uiuimus et in deum credimus et Christum passum esse pro nobis et resurrexisse confidimus in Christo manentes et per ipsum atque in ipso resurgentes ...* (CCSL 3A, 28), *ad Demetrianum* (CPL 46) 24: *In aeternam poenam sero credunt qui in uitam aeternam credere noluerunt* (CCSL 3A, 50), and the chapter titles of the *testimonia ad Quirinum* (CPL 39) II 20-28: *Quod cruci illum fixuri essent Iudaei, Quod in passione crucis et signo uirtus omnis sit et potestas, Quod a morte non uinceretur nec apud inferos remansurus esset, Quod ab inferis tertio die resurgeret, Quod cum resurrexisset acciperet a patre omnem potestatem et potestas eius aeterna sit, ..., Quod ipse iudex uenturus sit* (CCSL 3, 57-66). See Kattenbusch 1900, 511n41, 638n255, 640n258, 650-651n271, and 654.

The first of these two letters seems at first sight to give an accurate quotation from the interrogatory form of the Creed as Cyprian knew it: *Nam cum dicunt: credis in remissionem peccatorum et uitam aeternam per sanctam ecclesiam* ... [203]. There are some problems, however. First of all, the presence of *Credis in* immediately before *Remissionem peccatorum* is strange. The explanation is fairly straightforward, however, when we realize that nothing in the context of this quotation suggests that Cyprian is going to quote the Creed. To make it clear, therefore, that he is referring to the Creed in its interrogatory form, he inserts the words *Credis in* immediately before those words that are of interest to him. The second difficulty is the absence of *Carnis resurrectionem*. Especially in combination with the presence of *Et uitam aeternam*, an addition to the original form of the Creed, it is very improbable that a variant would ever have lacked this basic element. However, Cyprian does not say that his quotation is complete. What matters for him here is to show that the Novatianists may use the same credal formulas as he does, but that identical formulas do not always have the same bearing. To bear this out, he only needs some examples, for which he chooses the Remission of Sins and Eternal Life. He shows that both Catholics and Novatianists have *Remissionem peccatorum* and *Et uitam aeternam* in their forms of the Creed, but that belief in the Remission of Sins and Eternal Life is true for a Catholic, whereas it amounts to a lie for a Novatianist, as the one belongs to the true church through which these goods are imparted (*Per sanctam ecclesiam*) and the other does not [204]. Maybe, therefore, Cyprian's credal

---

[203] Cyprian of Carthage, *epistula 69* VII 2; CCSL 3C, 480. Probably because Cyprian is addressing the Roman schismatic Novatian, Kinzig treats these words as possibly testifying to **Roman** baptismal questions: see Kinzig 1999a, 87-88 and 1999b, 542-543. The fact that Novatianists apparently claimed to use the same *symbolum* for baptism as Catholics cannot be taken to mean that their form of the Creed was literally identical with Cyprian's: see above, chapter 2.3, particularly pp. 84-85 with footnote 43. Moreover, even a literal identity of the baptismal questions that were used by Carthaginian Novatianists with those used by Cyprian leaves open the possibility that Roman Novatianists favoured a different formula.

[204] *Quodsi aliquis illud opponit ut dicat eandem Nouatianum legem tenere quam catholica ecclesia teneat, eodem symbolo quo et nos baptizare ... ac propter hoc usurpare eum potestatem baptizandi posse, quod uideatur interrogatione baptismi a nobis non discrepare, sciat quisque hoc opponendum putat primum non esse unam nobis et*

quotation could better be printed thus: *Credis in ... remissionem peccatorum ... et uitam aeternam per sanctam ecclesiam?* [205]

Although this seems to be a reliable, though only fragmentary, credal quotation, Cyprian's next letter undermines this assumption by saying *Nam cum dicimus: Credis in uitam aeternam et remissionem peccatorum per sanctam ecclesiam?* [206] The best solution seems to be to assume that Cyprian apparently feels free to change the word order of the Creed when quoting [207]. Since he says, however, that he is quoting the *symbolum*, it seems at least certain that his form of the Creed contained the phrases *Remissionem peccatorum*, *Vitam aeternam*, and *Per sanctam ecclesiam* [208].

CY-C, therefore, can be taken to yield the following formulation of the Creed:

*schismaticis symboli legem neque eandem interrogationem. Nam cum dicunt ... mentiuntur interrogatione quando non habeant ecclesiam* (Cyprian of Carthage, *epistula 69* VII 1-2; CSEL 3C, 480, reproduced in Kinzig 1999a, 127-128).

[205] Eichenseer (1960, 400-401) reaches a similar conclusion. That Cyprian left out precisely the Resurrection of the Flesh is quite logical, since practically all early commentators on the Creed emphasize that everyone (thus even Novatianists) will rise again at the end of time. Compare Optatus of Mileve, *contra Parmenianum Donatistam* V 10, quoted in footnote 197 above. Kattenbusch (1900, 950) seems to claim that Cyprian has **replaced** *Carnis resurrectionem* with *Vitam aeternam*. Clarke (1989, 183-184), in his commentary on Cyprian's letters, does not see any reason to reconstruct the baptismal questions other than the way Cyprian quotes them here.

[206] Cyprian of Carthage, *epistula 70* II 1; CCSL 3C, 505-507, reproduced in Kinzig 1999a, 128. Since 1963, a Greek version of this letter has been known as well (Joannou 1963, 303-313, reproduced in CCSL 3C, 498-514). In this Greek version, the words *Per sanctam ecclesiam* have no counterpart: see Joannou 1963, 308 (Diercks fails to mention this in CCSL 3C, 497).

[207] In the light of Kinzig's assumption (see above, footnote 203), the possibility could also be envisaged that in this letter, in which the quotation is introduced by *dicimus*, Cyprian is quoting according to his own practice, whereas the quotation in *epistula 69*, introduced by *dicunt*, refers to the Novatianist formula. In such a case, however, the Novatianist claim that both groups asked the same questions at baptism (see above, footnote 204) would be false, and Cyprian would doubtless have said so. Clarke (1989, 199-200) does not seem to be aware of the difference between the two quotations: "The argument presupposes uniformity in liturgical formula, at least among the African churches ...".

[208] Compare Kattenbusch 1894, 135-136. Anyhow, *Per sanctam ecclesiam* seems to be the last element of Cyprian's form of the Creed. For a possible explanation of Cyprian's loose way of handling the relative order of the Holy Church and Remission of Sins, see below, chapter 3.7, footnote 544.

...

...

*remissionem peccatorum*

...

*(...?) uitam aeternam* [209]
*per sanctam ecclesiam.*

AU-H   Augustine of Hippo's (354-430) *sermo 215 de symbolo* (CPL 284) [210].

It is generally agreed that, when speaking about the Creed, Augustine usually refers to the form with which he was baptized in Milan, but that his *sermo 215* comments upon the form of his African bishopric Hippo [211]. When we try to reconstruct a Hipponic variant of the Creed from this sermon, we should be cautious, how-

---

[209] There is no certainty about the order of the parts of the Creed that precede *Per sanctam ecclesiam.*

[210] The date of this sermon seems to be entirely unknown: see Verbraken 1976, 105. However, because the underlying form of the Creed of this sermon clearly contains a number of elements that were absent from the Creed as Augustine had learnt it and used to quote it on most occasions (see chapter 3.5, pp. 189-196), it seems safe to assume that this form of the Creed was already in use in Hippo before Augustine became bishop of the town in 396. See above, chapter 2.3, pp. 81-84, for a more elaborate discussion.

[211] See Kattenbusch 1894, 135, Hahn 1897, 58n107, Nerney 1953a, 275, Verbraken 1958, 6n1, Eichenseer 1960, 105-107 and *passim*, Kelly 1976, 175, O'Callaghan 1992, 285, and Harmless 1995, 275. See also above, chapter 2.3, footnote 38. All these authors except Kattenbusch make a reconstruction of this African form (Verbraken does not explicitly say so, but clearly marks those parts of the text which he considers to be quotations from the Creed by printing them in a different fount). Eichenseer reconstructs the Italian and the African form for each article, and at the end of his book presents a reconstruction of these two forms that is not always identical with what he has said before. Kelly, surprisingly, still uses Migne's edition. Poque, who also makes a reconstruction of this Hipponic form of the Creed in the introduction to her edition of a number of Augustinian sermons, believes that *sermo 212* also refers to the Hipponic form of the Creed (see SChr 116, 63-64). This may be probable enough, but does not shed any light on the wording of this form of the Creed because *sermo 212* does not contain any direct quotations. Mountain, in an appendix to his edition of Augustine's *de trinitate* (CCSL 50A, 558-563), under the heading "Symbolum Africanum" offers a reconstruction on the basis of those by Hahn and Eichenseer.

ever. It seems to be Augustine's intention to present the whole Creed [212], but he hardly gives any certain quotations. Practically all passages in which a new article is introduced must therefore be regarded as indications of the content of the Creed or at best grammatically imbedded quotations [213]. On the other hand, when one puts all these indications together, a coherent form of the Creed does emerge, so that it is possible to reconstruct an Hipponic form of the Creed in some detail. When we do so, however, we should bear in mind that such a reconstruction rests on the assumption that Augustine wanted to give the exact wording of the Creed in his *sermo 215*, and that this is an assumption only.

Augustine, then, starts his exposition with the words *Fides ergo haec et salutis est regula, credere nos in deum patrem omnipotentem, uniuersorum creatorem, regem saeculorum, immortalem et inuisibilem* [214]. Of course, the words *In deum patrem omnipotentem* can safely be taken to belong to the first article of the credal variant Augustine alludes to here. It is already more difficult to decide about the addition of *Vniuersorum ... inuisibilem*. However, since Augustine seems to comment upon just these terms in what follows [215], the best decision is probably to take them as a credal quotation [216]. In addition, an explicit quotation of the first words of the Creed is offered by Augustine's *sermo 56*: *Memento quod in symbolo reddidisti: Credo in deum patrem omnipotentem* [217].

---

[212] The Session at the Right Hand, Remission of Sins, Resurrection of the Flesh, and Eternal Life are mentioned, but not commented upon.

[213] This point is made very forcefully by Kattenbusch 1894, 136-138.

[214] Augustine of Hippo, *sermo 215* 2; Verbraken 1958, 19.

[215] *Ipse est quippe deus omnipotens qui in primordio mundi cuncta ex nihilo fecit, qui est ante saecula, et qui fecit et regit saecula. Non enim tempore augetur aut loco distenditur aut aliqua materia concluditur aut terminatur, sed manet apud se et in se ipso plena et perfecta aeternitas quam nec comprehendere humana cogitatio potest nec lingua narrare. Nam si munus quod promittit sanctis suis nec oculus uidit nec auris audiuit nec in cor hominis ascendit, quomodo potest ipsum qui promittit aut mens concipere aut cor cogitare aut lingua narrare?* (Augustine of Hippo, *sermo 215* 2; Verbraken 1958, 19).

[216] Kattenbusch (1894, 136), Hahn (1897, 58-59n108), Eichenseer (1960, 192 and 199), Kelly (1976, 176), Verbraken (1958, 19), Poque (SChr 116, 63), and Mountain (CCSL 50A, 561) come to the same conclusion. Mountain, however, seems to doubt the presence of *Patrem*, which he puts between brackets.

[217] Augustine of Hippo, *sermo 56* 7; Verbraken 1958, 29. Since Augustine held this sermon as a bishop of Hippo (see Verbraken 1976, 66), these words must

The second article is introduced thus: *Credimus et in filium eius Iesum Christum, dominum nostrum, deum uerum de deo uero, dei patris filium deum, sed non duos deos* ... [218]. Although the use of the plural *Credimus* must be due to stylistic reasons, it is not clear whether the Hipponic form of the Creed to which Augustine refers started with *Credo* or with *Et* [219]. Further, it is not absolutely clear where the article ends and the commentary starts. The words *deum uerum de deo uero*, which are apparently taken from the Nicene or Nicaeno-Constantinopolitan Creed, seem to be explained best as part of the commentary [220], but *dominum nostrum* could belong to either. However, Augustine seems to quote this article again in shortened form further below: *Credamus ergo in Iesum Christum dominum nostrum, natum de spiritu sancto et uirgine Maria* [221], which makes it probable that *Dominum nostrum* was part of the second article of the credal variant that was in use in Hippo [222].

For the third article, we have an unambiguous quotation: *Audi et crede: Natum de spiritu sancto et uirgine Maria* [223], which is confirmed by the combined quotation of the second and third articles in the next paragraph (see above) [224]. For the fourth, there is one

refer to local practice (Poque [SChr 116, 63n2] seems to be the first to have pointed this out). Thus, the common assumption that Augustine testifies in his *sermo 215* to an African form of the Creed that contains a threefold *Credimus*, probably because of his introduction to the second and ninth articles (see below), is erroneous. See Hahn 1897, 58-59, Verbraken 1958, 19n (!), Eichenseer 1960, 200 and 337-338, and Kelly 1976, 176. Later on, Eichenseer (1960, 474) is a little more cautious and leaves some room for a form with a threefold *Credo* as well, as do Mountain (CCSL 50A, 561-563) and Smulders 1970, 243n1. Kattenbusch (1894, 136) reconstructs *Credo*, but does not refer to *sermo 56* for this point.

[218] Augustine of Hippo, *sermo 215* 3; Verbraken 1958, 19.

[219] See above, footnote 217, for earlier scholarship on this point. Poque (SChr 116, 63+n3) omits *Et* from her reconstruction and deems the presence of *Credo* certain.

[220] Thus also Hill 1993, 165n5. Compare Verbraken 1958, 19n and Kattenbusch 1894, 136.

[221] Augustine of Hippo, *sermo 215* 4; Verbraken 1958, 21.

[222] Kattenbusch (1894, 136-137), Hahn (1897, 159n110), and Eichenseer (1960, 200-201), who still took *R* as the common ancestor of all variants of the Apostles' Creed, all doubt the absence of *Vnicum* in this article. Mountain (CCSL 50A, 561) prints it between brackets.

[223] Augustine of Hippo, *sermo 215* 3; Verbraken 1958, 20. There is an important variant *Ex* for *Et*.

[224] Two further Augustinian passages seem to testify to this formulation as well: ... *per quam credimus dominum nostrum Iesum Christum non solum natum*

partial but not very informative quotation: *Audi quo tempore: sub Pontio Pilato*. The whole article could very well be indicated some lines below (*Credite ergo filium dei crucifixum sub Pontio Pilato et sepultum*), though a little earlier we read *Crucifixus insuper, mortuus et sepultus est* [225]. However, as the accusative construction seems to fit in better with the third article as Augustine presents it, we should probably choose the formulation without *mortuus* as the more probable one. This is also the form which is supported by the introduction to the next article: *Qui enim crucifixus sub Pontio Pilato et sepultus est tertia die a mortuis resurrexit* [226].

That such is indeed the wording of the fifth article in the Hipponic form of the Creed is proved by a direct quotation a little further on: *Nunc quia dicitur: Tertia die a mortuis resurrexit* ... and confirmed by even a third instance: *Quia uero tertia die a mortuis resurrexit* ... [227]. The reconstruction of the next three articles seems again

---

*de deo sempiterno ... sed etiam iam natum de spiritu sancto et uirgine Maria, quod pariter confitemur* and *Non tamen interrupit ordinem et textum fidei nostrae, qua confitemur: Natum de Spiritu sancto et uirgine Maria* (Augustine of Hippo, *sermo 51* 8 and 18; Verbraken 1981, 28-29 and 34). A third instance is said by Morin to testify to this article of the "Symbolum Hipponense", but rather looks like a free formulation by Augustine himself: *Ergo, fratres, quando auditis: Natus est de spiritu ex uirgine Maria, passus est, uapulauit, alapas accepit, quando auditis: Passus est haec Christus ...* (Augustine of Hippo, *sermo 375B* [= *sermo Denis 5*; CPL 285] 6; Morin 1930, 27).

[225] Augustine of Hippo, *sermo 215* 5; Verbraken 1958, 22.

[226] Augustine of Hippo, *sermo 215* 6; Verbraken 1958, 23. The construction with *Qui ... est* is, as Kattenbusch (1894, 137) already saw, due to the fact that Augustine wants to link up two articles in one grammatical sentence. Nevertheless, Hahn (1897, 59) has *Qui crucifixus sub Pontio Pilato et sepultus est* in his reconstruction. Eichenseer (1960, 280) says that he follows Kattenbusch in the opinion that *Qui sub Pontio Pilato crucifixus est et sepultus* could have been the wording of the fourth article in this form of the Creed, but he just misunderstands Kattenbusch (surprisingly, he chooses the accusative construction after all in his final reconstruction [Eichenseer 1960, 474]). Kelly (1976, 176) has the accusative construction with *Mortuum* added. Poque (SChr 116, 63) has *Crucifixus est sub Pontio Pilato et sepultus est*.

[227] Augustine of Hippo, *sermo 215* 6; Verbraken 1958, 23-24. Compare *sermo 227: Quid reddidistis in symbolo? Tertia die resurrexit a mortuis, ascendit in caelum, sedet ad dexteram patris* (SChr 116, 238). As they did not yet know Verbraken's critical edition, Hahn (1897, 59) and Kattenbusch (1894, 137) also have the word order *Resurrexit a mortuis*. Poque (SChr 116, 63) and Kelly (1976, 176) still do the same, whereas Eichenseer (1960, 474) and Mountain (CCSL 50A, 563) surprisingly give *[Qui] tertio die a mortuis resurrexit*, for which Eichenseer

to present few difficulties as we read *Postquam ergo resurrexit a mortuis ascendit in caelos, sedet ad dexteram patris* and *Nam qui modo sedet ad dexteram patris aduocatus pro nobis inde uenturus est iudicare uiuos et mortuos* [228]. There is, however, a quotation in *sermo 227* which clearly refers to the Creed as it was recited by the catechumens during the *redditio symboli*, where the sixth article is explicitly quoted as *Ascendit in caelum* [229]. It will be better, therefore, to take this explicit quotation seriously and to consider the words of *sermo 215*, which lays no claims to rendering the Hipponic form of the Creed in a literal way, as a more free formulation here [230].

The ninth article is introduced with the words *Credamus ergo et in spiritum sanctum* [231]. Again, it is impossible to decide whether this article started with *Credo* or with *Et* [232]. It is even more difficult to reconstruct the articles on Forgiveness of Sins, Resurrection of the Flesh, and Eternal Life. First we read *Per ipsum remissionem accepimus peccatorum, per ipsum resurrectionem credimus carnis, per ipsum uitam speramus aeternam*, and more below *Quo remissionem peccatorum et resurrectionem carnis et uitam aeternam ... apprehendere ualeatis* [233]. Verbraken seems to take these articles as simply running *Remissionem peccatorum, resurrectionem carnis, uitam aeternam* [234].

(1960, 474n8) refers to the anonymous sermon CPL 846 (see for this text below, chapter 4.6). The different word order in *sermo 227* is probaby best explained as a scribal error due to the influence of *T*.

[228] Augustine of Hippo, *sermo 215* 7; Verbraken 1958, 24.

[229] See above, footnote 227. This sermon was delivered in Hippo: see Verbraken 1976, 109.

[230] I did not yet recognize the importance of *sermo 227* for the reconstruction of the credal variant of Hippo in Westra 1996a, 74. For some unknown reason, Poque (SChr 116, 63) has *Ad caelos* in the sixth article. In the seventh article, Hahn (1897, 59) reads *Dei* before *Patris*, something which Kattenbusch (1894, 139-140) thinks just possible. Although this possibility has now been discarded by Verbraken's edition and moreover by the passage in *sermo 227*, Poque (SChr 116, 63) and Kelly (1976, 176) still agree with Hahn here. Our reconstruction of the formulation of the eighth article is probably supported by two quotations in *sermones 79A* and *110*: see below, chapter 3.5, footnote 344.

[231] Augustine of Hippo, *sermo 215* 8; Verbraken 1958, 24.

[232] For the opinions of other scholars, see above, footnote 217, and Verbraken 1958, 24.

[233] Augustine of Hippo, *sermo 215* 8-9; Verbraken 1958, 24-25.

[234] Similarly Kelly 1976, 176. Poque (SChr 116, 63) inserts *In* before *Remissionem peccatorum*. Hahn (1897, 59), Kattenbusch (1894, 138), Eichenseer (1960, 400-401), and Poque (SChr 116, 63) all read *Et uitam aeternam*. This is indeed

This is possible, but a reconstruction on the basis of indications that are so loosely formulated cannot be given too much weight. Moreover, in his *de symbolo ad catechumenos* (CPL 309) Augustine probably refers to the Hipponic form of the Creed when he says ... *additum est: In uitam aeternam* [235]. If this is true, the last article but one of the Hipponic variant of the Creed may well have run *Carnis resurrectionem in uitam aeternam.* The last article, finally, is quoted clearly again: ... *ut diceretur: Per sanctam ecclesiam* [236].

All in all, we can take the underlying form of the Creed of AU-H to run as follows:

> *Credo in deum patrem omnipotentem, uniuersorum creatorem, regem*
> *saeculorum, immortalem et inuisibilem*
> *(credo?) et in filium eius Iesum Christum, dominum nostrum*
> *natum de spiritu sancto et uirgine Maria*
> *crucifixum sub Pontio Pilato et sepultum*
> *tertia die a mortuis resurrexit*
> *ascendit in caelum*
> *sedet ad dexteram patris*
> *inde uenturus est iudicare uiuos et mortuos*
> *(credo?) (et?) in spiritum sanctum*
> *[remissionem peccatorum*
> *resurrectionem carnis]*
> *in uitam aeternam*
> *per sanctam ecclesiam.*

QU  Quodvultdeus of Carthage's (bishop from 437 to 453, but expelled from his see in 439) three *sermones de symbolo* (CPL 401-403) and *contra Iudaeos paganos et Arrianos* (CPL 404) [237].

possible, but cannot be proved. In his final reconstruction, Eichenseer (1960, 474) omits *Et* again. Mountain (CCSL 50A, 563) gives *(Et) uitam aeternam.*

[235] Augustine of Hippo, *de symbolo ad catechumenos* IX 17; CCSL 46, 199. See for more details below, chapter 3.5, p. 195. Eichenseer (1960, 467-468) considers the possibility that the words *Additum est* refer to some African synod or church council.

[236] Augustine of Hippo, *sermo 215* 9; Verbraken 1958, 25.

[237] All four works have been transmitted under the name of Augustine, but they have figured under Quodvultdeus's works ever since Morin 1914 and Franses 1920 tried to reconstitute the literary legacy of that author. Morin and Franses's thesis was opposed by Kappelmacher 1931, Simonetti 1950, 412-424,

Although we have four sources for the form of the Creed of Quodvultdeus, its reconstruction is even more problematic than that of AU-H. The three sermons *de symbolo* seem to treat the Creed in its entirety but in most places do not pretend to give the exact wording of the Creed as Quodvultdeus knew it. Even more evasive is the tractate *contra Iudaeos paganos et Arrianos*, where the Creed is used to yield material for the polemic with the author's adversaries. Nevertheless, with the few direct quotations and the many indirect, incomplete, or expanded ones, it is possible to reconstruct the form of the Creed that was used by Quodvultdeus with some probability.

A first difficulty is the fact that Quodvultdeus nowhere makes clear whether he is referring to the Creed in its declaratory or in its interrogatory form. At first sight we seem to possess an unambiguous quotation of the beginning of the Creed (*Sic accepistis, sic uos credere dixistis: Credo* [238]), but this may equally well refer to the catechumens' answers to the baptismal questions as to a complete declaratory form of the Creed [239]. For the rest, we find formulations of the first, second, and ninth articles in the first person singular, first person plural, and second person plural [240]. Of these, only the

and Lippold 1963 (see for a more detailed overview Müller 1956, 10-20), but most of their arguments were demolished by Braun in his 1964 edition of Quodvultdeus's *liber promissionum et praedictorum dei* (CPL 413; see SChr 101, 13-113). This was admitted by Simonetti himself, though he retained some doubts (Simonetti 1978), and the reconstitution of Quodvultdeus's work is nowadays generally accepted (see Mandouze 1982, 947-949, Dekkers 1995, 156, and Frede 1995, 725-728). Even before the identification by Morin and Franses, it was generally acknowledged that at least the four texts which interest us here were the product of one and the same author. Kattenbusch, Hahn, and Morin have all already tried their hands at a reconstruction of this unknown author's form of the Creed. Their conclusions will be mentioned in the footnotes below. Kelly (1976, 176) follows Morin in practically every detail.

[238] Quodvultdeus of Carthage, *de symbolo 3* IV 1; CCSL 60, 354.

[239] An interesting instance can also be found in another work of Quodvultdeus's: *Dic mihi ergo quod te interrogo: Credis in deum patrem omnipotentem? Credo, inquis. Interrogo: Credis et in Iesum Christum filium eius deum et dominum nostrum? Credo, inquis. Interrogo: Credis deum et hominem natum de spiritu sancto ex uirgine Maria? Credo, inquis* (Quodvultdeus of Carthage, *aduersus quinque haereses* (CPL 410) VI 7; CCSL 60, 280). Here we seem to have a set of questions that is clearly inspired by the form of the baptismal questions, but the wording of which has been adapted to the doctrinal points under discussion. This set of questions remains unmentioned in Kinzig 1999a.

[240] See below, pp. 170, 171 and 175, with footnotes 245, 251, 275, and 276.

phrase *Credo in spiritum sanctum* in the third sermon on the Creed can lay reasonable claim to being a literal quotation [241]. This means that the most we can say is that Quodvultdeus probably used a declaratory form of the Apostles' Creed in which the first and ninth articles started with *Credo*, but that we should leave the question of the exact formulation of the second article in that variant of the Creed open [242].

Despite the absence of any direct quotations of the first article in our four sources, it seems possible to say something about its wording in the form of the Creed that was used by Quodvultdeus. First of all, doctrinal changes may well be absent from the first of the three questions in Quodvultdeus's polemic work *aduersus quinque haereses* [243], since not God's being Father or Almighty is the author's main theme here, but rather the Son's equality with the Father [244]. This impression is reinforced by the introduction to the first article in the first sermon on the Creed (*Fideliter credite in deum patrem omnipotentem. Omnipotentem deum credimus ...*) and by a section in the next sermon (*nec solem credamus deum ... sed credamus in deum patrem omnipotentem ...*) [245]. What could be additions to the first article in one of these places (*... sed credamus in deum patrem omnipotentem, uniuersorum creatorem, regem caelorum* [246]) are probably not real additions at all. Not only do we not find any trace of the words *uniuersorum creatorem, regem caelorum* in quotations in one of the other two sermons *de symbolo*, but their presence here can also very well be explained as deliberately chosen by the author. In *de sym-*

[241] See below, pp. 175-176.

[242] Kattenbusch (1894, 138-139) takes a similar view. Morin (1923, 242-244) has *Credo* in the first, second, and ninth articles of his reconstruction. Hahn (1897, 60n115) opts for a threefold *Credimus*.

[243] See above, footnote 239.

[244] See especially *aduersus quinque haereses* VI 14-15, 25, and 39-40; CCSL 60, 282-287.

[245] Quodvultdeus of Carthage, *de symbolo 1* III 1 and *de symbolo 2* III 1-2; CCSL 60, 310 and 337. Compare also the words *Et quid est: Induite uos arma lucis, nisi: Credite in deum patrem omnipotentem?* and *Credite in deum patrem omnipotentem. Mutantes patrem, mutate haereditatem*, and *... posteaquam credimus in deum patrem omnipotentem, credamus et in filium eius Iesum Christum* (Quodvultdeus of Carthage, *contra Iudaeos paganos et Arrianos* I 11, V 1, and IX 3; CCSL 60, 228, 232, and 238).

[246] Quodvultdeus of Carthage, *de symbolo 2* III 2; CCSL 60, 337.

*bolo 2* III 1-2, Quodvultdeus wants to stress in what kind of God Christians ought to believe: ... *nec solem credamus deum uel regem caeli, nec mare aut nescio quem regem eius Neptunum ... nec terram et Plutonem, sed credamus* ..., and the predicates *uniuersorum creatorem, regem caelorum* serve to stress the difference between God Father Almighty and any other pseudo-god. Compare in the same sermon *Credimus ergo deum immortalem et inuisibilem* [247], and in the other two *Fides itaque catholica haec est: omnipotentem immortalem atque inuisibilem credere deum patrem, omnipotentem immortalem atque inuisibilem credere deum filium ... omnipotentem immortalem atque inuisibilem credere spiritum sanctum* ..., *Rex terrenus ideo mortalis quia uisibilis, rex caelestis immortalis et inuisibilis*, and *Confiteamur, intelligamus habere nos regem immortalem et inuisibilem* [248]. We conclude, therefore, that the first article in the form of the Creed of Quodvultdeus of Carthage was the same as in *R* [249].

When we turn to the second article, the sources are even more parsimonious. The form of the second question of the section in *aduersus quinque haereses* [250] is probably already influenced by the author's doctrinal purposes, so that we should abstain from drawing conclusions from it about Quodvultdeus's form of the Creed. In the *sermones de symbolo*, we only find two possible free quotations. In the introduction to the third article in the first sermon, we read *Credimus in filium eius Iesum Christum, natum de spiritu sancto ex uirgine Maria. Hanc natiuitatem ...* [251] and the section on the second

[247] Quodvultdeus of Carthage, *de symbolo 2* III 14; CCSL 60, 338.

[248] Quodvultdeus of Carthage, *de symbolo 1* IV 35-37 and *de symbolo 3* II 15 and 22; CCSL 60, 316 and 352.

[249] Kattenbusch (1894, 138), Hahn (1897, 60+n116), and Morin (1923, 242-243) all consider the words *uniuersorum creatorem, regem caelorum* (which Morin takes as a corruption for *saeculorum*) as well as *immortalem et inuisibilem* as real additions to the first article of Quodvultdeus's form of the Creed. This is probably because of their much more certain presence in Augustine's and Fulgentius's forms of the Creed. The fact that an addition was present in the Hipponic form of the Creed in no way necessitates its use in Carthage, however. It may well be that the Carthaginian church was more conservative in its formulation of the Creed than its daughter churches, just as the church of Rome continued to use *R* long after other churches had begun to employ more elaborate formulae. Compare for the case of Rome below, chapter 3.6, pp. 210-211, and Kelly 1976, 346-348.

[250] See above, footnote 239.

[251] Quodvultdeus of Carthage, *de symbolo 1* V 1; CCSL 60, 317.

article in the second sermon starts *Filium eius Iesum Christum olim promissum per prophetas tenemus* ...[252]. These two instances, together with *aduersus Iudaeos paganos et Arrianos* IX 3 [253], seem to indicate that Quodvultdeus knew a relatively short second article without additions like *Vnicum* or *Dominum nostrum* [254], which probably ran ... *in filium eius Iesum Christum* [255].

Most clues for the wording of Quodvultdeus's third article are again found in *contra Iudaeos paganos et Arrianos* and *de symbolo 1*. In both texts, we probably find a literal quotation: *Hoc quippe nobis etiam ordo huius sacramenti declarat, quod posteaquam credimus in deum patrem omnipotentem, credamus et in filium eius Iesum Christum, natum de spiritu sancto ex uirgine Maria. Haec natiuitas* ... and *Credimus in filium eius Iesum Christum, natum de spiritu sancto ex uirgine Maria. Hanc natiuitatem* ...[256]. Other formulations (*Diximus et ... exposuimus has tres sententias: quod natus sit de uirgine Maria, crucifixus sub Pontio Pilato et sepultus, tertia die a mortuis resurrexit, Fides autem et ueritas hoc praedicat, quod Christus sit natus ex uirgine*, and *Non uobis denegauit pignora qui natus est de uirgine Maria* [257]) should be classified as loose credal quotations or just indications of the contents of the Creed [258].

For the fourth article, there is one clear quotation: *Crucifixum sub Pontio Pilato et sepultum. Et hoc credimus* ...[259]. This place,

---

[252] Quodvultdeus of Carthage, *de symbolo 2* IV 1; CCSL 60, 338.

[253] See above, footnote 245.

[254] This conclusion is supported by the fact that Quodvultdeus nowhere comments upon these or similar terms in his *sermones de symbolo*.

[255] Hahn (1897, 60) and Morin (1923, 243) take the presence of *Et* before *In* for certain. Kattenbusch (1894, 138 and 141) believes that our author used the same form of the second article as *R*, though later on he does not exclude the possibility that *Vnicum* and *Dominum nostrum* were lacking in Quodvultdeus's form of the Creed (see Kattenbusch 1900, 587 and 594n189). For these scholars' opinions on the first word of the second article see above, footnote 242. In Westra 1996a, 70, I was too optimistic about the possibility of giving an exact reconstruction of this article from Quodvultdeus's writings.

[256] Quodvultdeus of Carthage, *contra Iudaeos paganos et Arrianos* IX 3-4 and *de symbolo 1* V 1; CCSL 60, 238 and 317.

[257] Quodvultdeus of Carthage, *de symbolo 1* VI 28 and *de symbolo 3* IV 1 and 22; CCSL 60, 323 and 354-355.

[258] Morin (1923, 243) reconstructs *Qui natus est de spiritu sancto ex uirgine Maria* but does not give any reasons for his choice. Kattenbusch (1894, 139) and Hahn (1897, 60) assume an accusative construction here.

which is supported by the free quotation in *de symbolo 1* VI 28 (see above), not only offers the wording of the fourth article of Quodvultdeus's form of the Creed but also strengthens our surmise that the third article was constructed with an accusative only [260].

For the next article, we even have two certain quotations: one partial one in the third sermon: *Tertia die. Triduana mors domini* ..., and one complete one in the second: *Tertia die a mortuis resurrexit. Quamuis multi sancti ...* [261]. Additional evidence that this was indeed the wording of the fifth article of Quodvultdeus's form of the Creed is again provided by *de symbolo 1* VI 28 (see above) [262]. There are a number of other formulations of Christ's Resurrection in our four source texts, but these all look more like personal formulations by the author himself [263].

Quodvultdeus's sermons *de symbolo* yield two clear quotations of the sixth article. In the first sermon we read: *Quia ergo diximus quousque ille altissimus descenderit propter nos, nunc dicamus quomodo id quod suscepit ex nobis in caelum leuauerit, ad dexteram patris collocauerit, ac fidei nostrae certum pignus dederit, ut secura sint membra de tanto capite, fideliterque sperent ad ipsum se posse peruenire,*

---

[259] Quodvultdeus of Carthage, *de symbolo 2* V 1; CCSL 60, 341.

[260] Morin (1923, 243) reconstructs *Crucifixus est sub Pontio Pilato et sepultus*; Hahn (1897, 60-61n117) reads *Qui crucifixus sub Pontio Pilato et sepultus* because of the free quotation in *de symbolo 1* VI 28 (see above). For the opinion of Kattenbusch, see above, footnote 258.

[261] Quodvultdeus of Carthage, *de symbolo 3* VI 1 and *de symbolo 2* VI 3; CCSL 60, 358 and 343.

[262] Kattenbusch (1894, 139n6) hesitates; Hahn (1897, 60) and Morin (1923, 243-244) agree with our reconstruction here.

[263] In *contra Iudaeos paganos et Arrianos* XVIII 7 (*Die tertio a mortuis resurgens, assumptus in caelos, sedet ad dexteram patris. Dispersit uos per uniuersas terras ...*; CCSL 60, 253), Quodvultdeus makes use of the Creed in a passage the intention of which is to rub in the victory of the Christians over the Jews. In *de symbolo 2* VI 18-VII 1 (*... quia dominus Iesus resurgens a mortuis assumptus est in caelos et sedet ad dexteram dei patris. Quis est qui sedet ad dexteram patris?* CCSL 60, 344), the author closes his treatment of Christ's Resurrection and passes over to the Session at the Right Hand of the Father; the Resurrection is therefore formulated with a subordinate clause. Something similar holds true for *de symbolo 2* VIII 1 (*Postea enim quam a mortuis resurrexit, conuersatus est ...*; CCSL 60, 345) and *de symbolo 3* VI 10 (*Die tertia Christus de sepulcro surgens super caelos est exaltatus*; CCSL 60, 359). Finally, we find another clearly personal formulation in *de symbolo 3* V 23 (*... dum de sepulcro surrexit, amore totus credidit mundus*; CCSL 60, 358).

*quem iam credunt ad dexteram patris sedere. Assumptus in caelos, ad dexteram patris sedet. Sessionem istam ...* [264]. The fact that the author expressly states that he intends to say something about the Ascension guarantees the reliability of the ensuing quotation. Next we have *Assumptus in caelum. Qui descendit, ait apostolus ...* [265]. The difficulty is, of course, that these two quotations are not exactly identical: one has *Caelos*, the other *Caelum*. However, in the case of the quotation in *de symbolo 3* many manuscripts offer the variant *Caelo* for *Caelum*. The best solution seems, therefore, to be that the original reading was *Caelos* here, which must have been corrupted into *Caelo* at an early stage of the transmission of the text, which form was again corrected to *Caelum* in most manuscripts of *de symbolo 3*. Our hypothesis is strengthened by the fact that Quodvultdeus, when introducing the sections on the Session at the Right Hand in *contra Iudaeos paganos et Arrianos* XVIII 7 and *de symbolo 2* VI 18 [266], refers to this article with the words *Assumptus (est) in caelos* as well [267].

Only the first sermon on the Creed offers a direct quotation of the next article: *Ad dexteram patris sedet* [268]. The position of *Sedet* after *Patris* is singular, but supported by the phrase *Regnat homo iam susceptus a Christo ad dexteram patris sedens* [269]. Other passages, referring to this article with *Sedet* in its more usual position [270], show that Quodvultdeus knew that formulation of the seventh article as well, but do not invalidate the evidence of the one certain quotation with *Sedet* at the end [271].

---

[264] Quodvultdeus of Carthage, *de symbolo 1* VII 1-2; CCSL 60, 323.

[265] Quodvultdeus of Carthage, *de symbolo 3* VII 1; CCSL 60, 359.

[266] See above, footnote 263. More personal formulations may be seen in *contra Iudaeos paganos et Arrianos* IX 7 (... *quia solus pro nobis super caelos ascendit ut sederet* ...; CCSL 60, 238), *de symbolo 1* VII 1-3 (... *quomodo id quod suscepit ex nobis in caelum leuauerit, ad dexteram patris collocauerit ... Ad hoc enim ascendit in caelum ut* ...; CCSL 60, 323), and *de symbolo 3* VI 10 (*Die tertia Christus de sepulcro resurgens super caelos est exaltatus*; CCSL 60, 359).

[267] Hahn (1897, 60) opts for *Caelum* instead of *Caelos*; Kattenbusch (1894, 139) and Morin (1923, 244) insert *Est* after *Assumptus*.

[268] See above, footnote 264. Although the quotation of this article is transmitted by one manuscript only, the sequel shows that it is in place here, whereas its omission can be explained by the preceding *ad dexteram patris sedere*.

[269] Quodvultdeus of Carthage, *de symbolo 3* VII 4; CCSL 60, 359.

[270] See above, footnote 263.

We do not have a clear and complete quotation of the eighth article. Only *de symbolo 3* gives *Inde uenturus. Quis est qui expectatur uenturus mortuos uiuosque iudicare* ... [272]. There is, however, one place where we seem to have an extended quotation: *Inde enim uenturus est iudicare uiuos et mortuos. Aduentum eius* ... [273]. This would yield the fairly usual *Inde uenturus est iudicare uiuos et mortuos* as the Carthaginian form of this article [274].

As we have already seen, Quodvultdeus introduces the ninth article in different ways in our four source texts. On the one hand, we read *Credimus in spiritum sanctum, quem nos deum credimus aequalem patri et filio ..., Credimus in spiritum sanctum. Spiritum sanctum deum credimus aequalem patri et filio ...*, and *Credimus in spiritum sanctum. Spiritum sanctum deum dicimus* ... [275]; on the other hand we find *Credo in spiritum sanctum. Spiritus sanctus deus est* ... [276]. At first sight, it seems impossible to determine whether one of these formulations constitutes a direct quotation, and if so, which one. However, in view of the circumstance that Quodvultdeus is using the first person plural in the paragraphs that immediately precede the chapter on the Holy Spirit in the third sermon on the Creed, it is extremely improbable that he would either have changed an original *Credimus* or an original *Et* into the first person singular *Credo*

---

[271] Hahn and Morin, who neither yet knew of the only direct quotation of this article, offer different reconstructions of this article. Hahn (1897, 60) has *Sedet ad dexteram patris*, Morin gives *Et in dextera patris sedet*. Kattenbusch is silent about this and most of the rest of the articles. Kelly (1976, 176) reconstructs *Et ad dexteram patris sedet*. Undoubtedly formulations of Quodvultdeus's own can be found in *de symbolo 1* VII 1 (see above, footnote 266) and *de symbolo 3* V 23 (... *quoniam caput nostrum iam sedet in caelo*; CCSL 60, 358).

[272] Quodvultdeus of Carthage, *de symbolo 3* VIII 1; CCSL 60, 360.

[273] Quodvultdeus of Carthage, *de symbolo 2* VIII 1; CCSL 60, 345.

[274] This is supported by the phrase ... *qui uenturus est iudicare uiuos et mortuos* (Quodvultdeus of Carthage, *contra Iudaeos paganos et Arrianos* XVIII 14; CCSL 60, 254. We should be aware, though, that Quodvultdeus may have inserted *est* quite as well as *enim* (compare the case of EUSh9; see above, chapter 3.2, p. 133). Other ways in which Quodvultdeus indicates this article are found in *de symbolo 1* IV 12, VIII 1, and VIII 6 (... *quem in symbolo etiam tu confiteris uenturum uiuos mortuosque iudicaturum* ... *Venturus est enim uiuos et mortuos iudicare* ... *eum qui sic uenturus est iudicare*; CCSL 60, 314 and 325).

[275] Quodvultdeus of Carthage, *contra Iudaeos paganos et Arrianos* XIX 1, *de symbolo 1* IX 1, and *de symbolo 2* IX 1; CCSL 60, 254, 326, and 345.

[276] Quodvultdeus of Carthage, *de symbolo 3* IX 1; CCSL 60, 360.

here. If, therefore, the formulation *Credo in spiritum sanctum* cannot be due to stylistic reasons, it has to be a direct credal quotation, which again implies that the thrice attested *Credimus in spiritum sanctum* in the other texts must be due to stylistic or rhetorical reasons as in the case of AU-H [277].

After treating the Holy Spirit, the bishop of Carthage does not immediately mention the Church, but comments upon the remaining articles first. The form of the first of these, the Forgiveness of Sins, is difficult to assess, since we find three clear quotations, all of which yield a different wording: ... *quod in isto sancto symbolo sequitur: Remissionem omnium peccatorum. Noli minorem ..., Remissionem peccatorum. Omnia prorsus delicta ...,* and *In remissionem peccatorum. Fortiter tenete ...* [278]. On the other hand, it seems improbable to assume that Quodvultdeus taught his catechumens three or more different versions of the Creed. The best solution seems to be, then, that in two of our three cases he quoted the article not exactly as he had taught it, but in a slightly extended form, and that *Remissionem peccatorum* was the form that Quodvultdeus really used. He may have added *in* once to make a smoother transition, and inserted *omnium* at another point because he deemed this an important theological point [279]. Although this solution is bound to remain hypothetical (the case is complicated by the fact that in the first sermon *Omnium* is omitted by a number of manuscripts, and that it is added by one in the third), it seems at least more probable than the possibility that Quodvultdeus's form of this article really

[277] See above, footnote 217.

[278] Quodvultdeus of Carthage, *de symbolo 1* IX 30 - X 1, *de symbolo 2* X 1, and *de symbolo 3* X 1; CCSL 60, 329, 346, and 361.

[279] This last surmise is strengthened by *contra Iudaeos paganos et Arrianos* XIX 4-6, where we read *Dicendo tale uerbum de uerbo, tale uerbum de spiritu sancto, non remittentur nec hic nec in futuro saeculo peccata tua, et tu rebaptizando pollicere te posse dimittere aliena? Nos donum spiritus sancti esse cognoscimus remissionem omnium peccatorum, suffragante nobis ipsa ueritate, quae post resurrectionem suam ait discipulis suis: Accipite spiritum sanctum; si cui remiseritis peccata, remittentur illi. Vos autem sacrilego ausu, quibus iam Christus dono spiritus sancti per baptismum et originalia et propria cuncta dimisit omnino peccata, in iam baptizatis exsufflatis Christum, respuitis spiritum sanctum, et renatum non abluere sed sordidare, non liberare sed obligare, non uiuificare sed mortificare contenditis* (CCSL 60, 254-255).

contained the word *Omnium*, but that he omitted this word in two out of three quotations.

For the next article there are once again three quotations, which this time yield two possible forms: *In carnis resurrectionem. Resurrecturam esse omnem carnem ...*, *Carnis resurrectionem. Omnis spes ...*, and *Carnis resurrectionem. Magna fides ...* [280]. In the light of what has just been said, it is logical to assume that *Carnis resurrectionem* was probably the form Quodvultdeus used. In conjunction with the Resurrection of the Flesh, Eternal Life is mentioned. Although a clear quotation of this addition cannot be found, passages like *Hoc sequitur etiam in isto sancto symbolo, quod post resurrectionem carnis credamus et in uitam aeternam* and *Hoc sequitur in sancto symbolo quod omnia quae credimus et speramus in uita aeterna percipiamus* [281] prove the presence of Eternal Life in some form or another in Quodvultdeus's credal variant. In both places it seems probable that Quodvultdeus used the wording *Vitam aeternam*, without *Et* or *In*: *Et* is not mentioned in *de symbolo 3* and we have seen that *In* is probably also absent before *Remissionem peccatorum* and *Carnis resurrectionem*. However, this argument is far from conclusive, so that we have to consider the possibility that *Et* or *In* or even both figured here [282]. Moreover, the word order *Vitam aeternam*, which is supported by the second sermon on the Creed (*Sed agnoscat etiam illic accepturam se gratiam pro gratia in uita aeterna* [283]), is contradicted by *contra Iudaeos paganos et Arrianos* (*... sine morte in aeterna uita uiuentem* [284]).

Finally, then, Quodvultdeus mentions the Holy Church as part of his form of the Creed: *Sancta ecclesia, in qua omnis huius sacramenti terminatur auctoritas ...* and *Ideo sacramenti huius conclusio per ecclesiam terminatur* [285]. There is one direct quotation: *Sanctam ecclesiam.*

---

[280] Quodvultdeus of Carthage, *de symbolo 1* XI 1, *de symbolo 2* XI 1, and *de symbolo 3* XI 1; CCSL 60, 331, 347, and 361.

[281] Quodvultdeus of Carthage, *de symbolo 1* XII 1 and *de symbolo 3* XII 1; CCSL 60, 332 and 362.

[282] Hahn (1897, 61) has only *Vitam aeternam*, Kattenbusch (1894, 139n6; 1900, 950) and Morin (1923, 243) prefix *In*.

[283] Quodvultdeus of Carthage, *de symbolo 2* XI 9; CCSL 60, 347-348.

[284] Quodvultdeus of Carthage, *contra Iudaeos paganos et Arrianos* XXI 5; CCSL 60, 256.

[285] Quodvultdeus of Carthage, *de symbolo 1* XIII 1 and *de symbolo 2* XII 7; CCSL 60, 333 and 348.

*Propterea huius conclusio sacramenti* ..., though with an important textual variant *Per sanctam ecclesiam* [286].

The wording of the Creed as it can be reconstructed from QU, then, is the following:

> *Credo in deum patrem omnipotentem*
> *(credo?) (et?) in filium eius Iesum Christum*
> *natum de spiritu sancto ex uirgine Maria*
> *crucifixum sub Pontio Pilato et sepultum*
> *tertia die a mortuis resurrexit*
> *assumptus in caelos*
> *ad dexteram patris sedet*
> *inde uenturus est (?) iudicare uiuos et mortuos*
> *credo in spiritum sanctum*
> *remissionem peccatorum*
> *carnis resurrectionem*
> *(et?) (in?) uitam aeternam*
> *(per?) sanctam ecclesiam.*

FU   Fulgentius of Ruspe's (*c.* 462-527) fragmentary *contra Fabianum* (CPL 824), which was written during the last four years of the author's life [287].

Although earlier scholars have suggested otherwise [288], the form of the Creed of Fulgentius of Ruspe cannot be reconstructed in its entirety in a reliable way. We have a complete exposition of the Creed from his hand in *fragmentum 36* of his *contra Fabianum*, but this clearly does not pretend either to treat all parts of the Creed (the words *Sub Pontio Pilato* and *Sedet ad dexteram patris* are missing [289]) or to present accurate quotations of the parts that are expounded.

---

[286] Quodvultdeus of Carthage, *de symbolo 3* XIII 1; CCSL 60, 363. Hahn (1897, 61) and Morin (1923, 243) both have *Per sanctam ecclesiam*; Kattenbusch (1894, 139) does not believe that this reconstruction is guaranteed by the text.

[287] See CCSL 91, VII.

[288] Hahn 1897, 61-62 and Kelly 1976, 175-176; but compare Kattenbusch 1894, 140-141.

[289] That the article on the Session at the Right Hand was nevertheless present in Fulgentius's form of the Creed seems to be proved by what most resembles a paraphrase of the middle part of the Creed in his *de fide ad Petrum 63*: *Firmissime tene et nullatenus dubites uerbum carnem factum eandem humanam carnem semper ueram habere qua de uirgine uerbum deus natus est, qua crucifixus et mor-*

Fortunately, however, some hard and fast quotations are yielded by *fragmentum 32* of the same work. Here we read ... *dicitur: Credo in Iesum Christum filium eius unicum dominum nostrum, qui natus est de spiritu sancto ex uirgine Maria* [290]. This not only yields the exact wording of the second and third articles of Fulgentius's form of the Creed [291], but also makes it fairly probable that the ninth article ran *Credo in spiritum sanctum* when we read in another fragment *Confitemur nos credere in spiritum sanctum* [292].

For the rest of Fulgentius's form of the Creed, *fragmentum 36* is our only source. Although, as we said above, this source does not contain any direct quotations, it is nevertheless possible to elicit some information on the credal variant that was used by Fulgentius of Ruspe from it. First, it appears that Fulgentius knew a form of the first article with the same additions that we met in the case of AU-H. The text reads: *Quapropter inaniter tibi uisum est, male intellegendo, ad tuum sensum uelle rectitudinem symboli retorquere, et inde praescribere sanctae fidei catholicae, quia in symbolo non omnia dicta sunt de filio, quae sunt dicta de patre; cum utique propterea plenitudo diuinitatis, quantum oportebat debuerit in origine commendari, quia non debuit aliter in prole cognosci. Cum enim quisque se dicit credere in deum patrem omnipotentem ... Proinde sufficiebat ut diceretur de patre solo quidquid aequaliter intellegendum esset in filio. Pater enim sic omnipotentem filium genuit sicut est ipse pater omnipotens, sic uniuersorum creatorem sicut ipse uniuersorum creator est, sic regem saecu-*

---

*tuus est, qua resurrexit et in caelum ascendit et in dextera dei sedet, qua etiam uenturus est iudicare uiuos et mortuos* (CPL 826; CCSL 91A, 751).

[290] Fulgentius of Ruspe, *contra Fabianum fragmentum 32* 3; CCSL 91A, 831.

[291] A free quotation can be found in *de fide ad Petrum* again: *Rursus si non ille qui proprius atque unigenitus dei patris filius est sed spiritus sanctus nasceretur ex uirgine, non ipsum filium qui factus est ex muliere, factus sub lege, natum de spiritu sancto ex uirgine Maria in symbolo acceptum et corde ad iustitiam crederet et ore ad salutem sancta confiteretur ecclesia* (Fulgentius of Ruspe, *de fide ad Petrum* 9; CCSL 91A, 717): see Kattenbusch 1894, 140 and 1900, 429. Compare also ... *dicentes autem natum de spiritu sancto ex uirgine Maria natiuitatem fatemur ...,* ... *propterea in symbolo ipsum unicum dei filium quem de spiritu sancto ex Maria uirgine natum fatemur ...,* and ... *symboli tenor Christum dixit dominum* (Fulgentius of Ruspe, *contra Fabianum fragmenta 32* 4, *36* 10, and *37* 1; CCSL 91A, 832, 857, and 860).

[292] Fulgentius of Ruspe, *contra Fabianum fragmentum 36* 13; CCSL 91A, 858. Nevertheless, some scholars still cling to a general African use of *Credimus* in the Creed. See above, footnote 217.

*lorum sicut ipse rex saeculorum est, sic immortalem et inuisibilem sicut ipse immortalis est et inuisibilis. Omnia igitur quae deo patri dantur in symbolo, ipso uno filii nomine naturaliter tribuuntur et filio* [293]. When we reconstruct a first article from this that runs *Credo in deum patrem omnipotentem, uniuersorum creatorem, regem saeculorum, immortalem et inuisibilem*, every single element is covered by Fulgentius's statement that it occurred in the Creed.

Secondly, it appears that the article on the Church concluded his form of the Creed: *Remissio uero peccatorum, carnis resurrectio et uita aeterna propterea in symbolo post commemorationem sanctae trinitatis adiungitur ... subiungitur autem sancta ecclesia ...* [294]. The exact wording of the third part of the Creed remains obscure, however [295], though it is tempting to reconstruct *Remissionem peccatorum, carnis resurrectionem, et uitam aeternam* because of the words *Non autem sic credimus in remissionem peccatorum, in carnis resurrectionem et in uitam aeternam, sicut credimus in spiritum sanctum* [296].

For the formulation of the rest of the Creed (articles four to eight), we do not have any reliable information. Fulgentius discusses all these articles but one in his *fragmentum 36*, but gives no hard and fast quotations of them: *Propterea in symbolo ipsum unicum dei filium quem de spiritu sancto ex Maria uirgine natum fatemur crucifixum quoque dicimus et sepultum ... ideo fatemur quia sepultus die tertia resurrexit ... deinde autem fatemur Christum ascendisse in caelum et inde uenturum iudicare uiuos et mortuos* [297]. Therefore, we will be able to use Fulgentius of Ruspe in our investigation of possible African credal peculiarities only for the first three and last four articles.

---

[293] Fulgentius of Ruspe, *contra Fabianum fragmentum 36* 2-3; CCSL 91A, 855.

[294] Fulgentius of Ruspe, *contra Fabianum fragmentum 36* 14; CCSL 91A, 859.

[295] One might be tempted to consider the passage from *fragmentum 36* 14 which is quoted above as a fairly exact quotation because of the singular *adiungitur*. Such a singular, however, after a subject that consists of several elements, is perfectly regular if the last item in the list is singular in form. See Rubenbauer 1977, 121-122.

[296] Fulgentius of Ruspe, *contra Fabianum fragmentum 36* 15; CCSL 91A, 859. It should be noted that this corresponds exactly with the indication in *fragmentum 36* 14 (see above, footnote 294).

[297] Fulgentius of Ruspe, *contra Fabianum 36* 10-12; CCSL 91A, 857-858. Similar indications can be seen in *de fide ad Petrum* 63 (see above, footnote 289).

Thus, FU witnesses to the following formulation:

*Credo in deum patrem omnipotentem, uniuersorum creatorem, regem*
   *saeculorum, immortalem et inuisibilem*
*credo in Iesum Christum, filium eius unicum dominum nostrum*
*qui natus est de spiritu sancto ex uirgine Maria*
*[crucifixum quoque dicimus et sepultum*
*die tertia resurrexit*
*fatemur Christum ascendisse in caelum*
*...*

*et inde uenturum iudicare uiuos et mortuos]*
*credo in spiritum sanctum (?)*
*[remissio peccatorum*
*carnis resurrectio*
*et uita aeterna*
*sancta ecclesia].*

## 3.5 North Italian Forms of the Creed

In addition to the witnesses for the earliest variants of the Apostles' Creed in Rome, several other variants of the Creed that stem from Italy have come down to us. With the exception of one or two later Roman testimonies which will be discussed in the next section of the present chapter, these variants all stem from Northern Italy [298]. It will be useful, then, to take a closer look at these texts as well in order to find out whether we can detect certain distinctive features of the form of the Creed in this region.

Unfortunately, not all of the texts that were adduced by earlier scholars as witnesses for the form of the Creed in Italy are equally useful for our purpose. First of all, a number of texts that do not yield any clear quotations of the Apostles' Creed should be excluded from our analysis. Under this heading we should place the creed of Auxentius of Milan [299], Eusebius of Vercelli's (d. 371) *epistula 2*

---

[298] See for earlier overviews Kattenbusch 1894, 78-134 ("Italische Symbole"), Hahn 1897, 22-54 ("Die Symbolformeln der Kirchen Italiens"), Smulders 1970, 237n10, Kelly 1976, 172-174, O'Callaghan 1992, 285-287. For a possible source for a Neapolitan form of the Creed, see below, p. 184 with footnote 306, and especially chapter 4.7.

[299] This creed, which belongs to the class of the doctrinal creeds and was submitted by Auxentius to two high officials with the express purpose of demonstrating his orthodoxy in 364 (see Meslin 1967, 43 and 291-294), is quoted by

(CPL 107) [300], and the *symbolum fidei* in the appendix to Gregory the Great's (*sedit* 590-604) *registrum epistularum* (CPL 1714) [301].

Hilary of Poitiers in his *contra Arrianos* 14: *Exposui amicis pietatis uestrae meam confessionem, primum satisfaciens quia numquam sciui Arium, non uidi oculis, non cognoui eius doctrinam, sed ex infantia quemadmodum doctus sum credidi et credo in unum solum uerum deum patrem omnipotentem, inuisibilem, impassibilem, immortalem, et in filium eius unigenitum dominum nostrum Iesum Christum, ante omnia saecula et ante omne principium natum ex patre ... qui descendit de caelis uoluntate patris propter nostram salutem, natus de spiritu sancto et Maria uirgine secundum carnem sicut scriptum est, et crucifixum sub Pontio Pilato, sepultum, tertia die resurrexisse, ascendisse in caelis, sedere ad dexteram patris, uenturum iudicare uiuos et mortuos* ... (CPL 462; PL 10, 617-618). For the impossibility of drawing conclusions from this creed for the wording of the Apostles' Creed in Milan, see already Kattenbusch 1894, 97-98. Nevertheless, Mountain (CCSL 50A, 358-362) simply treats this creed as a local variant of the Apostles' Creed. Hahn (1897, 148-149+n422) presents this creed as a baptismal creed from Cappadocia, Auxentius's native area. Vinzent (1995, 395n123) astonishingly designates the Christological part of this creed as a "weitgehendes Zitat" of *R* as it occurs in Marcellus's *epistula ad Iulium papam* (see above, chapter 1.5, footnote 41).

[300] This letter contains an oath which refers to the contents of the Creed, but does not allow any reconstruction of its wording: *Nouit hoc omnipotens deus, nouit et eius unigenitus inenarrabiliter de ipso natus filius, qui salutis nostrae causa deus sempiternae uirtutis hominem perfectum induit, pati uoluit, morte triumphata tertio die resurrexit, ad dexteram patris sedet uenturus iudicare uiuos et mortuos, nouit et spiritus sanctus, testis est ecclesia catholica quae sic confitetur, quia non ego in me reus ero, sed uos qui conseruos meos necessaria ministraturos prohibere uoluistis* (Eusebius of Vercelli, *epistula 2* V 1; CCSL 9, 106-107). Compare Kattenbusch 1894, 205n7 and 1900, 329n105. As a matter of fact, the author could just as well have had the Nicene Creed in mind as the Apostles' Creed.

[301] This formula, which is, moreover, not yet available in a critical edition, again looks most like a doctrinal creed: *Credo in unum deum omnipotentem, patrem et filium et spiritum sanctum, tres personas, unam substantiam, patrem ingenitum, filium genitum, spiritum uero sanctum nec genitum nec ingenitum sed coaeternum de patre et filio procedentem. Confiteor unigenitum filium consubstantialem ... qui manens uerbum ante saecula perfectus homo creatus est iuxta finem saeculorum, conceptus et natus ex spiritu sancto et Maria uirgine qui naturam nostram suscepit absque peccato, et sub Pontio Pilato crucifixus est et sepultus, tertia die resurrexit a mortuis, die autem quadragesimo ascendit in caelum, sedet ad dexteram patris, unde uenturus est iudicare uiuos et mortuos* ... (PL 77, 1327-1329; reproduced in Hahn 1897, 337-338). A slightly different variant of the same creed is contained in John the Deacon's *uita Gregorii* 2 (PL 75, 87-88). Hahn's claim that the Christological part reflects the wording of the Apostles' Creed as it was in Roman use in Gregory's days (see Hahn 1897, 28n15) is impossible to prove; Kattenbusch (1900, 807-808) ventures the surmise that Gregory's creed is a combination of *C* and *R*.

Next, we have to discard the sixth-century writer Venantius Fortunatus's *expositio symboli* (CPL 1035). This text is an adaptation of Rufinus's *expositio* and takes over substantial parts of the original. This circumstance makes it impossible to decide whether the credal quotations stem from Rufinus's original or flow from Venantius's pen, and if the latter is the case, whether he is quoting the credal variant of his native town in Northern Italy or that of his bishopric Poitiers [302].

Then, the Italian origin of a number of texts is by no means certain. This holds true for two works that were formerly ascribed to the early fifth-century bishop Maximus of Turin but are nowadays no longer considered genuine, viz. *homilia 83 de symbolo* (CPL 220) [303] and *tractatus de baptismo 2* (CPL 222) [304]. Similarly, Nicetas

---

[302] Venantius Fortunatus, *carmina* XI 1: *Summam totius fidei catholicae recensentes ... Credo in deum patrem omnipotentem. Praeclarum in primordio ponitur fidelis testimonii fundamentum ...* (MGH AA IV 1, 253-258). Like Rufinus, Venantius interlards his exposition with direct quotations, but unlike his model, he omits a number of phrases. The circumstance that in some five cases Venantius's quotations differ from those of (our text of) Rufinus does not automatically mean that Venantius consistently used his own form of the Creed. In the light of the treatment of different forms of the Creed by most ancient Christian writers (see above, chapter 2.3, in particular pp. 84-86 with footnote 43), it is perfectly conceivable that Venantius in one case simply took over Rufinus's formulation, but substituted it for one of his own in another. See also Kattenbusch 1894, 130-132 and 1900, 458-459+n42, 482n13, and 594n189. Hahn (1897, 45-46) takes Venantius as a witness for the Aquileian form of the Creed (rather surprisingly, Kattenbusch [1894, 92] once makes a similar statement). For the evidence of Rufinus's *expositio*, see below, pp. 196-199.

[303] Nevertheless, this sermon appears as an important witness to the form of the Creed, as it offers literal quotations of each article: *Quod beati apostoli ... mysterium symboli tradiderunt ... Credis, inquit, in deum patrem omnipotentem. Credendus sine dubio ... Et in Iesum Christum, filium eius unicum dominum nostrum. Quod Christus ...* (PL 57, 433-440). Although a critical edition and a special study of its credal variant are therefore badly needed, we have abstained from including it in our appendix as the separate edition of only one sermon from a larger collection seems hardly sensible (see below and Étaix 1987, 38). See for the question of the authorship Mutzenbecher 1961, 290-293. Quite possibly, this sermon was written by a North Italian bishop in the middle of the fifth century: see Étaix 1987, 37-39, Dekkers 1995, 78 and 80, and Frede 1995, 628 and 631. For earlier studies of the underlying credal variant, see Kattenbusch 1894, 100-101, Hahn 1897, 40-41, and Kelly 1976, 174.

[304] This work contains a set of baptismal questions: *In hoc ergo fonte antequam uos toto corpore tingueremus interrogauimus: Creditis in deum patrem omnipoten-*

of Remesiana (*libellus 5 de symbolo*; CPL 647) cannot be claimed any more as an Italian author [305].

Also, some four sources for the form of the Creed that have been connected with Italy will be discussed in the next chapter. This group comprises two pseudo-Chrysostomic sermons on the Creed of some unknown Latin author (CPL 915) [306] and the anonymous *expo-*

*tem? Respondistis: Credo. Et rursus interrogauimus: Creditis in Christum Iesum filium eius, qui natus est de spiritu sancto et Maria uirgine? Respondistis singuli: Credo. Iterum interrogauimus: Et in spiritum sanctum? Respondistis similiter: Credo ... Quod autem interrogauimus: Credis in sanctam ecclesiam et remissionem peccatorum et carnis resurrectionem? ...* (pseudo-Maximus *tractatus de baptismo* 2 [Anonymus Veronensis, *homilia 6*] 3-4; Sobrero 1992, 119-121 [Migne 57, 775-776 = 40, 1209-1210; reproduced in Kattenbusch 1894, 101n1, Hahn 1897, 41n52, and Kinzig 1999a, 172]). Unfortunately, the critical edition of Sobrero 1992 came to my notice too late to include this interesting text in the present study. Nowadays, this work is thought to belong to a small collection that may stem from sixth-century Verona: see Dekkers 1995, 84 and 138 and Frede 1995, 174, following Sobrero 1992, 31-40 and 231-241. Within this same collection, the pseudo-Augustinian *sermo 238* (CPL 368) also contains at least two more credal quotations: *Postquam enim dixerimus in symbolo: Credo in deum patrem omnipotentem, sequitur: Et in Iesum Christum filium eius unicum dominum nostrum, qui natus est de spiritu sancto et Maria uirgine ...* (pseudo-Augustine, *sermo 238* [Anonymus Veronensis, *homilia 2*] 1; Sobrero 1992, 91 [PL 39, 2185]). The pseudo-Augustinian *sermones 237* and *239 de symbolo* belong to the same series, but do not contain any unambiguous quotations from the Creed. For credal scholarship concerning both the pseudo-Maximian baptismal questions and the pseudo-Augustinian credal quotations, see Kattenbusch 1894, 190+n2, Kattenbusch 1900, 449, 485n15, 594n189, and 894, Kinzig 1999a, 95n335, and especially Sobrero 1992, 197-205.

[305] Kattenbusch (1894, 107-108) and Hahn (1897, 47-49) still refer to the author as Nicetas of Aquileia, though Kattenbusch (1894, 121-130) already has his doubts about his Italian provenance. See below, chapter 3.6, pp. 212-216 for more information on this text, its authorship, and its testimony for the form of the Creed.

[306] Both of these sermons quote and comment upon the Creed article by article: *Vniuersalis ecclesia congaudet in una regula caritatis Christi ... Ergo audite hanc ut dixi regulam uestrae confessionis. Credo in deum patrem omnipotentem. Videte qui, cui loquimini ...* and *Super fabricam totius ecclesiae nihil aliud in fundamento ponunt sapientes architecti qui sunt uerbi praedicatores nisi Iesum Christum, de quo fundamento credulitas surgit ... Quid enim dicturi estis? Audite et intellegite, quia cum audieritis et intellexeritis laetitiam uobis acquiretis, dicente propheta: Auditui meo dabis exsultationem et laetitiam. Dicite ergo quod a nobis auditis: Credo in deum patrem omnipotentem. Videte: unde coepistis? Credo, dixistis. Haec credulitas ...* (Chrysostomus Latinus C, *sermo 26* 1-2 and *sermo 28* 1-2). Kattenbusch

*sitiones symboli* CPL 229a [307] and CPL 1751 [308]. As all four of these texts will be duly investigated in the next chapter, we abstain from discussing them here [309].

Finally, Hahn mentions a Greek text of the Apostles' Creed from a fifteenth-century manuscript, which is clearly too late for our study [310].

The texts that remain to provide information on the form of the Apostles' Creed in Northern Italy are the following.

AM    Ambrose    of    Milan's    (340-397)    *explanatio    symboli*    (CPL 153) [311].

---

(1894, 207-209) and Hahn (1897, 50) consider that these sermons stem from Italy, but compare Kattenbusch 1900, 456-457n39. Morin (1894, 398-402) has ventured the guess that they were written by John of Naples (c. 533-553). Although Morin later took another view, Frede (1995, 570) assigns them to this author again; Dekkers (1995, 301) is more sceptical. See for an elaborate discussion of these two sermons chapter 4.7 below.

[307] This text, which contains quotations of the complete Creed accompanied by short explaining remarks (*Credo in deum patrem omnipotentem. Si credidisti dubitare noli ...*; *expositio symboli* 1), occurs in a liturgical manuscript that was in use in Aquileia. Kattenbusch (1894, 107) and Hahn (1897, 43-44) both discuss the *expositio* among their Italian sources for the form of the Creed. This text has been attributed to Peter Chrysologus more than once (see for example Dekkers 1995, 91 and Frede 1995, 678), but, in our opinion, erroneously: see Westra 1996b. See below, chapter 4.3, for a discussion of this text.

[308] This *expositio* occurs in two Tuscan manuscripts, and offers a complete form of the Creed: *Sed nunc iam et ipsa uerba quorum rationem audistis accipite. Iterum adnuntiat diaconus: Signate uos, audite symbolum. Et sequitur presbyter: Credo in deum patrem omnipotentem, et in Iesum Christum, filium eius unicum dominum nostrum, qui natus est ...* (*tractatus symboli* 7). Kattenbusch (1894, 133-134) and Hahn (1897, 46-47) again both assign this text to Italy; Dekkers (1995, 572) and Frede (1995, 474) are silent about its region of origin. This text will also be discussed below: see chapter 4.10.

[309] Hahn (1897, 50-52) also designates the pseudo-Augustinian *sermones 240-242* as probably Italian texts. See for a short discussion of these three sermons above, chapter 3.2, footnote 45.

[310] This text was first edited by Caspari, and was apparently intended for the Council of Ferrara and Florence in 1438-1439: see Caspari 1875, 24-25. Hahn (1897, 53-54+n88) reproduces the text and offers a short discussion; but compare Kattenbusch 1900, 975n21.

[311] The authenticity of this text seems to be certain since Faller's edition of 1955 (see CSEL 73, 6*-19*; Gamber, who wanted to ascribe it to Nicetas of Remesiana, has not found any followers [see Gamber 1967; the same opinion already in Gamber 1960, 131 and 1964, 5]); compare SChr 25bis (Botte, 1961),

Ambrose's *explanatio symboli* clearly indicates where the credal quotations begin and end. However, these quotations are usually far from complete [312]. Moreover, Ambrose is not concerned with commenting upon each individual article of the Creed.

Of the first nine articles, only the following elements are secured by real quotations: *Credo ... et in ... filium eius unicum dominum nostrum* [313], *qui natus ... spiritu sancto ex Maria uirgine, sub ... et sepultus, tertia die ... a mortuis, ascendit ... sedet ad dexteram patris, unde ... et mortuos, et in spiritum sanctum* [314]. For the final three arti-

21-25, Rodomonti 1995, 135n60, Dekkers 1995, 46, Frede 1995, 108, and Markschies 1998, 19. Only Vinzent (1995, 400-401) again doubts the Ambrosian authorship of this text, but he does not say why he does so (he fails to mention the *explanatio* in Vinzent 1999). Faller in his introduction (see above) is entirely silent about the date of the *explanatio* (which must at least have been composed within the terms of Ambrose's episcopate from 373 to 397), and Frede (1995, 108) states: "Zeit ungewiß"; nevertheless, Markschies (1995, 198n622 and 165) seems to be certain that the *explanatio* is later than 380, although in a later publication, he stamps the work as "nicht datierbar": see Markschies 1998, 19. Kattenbusch (1900, 393-395+n64) and Connolly (1952, 17) offer a number of additional examples where Ambrose is possibly quoting the Creed or referring to its contents.

[312] Whether this is to be explained by the *disciplina arcani* or by the haste of the *notarius* cannot be decided here, and is not important for our purposes either. Compare CSEL 73, 17* and SChr 25bis, 22-23.

[313] *Hinc symbolum: Credo ... unicum, dominum nostrum. Sic dicite: Filium eius unicum. Non unicus dominus? Vnus deus est, unus et dominus. Sed ne calumnientur et dicant quia unam personam dicamus filium: Et in ... unicum, dominum nostrum* (Ambrose of Milan, *explanatio symboli* 5; CSEL 73, 6-7). The last quotation seems to make it certain that Ambrose began the second article with *Et* and closed it with *Nostrum*. In the preceding paragraph, Faller seems to consider the words *patrem omnipotentem* as a quotation as well, but there are no indications for such a hypothesis. See Ambrose of Milan, *explanatio symboli* 4: *Patripassiani cum emersissent, putauerunt etiam catholici in hac parte addendum: Inuisibilem et impassibilem ... Ex illo remedio Ariani inuenerunt sibi genus calumniae, et quoniam symbolum Romanae ecclesiae nos tenemus, ideo inuisibilem et impassibilem illi patrem omnipotentem aestimarent et dicerent: Vides quia symbolum sic habet, ut uisibilem filium et passibilem designarent* (CSEL 73, 5-6).

[314] *Quia dixi de diuinitate patris et filii, uenitur ad incarnationem ipsius: Qui natus ... et sepultus. Habes et passionem ipsius et sepulturam. Tertia die ... a mortuis. Habes et resurrectionem eius. Ascendit ... sedet ad dexteram patris. Vides ergo ... Sedet ad dexteram patris ... et mortuos. Audi, homo ... Et qui amat, habet quid timeat: Vnde ... et mortuos. Ipse de nobis iudicaturus est ... Ergo uide: Credis in patrem, credis in filium. Et quid tertio? Et in spiritum sanctum. Quaecumque accipies sacramenta ...* (Ambrose of Milan, *explanatio symboli* 5; CSEL 73, 7-8). See

cles, the evidence is rather ambiguous. The most extensive quotation reads *Sane accipe rationem, quemadmodum credimus in auctorem, ne forte dicas: Sed habet et: In ecclesiam, sed habet et: In remissionem peccatorum, sed habet et: In resurrectionem. Quid ergo? Par causa est: Sic credimus in Christum, sic credimus in patrem, quemadmodum credimus et in ecclesiam et in remissionem peccatorum et in carnis resurrectionem. Quae ratio est? Quia, qui credit in auctorem credit et in opus auctoris ... Nunc fides tua amplius elucebit, si in opus auctoris tui fidem ueram et integram putaueris deferendam, in ecclesiam sanctam et in remissionem peccatorum* [315]. At first sight, this seems to lead to the inevitable conclusion that Ambrose thrice repeated the preposition *In* in the final articles of his form of the Creed. However, this quotation bears a different character from those of the first nine articles. That it is in fact a free quotation is revealed by two absolutely literal quotations a number of lines further below: *Remissionem ... resurrectionem. Crede, quia resurget et caro* and *Et in spiritum sanctum ... resurrectionem. Ecce secundum duodecim apostolos et duodecim sententiae comprehensae sunt* [316]. The first of these in particular seems to point towards a credal variant without a repeated preposition. In that case, one should explain the words of the longer quotation as meaning only that the preposition *In* in the ninth article also governed the accusative of the following articles. It seems better, therefore, to reconstruct the final articles of Ambrose's form of the Creed as ... *ecclesiam* [317] , *remissionem ... resurrectionem* [318].

---

also *explanatio symboli* 3 (*Non enim ex uirili natus est semine sed generatus a spiritu, inquit, sancto ex Maria uirgine*; CSEL 73, 5) and *explanatio symboli* 8 (*Signate uos. Credo ... uirgine. Habes diuinitatem patris, diuinitatem filii, habes incarnationem filii, quemadmodum dixi. Sub ... sepultus. Habes passionem, mortem et sepulturam. Ecce quattuor istae sententiae. Videamus alias: Tertia die ... et mortuos. Ecce aliae quattuor sententiae. Hoc est octo sententiae. Videamus adhuc alias quattuor sententias: Et in spiritum sanctum ... resurrectionem*; CSEL 73, 10-11).

[315] Ambrose of Milan, *explanatio symboli* 6; CSEL 73, 8-9.

[316] Ambrose of Milan, *explanatio symboli* 6 and 8; CSEL 73, 9 and 11.

[317] The presence of *Sanctam* before *Ecclesiam* is obvious enough, but we should be aware that nothing contradicts the presence of the addition *Catholicam* either. On the other hand, the enumeration in *explanatio symboli* 6 seems to exclude the possibility that the Communion of Saints had a place in Ambrose's form of the Creed. The free quotation in *explanatio symboli* 6 (see above, footnote 314) is not proof that *Sanctam* really followed *Ecclesiam*, as is supposed by Hahn (1897, 37).

[318] That no addition followed the Resurrection of the Flesh is proved by the quotation in *explanatio symboli* 8 (see above, footnote 314). Hahn (1897, 37),

As the author of the *explanatio* states that he keeps to the
Roman form of the Creed (... *et quoniam symbolum Romanae ecclesiae nos tenemus ... Hoc autem est symbolum quod Romana ecclesia
tenet* [319]), it is tempting to fill up the gaps with the corresponding
parts of the Old Roman Creed [320] or from the text of the commentary to reconstruct the credal variant [321]. But the avowal to keep to
the Roman text need say no more than that the author's variant
did not contain any substantial additions that were absent from
*R* [322]. Moreover, what is treated in a commentary does not always
correspond exactly with the wording of the form of the Creed that
is commented upon. Accordingly, a sound basis for a complete
reconstruction of Ambrose's form of the Creed is lacking, and we
should therefore refrain from trying to make one [323].

What we can elicit from AM for the Milanese form of the Creed
amounts to the following:

> *Credo* ...
> *et in ... filium eius unicum dominum nostrum*
> *qui natus ... spiritu sancto ex Maria uirgine*
> *sub ... et sepultus*
> *tertia die ... a mortuis*
> *ascendit ...*
> *sedet ad dexteram patris*
> *unde ... et mortuos*
> *et in spiritum sanctum*
> *... ecclesiam (...?)*

Faller (CSEL 73, 19*), and Kelly 1976, 173 omit *In* in the three final articles;
Kattenbusch (1894, 91 and 1900, 484-485) and Connolly (1952, 10) seem to agree
with them. Eichenseer (1960, 358) retains it, Mountain (CCSL 50A, 562) puts it
between brackets.

[319] Ambrose of Milan, *explanatio symboli* 4 and 7; CSEL 73, 6 and 10. This
claim is repeated by Botte in SChr 25bis, 24.

[320] On the basis of earlier editions, this is done by Hahn 1897, 36-37 and Kelly
1976, 173; compare Connolly 1952, 1-3.

[321] As do Faller (CSEL 73, 19*) and Mountain (CCSL 50A, 360-362). Kattenbusch (1894, 90-91) and Vinzent (1995, 401n148) rightly point out the hazardous
nature of this procedure.

[322] See above, chapter 2.3, pp. 84-85.

[323] Thus also Kattenbusch 1894, 90-91 and 100n17.

*remissionem [peccatorum*
*carnis] resurrectionem.*

AU-M    Augustine of Hippo's (354-430) *sermo 213 de symbolo*
(CPL 284) and *sermo de symbolo ad catechumenos* (CPL
309) [324].

For more than a century already, there has been a scholarly consensus that these two sermons do not refer to the form of the Creed
of Augustine's bishopric Hippo, but rather to the form which he
learnt as a catechumen in the Milanese church [325]. In this context,
Augustine's *sermo 212 de symbolo, sermo 214 de symbolo, de fide et
symbolo* (CPL 293), *de agone christiano* (CPL 296), *enchiridion ad
Laurentium de fide spe et caritate* (CPL 295), as well as other Augustinian texts, are often said to contain Augustine's Milanese form of
the Creed as well [326]. In most cases, however, these texts just give
the contents of the Creed or even only allude to it [327]. The same
holds true for the many other examples adduced by Eichenseer

---

[324] The first is generally dated before 410 (see Verbraken 1976, 104), the second after 418 (see Frede 1995, 255).

[325] See Kattenbusch 1894, 91-97, Hahn 1897, 38-39n41, Nerney 1953a, 275,
Eichenseer 1960, 472-473, Smulders 1970, 237n10, Kelly 1976, 172-173, and
Vokes 1978, 535. Of these, Kattenbusch and Smulders consider *sermo de symbolo
ad catechumenos* to be a spurious work, but it is accepted as genuine by Dekkers
(1995, 125) and Frede (1995, 255). It should be noted that only as late as 1917
did a critical edition of *sermo 213* become available (reprinted in Morin 1930)
with credal quotations that were not adapted to *T*; Kattenbusch's and Hahn's
reconstructions have therefore lost most of their value. Kelly (1976, 172-173),
surprisingly, does not use Morin's edition yet either. Vander Plaetse (CCSL 46,
181-182) gives a rather slavish reconstruction of the form of the Creed that is
commented upon in *sermo de symbolo ad catechumenos*; Rodomonti does the
same, though with slightly different results, and claims that this credal variant
is distinctly different from Augustine's Milanese as well as his Hipponic formulation of the Creed: see Rodomonti 1995, 135-137. In his notes to this sermon, Hill
(1993, 147n1) seems to be unaware of the *communis opinio* and claims *sermo 213*
as a source for the wording of the Creed in Hippo. See above, chapter 2.4, pp.
87-90, for a discussion of the relationship between the two Milanese forms of the
Creed that are yielded by AM and AU-M.

[326] See Kattenbusch 1894, 91-92, Hahn 1897, 38-39n41, and Eichenseer 1960,
*passim*.

[327] Compare Augustine's own statement concerning *de fide et symbolo* in his
*retractationes* I xvii (xvi) 1: *In quo de rebus ipsis ita disseritur ut tamen non fiat*

when discussing the wording of the several articles of Augustine's form of the Creed [328]. The five pages of instances in the *index scriptorum* to Mountain's edition of Augustine's *de trinitate* (CPL 329) which are claimed to refer to either Augustine's Milanese or his African form of the Creed say, with the exception of some four or five instances, nothing whatsoever about either the form or the contents of Augustine's credal variants [329]. In *sermo 213 de symbolo* and *sermo de symbolo ad catechumenos*, however, Augustine clearly intends to comment upon each article of the Creed and interlards his commentary with quotations that are usually literal. We shall therefore limit ourselves to these two texts for our reconstruction of Augustine's Milanese form of the Creed, though hard and fast quotations of this variant which occur in other Augustinian works will be noted in due course as well.

When trying to reconstruct Augustine's Milanese form of the Creed one should be cautious because, just as in the case of AU-H, credal quotations are as a rule not marked as such in the two source texts. Fortunately, however, the quotations in *sermo 213* and *sermo de symbolo ad catechumenos* support each other for most articles. Where they seem to part company, the reading of *sermo 213* will have to be preferred as Vander Plaetse designates his edition of *sermo de symbolo ad catechumenos* as not yet completely critical [330].

No real difficulties are met with in reconstructing the first two articles of the Milanese credal variant of Augustine. In *sermo 213* we find some clear quotations: *Credo in deum patrem. Vide quam cito dicitur ... Posthoc quid? Et in Iesum Christum. Credo, dicis, in deum patrem omnipotentem, et in Iesum Christum filium eius unicum dominum nostrum. Si filium unicum ...* [331]. These quotations are supported by *sermo de symbolo ad catechumenos*: *... ut dicatis: Credo in deum patrem omnipotentem ... Ideo credimus et in filium eius, id est dei patris omnipotentis, unicum dominum nostrum. Quando audis ... et*

---

*uerborum illa contextio quae tenenda memoriter competentibus traditur* (CPL 250; CCSL 57, 552).

[328] Eichenseer 1960, *passim*.

[329] CCSL 50A, 761-765. See for a concrete example above, chapter 3.1, pp. 105-106.

[330] See CCSL 46, 183.

[331] Augustine of Hippo, *sermo 213* 2-3; Morin 1930, 443-444.

*sic credere debetis, quia credimus in deum patrem omnipotentem, et in Iesum Christum filium eius unicum. Iam quando ...* [332].

One instance where the two texts offer different readings is the third article of the Creed. There seem to be three possibilities. First, in *sermo 213* we read: *Propter nos quid? Ad nos quid? Qui natus est de spiritu sancto et uirgine Maria ... et tamen confiteris Iesum Christum filium eius unicum dominum nostrum, qui natus est de spiritu sancto et uirgine Maria. Ecce ...* [333]. Next we have two quotations in our second source text: *Sed ... uideamus quid fecit propter nos, quid passus est propter nos. Natus de spiritu sancto et uirgine Maria* and *Ergo inclinatio ipsius haec est: Natus de spiritu sancto et uirgine Maria* [334]. In the third place, it can be observed that in the first of these two quotations all, and in the second some, of the manuscripts that were consulted by Vander Plaetse insert *Est* after *Natus*. All in all, it seems best to take the formulation with *Natus est* as the genuine reading in *sermo de symbolo ad catechumenos* and to interpret this as a slightly abbreviated quotation for the one with *Qui natus est*, the form that is found in *sermo 213* [335]. The deviant reading in this sermon may be an instance of another abbreviated quotation, or *dictum* may be corrupt for *dictus*, which would mean it is not a quotation at all.

For the next article the two sources are not quite unanimous either. Our main source gives *Sequitur: Sub Pontio Pilato crucifixus*

---

[332] Augustine of Hippo, *sermo de symbolo ad catechumenos* I 2 - II 3; CCSL 46, 185-187. Vander Plaetse (CCSL 46, 181) surprisingly reconstructs the first article with *Credimus*, probably on the basis of the last phrase. Compare for the second article also the (probably) Augustinian *sermo 375C* (= *sermo Mai 95*) 7: *Sed mementote cum dixerimus: Et Iesum Christum filium eius unicum dominum nostrum* (CPL 285; Morin 1930, 346).

[333] Augustine of Hippo, *sermo 213* 3-4; Morin 1930, 444-445. This formulation seems to be supported by Augustine's *sermo 375C* (= *sermo Mai 95*) 7: *Mementote quod sequitur: Qui natus est de spiritu sancto et Maria uirgine* (Morin 1930, 346), where Morin is prepared to assume a scribal error to account for the word order *Maria uirgine*.

[334] Augustine of Hippo, *sermo de symbolo ad catechumenos* III 6; CCSL 46, 189. This form without *Est* is supported by *sermo 213* 4: *Cum enim dictum esset in symbolo: Natus de spiritu sancto et uirgine Maria, iam quid ...* (Morin 1930, 444).

[335] Kattenbusch seems to reach the same conclusion when he states that the credal variant of the *sermo de symbolo ad catechumenos* "hat ganz ohne Zweifel gelautet" *(qui) natus (est) de spiritu sancto et uirgine Maria* (Kattenbusch 1900, 455n38).

*et sepultus ... Sub Pontio Pilato crucifixus. Quis? Iesus Christus, uni-
cus dei filius, dominus noster. Et sepultus. Quis?* [336]. In the other text,
however, *Passus* seems to be prefixed to the article: *Quid deinde?
Passus sub Pontio Pilato. Praesidatum agebat et iudex erat ipse Pontius Pilatus quando passus est Christus. Iudicis nominis signata sunt
tempora quando passus est: Sub Pontio Pilato. Quando passus est,
crucifixus et sepultus. Quis, quid, pro quibus? Quis? Filius dei unicus
dominus noster. Quid? Crucifixus et sepultus. Pro quibus?* [337], but this
is only apparent. First of all, it should be noted that after *Quid
deinde?* it is not a complete quotation of the fourth article that follows, as one would perhaps expect, but only the words *Passus sub
Pontio Pilato*, in which the form *Passus* seems to be short for *Crucifixus et sepultus*. Augustine first indicates the whole fourth article,
and then continues to explain the several elements of it. That *Passus* was not really part of the credal variant that is expounded here
is also revealed by the fact that after the question *Quid?* we only
have *Crucifixus et sepultus*. When we combine this interpretation
with the testimony of *sermo 213*, it becomes practically certain that
Augustine's Milanese form of the Creed simply read *Sub Pontio
Pilato crucifixus et sepultus* [338].

The fifth article is quoted in *sermo 213* only [339], where we read
*Tertia enim die resurrexit a mortuis. Hoc sequitur in symbolo ...* [340].

[336] Augustine of Hippo, *sermo 213* 4; Morin 1930, 444-445.

[337] Augustine of Hippo, *sermo de symbolo ad catechumenos* III 7; CCSL 46, 189-
190.

[338] Vander Plaetse accepts *Passus* as part of the underlying credal variant of
*sermo de symbolo ad catechumenos*, though he is aware of the difference with *sermo 213* in this respect: see CCSL 46, 181-182. Rodomonti reconstructs: *Passus
sub Pontio Pilato*. She does not comment upon the omission of *Crucifixus et sepultus*, but is prepared to assume the influence of *C* to explain the addition of
*Passus*. Kelly (1976, 173) also assumes the presence of *Passus* in Augustine's Milanese form of the Creed, whereas Eichenseer's (1960, 279-283 and 473) opinion
remains unclear.

[339] Curiously enough, both Vander Plaetse and Rodomonti also omit this article from their reconstructions (see CCSL 46, 181 and Rodomonti 1995, 135),
though the text of *sermo de symbolo ad catechumenos* clearly presupposes it. See
for example *sermo de symbolo ad catechumenos* III 9 (*Ibi opus, quia crucifixus exemplum operis, crux, praemium operis resurrectio*; CCSL 46, 192) and III 10 (*Sic
enim legimus: Christus surgens ex mortuis iam non moritur*; CCSL 46, 195).
Neither Vander Plaetse nor Rodomonti comment upon this omission.

[340] Augustine of Hippo, *sermo 213* 5; Morin 1930, 445.

Although this can hardly be a pure quotation, the phrase *Hoc sequitur in symbolo* seems to suggest that the wording of the underlying form of the Creed was not too different either. Therefore, it seems best to consider it as a slightly extended quotation and to assume that the fifth article in Augustine's Milanese form of the Creed simply read *Tertia die resurrexit a mortuis* [341].

The following two articles are yielded without any problems as *Ascendit in caelum, sedet ad dexteram patris* [342], but for the eighth article the two witnesses again contradict each other. *Sermo 213* has *Inde uenturus iudicaturus uiuos et mortuos* and *sermo de symbolo ad catechumenos* reads *Inde uenturus est iudicare uiuos et mortuos* [343]. There are two reasons, however, for adopting the reading of *sermo 213* here. First of all, this text has been edited critically and *de symbolo ad catechumenos* not yet (or at least not yet completely), and, secondly, a change in the manuscript tradition from *Iudicaturus* to *Iudicare* is easier to imagine than the opposite, as *Iudicare* is the form which eventually found a place in *T* [344].

When we turn to the ninth article, both witnesses yield the formulation *Et in spiritum sanctum* [345]. As far as the last three articles of the form of the Creed to which Augustine testifies in these texts

[341] This solution is also chosen by Morin 1930, 445.

[342] *Sed quid sequitur? Ascendit in caelum. Et modo ubi est? Sedet ad dexteram patris. Intellege dexteram* ... (Augustine of Hippo, *sermo 213* 5; Morin 1930, 445) and *Ascendit in caelum. Credite. Sedet ad dexteram patris. Credite* (Augustine of Hippo, *sermo de symbolo ad catechumenos* IV 11; CCSL 46, 195). Compare also *sermo 375C* (= *sermo Mai 95*) 5: ... *qui confessi sunt: Ascendit in caelum, sedet ad dexteram patris* (Morin 1930, 344).

[343] *Quid? Inde uenturus iudicaturus uiuos et mortuos. Confiteamur saluatorem* ... (Augustine of Hippo, *sermo 213 de symbolo* 6; Morin 1930, 446) and *Inde uenturus iudicare uiuos et mortuos. Viuos, qui superfuerint* ... (Augustine of Hippo, *sermo de symbolo ad catechumenos* IV 12; CCSL 46, 195).

[344] The quotation of the eighth article in *sermo 110* 1 (*Veniens quando? Inde uenturus est iudicare uiuos et mortuos*; Morin 1930, 641) is then best explained as referring to Augustine's Hipponic variant. The same holds true for the indirect quotation in *sermo 79A* (= *sermo Lambot 15*; CPL 284), where we read: *Qui sicut credimus et confitemur uenturus est iudicare uiuos et mortuos*; Lambot 1939, 28). Vander Plaetse (CCSL 46, 181) and Rodomonti (1995, 135) of course both reconstruct *Inde uenturus iudicare uiuos et mortuos*.

[345] *Sequitur: Et in spiritum sanctum. Trinitas* ... (Augustine of Hippo, *sermo 213* 7; Morin 1930, 446) and *Sequitur in symbolo: Et in spiritum sanctum. Ista trinitas* ... (Augustine of Hippo, *de symbolo ad catechumenos de symbolo* V 13; CCSL 46, 196).

are concerned, the question is whether they did or did not begin
with the preposition *in*. The first possibility is supported by *sermo
213*, which gives *in* at the beginning of the tenth and eleventh articles: *Iam quod sequitur ad nos pertinet: In sanctam ecclesiam. Sancta
ecclesia nos sumus ... In remissionem peccatorum. Haec in ecclesia
...* [346]. *Sermo de symbolo ad catechumenos* pleads against the presence
of *In* with *Sequitur post trinitatis commendationem: Sanctam ecclesiam. Demonstratus est ... Remissionem peccatorum. Habetis symbolum
... Credimus etiam resurrectionem carnis ...* [347], though the last passage is an indirect quotation at best. Moreover, certain places in
*sermo 213* also plead against the presence of *in*: *... ut cum dixerimus: Sanctam ecclesiam, adiungamus: Remissionem peccatorum. Post
haec: Carnis resurrectionem. Iste iam finis est ...* [348], where at least
the words *Carnis resurrectionem* constitute an unambiguous quotation. Thus, if Augustine testifies to a Milanese form of the Creed in
which the twelfth article was constructed without *in*, it is difficult
to assume the presence of this preposition in the preceding two articles. This fact in combination with the information from *sermo de
symbolo ad catechumenos* seems to tip the scales in favour of the
absence of *in* in his Milanese credal variant. Its presence in two
places in *sermo 213* is probably best explained by the assumption
that Augustine, just like his teacher Ambrose, used the device of
putting *in* in front of the final articles of the Creed to introduce
these in his exposition [349].

As far as the exact wording of the twelfth article is concerned,
finally, there still are two problems. First of all, *sermo 213* and
*sermo de symbolo ad catechumenos* do not agree whether Augustine
testifies to a Milanese form of the Creed with *Carnis resurrectionem*
or with *Resurrectionem carnis* [350]. In this question, it seems better to
follow the explicit quotation and to reconstruct *Carnis resurrectio-*

---

[346] Augustine of Hippo, *sermo 213* 8-9; Morin 1930, 447-448.

[347] Augustine of Hippo, *sermo de symbolo ad catechumenos* VI 14 - IX 17;
CCSL 46, 197-199. Vander Plaetse (CCSL 46, 181-182) does not say anything
about the fact that this testimony is not identical with that of *sermo 213*.

[348] Augustine of Hippo, *sermo 213*, 9-10; Morin 1930, 449.

[349] Hill (1993, 148n10) seems to assume the presence of a threefold *In* in the
final articles of the underlying form of the Creed in AU-M.

[350] See the quotations above of *sermo de symbolo ad catechumenos* IX 17 and
*sermo 213* 10. Vander Plaetse (CCSL 46, 181-182) does not note this difference.

*nem* [351]. Then there is the question of whether Eternal Life did or did not figure in Augustine's Milanese credal variant. It is not mentioned by *sermo 213* as part of the Creed, though this text seems to quote all articles completely, but *sermo de symbolo ad catechumenos* reads: *Ne forte putet aliquis quomodo Lazari. Vt scias non sic esse additum est: In uitam aeternam. Regeneret uos* ... [352]. The phrase *Additum est* seems to indicate that Augustine was aware that *In uitam aeternam* had not always been part of the Creed. It could also mean that Augustine had added it himself to the Milanese variant that he continued to use in Africa at some date between the occasions for which he composed our two source texts [353]. If such a thing was the case, it would be probably under influence of the Hipponic form of the Creed which, like all African forms of the Creed that we know of, mentioned Eternal Life in some form or another. The most probable solution, however, seems to be that Augustine in *de symbolo ad catechumenos* IX 17 is simply referring to the Hipponic form of the Creed as he knew and used it [354].

All in all, the Milanese form of the Creed as it was known to Augustine can be reconstituted as follows:

*Credo in deum patrem omnipotentem*
*et in Iesum Christum, filium eius unicum dominum nostrum*
*qui natus est de spiritu sancto et uirgine Maria*
*sub Pontio Pilato crucifixus et sepultus*
*tertia die resurrexit a mortuis*
*ascendit in caelum*
*sedet ad dexteram patris*
*inde uenturus iudicaturus uiuos et mortuos*

---

[351] Vander Plaetse (CCSL 46, 181) and Rodomonti (1995, 135) both offer the reconstruction *Resurrectionem carnis*. As in the case of the eighth article (see above, footnote 344), they are silent about the difference with the testimony of *sermo 213*.

[352] Augustine of Hippo, *sermo de symbolo ad catechumenos* IX 17; CCSL 46, 199.

[353] The interval seems to have been at least eight years: see footnote 324 above. Rodomonti (1995, 136-139) explains *In uitam aeternam* as a deliberate insertion on Augustine's part against Pelagianism to emphasize that no other eternal life is possible than that which is imparted by means of baptism in the Church.

[354] See also above, chapter 3.4, footnote 235.

*et in spiritum sanctum*
*sanctam ecclesiam*
*remissionem peccatorum*
*carnis resurrectionem.*

RUF   Rufinus of Aquileia's (*c.* 345-410) *expositio symboli* (CPL
196; *c.* 404) [355].

Rufinus's *expositio symboli*, an extensive commentary on the
Creed in which its clauses are cited one by one, seems to yield a
complete credal variant without many problems, about which the
author himself expressly states that it is the local variant of the
Aquileian church [356].

The first article of this Aquileian form of the creed ran *Credo in*
*deum patrem omnipotentem, inuisibilem et impassibilem.* The unique
addition is guaranteed by secure quotations [357]. Next, the second
article reads *Et in Iesum Christum, unicum filium eius, dominum*
*nostrum,* as is borne out by three quotations [358]. In the first two of

---

[355] For the date, see CCSL 20, VIII-IX. Vinzent has recently started to doubt
Rufinus's authorship of the text (see Vinzent 1999, 186 and Kinzig 1999b,
554n70, as opposed to Vinzent 1995, 390 and 402), but does not mention any
arguments for this new position.

[356] See above, chapter 2.3, footnote 26. The last reconstruction of this variant
was made by Kelly (1976, 174). Strangely, although Kelly (1976, 173n1) says
that he bases his reconstruction on Simonetti's critical edition for *Corpus Chris-*
*tianorum,* he appears simply to be using his own earlier reconstruction (Kelly
1955, 15) again. Another reconstruction is found in Hahn 1897, 42-43. Kattenbusch (1894, 106-107) is remarkably reserved and only discusses the substantial
differences between Rufinus's form of the Creed and *R.*

[357] ... *cum dicitur: Credo in deum patrem omnipotentem. Verum priusquam* ...
*Credo, inquit, in deum patrem omnipotentem. Orientales ecclesiae* ... *His additur:*
*Inuisibilem et impassibilem. Sciendum quod duo isti sermones in Romanae ecclesiae*
*symbolo non habentur* and ... *eo modo quo in principio dicitur: Credo in deum pa-*
*trem omnipotentem, et post haec* ... (Rufinus of Aquileia, *expositio symboli* 3-5 and
33; CCSL 20, 135-140 and 169).

[358] *Et rursus in sequenti sermone, ubi nos dicimus: Et in Iesum Christum, uni-*
*cum filium eius, dominum nostrum, ita illi tradunt* ...; *Sequitur post hoc: Et in*
*Iesum Christum, unicum filium eius, dominum nostrum. Iesus Hebraei uocabuli*
...; ... *eo modo quo in principio dicitur: Credo in deum patrem omnipotentem, et*
*post haec: In Iesum Christum, unicum filium eius, dominum nostrum* ... (Rufinus
of Aquileia, *expositio symboli* 4, 6, and 33; CCSL 20, 137, 141, and 169). The last
of these quotations is slightly shortened, as is the one in *expositio symboli* 34:
*Nunc autem in illis quidem uocabulis ubi de diuinitate fides ordinatur, In deum*

these, there is an important *uaria lectio* with the word order *Christum Iesum*, but in the third, the tradition is practically unanimous. Moreover, in the exposition of the second article the name *Iesus* is explained before *Christus*. This seems to make it certain that the actual wording of Rufinus's form of the Creed had *Iesum Christum* rather than *Christum Iesum*, which is read in the first two quotations according to Migne's edition and thus far has been universally assumed to be genuinely Aquileian [359].

The third and fourth articles are again yielded in an unproblematic way as *Qui natus est de spiritu sancto ex Maria uirgine, crucifixus sub Pontio Pilato et sepultus* [360]. Although it is certain that the Descent to Hell was added to the fourth article of Rufinus's form of the Creed, its exact formulation has been subject to some scholarly dissension. Earlier editors all read *Descendit ad inferna*, but Simonetti has shown that the manuscript tradition yields *Descendit in inferna* as the more probable formulation of this addition as Rufinus knew it [361].

As far as the fifth article is concerned, this seems just to have run *Tertia die resurrexit* and to have lacked *A mortuis*. The only quotation of this article reads *Sequitur post hoc: Tertia die resurrexit. Resurrectionis gloria* ... [362]. Next, the sixth article is given as *Ascendit ad caelos* in the Migne edition and the various reconstructions

*patrem dicitur, et: In Iesum Christum filium eius, et: In spiritum sanctum. In ceteris uero* ... (CCSL 20, 170).

[359] See above, footnote 356. Only Hahn (1897, 42n62) is aware of the fact that this is not wholly unproblematic. Kattenbusch (1894, 106) is reluctant to accept that *Vnicum* really stood before *Filium*, though this is supported by the threefold quotation.

[360] *Qui natus est de spiritu sancto ex Maria uirgine. Haec iam inter homines dispensationis natiuitas est* ... and *Crucifixus sub Pontio Pilato et sepultus descendit in inferna. Docet apostolus Paulus* ... (Rufinus of Aquileia, *expositio symboli* 8 and 12; CCSL 20, 144 and 149).

[361] Simonetti 1958, 36. Kattenbusch (1894, 106) and Hahn (1897, 42) also already read *Descendit in inferna*. The relevant quotations are found in *expositio symboli* 12 (see previous footnote) and 16: *Sciendum sane est quod in ecclesiae Romanae symbolo non habet additum: Descendit in inferna, sed neque* ... (CCSL 20, 152).

[362] Rufinus of Aquileia, *expositio symboli* 27; CCSL 20, 161. Only one late manuscript adds *A mortuis* here, but it has nevertheless found its way into the Migne edition and the reconstructions by Hahn and Kelly (see above, footnote 356).

that depend from it, but Simonetti reads *Ascendit in caelos*[363]. The seventh article is given in both as *Sedet ad dexteram patris*, but the eighth is found in Simonetti's edition as *Inde uenturus iudicare uiuos et mortuos*, whereas earlier scholars inserted *Est* after *Inde*[364].

The rest of the Aquileian form of the Creed does not yield any problems and can safely be reconstructed as *Et in spiritum sanctum, sanctam ecclesiam, remissionem peccatorum, huius carnis resurrectionem*[365].

The underlying credal variant of RUF, therefore, runs thus:

*Credo in deum patrem omnipotentem, inuisibilem et impassibilem*
*et in Iesum Christum, unicum filium eius, dominum nostrum*
*qui natus est de spiritu sancto ex Maria uirgine*
*crucifixus sub Pontio Pilato et sepultus*
*descendit in inferna*
*tertia die resurrexit*
*ascendit in caelos*
*sedet ad dexteram patris*
*inde uenturus iudicare uiuos et mortuos*
*et in spiritum sanctum*
*sanctam ecclesiam*

---

[363] *Ascendit in caelos, sedet ad dexteram patris, inde uenturus iudicare uiuos et mortuos* (Rufinus of Aquileia, *expositio symboli* 29; CCSL 20, 164).

[364] See previous footnote.

[365] *Post hoc ponitur in symbolo: Et in spiritum sanctum. Ea quae ... ita iungetur: Et in spiritum sanctum. Illa uero omnia ... Sequitur namque post hunc sermonem: Sanctam ecclesiam, remissionem peccatorum, huius carnis resurrectionem. Non dixit: In sanctam ecclesiam, nec: In remissionem peccatorum, nec: In carnis resurrectionem. Si enim addidisset 'in' praepositionem, una cum superioribus eademque uis fuerat. Nunc autem in illis quidem uocabulis ubi de diuinitate fides ordinatur, In deum patrem dicitur, et: In Iesum Christum, filium eius, et: In spiritum sanctum. In ceteris uero ...* (Rufinus of Aquileia, *expositio symboli* 33-34; CCSL 20, 169-170). Compare also *expositio symboli* 41 and 43: *Et ideo satis cauta et prouida adiectione ecclesia nostra symboli docet, quae in eo quod a ceteris traditur: Carnis resurrectionem, uno addito pronomine tradit: Huius carnis resurrectionem. Huius sine dubio ...* and *Haec quidem dicta sint ad comprobationem professionis nostrae, qua confitemur in symbolo: Huius carnis resurrectionem. Quod enim adiunctum est 'huius', uide quam ...* (CCSL 20, 177 and 179). Rufinus also mentions this addition of *Huius* in his slightly earlier *apologia contra Hieronymum* I 5 (CPL 197; see above, chapter 2.5, p. 92). An interesting formulation of the contents of the Creed can be seen in *expositio symboli* 37 (CCSL 20, 173-174).

*remissionem peccatorum*
*huius carnis resurrectionem.*

PC   Peter Chrysologus of Ravenna's (d. *c.* 450) *sermones 57-62 de symbolo* (CPL 227).

Next, we have Peter Chrysologus's *sermones de symbolo*. Here, as in the case of Rufinus's *expositio*, the very unreliable Migne text has only recently been replaced by a critical edition in the *Corpus Christianorum* series [366]. Each of our source sermons discusses the Creed in a clear and systematic way, in which the Creed is quoted and explained article by article. This circumstance makes the task of reconstructing a Chrysologan form of the Creed at least in principle an easy one, but there are nevertheless some difficulties where the testimony of all six sermons is not unanimous. Olivar, the new editor of the sermons, offers a reconstruction of Chrysologus's credal variant which is reasonably accurate, though his explanatory remarks are thoroughly unreliable [367]. For that reason and because of the fact that we do not agree in every detail with Olivar's conclusions, it will be advisable to provide a fresh reconstruction here of the form of the Creed as it is yielded by Peter Chrysologus's *sermones de symbolo*.

The first article is given by all six sermons as *Credo in deum patrem omnipotentem* [368]. For the second article, we usually find *Et in Christum Iesum, filium eius unicum dominum nostrum* [369], but

---

[366] Reconstructions of Peter Chrysologus's form of the Creed on the basis of the Migne edition can be found in Kattenbusch 1894, 101-102, Hahn 1897, 41-42, and Kelly 1976, 173-174. Although Olivar's edition is vastly superior to Migne's, it seems in places to betray signs of a certain carelessness.

[367] CCSL 24, 312-313.

[368] *Credo in deum patrem omnipotentem. In deum ... Credo in deum patrem. Iam confiteatur ..., Credo in deum patrem omnipotentem. Qui confessus est ..., Credo in deum patrem omnipotentem. Credimus ..., Credo in deum patrem omnipotentem. Haec uox ... Mox addidit: Patrem. Qui credit ..., Credo in deum patrem omnipotentem. Qui credit ... quia dixisti: Credo in deum patrem omnipotentem. Omnipotens ...,* and *Credo in deum. Quae diu ... Credo in deum patrem. Inest deo ... Credo, dixisti ... Credo, dixisti, in deum patrem omnipotentem. Si est ... Credo in deum patrem omnipotentem, et in Christum Iesum ...* (Peter Chrysologus, *sermones 57* 3-4, *58* 3, *59* 3, *60* 3-4, *61* 3, and *62* 5-6 and 8; CCSL 24, 319-320, 326, 331, 336, 342, and 348-349).

[369] *Et in Christum Iesum, filium eius unicum dominum nostrum. Sicut reges ... Et in Christum Iesum, filium eius unicum. Quia et si sunt multi filii per gratiam, iste unus et singularis est per naturam. Vnicum dominum nostrum. Qui nos de tan-*

Chrysologus's *sermo de symbolo 60* once reads *Et in Iesum Christum, filium eius unicum dominum nostrum*. This, however, is either an instance of a free quotation or a scribal error [370], since the same sermon exhibits the word order *Christum Iesum* in two other quotations of this article and, moreover, the author discusses the meaning of the name *Christus* before that of *Iesus* [371].

Next, the third and fourth articles are again given in a uniform way as *Qui natus est de spiritu sancto et Maria uirgine* and *Qui sub Pontio Pilato crucifixus est et sepultus* [372]. The reconstruction of the

---

*torum ..., In Christum Iesum, unicum dominum nostrum. Christum unctum ..., Et in Christum Iesum, filium eius unicum dominum nostrum. Ab unctione Christus ... Et in Christum Iesum, filium eius unicum dominum nostrum. Ipse est ..., Et in Christum Iesum, filium eius. Christus a superno uocatur unguento ... Et in Christum Iesum, filium eius unicum dominum nostrum. Vt patris ...,* and *Et in Christum Iesum, filium eius unicum dominum nostrum. Attende qua reuerentia ... Credo in deum patrem omnipotentem, et in Christum Iesum filium eius unicum dominum nostrum, qui natus est de spiritu sancto et Maria uirgine. Age homo ...* (Peter Chrysologus, *sermo 57* 5, *58* 4, *59* 5-6, *61* 4, and *62* 7-8; CCSL 24, 320-321, 327, 331-332, 342-343, and 348-349. The quotation in *sermo 58* has clearly been abbreviated.

[370] This possibility gains in probability when one considers the fact that in practically all the instances enumerated in the previous footnote, one or more manuscripts show the word order *Iesum Christum*.

[371] *Et in Iesum Christum, filium eius unicum dominum nostrum. Posteaquam dei filius sicut pluuia in uellus toto diuinitatis unguento nostram se fudit in carnem, ab unguento nuncupatus est Christus, et huius nominis extitit solus auctor qui sic deo superfusus est et infusus, ut homo deusque esset unus deus. Hoc ergo unguento nomen effudit in nos, qui a Christo dicimur Christiani, et impletum est illud quod cantatur in Canticis Canticorum: Vnguentum effusum est nomen tuum. Et in Christum Iesum, filium eius. Illud sacramenti nomen est, hoc triumphi, nam sicut deo unctus nomen sortitur ex unguine, ita cum salutem mundo perditam reddidit a saluando nomen saluatoris assumit. Saepe iam diximus, quod Iesus Hebraica lingua dicitur, saluator dicitur hoc Latina. Et in Christum Iesum, filium eius. Cuius? Vtique dei patris. Cum dicis ergo: In Iesum filium eius ...* (Peter Chrysologus, *sermo 60* 5-6; CCSL 24, 337-338).

[372] *Qui natus est de spiritu sancto. Item et aliter ... Qui natus est de spiritu sancto et Maria uirgine. Vbi spiritus generat ... Qui sub Pontio Pilato crucifixus est et sepultus. Audis iudicis nomen ..., Qui natus est de spiritu sancto. Tali natiuitate ... Qui natus est de spiritu sancto et Maria uirgine. Virginitas deum credidit ... Qui sub Pontio Pilato crucifixus est et sepultus. Iudicem indicat ... Crucifixus. In cruce, in editis, coram omnibus ... mortem suscepit. Sepulturam patitur ne mortem non adisse ut uinceret, sed simulasse ut eluderet ab impiis iactaretur. Crucifixus est et sepultus, Qui natus est de spiritu sancto et Maria uirgine. Quid terrenum ... Qui sub Pontio Pilato crucifixus est et sepultus. Nomen persecutoris dicimus ..., Qui*

fifth article is somewhat more difficult. It is offered as *Tertia die surrexit a mortuis* [373], *Tertia die resurrexit* [374], *Tertia die surrexit* [375], and *Tertio die resurrexit* [376]. Apart from the masculine ordinal *Tertio*, all of these different quotations are transmitted in an almost unanimous way, so that it appears that Chrysologus quotes this article in three or four different ways. On the other hand, it is not very probable that Peter Chrysologus also used three or four different forms of the Creed during the *traditio symboli*. It is difficult to arrive at a satisfactory solution here. If we take the textual tradition to be reliable in this respect, the best way to account for the different forms will, therefore, be to assume that Peter Chrysologus gave an abbreviated quotation of this article in practically all these sermons, which in its full form probably ran *Tertia die resurrexit a mortuis* [377]. The fact that Chrysologus sometimes gives partial quotations of the first three articles as well can be used as an argument in support of this possibility [378]. On the other hand, one can well imagine that a possible Chrysologan fifth article in the form *Tertia die surrexit* would soon have given rise to scribal errors or supposed corrections that added *A mortuis* or replaced *Surrexit* with the more usual *Resurrexit*. In this light one can point to the circumstance that the free formulation in *sermo 60*, which precisely for

---

*natus est de spiritu sancto et Maria uirgine. Si iuxta euangelistam ... Qui sub Pontio Pilato crucifixus est et sepultus. Nomen iudicis audis ..., Qui natus est de spiritu sancto et Maria uirgine. Spiritus et uirgo ... Qui sub Pontio Pilato crucifixus est et sepultus. Iudicis nomen audis ...,* and *... qui natus est de spiritu sancto et Maria uirgine. Age homo ... Qui sub Pontio Pilato crucifixus est et sepultus. Quare, homo ...* (Peter Chrysologus, *sermo 57* 6-7, *58* 5-6, *59* 7-8, *60* 7-8, *61* 5-6, and *62* 8-9; CCSL 24, 321, 327, 332, 338, 343, and 349-350). Note that in many cases the variant *Ex Maria uirgine* is almost equally as well attested as *Et Maria uirgine*.

[373] *Tertia die surrexit a mortuis. Tres dies ...* (Peter Chrysologus, *sermo 57* 8; CCSL 24, 322).

[374] *Tertia die resurrexit. Et si in passione ...* and *Tertia die resurrexit. Quia hominis est quod moritur, trinitatis est quod resurgit* (Peter Chrysologus, *sermo 58* 7 and *61* 7; CCSL 24, 328 and 343).

[375] *Tertia die surrexit. Vt tribus in diebus ...* (Peter Chrysologus, *sermo 59* 9; CCSL 24, 333).

[376] *Tertio die resurrexit. Vt esset nostri corporis resurrectio uirtus, gratia, beneficium trinitatis* (Peter Chrysologus, *sermo 62* 10; CCSL 24, 351).

[377] This seems to be the solution that has been chosen by Olivar: see CCSL 24, 312. I did the same in Westra 1996a, 73 and 1996b, 528.

[378] See footnotes 368, 369, and 372 above.

that reason would be adapted less soon, supports the short formulation with *Surrexit* [379]. Moreover, to quote an article in three or four different ways would ill accord with Peter Chrysologus's normal usage, especially where the articles in the middle part of the Creed are concerned. Therefore, we prefer, though hesitantly, the short reconstruction of the Chrysologan fifth article as *Tertia die surrexit*.

Concerning the wording of the next article, our source sermons do not exactly agree either. Three of the six give a practically unanimously transmitted *Ascendit in caelos* [380], one has *Ascendit in caelum* [381], and in one sermon the manuscripts are more or less equally divided [382]. It seems most obvious, therefore, to choose the variant with *Caelos* for our reconstruction [383]. The seventh article is given by all six sermons as *Sedet ad dexteram patris* [384].

When we turn to the eighth article, there seem to be two main possibilities: *Inde uenturus iudicare uiuos et mortuos* [385] and *Inde uenturus est iudicare uiuos et mortuos* [386], each of which is supported by

---

[379] *Confiteris die tertia surrexisse. Die tertia, ut intelligas in resurrectione Christi totius trinitatis fuisse uictoriam* (Peter Chrysologus, *sermo 60* 9; CCSL 24, 339).

[380] *Ascendit in caelos. Ascendit nos perferens ..., Ascendit in caelos. Hominem ferens illo ubi semper ipse permansit,* and *Ascendit in caelos. Per me, qui per se numquam defuit caelo* (Peter Chrysologus, *sermo 58* 8, *61* 8, and *62* 11; CCSL 24, 328, 343, and 351).

[381] *Ascendit in caelum. Ascendit non ut se ...* (Peter Chrysologus, *sermo 57* 9; CCSL 24, 322).

[382] *Ascendit in caelos (caelum). Non petens, sed reppetens caelos (caelum) ...* (Peter Chrysologus, *sermo 59* 10; CCSL 24, 333).

[383] Our choice is supported by the indirect quotation in Chrysologus's *sermo 60* 10: *Dicis ascendisse caelos, ut caeli dominum credas ...* (CCSL 24, 339). Olivar (CCSL 24, 312-313) reaches the same conclusion.

[384] *Sedet ad dexteram patris. Sed suis patrem ..., Sedet ad dexteram patris. Ordo ibi diuinus ..., Sedet ad dexteram patris. Sed patrem ..., Clamas: Sedet ad dexteram patris. Vt quia patris et filii ..., Sedet ad dexteram patris. Ad dexteram sedet quia habet deitas nil sinistrum,* and *Sedet ad dexteram patris. Diuinae uirtutis ordine ...* (Peter Chrysologus, *sermo 57* 10, *58* 9, *59* 11, *60* 11, *61* 9, and *62* 12; CCSL 24, 322, 328, 333, 339, 343, and 351).

[385] *Inde uenturus iudicare uiuos et mortuos. Esto uiuos ...* and *Inde uenturus iudicare uiuos et mortuos. Si credimus ...* (Peter Chrysologus, *sermo 57* 11 and *59* 12; CCSL 24, 322 and 333).

[386] *Inde uenturus est iudicare uiuos et mortuos. Desinant homines ...* and *Inde uenturus est iudicare uiuos et mortuos. Iudicabit uiuos ...* (Peter Chrysologus, *sermo 58* 10 and *61* 11; CCSL 24, 328 and 343). In both places, there is an important *uaria lectio* without *Est*.

two sermons [387]. The first possibility, however, is also supported by some important manuscripts in the two sermons which witness to the second. This circumstance, together with the fact that *Est*, which has a place in *T*, was probably more apt to be added than omitted, seems to tip the balance in favour of a Chrysologan eighth article without *Est* [388].

More hazardous is the choice between the two possible forms *Credo in sanctum spiritum* and *Credo in spiritum sanctum* in the ninth article. The first is found in three of the six sermons, in all cases with the other possibility as a textual variant [389]. The other form is found in two of the other three sermons *de symbolo*, of which only one does not offer the word order *sanctum spiritum* in the apparatus [390]. Again, it seems very improbable that Peter Chrysologus would really have used two different formulations of the ninth article during the rites of *traditio symboli* and baptism. Since both variants are supported by the manuscript tradition in an almost equal way, it seems best to apply the argument again that the reading of *T* (*Credo in spiritum sanctum*) would be more apt to displace an original *Credo in sanctum spiritum* than the other way round, and thus to reconstruct *Credo in sanctum spiritum*.

For Chrysologus's form of the tenth article, the source material yields an almost bewildering variety. We once find the simple *Sanctam ecclesiam* [391], but in most cases slightly longer variants can be seen: *Et sanctam ecclesiam* [392], *Credimus sanctam ecclesiam* [393], *Credo*

---

[387] Of the other two sermons, *sermo 60* 12 puts *Est* before *Venturus* (*Inde est uenturus uiuos et mortuos. Quia ueniente Christo* ...; CCSL 24, 339) and *sermo 62* 13 does not provide much information (*Iudicare uiuos et mortuos. Et quid* ...; CCSL 24, 351).

[388] Olivar (CCSL 24, 312), however, reconstructs the eighth article with *Est*.

[389] *Credo in sanctum spiritum. Nunc perfecta* ..., *Credo in sanctum spiritum. Nunc usque dominicae* ..., and *Credo in sanctum spiritum. Hic in quem* ... (Peter Chrysologus, *sermo 58* 11, *59* 13, and *62* 14; CCSL 24, 328, 333, and 351).

[390] *Credo in spiritum sanctum. Postquam susceptae carnis* ... and *Credo in spiritum sanctum* (*sanctum spiritum*). *Vt in patre* ... (Peter Chrysologus, *sermo 57* 12 and *61* 12; CCSL 24, 323 and 344). Compare also *Credimus in spiritum sanctum* (*sanctum spiritum*), *quem deus nobis* ... (Peter Chrysologus, *sermo 60* 13; CCSL 24, 339).

[391] *Sanctam ecclesiam. Quia neque* ... (Peter Chrysologus, *sermo 57* 13; CCSL 24, 323). A number of manuscripts prefix *in*.

[392] *Et sanctam ecclesiam. Quasi coniuncta* ... and *Et sanctam ecclesiam. Credimus et* ... (Peter Chrysologus, *sermo 58* 12 and *59* 14; CCSL 24, 328 and 333). In both sermons, the reading *In sanctam ecclesiam* is an important variant.

*in sanctam ecclesiam* [394], and *In sanctam ecclesiam* [395]. The most probable explanation for this state of affairs is that Chrysologus's form
of the Creed just had *Sanctam ecclesiam* here, but that the author
thought this too harsh an introduction for a new section of his sermon, and therefore usually introduced the article by means of *et, in,*
or a form of *credo* [396].

The next two articles present a similar picture. The eleventh article can be seen in the formulations *Et in remissionem peccatorum* [397],
*In remissionem peccatorum* [398], *Credimus remissionem peccatorum* [399],
and *Credo in remissionem peccatorum* [400]. As far as the first words
of the twelfth are concerned, we find *Carnis resurrectionem* [401], *In resurrectionem mortuorum* [402], and *Credimus carnis resurrectionem* [403]. A
reconstruction with just *Remissionem peccatorum, carnis resurrectionem* again seems to be most natural and is moreover supported by
the two instances where we find the sequel (*Credo*) *in remissionem*

---

[393] *Credimus sanctam ecclesiam, quam sic in se* ... (Peter Chrysologus, *sermo 60*
14; CCSL 24, 340). Some manuscripts insert *In* after *Credimus*.

[394] *Credo in sanctam ecclesiam. Vt confitearis* ... (Peter Chrysologus, *sermo 61*
13; CCSL 24, 344). One manuscript omits *In*.

[395] *In sanctam ecclesiam. Quia ecclesia* ... (Peter Chrysologus, *sermo 62* 15;
CCSL 24, 351). Only in this case is the manuscript tradition unanimous.

[396] Olivar (CCSL 24, 312-313) chooses the formulation *Et sanctam ecclesiam* for
his reconstruction.

[397] *Et in remissionem peccatorum. Ipse sibi* ... (Peter Chrysologus, *sermo 57* 14;
CCSL 24, 323). The preposition is omitted by one important manuscript.

[398] *In remissionem peccatorum. Acquire tibi* ..., *In remissionem peccatorum. In
nouo homine* ..., and *In remissionem peccatorum. Da tibi homo* ... *In remissionem
peccatorum, carnis resurrectionem. Hoc est totum* ... (Peter Chrysologus, *sermo 58*
13, *59* 15, and *62* 16-17; CCSL 24, 328, 334, and 351).

[399] *Credimus remissionem peccatorum, quia per Christum* ... (Peter Chrysologus,
*sermo 60* 15; CCSL 24, 340).

[400] *Credo in remissionem peccatorum, carnis resurrectionem. Qui remissionem* ...
(Peter Chrysologus, *sermo 61* 14; CCSL 24, 344). The preposition is omitted by
two manuscripts.

[401] *Carnis resurrectionem. Bene credit* ... and *Carnis resurrectionem. Quia qui* ...
(Peter Chrysologus, *sermo 57* 15 and *58* 14; CCSL 24, 323 and 328). See also
footnotes 398 and 400 above.

[402] *In resurrectionem mortuorum. Crede homo in morte resurgere te posse* ... (Peter Chrysologus, *sermo 59* 16; CCSL 24, 334).

[403] *Credimus carnis resurrectionem, ut credamus passionis* ... (Peter Chrysologus,
*sermo 60* 16; CCSL 24, 340).

*peccatorum, carnis resurrectionem* in one quotation [404]. The deviating quotation *In resurrectionem mortuorum* is probably best explained as caused by the Nicaeno-Constantinopolitan Creed.

A final problem concerning Chrysologus's credal variant, about which Olivar does not say a word, is the possible presence of *Vitam aeternam*. Kattenbusch already noted that this element is treated rather cursorily in the six Chrysologan sermons that expound the Creed, and therefore ventured the hypothesis that these parts had been added by an interpolator and that *Vitam aeternam* did not yet figure in Chrysologus's form of the Creed [405]. However, this explanation is not very satisfying since *Vitam aeternam* is entirely absent from *sermo 61*, is only mentioned but not expounded in *sermo 57* [406], and is introduced with stylistic variation in *sermo 60* [407]. This seems to be a strange procedure for an interpolator who only wanted to fill an apparent gap in Chrysologus's credal sermons. Moreover, in *sermo 83*, where Peter Chrysologus formulates a *regula fidei* in which most elements of the Apostles' Creed seem to occur, the presence of *Vitam aeternam* in Chrysologus's form of the Creed seems to be presupposed: *Credat homo etiam peccatorum remissionem, quia caelestis ... Credat et carnis resurrectionem, ut sit homo ... Credat aeternam uitam, ne locum habeat mors secunda* [408]. Therefore,

---

[404] See footnotes 398 and 400 above.

[405] Kattenbusch 1894, 101-102 and 1900, 953n154.

[406] *Carnis resurrectionem. Bene credit ... nec difficile est deo facere de te sene, quod tu facis semper ipse de semine. Vitam aeternam. Haec fides, hoc sacramentum non est committendum chartis ...* (Peter Chrysologus, *sermo 57* 15-16; CCSL 24, 323-324).

[407] *Aeternam credimus uitam, quia post resurrectionem nec bonorum finis est nec malorum* (Peter Chrysologus, *sermo 60* 17; CCSL 24, 340). The other Chrysologan instances are: *Vitam aeternam. Manifestum est quia uita aeterna ipsa morte moriente succedit, Vitam aeternam. Necesse est ut qui resurgit uiuat in aeternum, quia nisi in aeternum uiueret, non uitae resurgeret sed morti,* and *Vitam aeternam. Bene addidit uitam aeternam, ut resurrecturum se crederet* (*sermo 58* 15, *59* 17, and *62* 18; CCSL 24, 328, 334, and 352).

[408] *... quia Christus sic homo factus est ut quod deus est permaneret, sic est mortuus ut mortuos totis saeculis sua resuscitaret ex morte, quod non sibi resurrexit ille sed nobis, quod nos caelo pertulit dum se sustulit caelo, quod sedet ad auctoritatem iudicis non ad requiem fatigati, quod ueniet non loco qui ubique est ad monendum neque ut mundum suum teneat qui mundum possidet totum, sed ut mundus iam semper uisionem sui mereatur auctoris. Credat homo etiam peccatorum remissionem, quia caelestis regio cum sit latissima non capit peccatorem, neque de suorum disperet*

Hahn's explanation that *Vitam aeternam* figured in Chrysologus's variant not as a separate article but as part of the twelfth [409] has much to say for it. In that case, the absence of *Vitam aeternam* in one sermon is paralleled by the instances where Chrysologus quotes the second, third, and eighth articles only partially [410]. Our conclusion is, therefore, that the twelfth article of Peter Chrysologus's form of the Creed reads *Carnis resurrectionem, uitam aeternam.*

The following formulation, then, emerges as the underlying wording of the Creed in PC:

*Credo in deum patrem omnipotentem*
*et in Christum Iesum, filium eius unicum dominum nostrum*
*qui natus est de spiritu sancto et Maria uirgine*
*qui sub Pontio Pilato crucifixus est et sepultus*
*tertia die surrexit (?)*
*ascendit in caelos*
*sedet ad dexteram patris*
*inde uenturus iudicare uiuos et mortuos*
*credo in sanctum spiritum*
*sanctam ecclesiam*
*remissionem peccatorum*
*carnis resurrectionem*
*uitam aeternam.*

CHRO    Chromatius of Aquileia's (d. 407) *tractatus in Mathaeum 41* (CPL 218A). This text was probably written after 397 [411].

Chromatius of Aquileia testifies only to the final part of the creed, but gives a clear and explicit quotation: ... *secundum quod*

---

*homo magnitudine peccatorum quia si est quod deus donare non potest omnipotens non est. Credat et carnis resurrectionem, ut sit homo ipse, ut accipiat ipse qui peccat poenam, ipse praemium qui laborat. Credat aeternam uitam ne locum habeat mors secunda* (Peter Chrysologus, *sermo 83* 4; CCSL 24A, 514-515).

[409] Hahn 1897, 42n58.

[410] See above, footnotes 369, 372, and 387.

[411] For the date, see above, chapter 2.5, footnote 64. For the relationship between Chromatius's testimony and that of Rufinus, see *ibidem*. Apart from Benvin (1989, 199n21), this source seems to have escaped the notice of credal scholars.

*in fide symboli in qua baptismum accipimus profitemur dicendo: Huius carnis resurrectionem in uitam aeternam* [412].

Thus, CHRO testifies to the following credal formulation:

...

...

*huius carnis resurrectionem
in uitam aeternam.*

## 3.6 Other Variants of the Creed

Thus far, we have inspected the various witnesses to the form of the Apostles' Creed in Gaul, Spain, Africa, and Northern Italy. The remaining source material for the form of the Creed in the Western Church is so scanty that it hardly seems justified to devote more than one section to it. Apart from two Roman texts, this material stems from the Latin Balkans and Ireland [413].

A number of texts that have been mentioned in this context should be excluded from our analysis, however. The earliest of these

---

[412] Chromatius of Aquileia, *tractatus in Mathaeum 41* 8; CCSL 9A, 396.

[413] See for earlier overviews Kattenbusch 1894, 184-188 ("Ein Symbol aus Irland"), Hahn 1897, 83-94 ("Symbolformeln der britischen Kirchen"), Smulders 1970, 237n10, Kelly 1976, 174-175, and O'Callaghan 1992, 285-286. Kattenbusch, Hahn, and O'Callaghan do not mention any forms of the Creed from the Balkans; Smulders and Kelly are silent about any witnesses from the British Isles. Burn (1909, 12) offers a short outline of a possible history of the Creed in "Britain". Nerney's (1952, 374-375) claim that the existence of a "Celtic family" of the Creed "is generally assumed" seems therefore to be rather exaggerated. Burn (1909, 12) offers a short outline of the possible history of the Creed in "Britain". Further, Hahn gives a series of "Symbolformeln der germanischen Kirche" (Hahn 1894, 95-124; see also O'Callaghan 1992, 285-287), but most of these are far too late for our purpose, and many of them are just translations of *T* (Amalarius of Trier's *epistula ad Carolum magnum* [see above, chapter 3.2, footnote 44], a deviating credal variant in the (now lost) Lambach manuscript of Ambrose's *explanatio symboli*, and two isolated forms of the Creed of unknown origin comprise the remainder). See also Barbian 1964, 12 and, for more details on these texts, Kattenbusch 1894, 183-184 and 1900, 592n186, 743n25, 764, 765n8, 766, 769, 803-804, 822n16, 823n17, and 864-866. Hahn's (1897, 125-126) two "Symbolformeln aus den nordischen (norwegischen und isländischen) Kirchen", neither of them in Latin, are of course even later. Compare Kattenbusch 1894, 199-202 ("Norwegische und isländische Formeln"). Creeds in Barbian 1964 (*Die altdeutschen Symbola*) stem from the eleventh and twelfth centuries, and mostly comprise doctrinal creeds.

are Victorinus of Poetovio's *commentarii in Apocalypsim Ioannis* (*c.* 260; CPL 80), which work contains a *regula fidei* rather than a form of the Creed [414]. On similar grounds, Saint Patrick's *confessio* (*c.* 450; CPL 1100) [415] and the creed of Gregory the Great (*sedit* 509-604) [416] should be excluded from our analysis. In this context, one could also point to the Venerable Bede's *retractatio in Actus Apostolorum* (*c.* 730; CPL 1358) [417].

---

[414] Victorinus of Poetovio, *commentarii in Apocalypsim Iohannis* XI 1: *Mensura autem fidei est mandatum domini nostri patrem confiteri omnipotentem ut didicimus, et huius filium dominum nostrum Iesum Christum ante originem saeculi spiritaliter apud patrem genitum* ... (CSEL 49, 96). Compare Kattenbusch 1894, 212-214 and Hahn 1897, 17-18. Hanson (1976, 27-30) offers some very sound remarks upon the text of this *regula*. Poetovio (other Latin variants of the name also occur) is modern Slovenian Ptuj, formerly Austrian Pettau. One also encounters the Italian name Petabio. For the date, see SChr 423, 15.

[415] Saint Patrick, *confessio* 4: *Quia non est alius deus nec umquam fuit nec ante nec erit post haec praeter deum patrem ingenitum, sine principio, a quo est omne principium, omnia tenentem ut dicimus, et huius filium* ... (SChr 249, 74 and Bieler 1950, 58-60). See for the date Hanson (SChr 249, 18-21 and 45) and Frede 1995, 662. This *regula* is reproduced in Hahn 1897, 331; compare Kattenbusch 1894, 188n6, 212-213, and 395 and Smulders 1970, 237n10. See Kattenbusch 1894, 212-213 and 395, Oulton 1940 (an extensive commentary on this text), Bieler 1948, and Hanson 1976 for a discussion of the relationship between the *regulae* of Saint Patrick and Victorinus of Poetovio (see previous footnote). Chapters 59-60 of Patrick's *confessio* (*Certissimi reor, si mihi hoc incurrisset, lucratus sum animam cum corpore meo quia sine ulla dubitatione in die illa resurgemus in claritate solis, hoc est in gloria Christi Iesu redemptoris nostri* ...; SChr 249, 130 and Bieler 1950, 89-90) also bear the features of a *regula fidei*.

[416] This formula is a clearly doctrinal creed again: ... *oris sui diuinissimo gladio et rectam fidem muniuit et cunctas haereses uno symbolo dissipauit. Quod uidelicet sacrae confessionis symbolum ita se habet: Credo in unum deum omnipotentem, patrem filium et spiritum sanctum, tres personas, unam substantiam* ... (PL 75, 87-88). It occurs in a ninth-century *uita Gregorii* that was written by John the Deacon. See for this *uita* and its different versions Dekkers 1995, 562. Hahn (1897, 337-338) reproduces the creed as well as a reconstruction of an underlying form of the Apostles' Creed (*ibid.* 28). Compare Kattenbusch 1894, 76-77 and 1900, 807+n74 and 826n22b.

[417] In this text, which comments upon Acts 3, 21, we find a rather free formulation of the contents of some of the articles of the Creed: *Hoc est quod eidem domino Iesu Christo a deo patre dictum psalmista testatur: Sede a dextris meis donec ponam inimicos tuos scabellum pedum tuorum. Assumptus namque est in caelum et sedet a dextris dei, in qua nimirum sede paternae maiestatis semper diuinitus manet neque inde umquam afuit, uerum in assumpta humanitate uenturus est de caelo ad iudicandos uiuos et mortuos, quando omnes inimici eius subdentur pedibus eius et*

Next, the *altercatio Luciferiani et orthodoxi* (probably written in 380; CPL 608) of Jerome, a native of Stridon in Dalmatia, seems to quote parts of the Creed in its interrogatory form, but cannot be used here as this work has not yet received a critical edition [418].

Again, the Book of Deer, a ninth-century Scottish manuscript which contains a form of the Apostles' Creed, will not be taken into account because this form of the Creed lacks any liturgical or literary context [419]. In addition, many texts that are adduced by Hahn, Kattenbusch, and O'Callaghan as witnesses to the form of the Creed in the British Isles just give *T* or a vernacular version of it [420].

---

*restituentur omnia quae locutus est deus per omnes prophetas ab initio saeculi* ... (Beda Venerabilis, *retractatio in Actus Apostolorum* III 21; CCSL 121, 119-120). In an earlier work (*c.* 710), we find a possible quotation of the third article: *Ob hoc eum confitemur natum de spiritu sancto et Maria uirgine* (Beda Venerabilis, *expositio Actuum Apostolorum* [CPL 1357] X 38; CCSL 121, 54). Kattenbusch is more positive about this second instance, but he quotes the phrase without the pronoun *eum*: see Kattenbusch 1900, 845n62. For the date of both works, see Frede 1995, 315.

[418] Jerome, *altercatio Luciferiani et orthodoxi* 12: *Praeterea cum sollemne sit in lauacro post trinitatis confessionem interrogare: Credis sanctam ecclesiam? Credis remissionem peccatorum? quam ecclesiam credidisse discis?* (PL 23, 175). See for the date Frede 1995, 511. Kattenbusch (1894, 77n33 and 1900, 486n15) quotes this passage without any discussion. Kattenbusch (1894, 63n11 and 1900, 395-396) as well as Hahn (1897, 25n8) draw attention to another Hieronymian place which is of interest for students of the Creed: *In symbolo fidei et spei nostrae, quod ab apostolis traditum non scribitur in carta et atramento sed in tabulis cordis carnalibus, post confessionem trinitatis et unitatem ecclesiae omne Christiani dogmatis sacramentum carnis resurrectione concluditur* (*contra Iohannem Hierosolymitanum* [CPL 612] 28; PL 23, 396). This work, which was written in 397 (see Frede 1995, 521), also still awaits a critical edition. Compare Jerome's *epistula 84* 5 ... *et quasi simpliciter credentes aiunt: Credimus in resurrectionem carnis. Hoc uero cum dixerint uulgus indoctum putat sibi posse sufficere, maxime quia id ipsum et in symbolo creditur* (CPL 620; CCSL 55, 126). The fact that Jerome was baptized in Rome and worked most of his life in Palestine is another complicating factor.

[419] Book of Deer (Cambridge University Library, Ii.VI.32), f. 85R: *Credo in deum patrem omnipotentem* ... See for the date (about which some confusion exists in the literature that is mentioned below) and history of the manuscript Ellis 1994, 11-16. Its form of the Creed is printed in Warren 1881, 166. See for earlier credal scholarship Hahn 1897, 86, Kattenbusch 1894, 188n6 and 1900, 750+n40 and 762-764, and O'Callaghan 1992, 285.

[420] Hahn 1897, 87-94 and O'Callaghan 1992, 286; compare Kattenbusch 1900, 807 and 820n12.

Finally, O'Callaghan (1992, 286-287) mentions two sets of baptismal questions that occur in martyr acts as witnesses for the form of the Creed in Rome [421]. Here, we encounter not only the difficulty of the lack of a critical edition, but also the circumstance that it is far from certain that these formulations are in any way historically reliable [422].

What remains, then, are two texts from Rome, three from the Latin Balkans, and two from Ireland, which testify in different degrees to the form of the Apostles' Creed.

LEO    Pope Leo the Great's (*sedit* 440-461) famous *tomus ad Flauianum* (449; CPL 1656).

Leo's *tomus* contains an indirect but explicit quotation of the first three articles of the Creed: *Qui ne ipsius quidem symboli initia comprehendit ... illam saltem communem et indiscretam confessionem sollicito recepisset auditu, qua fidelium uniuersitas profitetur credere se in deum patrem omnipotentem, et in Christum Iesum filium eius unicum dominum nostrum, qui natus est de spiritu sancto et Maria uirgine. Quibus tribus sententiis ...* [423].

---

[421] See for the text of these and similar sources Hahn 1897, 34-35 and in particular Kinzig 1999a, 128-132. The relevant acts are those of Calixtus (Callistus; CPL 2173), Stephanus (CPL 2236), Pope Marcellus, and Susanna (CPL 2237). See for more details Dekkers 1995, 705 and 715 and Frede 1995, 56 and 87.

[422] Compare Kattenbusch 1894, 77n33: "Zu lernen ist aus diesen ... Stücken ... nichts, sie sind keine "Quellen" weder für noch wider irgendeinen Wortlaut von R"; similarly Kattenbusch 1900, 486n15.

[423] Leo the Great, *tomus ad Flauianum* (*epistula 28*) 11-15; Silva-Tarouca 1959, 21 (Schwartz 1932a, 25). Compare *ibid.* 131: *Vnde unigenitum filium dei crucifixum et sepultum omnes etiam in symbolo confitemur ...* (Silva-Tarouca 1959, 28; Schwartz 1932a, 29). For earlier credal scholarship, see Kattenbusch 1894, 76 and Hahn 1897, 27+n14; see for the date Denzinger 1991, 135. See for an echo of Leo's words above, chapter 1.6, footnote 59. The Creed is mentioned, but not quoted, in Leo's *epistula 31* 4 (Silva-Tarouca 1934, 12; Schwartz 1932b, 14-15). Several allusions to the contents of the Creed can be found in Leo's works, see for example *tractatus 72* 3 and 7: *Si incunctanter itaque, dilectissimi, corde credimus quod ore profitemur, nos in Christo crucifixi, nos sumus mortui, nos sepulti, nos etiam cum ipso die tertio suscitati ... Implet ergo Iesus proprietatem nominis sui, et qui ascendit in caelos non deserit adoptatos, qui sedet ad dexteram patris ipse totius habitator est corporis, et ipse deorsum confortat ad patientiam qui sursum inuitat ad gloriam* and *Cuius unitatis nullum poterunt habere consortium qui in dei filio deo uero humanam negant manere naturam ... quia ab Euangelio dissentiunt et symbolo contradicunt ... quia etsi audent sibi Christianum nomen assumere ab omni*

LEO    therefore testifies to the following credal formulation:

*Credo in deum patrem omnipotentem*
*et in Christum Iesum, filium eius unicum dominum nostrum*
*qui natus est de spiritu sancto et Maria uirgine*

...

...

ARN    Arnobius the Younger's *conflictus cum Serapione Aegyptio* (CPL 239; *c.* 454).

This text exhibits a similar indirect quotation: *Et ubi est quod symbolo uniuersalis ecclesiae confitemur nos credere Christum Iesum filium eius unicum dominum nostrum, qui natus est de spiritu sancto et Maria uirgine? Qui sibi ante saecula ...* [424] It is to be noted, however, that this quotation does not allow any conclusions concerning the beginning of the second article of the Creed.

The testimony of ARN to the wording of the Creed can therefore be distilled to this:

...

... Christum Iesum, filium eius unicum dominum nostrum
*qui natus est de spiritu sancto et Maria uirgine*

...

...

---

*tamen creatura cui Christus caput est repelluntur, uobis in hac sollemnitate merito exsultantibus pieque gaudentibus qui nullum recipientes in ueritate mendacium, nec de natiuitate Christi secundum carnem, nec de passione ac morte, nec de corporali resurrectione eius ambigitis, quoniam sine ulla separatione deitatis uerum Christum ab utero uirginis, uerum in ligno crucis, uerum in sepulcro carnis, uerum in gloria resurrectionis, uerum in dextera paternae maiestatis agnoscitis* (CPL 1657; CCSL 138A, 443-444 and 448) and *epistula 124* 4: *... cum inter filios hominum unus solus dominus noster Iesus Christus extiterit in quo omnes crucifixi, omnes mortui, omnes sepulti, omnes sunt etiam suscitati ...* (Schwartz 1932b, 160-161). Many other instances are mentioned in Kattenbusch 1894, 76n31, Hahn 1897, 27n14, and Kattenbusch 1900, 425n94 and 810n78.

[424] Arnobius the Younger, *conflictus cum Serapione Aegyptio* II 8; CCSL 25A, 101. For the date, see CCSL 25A, 14-15. Kattenbusch (1900, 625n235 and 977) seems to be the only earlier student of the Creed who has noticed this text. He assumes the influence of Leo's *tomus* here, but Daur, the editor of the *Corpus Christianorum* text, does not mention Leo in his *apparatus fontium*. Daur connects a number of other instances in the *conflictus* with the Creed (I 3, II 21 and 26; CCSL 25A, 45, 145, 154-155), but these are allusions at best.

NIC   Nicetas of Remesiana's *libellus V de symbolo* of his *instruc-
      tiones ad competentes* (CPL 647; probably written between
      370 and 375) [425].

This text seems to discuss each article of the Creed, but only
incidentally gives hard and fast quotations. Most of the time, Nicetas either renders the wording of an article in a free way, or just
indicates its content. It is best, therefore, to investigate briefly all
those instances which may inform us about the wording of the several articles of the Apostles' Creed as it was used by Nicetas.

The first article, then, is quoted in an explicit and direct way: ...
*iam sincera uoce pronuntiat: Credo in deum patrem omnipotentem.
Bene incipit a credulitate confessio* ... [426]. According to Burn, the
words *Creatorem caeli et terrae* also occur in Nicetas's form of the
Creed [427]. However, these are found only in one of the two manuscripts of Burn's 'second' recension, whereas all other manuscripts
omit it, and are therefore most probably explained as a scribal addi-

---

[425] The authorship of this work used to be heavily disputed (see for example
Hahn 1897, 47-49n72 and Kattenbusch 1894, 107-108 and 112-130), but seems to
be certain since the edition of Burn in 1905: see Dekkers 1995, 228-229 and
Frede 1995, 648. For the date, see Burn 1905, lxvii-lxx. Burn prints those parts
of the text which he considers to be credal quotations in capitals and discusses
Nicetas's form of the Creed in more detail on pp. lxxiv-lxxix. Burn's text, though
without critical apparatus, has been reprinted in Gamber 1964, 115-122. Gamber
uses the same device to denote the credal quotations (though he marks them as
not very reliable: see Gamber 1964, 6n1), but sometimes adapts them to those in
Ambrose's *explanatio symboli* (CPL 153; he considers this text to stem from Nicetas as well: see above, chapter 3.5, footnote 311). Note that the complete text
exists in two recensions, with fragments of a third. Burn refers to these as the
'first recension' (the fragmentary one), 'second recension', and 'Austrian recension'. As far as I can see, Burn only uses the 'second' and 'Austrian' recensions
in his edition of *libellus V*. Of these, the 'second' recension seems to be more
original than the 'Austrian' one, which Burn designates as "mutilated": see Burn
1905, lxv-lxvii. Thus, as a rule it seems best to follow the 'second' recension
when the two part ways where the credal quotations are concerned. Ancient Remesiana is modern Serbian Bela Palanka.

[426] Nicetas of Remesiana, *libellus V de symbolo* 1-2; Burn 1905, 39. Another
quotation of the first article is offered by a fragment of Nicetas's *libellus II*: ...
*iam sincera uoce pronuntiat: Credo in deum patrem omnipotentem et reliqua. De
fide enim sicut in eodem symbolo continetur* ... (Burn 1905, 8).

[427] Burn 1905, lxxv. Hahn (1897, 49n75) and especially Kattenbusch (1894,
112n14a and 118n24; 1900, 878) and Kelly (1976, 175) come closer to our position.

tion, as the clause *Creatorem caeli et terrae* had a place in *T*, the form of the Creed that most Christian writers since the ninth century knew by heart. The occurrence of the same words some lines below (... *qui non in tempore coepit uiuere, sed semper uiuens nullum patitur successorem, deum bonum et iustum, caeli et terrae creatorem* [428]) does not mean much because they are clearly part of the explanation of the word *Deum*. Because of Nicetas's apparently complete discussion of all parts of the Creed, the best conclusion seems to be here that the phrase *Creatorem caeli et terrae* did not figure in his credal variant.

Nicetas moves on to the second article with the words: *Credens ergo in deum patrem, statim te confiteberis credere et in filium eius Iesum Christum* [429], after which a short explanation ensues. In fact, any form of the second article may be represented by this indirect quotation, though the absence of *Vnicum* strikes one as significant. More information is provided by a summary of belief in the three persons of the Trinity in which words are used that are clearly inspired by the Creed: *Hanc trinitatis fidem, fratres, in cordibus firmate uestris, credentes in unum deum patrem omnipotentem et in filium eius Iesum Christum dominum nostrum et in spiritum sanctum* [430]. As the formulation *Et in filium eius Iesum Christum*, without *Vnicum*, recurs here, Nicetas's indirect quotation of the second article in *libellus V* 3 is probably indeed reliable. Since the words *Dominum nostrum* in the later quotation can hardly come from any other source than the author's form of the Creed either, we conclude that Nicetas's form of the second article probably ran as follows: *Et in filium eius Iesum Christum, dominum nostrum* [431].

Similarly, the third article may well be quoted accurately, though this is not explicitly indicated by the text: *Hic propter nostram salutem descendit a patre de caelis et simile nobis corpus accepit. Natus ex*

---

[428] Nicetas of Remesiana, *libellus V de symbolo* 2; Burn 1905, 39-40.

[429] Nicetas of Remesiana, *libellus V de symbolo* 3; Burn 1905, 41.

[430] Nicetas of Remesiana, *libellus V de symbolo* 8; Burn 1905, 46.

[431] Hahn (1897, 49n75) takes Nicetas's form of the second article without *Dominum nostrum*, whereas Kattenbusch concurs first with Hahn's (Kattenbusch 1894, 110-111) and then with our interpretation (Kattenbusch 1900, 594n189). Burn (1905, lxxv) accepts Kattenbusch's later view, whereas Kelly (1976, 175) again doubts the presence of *Dominum nostrum*.

*spiritu sancto et ex Maria uirgine. Sine ulla uiri operatione corpus ex corpore spiritus sancti uirtute generatum est* [432].

About the formulation of the fourth article, on the other hand, we are left totally in the dark. The section on this article clearly starts with an indication of its contents [433]. There is one possible quotation in the ensuing commentary (*Sub Pontio ergo Pilato passus est. Tempus designatur ...* [434]), but this is probably just a deliberately abbreviated formulation. Only the words *Sub Pontio Pilato*, which are explained in what follows, can lay some reasonable claim to being a quotation, but that does not say very much [435].

The fifth article again seems to be quoted in a direct way: *Tertia die resurrexit uiuus a mortuis. Sicut ait propheta ...*, and the same holds true for the next three articles: *Ascendit in caelos, unde et descenderat ... Sedet ad dexteram patris, secundum quod dictum est ... Inde uenturus iudicare uiuos et mortuos. Crede quoniam hic ipse Christus ...* [436]. Next, the ninth article is introduced with the words *Credis et in spiritum sanctum* [437]. Because of the summary of Trini-

---

[432] Nicetas of Remesiana, *libellus V de symbolo* 3; Burn 1905, 41. Burn connects *Natus* with *sine ulla uiri operatione* and places a full stop before *corpus*, which is thus connected with *generatum est*. But the phrase *sine ulla uiri operatione* makes more sense in combination with *generare* than with *nasci*, so that a stop should be placed before *sine ulla ...* This implies again that the words *Natus ex spiritu sancto et ex Maria uirgine* constitute a literal quotation. Instead of *Natus*, the manuscripts of the 'Austrian' recension read *Natum*, which is also what we find in the reconstructions of Hahn (1897, 48) and Kelly (1976, 175). Compare Kattenbusch 1894, 111.

[433] *Sequitur ut credas dominicae passioni et passum confitearis Christum, crucifixum a Iudaeis, secundum praedicta prophetarum* (Nicetas of Remesiana, *libellus V de symbolo* 5; Burn 1905, 43). As Nicetas seems to have something to say about every element of the Creed, this seems to exclude the possibility that his variant contained the Descent to Hell.

[434] Nicetas of Remesiana, *libellus V de symbolo* 5; Burn 1905, 44.

[435] Hahn (1897, 49) reconstructs *Sub Pontio Pilatus passum, crucifixum et mortuum*; Burn prints the phrase *Sub Pontio Pilato passus est* as a quotation in his edition; Kelly (1976, 175) gives *Passum sub Pontio Pilato, crucifixum, mortuum*. But compare Kattenbusch 1894, 111-112 and especially 1900, 889n30.

[436] Nicetas of Remesiana, *libellus V de symbolo* 6; Burn 1905, 44-45. It is to be noted, however, that this form of the sixth, seventh and eighth articles is to be found in the 'second' recension only. The 'Austrian' recension has *In caelum ascendit ... Sedet ad dexteram dei patris ... Inde uenturus est iudicare uiuos et mortuos*. This was of course not yet known to Hahn and Kattenbusch.

[437] Nicetas of Remesiana, *libellus V de symbolo* 7; Burn 1905, 45.

tarian belief in the next paragraph (see above), it seems best to reconstruct *Et in spiritum sanctum* here [438].

After treating the doctrine of the Trinity, Nicetas proceeds as follows: *Post confessionem beatae trinitatis iam profiteris te credere sanctam ecclesiam catholicam* [439]. That *Catholicam* really belonged to Nicetas's form of the Creed is made extremely probable by the fact that, after explaining the church's holiness, he continues by explaining its catholicity: *Ecclesia quid est aliud quam sanctorum omnium congregatio? Ab exordio enim saeculi siue patriarchae Abraham et Isaac et Iacob siue prophetae siue apostoli siue martyres siue ceteri iusti qui fuerunt, qui sunt, qui erunt, una ecclesia sunt, quia una fide et conuersatione sanctificati, uno spiritu signati, unum corpus effecti sunt, cuius corporis caput Christus esse perhibetur et scriptum est ... Ergo in hac una ecclesia credis te communionem consecuturum esse sanctorum. Scito unam hanc esse ecclesiam catholicam in omni orbe terrae constitutam, cuius communionem debes firmiter retinere. Sunt quidem et aliae pseudoecclesiae ...* [440]. More problematic is the presence of the clause *Communionem sanctorum* in Nicetas's form of the Creed. Nicetas closes his explanation of *Sanctam ecclesiam* with the words: *Ergo in hac una ecclesia credis te communionem consecuturum esse sanctorum*, after which the explanation of *Catholicam* follows (see above). This state of affairs makes the presence of *Communionem sanctorum* in Nicetas's variant of the Creed very improbable. The phrase *communionem ... sanctorum* only occurs in a sentence that is clearly meant to round off the commentary on *Sanctam ecclesiam*, and even if one were inclined to read it as an indirect quotation from the Apostles' Creed, its position before, instead of after, the explanation of *Catholicam* would make such an interpretation highly questionable [441].

---

[438] Similarly Hahn (1897, 49), Kattenbusch (1900, 458n41), Burn (1905, lxxiv and lxxvi), and Kelly (1976, 175).

[439] Nicetas of Remesiana, *libellus V de symbolo* 10; Burn 1905, 48.

[440] Nicetas of Remesiana, *libellus V de symbolo* 10; Burn 1905, 48. Kattenbusch (1894, 110 and 1900, 918), Hahn (1897, 49), Burn (1905, lxxiv), and Kelly (1976, 175) also reconstruct *Sanctam ecclesiam catholicam*.

[441] Nevertheless, Kattenbusch (1894, 110 and 1900, 927), Hahn (1897, 49), Burn (1905, lxxvi-lxxvii), and Kelly (1976, 175) all assume the presence of *Communionem sanctorum* in the form of the Creed that was used by Nicetas.

After the section on the Church, Nicetas continues: *Credis deinde remissionem peccatorum ... Consequenter credis et carnis tuae resurrectionem et uitam aeternam* [442]. Here, the most natural conclusion seems to be that Nicetas's variant ended with the words *Remissionem peccatorum, carnis resurrectionem, et uitam aeternam*, though it is important to bear in mind that there is nothing to guarantee this wording [443].

All in all, then, NIC can be taken to witness to the following variant of the Creed:

> *Credo in deum patrem omnipotentem*
> *et in filium eius Iesum Christum, dominum nostrum*
> *natus (natum?) ex spiritu sancto et ex Maria uirgine*
> ...
> *tertia die resurrexit uiuus a mortuis*
> *ascendit in caelos (in caelum ascendit?)*
> *sedet ad dexteram (dei?) patris*
> *inde uenturus (est?) iudicare uiuos et mortuos*
> *et in spiritum sanctum*
> *sanctam ecclesiam catholicam*
> *remissionem peccatorum (?)*
> *carnis resurrectionem*
> *et uitam aeternam (?).*

ARR     *Fragmentum 10* of the nineteen Arian fragments (CPL 705) in a Bobbio palimpsest that were first edited by Mai. According to their latest editor, these fragments stem from late fourth-century or early fifth-century Illyria [444].

---

[442] Nicetas of Remesiana, *libellus V de symbolo* 10; Burn 1905, 49.

[443] Thus also Burn 1905, lxxvii and 49n and Kelly 1976, 175. Kattenbusch (1894, 108-110 and 1900, 952) reconstructs *Remissionem peccatorum, carnis resurrectionem, in uitam aeternam*; Hahn (1897, 49) has *In remissionem peccatorum, huius* (because of *tuae*) *carnis resurrectionem, et in uitam aeternam*.

[444] For the date, see CCSL 87, XXII-XXV. Compare Hahn 1897, 41n52 and Kattenbusch 1900, 753-754 for earlier credal scholarship. Kinzig (1999a, 140) doubts the early date. It should noted that this fragment was first printed as *fragmentum VII* by Mai: see Mai 1818, 222-223 (= PL 13, 611-612). The part which contains the credal quotations may also be found in Mohlberg 1966, 201.

This fragment contains the first article and either the beginning of or the entire second article of the Apostles' Creed in interrogatory form: *Item nullo modo praeponunt in scriptis suis patrem filio, insuper et damnant omnes qui praeponunt patrem filio, et tamen ipsi praeponunt patrem filio in symbolo dum dicunt: Credis in deum patrem omnipotentem creatorem caeli et terrae? Credis et in Christum Iesum filium eius?* [445] It is to be observed that from these questions nothing can be inferred about the beginning of the second article in declaratory form. Further, this quotation does not exclude the possibility of *Dominum nostrum* or a similar phrase at the end of the article, though this is not very probable since the first article has not been abbreviated either.

ARR, then, yields the following formulation:

*Credo in deum patrem omnipotentem, creatorem caeli et terrae (credo?) et in Christum Iesum filium eius (...?)*

...

...

APS    A fifth or sixth-century inscription from ancient Apsarus on the Croatian island of Kres (Italian Cherso), which was published as containing parts of the Apostles' Creed by Piero Sticotti in 1914. It was re-edited by Anton Benvin in 1989 [446].

---

[445] *Fragmenta theologica Arriana, fragm. 10*; CCSL 87, 244, reproduced in Kinzig 1999a, 140. In some of the other fragments, we find portions that make use of the Creed in the way of a *regula fidei*. See especially *fragmentum 2 (Mai XVII)*: ... *ut per suam doctrinam et passionem et mortem crucis et tertia die resurrectionem et ascensionem in caelis cum carnem illuc unde sine carne descenderat et per donum baptismi omnem genus hominum in se integra fide credentium saluaret, quos etiam ecclesiam cognominauit* ... (CCSL 87, 232), *fragmentum 5 (Mai XV)*: *Per filium legem tradidit, filius spiritum sanctum dedit et dat semper sanctis, prophetas instruxit, templum suum quod sumpsit ex Maria uirgine et in cruce dimisit ipse filius suscitauit, mundum patri suo et sibi reconciliauit, pecccata dimisit et dimittit cottidie, omnes mortuos resuscitaturus et iudicaturus omnes uiuos et mortuos* ... *Vnum autem deum et patrem omnium sic dicimus et credimus, ut istum spiritum sanctum quem tertio loco a patre post filium in symbolo et in baptismo tradimus* ... (CCSL 87, 236-237), also *fragmenta 14, 17*, and *20 (Mai II, IV*, and *XIII*; CCSL 87, 250, 255, and 260-261). Compare Kattenbusch 1900, 753-754 and Burn 1905, lxxiv-lxxv.

[446] The inscription has been preserved in two fragments, which were discovered in the nineteenth and early twentieth centuries. The first part, still uniden-

In two fragments, parts of all articles except the first have been preserved, so that a fairly complete variant of the Creed can be reconstructed from it with some reliability.

As far as we can see, then, the form of the Creed of APS runs thus [447]:

> ...
> ... *domiNUM NOStrum (...?)*
> *qui (?) nATVS ESt ... SPIRITV SANCTO Et (Ex?) mariA*
>    *VIRGINe*
> *(...?) passuS SVB POntio pilATO Crucifixus ...* [448]
> *... A MORtuis (...?)*
> *asCENDIT In ...*
> *sEDET Ad dexteRAM PATris* [449]
> *INDE VENTurus (est?) DIIVDICARE* [450] *VIuos ...*

tified, was edited in 1880 (Benndorf 1880, 80) and re-edited in 1902 (CIL III Suppl. 1, 10144). Later, the two fragments were recognized as a source for the form of the Apostles' Creed by Piero Sticotti: see Sticotti 1914, 137 and Benvin 1989, 188-189. Sticotti (1914, 138-141) reproduced the two fragments, offered a reconstruction of the complete credal variant, and made a few remarks on its form, but his conclusions seem to have remained unnoticed by students of the Creed until 1989. In that year, Anton Benvin dedicated a fresh study to the two fragments, offering Sticotti's facsimile again, a reconstruction of his own, and a detailed study of the inscription: see Benvin 1989, 189-207 (this seems to be a translation or adaptation of an earlier study in Croatian: see Benvin 1989, 188n6). It should be observed that Benvin's reconstruction is coloured by the fact that he connects APS in particular with the anonymous *expositio symboli* that is ascribed to Peter Chrysologus by Olivar (CPL 229a; see above, chapter 3.5, footnote 307, and below, chapter 4.3) and with the *codex Laudianus* of R (see above, chapter 1.4, pp. 28-29). Benvin dates the inscription to the sixth century, but thinks that its credal variant goes back to the fifth: see Benvin 1989, 204-207. This position is taken over by Vinzent 1999, 191n679. Sticotti is even prepared to date the inscription to the fourth century: see Sticotti 1914, 140-141. Sticotti's reconstruction (*ibid.*, 138) is rather arbitrary.

[447] As in the case of TOL, the parts of words that have actually been preserved are printed in capitals.

[448] At this point, the first fragment of APS breaks off, so that nothing certain can be said about the possible presence of the Descent to Hell in its form of the Creed.

[449] The available space between *Pat/ris* and *Inde* ... excludes the possibility that *Omnipotentis* had a place in the inscription: see Benvin 1989, 200.

[450] This interpretation of the form *Diudicare* in the inscription, which is defended by Benvin (1989, 195n15) with a reference to the use of *Diiudicare* in

*CREDO IN SANCTUM SPIRITVM*
*ET SANCTAM ECclesiam CATHOLICAM*
*ReMISSIONEM PEccatoRVM*
*CAR...*

BAN   The so-called Antiphonary of Bangor (CPL 1938), an Irish
      liturgical manuscript that was written between 680 and
      691 [451].

This manuscript contains a form of the Apostles' Creed on ff.
19R-19V [452]. What immediately leaps to the eye when one studies
this variant is the extent to which it deviates from other forms of
the Apostles' Creed. All its students seem to agree that this variant
is a deliberate composition, although based on the Apostles' Creed,
rather than just a local form of the Creed with some peculiarities [453].
Reformulations like *Credo et in spiritum sanctum, deum omnipoten-*

certain Latin pre-Vulgate Bible manuscripts, seems to be more probable than
Sticotti's (1914, 139-140) interpretation as *AJd iudicare*, as the *D* seems to be
written as the first letter of the line (see the facsimile in Sticotti 1914, 138 and
Benvin 1989, 194). A third possibility is that *Diudicare* is just a vulgar spelling
for *Iudicare*: see Väänänen 1981, 52-53.

[451] On place and date of origin, see Warren 1893, viii-xii, Nerney 1952, 369-
372, and O'Callaghan 1992, 255-256.

[452] *Antiphonarium Benchorense* 35; Warren 1895, 21. The Creed is preceded by
the words *Incipit symbolum* and rounded off with *Haec omnia credo in deum.
Amen.* A facsimile with transcription is offered by Warren 1893. See for earlier
credal scholarship Hahn 1897, 83-85, Kattenbusch 1894, 184-186 (both still ignorant of Warren's 1893 edition), and Kelly 1976, 402-403. Warren (1895, 62-
63), Nerney (1952, 1953a, 1953b), and O'Callaghan (1992) discuss the credal variant of BAN in some detail as well; Nerney (1952, 372-373) and O'Callaghan
(1992, 259-260) adopt Warren's text. On the basis of antiheretical formulations
in the text and parallels with Gallican forms of the Creed, Nerney (1952, 375-385
and 1953b) contends that this variant was composed in Burgundy around 500,
but most of his arguments lose their value when one realizes that changing the
wording of a form of the Apostles' Creed is not the most suitable way of combatting heresies. On the other hand, heresies may influence the wording of orthodox
documents, even in places where they never gained any foothold at all, long
after they ceased to play a role. O'Callaghan (1992, 284) calls the form of the
Creed of BAN "one of the few original theological works of the early Irish
Church". But even if Nerney's position were true, the fact would remain that
only the liturgical use of this text in seventh-century Ireland is certain.

[453] See for example Kattenbusch 1894, 184-186, Warren 1895, 62, Hahn 1897,
85n22, Kattenbusch 1900, 747n34, Nerney 1952, 375-376 and 1953b, 393, and
O'Callaghan 1992, 258.

*tem, unam habentem substantiam cum patre et filio* and *Credo uitam post mortem et uitam aeternam in gloria Christi* probably pertain to the author's theological concerns, and need say nothing at all about a local Irish form of the Creed. Even details like the repetition of *Credo* in the second and ninth articles, the construction with *Qui* in the fourth and the unique *Exinde* instead of *Inde* in the eighth may be deliberate alterations that are intended to underline the twelve-fold structure of the Creed, as Kattenbusch points out [454]. Therefore, when discussing the features of the credal variant of the Antiphonary of Bangor, we shall have to be very careful if we want to explain a certain detail as local Irish usage.

What we find in BAN, then, is the following credal variant:

> *Credo in deum patrem omnipotentem, inuisibilem, omnium creaturarum uisibilium et inuisibilium conditorem*
> *credo et in Iesum Christum, filium eius unicum dominum nostrum, deum omnipotentem*
> *conceptum de spiritu sancto, natum de Maria uirgine*
> *passum sub Pontio Pilato, qui crucifixus et sepultus*
> *descendit ad inferos,*
> *tertia die resurrexit a mortuis*
> *ascendit in caelis*
> *sedetque ad dexteram dei patris omnipotentis*
> *exinde uenturus iudicare uiuos ac mortuos*
> *credo et [455] in spiritum sanctum, deum omnipotentem, unam habentem substantiam cum patre et filio [456]*
> *sanctam esse ecclesiam catholicam*
> *abremissa [457] peccatorum*
> *sanctorum communionem*
> *carnis resurrectionem*
> *credo uitam post mortem et uitam aeternam in gloria Christi.*

---

[454] Kattenbusch 1894, 184-186.

[455] Nerney 1952, 372 omits *Et*.

[456] Warren (1895, 62) thinks that the words *Et filio* should perhaps be deleted. Nerney 1952, 377n3 gives some good reasons why they should be retained, however.

[457] Warren (1895, 21) erroneously reads *Abremissam*.

DIM     Another manuscript of Celtic provenance, the so-called
        Book of Dimma, which stems from eighth-century Ire-
        land [458].

Here, a form of the Creed crops up in a *missa de infirmis*: *Diuino
magisterio edocti et diuina institutione formati audemus dicere: Credo
in deum patrem omnipotentem ... Credo me resurgere. Vngo te de oleo
sanctificato ...* [459]. Since this form of the Creed contains only articles
1, 2, 9, and 12, it seems certain that it is a deliberately abbreviated
formula. A question that cannot be resolved is whether the compos-
er also abbreviated these four articles. Similarly, the fivefold use of
*Credo* may or may not hark back to a local Irish form of the Creed.
We shall have to be very careful, therefore, if we want to use this
variant to draw conclusions about the form of the Creed in Ireland [460].

DIM, then, testifies to the following variant of the Creed.

*Credo in deum patrem omnipotentem (...?)*
*credo et in Iesum Christum filium eius (...?)*
...
...
*credo et in spiritum sanctum*
...
...
*credo uitam post mortem*
*credo me resurgere.*

---

[458] Dublin, Trinity College 59. For the date, see for example Lowe 1935, 44
and Colker 1991, 58-59. With the exception of O'Callaghan (1992, 285), this text
seems to have been overlooked by students of the Creed.

[459] Warren 1881, 169. This mass is a later addition to the manuscript.
Although its date of insertion is unknown, the fact that this mass represents local liturgical material seems undisputed (see for example Warren 1881, 167 and
xi-xii).

[460] Another Irish *missa de infirmis*, which is found in the so-called Book of
Mulling (Dublin, Trinity College, 60; eighth century), contains only the first
words of the Creed: *Credo in deum patrem.* See Warren 1881, 171-172.

3.7 Comparison and Analysis

Now that we have listed 38 complete or partial variants of the Apostles' Creed that testify to its form before the rise of *T* as a single standard, we shall investigate what they say about the formulation of the Creed in the regions of Gaul, Spain, Africa, Northern Italy, Rome, the Latin Balkans, and Ireland. In order to do so it will first be useful to compare the testimony of our 38 source texts for each single article. The additions of Descent to Hell, Communion of Saints, and Eternal Life will not be treated as parts of articles but will each receive a separate discussion. To present our data in as clear a way as possible, we shall list the different formulations for each region that are found in the relevant source texts, followed by the abbreviations of the relevant texts. Although this will involve many formulations being mentioned more than once, this procedure has the advantage that it can be seen at a glance which formulations are attested in which regions and since when. This again will help us to make a detailed article-by-article comparison of all variants of the Creed and to draw as precise a picture as possible of the history of the formulation of each article in the period from the third to the eighth century. When that has been done, we shall probably be in a position that allows us to say something about the possible existence of regional types of the Apostles' Creed.

### The first article

#### Gallican formulations

| | |
|---|---|
| *Credo in deum ...* | FAU, EUSh10 |
| *Credo in deum patrem omnipotentem* | SAL, CAE-B, CY-T, |
| | EUSh9 |
| *Credo in deum patrem omnipotentem, creatorem caeli et terrae* | |
| | CAE-A, CAE-C, PIRM, MGV, Bobbio A, Bobbio C |
| *Credo in deum patrem (...?)* | FAU-R |
| *Credo in deum ... omnipotentem (...?)* | Bobbio B |

#### Spanish formulations

| | |
|---|---|
| *Credo in deum patrem omnipotentem* | MART, MM, LO, ILD, EB |
| *Credo (in?) unum deum patrem omnipotentem* | PRIS |

African formulations

*Credo in deum patrem omnipotentem* QU

*Credo in deum patrem omnipotentem, uniuersorum creatorem, regem*
  *saeculorum, immortalem et inuisibilem* AU-H, FU

North Italian formulations

*Credo ...* AM

*Credo in deum patrem omnipotentem* AU-M, PC

*Credo in deum patrem omnipotentem, inuisibilem et impassibilem*
  RUF

Other formulations

*Credo in deum patrem omnipotentem* LEO, NIC

*Credo in deum patrem omnipotentem (...?)* DIM

*Credo in deum patrem omnipotentem, creatorem caeli et terrae*
  ARR

*Credo in deum patrem omnipotentem, inuisibilem, omnium creatu-*
  *rarum uisibilium et inuisibilium conditorem* BAN

It appears that the original wording of the first article, *Credo in deum patrem omnipotentem* (attested by *R* and almost certainly already present in proto-*R* as well), found its way to Gaul (SAL, CAE-B, CY-T, EUSh9; perhaps also FAU-R), Spain (MART, MM, LO, ILD, EB), Africa (QU), Northern Italy (AU-M, PC), the Balkans (NIC), and probably Ireland (DIM) too. Soon, however, additions start to appear. The first of these occurs in Spain, where PRIS inserts *Vnum* before *Patrem* between 380 and 390. Since all of the other Spanish witnesses to the wording of this article retain the formulation of proto-*R*, and *Vnus* is not found outside Spain either, this insertion looks like a deliberate addition to accentuate God's transcendence and indivisibility, something that would accord well with what we know of Priscillian's theology [461].

Next is Rufinus with the addition *Inuisibilem et impassibilem*. Rufinus states himself that these words were deliberately added by the Aquileian church to combat the heresy of Sabellianism [462]. The difference with the case of PRIS seems to be that this addition was

---

[461] See Chadwick 1976, 75-77 and 89 and Burrus 1995, 72-73. The wording of *N* (see below, footnote 472) may also have played a role here. Compare also above, chapter 2.3, footnote 43.

[462] See above, chapter 2.3, footnote 33.

certainly part of the Creed as it was used in its liturgical context of
*traditio* and *redditio symboli*. Not everyone was equally satisfied
with this procedure, however, as is proved by the testimony of
Ambrose [463]. It is perhaps for this reason that we do not find any
similar additions in the other three North Italian witnesses. Nevertheless, the need to mention God's invisibility does not seem to have
been limited to the church of Aquileia, as we find the predicates
*Vniuersorum creatorem, regem saeculorum, immortalem et inuisibilem*
added in AU-H. Since this addition was almost certainly already
present in the Hipponic form of the Creed as Augustine found it in
396 [464], and Rufinus explicitly refers to the Aquileian form of the
Creed with which he was baptized in around 370 [465], it seems logical
to surmise that the two churches each responded to the same theological need in their own way at some date in the fourth century.
At any rate, the church of Hippo was not the only place where the
addition *Vniuersorum ... inuisibilem* could be heard, since we meet
it again in the testimony of FU in the first half of the sixth century. It remained absent, however, in the metropolitan church of
Carthage, as Quodvultdeus, one of the last resident bishops of the
city, still shows the original wording in the first half of the fifth
century.

The difference between the additions of RUF on the one hand
and AU-H and FU on the other does not pertain to points of formulation, as the African insertion is not only concerned with God's
invisibility but also explicitly mentions God's creating activity with
the words *Vniuersorum creatorem*. Although this formulation is not

---

[463] See above, chapter 2.3, footnote 41, and in particular *explanatio symboli* 4:
*Patripassiani cum emersissent putauerunt etiam catholici in hac parte addendum:
Inuisibilem et impassibilem, quasi filius dei uisibilis et passibilis fuit! ... Ergo esto,
medici fuerint maiores nostri, uoluerint addere aegritudini sanitatem medicina. Non
quaeritur ergo si medicina non fuit eo tempore necessaria quo erat haereticorum quo-
rundam grauis aegritudo animarum. Et si fuit tunc temporis quaerenda, nunc non
est. Qua ratione? Fides integra aduersus Sabellianos, exclusi sunt Sabelliani, maxime de parte occidentis. Ex illo remedio Arriani inuenerunt sibi genus calumniae, et
quoniam symbolum Romanae ecclesiae nos tenemus, ideo inuisibilem et impassibilem
patrem omnipotentem illi aestimarent et dicerent: Vides quia symbolum sic habet? ut
uisibilem filium et passibilem designarent. Quid ergo? Vbi fides integra est sufficiunt
praecepta apostolorum, cautiones, licet sacerdotum, non requirantur* (CSEL, 73, 5-6).

[464] See above, chapter 3.4, footnote 210.

[465] See chapter 2.3, footnote 26.

found elsewhere, the same thought is expressed in Gaul (CAE-A, CAE-C, PIRM, MGV, Bobbio A, Bobbio C) and the Latin Balkans (ARR) by means of the addition *Creatorem caeli et terrae*. The Balkan churches seem to be earlier in the field in this respect, since the testimony of ARR can be dated to around 400, whereas the first Gallican witness to this wording, CAE-A, appears a hundred years later or more [466]. Since we have quite a number of earlier Gallican witnesses which still show the wording of proto-*R* here, it seems certain that the phrase *Creatorem caeli et terrae* was deliberately imported into Gaul from the East at some date [467].

Finally, we have the Irish addition *Inuisibilem, omnium creaturarum uisibilium et inuisibilium conditorem*. Although this comes close to the African insertion of *Vniuersorum ... inuisibilem* in content, its wording is quite different [468]. As far as we can determine, this may well be an originally Irish extension of the first article.

We can thus sum up the evidence as follows - the original formulation of the first article of the Creed can be found in all regions. In the course of the fourth century, however, the apparent need arose to say something more about God than just that he was Father Almighty. This led to different additions in Africa, Northern Italy, the Latin Balkans and, though perhaps only towards the end of the seventh century, Ireland. In the course of the fifth century or even later, Gallican churches adopted the Balkan addition. Apart from Priscillian's idiosyncratic insertion of *Vnum*, Spain kept clear of this tendency.

The second article

Gallican formulations

*Et in Iesum Christum, filium eius (...?)*                    SAL

---

[466] That is to say, if the credal variant of CAE-A goes back to Caesarius himself, and not to one of the compilers of the *Missale Gallicanum Vetus*. In the latter case, the phrase *Creatorem caeli et terrae* would only be attested for Gaul as late as the seventh century. It should be noted, however, that its absence in the fifth-century FAU-R is not certain.

[467] The formulation of the first article in the Nicaeno-Constantinopolitan Creed (Πιστεύω εἰς ἕνα θεὸν πατέρα παντοκράτορα, ποιητὴν οὐρανοῦ καὶ γῆς, ὁρατῶν τε καὶ ἀοράτων) may have contributed to this process. See for a fanciful historical account of such a borrowing Burn 1909, 4-5.

[468] Nerney (1952, 274-275) lays a link with the Nicene Creed; O'Callaghan (1992, 262-263) is more sceptical about this possibility.

*Et in filium eius (...?) Iesum Christum (...?)*                EUSh9
*Et in Iesum Christum, filium eius unicum dominum nostrum*
                                                        T, MGV
*Et in Iesum Christum, [filium eius] unicum dominum nostrum*
                                                        Bobbio B
*Credo et in filium dei Iesum Christum, unicum dominum nostrum*
                                                        FAU-R
*Credo et in filium eius Iesum Christum, dominum nostrum*   FAU
*Credo et in Iesum Christum, filium eius unigenitum sempiternum*
                                          CAE-A, CAE-B, CAE-C [469]
*Credo et in Iesum Christum, filium eius unigenitum, dominum nos-*
*trum*                                                   CY-T
*Credo et in filium eius unicum dominum nostrum Iesum Christum*
                                                        EUSh10
*Credo in filium eius Iesum Christum, dominum nostrum*
                                                        PS-AU [470]
*Credo in Iesum Christum, filium eius unigenitum sempiternum*
                                                        Bobbio A
*(Credo?) et in Iesum Christum, filium eius unicum dominum nos-*
*trum*                                                   Bobbio C

Spanish formulations

*Et in Iesum Christum, filium eius unicum dominum nostrum*   MM
*Et in Iesum Christum, filium eius unicum, deum et dominum nos-*
*trum*                                            MART, LO, EB
*(Credo?) et in Iesum Christum, filium dei unicum, deum et domi-*
*num nostrum*                                            ILD
*Et (in?) unum dominum Iesum Christum*                   PRIS

African formulations

*(Credo?) (et?) in filium eius Iesum Christum*           QU
*(Credo?) et in filium eius Iesum Christum, dominum nostrum*
                                                        AU-H
*Credo in Iesum Christum, filium eius unicum dominum nostrum*
                                                        FU

[469] The presence of *Et* in CAE-C is not certain.
[470] The expository part of MGV also testifies to a form of the second article that begins with *Credo in filium eius ...*

North Italian formulations

*Et in Christum Iesum, filium eius unicum dominum nostrum*     PC

*Et in Iesum Christum, filium eius unicum dominum nostrum*

AU-M

*Et in Iesum Christum, unicum filium eius, dominum nostrum*

RUF

*Et in ... filium eius unicum dominum nostrum*     AM

other formulations

*(Credo?) et in Christum Iesum, filium eius (...?)*     ARR

*Credo et in Iesum Christum, filium eius (...?)*     DIM

*Et in filium eius Iesum Christum, dominum nostrum*     NIC

*Et in Christum Iesum, filium eius unicum dominum nostrum*

LEO

*... Christum Iesum, filium eius unicum dominum nostrum*     ARN

*Credo et in Iesum Christum, filium eius unicum dominum nostrum,*
  *deum omnipotentem*     BAN

*... dominum nostrum ...*     APS

We have seen that proto-*R* probably had quite a short second article, something not too unlike *Et in Christum Iesum, filium eius* [471]. Two features of this formulation were soon obliterated by later developments - the word order *Christum Iesum* and the absence of any predicates but *Filium eius*. The word order *Christum Iesum*, still present in *R* and *H*, can for the rest only be found in LEO, ARN, PC, and ARR, which means that, outside Rome, it only gained a foothold in Northern Italy and the Latin Balkans. All other witnesses unanimously exhibit the word order *Iesum Christum*.

As far as the addition of predicates is concerned, our source texts are more divided. Formulations without any additions at all can still be seen in SAL, EUSh9, QU, ARR, and DIM. Although most of these witnesses do not necessarily give complete quotations here, their cumulative evidence seems to indicate that at least a number of regions knew a form of the Creed with a short second article like proto-*R* or *H*. This impression is reinforced by the fact that two of these four sources, SAL and ARR, give very early evidence for their regions, and that QU, though later than AU-H, nevertheless

---

[471] See above, chapters 1.15 and 1.16, pp. 63-64 and 68.

represents a more conservative state of affairs concerning the wording of the first article as well [472].

When we turn to the texts that do exhibit additions to the second article, we can distinguish the predicates *Vnicum* (or *Vnigenitum* [473]), *Sempiternum*, *Dominum nostrum*, *Deum et dominum nostrum*, and *Deum omnipotentem*. Of these, *Vnicum* and *Dominum nostrum* have received the most general acceptance. The latter is found in FAU-R, FAU, CY-T, PIRM, MGV, Bobbio B, MM, AU-H, FU, AM, AU-M, RUF, PC, LEO, ARN, NIC, APS, and BAN. It is substituted by the more elaborate *Deum et dominum nostrum* in MART, LO, ILD, and EB [474]. *Vnicum* is attested by FAU-R, EUSh10, PIRM, MGV, Bobbio B, Bobbio C, MART, MM, LO, ILD, EB, FU, AM, AU-M, RUF, PC, LEO, ARN, and BAN. In a number of witnesses *Vnigenitum* takes the place of *Vnicum* (CAE-A, CAE-B, CAE-C, CY-T, Bobbio A [475]). The addition *Sempiternum* only occurs in combination with *Vnigenitum* and can be found in CAE-A, CAE-B, CAE-C, and Bobbio A. Lastly, the addition *Deum omnipotentem* is found in BAN only. A detail is the use of *Dei* instead of *Eius* after *Filium*. This usage is found in FAU-R and ILD.

A special feature of the second article in its different forms is the fact that the order of its elements tends to vary rather freely. Designating the four main elements for the moment with the abbreviations IC (*Iesum Christum* or *Christum Iesum*), F (*Filium* ...), V (*Vnicum*, *Vnigenitum*, or *Vnigenitum sempiternum*), and D (*Dominum* ...), we can distinguish eight types:

IC + F  (SAL, ARR, DIM)

IC + F + V (CAE-A, CAE-B, CAE-C, Bobbio A)

IC + F + V + D (CY-T, PIRM, MGV, Bobbio C, MART, MM, LO, ILD, EB, FU, AM, AU-M, PC, LEO, ARN, BAN [476])

---

[472] Priscillian's curious *Et unum dominum Iesum Christum* again seems to be due to an idiosyncrasy. See Burrus 1995, 58 for Priscillian's stress on the unity of Christ and God. *N* has a similar formulation: Καὶ εἰς ἕνα κύριον Ἰησοῦν Χριστόν.

[473] I shall treat *Vnicum* as a separate predicate because it appears in different positions in different formulations of the second article.

[474] The same could also have happened in the form of the Creed of APS.

[475] Compare also the use of *unigenitum* in Bobbio B: see above, chapter 3.2, p. 140.

[476] Bobbio B may well belong to this group, too.

IC + V + F + D (RUF)
F + IC (EUSh9, QU)
F + IC + D (FAU, PS-AU, AU-H, NIC)
F + IC + V + D (FAU-R)
F + V + D + IC (EUSh10) [477].

Lastly, we can identify the use of *Credo* to introduce the second article. This repeated *Credo* can occur both with and without *Et*. The introduction with *Credo et* is found in FAU-R, FAU, CAE-A, CAE-B, CAE-C, CY-T, EUSh10, DIM, and BAN, the formulation with *Credo* only can be seen in PS-AU, Bobbio A, and FU, whereas the original introduction by means of *Et* is still yielded by SAL, EUSh9, PIRM, MGV, Bobbio B, PRIS, MART, MM, LO, EB, AM, AU-M, RUF, PC, LEO, and NIC [478].

All of these facts make it crystal clear that no part of the Creed has known so many different formulations as the second article. Nevertheless, certain patterns seem to be discernable in the mass of detail. First of all, it appears that some regions still knew the original short form of the second article (Gaul, Africa, the Latin Balkans, Ireland). It seems to be no accident that one of these, Gaul, exhibits the greatest number of different 'order types', no less than seven. The idea that *Vnicum* and *Dominum nostrum* were missing in their form of the Creed probably started to cause many Gallican churches a certain uneasiness, which led them to insert one or both of these additions at different points in the second article [479]. This, again, must have doubtless led to a good deal of uncertainty with respect to the exact word order in the article, which was probably reinforced by the fact that even before the various additions made their appearance in Gaul, different word orders could already be met with there, as is proved by SAL and EUSh9. The fact that the short form with the word order *Filium eius Iesum Christum* also occurs in Africa (QU) seems to prove that the word order of the second article already varied in Rome. A similar development as in Gaul may have taken place in Africa, where we meet three 'order types' in the same number of source texts [480].

---

[477] APS does not yield any information on this point.

[478] The testimony of Bobbio C, ILD, AU-H, QU, ARN, ARR, and APS is ambiguous on this point.

[479] Thus also Smulders 1970, 247n31.

[480] The Latin Balkans and Ireland offer too little material to make a comparison in this respect useful.

The second article seems to have reached the regions of Northern Italy and Spain in a more complete form. Spain stands out, however, because of its peculiar formulation *Deum et dominum nostrum.* In a similar way, Gaul is unique with its variants *Vnigenitum* and *Vnigenitum sempiternum* and Ireland with its addition of *Deum omnipotentem.* The word order *Iesum Christum*, which is practically universal in all regions, is for that reason probably also of Roman origin.

Finally, variations which seem to have risen independently in more than one region include the use of *Dei* instead of *Eius* (Gaul and Spain [481]). From there, it may have travelled to Ireland, where this variation is even general, though not too much weight should be attached to this observation in view of the scantity of our Irish material. The repetition of *Credo*, which is found in Gaul, Africa, and Ireland, may well also have been introduced independently in Gaul and Africa at an early date, though the possibility of mutual influence or common origin should not be excluded too soon. At any rate, it seems probable that the Irish churches inherited this feature from Gaul. It should be noted that it does not show itself in Spain, Northern Italy, or the Latin Balkans.

The third article

Gallican formulations

*Qui conceptus est de spiritu sancto, natus ex Maria uirgine*
                    FAU-R, EUSh10, PIRM, MGV, Bobbio B
*[Qui conceptus est de spiritu sancto,] natus ex Maria uirgine*
                                                    EUSh9
*Qui conceptus est de spiritu sancto, natus est de Maria uirgine*
                                                    CAE-A
*Qui conceptus de spiritu sancto, natus ex Maria uirgine*     CY-T,
                                                    PS-AU
*Conceptus de spiritu sancto, natus ex Maria uirgine*         FAU
*Conceptus de spiritu sancto, natus de Maria uirgine*         CAE-B,
                                                    CAE-C

---

[481] Although the possibility cannot be excluded that *H* or a related Roman form of the Creed played a role here.

| | |
|---|---|
| *Conceptum de spiritu sancto, natum ex Maria uirgine* | Bobbio A, Bobbio C [482] |

Spanish formulations

| | |
|---|---|
| *Qui natus est de spiritu sancto et Maria uirgine* | LO, ILD, EB |
| *Qui natus est de spiritu sancto ex Maria uirgine* | MART |
| *Natum ex Maria uirgine ex spiritu sancto* | PRIS [483] |
| *Natum de spiritu sancto ex utero Mariae uirginis* | MM |

African formulations

| | |
|---|---|
| *Qui natus est de spiritu sancto ex uirgine Maria* | FU |
| *Natum de spiritu sancto ex uirgine Maria* | QU |
| *Natum de spiritu sancto et uirgine Maria* | AU-H |

North Italian formulations

| | |
|---|---|
| *Qui natus est de spiritu sancto et Maria uirgine* | PC |
| *Qui natus est de spiritu sancto et uirgine Maria* | AU-M |
| *Qui natus est de spiritu sancto ex Maria uirgine* | RUF |
| *Qui natus ... spiritu sancto ex Maria uirgine* | AM |

other formulations

| | |
|---|---|
| *Qui natus est de spiritu sancto et Maria uirgine* | LEO, ARN |
| *(Qui?) natus est ... spiritu sancto et/ex Maria uirgine* | APS |
| *Natus ex spiritu sancto et ex Maria uirgine* | NIC [484] |
| *Conceptum de spiritu sancto, natum de Maria uirgine* | BAN |

Several variations can be found of the third article of the Creed. Most of these concern details of wording and grammatical construction. First of all, our witnesses vacillate between the use of *Et* (as in *R*) and *Ex* (as in *H*) before *Maria uirgine*. The formulation with *Et* can be found in LO, ILD, EB, AU-H, AU-M, PC, LEO, and ARN. *Ex* is offered by PRIS, MART, QU, FU, AM, and RUF. Less frequent variations are *Ex utero Mariae uirginis* (MM) and *Et ex Maria uirgine* (NIC) [485].

---

[482] Compare also chapter 3.2, footnotes 48 and 96 for two more possible Gallican quotations of this article.

[483] The grammatical construction of this article in Priscillian's form of the Creed is uncertain.

[484] The 'Austrian' recension of NIC has *Natum* instead of *Natus*.

[485] APS may offer either *Ex* or *Et*; AM does not yield any information on this point. For the Gallican witnesses, see below.

Similarly, the word order *Maria uirgine* may occasionally be replaced by *Virgine Maria* (AU-H, QU, FU, AU-M). Twice we find the expression *Ex spiritu sancto* (PRIS, NIC) instead of *De spiritu sancto* [486].

As far as the construction of the article is concerned, three possibilities can be distinguished - a relative clause with *Qui*, a participle construction in the nominative case, and a participle construction in the accusative case. The first of these is presented by FAU-R, CAE-A, CY-T, PS-AU, EUSh10, PIRM, MGV, Bobbio B, MART, LO, ILD, EB, FU, AM, AU-M, RUF, PC, LEO, and ARN. The second possibility is found in FAU, CAE-B, CAE-C, and NIC [487]. Finally, the third option can be seen in Bobbio A, Bobbio C, MM, AU-H, QU, and BAN [488].

Of a quite different nature is the insertion of a form of *Conceptus* to the effect that the third article is divided into two halves, one stating that Jesus Christ was begotten of the Holy Spirit and one that he was born of the Virgin Mary. This phenomenon can be observed in FAU-R, FAU, CAE-A, CAE-B, CAE-C, CY-T, PS-AU, EUSh9, EUSh10, PIRM, MGV, Bobbio A, Bobbio B, Bobbio C, and BAN. Of these, CAE-A, CAE-B, and CAE-C construct both *Conceptus* and *Natus* with *De*, whereas FAU-R, FAU, CY-T, PS-AU, EUSh9, EUSh10, PIRM, MGV, Bobbio A, Bobbio B, and Bobbio C use *De* with *Conceptus* (*Conceptum*) and *Ex* with *Natus* (*Natum*). Further variation is effected by the absence or presence of *Est* - FAU-R, CAE-A, EUSh10, PIRM, MGV, and Bobbio B exhibit *Est* only after *Conceptus*, CAE-A has it both after *Conceptus* and after *Natus*, whereas CY-T, PS-AU, FAU, CAE-B, and CAE-C omit it altogether.

The picture that emerges from all this is the following. On the one hand, we find an almost general uncertainty concerning the exact formulation of the end of the article. Already in Rome, we find both *Et Maria uirgine* (*R*) and *Ex Maria uirgine* (*H*). This variation was apparently inherited by the churches of Spain, Africa,

---

[486] Priscillian's unique way of mentioning the Holy Spirit only after the Virgin Mary perhaps again reflects a theological idiosyncrasy, as is assumed by Kelly: see Kelly 1976, 178.

[487] EUSh9 and APS may represent either of the first two possibilities.

[488] It is also read in PRIS, but may equally well represent one of the other constructions there.

and Northern Italy. Although this variation at first need not have had any theological implications, it may well be that these were connected with it over the course of time [489]. The use of *Ex* could at least suggest that Christ was not born of Mary in the same way as he was born of the Holy Spirit. Once such an idea had established itself, it would only be a matter of time before the use of *Et* would be taken to mean the opposite, viz. that Christ was born of the Holy Spirit and of his mother in exactly the same fashion. In this way, the fact that both *Et* and *Ex* can be found in one and the same region would soon be considered a theological problem.

That such a thing did indeed happen seems to be indicated by a number of formulations that may well have been coined to solve the ambiguity. On the one hand, we find the wording *Natus ex spiritu sancto et ex Maria uirgine* (NIC), which explicitly juxtaposes the role of Mary with that of the Holy Spirit. Equally explicit differentiations between them, however, are made by the Spanish formulation *Natum de spiritu sancto ex utero Mariae uirginis* (MM) and the Gallican use of *Conceptus*. Even Priscillian's unconventional formulation could be explained as a solution for the same problem. At any rate, the testimony of NIC places this problem firmly in the fourth century, a conclusion that is reinforced by the fact that each and every Gallican form of the Creed from the fifth century onwards exhibits the double formulation with *Conceptus* and *Natus*. The length of time of one century seems hardly long enough for such an explicit change to have acquired universal adoption in a region.

It should be noted that although the problem seems to have been present in most of our regions, each solution tends to remain restricted to one region only. Even the Gallican insertion of *Conceptus* which proved to be the most successful, is only found outside Gaul in Ireland, where it may well have been introduced together with the problem. Again, the word order *Virgine Maria*, apart from the testimony of AU-M, is not found outside Africa. It seems logical here to assume an influence of the Hipponic form of the Creed on Augustine's way of quoting the variant with which he was baptized.

---

[489] Compare Holland 1965, 274 and Smulders 1970, 244. See also above, chapter 2.3, footnote 34.

On the other hand, the variation in grammatical construction can be seen in Gaul, Spain, and Africa, where it may well have played a role from the start. Northern Italy, however, seems to stick to the use of the relative *Qui*.

The fourth article

Gallican formulations

| | |
|---|---|
| *[Crucifixus et sepultus]* | EUSh10 |
| *Passus sub Pontio Pilato, crucifixus et sepultus* | CY-T, PS-AU |
| *Passum sub Pontio Pilato, crucifixum et sepultum* | Bobbio C |

*Passus sub Pontio Pilato, crucifixus, mortuus et sepultus*

CAE-B, CAE-C, PIRM, MGV

*Passus est sub Pontio Pilato, crucifixus, mortuus et sepultus*

CAE-A

*Passum sub Pontio Pilato, crucifixum, mortuum et sepultum*

Bobbio A, Bobbio B

Spanish formulations

| | |
|---|---|
| *Passus sub Pontio Pilato, crucifixus et sepultus* | MART, MM, LO, EB |
| *Passum sub Pontio Pilato, crucifixum et sepultum* | PRIS [490] |
| *... sub Pontio Pilato crucifixus/crucifixum ...* | TOL |

African formulations

| | |
|---|---|
| *Crucifixum sub Pontio Pilato et sepultum* | AU-H, QU |
| *[Crucifixum quoque dicimus et sepultum]* | FU |

North Italian formulations

| | |
|---|---|
| *Qui sub Pontio Pilato crucifixus est et sepultus* | PC |
| *Sub Pontio Pilato crucifixus et sepultus* | AU-M |
| *Crucifixus sub Pontio Pilato et sepultus* | RUF |
| *Sub ... et sepultus* | AM |

other formulations

| | |
|---|---|
| *Passum sub Pontio Pilato, qui crucifixus et sepultus* | BAN |
| *(...?) passus sub Pontio Pilato, crucifixus ...* | APS |

---

[490] In the credal variant to which PRIS testifies, the grammatical construction of this article is again uncertain.

A more or less similar picture to that of the third article can be gained from the various forms of the fourth. On the one hand, we find four different grammatical constructions - a relative clause with *Qui* (PC), a clause with finite verb (CAE-A), a participle construction in the nominative (CAE-B, CAE-C, CY-T, PS-AU, PIRM, MGV, MART, MM, LO, EB, AU-M, RUF [491]), and a participle construction in the accusative (Bobbio A, Bobbio B, Bobbio C, AU-H, QU [492]). BAN stands out with its curious mixed form - *Passum sub Pontio Pilato, qui crucifixus et sepultus.* Similarly, we find the words *Sub Pontio Pilato* both before (the usual practice) and after *Crucifixus* (thus AU-H, QU, and RUF).

On the other hand, there are two possible additions to the contents of the article, the participles *Passus* and *Mortuus.* These occur together in CAE-A, CAE-B, CAE-C, PIRM, MGV, Bobbio A, and Bobbio B. *Passus* alone is added in CY-T, PS-AU, Bobbio C, PRIS, MART, MM, LO, EB, and BAN. Both additions are absent from AU-H, QU, AU-M, PC, and RUF [493].

It leaps to the eye at once that *Passus* is, as far as one can see, general in Spain and Gaul. Since this addition is only found in two other, rather later isolated witnesses, it seems logical to assume that it originated either in Spain or in Gaul in the fourth century (when it is already attested by PRIS). In Gaul, *Passus* seems to have triggered the insertion of *Mortuus* as well, perhaps out of a concern for completeness [494]. This second addition is first attested in CAE-B, which represents a form of the Creed that can be dated to the first half of the sixth century at the latest, and becomes almost general in later Gallican variants (Bobbio C is the exception). It apparently did not penetrate into other regions. The addition of *Passus* prob-

[491] AM lacks *Qui* and has its participles in the nominative case, but it is uncertain whether its form of the Creed did or did not contain a finite verb. APS might even represent any of the first three constructions.

[492] Again, the presence of the same construction in PRIS does not say much about Priscillian's form of the Creed. Nor can anything definite be said about the construction of the fourth article in EUSh10, TOL, and FU.

[493] Nothing can be said in this respect about EUSh10, TOL, FU, or AM. Whether the form of the Creed to which APS testifies contained both additions or only *Passus* cannot be ascertained.

[494] The wording of *H*, in which *Mortuus* seems to occur as a variant for *Sepultus*, probably has nothing to do with this process.

ably reached Ireland and the Latin Balkans either from Spain or from Gaul [495]. If Gaul was the intermediary for Ireland, the borrowing probably took place in the sixth century or earlier, since *Mortuus* is absent from BAN.

As far as the other variations are concerned, these may well go back to some original Roman uncertainty that is reflected by the difference between *R* (*Qui sub Pontio Pilato crucifixus est et sepultus*) and *H* (*Et crucifixus sub Pontio Pilato et mortuus est*). This time, even Northern Italy exhibits two different constructions as well as two different variants concerning word order. In Gaul and Spain, the early introduction of *Passus* (or *Passum*) seems to have fixed the word order of the article, though three different grammatical constructions can still be observed there. Our two African witnesses to the fourth article both show the same formulation. The typical construction that is found in BAN, finally, is probably best explained as a deliberate change that cuts the article in two in order to safeguard the total number of twelve articles [496].

The Descent to Hell

Gallican formulations

-- CAE-B, CAE-C, CY-T, PS-AU, MGV

*Descendit ad inferna,* CAE-A, PIRM, Bobbio A, Bobbio B, Bobbio C [497]

Spanish formulations

-- PRIS, MART, MM

*Descendit ad inferna*

LO, ILD, EB, TOL

---

[495] It is very unfortunate that we cannot know whether Nicetas did or did not read *Passus* in his form of the Creed. If he did, the addition could equally well stem from the Latin Balkans.

[496] See Kattenbusch 1894, 185. Nerney (1953a, 277) quotes the article with *Passus* in his commentary. O'Callaghan (1992, 267-268) thinks that the use of a participle in the accusative case (as in the third article) "does not refer only to a past action ... but to something which has supra-temporal (or divine) value." This interpretation is new to me, and seems hard to defend in view of the combination of *Passum* with *Sub Pontio Pilato*.

[497] The presence of the Descent to Hell in FAU, EUSh9, and EUSh10 can be neither proved nor disproved.

African formulations

--                                    AU-H, QU [498]

North Italian formulations

--                                    AM, AU-M, PC

*Descendit in inferna* RUF

other formulations

--                                    NIC

*Descendit ad inferos* BAN [499]

Three different formulations of the Descent to Hell are found - *Descendit ad inferna* (CAE-A, PIRM, Bobbio B, Bobbio C, LO, ILD, EB, TOL), *Descendit in inferna* (RUF), and *Descendit ad inferos* (BAN). The addition is absent from CAE-B, CAE-C, CY-T, PS-AU, MGV, PRIS, MART, MM, AU-H, QU, AM, AU-M, PC, and NIC.

This addition, which is already found in the late fourth-century form of the Creed about which Rufinus informs us, was apparently adopted from Northern Italy by a number of other churches, though in different formulations. It may well be that the Spanish churches adopted it from the Gallican ones or vice versa, since we find the same wording for the addition in both regions. It seems impossible to ascertain where the addition was first adopted, since all Spanish and Gallican occurrences are found in material that is rather difficult to date. It is unlikely, however, that it made a very early entrance in either Gaul or Spain, as our earliest witnesses for the wording of the Creed there (CY-T, CAE-B, PRIS, MART) all lack it. The Descent to Hell also found its way to Ireland, where it received a third formulation, but because of the scantity of Irish credal material nothing whatsoever can be said about the circumstances of this process.

It is to be observed that, as far as we can see, other regions of the Latin Church did not take over this addition, and that it did not even spread over the rest of Northern Italy.

---

[498] FU does not mention the Descent to Hell, but that does not prove its absence in Fulgentius's form of the Creed.

[499] The presence or absence of the Descent to Hell in APS is a matter of conjecture.

The fifth article

Gallican formulations

| | |
|---|---|
| *Tertia die resurrexit* | CAE-B, CAE-C, EUSh10 |
| *Tertia die resurrexit (...?)* | FAU |
| *Tertia die resurrexit a mortuis* | CAE-A, CY-T, MGV, Bobbio A,         Bobbio B, Bobbio C |
| *Tertia die surrexit a mortuis* | PIRM |

Spanish formulations

| | |
|---|---|
| *Tertia die resurrexit* | PRIS |
| *Tertia die resurrexit uiuus a mortuis* | MART, MM, LO, ILD, EB |
| *(...?) Resurrexit (surrexit?) uiuus ...* | TOL |

African formulations

| | |
|---|---|
| *Tertia die a mortuis resurrexit* | AU-H, QU |
| *[Die tertia resurrexit]* | FU |

North Italian formulations

| | |
|---|---|
| *Tertia die surrexit* | PC [500] |
| *Tertia die resurrexit* | RUF |
| *Tertia die resurrexit a mortuis* | AU-M |
| *Tertia die ... a mortuis* | AM |

other formulations

| | |
|---|---|
| *Tertia die resurrexit uiuus a mortuis* | NIC |
| *Tertia die resurrexit a mortuis* | BAN |
| *... a mortuis (...?)* | APS |

When we turn to the fifth article, it is possible to distinguish again between variations in wording and substantial additions. As far as the former are concerned, we seem to meet *Surrexit* (PIRM, PC) as well as *Resurrexit* (FAU, CAE-A, CAE-B, CAE-C, CY-T, EUSh10, MGV, Bobbio A, Bobbio B, Bobbio C, PRIS, MART, MM, LO, ILD, EB, AU-H, QU, AU-M, RUF, NIC, BAN [501]). On the other hand, the additions *A mortuis* and *Viuus* can be noted. *A mortuis* is present in CAE-A, CY-T, PIRM, MGV, Bobbio A,

---

[500] This reconstruction is not very certain.

[501] The exact form of the verb in TOL, AM, FU, and APS cannot be ascertained.

Bobbio B, Bobbio C, MART, MM, LO, ILD, EB, AU-H, QU, AM, AU-M, NIC, APS, and BAN, *Viuus* can be found in MART, MM, LO, ILD, EB, and TOL (as far as we can see, always in combination with *A mortuis*), whereas both additions are absent from CAE-B, CAE-C, EUSh10, PRIS, RUF, and PC[502]. It should be noted that *A mortuis* usually follows *Resurrexit*, but that the word order *Tertia die a mortuis resurrexit* occurs in AU-H and QU.

A distinctive feature of the wording of the fifth article in the Western church as compared with that of the second, third, and fourth articles is the fact that we only find variations of wording on a very limited scale. We only have the instance of *Surrexit* in one Gallican and possibly in one Spanish and one North Italian variant, and a deviating word order that occurs in Africa and only there. Apparently, the Roman variation of wording as reflected by *H* (*Et resurrexit tertia die uiuus a mortuis*; the use of *Et* and the word order *Resurrexit tertia die* are not found in any of the other witnesses) and *R* (*Tertia die resurrexit a mortuis*) had already given way to a more uniform formulation when the Creed began to spread over Europe.

The addition of phrases seems to be a more general phenomenon, however. First of all, there are the words *A mortuis*. Although these are already present in *R* as well as in *H*, their absence in four Gallican, one Spanish, and two Italian forms of the Creed makes the assumption that the fifth article reached these regions in the short form *Tertia die resurrexit* extremely plausible. Shortly afterwards, or even simultaneously, however, people must have become aware that a longer formulation with *A mortuis* added was in Roman use too, so that they started to add that phrase themselves as well. In Gaul, where we lack any certain fourth or fifth-century witnesses for the wording of this article, the longer formulation seems to become general in the seventh century, whereas both can still be met with in the sixth. In Spain, only the fourth-century witness PRIS lacks *A mortuis*, whereas it is probably present in all later texts. In Northern Italy both formulations can be seen from the fourth century onwards. Lastly, the African variation of word order might well be

---

[502] Nothing can be said about the possible presence of *A mortuis* in TOL. The same holds true for the presence of *Viuus* in AM and APS. In FAU and FU, neither addition is attested, although the possibility cannot be excluded that either or both figured in their credal formulations.

an indication that *A mortuis* was added there at a later date as well, rather than that these words were part of the African form of this article right from the start.

As far as the other Roman addition is concerned, *Viuus*, this had a more limited influence. It seems to have reached only Spain and the Latin Balkans. In Spain, it met with considerable success, just as *A mortuis* did. It is certainly possible that both additions found their way there together.

The sixth article

Gallican formulations

| | |
|---|---|
| *Ascendit in caelos* | CY-T |
| *Ascendit in caelis* | Bobbio B, Bobbio C |
| *Ascendit in caelum* | FAU |
| *Ascendit ad caelos* | CAE-A, CAE-B, EUSh9, EUSh10, PIRM, Bobbio A |
| *Ascendit ad caelum* | CAE-C |
| *Ascendit uictor ad caelos* | MGV |

Spanish formulations

| | |
|---|---|
| *Ascendit in caelos* | PRIS, MART, LO, EB |
| *Ascendit in caelum* | MM, ILD |
| *... caelos* | TOL |

African formulations

| | |
|---|---|
| *Ascendit in caelum* | AU-H |
| *Assumptus in caelos* | QU |
| *[Fatemur Christum ascendisse in caelum]* | |
| | FU |

North Italian formulations

| | |
|---|---|
| *Ascendit ...* | AM |
| *Ascendit in caelos* | RUF, PC |
| *Ascendit in caelum* | AU-M |

other formulations

| | |
|---|---|
| *Ascendit in caelos* | NIC [503] |
| *Ascendit in caelis* | BAN |
| *Ascendit in ...* | APS |

[503] The 'Austrian' recension of NIC reads *In caelum ascendit.*

A great variety of wording is offered by the sixth article. This is for the most part due to an apparent uncertainty concerning the number and case of *Caelum* and its accompanying preposition. To start with the latter, one can meet both *In* (FAU, CY-T, Bobbio B, Bobbio C, PRIS, MART, MM, LO, ILD, EB, AU-H, QU, AU-M, RUF, PC, NIC, APS, BAN) and *Ad* (CAE-A, CAE-B, CAE-C, EUSh9, EUSh10, PIRM, MGV, Bobbio A [504]). Similarly, the noun *Caelum* can be used in the singular (FAU, CAE-C, MM, ILD, AU-H, AU-M) as well as in the plural. In the latter case, we find either an accusative (CAE-A, CAE-B, CY-T, EUSh9, EUSh10, PIRM, Bobbio A, PRIS, MART, LO, EB, TOL, QU, RUF, PC, NIC) or an ablative (Bobbio B, Bobbio C, BAN [505]).

The only addition that we can find to the wording of this article is the word *Victor* after *Ascendit* in MGV. Further, QU replaces *Ascendit* with *Assumptus*. Neither change seems to have known a wide diffusion.

As far as we can see, the wavering between the ablative and accusative cases goes back to the period before the spread - *H* has *Caelis*, whereas *R* has *Caelos*. This uncertainty seems to have influenced the form of the Creed in Gaul, but not elsewhere. Only in Ireland do we find another case of the use of the ablative *Caelis*, which may well be due to Gallican influence. The confusion concerning case probably soon caused a similar confusion in number, as this has left its traces not only in Gaul, but in Spain, Africa, and Northern Italy as well, although in the latter case it again seems logical to assume some influence from the Hipponic form of the Creed on Augustine's way of quoting his baptismal Milanese variant. The use of the preposition *Ad*, finally, appears to have been limited to Gaul.

The seventh article

Gallican formulations

| | |
|---|---|
| *Sedet ad dexteram patris* | CY-T |
| *Sedet ad dexteram patris omnipotentis* | Bobbio B |
| *Sedet ad dexteram dei* | FAU |

---

[504] TOL and AM do not yield any information on this point.

[505] As far as the number and case of *Caelum* are concerned, AM and APS are silent.

*Sedet ad dexteram dei patris omnipotentis*     CAE-A, CAE-B, CAE-C,
               EUSh9, EUSh10, PIRM, MGV, Bobbio A, Bobbio C

Spanish formulations
*Sedet ad dexteram patris*                 MART
*Sedet ad dexteram dei patris omnipotentis*  PRIS, MM, LO,
                                           ILD, EB
*Sedet ad ...*                             TOL

African formulations
*Sedet ad dexteram patris*                 AU-H
*Ad dexteram patris sedet*                 QU

North Italian formulations
*Sedet ad dexteram patris*                 AM, AU-M, RUF, PC

other formulations
*Sedet ad dexteram patris*                 NIC [506], APS
*Sedetque ad dexteram dei patris omnipotentis* BAN

Not much variation in wording can be seen in the formulation of
the seventh article. QU stands apart with the word order *Ad dexteram patris sedet*, whereas all other witnesses have *Sedet* before *Ad
dexteram* (FAU, CAE-A, CAE-B, CAE-C, CY-T, EUSh9, EUSh10,
PIRM, MGV, Bobbio A, Bobbio B, Bobbio C, PRIS, MART, MM,
LO, ILD, EB, TOL, AU-H, NIC, APS, BAN). Further, BAN offers
the unique *Sedetque*.

What we do find, however, are two substantial and rather wide-
spread additions - *Dei* and *Omnipotentis*. *Dei* is inserted before
*Patris* in CAE-A, CAE-B, CAE-C, EUSh9, EUSh10, PIRM, MGV,
Bobbio A, Bobbio C, PRIS, MM, LO, ILD, EB, and BAN, *Omnipo-
tentis* is added after *Patris* by the same texts as well as by Bobbio
B. Finally, *Dei* has replaced *Patris* in FAU [507].

The conclusion seems to be justified that, although *H* testifies to
a Roman variation *Et sedet ad dexteram patris*, the seventh article
reached all regions in the wording of proto-*R* and *R* (*Sedet ad dexteram patris*), and was to remain relatively stable. A variation in
word order seems to be limited to Africa, whereas the additions of

[506] The 'Austrian' recension inserts *Dei* before *Patris*.
[507] Whether one or both of these additions were present in the form of the
Creed of TOL cannot be ascertained.

*Dei* and *Omnipotentis* remain confined to the regions Gaul, Spain, and Ireland [508]. The question arises, of course, of where these additions first saw the light. As long as we do not have more information about the wording of the Creed there, it seems best to assume that Ireland received the double addition either from Spain or from Gaul. The arguments for Gaul and Spain more or less balance each other, however. On the one hand, we meet both additions together as early as the fourth century in Spain (PRIS), whereas we have to wait for the sixth century to find a similar formulation in Gaul. On the other hand, Spain exhibits the two additions together in a fixed wording, but no less than three different formulations are found in Gaul: *Sedet ad dexteram dei*, *Sedet ad dexteram patris omnipotentis*, and the familiar *Sedet ad dexteram dei patris omnipotentis*. Perhaps the most plausible solution is to assume that both *Dei* and *Omnipotentis* originated in a number of Gallican churches at a very early date as two distinct additions, which led to a certain fluidity in the formulation of the article, so that they could occur together as well as alone and occasionally ousted *Patris*, and that they made their combined entrance in Spain soon afterwards, where their presence became universal but for MART [509]. The alternative, that *Dei ... omnipotentis* arose as a single addition in fourth-century Spain and that it was imported to Gaul, where it was suddenly shortened again in a number of different ways, is possible, but nevertheless seems a less likely explanation.

## The eighth article

### Gallican formulations

| | |
|---|---|
| *Inde uenturus iudicare uiuos et mortuos* | FAU, CAE-A, CAE-B, EUSh10, PIRM, MGV, Bobbio A, Bobbio B |
| *Inde uenturus iudicare uiuos ac mortuos* | CAE-C, Bobbio C |
| *Inde uenturus iudicaturus uiuos ac mortuos* | CY-T |

---

[508] The use of the particle *-que* in BAN is probably intended to tie the fifth, sixth, and seventh articles together: see Kattenbusch 1894, 185. O'Callaghan (1992, 274) considers its function "probably purely stylistic".

[509] Another possibility is that *Dei* started as a Gallican alternative for *Patris* but soon became a set addition to it, whereupon the formulation *Dei patris* was felt to be defective without *Omnipotentis* because of the wording of the first article of the Creed.

*Inde uenturus est iudicare uiuos et mortuos* EUSh9 [510]

Spanish formulations

*Inde uenturus iudicare uiuos et mortuos* MART, LO, ILD, EB
*Inde uenturus iudicaturus uiuos et mortuos* MM
*Inde uenturus et iudicaturus de uiuis et mortuis* PRIS [511]
*... iudicare ...* TOL

African formulations

*Inde uenturus est iudicare uiuos et mortuos* AU-H, QU [512]
*[Et inde uenturum iudicare uiuos et mortuos]* FU

North Italian formulations

*Vnde ... et mortuos* AM
*Inde uenturus iudicare uiuos et mortuos* RUF, PC
*Inde uenturus iudicaturus uiuos et mortuos* AU-M

other formulations

*Inde uenturus iudicare uiuos et mortuos* NIC [513]
*Inde uenturus (...?) diiudicare uiuos ...* APS
*Exinde uenturus iudicare uiuos ac mortuos* BAN

No substantial additions are found in the formulation of the eighth article. As far as variation of wording is concerned, we can point out the isolated use of *Vnde* in AM and *Exinde* in BAN, all other texts reading *Inde* (FAU, CAE-A, CAE-B, CAE-C, CY-T, EUSh9, EUSh10, PIRM, MGV, Bobbio A, Bobbio B, Bobbio C, PRIS, MART, MM, LO, ILD, EB, AU-H, QU, AU-M, RUF, PC, NIC, APS [514]). Then there is the (possible) presence of *Est* after *Venturus* in EUSh9, AU-H, and QU, but not in the other texts [515]. Again, *Iudicare* is substituted by *Iudicaturus* in CY-T, MM, and AU-M, and by *Diiudicare* in APS [516]. Then, PRIS changes the nor-

[510] The formulation of this article in EUSh9 is not entirely certain.
[511] The grammatical construction of the article is uncertain here.
[512] The presence of *Est* in QU is not certain.
[513] The 'Austrian' recension adds *Est* after *Venturus*.
[514] TOL does not yield any information concerning this point.
[515] PRIS, TOL, QU, AM, and APS do not allow any conclusions here.
[516] But compare chapter 3.6, footnote 450 above. AM is silent again; PRIS may represent a form of the Creed with *Iudicaturus*, but this cannot be ascertained.

mal construction with the accusative for one with *De*[517]. CAE-C, CY-T, Bobbio C and BAN, finally, replace *Et* with *Ac*[518].

It seems fairly certain that the eighth article reached most regions of the Western church in the form *Inde uenturus iudicare uiuos et mortuos*, a wording that takes a middle position between *R* (*Vnde uenturus est iudicare uiuos et mortuos*) and *H* (*Venturus iudicare uiuos et mortuos*). Only in Northern Italy do we find a possible trace of a formulation that betrays the influence of *R* with its use of *Vnde*. It seems too far-fetched to ascribe the presence of *Est* in EUSh9, AU-H, and QU to a similar cause; it is more probable that *Est* was added spontaneously in Gaul and Africa. The other variations that occur (*Exinde, Iudicaturus, Diiudicare, De, Ac*) also look rather like local changes, though *Ac* gained a certain popularity in Gaul and may have travelled from there to Ireland, and the use of *Iudicaturus* may have been more frequent in Spain, something which could also hold true for the use of *Est* in Africa.

The ninth article

Gallican formulations

| | |
|---|---|
| *Credo et in spiritum sanctum* | FAU-R |
| *Credo in spiritum sanctum* | FAU, CAE-C, EUSh10, PIRM, Bobbio B |
| *Credo in sanctum spiritum* | CAE-A, CAE-B, EUSh9, MGV, Bobbio A |
| *(Credo? Et?) in sanctum spiritum* | Bobbio C [519] |

Spanish formulations

| | |
|---|---|
| *Credo in spiritum sanctum* | MART, EB |
| *Credo in sanctum spiritum* | MM, LO, ILD |
| *... sanctum (...?)* | TOL |
| *Sanctum spiritum, baptismum salutare* | PRIS [520] |

---

[517] The witness of TOL leaves room for either possibility.

[518] On this point, TOL and APS are silent.

[519] Perhaps a Gallican wording *Credo et in sanctum spiritum* should be added to the extant formulations of the ninth article: see above, chapter 3.2, footnote 96.

[520] PRIS inverts the order of the ninth and tenth articles; Kattenbusch (1894, 157-158), however, doubts that this really reflects Priscillian's use of the Creed.

African formulations

| | |
|---|---|
| *Credo in spiritum sanctum* | QU, FU [521] |
| *(Credo?) (Et?) et in spiritum sanctum* | AU-H |

North Italian formulations

| | |
|---|---|
| *Et in spiritum sanctum* | AM, AU-M, RUF |
| *Credo in sanctum spiritum* | PC |

other formulations

| | |
|---|---|
| *Et in spiritum sanctum* | NIC |
| *Credo et in spiritum sanctum* | DIM |
| *Credo et in spiritum sanctum, deum omnipotentem, unam habentem substantiam cum patre et filio* | BAN |
| *Credo in sanctum spiritum* | APS |

As in the case of the eighth article, the ninth mainly presents variations in wording. The exceptions include the quite extensive formulation that is offered by BAN (*Credo et in spiritum sanctum, deum omnipotentem, unam habentem substantiam cum patre et filio*) and the addition of *Baptismum salutare* in PRIS. For the rest, there are only two variations - one concerning the construction of the article, and one concerning its word order. With regard to the latter, we find both *Spiritum sanctum* (FAU-R, FAU, CAE-C, EUSh10, PIRM, Bobbio B, MART, EB, AU-H, QU, FU, AM, AU-M, RUF, NIC, BAN, DIM) and *Sanctum spiritum* (CAE-A, CAE-B, EUSh9, MGV, Bobbio A, Bobbio C, MM, LO, ILD, PRIS, PC, APS [522]). Turning to the former, one can distinguish between formulations of the ninth article that start with *Et in* (AM, AU-M, RUF, NIC), *Credo et in* (FAU-R, BAN, DIM), and *Credo in* (FAU, CAE-A, CAE-B, CAE-C, EUSh9, EUSh10, PIRM, MGV, Bobbio A, Bobbio B, MART, MM, LO, ILD, EB, QU, FU, PC, APS [523]).

It seems obvious that the two unique additions that can be seen in PRIS and BAN were done for theological reasons. The extensive

---

[521] The reconstruction from FU is probable, but not certain.

[522] The testimony of TOL allows either possibility.

[523] Bobbio C, TOL, and AU-H do not yield any information on this point. Priscillian makes his form of the ninth article depend on *Credentes in*, which seems to rank him among the other Spanish witnesses.

formulation of BAN is probably as old or as young as the credal variant in which it occurs, which shows various traces of redaction. As far as Priscillian's *Baptismum salutare* is concerned, one might be tempted to consider it an old Spanish pendant to *Sanctorum communionem* [524], but this becomes less probable when one considers the comparatively late date at which that addition appears in other regions and the fact that no trace of such an addition is to be found in the other Spanish variants of the Creed except one (see below). Moreover, the importance of baptism seems to have loomed large in Priscillian's thought [525], so that his credal formulation may just as well be explained as a deliberate doctrinal adaptation of the text of the Creed.

When we turn to the theologically less significant variations, it leaps to the eye that in practically all regions *Credo* has replaced *Et*. This seems to indicate that such a change had already taken place when the Creed started to travel to Gaul, Spain, Africa, and Ireland [526]. Apart from Rome, only Northern Italy and the Latin Balkans still show traces of the (probably older) introduction by means of a simple *Et*. It is impossible to say whether these two regions received the formulation with *Credo in* from Rome or from one of the regions where this formulation had become general. Similarly, the fifth-century occurrence of *Credo* together with *Et* in Gaul (FAU-R) and Ireland (DIM, BAN) could be due to a wish to combine both Roman forms, though it is equally probable that we just have local developments here. It is worth noting that this formulation is, as far as we can see, general in Ireland.

As far as the use of the word order *Sanctum spiritum* is concerned, this is found fairly early in Spain (PRIS) and Northern Italy (PC), and later on in Gaul and the Latin Balkans as well. Most probably, this change took place independently in all these regions, though the possibility that it travelled from Spain to Gaul is certainly real.

---

[524] See below, footnote 535.

[525] See Burrus 1995, 74 and 193n61.

[526] Because of the interrogatory character of *H*, it cannot be ascertained whether this change had already influenced its declaratory form of the Creed or not, but the absence of *Et* at least suggests so.

The tenth article

Gallican formulations

| | |
|---|---|
| *Sanctam ecclesiam catholicam* | FAU, CAE-A, EUSh10, PIRM, MGV, Bobbio6 A, Bobbio B, Bobbio C |
| *Credo sanctam ecclesiam catholicam* | FAU-R, CAE-B, CAE-C, EUSh9 |

Spanish formulations

| | |
|---|---|
| *Sanctam ecclesiam catholicam* | MART, MM, LO, ILD, EB |
| *Credo in sanctam ecclesiam* | PRIS [527] |

African formulations

| | |
|---|---|
| *Per sanctam ecclesiam* | CY-C, AU-H, QU |
| *[Sancta ecclesia]* | FU [528] |

North Italian formulations

| | |
|---|---|
| *Sanctam ecclesiam* | AU-M, RUF, PC |
| *... ecclesiam (...?)* | AM |

other formulations

| | |
|---|---|
| *Sanctam ecclesiam catholicam* | NIC |
| *Et sanctam ecclesiam catholicam* | APS |
| *Sanctam esse ecclesiam catholicam* | BAN |

A great variety is offered by the tenth article, not only with regard to points of formulation and more substantial additions, but also with respect to its position. PRIS is unique in placing the tenth article before the ninth (*Credentes in sanctam ecclesiam, sanctum spiritum ...*), but no less than four texts witness to a form of the Creed in which the tenth article comes last of all: CY-C, AU-H, QU, and FU. Of these, CY-C, AU-H, and QU offer the formulation *Per sanctam ecclesiam*, which is not found elsewhere [529].

[527] Compare footnote 520 above for PRIS. Nothing certain can be said about the wording of this article in the form of the Creed of TOL.

[528] All four African witnesses place this article after Eternal Life at the end of the Creed. The use of *Per* in Quodvultdeus's variant is not entirely certain.

[529] The testimony of FU does not allow a reconstruction of the exact wording of the article.

When we turn to the texts which offer the tenth article in its more usual position, a number of peculiarities can be noted. First of all, there is the tendency to introduce the article with *Credo*. Apart from PRIS, where it has been caused by a transposition of the ninth and tenth articles, this phenomenon can be observed in FAU-R, CAE-B, CAE-C, and EUSh9. Similarly, BAN reads *Sanctam esse ecclesiam catholicam* and APS *Et sanctam ecclesiam catholicam*. The other witnesses just juxtapose the article (FAU, CAE-A, EUSh10, PIRM, MGV, Bobbio A, Bobbio B, Bobbio C, MART, MM, LO, ILD, EB, AU-M, RUF, PC, NIC [530]). A second important change is the addition of *Catholicam*. This can be observed in FAU-R, FAU, CAE-A, CAE-B, CAE-C, EUSh9, EUSh10, PIRM, MGV, Bobbio A, Bobbio B, Bobbio C, MART, MM, LO, ILD, EB, NIC, APS, and BAN. Only PRIS, AU-M, RUF, and PC have retained the more sober *Sanctam ecclesiam*.

Most if not all variations that have just been enumerated seem to be due to more or less theological reasons. The position of the article on the Church before that on the Holy Spirit in PRIS was probably caused by Priscillian's concern for the holiness of the Church [531], a change that did not gain much influence. This is different with the tendency to put the tenth article last, which we encounter in all African texts. It may well be that this variation was bound up with the use of *Per*, which indicates that the believer can receive Forgiveness of Sins, Resurrection of the Flesh, and Eternal Life through the Holy Church only. Since no traces of similar variations can be found in Rome or any of the other regions, the closing of the Creed by means of *Per sanctam ecclesiam* is probably a quite early African development that may well have affected all forms of the Creed there.

Next, the use of *Credo* (without *In*) to introduce the tenth article should probably be connected with the concern to distinguish the three divine persons from the Church, and probably from the Communion of Saints, Forgiveness of Sins, Resurrection of the Flesh, and Eternal Life as well [532]. The insertion of *Esse* in BAN can be

---

[530] Nothing can be said about the formulation of this article in AM.

[531] See Chadwick 1976, 71-74 and Burrus 1995, 14.

[532] See Oulton 1938; compare the quotation by Faustus of Riez in chapter 3.2, pp. 117-118.

explained in a similar way [533], and the use of *Et* (not *Et in!*) in APS might be due to the same concern [534]. Since this last variant is already present in *H*, it seems justified to conclude that the concern to indicate that belief in the three divine persons is different from belief in the Church and its gifts was directly inherited from Rome by the Gallican, Balkan, and possible also African churches. It cannot be ascertained whether Ireland became acquainted with it by way of Gaul or in a direct way. At any rate, all three or four regions developed their own way of expressing this theological concern - Gaul by means of *Credo*, the Balkans by means of *Et*, Ireland by means of *Esse*, and Africa possibly by coining the phrase *Per sanctam ecclesiam* and putting this last. It should be noted that the Gallican use of *Credo* is, as far as we can see, particularly popular in the earlier Gallican witnesses to this article, whereas all Gallican variants that stem more or less certainly from the seventh century lack it. The fact that this formulation did not succeed in conquering the whole region, and perhaps eventually fell in disuse again, clearly indicates that at least in Gaul the wording of *R*, which simply juxtaposes the three last articles with the ninth, must have played a role from the start as well. This wording seems to have completely conquered Spain and Northern Italy.

The addition of *Catholicam* presents a different picture. We meet it for the first time in fourth-century Illyria (NIC), whence it seems to have reached Gaul, Spain, and Ireland. The Gallican churches may well have played the role of intermediary in this process, though a direct influence from the Balkans on Spain or Ireland cannot be excluded. In Gaul, the use of *Catholicam* became universal, which suggests a rather early entry of that addition there. In Spain, the addition may still have been absent in the fourth century (PRIS), but it is present in all our later Spanish sources. This seems to suggest that *Catholicam* cannot have reached Spain very much later than Gaul. As far as we can see, it never gained a foothold in Africa or in Northern Italy.

---

[533] See Kattenbusch 1894, 186 and Oulton 1938, 241.

[534] Although this does not look like the primary cause of the African peculiarity of closing the Creed with the words *Per sanctam ecclesiam*, it should be noted that this construction answers the need to distinguish the Holy Church from the Holy Spirit equally well.

The Communion of Saints

Gallican formulations

| | |
|---|---|
| -- | Bobbio B |
| *Sanctorum communionem* | CAE-A, CAE-B, CAE-C, EUSh10, PIRM, MGV, Bobbio A, Bobbio C |
| *[Sanctorum communionem]* | FAU-R, FAU |

Spanish formulations

| | |
|---|---|
| -- | PRIS [535], MART, LO, ILD, EB |
| *Sanctorum communionem* | MM [536] |

African formulations

| | |
|---|---|
| -- | AU-H, QU [537] |

North Italian formulations

| | |
|---|---|
| -- | AM, AU-M, RUF, PC |

other formulations

| | |
|---|---|
| -- | NIC, APS |
| *Sanctorum communionem* | BAN [538] |

The addition *Sanctorum communionem* does not show any variations in wording in our source texts [539]. It is absent from Bobbio B, PRIS, MART, LO, ILD, EB, AU-H, QU, AM, AU-M, RUF, PC, NIC, and APS, but can be seen in FAU-R, FAU, CAE-A, CAE-B, CAE-C, EUSh10, PIRM, MGV, Bobbio A, Bobbio C, MM, and BAN.

Since this addition is already present in fifth-century Gaul, gains almost universal acceptance there, and is with the exception of two

[535] There is as yet no consensus about the original meaning of *Sanctorum communionem*. One of the possibilities is 'partaking in the holy things' (see Vokes 1978, 550-551). If this were somehow near the truth, it would be attractive to explain the addition *Baptismum salutare* in PRIS as having a similar meaning. But compare also pp. 246-247 above.

[536] Nothing certain can be said about the presence or absence of this addition in TOL.

[537] The presence of the Communion of Saints in Fulgentius's form of the Creed can be neither proved nor disproved from the text of FU.

[538] In BAN, the Communion of Saints appears as an addition to the eleventh article.

[539] Although no exact formulation can be gained from FAU-R and FAU.

rather late Spanish and Irish sources not found elsewhere, the conclusion seems justified that the phrase *Sanctorum communionem* is of Gallican origin.

The eleventh article

Gallican formulations

| | |
|---|---|
| -- | CAE-B, CAE-C |
| *Remissionem peccatorum* | CAE-A, PIRM, Bobbio A, Bobbio B, Bobbio C |
| *Abremissionem peccatorum* | MGV |
| *[Abremissio peccatorum]* | FAU |
| *Abremissa peccatorum* | EUSh10 |
| *[Abremissa peccatorum]* | FAU-R |

Spanish formulations

| | |
|---|---|
| *Remissionem peccatorum* | PRIS, ILD |
| *Remissionem omnium peccatorum* | MART, MM, LO, EB |

African formulations

| | |
|---|---|
| *Remissionem peccatorum* | CY-C [540], QU |
| *[Remissionem peccatorum]* | AU-H |
| *[Remissio peccatorum]* | FU |

North Italian formulations

| | |
|---|---|
| *Remissionem peccatorum* | AU-M, RUF, PC |
| *Remissionem [peccatorum]* | AM |

other formulations

| | |
|---|---|
| *Remissionem peccatorum* | NIC [541], APS |
| *Abremissa peccatorum* | BAN |

This article is entirely absent from CAE-B and CAE-C. Most other witnesses testify to the wording *Remissionem peccatorum* (CAE-A, PIRM, Bobbio A, Bobbio B, Bobbio C, PRIS, ILD, CY-C, QU, AU-M, RUF, PC, NIC, APS). Deviating formulations include *Abremissionem peccatorum* (MGV), *Abremissa peccatorum*

---

[540] The exact place of this article in the form of the Creed of CY-C is uncertain.

[541] This reconstruction from NIC is not certain.

(EUSh10, BAN), and the fuller *Remissionem omnium peccatorum* (MART, MM, LO, EB) [542].

We have seen that the eleventh article probably did not yet figure in proto-$R$, and that it was subsequently added by the redactor(s) of $R$ or one of its predeccesors [543]. Nevertheless, at least one early variant of the Creed that still lacked this article must have found its way abroad, as it is absent in two Gallican forms of the Creed, one of which is probably fairly early [544]. It is striking, moreover, that it is precisely in Gaul that we meet the greatest variety in the wording of this article. It seems probable that, more or less in the same way as in the case of the second article, Gallican churches became aware of the fact that their form of the Creed lacked an element between the article on the Holy Church and that on the Resurrection of the Flesh, and that they started to make up for this defect in different ways. Whether Ireland also once knew a form of the Creed without Remission of Sins cannot be ascertained [545], but the use of *Abremissa* in BAN at least seems to betray Gallican influence on its formulation of this article.

The addition of *Omnium*, which is rather popular among forms of the Creed from Spain, is probably an original Spanish contribution to the wording of the eleventh article. Since we do not yet find it in PRIS, and MM is also free from it, this insertion is probably not a very early one.

The twelfth article

Gallican formulations

| | |
|---|---|
| *Carnis resurrectionem* | FAU, CAE-A, CAE-B, CAE-C, EUSh10, PIRM, MGV, Bobbio A, Bobbio B, Bobbio C |

[542] FAU, FAU-R, AU-H, FU, and AM do not permit certain reconstructions of this article. It is nevertheless clear that the form of the Creed of AM used *Remissionem* and not *Abremissa* or some other term.

[543] See above, chapter 1.16, pp. 66 and 68.

[544] The fact that the exact position within the Creed of the Remission of Sins in CY-C seems uncertain, or at any rate not very important to the author, at least suggests the possibility that the phrase *Remissionem peccatorum* was imported to Africa after the introduction of the Creed there.

[545] The fact that BAN has the eleventh article between the article on the Church and the Communion of Saints could be taken to point in that direction. On the other hand, it can also be explained as a deliberate change to mirror the sequence of the sacraments of baptism (Remission) and eucharist (Communion).

*[Carnis resurrectionem]*      FAU-R

Spanish formulations

| | |
|---|---|
| *Carnis resurrectionem* | MART, ILD, EB |
| *Carnis huius resurrectionem* | MM, LO |
| *(...?) carnis resurrectionem* | TOL |
| *Resurrectionem carnis* | PRIS |

African formulations

| | |
|---|---|
| *Carnis resurrectionem* | QU |
| *[Carnis resurrectio]* | FU |
| *[Resurrectionem carnis]* | AU-H |

North Italian formulations

| | |
|---|---|
| *Carnis resurrectionem* | AU-M, PC |
| *[Carnis] resurrectionem* | AM |
| *Huius carnis resurrectionem* | RUF, CHRO |

other formulations

| | |
|---|---|
| *Carnis resurrectionem* | NIC [546], BAN |
| *Carnis ...* | APS |
| *Credo me resurgere* | DIM [547] |

Most sources yield the twelfth article in the form *Carnis resurrectionem* (FAU, CAE-A, CAE-B, CAE-C, EUSh10, PIRM, MGV, Bobbio A, Bobbio B, Bobbio C, MART, ILD, EB, QU, AU-M, PC, NIC, BAN). Only once do we find the inverse word order *Resurrectionem carnis* (PRIS) [548]. The only substantial addition is the word *Huius*, which is responsible for two more formulations: *Huius carnis resurrectionem* (RUF, CHRO) and *Carnis huius resurrectionem* (MM, LO) [549]. Finally, DIM offers an entirely different form of the twelfth article with the words *Credo me resurgere*, which is, moreover, put after the clause on Eternal Life.

[546] This reconstruction is uncertain again.

[547] DIM mentions the Resurrection of the Flesh only after Eternal Life.

[548] FAU-R, FU, and AU-H do not provide any information on this point. In AM, *Resurrectionem* is certainly the last word of the Creed, but we cannot know what preceded it. Similarly, APS makes clear that it started the twelfth article with *Carnis*, but that is where its information stops.

[549] FAU-R, FU, AU-H, and AM are silent on this point. TOL admits the presence of *Huius* before *Carnis*, but not after it, whereas the reverse holds true for APS.

The picture that emerges from the evidence is one of relative uniformity. The twelfth article probably reached all regions in the form
*Carnis resurrectionem*, which implies that the formulation of *H* (*Et
carnis resurrectionem*) had already ceased to exert any influence
when the process of dissemination began. The occasional inversion
of the word order in Spain is probably quite accidental. As far as
the addition of *Huius* is concerned, this may have travelled from
Northern Italy, where it must already have occurred in the fourth
century, to Spain. Nevertheless, the two Spanish cases of this addition exhibit a slightly different formulation. The unique wording of
the twelfth article that we find in DIM can partly be explained as
born of the wish to create a shortened form of the Creed with a
fivefold *Credo* [550], but may also have been chosen for the reason that
this short credal variant was to be used in a service for the visita-
tion of the sick. The same reason may apply to the fact that such a
confession of belief in a personal resurrection closes this particular
form of the Creed.

Eternal Life

Gallican formulations

| | |
|---|---|
| *Vitam aeternam* | FAU, CAE-A, CAE-B, EUSh10, PIRM, MGV, Bobbio A, Bobbio B |
| *[Vitam aeternam]* | FAU-R |
| *In uitam aeternam* | CAE-C |
| *Vitam habere post mortem, in gloriam Christi resurgere*    Bobbio C | |

Spanish formulations

| | |
|---|---|
| -- | PRIS |
| *Et uitam aeternam* | MART, MM, LO, ILD, EB |

African formulations

| | |
|---|---|
| *(...?) uitam aeternam* | CY-C [551], QU |
| *In uitam aeternam* | AU-H |
| *[Et uita aeterna]* | FU |

---

[550] Compare the formulation of Eternal Life in DIM, below.

[551] The exact place of this addition in the form of the Creed of CY-C is uncertain.

North Italian formulations

|                      | -- AM, AU-M, RUF |
|----------------------|------------------|
| *Vitam aeternam*     | PC               |
| *In uitam aeternam*  | CHRO             |
| other formulations   |                  |

| *Et uitam aeternam*      | NIC [552] |
|--------------------------|-----------|
| *Credo uitam post mortem* | DIM      |

*Credo uitam post mortem et uitam aeternam in gloria Christi*
BAN [553]

Finally, we come to Eternal Life, an addition to the last article of the Creed that is absent only in PRIS, AM, AU-M, and RUF. Its shortest formulation is just *Vitam aeternam*, which is found in FAU, CAE-A, CAE-B, EUSh10, PIRM, MGV, Bobbio A, Bobbio B, and PC. Slightly longer are the wordings *Et uitam aeternam* (MART, MM, LO, ILD, EB, NIC), *In uitam aeternam* (CAE-C, AU-H, CHRO), and *Credo uitam post mortem* (DIM). Quite elaborate variants are offered by Bobbio C (*Vitam habere post mortem, in gloriam Christi resurgere*) and BAN (*Credo uitam post mortem et uitam aeternam in gloria Christi*).

Since this addition is already present in a third-century text (CY-C), a late fourth-century one (NIC), and an early fifth-century one (CHRO), all from different regions, it is difficult to assess where and how it originated. As far as we can see, it is general in Gaul, Africa, and Ireland. Wherever it originated, it must have become almost obligatory in all these regions. Only Spain and Northern Italy seem to have resisted for a while, but this resistance probably did not outlast the fourth century.

The original wording of this addition was most probably the concise *Vitam aeternam*. The use of an introductory *Et* may have been invented independently in various regions, but it should be noted that its use became general in Spain. A similar use of *In* remained incidental in Gaul, Africa, and Northern Italy. Again, this was probably a variation that could occur more or less spontaneously in different regions.

---

[552] This reconstruction is not certain.

[553] The presence or absence of Eternal Life in APS is a matter of conjecture.

Things are otherwise with the formulations that are offered by Bobbio C, BAN, and DIM. The phrases *Vitam post mortem* and *In gloria(m) Christi* look like attempts to leave no doubt that Eternal Life was only to be enjoyed after death. They may well have travelled from Gaul to Ireland, though the opposite route should not be excluded. The formulation of BAN seems to aim at the greatest possible clarity by adding *Et uitam aeternam* again. Why the redactor(s) of the form of the Creed that we find in Bobbio C added *Resurgere* after *In gloriam Christi* is once more a more difficult question to answer. The use of *Credo* in DIM, finally, will doubtless have been chosen to attain a formula with a five-fold anaphora of that verb, but its presence in BAN at least suggests that the resulting formulation enjoyed a certain popularity in Ireland.

## 3.8 The Question of Regional Types of the Apostles' Creed

Now that we have compared a number of Western European witnesses to the wording of the Apostles' Creed and tried to reconstruct the history of the form of each separate article in some detail, it is time to present an overview of what we know of the development of the Creed in the various regions. This will probably enable us to assess whether one can indeed speak of regional credal types and, if so, what their characteristics are.

We are well aware that it is hardly possible to reconstruct in any convincing way the history of the formulation of the Creed in a certain region for the period between its arrival there and our first witness. Therefore, we shall start our discussion of each region with a reconstruction of a form of the Creed that can reasonably be considered the ancestor of each separate credal variant in that region. As a matter of fact, the aim is to reveal for each separate article which changes it already had or had not undergone before its arrival in a certain region. Here, there are four possibilities.

1) First of all, an article may have arrived in a certain region in the formulation of proto-*R*. This seems to be the case with the first article in Africa. The formulation of proto-*R*, without any additions, is still found in QU, so that we assume that, in Africa, changes in that article only came about after the arrival of the Creed there.

2) Next, an article (or part of it) may have arrived in a somewhat later Roman formulation. Thus, the word order *Iesum Christum*, which probably originated as a later Roman variant of the proto-*R* formulation *Christum Iesum*, is general in Gaul, so that we assume that the Creed arrived there in a form that had already substituted *Iesum Christum* for *Christum Iesum*.

3) Again, an article (or part of it) may have arrived more or less simultaneously in two different formulations. Thus, *H* and *R* show that in Rome already, the construction of the fourth article fluctuated between one with a participle in the nominative case and one with *Qui*. As both constructions also occur in Northern Italy, we assume that this uncertainty in the formulation of the Creed played a role there from the start.

4) Finally, substantial additions to the Creed that originated in Rome may have arrived in a certain region together with the Creed itself. A good example is the Forgiveness of Sins in Spain. It must have been added to the Creed in Rome between the birth of proto-*R* and the formulation of *R*. Since, however, all Spanish witnesses exhibit this element in the same place, we may assume that it could already be seen in the form of the Creed that was first brought to Spain.

After the presentation of such a reconstruction, it will be possible to say something more about the other variations and additions that were made in a certain region. Soon after the Creed first arrived somewhere, new changes will have begun to occur in its wording, as they had begun to occur in Rome before. One should be aware that this process was probably not an organized one in any sense of the word, but rather a local phenomenon that could occur quite spontaneously. One church could adopt some newer formulation from Rome while its neighbour refused to do so, and individual churches could make changes to the wording of the Creed of their own invention as well. What is important to bear in mind here, is the fundamental difference between innovations that were present in a certain region from the start and innovations that started to occur there later (either spontaneously or under influence from outside), as the first group is bound to leave its traces in all later forms of the Creed of that region, whereas innovations of the latter group may have exerted a more limited influence.

When describing the various changes that must have taken place after a region had received its first form of the Creed, we shall try to give the date of entrance and the provenance of each change as well. It should be remembered, however, that these are often completely hypothetical. It is nevertheless the closest we can get to a somewhat detailed history of the form of the Apostles' Creed before the use of the *textus receptus* became common practice.

Gaul

We can reconstitute the following parent formulation for all our Gallican witnesses.

*Credo in deum patrem omnipotentem*
*et in Iesum Christum, filium eius*
*qui natus est de spiritu sancto et/ex Maria uirgine*
*sub Pontio Pilato crucifixus et sepultus*
*tertia die resurrexit*
*ascendit in caelos/caelis*
*sedet ad dexteram patris*
*inde uenturus iudicare uiuos et mortuos*
*credo in spiritum sanctum*
*sanctam ecclesiam*
*carnis resurrectionem.*

Notes: the first article must have been directly inherited from proto-*R*; the second article probably arrived with the word order *Iesum Christum* but otherwise identical to its form in proto-*R*; in the third article, both *Et* and *Ex* seem to have played a role from the start; the fourth article probably had already lost *Qui* and *Est*; the fifth article arrived in its original form; the uncertainty concerning the use of *Caelos* or *Caelis* in the sixth article probably entered Gaul together with the article itself; the seventh article is identical with the form in proto-*R*; *Inde* had already been prefixed to the eighth article; *Credo* was already part of the ninth; the tenth and twelfth articles arrived in their original form.

We have seen that many of the formulations that we find in the Gallican witnesses to the wording of the Creed were probably taken over from Rome when a shorter Roman variant had already begun to spread in Gaul. Changes of this kind were probably among the first to occur on Gallican soil. Here, we can point to the additions of *Vnicum* and *Dominum nostrum*, which appear to have caused a great variety of word order in the second article. The occasional Gallican replacement of *Eius* with *Dei* may also be connected with these phenomena. Again, the phrase *A mortuis* and the complete eleventh article were probably inserted when members of the Gallican churches became aware that it figured in other Roman forms of the Creed than the one they had taken over first. When we date the spread of the Creed over the Western churches to the third century [554], all these changes would probably have taken place before the first third of the fourth century had elapsed.

Next, we encounter a number of innovations that were probably invented in Gaul itself. Of these, the introduction of *Conceptus* in the third article, the insertion of *Dei* and *Omnipotentis* in the seventh and the repetition of *Credo* in the tenth article may well go back to the middle of the fourth century or an earlier date. The use of *Conceptus* and of *Credo* (in the tenth article) were probably original Gallican answers to theological questions that were already connected with the Creed when it found its way to Gaul, whereas the additions of *Dei* and *Omnipotentis*, of which *Dei* is probably the older one, seem to have been introduced at such an early date that they could influence Priscillian's form of the Creed in the period between 380 and 390. These three (or four) changes, however, did not affect all subsequent Gallican variants.

In the same period, the spread of the (originally Roman) additions *Vnicum*, *Dominum nostrum*, and *Remissionem peccatorum* probably gave rise to formulations of the second article with *Vnigenitum* and *Sempiternum* and to formulations of the eleventh article with *Abremissa* and *Abremissionem* in the eleventh. Similarly, the use of *Conceptus* will have tended to influence the construction of the third and fourth articles as well as details of wording in the third only. Again, the use of *Credo* in the ninth article (or in the ninth and tenth articles) may have triggered the repetition of *Credo* in the second article as well.

Next, a number of additions were taken over from other regions. *Passus* was probably introduced from Spain, the additions of *Crea-*

---

[554] See above, chapter 1.16, p. 67.

*torem caeli et terrae*, of the Descent to Hell, and of *Catholicam* probably came from the Latin Balkans or Northern Italy, and that of Eternal Life may have come from Africa, the Balkans, or Northern Italy. *Mortuus* and *Sanctorum communionem* were coined as additions to the Creed in Gaul itself. All these additions probably hark back to the end of the fourth or the beginning of the fifth century, except *Creatorem caeli et terrae* and the Descent to Hell, which are not attested in Gaul before the sixth. It should be noted that not all these additions were equally successful - whereas *Passus*, *Catholicam*, and *Vitam aeternam* found their way into all extant Gallican forms of the Creed and *Sanctorum communionem* into all but one, *Creatorem caeli et terrae*, *Mortuus*, and *Descendit ad inferna* are only found in about half of our sources.

Some changes in details of wording crop up with only a limited range of influence, i.e. the insertion of *Credo* in the second article, the use of *Victor*, *Ad*, and the singular *Caelum* in the sixth article, the form *Iudicaturus* and the particle *Ac* in the eighth, the use of *Et* and the word order *Sanctum spiritum* in the ninth, and the formulations *In uitam aeternam* and *Credo uitam post mortem, in gloria Christi resurgere*. Apart from the last, which could also be due to Irish influence, these innovations were probably invented in Gallican churches in the fifth, sixth, and seventh centuries.

It can be observed, finally, that towards the end of this period the additions of *Creatorem caeli et terrae*, *Vnicum*, *Dominum nostrum*, *Mortuus*, *Descendit ad inferna*, *A mortuis*, and *Dei ... omnipotentis* are fairly general, whereas those of *Vnigenitum*, *Sempiternum*, and *Credo* (in the tenth article) seem to become less common.

Spain

For Spain, the following 'original' form of the Creed can be reconstituted.

*Credo in deum patrem omnipotentem*
*et in Iesum Christum, filium eius unicum dominum nostrum*
*qui natus est de spiritu sancto et/ex Maria uirgine*
*sub Pontio Pilato crucifixus et sepultus*
*tertia die resurrexit*
*ascendit in caelos*
*sedet ad dexteram patris*
*inde uenturus iudicare uiuos et mortuos*

*credo in spiritum sanctum*
*sanctam ecclesiam* [555]
*remissionem peccatorum*
*carnis resurrectionem.*

Notes: the first article is identical with the formulation of proto-*R*; the second represents a later Roman development; in the third, the Roman uncertainty concerning *Et* and *Ex* has been taken over; the fourth article agrees with proto-*R* or some later Roman variant; the fifth, sixth, and seventh articles agree with proto-*R*; the eighth and ninth represent a later Roman variant; the tenth article comes from proto-*R* again; the eleventh article is a Roman addition to the Creed; the twelfth agrees with proto-*R*.

As far as we can see, the form of the Creed in Spain is much more stable than in Gaul. Most articles are found in the wording that we have just reconstructed when they crop up in our source texts in the sixth and seventh centuries. This relative stability seems to be due to two reasons. On the one hand, Spain proved less open to credal additions than Gaul, as will emerge from our discussion below. But at least equally important seems to be the fact that the Creed reached Spain in a form that is decidedly more complete than the form that first reached Gaul - *Vnicum, Dominum nostrum,* and *Remissionem peccatorum* all seem to have been present from the beginning, so that no alternative versions of the second article or synonyms for *Remissionem* had a chance. Although this may well mean that the Creed arrived later in Spain than in Gaul, we know so little about the first spread of the Creed that it is safer to stick to a third-century date.

In the period that immediately followed the entrance of the Creed to Spain, the words *Dei, Viuus,* and *A mortuis* must have been introduced to the second and fifth articles respectively. They are found in only some of our witnesses, and therefore can only have been imported when more conservative variants of these arti-

---

[555] The testimony of PRIS is clear on the point of the absence of *Catholicam.* Its inversion of the ninth and tenth articles at least suggests that in Priscillian's original these two articles were juxtaposed, and that the ninth was introduced by means of *Credo in.*

cles had already received a place in a number of Spanish churches. Nevertheless, they still betray Roman influence on the form of the Creed in Spain.

When we turn to later innovations that were made in the Spanish churches, it appears that the addition of *Passus* to the fourth article must have been one of the very first, as it is already present in PRIS. It was not only an early addition, however, but also a successful one, since it can be seen in all our later sources for the form of the Creed in Spain. Although we cannot achieve any certainty on this point, *Passus* looks most like an original Spanish addition. The phrase *Deum et dominum nostrum*, which is found in all Spanish witnesses after Priscillian except one, is certainly Spanish. Although it is impossible to provide it with an exact date, its later popularity strongly suggests a fourth or early fifth-century origin. Similarly, the word order *Sanctum spiritum* in the ninth article is already attested in the fourth century and recurs regularly in our later sources. As far as borrowings from other regions are concerned, the addition of *Dei ... omnipotentis*, if it is not an original Spanish formulation, must have been taken over from Gaul before the eighties of the fourth century. The addition of *Et uitam aeternam* (possibly imported from Africa) cannot be much younger, though it is still absent from PRIS. The additions *Descendit ad inferna* and *Catholicam* (in the tenth article) are probably fifth-century borrowings, one from Northern Italy and one from the Balkans (possibly by way of Gaul). The insertion of *Huius* in the twelfth article, probably taken over from Northern Italy, and the addition of *Omnium* in the eleventh article, probably original, may both go back to the same period, though their modest diffusion suggests that they are slightly younger.

Finally, a number of innovations are found on such a limited scale that they are very probably rather late. This applies to the participle construction in the accusative and the use of *Ex utero* in the third article, the singular *Caelum* in the sixth, and the participle *Iudicaturus* in the eighth article. All these changes are probably due to sixth or seventh-century Spanish developments. In the same period, *Sanctorum communionem* will have been introduced from Gaul to a small number of Spanish churches. Two isolated fourth-century variants are the occurrence of *De* in the eighth article and the word order *Resurrectionem carnis*.

Africa

When we try to give a reconstruction of a first African form of
the Creed, we encounter the difficulty that for many of the articles
we possess only two witnesses. Our reconstruction must therefore be
considered even more hypothetical than the two preceding ones.
Nevertheless, the following form of the Creed may well resemble
the formulation that first came to Africa.

*Credo in deum patrem omnipotentem*
*et in filium eius Iesum Christum*
*(qui) natus/natum est de spiritu sancto et/ex Maria uirgine*
*(qui) crucifixus/crucifixum sub Pontio Pilato et sepultus/sepultum*
*tertia die resurrexit*
*ascendit in caelos*
*sedet ad dexteram patris*
*inde uenturus est iudicare uiuos et mortuos*
*credo in spiritum sanctum*
*sanctam ecclesiam*
*remissionem peccatorum* [556]
*carnis resurrectionem.*

Notes:  The formulation of the first article is according to proto-*R*;
the second article arrived in a slightly later Roman
variant; the third and fourth articles seem to have been
present in two or more rival formulations from the start;
the fifth and sixth articles agree with proto-*R* again; the
eighth article agrees with *R*; the ninth article shows yet
another Roman formulation; the final three articles probably arrived in the wording of proto-*R*.

When we examine the various changes that occurred in the formulation of the Creed after its arrival in Africa, we can point to at
least two third-century innovations - the addition of *Vitam aeternam*
and the conclusion of the Creed by means of *Per sanctam ecclesiam*.
Both are probably African inventions. A number of other changes
can be dated to approximately the same period because of their
obvious Roman provenance - the introduction of *Vnicum* and *Do-*

---

[556] Although there is a possibility that CY-C testifies to a stage when this article had only just been introduced.

*minum nostrum* as well as a rival word order in the second article and the addition of *A mortuis* to the fifth.

Next, we have a group of changes which are already testified to in the fourth century and seem to have gained a certain African popularity. This group comprises the extensive addition *Vniuersorum creatorem, regem saeculorum, immortalem et inuisibilem*, the word order *Virgine Maria*[557], the participle construction in the accusative case in the third and fourth articles, and the use of the singular *Caelum* in the sixth article. All these features are probably original African innovations again.

Finally, the introduction of the second article with *Credo in*, the use of *Assumptus* in the sixth article, and the word order *Ad dexteram patris sedet* probably originated later, and seem not to have gained much influence.

Northern Italy

Fortunately, our source material is a little more abundant in Northern Italy. When we try to elicit a first North Italian form of the Creed from it, the following reconstruction seems to be most likely.

*Credo in deum patrem omnipotentem*
*et in Christum Iesum/Iesum Christum, filium eius unicum dominum nostrum*
*qui natus est de spiritu sancto et/ex Maria uirgine*
*(qui) sub Pontio Pilato crucifixus (est) et sepultus/ crucifixus sub Pontio Pilato et sepultus*
*tertia die resurrexit*
*ascendit in caelos*
*sedet ad dexteram patris*
*unde/inde uenturus iudicare uiuos et mortuos*
*et in spiritum sanctum*
*sanctam ecclesiam*
*remissionem peccatorum*
*carnis resurrectionem.*

Notes: the first article agrees with proto-*R*; the second, third, and fourth articles probably arrived in two or more dif-

---

[557] Kattenbusch (1900, 455n38) already stamped this peculiarity as "anscheinend gemein afrikanisch".

ferent versions; the fifth, sixth, and seventh articles show the wording of proto-$R$ again; the eighth was present in two formulations from the start; the ninth and tenth articles agree with proto-$R$; the eleventh shows the wording of $R$; the twelfth article arrived in the wording of proto-$R$.

Shortly after the Creed had begun to spread over Northern Italy, the phrase *A mortuis* and the use of *Credo* instead of *Et* in the ninth article must have been imported from Rome. The fact that these two additions arrived when more conservative formulations had already established themselves in a number of churches, and the many cases of articles being introduced to Northern Italy in two or even three rival forms account for most of the North Italian credal variety. Not many phrases were newly coined or taken over from other regions, and none of the changes that took place met with general acceptance. The only addition that has probably been taken over from another region is that of Eternal Life (around 400). Other innovations seem to have originated in the region itself, mostly in the fourth century. We can point to the addition of *Inuisibilem et impassibilem*, the word order *Vnicum filium eius* [558], the addition of *Descendit in inferna*, the use of the verb *Surrexit* and of the participle *Iudicaturus*, the word order *Sanctum spiritum*, and the addition of *Huius* in this context [559].

Rome

Our only two witnesses for the form of the Creed in Rome after the fourth century both give the wording of $R$, though for the first three articles only. At any rate, this confirms the generally accepted thesis that $R$ remained in Roman use down to the sixth century [560].

[558] One could also envisage the possibility that in Northern Italy, as in Gaul, the second article first entered in the short form *Et in Christum Iesum filium eius*, and that the introduction of additions caused a certain confusion afterwards.

[559] The use of the word order *Virgine Maria* and the singular *Caelum* in AU-M may well be due to the influence of the Hipponic form of the Creed on Augustine's formulation of the variant with which he was baptized.

[560] See for example Kelly 1976, 427.

## The Latin Balkans

Although our source material for the form of the Creed becomes exceedingly scanty when we turn to the Latin Balkans, it nevertheless allows us to reconstitute a form of the Creed that cannot be too different from the variant that first arrived there.

*Credo in deum patrem omnipotentem*
*et in Christum Iesum, filium eius/filium eius Iesum Christum*
*qui (?) natus est ex (de?) spiritu sancto et/ex Maria uirgine*
*...*
*tertia die resurrexit uiuus a mortuis*
*ascendit in caelos*
*sedet ad dexteram patris*
*inde uenturus iudicare uiuos et mortuos*
*et in spiritum sanctum*
*sanctam ecclesiam*
*remissionem peccatorum*
*carnis resurrectionem.*

Notes: the first article arrived in its original wording; the second and third articles seem to have known at least two different formulations from the start; no information can be gained concerning the first Balkan wording of the fourth article; the fifth article may have arrived in a formulation that comes close to that of *H*; the sixth and seventh articles agree with proto-*R*; the eighth article arrived in a slightly younger Roman form; the ninth and tenth articles agree with proto-*R* again; the eleventh appeared according to the wording of *R*; the twelfth article shows its original formulation.

While the Creed was already finding its way to Latin churches all over the Balkans, the additions of *Vnicum* and *Dominum nostrum* in the second article and the use of *Credo* instead of *Et* in the ninth article were probably introduced. Additions that may go back to the same period, but certainly are not younger than the middle of the fourth century, are *Creatorem caeli et terrae*, *Catholicam*, and *Et uitam aeternam*. The first two are probably original Balkan inventions; the third may well have been imported from Africa. The use of *Ex ... et ex* in the third article probably belongs to the same period. Formulations with *Diiudicare* and *Sanctum spiritum* may be younger. The same seems to hold true for the addition of *Passus*. All these innovations are again probably original except *Passus*, which must be considered a Gallican or Spanish innovation as long as no additional source material is available.

Ireland

Finally, we come to the two Irish witnesses to the form of the Creed. Since these are both the, rather late, products of a great deal of stylistic and theological revision, it is extremely difficult to say anything about the original formulation of the Creed in Ireland. What strikes one as significant, however, is the similarity of BAN and DIM with each other on the one hand, and with the Gallican formulations of the Creed on the other. This at least suggests that Ireland received the Creed by way of Gaul. The following points of resemblance are worth mentioning - the use of the word order *Iesum Christum* and the addition of *Vnicum* and *Dominum nostrum* in the second article, the term *Conceptus* in the third (together with the use of a participle construction and the combination of *Natus* with *De*), the addition of *Passus* (though without *Mortuus*; it may therefore have come from Spain as well), the addition of the Descent to Hell, the addition of *A mortuis* to the fifth article, the use of the ablative *Caelis* in the sixth, the addition of *Dei ... omnipotentis* in the seventh article (again, Spanish influence cannot be excluded here), the use of *Ac* in the eighth article, the use of *Credo* in the ninth (also very common in Spain), the addition of *Catholicam* in the tenth (ditto), the addition of *Sanctorum communionem*, the use of the form *Abremissa* in the eleventh article, and the formulation *Vitam post mortem*.

In addition, a few details of wording that can hardly be explained as deliberate changes can be seen - the formulation *Descendit ad inferos* and the use of *Exinde* in the eighth article. Since both our Irish sources stem from the seventh century, it is impossible to say anything more precise about the development of the form of the Creed in Ireland.

One conclusion now seems crystal clear - between the third and the seventh centuries, the Apostles' Creed developed differently in Gaul, Spain, Africa, Northern Italy, and the Latin Balkans. The question is, of course, did these more or less separate developments lead to regional types of the Creed? The answer depends largely on our definition of such a concept. If one wants one concrete form of the Creed that is or tends to be general in a certain region, we shall have to respond in the negative. As far as we could ascertain, no regional development of the Creed has resulted in one form of the Creed to the exclusion of the others. In other words, until the spread of *T* as a uniform standard, we meet different credal variants in all regions.

Nevertheless, the hypotheses that were formulated at the end of the second chapter [561] are largely corroborated by the source material. It will be remembered that we expected changes in wording to remain limited to their regions of origin, whereas, in our opinion, changes in content would travel from one region to another much more easily. Our analysis and subsequent reconstruction has revealed that, to understand the development of the Creed in the several regions, it is essential to distinguish not only between changes in wording and of content, but also between changes that originated in Rome and those that first occurred elsewhere. It appears that changes of Roman origin, and in particular the changes in content, have left their traces in most if not all regions. This holds true for the additions of *Vnicum* and *Dominum* in the second article, the use of *Ex* in the third, the additions of *A mortuis* and *Viuus* to the fifth, and the entire eleventh article, all credal innovations of content that originated in Rome but found their way to all other regions. Similarly, the word order *Iesum Christum* in the second article, the construction of the third and fourth articles, the use of *Resurrexit* in the fifth, the use of *Inde* in the eighth, and the formulation with *Credo* in the ninth, all Roman changes in form, have left their traces in each region. Only the use of *Credo* in the second article (Gaul, Africa, Ireland) and that of *Dei* in the seventh (Gaul, Spain, Ireland) remain confined to three regions, whereas the use of *Caelis* in the sixth article appears to be limited to Gaul and Ireland.

When the changes of Roman origin have thus been subtracted, the remaining ones [562] clearly respond to our expectations. Of the changes in form, the formulation with *Natus (est) de Maria uirgine*

---

[561] See above, chapter 2.7, pp. 97-98.

[562] Here, we exclude those changes that are attested only once, as they logically also occur in one region only.

in the third article, the use of *Ad* in the in sixth article, the addition of *Omnipotentis* in the seventh, and the formulation with *Abremissam* in the eleventh all remain confined to Gaul. In the same way, the word order *Virgine Maria* in the third article, that is, if its occurrence in AU-M is indeed due to African influence, is confined to Africa. A spread over two adjacent regions can be observed for the use of *Ac* in the eighth article, *Credo et* in the ninth, and *Abremissa* in the eleventh (Gaul and Ireland) as well as the use of *Credo* in the tenth article (Gaul and Spain). Nevertheless, a number of regional changes in form have succeeded in gaining access to three regions or more - the singular *Caelum* in the sixth article (Gaul, Spain, Africa, and perhaps Italy as well), the formulation with *Iudicaturus* in the eighth (Gaul, Spain, Italy), the use of *Credo* in the ninth article (all regions), and the word order *Sanctum spiritum* in the same (Gaul, Spain, Italy, Latin Balkans).

When we turn to changes in content that originated in one of the regions, our surmise that these will know a wider diffusion is confirmed. First of all, we can point to the addition of *Passus* in the fourth article (Gaul, Spain, Latin Balkans, Ireland), the addition of *Catholicam* to the tenth article (Gaul, Spain, Latin Balkans, Ireland), and the Communion of Saints (Gaul, Spain, Ireland). Secondly, there are a number of changes in content that, rather surprisingly, tend to be accompanied by differences in wording that remain limited to one or two regions only. Thus, additions to the first article that profess God's sovereignty over heaven and earth are found in all regions except Spain, but whereas Gaul and the Latin Balkans have *Creatorem caeli et terrae*, Africa yields *Vniuersorum creatorem, regem saeculorum, immortalem et inuisibilem*, Italy *Inuisibilem et impassibilem*, and Ireland *Inuisibilem, omnium creaturarum uisibilium et inuisibilium conditorem*. Again, the addition of Eternal Life can be seen in all our regions, but Gaul and Ireland stand apart with the formulation *Vitam post mortem* ..., and Spain and the Balkans with *Et uitam aeternam*. Similarly, the Descent to Hell (Gaul, Spain, Italy, Ireland) exhibits a unique formulation with *In* (elsewhere *Ad*) in Italy, and the addition of *Huius* to the twelfth article causes two distinct formulations in Spain and Italy [563].

---

[563] Variations to Roman changes that remain limited to one or two regions seem to be best explained in the same light. Thus, in the second article, we find the Gallican *Vnigenitum* (*sempiternum*) as a variant for *Vnicum*, as well as a

Finally, only a few changes in content seem to have been confined to their regions of origin. Thus, the formulation *Per sanctam ecclesiam* is, at least as far as we can tell from our sources, exclusive to Africa, as are the use of *Conceptus* in the third article, the addition of *Mortuus* to the fourth, and that of *Victor* to the sixth for Gaul, as well as the addition of *Omnium* to the eleventh article for Spain.

Thus it seems safe to conclude that credal change indeed gave rise to regional variety, and that this was favoured by changes in both wording and content, though more so by the former than by the latter. Thus, of the changes in wording that, according to our analysis, originated in one of the regions of the Western Church, five remained confined to their region of birth, four spread to one adjacent region as well, and three gained access to three regions or more. Of the changes in content, on the other hand, three became fairly general in a uniform way, four spread over more than one region but at the same time gave birth to new regional peculiarities of wording, and five remained confined to their regions of origin. The exception to the rule that credal change favours regional diversity is constituted by changes that are of Roman origin. Of these, six changes in content and six in wording found a welcome in almost all our regions, two changes in wording were accepted in three regions, and only one change in wording remained confined to two regions only. Nevertheless, two Roman changes in content gave also rise to further regional peculiarities.

Now that it has been shown that each region of the Western church has its own history of the form of the Apostles' Creed, and, moreover, that credal change favoured further regional diversity, it is possible to present the features of the form of the Creed for each of our five main regions. This is, of course, particularly helpful with a view to the task of assigning a number of anonymous credal texts to some more definite date and place. To facilitate this task, it will be useful to distinguish between 1) formulations that can be found in all forms of the Creed of one region ('general features'), 2) formulations that occur in one region only, and not in any other ('unique features'), and 3) formulations that occur in some of the credal variants of a region but are not confined to that region ('other fea-

Spanish (*Deum et* ...) and an Irish addition (... *Deum omnipotentem*) to *Dominum nostrum.*

tures'). Of course, certain formulations may represent features of the first kind for one region and features of the third for another. When one tries to assign a form of the Creed of unknown origin to its region of provenance, features of all three kinds can be helpful. Features of the third kind indicate one or more possible regions, features of the second kind point to one region only, and features of the first kind are obligatory for a form of the Creed to belong to a certain region. When understood as the sum of a number of features of all three kinds, it is indeed possible to reconstruct five regional types of the Creed.

We shall thus conclude this chapter with the enumeration of a Gallican, Spanish, African, North Italian, and Balkan type of the Creed.

The Gallican type of the Creed
    general features
      unique features
        other features

1   *Credo in deum patrem omnipotentem*
      *Creatorem caeli et terrae*
2   word order *Iesum Christum*
      *Vnigenitum*
      *Sempiternum*
        *Filium eius/dei unicum*
        *Dominum nostrum*
        great variety of word order
3   use of *Conceptus*
        great variety of construction
4   use of *Passus*
      use of *Mortuus*
        variety of construction
4a      *Descendit ad inferna*
5   *Tertia die resurrexit*
      *A mortuis*
6   *Ascendit*
      *Victor*
      *Ad caelos/caelum*
        *In caelos/caelis/caelum*
7   *Sedet ad dexteram*

    *Dei*
    *Patris omnipotentis*
      *Patris*
      *Dei patris omnipotentis*

8   *Inde uenturus*
    *Iudicaturus uiuos ac mortuos*
      *Est*
      *Iudicare uiuos et mortuos*
      *Iudicare uiuos ac mortuos*

9   *Credo*
      *Et in spiritum sanctum*
      *In spiritum sanctum*
      *In sanctum spiritum*

10    *Credo*
  *Sanctam ecclesiam catholicam*

10a     *Sanctorum communionem*

11    --
    *Remissionem peccatorum*
    Abremissa peccatorum
    *Abremissionem peccatorum*

12  *Carnis resurrectionem*

12a Eternal Life
    *Vitam habere post mortem, in gloria Christi resurgere*
    *Vitam aeternam*
    *In uitam aeternam.*

The Spanish type of the Creed
  general features
    unique features
      other features

1   *Credo in deum patrem omnipotentem*
2   *Et in Iesum Christum, filium eius unicum*
    *Deum et dominum nostrum*
     *Dominum nostrum*
3   *Ex utero Mariae uirginis*
    variety of construction
4   *Passus sub Pontio Pilato, crucifixus et sepultus*
4a    *Descendit ad inferna*

5    *Tertia die resurrexit*
          *Viuus*
          *A mortuis*
6    *Ascendit in*
          *Caelos/Caelum*
7    *Sedet ad dexteram*
          *Patris*
          *Dei Patris omnipotentis*
8    *Inde uenturus*
          *Et iudicaturus de uiuis et mortuis*
          *Iudicare uiuos et mortuos*
          *Iudicaturus uiuos et mortuos*
9    *Credo in*
          *Spiritum sanctum*
          *Sanctum spiritum*
          *Baptismum salutare*
10    *Credo in*
      *Sanctam ecclesiam*
          *Catholicam*
10a       *Sanctorum communionem*
11    *Remissionem omnium peccatorum*
          *Remissionem peccatorum*
12    *Carnis huius resurrectionem*
          *Carnis resurrectionem*
          *Resurrectionem carnis*
12a       --
          *Et uitam aeternam.*

The African type of the Creed

    general features
        unique features
            other features

1    *Credo in deum patrem omnipotentem*
          *Vniuersorum creatorem, regem saeculorum, immortalem et*
          *inuisibilem*
2    word order *Iesum Christum*
          *Filium eius unicum*
          *Dominum nostrum*

variety of word order
3     word order *Virgine Maria*
      variety of construction
4     *Crucifixum sub Pontio Pilato et sepultum*
4a    --
5     *Tertia die a mortuis resurrexit* (also 'unique')
6     *Assumptus in caelos*
      *Ascendit in caelum*
7     *Ad dexteram patris sedet*
      *Sedet ad dexteram patris*
8     *Inde uenturus est iudicare uiuos et mortuos*
9     *Credo in spiritum sanctum*
10    *Per sanctam ecclesiam* (at the end of the Creed; also 'unique')
10a   --
11    *Remissionem peccatorum*
12    *Carnis resurrectionem*
12a   *In uitam aeternam.*

The North Italian type of the Creed

general features
      unique features
           other features

1     *Credo in deum patrem omnipotentem*
      *Inuisibilem et impassibilem*
2     *Et in ...*
      *Vnicum*
      *Dominum nostrum*
           variety of word order
3     *Qui natus est de spiritu sancto et/ex Maria uirgine*
4     *Qui*
           variety of construction
4a    *Descendit in inferna*
5     *Tertia die*
      *Surrexit*
         *Resurrexit*
         *A mortuis*
6     *Ascendit in*
           *Caelos/Caelum*
7     *Sedet ad dexteram patris*

8   *Vnde*
          *Inde*
          *Venturus iudicare uiuos et mortuos*
          *Venturus iudicaturus uiuos et mortuos*
9          *Et in spiritum sanctum*
          *Credo in sanctum spiritum*
10  *Sanctam ecclesiam*
10a --
11  *Remissionem peccatorum*
12      *Huius carnis resurrectionem*
          *Carnis resurrectionem*
12a        --
          *Vitam aeternam*
          *In uitam aeternam.*

The Balkan type of the Creed
     general features
          unique features
          other features

1   *Credo in deum patrem omnipotentem*
          *Creatorem caeli et terrae*
2          *Dominum nostrum*
          variety of word order
3   construction with the nominative case
4   *Passus sub Pontio Pilato, crucifixus ...*
4a  --
5   *Tertia die resurrexit uiuus a mortuis*
6   *Ascendit in caelos*
7   *Sedet ad dexteram patris*
8      *Diiudicare*
          *Inde uenturus iudicare uiuos et mortuos*
9          *Et in spiritum sanctum*
          *Credo in sanctum spiritum*
10      *Et*
     *Sanctam ecclesiam catholicam*
10a --
11  *Remissionem peccatorum*
12  *Carnis resurrectionem*
12a      *Et uitam aeternam.*

CHAPTER FOUR

Anonymous Witnesses to the Form of the Creed

4.1 Introduction

In the present chapter, we shall test whether our regional typology can help to assign anonymous texts that contain a form of the Creed to a certain region and period. Several anonymous witnesses to the form of the Creed have survived, and it will be a good idea to set out again some criteria to make the total amount of source material as uniform as possible.

First of all, we shall not attempt to date isolated forms of the Creed but only those forms of the Creed that are embedded in some way or another in a longer text. There are two reasons for excluding the isolated forms of the Creed. The first is that there is as yet no overview of these isolated variants, which often occur at the end of manuscripts or at some other place where some space was available[1]. These isolated witnesses certainly deserve a separate study but this would exceed the limits of this book. A second reason, of a different nature, is that the non-isolated forms have the advantage that the texts in which they occur have often already been subject to a certain amount of discussion about their provenance,

---

[1] Those cases where a later scribe has replaced the original form of the Creed in a work with another one, presumably his own, also come under this heading as these variants lack their **proper** context. Examples include the Sankt Gallen and Lambach manuscripts of Ambrose's *explanatio symboli* (see above, chapter 3.2, footnote 48, chapter 3.6, footnote 413, and CSEL 73, 17*), the anonymous adaptation of Fulgentius of Ruspe's *fragmentum 36 contra Fabianum* (see above, chapter 3.4, footnote 198), the Wrocław and Munich manuscripts of Augustine's *sermo 213* (see above, chapter 3.5, footnote 325 and Morin 1917, V), the variant of the Creed in the introductory part of CAE-C (see above, chapter 3.2, p. 127), and the fourth credal variant of the Bobbio Missal (see above, chapter 3.2, footnote 141). In fact, this last credal variant is not completely isolated, as a short commentary ensues: *Haec est quod a duodecinario numero apostolorum cum magna cautela collecta est et credentibus assignatum, quia fides † sanctarum deo ad homenibus nominibus † nomen est, fides diuini muneris portio est, fides deo hominem sociat, fides praesentia et futura coniungit, fides etiam quae inuisibilia sunt facit uidere, fides post sepulcrum cineris caelum atque regna caelorum promittit. Ideoque qui in tali confessione permanserit [ad] superuenientem iram timere non potest* (*Missale Bobiense*, 591; Lowe 1920, 181).

so that we are in a position to compare our conclusions with the findings of earlier credal scholars.

In the second place, as in the case of the texts that have been discussed in the previous chapter [2], a critical edition of the source text is necessary to obtain reliable information concerning the formulation of a credal variant. Since many anonymous *expositiones symboli* do not yet meet this criterion, we have chosen to offer a new edition of these in the appendix when possible, but to leave aside those texts for which such a procedure proved to be impracticable. Thus, according to the latest edition of the *Clauis Patrum Latinorum*, pseudo-Maximus of Turin's *homilia 83 de symbolo* (CPL 220) belongs to a distinct collection, the author of which has conveniently been baptized 'Maximus II'. Here, an edition of only one sermon out of a collection of some 80 would not be very useful [3]. For a more or less similar reason, the pseudo-Augustinian *sermo 243 de symbolo* (CPL 368) has been left out of account as well [4]. Although an edition of this sermon would in itself be feasible, the

---

[2] See chapter 3.1, p. 101.

[3] See Dekkers 1995, 77na and 78 and Frede 1995, 628-629. For earlier credal scholarship on the pseudo-Maximian *homilia 83* (CPL 220), see above, chapter 3.5, footnote 303. Unfortunately, the important work of G. Sobrero on two other pseudonymous sources for the form of the Creed (pseudo-Maximus, *tractatus de baptismo 2* [CPL 222] and pseudo-Augustine, *sermo 238* [CPL 368]: see above, chapter 3.5, *ibidem*) came to my notice too late to discuss them in this study. The same holds true for the anonymous *ordo scrutiniorum* CPL 2003. This liturgical text contains a variant of the Creed that is first quoted in full and then phrase by phrase as part of an expository sermon: *Signate uos, competentes, et audite symbolum. Credo in deum patrem omnipotentem ... Credo in deum patrem omnipotentem. Si de dei magnitudine, si de potestate turbatus es ... Remissionem peccatorum, carnis resurrectionem, uitam aeternam. Haec si decreueritis dum transmissa per aures intus cordis uestri secreta purificant, peccatorum remissione gaudebitis. Haec non litteris committendum est, sed in tabulis carnalibus insitum pro animarum tutela gestandum. Est enim talis medicina sacramenti quam et retinere debetis et reddere. Per dominum ...* (Lambot 1931, 25-27). For a study of the credal variant see Morin 1927, 67-74 and Lambot 1931, 25n10 and 26n4. Compare also Morin 1934b and Frede 1995, 168.

[4] This sermon contains literal quotations of the complete Creed except for the first article: *Et in Iesum Christum, filium eius unicum dominum nostrum. Nisi enim eundem ... Carnis resurrectionem, et uitam aeternam. Quod in Christi gloriosa resurrectione audisti completum ...* (pseudo-Augustine, *sermo 243* 2-4; PL 39, 2193-2194). See for earlier scholarship on this sermon Kattenbusch 1894, 191-193, Hahn 1897, 51-52n86, and Kattenbusch 1900, 462+n45, 777n29a-b, and 982.

circumstance that it has, at least traditionally, often been connected with the pseudo-Augustinian *sermones 240-242* [5] made me decide to leave it aside for the time being. All four sermons badly need a critical edition, and that would be beyond the scope of the present study. Further, the pseudo-Ambrosian work *de trinitate* or *tractatus in symbolum apostolorum* (CPL 171) is awaiting its critical edition by Martien Parmentier, and doubling his work only for the purpose of rendering our study more complete seemed hardly appropriate [6]. Finally, as is probably inevitable when writing studies like the present one, we encountered a number of new credal texts at too late a stage of the work to be able to include them without considerable loss of time [7].

The texts that remain are the following:
- a pseudo-Ambrosian *exhortatio de symbolo ad neophytos* (CPL 178)
- an anonymous *expositio symboli*, usually ascribed to Peter Chrysologus (CPL 229a)
- a pseudo-Augustinian *sermo super symbolum* (CPL 365)
- an anonymous *expositio de fide catholica* (CPL 505)
- a pseudo-Fulgentian *sermo de symbolo* (CPL 846)
- two pseudo-Chrysostomic *sermones de symbolo* (CPL 915)

---

[5] See above, chapter 3.2, footnote 45.

[6] This text contains a number of credal quotations and some other points of interest as well: see pseudo-Ambrose *de trinitate* 12 (*Ipse est qui nobis Christi domini natiuitatem, mirabilia, persecutionem, passionem, crucem, mortem, sepulturam, resurrectionem, in caelis ascensionem, et ad iudicum uenturum ante plurimos praenuntiauit annos ... sed ista mirabilis et singularis natiuitas qua Christus genitus est et [est,] de spiritu sancto et Maria uirgine facta est, sicut fides sancti symboli testatur ... De sancto ergo spiritu et Maria uirgine secundum carnem eum natum fatemur ... Qui filius dei pro nostra salute sub Pontio Pilato crucifixus est ac sepultus*; PL 17, 552-553 [523-524]) and in particular 14-15 (*Ecce Pilati iudicis facio mentionem ... sed quid sequatur accipito: Tertia die resurrexit a mortuis, ascendit in caelis [caelos], sedet ad dexteram patris, inde uenturus est iudicare uiuos et mortuos, id est ... uerum quoniam in fine dogmatis nostri carnis nostrae ponitur resurrectio eadem a nobis sunt firmius propter haereticos ac saepius repetenda*; PL 17, 555-557 [527-528]). Despite the attention of earlier credal scholarship (see Kattenbusch 1894, 98-100, Hahn 1897, 37-38n40, and Kattenbusch 1900, 423n93), more recent authors seem to have lost interest in this work: see Dekkers 1995, 54 and Frede 1995, 116.

[7] See below, p. 480, footnote 2.

- a pseudo-Augustinian *excarpsum de fide catholica*, usually ascribed to Caesarius of Arles (CPL 368, 244; CPL 1008, 10)
- a pseudo-Athanasian *enarratio in symbolum apostolorum* (CPL 1744a)
- an anonymous *tractatus symboli* (CPL 1751)
- an anonymous *symbolum apostolorum* (CPL 1758)
- an anonymous *sermo de symbolo* (CPL 1759)
- an anonymous *expositio super symbolum* (CPL 1760)
- an anonymous *expositio symboli* (CPL 1761)
- an anonymous *de fide trinitatis quomodo exponitur* (CPL 1762)
- an anonymous *expositio fidei* (CPL 1763)
- a newly discovered anonymous *expositio symboli* (no CPL number)

The following paragraphs will discuss these sixteen witnesses one by one. We shall first try to reconstruct a variant of the Apostles' Creed from each. Next, we shall give a short overview of what has been said by earlier scholars about the possible provenance of a text. Each paragraph will close with an attempt to make the reconstructed credal variant fit our regional typology of the Creed. Thus, it will become clear whether or not our typology is helpful for the task of determining the date and place of origin of anonymous source texts of the Apostles' Creed.

## 4.2 The Pseudo-Ambrosian *exhortatio de symbolo ad neophytos* CPL 178

This text, like so many others, was discovered and first edited by Caspari[8]. His edition provides the text as well as a considerable amount of commentary. Caspari edited it again after discovering a new manuscript of the text[9]. This new text was reprinted in the Supplement Series to Migne's *Patrologia Latina*[10]. Since more manuscripts of this text have come to light since Caspari's second edition, a new edition of this text will be offered in the appendix to this study.

It is not difficult to extract a form of the Creed from the text as the Creed is quoted in full after a short introduction: *Credimus ita-*

---

[8] Caspari 1869, 128-182.
[9] Caspari 1879, 186-195.
[10] PLS 1, 606-611 and 1749.

*que in deum patrem omnipotentem ... carnis resurrectionem. Huius symboli forma ...* [11] It seems obvious that the words *Credimus itaque* have been chosen to introduce the Creed and that the 'normal' declaratory form of this variant started *Credo in ...* [12].

For the rest, the quotation is quite clear. Articles five to eight are quoted again towards the end of the text: *Sepultus tertia die resurrexit a mortuis et cum resurrexisset ...* and *... quo crucifixus fuerat et sepultus. Ascendit in caelos, sedet ad dexteram dei patris, inde uenturus iudicare uiuos et mortuos. Hunc ordinem ...* [13]. The only difference with the complete quotation of the Creed at the beginning of the *exhortatio* consists in the absence of *Est* in the eighth article. This means that the author is either quoting loosely the second time, or that the text has been slightly corrupted in either the first or the second quotation. The first solution seems more natural, but the second cannot be dismissed out of hand, so that it is best not to take the presence of *Est* in the eighth article for absolutely certain.

Finally, we can point to a number of places where we meet loose or embedded quotations. Clear examples of the first are *Credimus itaque et in Iesum Christum filium dei omnipotentem aequalem deo ...* and *Credite ergo et confitemini deum patrem omnipotentem et filium coomnipotentem, coopificem ...* [14]. A more difficult instance is found towards the end of the *exhortatio*: *De humano corpore uestimentum carnis assumpsit, iuxta symboli ordinem crucifixum sub Pontio Pilato, per illud tempus Iudaeae prouinciae legato ...* [15]. Although the words *crucifixum sub Pontio Pilato* at first sight look like a literal quotation because of the phrase *iuxta symboli ordinem*, it is possible to take them as an apposition to *uestimentum carnis*. The second interpretation is supported by the fact that the words *sub Pontio Pilato* are directly connected with the rest of the sentence by means of an apposition as well. At any rate, it is not necessary to take *crucifixum sub Pontio Pilato* as a literal credal quotation here, so that there is no difficulty in the fact that it does not exactly agree with

[11] *Exhortatio de symbolo ad neophytos* 3-4; see below, p. 415.

[12] Compare the cases of AU-H and FU: see above, chapter 3.4, footnote 217 and p. 179.

[13] *Exhortatio de symbolo ad neophytos* 25-26; see below, p. 419.

[14] *Exhortatio de symbolo ad neophytos* 12 and 14; see below, p. 417.

[15] *Exhortatio de symbolo ad neophytos* 24; see below, p. 419.

the complete quotation at the beginning of the text, which gives the third article as *Qui sub Pontio Pilato crucifixus et sepultus* [16].

Our *exhortatio de symbolo ad neophytos* can thus be taken to witness to the following form of the Creed.

> *Credo in deum patrem omnipotentem, saeculorum omnium et crea-*
>     *turarum regem et conditorem*
> *et in Iesum Christum, filium eius unicum dominum nostrum*
> *qui natus est de spiritu sancto et ex Maria uirgine*
> *qui sub Pontio Pilato crucifixus et sepultus*
> *tertia die resurrexit a mortuis*
> *ascendit in caelos*
> *sedet ad dexteram dei patris*
> *inde uenturus est (?) iudicare uiuos et mortuos*
> *et in spiritum sanctum*
> *et sanctam ecclesiam catholicam*
> *remissionem peccatorum*
> *carnis resurrectionem.*

There has been considerable discussion about the origin of the pseudo-Ambrosian *exhortatio*, though scholars seem to have lost interest in this text after the Great War. A consensus has not yet been reached, and the question can still be considered as open as when Caspari first edited the text in 1869. It will therefore be a good idea to provide an overview of the various arguments that have been brought into the field before we try to assign the *exhortatio* to a certain region and period on the basis of its form of the Creed.

Caspari gives a learned and detailed commentary in his first edition. He discusses genre and composition, date and place of provenance as well as the possible authorship of the *exhortatio*. As far as its date of composition is concerned, Caspari gives various arguments for dating the text fairly early. Data to establish the *terminus ante quem* are (1) the conversion of the Langobards, the last Arian force in the Roman Empire, in 675, whereas the *exhortatio* is vehemently anti-Arian, (2) the general use of the Vulgate in 600, whereas this text makes use of an older Latin translation, and,

---

[16] Caspari (1869, 174-176n150) offers an extensive discussion of these isolated quotations; his conclusions are essentially the same as ours.

especially, (3) the beginning of the debate about the status of the Holy Spirit in around 370, something which our *exhortatio* seems to be completely unaware of [17]. More general indications for an early date, according to Caspari, are the fact that the *exhortatio* does not borrow, like many later sermons for the same occasion, phrases from sermons by Ambrose, Augustine, or Peter Chrysologus, the "Kürze und Gedrängtheit" which give it an "alterthümliches Gepräge", and the fact that no 'free sermons', that is, sermons that were first preached and then written down, as Caspari thinks is the case with the *exhortatio*, for the occasion of the *traditio symboli* are found after 550 [18]. In addition, there is the close relationship between the credal variant in our *exhortatio* and forms of the Creed which are found in the fourth and fifth centuries [19]. All this brings Caspari to the conclusion that the sermon was probably written between 340 (when Arianism first became a threat [20]) and 370 (the outbreak of the Pneumatomachic struggle) [21]. He does not credit the *disciplina arcani*, which in his opinion would forbid any writing down of the creed before 450, with sufficient weight to make a later date necessary [22].

The closeness of the credal form in the *exhortatio* to fourth and fifth-century Italian forms of the Creed leads Caspari to the conclusion that our text was probably written in Italy [23]. After discussing and excluding a number of possible authors, Caspari tentatively proposes Lucifer of Cagliari because of his vehement style and his predilection for adjectives composed with *con-*. He admits immediately, however, that these arguments are far from conclusive [24].

In his monograph on Lucifer of Cagliari, Krüger indeed devotes some ten pages to the *exhortatio de symbolo* but, for reasons of style, he does not follow Caspari's suggestion [25]. Instead, Krüger proposes Eusebius of Vercelli as the possible author. His arguments are the

---

[17] Caspari 1869, 156-159; 162-167.
[18] Caspari 1869, 152-154. Compare Kattenbusch 1900, 453.
[19] Caspari 1869, 154-156.
[20] Caspari 1869, 151-152.
[21] Caspari 1869, 168.
[22] Caspari 1869, 168-169.
[23] Caspari 1869, 171-174.
[24] Caspari 1869, 177-182.
[25] Krüger 1886, 118-122.

following: (1) the form of the Creed might be that of Vercelli, (2) there are some similarities between our *exhortatio* and two sermons by Maximus of Turin that were written in honour of Eusebius, and (3) what we know about Eusebius's theology and character does not contradict the identification [26].

The next person to say something about the authorship of the *exhortatio* was Morin. In a short but influential article he mentions a previously unknown manuscript of our text from Reims, which (among other things) contains seven additional pieces: an anonymous work *regulae definitionum* (CPL 560; nowadays usually ascribed to Syagrius) and the pseudo-Augustinian *sermones 113, 232*, and *236-239* (CPL 368). On the basis of a description by Gennadius of the works of Syagrius as a treatise *de fide* and *septem de fide et regulis fidei libri praetitulati*, he identifies the eight pieces in the Reims manuscript with Syagrius's work as Gennadius knew it. As Gennadius already had his doubts about the genuineness of all the *septem libri*, Morin does not go so far as to claim Syagrius directly as the author of our *exhortatio* [27].

In the first volume of his monograph on the Apostles' Creed, Kattenbusch discusses the credal variant of the *exhortatio de symbolo ad neophytos* among the "unbestimmbare Symbole". He agrees with Caspari that the text must hark back to the middle of the fourth century, but he rejects the identification of the author with Lucifer of Cagliari on the grounds that were brought forward by Krüger [28]. He considers Krüger's guess equally unsatisfactory, however, as no positive indications for Eusebius's authorship can be found [29]. Kattenbusch is nevertheless convinced that one of the authors we know from the relevant period must be the one he is looking for, and proposes Gregory of Elvira - his theological character fits the text, and an *elegans liber de fide* is ascribed to him by Jerome. Other possible authors are ruled out by the style of their known works or by their form of the Creed [30]. Nevertheless, in the

---

[26] Krüger 1886, 118-129.

[27] Morin 1893, 392-394. Curiously, Hamman, when reprinting the text of the *exhortatio*, understood Morin to be denying Syagrius's authorship (see PLS 1, 600).

[28] Kattenbusch 1894, 202-204.

[29] Kattenbusch 1894, 204-205.

[30] Kattenbusch 1894, 205-207.

"Nachträge" to his volume Kattenbusch deems the identification of the eight theological treatises to which Morin called attention with the works ascribed to Syagrius in Gennadius's time probable [31].

The third edition of Hahn's *Bibliothek der Symbole* gives the text of the form of the Creed that is offered by our *exhortatio* in § 45. Hahn situates this creed in Africa because of the addition *Saeculorum omnium et creaturarum regem et conditorem* in the first article [32].

In the second volume of his monograph, Kattenbusch frequently returns to the pseudo-Ambrosian *exhortatio*. Among other observations, he mentions a number of similarities with Ambrose's *explanatio* [33] and reflects on the possibility that the Creed was later inserted into the text of the *exhortatio* [34]. Nevertheless, after considering Morin's thesis anew, Kattenbusch arrives at the conclusion that the *septem de fide et regulis fidei libri praetitulati* are perhaps earlier works against Arianism that were collected by Syagrius, and that our *exhortatio* is indeed one of these. This strengthens his belief that Gregory of Elvira could be its author [35]. Further, Kattenbusch comments upon the absence of *In* before *Ecclesiam*, the absence of *Mortuus*, and the insertion of *Dei* before *Patris*, and suggests that the last two features could be characteristic for Spanish forms of the Creed [36]. As an additional argument for an early date, he mentions the absence of any thoughts on the origin of the Creed in the *exhortatio* [37].

Next, Karl Künstle pays attention to this text in a work that, similarly to Hahn's, is entitled *Eine Bibliothek der Symbole* .... Künstle applauds Morin's thesis and gives a number of reasons for dating the *exhortatio* later than the fourth century. This fact and several "positive Merkmale des Gegensatzes zum Priscillianismus" (among

---

[31] Kattenbusch 1894, 408.

[32] Hahn 1897, 56-57+n98.

[33] Kattenbusch 1900, 437-439.

[34] Kattenbusch 1900, 440n19.

[35] Kattenbusch 1900, 449-450n30.

[36] Kattenbusch 1900, 481-482n13, 889n32, and 916-917. In a later publication, Krüger (1902, 666) abandons his thesis that Eusebius of Vercelli is the author of the *exhortatio*, and lends cautious support to Kattenbusch's opinion.

[37] Kattenbusch 1900, 18n15.

them various similarities with Spanish texts) lead Künstle to the conclusion that Syagrius is indeed the author of our *exhortatio* [38].

Brewer devotes a significant number of pages in an appendix to his monograph on the Athanasianum to the question of the authorship of our *exhortatio*. He detects some Ambrosian reminiscences in the text as well as allusions to Apollinarism and Jovinianism. All this leads Brewer to date the text after 390 [39]. With regard to its place of origin, Brewer opts for Northern Italy. Indications are Caspari's classification of the credal form as Italian, the fact that in the period in question Arianism was only a force in Illyria, and that Psalm 34 (*Venite, filii, audite*) was still in use in the Milanese liturgy for the *traditio symboli* in the eleventh century [40]. Various similarities between our *exhortatio*, the treatise *de fide orthodoxa contra Arianos* (CPL 551), and the so-called *tractatus Origenis* (CPL 546; both works are nowadays firmly ascribed to Gregory of Elvira) lead Brewer to the conclusion that these three works stem from the same author, whom he identifies with Rufinus of Aquileia. Brewer finds an explanation for the fact that Rufinus uses a quite different form of the Creed in his *expositio symboli* by assuming that this work was written for a friend, and that Rufinus therefore did not expound his own baptismal form of the Creed, but rather the one that was used by that friend [41].

After Brewer's substantial contribution, scholars seem to have lost interest in the pseudo-Ambrosian *exhortatio de symbolo ad neophytos*. Apart from some short references [42], the discussion about its origin seems to have come to a standstill, although no conclusion had been reached yet. Badcock cautiously follows Morin's suggestion in the second edition of his *The History of the Creeds* [43], as does

[38] Künstle 1900, 60-69. The same position in Künstle 1905, 128n1.

[39] Brewer 1909, 142-145.

[40] Brewer 1909, 146-147.

[41] Brewer 1909, 147-175.

[42] The *exhortatio* is mentioned in § 33 of Bardenhewer's *Geschichte der altchristlichen Literatur*. This paragraph is entitled "Luzifer von Calaris und seine Freunde ...", but Bardenhewer (1912, 474-475) does not state explicitly that Lucifer or one of his friends is the author. Schanz's *Geschichte der römischen Litteratur* mentions the *exhortatio* twice: in § 906 ("Die Schriftstellerei des Eusebius von Vercelli) and in § 939 (on Ambrose's "Andere dogmatische Schriften". But Schanz (1914, 311-312 and 347) does not identify the author either.

[43] Badcock 1938, 91-92.

O'Callaghan, more recently and less cautiously [44]. Frede agrees with Caspari in dating the text between 340 and 370 but denies Syagrius's authorship [45], and Dekkers pronounces a *non liquet* [46].

In these circumstances, it is all the more interesting to investigate whether our regional typology of credal forms might help to establish when and where the pseudo-Ambrosian *exhortatio* could have been written. In order to do so, it seems best to look for formulations in the credal variant of the *exhortatio* that have been classed as 'unique features' in our typology. In theory, the presence of only one such feature would already attribute an anonymous text to a certain region. However, formulations that we have classed as 'unique features' may well have known a wider diffusion in reality, and precisely such a thing could be the case if we find 'general' or 'other' features from one region together with a 'unique' feature from another. It will thus be advisable to take a look at the formulations of the other two categories as well. When we have thus gained an impression of the possible origin of the anonymous form of the Creed, we shall conclude the investigation by checking that no 'general' features that should be present if our impression is correct are absent. This can result again in either an adaptation of the typology or a new conclusion concerning the *exhortatio*.

A search for formulations that we have found to be confined to one region yields only one such feature in our pseudo-Ambrosian text - the use of *Et* to introduce the tenth article. This feature is only seen in APS, and is therefore unique for the Balkan type of the Creed. Since the introduction of the tenth article by means of the particle *Et* may well be due to theological reasons [47], we cannot dismiss its occurrence here lightly. A Balkan origin of the form of the Creed of our *exhortatio* will therefore serve as a working hypothesis. Before we proceed by looking for what we have designated 'other features', we should note that, apart from the one 'unique feature', we also find no less than four articles that are formulated in a way that we have not encountered before. These are the first, the third, the fourth, and the seventh articles.

[44] O'Callaghan 1992, 287.
[45] Frede 1995, 115.
[46] Dekkers 1995, 55.
[47] See above, chapter 3.7, pp. 249-250.

The first article offers the uniqe addition *Saeculorum omnium et creaturarum regem et conditorem*. This is apparently a variant on the theme 'creator of heaven and earth'. It comes closer to the African *Vniuersorum creatorem, regem saeculorum, immortalem et inuisibilem* and the Irish *Inuisibilem, omnium creaturarum uisibilium et inuisibilium conditorem* than the Balkan *Creatorem caeli et terrae* and the North Italian *Inuisibilem et impassibilem*, but that need not imply that our text stems form Ireland or Africa. All these parallel formulations probably stem from the fourth century (only the Irish addition can hardly be dated), so that our text may indeed be as old as that.

In the third article we find the combination *De ... et ex*, which is not present in the credal variants that we have examined so far. The formulation it resembles most is the fourth-century Balkan *Ex ... et ex*. As we have seen that this use is probably more than just a variation in wording and may well have been caused by the same ambiguity which gave rise to the use of *Conceptus* in Gaul and *Ex utero* in Spain [48], this resemblance can safely be taken as a confirmation of our working hypothesis.

Next, the fourth article is unique because of the construction with *Qui* and without *Est*. As far as we know, the use of the relative in the fourth article is confined to Rome (*R*) and Northern Italy. This does not say much, however, because the presence or absence of *Qui* concerns the formulation only. There is, moreover, no reason to exclude the possibility that the relative in the fourth article found its way to other regions than Northern Italy, though this is not very probable in the case of Gaul and Spain.

Again, the seventh article exhibits the addition of *Dei* without *Omnipotentis* [49]. The use of *Dei* (together with *Omnipotentis*) is found first in fourth-century Spain, but we have seen that there are reasons to assume that it originated in Gaul because of the later Gallican formulations *Sedet ad dexteram dei* and *Sedet ad dexteram patris omnipotentis*. We should therefore also take into account the possibility that the pseudo-Ambrosian *exhortatio de symbolo ad neophytos* is of Gallican origin. In that case, the prefixed particle *Et* in the

---

[48] See above, chapter 3.7, pp. 232-233.

[49] This confirms our hypothesis that these two additions originated separately. See above, chapter 3.7, pp. 242-243.

tenth article would be a variant of the more usual Gallican *Credo*. The presence of the unique addition *Saeculorum omnium* ... in the first article is more difficult to explain, since we have found that when the Gallican churches started to make additions to the fourth article, they borrowed the phrase *Creatorem caeli et terrae* from the Latin Balkans. On the other hand, if we want to stick to a more Eastern origin for the *exhortatio*, we shall have to assume that the addition of *Dei* had travelled already from the Balkans to Gaul and Spain in the fourth century.

When we turn to formulations in the form of the Creed of the *exhortatio* that are found in more than one region, we can point to the following features - the word order *Iesum Christum* and the addition of *Vnicum* and *Dominum nostrum* in the second article, the addition of *A mortuis* in the fifth article, the use of *Est* in the eighth article, the addition of *Catholicam* in the tenth article, and the presence of the eleventh article. Most of these can be found in all regions. The use of *Est* occurs in Gaul and Africa only, but is in itself such an insignificant feature that that does not carry much weight. More important is the presence of *Catholicam*. This addition is found in the Balkans from the fourth century on, whence it soon travelled to Gaul, Spain, and Ireland. Our anonymous *exhortatio* may therefore just as easily stem from Gaul as from the Balkans.

We shall now ascertain whether the study of features that are general for certain regions can take us any further. If our *exhortatio* were a Gallican text, it would lack the following 'general features' - the formulation with *Conceptus* in the third article, the insertion of *Passus* in the fourth article, and the use of *Credo* in the ninth article. Of these, the use of *Conceptus* and the repetition of *Credo* are probably very early Gallican inventions, whereas *Passus* seems to have been probably taken over from Spain. If the text stems from the Balkans, we should miss *Passus* as well as the insertion of *Viuus* in the fifth article. The latter may have been imported from Rome together with the Creed itself, whereas the former was probably taken over from Spain [50].

---

[50] The absence of no less than six 'general features', the word order *Virgine Maria* in the third article, the formulation *Crucifixum sub Pontio Pilato et sepultum* in the fourth, the word order *A mortuis resurrexit* in the fifth, the use of *Credo in* in the ninth article, the addition of *In uitam aeternam*, and the position of the tenth article at the end of the Creed, pleads against an African origin for

At this point, it is important to remember that the designation of *Passus* as a 'general feature' for the Latin Balkans is based on its occurrence in APS only, because the other two Balkan texts do not witness to the form of the fourth article. This consideration makes a Balkan origin of the *exhortatio* already more probable than a Gallican one. The absence of *Viuus* can be explained by the assumption that the fifth article crossed the Adriatic not in one form but in two, one corresponding to *H* and one to *R*. Further, the formulation of the seventh article as *Sedet ad dexteram dei patris*, as we have seen, would force us to assume that *Dei* was not a Gallican but a Balkan invention which had already travelled to Spain and Gaul in the fourth century. Although this would mean that we should have to revise our reconstruction of the history of the seventh article, it is in itself perfectly possible.

A Gallican origin for our anonymous text, however, is more difficult to support. First of all, we should have to explain the absence of no less than three Gallican 'general features'. This can be achieved by dating the *exhortatio* extremely early, but that would ill accord with the presence of *Catholicam* in the tenth article, which we took to be imported from the East at the end of the fourth century. Of course, we can abandon this view and make *Catholicam* an original Gallican addition to the tenth article, but that does not seem very congruent with the early date that is necessary because of the absence of *Conceptus*, *Passus*, and *Credo* (in the ninth article). Moreover, even if we accept an early Gallican origin of the *exhortatio* on these terms, it would be strange that the addition *Saeculorum omnium et creaturarum regem et conditorem* did not leave any traces in Gaul, and that one or two centuries later the Gallican churches started to borrow the alternative *Creatorem caeli et terrae* instead.

If we accept the Latin Balkans as the most probable home for the pseudo-Ambrosian *exhortatio de symbolo ad neophytos*, we still have to answer the question of its date. Since the sources for the form of the Creed East of the Adriatic are rather few, however, we can hardly hope to reach anything like certainty on this point. Nothing prohibits a fourth-century origin, since two of the three

the *exhortatio*. Nor are there any very strong arguments against a Spanish provenance, but there is nothing to suggest that possibility either. The presence of *Catholicam* makes a North Italian provenance rather unlikely.

youngest elements of its credal variant (*Dei* and *Catholicam*) are already attested by then, whereas the third (*Saeculorum ... conditorem*) has a fourth-century parallel in the phrase *Creatorem caeli et terrae*. A possible argument in favour of such an early date is the use of *Qui* in the fourth article, which has at least a rather conservative flavour [51], but that can hardly be decisive. It is best, therefore, to conclude that our anonymous *exhortatio* presents a fourth-century or later form of the Apostles' Creed from the Latin Balkans.

## 4.3 The Anonymous *expositio symboli* CPL 229a

This *expositio* is part of the rite for the *traditio symboli* as given in a liturgical manuscript that is preserved in the North Italian Cividale del Friuli or Cividât. It was discovered and edited by the Italian humanist Joannes Franciscus Bernardus Maria de Rubeis [52]. The Catalan editor of the sermons of Peter Chrysologus, Alejandro Olivar, published the text of the *expositio symboli* anew in 1962, though he did not inspect the manuscript himself [53]. Although this *expositio* is one of the shortest to have come down to us, Olivar's edition contains a significant number of errors, so that it is advisable to present this text in an edition of our own as well.

With one exception, all the articles of the Creed are first quoted and then expounded in the *expositio*; in two instances, an article is cut in two. In view of the author's meticulous way of saying something, however short, about each article, it is probably safe to reconstruct his form of the Creed from the *expositio*. The one exception to the rule mentioned above is provided by the addition of Eternal Life, which is presented thus: *Credimus et uitam aeternam,*

---

[51] As far as we can tell, it did not find its way from Rome to the other churches of the West except that of Ravenna.

[52] De Rubeis 1754, 236-245; the *expositio* is found on p. 242. One can find De Rubeis's name in more than one form. Sometimes his first two Christian names are omitted, and sometimes his surname is written De Rossi. De Rubeis presented the text of the *expositio* once more in a later work: De Rubeis 1762, 19-20.

[53] Olivar 1962, 494-495. This text was adopted by Olivar in CCSL 24, 354-355. Before making his own edition of the *expositio*, he had already offered its text in De Rubeis's edition: Olivar 1961, 310-312.

*quia homo* ... [54]. Since the first and ninth articles of the author's form of the Creed begin with *Credo*, it is extremely improbable that the plural *Credimus* would represent a literal quotation here. The author of the sermon probably inserted this verb form to introduce the final topic of his form of the Creed [55]. This implies, however, that we cannot know whether he is really quoting this final topic or only indicating it. Although it is tempting to assume that he is quoting here just as in the rest of the *expositio*, which would yield *Et uitam aeternam* for our reconstruction, it is better not to do so and to confine ourselves to saying that our anonymous *expositio* testifies to a form of the Creed in which the addition of Eternal Life is present [56].

Therefore, the anonymous *expositio symboli* CPL 229a provides the following credal variant:

*Credo in deum patrem omnipotentem*
*et in Iesum Christum, filium eius unicum dominum nostrum*
*qui natus est de spiritu sancto et Maria uirgine*
*qui sub Pontio Pilato crucifixus est et sepultus*
*tertia die resurrexit uiuus a mortuis*
*ascendit in caelum*
*sedet ad dexteram patris*
*inde uenturus est iudicare uiuos et mortuos*
*credo in sanctum spiritum*
*sanctam ecclesiam catholicam*
*remissionem peccatorum*
*carnis resurrectionem*
*[credimus et uitam aeternam].*

The *ordo* in which this form of the Creed occurs was in use in the church of Aquileia in the second half of the ninth century, as is

---

[54] *Expositio symboli* 14; see below, p. 425.

[55] The syntactic break and the formulation with *Credimus et* exclude the possibility that the sentence still belongs to the exposition of *Carnis resurrectionem*.

[56] De Rubeis first (1754, 249) reconstructs *Vitam aeternam* and later (1762, 20) *Et uitam aeternam*. Hahn (1897, 44) and Olivar (1961, 312 and CCSL 24, 355) also opt for *Et uitam aeternam*; I did so myself in Westra 1996b, 528. Kattenbusch (1894, 107), however, rightly signals that *Et* need not belong to the quotation.

borne out by the text itself [57]. This does not mean, however, that all its parts are originally Aquileian, especially since the form of the Creed differs in a number of places from the Aquileian form as it is presented by Rufinus. De Rubeis calls attention to Roman (that is, Gelasian) as well as Gallican elements in the *ordo*, but leaves the question of its origin essentially open [58]. When turning to the form of the Creed that is contained in the *expositio symboli*, De Rubeis observes that it is essentially identical with the Old Roman Creed. He assumes a liturgical 'reformation' in the Aquileian church which would have implied, among other things, a return to the use of the Roman form of the Creed which, according to him, was in use in the rest of Italy [59]. De Rubeis was aware of the fact that the addition of Eternal Life did not yet figure in the Old Roman Creed but, he states, it did in the credal variant of Peter Chrysologus. This fact, together with numerous parallels between the anonymous *expositio* and the Chrysologan sermons *de symbolo*, leads him to the conclusion that Peter Chrysologus was the author of our anonymous *expositio symboli* [60].

Kattenbusch, the next to turn his attention to this *expositio*, is more cautious. First of all, he doubts Chrysologus's authorship of the *expositio*. In his opinion, the text looks more like a cento of Chrysologan phrases than a genuine product of Peter Chrysologus's pen. Consequently, he denies the identity of the form of the Creed in the anonymous *expositio* with the variant that was used by the

[57] See De Rubeis 1754, 229-230. The relevant passage is repeated in Olivar 1961, 295-296 and 1962, 369-370. Compare also the statement in De Rubeis 1762, 18, repeated in Olivar 1962, 371.

[58] De Rubeis 1754, 246-250; see also De Rubeis 1762, 21. Gamber (1958, 53-56) thinks that the Gelasian liturgical texts go back to a Ravennatic collection of Roman material.

[59] De Rubeis 1762, 18-22, especially 21: "... ita primaevam Symboli Apostolorum Romanam formulam deduxerunt in usum, additamentis praetermissis, quae *Rufini aetate* vigebant. Quidni enim Romanam praedictam formulam adoptassent, quae caeteris Ecclesiis in Italia communis erat?"

[60] De Rubeis 1762, 20-21. Another conspicuous addition in the credal variant of the *expositio* that is absent from Chrysologus's form of the Creed, viz. the addition of *Viuus* to the fifth article (which was, as a matter of fact, misread by De Rubeis as *Viuens*, an error which has been copied by Olivar in CCSL 24, 312), is briefly discarded by De Rubeis (1754, 249): "Vox illa, *vivens*, redundat in illo versiculo: *Tertia die resurrexit* vivens *a mortuis*". He does not comment upon the word order *Iesum Christum* or the addition *Catholicam*.

bishop of Ravenna. Finally, he thinks that the *ordo* in which the *expositio* occurs need not absolutely have been in use in Aquileia, but that it may represent the usage of one of its neighbouring bishoprics as well [61]. In this last respect, he is followed by Hahn [62].

In the twentieth century, the anonymous *expositio symboli* has been the subject of repeated study by Olivar. Following the cue given by De Rubeis in 1762, he finds a great number of parallels with the Chrysologan sermons *de symbolo*. Like De Rubeis, he states, moreover, that Peter Chrysologus and the author of the *expositio* use the same form of the Creed. Finally, Olivar points out certain resemblances between the style of the *expositio* and that of Peter Chrysologus. He concludes that the anonymous *expositio symboli* is in fact a genuine Chrysologan sermon [63]. Olivar's identification of the anonymous author with Peter Chrysologus has found practically universal acceptance [64].

As we have endeavoured to show elsewhere in more detail, there are at least two reasons for doubting Olivar's identification. First, there are some real differences between Peter Chrysologus's form of the Creed and the one found in the anonymous *expositio* [65]. Second, there are a number of differences in structure, formulation and emphasis between the *expositio* and the Chrysologan sermons *de symbolo* [66]. In that light, the numerous parallels, which indeed cannot be denied, seem to be explained better by Kattenbusch's thesis that we have here a cento of Chrysologan phrases than by Olivar's ascription of the text to Chrysologus himself.

---

[61] Kattenbusch 1894, 107.

[62] Hahn 1897, 44n66. Nevertheless, Hahn (1897, 42) presents the form of the Creed of the *expositio* as one in use "In der Kirche zu Aquileia".

[63] Olivar 1961, 301-309. This argument, in much the same form, is repeated in Olivar 1962, 376-382. Olivar has included the text of the *expositio symboli* as *sermo 62bis* in his edition of the sermons of Peter Chrysologus (CCSL 24, 354-355).

[64] See Dekkers 1995, 91 and Frede 1995, 677-678. The only critical note I could find is Bouhot's review of Olivar's edition in the *Revue des Études Augustiniennes* 29, 1983, 352-353.

[65] Compare our reconstruction of the underlying credal variant of PC (see above, chapter 3.5, p. 206) with the form of the Creed that has been offered in this paragraph; see also Westra 1996b, 527-530.

[66] See Westra 1996b, 530-538.

If the question of the origin of the *expositio symboli* CPL 229a is considered an open one again, it will be all the more interesting to see whether our regional typology of Creed forms can help us any further. As in the case of the anonymous *exhortatio ad neophytos de symbolo*, we shall first look for 'unique features' and then for 'other' and 'general features'. When we have gained a first impression of the place of origin of the text in that way, we shall have to see whether any 'general features' are absent that should be present if our impression is correct. Finally, it will be advisable to examine those features that might say something about the date of the text.

The only 'unique feature' in the form of the Creed under discussion is the use of *Qui* in the fourth article, which is only found in PC, one of our North Italian witnesses. For the rest, almost all of the articles are formulated in such a way that they have parallels in three or more regions. The two exceptions are the fifth and the eighth articles. The formulation of the fifth article (*Tertia die resurrexit uiuus a mortuis*) seems to be confined to Spain (MART, MM, LO, ILD, EB, and possibly TOL) and the Latin Balkans (NIC), whereas that of the eighth (*Inde uenturus est iudicare uiuos et mortuos*) is only found in Gaul (EUSh9; not entirely certain) and Africa (AU-H, QU; the presence of *Est* in the latter is not entirely certain either). This relative uniqueness of the formulation of the eighth article is caused by the presence of the auxiliary *Est* only, so that it should not be credited with too much weight. But even when this feature is discarded, the fact remains that the unique use of *Qui* and the relatively rare addition of *Viuus* do not point in the same direction. It will thus be advisable to take a closer look at the three possibilities of a Spanish, a North Italian, or a Balkan provenance for the credal variant of the anonymous *expositio*.

A Spanish 'general feature' that is lacking in this credal variant is the typical formulation of the fourth article: *Passus sub Pontio Pilato, crucifixus et sepultus*. In particular, the absence of *Passus* is significant here, as we have seen that this was one of the first additions to the Creed in Spain. If we want to assume a Spanish provenance for our anonymous *expositio*, we should have to date it very early, since *Passus* is already found in PRIS. This, however, would ill accord with the presence of *Catholicam*, which was probably first introduced into Spanish forms of the Creed in the fifth century.

When we consider the possibility of a North Italian origin for our anonymous text, it is again the presence of *Catholicam* that constitutes a difficulty, as all our North Italian witnesses to the form of the Creed lack this addition. In this case, however, the difficulty tends to disappear when we consider the fact that our latest North Italian witness to the form of the Creed is the mid-fifth-century PC. Nothing precludes the possibility of assuming that *Catholicam* was added to some North Italian form of the Creed in the course of the fifth, sixth, or even seventh centuries. This is all the more probable in the light of our assumption that the addition *Catholicam* travelled westward from the Latin Balkans. A second objection against a possible North Italian origin of the credal variant we are investigating, viz. the absence of *Viuus* in the North Italian witnesses, can be answered on similar lines. Moreover, the fifth article can already be seen in three different North Italian formulations, so that the addition of *Viuus*, presumably again borrowed from the Latin Balkans, cannot really be called surprising in a later North Italian form of the Creed.

The third possibility that is suggested by our study of 'unique' and 'other features' in the form of the Creed of the anonymous *expositio symboli* CPL 229a is that of a Balkan origin. In this case, we should miss *Passus* again, whereas the use of *Caelum* instead of *Caelos* would also lack any Balkan parallels. Both objections are not very serious, however. Formulations of the sixth article with *Caelos* and *Caelum* have been found to alternate in Gaul, Spain, Africa, and Northern Italy, so that there is no reason to assume that things were any different east of the Adriatic. As far as the absence of *Passus* is concerned, it has been observed before that its designation as a 'general feature' of the form of the Creed in the Latin Balkans rests on one witness only. Moreover, we have already assigned another anonymous credal text without *Passus* in the fourth article to the Balkans.

We are left, then, with two possible regions of origin for the anonymous *expositio symboli* CPL 229a: Northern Italy and the Latin Balkans [67]. Of course, a North Italian origin seems more prob-

---

[67] The absence of *Conceptus* and *Passus* makes a Gallican provenance less likely; to take an African origin into account, we should need the word order *Virgine Maria*, the formulations *Crucifixum sub Pontio Pilato et sepultum* and

able in the light of its occurrence in a missal that was in use in ninth-century Aquileia (or perhaps a neighbouring church), but it is important to bear in mind that Illyria was not very far away from that city. It is certainly possible, for example, that after the destruction of Aquileia by the Huns in 452 new liturgical texts were needed because the old ones had been lost [68], and nothing precludes the possibility that the new material came from the East.

One consideration seems to speak against such a hypothesis, however. We know that from the fourth century onwards, the addition *Creatorem caeli et terrae* [69] could be found in Balkan variants of the Creed. If our anonymous text were to stem from the Balkans as well, it could for that reason hardly be dated later than the first half of the fifth century. We have indicated above that our anonymous *expositio symboli* was probably composed by someone who had Peter Chrysologus's sermons *de symbolo* to hand, which would result in 450 as the earliest possible *terminus post quem*. It is more likely that a cento-like text like our anonymous *expositio* would be composed only after some time had elapsed after the death of the author of the sources, so that our *expositio* was probably not written before the beginning of the sixth century. On the other hand, if we assume a North Italian origin for the credal variant, it can only be dated rather late because of the presence of *Catholicam*, which probably did not enter Northern Italy before the second half of the fifth century. This again would fit perfectly with what we already know of the *expostio*.

Our conclusion, therefore, is that the anonymous *expositio symboli* CPL 229a is a fifth, sixth, or seventh-century North Italian text.

## 4.4 The Pseudo-Augustinian *expositio super symbolum* CPL 365

Like the pseudo-Ambrosian *exhortatio de symbolo ad neophytos*, this text was first edited by Caspari [70]. He found the *expositio*, so he states, in a Bamberg incunabulum and a Munich half-incunabulum [71]. In the critical apparatus to his edition, he lists a number of

---

*Tertia die a mortuis resurrexit*, the word order *Spiritum sanctum*, and the closing of the Creed with *In uitam aeternam per sanctam ecclesiam*.

[68] Such a possibility was envisaged by Kattenbusch 1894, 107.

[69] Or, for that matter, *Saeculorum omnium et creaturarum regem et conditorem*: see above, chapter 4.2, p. 288.

[70] Caspari 1883a, 290-292.

[71] Caspari 1883a, 290n1.

instances where both sources part ways. Caspari, however, is a victim of the fact that he was not in a position to order microfilms of the material he studied in various European libraries. As a matter of fact, the variants in his apparatus do not represent two different manuscripts or incunabula but are rather differences between his collations, since the Bamberg and Munich versions of the sermon are exactly identical printed texts. There is even a third copy of the same incunabulum in Bamberg, but this was not noticed by Caspari.

The text of the pseudo-Augustinian *expositio super symbolum* consists of a double introduction and a commentary which follows the articles of the Creed. The first introduction stems from another pseudo-Augustinian text, *sermo 242 de symbolo* (CPL 368). For that reason, Caspari omitted this introduction, which can be found in several other credal texts as well[72]. In his edition, accordingly, the sermon begins with the quotation of the opening words of the Creed *Credo in deum patrem omnipotentem et cetera*. This has again been taken as the *incipit* of the *expositio* by Dekkers[73]. Nevertheless, the anonymous author and compiler probably intended his sermon to begin with the traditional *Quaeso uos, fratres*. Therefore, it seems appropriate to offer a new edition of the complete text of this pseudo-Augustinian *expositio super symbolum* in the appendix to this study.

When we study the form of the Creed that was used by the author of the *expositio*, things are not quite so straightforward as in the case of the two previous texts. No explicit quotations occur, with the exception of the first words of the Creed, which are announced thus: ... *iam ad ipsius symboli perfectionis sacramentum textumque ueniamus. Credo in deum patrem omnipotentem et cetera*[74]. Since some general statements about the relationship between believing and professing one's faith follow, it seems certain that *et cetera* indicates the whole rest of the Creed[75]. Although explicit quo-

---

[72] See Caspari 1883a, XVIII.

[73] Dekkers 1995, 136.

[74] Pseudo-Augustine, *expositio super symbolum* 3; see below, p. 428

[75] See for a different opinion Kattenbusch (1900, 762-763n5), who thinks that *et cetera* can only mean *Creatorem caeli et terrae* here.

tations like this one are absent from the ensuing commentary, it is clear that the author is quoting at least some of the articles literally. This certainly holds true for articles 3, 4, 6, and 7. After the discussion of the second article, the anonymous author continues: *Qui conceptus est de spiritu sancto, natus ex Maria uirgine. Qui de deo patre natus est deus ante omnia tempora, ipse in tempore ex Maria uirgine natus est homo, ut idem* ... [76]. There is a syntactic break before and after *Qui conceptus ... uirgine*, and it is clear that with the words *Qui de deo patre* the commentary on the third article begins. Similarly, the section on the fourth article opens thus: *Passus sub Pontio Pilato, crucifixus, mortuus et sepultus. Ecce quanta pro nobis pertulit unigenitus deus* ... [77]. Here we find two syntactic breaks again, one of them marking the beginning of the entire section on the fourth article and one marking the beginning of the commentary. It is therefore safe to conclude that the phrase between the two breaks is a literal quotation. The same procedure is used for the sixth and seventh articles. After the commentary on the Resurrection of Christ, we read: *Ascendit in caelum, sedet ad dexteram dei patris omnipotentis, ut nos crederemus, si eum ex toto corde sequeremur* ... [78]. Here, the transition from quotation to commentary is clearly indicated by the use of *ut*. This makes it extremely probable that the reference to the Descent to Hell also constitutes a literal quotation, as we read: *Descendit ad infernum, ut nos misericordia sua eleuaret in caelum* [79].

In other places, however, the author has chosen to introduce a new article in a more elaborate way. Turning to the fifth article, he states: *Deinde tertia die resurrexit a mortuis. Ipse pro nobis pertulit mortem, ut* ... [80] It is clear that the words *Deinde ... mortuis* serve to introduce the article and that its exposition only starts with *Ipse pro nobis* ... At least the word *Deinde*, however, seems unlikely as part of a literal quotation from the Creed. This means that there are two possibilities: either the whole phrase *Deinde ... mortuis* is a product of the author's pen, or the author has inserted *Deinde*, but for the rest offers a faithful quotation of the fifth article as it was

[76] Pseudo-Augustine, *expositio super symbolum* 9; see below, p. 429.
[77] Pseudo-Augustine, *expositio super symbolum* 10; see below, p. 429.
[78] Pseudo-Augustine, *expositio super symbolum* 14; see below, p. 430.
[79] Pseudo-Augustine, *expositio super symbolum* 12; see below, p. 430.
[80] Pseudo-Augustine, *expositio super symbolum* 13; see below, p. 430.

formulated in his form of the Creed. Similarly, the section concerning the eighth article begins thus: *Christus sicut ascendit in caelum, ita inde uenturus est iudicare uiuos et mortuos. Qui uenerat cum mansuetudine ...* [81] Here, however, the words *Christus ... ita* seem to serve to make clear that *Inde* in the Apostles' Creed does not refer to the right hand of God, but to heaven. If this is true, the phrase *Inde ... mortuos* is probably best taken as a literal quotation of the eighth article. An additional argument to support the assumption that our anonymous author is offering literal quotations of both the fifth and the eighth articles is the fact that not all elements of these phrases are commented upon. Thus, the words *Tertia die* and *Viuos et mortuos* receive no explanation whatsoever. The same phenomenon can be observed in the portions concerning the third, fourth, and seventh articles. The Conception by the Holy Spirit, the role of Pontius Pilate, and the Sitting at the Right Hand are not commented upon, although they are present in the introductory quotation. This state of affairs strongly suggests that the author is concerned with quoting the articles in their complete forms but that he does not go out of his way to say something about every single element of the Creed in his exposition.

This impression can help us to evaluate the evidence concerning the other articles of the pseudo-Augustinian *expositio super symbolum*. Apart from the literal quotation that is mentioned above, there are two relevant passages for the form of the first article. After the author's own introduction, we read: *Ideo autem credamus in deum patrem omnipotentem creatorem omnium* [82] *quae sunt uisibilium et inuisibilium. Ipse est deus pater*, and further on: *Proinde, desiderantissimi, credentes in deum patrem omnipotentem omnium creatorem, credamus et in Iesum Christum, filium eius unicum domi-*

---

[81] Pseudo-Augustine, *expositio super symbolum* 16; see below, p. 430.

[82] Note that the words *Creatorem omnium* are probably a conjecture by Caspari (he claims that he has found them in one of his two sources, but that is demonstrably untrue: see above, pp. 297-298). *Creatorem* is therefore not absolutely certain, but at least as equally probable as *Conditorem* or *Factorem*, whereas the words *Quae sunt uisibilium et inuisilium* almost demand *Omnium* as an antecedent. One could also consider the possibility that *Omnium creatorem* should be supplied, which would tally better with the formulation in the introduction to the second article (see below), but *Creatorem omnium* is slightly more probable from a palaeographic point of view (the scribe or editor's eye may have jumped from *Omnipotentem* to *Omnium*) and also much more natural Latin.

*num nostrum. Ipse est enim unigenitus deus* ... [83] That the first *credamus* represents *Credo* and thus introduces an embedded quotation is certain because of the initial explicit quotation that has been discussed above. The problem is, of course, whether the words *creatorem* ... *inuisibilium* still belong to the embedded quotation or to the expository part. There are two considerations that speak in favour of the first possibility. First, the phrase *Ipse est deus pater* ... looks more like the beginning of the commentary on the first article than the words *Creatorem omnium* ... [84]. Moreover, the two words *omnium creatorem* in the introduction to the embedded quotation of the second article (see below) seem to be perfectly in place as an abbreviation of the complete phrase *Creatorem* ... *inuisibilium*. On the other hand, the words *Creatorem omnium quae sunt uisibilium et inuisibilium* have no direct parallel as an addition to the first article in other forms of the Creed that we know of, and can also be read as a commentary to the word *Omnipotentem*. In that case, however, the words *omnium creatorem* in the introduction to the second article would be rather illogical. Moreover, there is a perfect parallel for the words *Creatorem omnium quae sunt uisibilium et inuisibilium* as part of the Creed in the Creed of Nicea: Πάντων ὁρατῶν τε καὶ ἀοράτων ποιητήν. We thus seem to have a case here of a borrowing from the Nicene Creed in a variant of the Apostles' Creed. The fact that this borrowing is shortened to *omnium creatorem* in a repeated quotation seems to indicate, however, that the author of our pseudo-Augustinian *expositio* was still aware that the words *Creatorem* ... *inuisibilium* were an addition to the original form of the first article. One could even imagine that these words were added by the author of the *expositio* himself because he thought his form of the Creed deficient in this respect. In that case, the words *creatorem* ... *inuisibilium* and *omnium creatorem* look somewhat like an afterthought, and would formally belong to the commentary. It is with some hesitation, therefore, that we recon-

---

[83] Pseudo-Augustine, *expositio super symbolum* 7-8; see below, p. 429.

[84] Especially in the light of the beginning of the commentary on the second and ninth articles: *Ipse est enim unigenitus deus* ... and ... *qui est uerus deus sicut pater et filius, quia ipse est unus patris et filii spiritus sanctus* (pseudo-Augustine, *expositio super symbolum* 8 and 18; see below, pp. 429 and 430). Compare also the commentary on the fifth article, which starts: *Ipse pro nobis* ... (see above, footnote 80).

struct the first article of the anonymous author's form of the Creed as *Credo in deum patrem omnipotentem, creatorem omnium quae sunt uisibilium et inuisibilium* [85].

In the case of the second and ninth articles, the problem is not where the quotations end but where they begin. Both articles are introduced in rather similar ways: *Proinde, desiderantissimi, credentes in deum patrem omnipotentem omnium creatorem, credamus et in Iesum Christum filium eius unicum dominum nostrum. Ipse est enim* ... and *Credentes itaque in deum patrem, et filium eius unicum dominum nostrum Iesum Christum, credamus et in spiritum sanctum, qui est uerus deus* ... [86]. The question is whether the second and ninth articles of the author's credal variant started with *Et* or with *Credo et*. Although either solution is possible, the latter seems the more likely one for two reasons. First, we have already seen that the author not only seems concerned with making smooth transitions when he turns from one article to another but also with offering exact quotations. Second, we know from his treatment of the first article that he uses *Credamus* to indicate the occurrence of the form *Credo*, which is somewhat difficult to work into a running commentary. Therefore, we reconstruct *Credo et in Iesum Christum, filium eius unicum dominum nostrum* and *Credo et in spiritum sanctum* [87].

Things again become more complicated when we turn to the final articles of the Creed. The tenth article, introduced with the words *Credamus ergo sanctam ecclesiam catholicam, sine qua et extra quam* ... [88], may still be reconstructed in an analogous way as *Credo sanctam ecclesiam catholicam*, though this is far from certain [89]. The Remission of Sins and the Resurrection of the Flesh, however, are only indicated: *In qua omnis qui crediderit et baptizatus fuerit*

---

[85] Caspari (1883a, 290) and Hahn (1897, 74+n171) present the first article of the credal variant under discussion as just *Credo in deum patrem onuipotentem*. See footnote 75 above for Kattenbusch's opinion.

[86] Pseudo-Augustine, *expositio super symbolum* 8 and 18; see below, pp. 429 and 430.

[87] Caspari (1883a, 290-292) and Hahn (1897, 74-75) make both articles start with *Et*. Kattenbusch (1894, 210) states that the credal variant "ist fast identisch mit T", which leaves both possibilities open.

[88] Pseudo-Augustine, *expositio super symbolum* 19; see below, p. 430.

[89] For example, one can put the comma before instead of after *catholicam*, which would make it part of the exposition.

*omnium peccatorum suorum remissionem consequetur et carnis resur-*
*rectionem* [90]. Eternal Life is indicated in an even more elusive way:
*Quapropter, dilectissimi, bene uiuamus, ut non ad poenam sed ad*

---

[90] Pseudo-Augustine, *expositio super symbolum* 19; see below, p. 430. That *ui-*
*tam aeternam*, the reading of the incunabulum, must be a mistake for *Carnis re-*
*surrectionem* (or some similar term) is shown by the following words: ... *quam in*
*semet ipso nobis demonstrauit Christus ut de illa nullatenus dubitemus.* Christ did
not show Eternal Life, but the Resurrection of the Flesh, as is also stated some
paragraphs earlier: *Resurrexit Christus a mortuis, ut nos resurrectionem certissime*
*crederemus* (*ibidem* 13; see below, p. 430). Compare the pseudo-Ambrosian *exhor-*
*tatio de symbolo ad neophytos* (CPL 178) 27: ... *ut resurrectionem nostram in cor-*
*pore suo, id est habitu nostrae fragilitatis nostrae, ostenderet nobis* (see below,
p. 419), the pseudo-Augustinian *excarpsum de fide catholica* 1: *Credite eum tertia*
*die a mortuis resurrexisse et nobis exemplum resurrectionis ostendisse* (CCSL 103,
51), the anonymous *tractatus symboli* (CPL 1751) 12: *Tertia die resurrexit a mor-*
*tuis, ut nobis futurae resurrectionis mysterium in suo corpore demonstraret* ... (see
below, p. 471), the anonymous *symbolum apostolorum* (CPL 1758) 6: *Tertia die*
*resurrexit ut nobis exemplum resurrectionis ostenderet* (see below, ), the anonymous
*sermo de symbolo* (CPL 1759) 24: *Ostendit uera prima resurrectione quia omnes ho-*
*mines resurgere habent cum corporibus suis* (see below, p. 492), and the anonymous
*expositio super symbolum* (CPL 1760) 8: *Sed sicut ipse tertia die resurrexit a mor-*
*tuis, ita et nos in die iudicii absque dubio resurrecturos nos esse credamus* (see below, p. 506). A possible counter-example is pseudo-Fulgentius, *sermo de symbolo*
(CPL 846) 28, where we read: *Quia uero Christus surgens a mortuis iam non mori-*
*tur et mors ei ultra non dominabitur, et quod in se ostendit hoc suis fidelibus repro-*
*misit, credite etiam uitam aeternam* ... (see below, p. 446). But here, Christ's 'show-
ing' of Eternal Life is not presented as a self-evident fact, but rather the product
of some preceding theological reflexion. Moreover, in the same sermon we also
read: *Christus resurgens ueram spem futurae resurrectionis ostendit* ... *resurrexit*
*Christus secundum carnem ut resurrectionem carnis certissime speraremus* and *Cre-*
*dite etiam carnis resurrectionem, quam in se ipso nobis demonstrauit Christus ut de*
*illa nullatenus desperemus* (pseudo-Fulgentius, *sermo de symbolo* 15 and 25; see
below, pp. 444 and 445). That Christ came to reveal our future resurrection
seems to be a very old piece of theology: see Rordorf 1995, 58. It also occurs
in a *regula fidei* by Cyprian of Carthage: *Numquid hanc trinitatem Marcion tenet?*
*Numquid eundem asserit quem et nos deum patrem creatorem? Eundem nouit filium*
*Christum de uirgine Maria natum, qui sermo caro factus sit, qui peccata nostra por-*
*tauerit, qui mortem moriendo uicerit, qui resurrectionem carnis per semet ipsum pri-*
*mus initiauerit et discipulis suis quod in eadem carne resurrexisset ostenderit?* (Cyprian of Carthage, *epistula* 73 [CPL 50] V 2; CCSL 3C, 535). See also Novatian *de*
*trinitate* X 8: *Qui dum in eadem substantia corporis in qua moritur resuscitatus ip-*
*sius corporis uulneribus comprobatur, etiam resurrectionis nostrae leges in sua carne*
*monstrauit, qui corpus quod ex nobis habuit in sua resurrectuione restituit* (CPL 71;
CCSL 4, 28).

*aeternam uitam resurgamus ...* [91] In fact, we can say nothing about the form of the final articles of the credal variant that is expounded in the pseudo-Augustinian *expositio super symbolum* CPL 365. As far as the contents are concerned, we can say that the Church was certainly mentioned (probably with the words *Credo sanctam ecclesiam catholicam*), that Remission of Sins and Resurrection of the Flesh were both probably present as well, and that Eternal Life possibly concluded the credal variant under discussion. Since nothing is said about the Communion of Saints, this addition was probably absent from the author's form of the Creed [92].

For the *expositio super symbolum*, then, we may reconstruct the underlying form of the Creed as follows:

> *Credo in deum patrem omnipotentem, creatorem omnium quae sunt*
>     *uisibilium et inuisibilium (Credo in deum patrem omnipotentem?)*
> *credo (?) et in Iesum Christum, filium eius unicum dominum nos-*
>     *trum*
> *qui conceptus est de spiritu sancto, natus ex Maria uirgine*
> *passus sub Pontio Pilato, crucifixus, mortuus et sepultus*
> *descendit ad infernum*
> *tertia die resurrexit a mortuis*
> *ascendit in caelum*
> *sedet ad dexteram dei patris omnipotentis*
> *inde uenturus* [93] *est iudicare uiuos et mortuos*
> *credo (?) et in spiritum sanctum*
> *credo sanctam ecclesiam catholicam (?)*
> *[... omnium peccatorum suorum remissionem consequetur*
> *et <carnis resurrectionem> ...]*
> *[ad aeternam uitam].*

Thus far, nothing particularly definite has been said about the pseudo-Augustinian *expositio super symbolum*. Caspari provided

---

[91] Pseudo-Augustine, *expositio super symbolum* 20; see below, p. 431.

[92] Caspari (1883a, 292) reconstructs *Sanctam ecclesiam catholicam, peccatorum remissionem, uitam aeternam*. Kattenbusch does not offer a reconstruction but thinks that *Sanctorum communionem* may well have been present in the Creed form (Kattenbusch 1894, 210 and 1900, 763n5). Hahn (1897, 75) reconstructs *Sanctam ecclesiam catholicam, peccatorum remissionem, et uitam aeternam*.

[93] The variant *Rediturus* that is given in Hahn (1897, 75) goes back to a copying error by Caspari (see above).

hardly any notes to accompany his edition as he intended to discuss the *expositio* more fully later [94] (which never happened), and limited himself to the observation that the text was written for the *traditio symboli*. He dates the text to the sixth or seventh century [95] and says nothing about its place of origin. Kattenbusch, who discusses the *expositio* among the "Unbestimmbare Symbole", leaves even more room for dating the text. In his opinion, it may be older than the sixth century but could also be as young as the tenth [96], and he is equally uninformative about its birthplace. Hahn considers the credal variant of the *expositio* to be Gallican but does not give any reason for this opinion. He follows Caspari in dating the text to the sixth or seventh century [97]. According to Frede, it is dependent on pseudo-Augustine, *sermo 242* and on the pseudo-Fulgentian *sermo de symbolo* CPL 846 [98].

Since none of these authors presents any arguments to ascribe either the underlying form of the Creed or the *expositio* itself to any certain place or region, it is all the more interesting to see whether our typology can bring the question any closer to a solution. Similarly, it will be worthwhile investigating whether Kattenbusch is right that the *expositio* could have been written at any date between 400 and 1000, or whether the opinion of Caspari and Hahn is nearer to the truth.

The credal variant of the pseudo-Augustinian *expositio super symbolum* yields no less than three 'unique features' - the formulation of the third article as *Qui conceptus est de spiritu sancto, natus ex Maria uirgine*, the formulation of the fourth with *Passus* and *Mortuus*, and the use of a prefixed *Credo* in the tenth article, all features that are not found outside Gaul. Even when we exclude the formulation *Credo sanctam ecclesiam catholicam*, which must remain hypothetical, the other two suffice to make a Gallican provenance of the text extremely probable. The use of *Conceptus* in the third article was, as we have seen, most likely an original Gallican invention that

[94] See Caspari 1883a, III.
[95] Caspari 1883a, XVII-XVIII+n2.
[96] Kattenbusch 1894, 210-211.
[97] Hahn 1897, 74n171.
[98] Frede 1995, 125; compare Dekkers 1995, 136. For pseudo-Augustine, *sermo 242*, see above, chapter 3.2, footnote p. 45; for the pseudo-Fulgentian *sermo de symbolo* CPL 846, see below, chapter 4.6.

may hark back to the middle of the fourth century. It should be
noted that the form of the Creed of the *expositio* retains the conservative *Qui*, which tends to disappear in later Gallican forms of
the Creed; it is also absent from BAN, the one non-Gallican variant
that uses *Conceptus*. The addition of *Credo* in the tenth article seems
to be equally old, but is only attested until the sixth century. The
use of *Passus* together with *Mortuus* probably stems from the beginning of the fifth century. All three 'unique features' together, therefore, seem to indicate a Gallican origin at some date between 450
and 600.

The wording of the other articles does not contradict this. Of
course, the phrase *Creatorem omnium quae sunt uisibilium et inusibi-*
*lium*, if it belongs to the credal variant and not to the commentary,
does not have any Gallican parallels, but it would be unique for any
region. One can only say that it would be difficult to imagine its
use in a Gallican form of the Creed once the Balkan addition *Crea-*
*torem caeli et terrae* had become general. This formulation may well
have made its entrance into Gaul in the fifth century or even earlier, but we find Gallican forms of the Creed that lack this addition
down to the sixth century. After 600, however, it is always present,
so that this form of the first article reinforces our impression that
the *expositio super symbolum* was probably written before the
seventh century.

The second article in its full form and introduced by *Credo et* or
by *Et* only is not found among our Gallican witnesses to the wording of the Creed [99], but they present such a variety in the formulation of this article that this is hardly an obstacle for a Gallican
origin of the *expositio*. The use of *Vnicum* and *Dominum nostrum* is
particularly popular in later Gallican variants, but it is already
attested by FAU-R in the second half of the fifth century.

The Descent to Hell, on the other hand, is not found in Gallican
forms of the Creed prior to the middle of the sixth century. The use
of the singular *Infernum* is not present in any other credal variant
we have met so far, and would therefore be a Gallican innovation.
This is not problematic, however, as we know that the Gallican
churches when taking over the Descent to Hell from Northern Italy

---

[99] The formulation *Credo et in Iesum Christum, filium eius unicum dominum*
*nostrum* is not found in any other region either.

probably did not cling to the wording of their example. Since the other Gallican witnesses to this addition are considerably later, our text may well stem from a church that was among the first in the field in this respect.

The wording of the fifth, sixth, seventh, and eighth articles (*Tertia die resurrexit a mortuis, ascendit in caelum, sedet ad dexteram dei patris omnipotentis, inde uenturus est iudicare uiuos et mortuos*) reflects more or less mainstream Gallican credal development. The combination *In caelum* and the formulation of the eighth article with *Est* are found only once in our other Gallican witnesses, but both cases comprise a question of wording only.

Finally, the formulation of the ninth article [100] as *Credo et in spiritum sanctum* is not very common in Gaul, but can nevertheless be seen in FAU-R. If we reconstruct the article without *Credo*, however, a Gallican origin would be more difficult to maintain, since *Credo* seems to have been part of the Gallican wording of this article from the start.

When all these considerations are taken together, a Gallican provenance for the pseudo-Augustinian *expositio super symbolum* can be assumed to be practically certain. The formulation of the first, third, and tenth articles on the one hand, and the presence of the Descent to Hell on the other, means that a date between 550 and 600 is more probable than any other, though the lower limit in particular cannot be taken as very rigid.

## 4.5 The Anonymous *expositio de fide catholica* CPL 505

This anonymous text was first edited by Burn in the *Zeitschrift für Kirchengeschichte* of 1898 [101] on the basis of three manuscripts. Künstle discovered the *expositio* in a fourth manuscript as well, and published the text of this manuscript in his *Bibliothek der Symbole* [102]. This last text has been faithfully reprinted in one of the supplements to Migne's *Patrologia Latina* [103]. Parts of the anonymous *expositio de fide catholica* recur in the equally anonymous

---

[100] The final two articles of the Creed are indicated too vaguely to draw any conclusions from them.

[101] Burn 1898, 180-182.

[102] Künstle 1900, 173-175.

[103] PLS 3, 57-58.

*expositio fidei* CPL 1763, which is preserved in two Parisian manuscripts [104]. Since no editor has hitherto made use of all six available manuscripts, we offer a new edition in the appendix.

When we turn to this text in order to reconstitute the author's form of the Creed, we meet with the difficulty that no explicit quotations can be found. What is worse, the majority of the articles are indicated in such a way that it seems certain that they are not quoted literally either [105]. Fortunately, however, the author more or less consistently indicates where the commentary begins and the introduction to one or more articles ends. It will be a good idea to investigate these cases first.

Up to and including the eighth article, the author clearly marks the beginning of his commentary by means of the tag *hoc est*. Moreover, he uses the imperative *Credite* to introduce most articles here. Thus we read: *Credite in deum Patrem omnipotentem inuisibilem uisibilium et inuisibilium conditorem, hoc est quia omnia creauit simul uerbo potentiae suae. Credite et in Iesum Christum filium eius unicum dominum nostrum, conceptum de spiritu sancto natum ex Maria uirgine, hoc est sine matre in caelo, sine patre carnali in terra. Crucifixum sub Pontio Pilato praeside et sepultum, tertia die resurgentem ex mortuis, hoc est in uera sua carne quam accepit ex Maria semper uirgine. Per ueram resurrectionem resurrexit, postquam diabolum ligauit et animas sanctorum de inferno liberauit. Victor ... sedet in dexteram dei patris. Inde credite uenturum iudicare uiuos ac mortuos, hoc est ...* [106] Since the author does not even comment upon half of the elements that are thus presented, the conclusion seems safe that he is concerned with quoting the complete Creed even if he does not feel the need to say something about each individual article, and that the introductions constitute embedded quotations [107].

---

[104] See below, pp. 432-435 and p. 529 for more details on the relationship between these manuscripts and on the question of whether the anonymous *expositio de fide catholica* CPL 505 or the related *expositio fidei* CPL 1763 is more original.

[105] Burn (1898, 180-182 and 1899, 243-244) treats all indications as literal quotations, whereas Kattenbusch (1900, 747+n33) considers a reconstruction of a credal variant impossible. Both positions are probably too rigid.

[106] *Expositio de fide catholica* 1-4; see below, pp. 436-437. For the lacuna after *Victor*, see below, p. 310.

[107] In his edition, Burn (1898, 180-181) does not take the words *Inuisibilem ... conditorem* as part of the author's form of the Creed but rather as an addition

The first of these is *Credite in deum patrem omnipotentem inuisibilem uisibilium et inuisibilium conditorem*. Although we do not have any exact parallels for this formulation, there seems to be no reason to reconstruct the author's form of the first article in any other way than *Credo in deum patrem omnipotentem inuisibilem uisibilium et inuisibilium conditorem*, especially as the commentary (*hoc est quia omnia creauit simul uerbo potentiae suae*) guarantees that the words *Inuisibilem ... conditorem* belong to the embedded quotation.

Next, the second and third articles are presented thus: *Credite et in Iesum Christum filium eius unicum dominum nostrum, conceptum de spiritu sancto natum ex Maria uirgine*. Apart from the introductory *Credite*, this looks like a faithful quotation. Since the author has *Credite* in at least one place where the occurrence of *Credo* in the Creed is out of the question (see the section on the eighth article), there is no way to decide whether the author's declaratory form of the second article began with *Credo et* or with *Et* [108].

The fourth and fifth articles seem to depend on the same *Credite*, as the text continues: *... hoc est sine matre in caelo, sine patre carnali in terra. Crucifixum sub Pontio Pilato praeside et sepultum, tertia die resurgentem ex mortuis*. The participle *Resurgentem* is probably caused by the author's concern to avoid a syntactic break within the quotation, so that we may reconstruct the more familiar *Resurrexit* from it [109]. The apposition *praeside* with *Pontio Pilato* is somewhat suspect. It may be part of the underlying form of the Creed, but it looks more like an explanatory gloss by the author [110]. It

from an Oriental creed. A year later, however, he reconstructs *Credo in deum patrem omnipotentem, inuisibilem, uisibilium et inuisibilium rerum conditorem* (Burn 1899, 243; *rerum* is only supported by part of the manuscript tradition: see below, p. 438). Künstle (1900, 87-88), following manuscript *A*, seems to reconstruct the first, second, and ninth articles as *Credo deum patrem omnipotentem (...?)*, *Credo et Iesum Christum, filium eius unicum dominum* and *Credo et spiritum sanctum (...?)*.

[108] Burn (1899, 243) opts for the second possibility. See the previous footnote for Künstle's opinion.

[109] Compare the case of PRIS (see above, chapter 3.3, footnote 152). If the form of the Creed had read *(Qui) crucifixus (est)* ..., this procedure would have been unnecessary, so that the form *Resurgentem* indirectly proves the use of an accusative construction in the fourth article. This again is a strong reason for assuming that the third article was constructed in the same way.

[110] Burn (1898, 181 and 1899, 243) does not consider it as part of the underlying form of the Creed either.

seems best to leave both possibilities open. Further, the fact that
the Descent to Hell is alluded to in the commentary (... *postquam
diabolum ligauit et animas sanctorum de inferno liberauit*) but is
absent from the embedded quotation, seems to point to a form of
the Creed in which this addition was still absent, although the
author knew that it could be found in other credal variants [111].

In the quotation of the next articles, we encounter a lacuna. The
manuscripts that testify to the text of the anonymous *expositio de
fide catholica* CPL 505 all omit the sixth article and continue *Victor
sedet ...* (*A*: *redit*; *BMW*: *sedit*) [112]. Since *Victor* is found in a number
of credal variants as an addition to the sixth article, the obvious
solution is that the scribe of a manuscript from which *ABMW* all
descend omitted the rest of the sixth article, and to place the
lacuna between *Victor* and *Sedet* [113]. Further, we again meet an
inserted *Credite* in the rest of the quotation: *Victor ... sedet in dexteram dei patris. Inde credite uenturum iudicare uiuos ac mortuos.* The
most natural reconstruction here is *Inde uenturus iudicare ...*, though
the presence of *Est* after *Venturus* cannot be excluded.

It is more difficult to reconstruct the ninth article, as the absence
of *hoc est* or a similar tag makes it impossible to locate the point
where the quotation ends and the commentary begins. The text
reads: *Credite et in spiritum sanctum, deum omnipotentem, unam
habentem substantiam cum patre et filio. Sed tamen intimare debemus
...* [114] It is clear that with the words *Sed tamen ...* we are well within
the expository part, but where exactly does it begin? The phrases
*deum omnipotentem* and *unam habentem substantiam cum patre et filio*

[111] This reasoning would also hold true if one wanted to construct ... *hoc est in
uera sua carne quam accepit ex Maria semper uirgine, per ueram resurrectionem
resurrexit. Postquam diabolum ligauit et animas sanctorum de inferno liberauit uictor ...*

[112] That a new quotation begins here seems to be guaranteed by the syntactical break between *liberauit* and *Victor*, though it is possible to link the clause
*postquam ... liberauit* with *Victor ...* (see previous footnote). In that case, however, the text would suggest that the Descent to Hell took place between the
Resurrection and the Ascension.

[113] This is also Burn's (1898, 180 and 1899, 243) position. Künstle (1900, 88)
defends the reading of *A*, which, in his opinion, deliberately combines the sixth
and seventh articles. Compare also Kattenbusch 1900, 746n30.

[114] *Expositio de fide catholica* 5; see below, p. 437.

may belong to both, and a decision is not easy. Apart from BAN, where both phrases are added to the ninth article, no such extensions occur in the credal variants that we have examined so far. Perhaps, therefore, the words *deum ... filio* are best explained as part of the commentary here, and their presence as part of the Creed in BAN is due to the fact that its redactor deliberately took them over from our anonymous *expositio* or a similar text [115].

In the rest of the sermon, the line between the introduction of the several articles and their exposition is clear again. The question of whether the author is offering more or less literal embedded quotations as in the first part of the text, or presenting the remaining articles more freely is more difficult, however. The tenth article is introduced thus: *Credite ecclesiam catholicam, hoc est uniuersalem uniuerso mundo ...* [116]. As in the case of the second and ninth articles, *Credite* may or may not represent the form *Credo* as part of the formulation of this article. One can point to parallels for both possibilities. More problematic is the absence of *Sanctam*, which, as far as we can see, is present in all forms of the Creed. All in all, it seems best to consider the phrase *Credite ecclesiam catholicam* as a free embedded quotation [117]. Nevertheless, the presence of *Catholicam* in the author's form of the Creed is certain, since the commentary focuses on this word.

The sermon also introduces the Remission of Sins with *Credite*: *Credite remissionem peccatorum, aut per baptismum ...* [118]. Again, the exact formulation cannot be certain, although the common *Remissionem peccatorum* strongly suggests itself.

The twelfth article is introduced in a more elaborate way: *Credite communem omnium corporum resurrectionem post mortem. Sine dubio enim ...* [119]. Although the possibility cannot be excluded that the author really knew a form of the Creed ending (*Credo*) *communem omnium corporum resurrectionem post mortem*, this formulation looks

---

[115] Burn first (1989, 181) omits the phrase *deum ... filio* from his reconstruction, but later (1899, 244) includes it. For Künstle's reconstruction of the ninth article, see above, footnote 107.

[116] *Expositio de fide catholica* 8; see below, p. 437.

[117] Burn (1898, 181 and 1899, 244) reconstructs *Ecclesiam catholicam*.

[118] *Expositio de fide catholica* 9; see below, p. 437.

[119] *Expositio de fide catholica* 10; see below, p. 437.

more like a free paraphrase of the article than anything else [120]. It seems best, therefore, to abstain from giving a reconstruction here. It should be observed, finally, that no mention is made of Eternal Life, so we may safely conclude that this addition was absent from the author's credal variant.

We can thus reconstruct the following form of the Creed from the anonymous *expositio de fide catholica* CPL 505:

> *Credo in deum patrem omnipotentem, inuisibilem uisibilium et inui-*
>     *sibilium conditorem*
> *(credo?) et in Iesum Christum, filium eius unicum dominum nos-*
>     *trum*
> *conceptum de spiritu sancto, natum ex Maria uirgine*
> *crucifixum sub Pontio Pilato (praeside?) et sepultum*
> *tertia die resurrexit ex mortuis*
> *uictor ...*
> *sedet in dexteram dei patris*
> *inde uenturus (est?) iudicare uiuos ac mortuos*
> *(credo?) et in spiritum sanctum*
> *... ecclesiam catholicam*
> *remissionem peccatorum (?)*
> *...*

Not much has been written about the origin of the anonymous *expositio de fide catholica* CPL 505, and the discussion that has taken place mainly centres around two questions. In the first place, this *expositio* is closely related not only to the anonymous *expositio fidei* CPL 1763, as has already been noted above, but also to the pseudo-Augustinian *sermo 244 de symbolo*, nowadays usually ascribed to Caesarius of Arles. Both texts will be studied below with respect to the form of the Creed to which they testify [121], but only after we have examined all three texts separately shall we be in a position to turn our attention to the problem of their mutual relationship. More promising for our purpose are the remarks that have been made about the credal variant of the *expositio*, which constitutes the second main topic in the scholarly discussion about this text.

---

[120] Burn first (1898, 182) reconstructs only *Omnium corporum resurrectionem post mortem*, but later (1899, 244) includes *communem*.

[121] See below, chapters 4.8 and 4.16.

According to Burn, Southern Gaul is the most probable home for our anonymous sermon because of the connection with the pseudo-Augustinian *sermo 244*, which he considers a Caesarian text. In his opinion, the use of *Conceptus* in the third article also points to a Gallican origin, while the fact that *Passus* and *Mortuus* are absent indicates a period prior to Caesarius, viz. the fifth century or even earlier. Moreover, he states, the phrases *Deum omnipotentem, unam habentem substantiam cum patre et filio* and *Post mortem* (in the final article) occur in the credal variant of the Bangor Antiphonary (BAN). He explains these similarities by assuming that BAN derives from a text similar to our anonymous *expositio* [122].

Kattenbusch examines the problem of the relationship between the three texts from more than one angle and notices a number of parallels with other texts as well. However, he does not doubt Burn's hypothesis that the *expositio de fide catholica* stems from Gaul. In the light of the parallels with BAN, he thinks that the monastery of Lérins may well be its home, and he suggests the authorship of Hilary of Arles (*sedit c.* 429-440) [123].

Künstle strikes a quite different note. Referring to one version of the text only and without paying attention to the form of the creed, he mentions a number of features that remind him of certain Spanish texts. This, together with the fact that his manuscript contains the *expositio* in the context of a (supposedly) Spanish collection, brings him to the conclusion that our *expositio* stems from Spain [124].

The most recent person to discuss the provenance of the *expositio de fide catholica* is Paul Lejay. He mainly studies the relationship between the *expositio* and its two sister texts, and arrives at the conclusion that all three texts represent successive stages in Caesarius of Arles's struggle for a concise summary of catholic faith [125]. He also mentions the parallels with BAN, and explains these by pointing out the close contacts between Southern Gaul and Ireland [126].

---

[122] Burn 1898, 180 and 1899, 244.

[123] Kattenbusch 1900, 745-748+nn29, 34.

[124] Künstle 1900, 89-90.

[125] Lejay 1906, 46-54. According to Lejay, the Athanasian Creed is the fourth and final product of this process.

[126] Lejay 1906, 48-50+nn1, 3, and 4.

Finally, it should be observed that, following Kattenbusch's suggestion, both Dekkers and Frede rank the anonymous *expositio* among the works of Hilary of Arles, though they give no reason for this decision [127].

It will be clear that the discussion about the origin of the anonymous *expositio de fide catholica* CPL 505 has fizzled out rather than been concluded. Most scholars opt for a Gallican origin of the text, but Künstle's suggestion of Spain as its birthplace has never really been discussed. Nor has any consensus been achieved among the defendants of a Gallican origin concerning the date of the text. According to Burn and Kattenbusch, it is prior to Caesarius of Arles, whereas Lejay wants to ascribe it to precisely that author. A fresh investigation of the underlying form of the Creed can perhaps throw new light on these questions.

When we take a closer look at this credal variant no less than three formulations can be noted that are not found in other forms of the Creed. These are the addition *Inuisibilem uisibilium et inuisibilium conditorem* in the first article, the use of *Ex mortuis* instead of *A mortuis* in the fifth, and the formulation of the seventh article with *In dexteram dei patris*, in which neither the preposition *In* nor the combination *Dei patris* without *Omnipotentis* are seen elsewhere.

Next, we encounter a number of 'unique features' - the formulation of the third article as *Conceptum de spiritu sancto, natum ex Maria uirgine* and the addition of *Victor* to the sixth article are only found in Gaul, though *Conceptus* also occurs in Ireland, whereas the formulation of the fourth article as *Crucifixum sub Pontio Pilato et sepultum* can only be seen in Africa, though the accusative construction also occurs in Gaul. An African origin, however, is rendered extremely improbable by the absence of African 'general features' such as the word order *Virgine Maria* in the third article, the formulation of the fifth article as *Tertia die a mortuis resurrexit*, the formulation of the eighth article with *Et*, the addition of Eternal Life, and the conclusion of the Creed by means of *Per sanctam ecclesiam*.

---

[127] Dekkers 1995, 179 and Frede 1995, 546 (with the remark "Echtheit zweifelhaft"). Morin (1937, 910) and Hamman (PLS 3, 56) refer to the earlier discussion, but do not take sides.

Many additional observations, however, favour a Gallican origin of the credal variant under discussion. First of all, one can point to the addition *Inuisibilem uisibilium et inuisibilium conditorem*, which rather resembles another addition to the first article, *Creatorem omnium quae sunt uisibilium et inuisibilium*, which is found in the pseudo-Augustinian *sermo super symbolum* CPL 365, a text that we have assigned to Gaul as well [128]. Secondly, the formulation *In dexteram dei patris* reflects a stage in the development of the sixth article in which *Dei* had already been added but *Omnipotentis* not yet. Since both additions probably stem from Gaul and reached other regions either together or not at all, this peculiar wording can, at least according to our credal typology, only be Gallican. Thirdly, the formulation of the fifth article with *Ex* instead of *A* tallies with our theory that this article reached Gaul in the shorter form *Tertia die resurrexit*. Finally, the use of *Ac* in the eighth article is limited to the regions of Gaul and Ireland.

On the other hand, the credal variant of the *expositio* lacks two important Gallican 'general features' - the use of *Passus* in the fourth article and the addition of Eternal Life at the end of the Creed. The absence of both, however, can be explained by our reconstruction of the history of the form of the Creed in Gaul. To start with *Passus*, it should be remembered that this addition was either a mid-fourth-century Gallican innovation or was introduced to Gaul from Spain in around 400. In either case, its introduction need not have erased all traces of the original shorter wording of the article in Gaul. As far as the addition of Eternal Life is concerned, we have postulated its first entrance into a Gallican form of the Creed towards the end of the fourth century, which implies that, at least in the fifth, credal variations could still be found in Gaul which ended with the Resurrection of the Flesh.

Perhaps a word or two should still be said about the possibility of an Irish origin for this form of the Creed. Although no author has positively connected either the anonymous *expositio de fide catholica* or its credal variant with Ireland, we have had opportunity to observe that there are nevertheless a number of points of resemblance between our text and its Creed form on the one hand and the credal variant of BAN on the other. Could it be the case, there-

---

[128] See above, chapter 4.4, pp. 305-307.

fore, that the form of the Creed under discussion indeed stems from Ireland? Although we know too little about the wording of the Creed in Ireland either to prove or to disprove this possibility, two considerations seem to speak against such a hypothesis. For one thing, we have seen that the most salient similarities, the phrases *deum omnipotentem, unam habentem substantiam cum patre et filio* and the use of *post mortem* in connection with the Resurrection of the Flesh, are probably not part of a credal quotation in the *expositio*, but rather belong either to the commentary or to a freely formulated indication of the content of the Creed, and that their presence in BAN as part of the Creed is probably best explained by assuming that the redactor deliberately adopted them from our *expositio* or a similar text. Moreover, we have seen that there is reason to assume that the Creed reached Ireland by way of Gaul, which would suffice to explain the resemblances that remain (the use of *Conceptus* in the third article and of *Ac* in the eighth are the most striking ones). That our *expositio* does indeed contain not an Irish but a Gallican variant is strongly suggested by a second consideration. We have seen that from the fourth century onwards, the Gallican combination *Dei ... omnipotentis* gradually spread over the other regions of the Western church, whereas our text yields the more conservative *In dexteram dei patris*. If the credal variant under discussion really stemmed from Ireland, we would have to assume that a Gallican form of the Creed travelled thither as early as the fourth century, which accords ill with the fact that Irish Christianity only began to take shape after 400 [129].

Since practically all the signs are that Gaul is the home of the credal variant in our anonymous *expositio de fide catholica* CPL 505, and no other region constitutes a serious alternative [130], the conclusion that we indeed have a Gallican form of the Creed here is obvious. The next question is, of course, that of the date of its origin.

Here, it should be recalled that this form of the Creed has preserved a number of markedly conservative traits. The most important of these are the absence of *Passus* and of Eternal Life, which

---

[129] Saint Patrick, d. 461, is the first Irish author to figure in Dekkers 1995.

[130] The use of *Conceptus* in the third article and of *Victor* in the sixth rule out Spain, Northern Italy, and the Latin Balkans. For the case of Africa, see above, p. 314.

reflect a fourth or early fifth-century stage in the Gallican development of the wording of the Creed. The formulation of the seventh
article with *In dexteram dei patris* at least represents an equally
early situation, as we have already had opportunity to observe. In
fact, the absence of the Communion of Saints constitutes an almost
equally strong argument for an early dating of the *expositio*. This
addition was almost certainly born in Gaul, to all probability at
some date not too remote from 400, and met with practically the
same success as *Conceptus*, *Passus*, and Eternal Life. Of course, an
originally fourth-century formulation may well have remained in
living use for a considerable time after 400, but the fact that the
credal variant of the anonymous *expositio* exhibits no less than four
such formulations, all having hardly any parallels in other Gallican
witnesses to the form of the Creed, makes a sixth or even seventh-
century origin very hard to imagine. These considerations are supported by the fact that the addition of the phrase *Inuisibilem uisibilium et inuisibilium conditorem* to the first article must precede the
time that *Creatorem caeli et terrae* became the obligatory extension
of the first article in Gaul [131].

On the other hand, there are a number of points that speak
against too early a date. First of all, the second article already exhibits *Vnicum* and *Dominum nostrum* and the fifth article has been
extended to *Tertia die resurrexit ex mortuis*. Although both phenomena probably go back to the beginning of the fourth century, it
should be borne in mind that no Gallican form of the second article
using the word order *Iesum Christum, filium (eius) unicum dominum nostrum* can be found before the second half of the sixth century (CY-T) and that such formulations occur more frequently only
towards the end of the development of the wording of the Creed in
Gaul (PIRM, MGV, Bobbio C). Similarly, the addition of *A mortuis*
to the Gallican form of the fifth article only becomes a rule towards
the end of the sixth century, whereas there is only one certain
instance of its use before that time (CY-T). Moreover, the addition
of *Catholicam*, which is certainly present in the form of the Creed
that underlies our anonymous text, probably did not arrive in Gaul
before the end of the fourth century. Finally, we have seen that,

---

[131] Compare the case of the credal variant of the pseudo-Augustinian *sermo
super symbolum* CPL 365. See above, chapter 4.4, p. 306.

although this addition did not yet figure in his credal variant, the anonymous author of the *expositio* was aware of the fact that other forms of the Creed could contain the Descent to Hell, an addition that is not attested in any Gallican form of the Creed before the sixth or even seventh century (CAE-A being the only possible sixth-century witness) and is still absent from at least one seventh-century one (MGV).

In the light of all these considerations, it seems best to date the anonymous *expositio de fide catholica* CPL 505 between 400 and 500. An earlier date would be incompatible with the wording of the first, second, fifth, and tenth articles and with the apparent awareness of the Descent to Hell, whereas a later one would be difficult to reconcile with the formulation of the third, fourth, and seventh articles or with the absence of the Communion of Saints and Eternal Life. This means that, as far as we can judge, Kattenbusch's suggestion of Hilary of Arles's authorship remains possible, but Lejay's claim for Caesarius should be rejected.

## 4.6 The Pseudo-Fulgentian *sermo de symbolo* CPL 846

This anonymous sermon on the Creed was only discovered and edited in the twentieth century by the well-known scholar Germain Morin [132]. Morin found it in one manuscript, nowadays in Vienna but originally written somewhere in Northern Italy [133]. Morin's edition is on the whole a very accurate one but nevertheless stands in need of correction in one or two places. For that reason and in order to facilitate reference in our discussion of its credal variant, we offer a new edition of this text in the appendix to our study.

When we turn to the pseudo-Fulgentian *sermo de sybolo* to elicit a credal variant from it, we encounter the difficulty that there are no explicit quotations of the Creed to be found in it. On the other hand, it is clear that the author follows the Creed closely [134]. Each article is first introduced and then discussed at some length. In each introduction, the phrase indicating the article that the author is

---

[132] Morin 1923, 236-242.

[133] See Grégoire 1980, 281.

[134] That the author is indeed commenting upon the Creed is not only indicated by the title but also borne out by a remark closing the exposition of the seventh article: *Audite quid in symbolo sequitur* (see below, with footnote 143).

going to discuss could be a literal quotation. We meet, therefore, the same procedure as with AU-H, so it will be best to proceed in the same way as we did when discussing that witness. That is to say, we shall treat these indications as literal quotations [135] but bear in mind that this depends on our assumption that the author was concerned with offering literal quotations, but that he does not say so himself in so many words.

Although Morin made the same choice when editing the text [136], we nevertheless arrive at a different reconstruction from his in three points - the first article, the construction of the second and ninth articles, and the Descent to Hell.

To start with the first article, this is introduced thus: *Renuntiantes autem diabolo fideliter atque indubitanter credite in deum patrem omnipotentem. Deus enim pater ...* [137]. After this introduction, the author makes a point of explaining that God is truly God and truly Father. Turning to the second article, he refers to the contents of the first again: *Ideo credentes in deum patrem omnipotentem uniuersorum creatorem, credite in filium eius Iesum Christum dominum nostrum. Ipse est enim ...* [138]. On the basis of this second instance, Morin reconstructs *Credo in deum patrem omnipotentem, uniuersorum creatorem*, referring to Quodvultdeus of Carthage and Fulgentius of Ruspe, who, in his opinion, both testify to a similar form of the first article [139]. There are two reasons, however, for doubting that the phrase *Vniuersorum creatorem* belonged to the form of the Creed of our anonymous author.

First of all, Morin's procedure of treating the introduction to the second article as a literal quotation of the first is rather questionable. It is indeed the case that our author likes to repeat the article he has just expounded before going on with the next, but in most cases this repetition is couched in different terms than the introductory quotations. Thus, the second article, introduced as ... *credite in*

---

[135] This decision is supported by the fact that in most cases a syntactic break follows such a quotation.

[136] Morin (1923) prints the credal quotations in capitals and discusses these on pp. 242-244.

[137] Pseudo-Fulgentius, *sermo de symbolo* 6; see below, p. 442.

[138] Pseudo-Fulgentius, *sermo de symbolo* 8; see below, p. 443.

[139] Morin 1923, 242. See above for our discussion of the relevant sections in QU and FU: chapter 3.4, pp. 170-171 and 179-180.

*filium eius Iesum Christum dominum nostrum* (see above), is
resumed with the words *Iste unigenitus dei filius ...* (before the third
article), as *Redemptor ergo noster Christus dei filius* (before the
fourth), and again with the words *Credentes itaque in deum patrem
omnipotentem, et in filium eius dominum nostrum Iesum Christum,
credite in spiritum sanctum* (before the ninth) [140]. Similarly, the
fourth article is presented as *... crucifixus est sub Pontio Pilato et
sepultus. Ecce quantum ...* and resumed as *Christus ergo dei filius crucifixus et sepultus descendit ...* [141]. The same procedure is followed for
the fifth article (first: *Deinde tertio die a mortuis resurrexit. Audisti,
homo ...*, then: *Non solum autem resurrexit, sed etiam in caelum
...* [142]), the sixth (first: *... sed etiam in caelum ascendit et in dextera
patris sedet*, then: *Christus qui ascendit in caelum, inde uenturus
...* [143]), Eternal Life (first: *... credite etiam uitam aeternam, quia nos
...*, then: *Accepimus itaque uitam aeternam per sanctam ecclesiam* [144]),
and the tenth article (first: *... per sanctam ecclesiam. Ipsa est ...*,
then: *In ecclesia ergo catholica permanete* [145]; more examples can be
found below). The sixth article excepted (see above), all these parts
of the Creed are resumed in a different formulation from that of
their introduction. If, then, we regard these introductions as literal
quotations, which nothing prohibits, it will be impossible to regard
the resuming references as quotations as well.

   That the introductions pretend to present not only the literal but
also the complete wording of an article is made extremely probable
by a second observation, which thus forms an additional argument
not to take the words *uniuersorum creatorem* in this sermon as part
of the author's form of the Creed. This is the fact that the introductory indications frequently contain elements that do not recur in
the commentary. Thus, the words *Dominum nostrum*, *De spiritu
sancto*, *Sub Pontio Pilato*, *Tertio die*, *Viuos et mortuos*, and in fact
the whole seventh article, are mentioned but not commented upon.
We have already had opportunity to observe that such a procedure
can be taken as a sure indication that an author is concerned with

---

[140] Pseudo-Fulgentius, *sermo de symbolo* 9, 11, and 21; see below, pp. 443 and 445.
[141] Pseudo-Fulgentius, *sermo de symbolo* 11 and 14; see below, pp. 443-444.
[142] Pseudo-Fulgentius, *sermo de symbolo* 15-16; see below, p. 444.
[143] Pseudo-Fulgentius, *sermo de symbolo* 16-18; see below, p. 444.
[144] Pseudo-Fulgentius, *sermo de symbolo* 28-29; see below, p. 446.
[145] Pseudo-Fulgentius, *sermo de symbolo* 29 and 32; see below, pp. 446-447.

offering complete quotations. That we find it used in the pseudo-Fulgentian *sermo de symbolo* as well not only strengthens our conclusion that the author provides quotations instead of mere indications of the contents of the Creed, but also makes it rather less probable that he has reserved part of his form of the first article for the introduction to his exposition of the second article [146].

A more probable explanation for the formulation that we find in the introduction to the second article is that the author was influenced by the way he had closed his exposition of the first: *Deus ergo uerus aequalem sibi genuit deum uerum, deus aeternus aequalem sibi deum genuit coaeternum ... omnipotens aequaliter omnipotentem, rerum omnium creator aequaliter rerum omnium creatorem* [147]. That he chose the phrase *uniuersorum creatorem* may well indicate that he was acquainted with forms of the Creed in which it did play a role, but that is, of course, something quite different from postulating such a form of the Creed for our anonymous author here.

A second point in respect to which we cannot agree with Morin's reconstruction is constituted by the beginnings of the second and ninth articles. Morin reconstructs these as *Credo et in filium eius Iesum Christum, dominum nostrum* and *Credo et in spiritum sanctum* on the basis of the phrases *... credite in filium eius Iesum Christum dominum nostrum* and *... credite et in spiritum sanctum* in pseudo-Fulgentius, *sermo de symbolo* 8 and 21 (see above) [148]. If we take our hypothesis that the anonymous author is concerned with following the wording of the Creed in as literal a way as possible seriously, a reconstruction of the second article as *Credo in filium eius Iesum Christum, dominum nostrum* is much more likely. If the second article of the author's credal variant really contained the particle *Et*, its absence in the introductory quotation would be hard to explain, especially since the immediately preceding words *Ideo credentes in deum patrem omnipotentem, uniuersorum creatorem* [149] would make its use quite natural. Matters are somewhat more complicated in the case of the ninth article, since the phrase *... credite in spiritum sanctum* is based upon a conjecture of Morin's. The manuscript

---

[146] This conclusion is reinforced by the fact that the phrase *uniuersorum creatorem* is absent from the introduction to the ninth article (quoted above).

[147] Pseudo-Fulgentius, *sermo de symbolo* 7; see below, pp. 442-443.

[148] Morin 1923, 238-239 and 243-244.

[149] See above, footnote 138.

reads ... *credite et spiritu sanctum.* To amend *spiritu* to *spiritum*
seems to be fully justified, and the preposition *in* can also hardly
be dispensed with, but both difficulties are solved equally well by
reading ... *credite in spiritum sanctum.* Here, as in the case of the
second article, the preceding phrase (*Credentes itaque in deum patrem
omnipotentem, et in filium eius dominum nostrum Iesum Christum* [150])
almost begs the use of *Et*, which could well explain its supplanting
an original *In*. If our explanation is right, then in the author's form
of the Creed both the second and the ninth article began with the
words *Credo in*, and neither contained the particle *Et*.

In the third place, the Descent to Hell is indicated thus: *Christus
ergo dei filius crucifixus et sepultus descendit etiam in infernum* [151],
after which a short commentary ensues. From this, Morin reconstructs *Descendit in infernum* [152]. First of all, it should be observed
that the fact that the author introduces the Descent to Hell by
recalling the Crucifixion and Sepulture of Christ is a very strong
indicaton that this addition was indeed part of his form of the
Creed, and that it is not merely mentioned in the exposition of the
fourth article. In the light of the author's usual concern to offer an
embedded but literal quotation of the article he is going to comment upon, it would be rather arbitrary on our part to exclude
*Etiam* from our reconstruction, especially as there is no compelling
reason why it could not be part of the Creed here [153].

For the rest, the pseudo-Fulgentian *sermo de symbolo* yields its
underlying form of the Creed without any problems. Most phrases
introducing, and therefore probably quoting, the several articles
have already been mentioned above. For the remaining parts of
the Creed, we can marshal the following passages: *Iste unigenitus
dei filius uerus et naturaliter deus et cum patre unus deus, ut quos*

---

[150] Pseudo-Fulgentius, *sermo de symbolo* 21; see above.

[151] Pseudo-Fulgentius, *sermo de symbolo* 14; see below, p. 444.

[152] Morin 1923, 239 and 243.

[153] Compare the phrase *Crucifixus etiam pro nobis* in the Latin translation of
the Nicaeno-Constantinopolitan Creed. On similar grounds, the presence of
*Deinde* in the fifth article (*Deinde tertio die a mortuis resurrexit*; see above, footnote 142) cannot be excluded, although it seems to be better explained as a short
introduction to the quotation. The use of *sed etiam* before the sixth article (see
below) is entirely caused by the preceding *Non solum*. Similarly, the form *Credite
etiam* introducing the twelfth article (see below) can hardly be taken as part of
the quotation.

*fecerat reficeret et quos creauerat recrearet natus est de spiritu sancto ex uirgine Maria. Qui enim ...* [154], *Non solum autem resurrexit sed etiam in caelum ascendit et in dextera patris sedet. Quod ergo ...* [155], *Christus qui ascendit in caelum, inde uenturus est iudicare uiuos et mortuos. Veniet iudicaturus ...* [156], *... in hac fide nobis tribuitur remissio peccatorum* [157], *Credite etiam carnis resurrectionem, quam in se ipso nobis demonstrauit Christus ...* [158], and *Accipiemus itaque uitam aeternam per sanctam ecclesiam* [159].

We thus may reconstruct the underlying credal variant of the pseudo-Fulgentian *sermo de symbolo* as follows:

*Credo in deum patrem omnipotentem*
*credo in filium eius Iesum Christum, dominum nostrum*
*natus est de spiritu sancto ex uirgine Maria*
*crucifixus sub Pontio Pilato et sepultus*
*descendit etiam in infernum*
*(deinde?) tertio die a mortuis resurrexit*
*in caelum ascendit*
*et in dextera patris sedet*
*inde uenturus est iudicare uiuos et mortuos*
*credo (et?) in spiritum sanctum*
*remissionem peccatorum*
*carnis resurrectionem*
*uitam aeternam*
*per sanctam ecclesiam.*

Since the moment of its publication, both the pseudo-Fulgentian sermon and the form of the Creed represented by it have been assigned to sixth-century Africa. Morin points in particular to the

---

[154] Pseudo-Fulgentius, *sermo de symbolo* 9; see below, p. 443.

[155] Pseudo-Fulgentius, *sermo de symbolo* 16; see below, p. 444.

[156] Pseudo-Fulgentius, *sermo de symbolo* 18; see below, p. 444.

[157] Pseudo-Fulgentius, *sermo de symolo* 23; see below, p. 445. This is the only case, apart from the use of *Credite* instead of *Credo*, where we are forced to assume that the quotation is not entirely literal, though the reconstruction of *Remissionem peccatorum* is obvious and does not pose any problems. It is all the more interesting, therefore, that number 127 in the Mondsee homiliary, borrowing from our pseudo-Fulgentian sermon, reads *In hac fide credamus nobis tribui remissionem omnium peccatorum*: see Lemarié 1993, 581.

[158] Pseudo-Fulgentius, *sermo de symbolo* 25; see below, p. 445.

[159] See above, with footnote 145.

form of the Creed, which shows numerous parallels with that found in QU, but also recognizes African features in the sermon itself. Although he does not explicitly discuss its date, Morin signals the influence of Fulgentius of Ruspe in the sermon, which would indeed make a sixth-century African origin rather obvious [160].

It will nevertheless be interesting to see whether Morin's conclusion is supported by our regional typology or not. Moreover, we can try to establish something more definite about the dating of the text. Of course, Morin may be right that our anonymous author borrows from Fulgentius of Ruspe, but as long as this question has not been studied more closely, the relationship could just as well have been the other way round, or both texts may draw from a common source. Let us see, then, where our theory about the history of the form of the Creed will take us.

First of all, we should note a number of formulations in the credal variant of the pseudo-Fulgentian *sermo de symbolo* that cannot be found in witnesses to the form of the Creed that we have examined so far. These comprise the wording of the third article with *Natus est* without *Qui* (though the testimony of APS admits of this possibility), the use of *Etiam* and *In infernum* in the Descent to Hell, the formulation of the fifth article with the masculine form *Tertio*, the word order in the sixth article (*In caelum ascendit*), and the use of *Et* and the ablative *Dextera* in the seventh article, though the latter feature cannot, in the light of the scribe's spelling habits [161], be assigned too much value. We shall have to come back to these peculiarities once we have formed a theory about the origin of the credal variant under discussion.

When we turn to the credal variant looking for 'unique features', no less than three of them crop up, all pointing to Africa: the word order *A mortuis resurrexit* in the fifth article, the word order *In dextera patris sedet* in the seventh article, and the use of the formula

---

[160] Morin 1923, 242-244. That Morin does not envisage a later origin is borne out by the title of the article containing his text: 'Deux sermons africains du Ve/ VIe siècle ...'. Morin's conclusion is applauded by Lambot (1958, 192), Lemarié (1993, 569+n2), Dekkers (1995, 281), and Frede (1995, 488). The latter two authors also connect the text with the pseudo-Augustinian *expositio super symbolum* CPL 365: see above, chapter 4.4, p. 305.

[161] See Lambot 1958, 190 and the critical apparatus to our edition of the text in the appendix.

*Per sanctam ecclesiam* to close the Creed. Of course, the wording of the fifth and seventh articles as we meet them in our pseudo-Fulgentian text does not agree completely with what we have postulated as 'unique features' for Africa (*Tertia die a mortuis resurrexit* and *Ad dexteram patris sedet*), but the important thing is the fact that the elements *Resurrexit* and *A mortuis* as well as *Sedet* and *Ad dextera(m) patris* have been reversed. Both are phenomena that, as far as we can see, do not occur outside Africa. Moreover, our author seems to know forms of the Creed that add *Vniuersorum creatorem* to the first article, which is another African 'unique feature'. Further, one should note the word order *Virgine Maria* in the third article. Since this also occurs in AU-M, it is not a 'unique feature' for the African form of the Creed in the strict sense of the word, but we have seen that its occurrence in AU-M may well be due to African influence. That we meet it again in the credal variant of the pseudo-Fulgentian *sermo de symbolo* can therefore be considered as another indication that this variant stems from Africa. Finally, one could point out the formulation of the second article as *Credo in filium eius Iesum Christum, dominum nostrum*. This has an exact parallel only in the Gallican witness PS-AU, but then this article presents itself in such a bewildering variety that this formulation can hardly be considered a compelling 'unique feature' for Gaul.

At first sight, therefore, the hypothesis of an African home for the credal variant under discussion seems to be the most likely possibility. This hypothesis is confirmed by the fact that practically all African 'general features' can be found in our anonymous author's form of the Creed as well. The first, second, third, eighth, ninth, tenth, eleventh, and twelfth articles all fit in with the picture of the form of the Creed in Africa as we have reconstructed it. On the other hand, our anonymous variant departs from this general African picture in some four places. Of these, three comprise points of wording. Thus, we have postulated the accusative construction *Crucifixum sub Pontio Pilato et sepultum* to be general in Africa, whereas the form of the Creed under discussion has *Crucifixus sub Pontio Pilato et sepultus*. We have seen, however, that two or more different constructions of the fourth article were probably in African use from the start. One can also point to the fact that the placing of the fourth article in an accusative construction as an African 'general feature' is based on the testimony of AU-H and QU only,

FU yielding no quotation of this article. It is more than probable, however, that the underlying form of the Creed in FU would yield the same construction as our pseudo-Fulgentian text, since FU offers the third article as *Qui natus est de spiritu sancto ex Maria uirgine*. Similarly, the addition of *Vitam aeternam* to the twelfth article shows a small difference with our African 'general feature' *In uitam aeternam*. In the light of the fact that *In uitam aeternam* is only read by one African witness, the other three not yielding any information concerning the use of *In* here, this can hardly be considered an objection to an African origin of the credal variant under discussion. The same thing holds true for the use of the conjunction *Et* and *Tertio* instead of the general African *Tertia*, since *Et* and *Tertio* would be strange for any region.

The most serious deviation from the African 'general features' is the addition of the Descent to Hell, which is absent, as far as we can see, from all other African witnesses. If we want to ascribe pseudo-Fulgentius's form of the Creed to Africa, therefore, we shall have to postulate that the Descent to Hell was adopted by some African church from one of the other regions. Such an assumption is, of course, quite possible and may even be supported by the fact that our text yields a different formulation here from those that we meet in other regions.

Since the other articles of the credal variant under discussion do not pose objections to its stemming from Africa [162], and no other region presents itself as a likely home for it [163], the conclusion seems safe that the pseudo-Fulgentian *sermo de symbolo* presents an African form of the Creed.

It is more problematic to be definite about its date. First of all, because of the paucity of Creed forms that certainly stem from Africa, it is difficult to gain an impression of any internal African

[162] *Credo in deum patrem omnipotentem* is also found in QU, *Credo in filium eius Iesum Christum, dominum nostrum* comes quite close to AU-H, *In caelum ascendit* is new but fits in with the African variety of wording in the sixth article and the formulations of the eighth, ninth, eleventh, and twelfth articles all belong to the 'general features' of the Creed in Africa.

[163] The absence of *Conceptus* and *Passus* in combination with the presence of the Descent to Hell and Eternal Life speak against a Gallican origin; for Spain, the absence of *Passus* is also a determining factor; for Northern Italy, the absence of *Qui* in the third article and for the Balkans, the absence of *Catholicam* is problematic.

developments. All we know for sure is that the addition of Eternal
Life and *Per sanctam ecclesiam* as the final clause of the Creed and
the introduction of *Vnicum, Dominum nostrum,* and *A mortuis* must
belong to the protohistory of the form of the Creed in Africa, and
that additions to the first article, the word order *Virgine Maria,* the
accusative construction in the third and fourth articles, the use of
*Assumptus est* and *Caelum* instead of *Ascendit* and *Caelos,* the word
order *Ad dexteram patris sedet,* and the use of *Credo in* for the second and ninth articles came later to the fore, though usually also
before the end of the fourth century. What we do not know is how
popular all these innovations became. Nevertheless, we can say that
our anonymous African credal variant seems to combine conservative features and innovations. Thus, it has not yet adopted the
addition of *Vniuersorum creatorem, regem saeculorum, immortalem et
inuisibilem* to the first article (already attested for the fourth century) or that of *Vnicum* to the second article (attested in the sixth
century only by FU, but probably present in Africa from the third
century onwards). On the other hand, we do find *Dominum nostrum*
in the second article, the word order *Virgine Maria* in the third, *A
mortuis* in the fifth, *Caelum* in the sixth, Eternal Life, the closing of
the Creed with *Per sanctam ecclesiam* (all already attested for the
fourth or even third centuries), or *Credo in* in the second and ninth
articles (first attested in the fifth century). Moreover, the addition
of the Descent to Hell cannot have taken place before the fifth century.

This last point provides a safe *terminus a quo* - our anonymous
form of the Creed will certainly not be older than the fifth century.
But what about a *terminus ad quem*? When one considers the fact
that substantial additions to the Creed tend to become general once
they have entered a certain region, it is rather unexpected that
pseudo-Fulgentius does not testify to *Vniuersorum ... inuisibilem*
and *Vnicum,* which already played a role in fourth-century African
forms of the Creed. More in line in this respect is FU, a sixth-century text in which both additions can be found. For that reason, we
are somewhat hesitant to state as boldly as Morin that our anonymous form of the Creed must be later than FU. In fact, looking
at the form of the Creed only, a fifth-century origin seems to be
most probable for the pseudo-Fulgentian *sermo de symbolo.* We
should be aware, however, that we know too little about the history

of the formulation of the Creed in Africa to exclude the possibility of a sixth-century origin altogether. Perhaps a new study of the exact relationship between Fulgentius's and pseudo-Fulgentius's commentaries can throw new light on this question, but that would fall beyond the scope of our study.

### 4.7 Two Pseudo-Chrysostomic *expositiones symboli* CPL 915

In 1869, Caspari called attention to two sermons on the Creed that he had found in two sixteenth-century Latin editions of John Chrysostom. He published their texts anew, partly from these editions, partly from two manuscripts [164]. Morin established beyond any reasonable doubt that both sermons, together with some twenty others, constituted a collection of sermons that stemmed from one and the same, albeit anonymous, Latin author [165]. The complete collection was reprinted from the Parisian 1536 edition of John Chrysostom (Erasmus - Hucherius) [166] in the Supplement Series to Migne's *Patrologia Latina* by Hamman [167]. Although Morin already called for a critical edition of the sermon collection in 1905 [168], this task was only tackled recently by François Joseph Leroy, who is preparing an edition for *Corpus Christianorum* [169]. It is by his kind permission that we are able to present his critical text of both sermons in the appendix to our study.

Although he discusses the several articles of the Creed more or less one by one, the author of our two *expositiones* does not always

[164] Caspari 1869, 225-234.

[165] Morin 1894.

[166] See for more extensive data concerning this edition the *Catalogue général des livres imprimés de la Bibliothèque Nationale. Auteurs ... Tome LXXVII ...*, Paris, 1923, 684-685.

[167] PLS 4, 741-834. It should be noted that there is more than one Latin pseudo-Chrysostomic sermon collection, which Hamman distinguishes from each other by Roman capitals. Following him, we shall indicate our anonymous author as 'Chrysostomus Latinus C'. Hamman offers 31 sermons, of which our two *expositiones* bear the numbers 27 and 29 (PLS 4, 814-817 and 821-825). There are, however, really only 30 sermons (see below, footnote 213), and the two *expositiones* are numbered 26 and 28 by Leroy (communication by letter). We shall use Leroy's numbering.

[168] Morin 1905b, 333.

[169] The edition by J.G. Lister, announced by Morin (1913, 38), never saw the light of day (kind communication from F.J. Leroy).

follow the same procedure when referring to them. He provides an occasional hard and fast quotation, but more often only indicates the part of the Creed he is going to comment upon. Sometimes he even skips certain parts of the Creed [170]. Fortunately, the fact that we have two *expositiones* from the same author enables us in most cases to gain a fairly accurate impression of his form of the Creed. Nevertheless, because of this methodical inconsistency, it will be best to discuss the information about the author's form of the Creed article by article.

We have several hard and fast quotations for the wording of the first article: *Ergo audite hanc ut dixi regulam uestrae confessionis: Credo in deum patrem omnipotentem* [171], *Ergo: Credo in deum patrem omnipotentem* [172], *Dicite ergo quod a nobis auditis: Credo in deum patrem omnipotentem. Videte, unde coepistis? Credo, dixistis ...* [173], *Sed in quo? Videte: In patrem. Quod dixistis in capite orationis: Pater noster qui es in caelis, hoc dicitis et in symboli confessione: Credo in deum patrem omnipotentem* [174]. More free references are found in *sermo 26* 3 (*Ergo creditis deo omnipotenti, quia ...*; see below, p. 450) and *26* 4 (*Ecce patrem deum uocatis ...*; see below, p. 450). That the words *Credo in deum patrem omnipotentem* constitute the complete first article cannot be considered absolutely certain, as the author sometimes skips parts of the Creed in his *expositiones*, but it is at least extremely probable in the light of two observations. First, our anonymous expositor presents no less than five literal quotations of the first article in its original shorter form. If the words *Creatorem caeli et terrae* or a similar addition belonged to his credal variant, one would expect at least a trace of them. A second, more positive argument is provided by the transition from the first to the second article in *sermo 26*. After the author has expounded the elements *Credo, Patrem* and *Omnipotentem*, he continues: *Ecce isti qui hoc faciunt libere dicunt: Credo in deum patrem omnipotentem.*

---

[170] Thus, we do not find any reference to the Descent to Hell or to the sixth article in *sermo 26*. The same holds true for the sixth, seventh, and eighth articles in *sermo 28*.

[171] Chrysostomus Latinus C, *sermo 26* 1-2; see below, p. 450.

[172] Chrysostomus Latinus C, *sermo 26* 3; see below, p. 450.

[173] Chrysostomus Latinus C, *sermo 28* 2; see below, p. 453.

[174] Chrysostomus Latinus C, *sermo 28* 3; see below, p. 453.

*Sequitur dicens: Et in unicum filium eius* ... [175]. The word *sequitur*, linking two successive quotations, seems to exclude the possibility that an addition of any kind had a place in the author's form of the first article of the Creed [176].

For the second article, we have one certainly literal quotation: *Sequitur dicens: Et in unicum filium eius, dominum nostrum Iesum Christum. Iste quare unicus?* ... [177], which is supported by two probable embedded quotations: *Ergo creditis in unicum filium eius, dominum nostrum Iesum Christum* [178] and *Ergo creditis in unicum dominum nostrum Iesum Christum, natum* ... [179]. The word *ergo* seems to serve as a quotation marker here, though the second quotation, lacking the words *Filium eius*, has been shortened, probably because of the fact that its only function is to introduce the next article [180]. There is, therefore, no reason to doubt that the author's form of the second article ran *Et in unicum filium eius, dominum nostrum Iesum Christum*.

Matters become more complicated when we turn to the third article. In the first *expositio*, it is introduced thus: *Ergo iste natus est de spiritu sancto et uirgine Maria* [181]. That the words *natus est* ... probably constitute an embedded quotation is suggested by the use of *ergo* and by their position in the introduction to the discussion of the third article. This suggestion is supported by two partial but literal quotations: *Ideo diximus ista quia dictum est: Natus de spiritu sancto* [182] and *Et quia deus spiritus est uenit in Mariam, dicente angelo: Spiritus sanctus ... uocabitur filius dei. Natus de spiritu sancto. Istum spiritum sanctum* ... [183] (the syntactic break vouches for a literal quotation here). It should be noted, however, that both quotations lack the auxiliary *est*, so that this was probably added by the author to our first, embedded, quotation in order to create smoother syntax. More free quotations or even indications are prob-

---

[175] Chrysostomus Latinus C, *sermo 26* 4-5; see below, p. 450.

[176] Thus also Caspari 1869, 239-n90. Hahn (1897, 50+nn82-84) and Morin (1894, 397-398) follow Caspari in his reconstruction of this and the other articles.

[177] Chrysostomus Latinus C, *sermo 26* 5; see below, p. 450.

[178] Chrysostomus Latinus C, *sermo 28* 4; see below, p. 453.

[179] Chrysostomus Latinus C, *sermo 28* 6; see below, p. 454.

[180] Similarly Caspari 1869, 239-240n91.

[181] Chrysostomus Latinus C, *sermo 26* 5; see below, p. 454.

[182] Chrysostomus Latinus C, *sermo 28* 4; see below, p. 454.

[183] Chrysostomus Latinus C, *sermo 28* 5; see below, p. 454.

ably found in *sermo 28* 4 (*Non dicatis minorem esse filium de patre genitum, sed istum qui natus est de spiritu sancto et Maria uirgine*; see below, p. 453), *28* 5 (*Ergo creditis in unicum dominum nostrum Iesum Christum, natum de spiritu sancto et uirgine Maria*; see below, p. 454), and *28* 8 (*Ergo natus de spiritu sancto et de uirgine Maria crucifixus* ...; see below, p; 455). All in all, it seems safe to reconstruct *Natus de spiritu sancto et uirgine Maria*. The first five words are vouched for by literal quotations, the word order *Virgine Maria* and the connection with a simple *Et* are each presented by three out of four free or embedded quotations.

When turning to the fourth article, we find that our author contents himself with just giving indications or embedded quotations at best. Thus we read in the first *expositio*, at the beginning of the section on the fourth article: *Iste ergo natus creuit, ad passionem peruenit, crucifixus est sub Pontio Pilato* [184]. The words *crucifixus est sub Pontio Pilato* just might be a partial quotaton, but apart from the fact that they serve to introduce a discussion of the importance of Christ's Crucifixion, nothing supports such a supposition. Some lines further on, we read: *Iste Pontius Pilatus praesidatum gerebat, iussit eum crucifigi. Sepultus est postquam mortuus, ut nobis uitam praestaret* ... [185]. Here, the phrase *Sepultus est postquam mortuus* looks like a free reference to the contents of the Creed, especially because of the gloss-like sequel introduced by *ut*. Next, the section on the fifth article opens thus: *Ergo iste crucifixus, sepultus, tertia die* ... [186]. Again, the fourth article is indicated, not quoted. In the other *expositio*, the author turns from the third to the fourth article with the words: *Ergo natus de spiritu sancto et de uirgine Maria crucifixus est sub Pontio Pilato. Quare hoc* ... [187]. Here, as in the other sermon, the words *crucifixus est sub Pontio Pilato* might be a quotation but there is nothing to corroborate such a hypothesis. Some lines further on, finally, we read: *Ergo iste crucifixus sub Pontio Pilato sepultus est, ut in morte sua* ... [188]. The use of *ut* again strongly suggests that the author is referring to the contents of the Creed, but the preceding words are as unhelpful for reconstructing a particular wording

---

[184] Chrysostomus Latinus C, *sermo 26* 6; see below, p. 451
[185] Chrysostomus Latinus C, *sermo 26* 6; see below, p. 451
[186] Chrysostomus Latinus C, *sermo 26* 7; see below, p. 451
[187] Chrysostomus Latinus C, *sermo 28* 8; see below, p. 455
[188] Chrysostomus Latinus C, *sermo 28* 9; see below, p. 455

of the fourth article as the other passages that we have just examined. All in all, then, it seems best to abstain from making any reconstruction at all here [189].

The Descent to Hell may well have been present in the credal variant under discussion. After treating the importance of Christ's death, the author continues in his second *expositio*: *Descendit ad infernum, ut et ibi a miraculo non uacaret* (*sermo 28* 9), connecting the Descent with the resurrection of many saints described in Matt. 27, 52. The clause *ut et ibi ...* looks like the start of a new piece of commentary, so that there is every reason to assume that *Descendit ad infernum* is a real quotation, though the possibility remains that the author used a different formulation in his credal variant, in which case we would only have an indication of the contents of the Creed here. That the Descent to Hell is not mentioned in the other *expositio* cannot be an argument against our conclusion because there are more credal elements than just this one that are left out by the author in one or even both sermons [190].

As far as the fifth article is concerned, we have a probable quotation in each sermon: *Ergo iste crucifixus, sepultus, tertia die a*

---

[189] Caspari (1869, 240-241n93) is more positive and reconstructs *Crucifixus est sub Pontio Pilato et sepultus*. He observes that the author expounds the fourth article in both sermons in a similar way: first he dwells on the importance of Christ's suffering, then he explains the presence of Pontius Pilate's name in the Creed, after which a mention of the Sepulture triggers an expositon of the importance of Christ's death. According to Caspari, this proves that our anonymous author used a form of the fourth article without either of the additions *Passus* and *Mortuus*. But the words ... *ad passionem peruenit* and *Sepultus postquam mortuus* in *sermo 26* could be taken to refer to a form of the fourth article in which both additions were already present.

[190] Caspari, though reading *Descendit ad infernum* in his reconstruction, nevertheless sees a strong argument against this in the fact that our anonymous author in his first *expositio* links Christ's Crucifixion and Sepulture on the one hand and his Resurrection on the other as two immediately successive credal elements (*Ergo iste crucifixus, sepultus, tertia die ...* [*sermo 26* 7; see below, p. 451]; compare also the reference to the contents of the Creed that is quoted in footnote 193 below): see Caspari 1869, 240-242n94. But the words *iste crucifixus, sepultus* clearly constitute a short indication, in which the Descent to Hell may well have been understood. Kattenbusch thinks that the words *Descendit ad infernum* in *sermo 28* may be a reference to *Sepultus*, but his argument does not sound very convincing: see Kattenbusch 1894, 208. Morin (1923, 243) is more positive about the presence of the Descent to Hell in the credal variant under discussion.

*mortuis resurrexit. Ecce* ... [191] and *Tertia die a mortuis resurrexit, ne caro eius* ... [192]. There is no reason to assume that the author's form of the fifth article was different from the formulation he uses to introduce it in his expositions.

A rather special case is provided by the sixth article, the Ascension to Heaven. It does not figure in either sermon, so that we cannot say anything whatsoever about its formulation in our anonymous author's credal variant. Its absence in the two sermons does not imply, however, that it was also absent in his credal variant too, since the author is clearly not concerned with treating every single article of the Creed [193].

The next article is present in the first *expositio* only, where it is quoted no less than three times in an unambiguous way: *Sedet ad dexteram patris. Cum auditis: Sedet, nolite credere* ... [194], *Ergo hoc nolite credere cum auditis: Sedet ad dexteram patris* [195], and *Ergo: Sedet ad dexteram patris* [196].

The article on the Second Coming and the Last Judgement is also represented in the first sermon only: *Inde uenturus est iudicare uiuos et mortuos. Hic geminum intellectum* ... [197]. Its position at the head of a new paragraph as well as the clearly commentary words *Hic geminum intellectum* ... make it fairly certain that the phrase *Inde uenturus est iudicare uiuos et mortuos* may be taken as a literal quotation here.

For the ninth article, we again have the testimony of both source texts. First we read: *Credo in spiritum sanctum. Iste spiritus* ... [198]. Here, the use of the first person singular *Credo* guarantees a literal quotation. The other sermon yields: *Videte ubique sacramentum trinitatis: ecce et in spiritum sanctum credimus. Qui spiritus* ... [199]. This

[191] Chrysostomus Latinus C, *sermo 26* 7; see below, p. 451
[192] Chrysostomus Latinus C, *sermo 28* 9; see below, p. 455.
[193] Morin (1894, 398 and 396n2), moreover, points out that the author refers to the Ascension as part of the Creed in *sermo 11* of the same collection: *Semper eum confitetur ecclesia natum ex uirgine Maria, crucifixum sub Pontio Pilato, sepultum, resurgentem, in caelis ascendentem* (PLS 4, 769).
[194] Chrysostomus Latinus C, *sermo 26* 8; see below, p. 451.
[195] Chrysostomus Latinus C, *sermo 26* 8; see below, p. 452.
[196] Chrysostomus Latinus C, *sermo 26* 8; see below, p. 452.
[197] Chrysostomus Latinus C, *sermo 26* 9; see below, p. 452.
[198] Chrysostomus Latinus C, *sermo 26* 10; see below, p. 452.
[199] Chrysostomus Latinus C, *sermo 28* 10; see below, p. 455.

looks most like an indication of the ninth article, although it could
also be a partial quotation. Either way, it fits in with the hard and
fast quotation in *sermo 26*, so that we may safely reconstruct the
author's form of the ninth article as *Credo in spiritum sanctum.*

The wording of the final articles of the credal variant to which
our anonymous author testifies poses the knottiest problems. The
passages which refer more or less directly to these articles are the
following. In *sermo 26* we read: *Ergo iste spiritus ... perducit ad sanctam ecclesiam. Quia uelut nauis ...* [200]. The fact that the author goes
on to explain the significance of the Holy Church may be taken as
an indication that the words *Sanctam ecclesiam* had a place in some
way or another in his form of the Creed. Next, we have: *Promittit
carnis resurrectionem, promittit uitam aeternam, quia mortale hoc
induet immortalitatem et corruptibile hoc induet incorruptionem. Credite carnis resurrectionem ... Credite uitam aeternam ...* [201]. The double
use of *promittit* and *credite* clearly implies that the author is indicating or even quoting parts of the Creed. *Sermo 28*, then, yields first
of all: *Ecce uidete alia tria: in carnis resurrectione fides, in uita
aeterna spes, in sancta ecclesia caritas* [202]. With *alia tria*, the author
refers to his introduction to the ninth article: *Videte ubique sacramentum trinitatis: ecce et in spiritum sanctum ...* (see above). When
the triad of Father, Son, and Holy Spirit is thus explicitly linked
with that of Resurrection, Eternal Life, and Holy Church, it is clear
that the author considers the latter as well as the former to belong
to the Creed. This conclusion is supported by the phrases *Credite
carnis resurrectionem ... Credite ergo uitam aeternam* [203] and by a second reference to the same triad: *Erunt homines in resurrectione, in
uita aeterna, sicut angeli in caelo, per sanctam ecclesiam peruenientes,
quae ...* [204].

The first thing one has to acknowledge is that none of these passages can lay claim to providing hard and fast quotations. At best,
the phrases beginning with *credite* could be partial quotations, but
nothing makes this possibility more probable than that of free indications. The passage *In carnis resurrectione fides ...* seems to be ren-

---

[200] Chrysostomus Latinus C, *sermo 26* 10; see below, p. 452.

[201] Chrysostomus Latinus C, *sermo 26* 11; see below, p. 452.

[202] Chrysostomus Latinus C, *sermo 28* 10; see below, p. 456.

[203] Chrysostomus Latinus C, *sermo 28* 10-11; see below, p. 456.

[204] Chrysostomus Latinus C, *sermo 28* 11; see below, p. 456.

dered best as "In the Creed, faith is presupposed because of the Resurrection of the Flesh ...", so that the preposition *in* cannot be taken as part of a credal quotation [205].

Second, the problem arises of whether the addition *Catholicam*, the Communion of Saints, and the Remission of Sins did or did not figure in the author's form of the Creed. In the light of the absence of any mention of the sixth article in either *expositio* and of the seventh and eighth in the second one, we should be prepared to admit the possibility of the presence of *Sanctorum communionem* and *Remissionem peccatorum* or similar phrases in the credal variant we are trying to reconstruct. On the other hand, both items are additions to the original form of the Creed, so that their absence in the sermons may correspond with their absence in the credal variant as well. Although at first sight a *non liquet* seems to be the only possible conclusion, the formulation in *sermo 28* may perhaps help to gain a more positive conclusion. As a matter of fact, the phrase *Ecce uidete alia tria* ..., linking faith with Resurrection of the Flesh, hope with Eternal Life, and love with the Church, would be very strange if Resurrection, Eternal Life, and the Holy Church did not, as elements of the Creed, belong together in some specific way, just as Father, Son, and Holy Spirit constitute a natural triad because they all depend on the phrase *Credo/Et in*. Now, the only natural link one could think of would be the circumstance that Resurrection, Eternal Life, and Church constituted the closing elements of the Creed. We conclude, therefore, that our anonymous author's credal variant did not contain any mention of the Communion of Saints or the Remission of Sins [206]. As far as the addition *Catholicam*

---

[205] In order to do so, one would have to deprive *fides*, *spes*, and *caritas* of all syntactic links, which would make very unnatural Latin.

[206] According to Caspari, the article on the Remission of Sins is clearly presupposed in the phrases *Ipsa* (viz. *ecclesia*) *est quae dimittit peccata, exonerat omnia pondera, eliquata corda perducit ad palmam promissam supernae uocationis* (Chrysostomus Latinus C, *sermo 26* 11; see below, p. 452), *Credulitas haec in toto mundo sparsa est: credit Christianus in ecclesia dimitti sibi peccata, credit moribus compositis deo placere, credit indulgentiam mereri, credit uitae aeternae promissionem, credit poenam promissam peccatoribus* (*sermo 26* 2; see below, p. 450) and *... per sanctam ecclesiam peruenientes, quae mittit perfectos, quae dimittit peccata, quae candidatos in martyrio acquisiuit, quae castos et pudicos perfecit, quae nescientes ad perfectam scientiam perduxit* (*sermo 28* 11; see below, p. 456). But this is based more on his assumption that the Remission of Sins cannot be absent

is concerned, it seems safest to state that nothing suggests its presence in the form of the Creed under discussion but that on the
other hand, no unambiguous quotations of the tenth article can be
found, so that its absence cannot be proved either [207].

Finally, there is the problem of the relative order of the final
three elements. The first *expositio* treats the article on the Church
before, but the second one after those on the Resurrection of the
Flesh and Eternal Life. Although we do indeed know a number of
other credal variants that close with the Holy Church (usually in
the wording *Per sanctam ecclesiam*), it seems better to follow *sermo
26* for our reconstruction. If the author used a form of the Creed
that ended with a mention of the Church, he would not have had
any reason to discuss the Church at the point he does in his first
*expositio*. On the other hand, the position of the section on the
Church in the second *expositio* is perfectly explained by the circumstance that the author connects the discussion of the final three elements in his credal variant with the triad *fides*, *spes*, and *caritas*, in
which the Church happens to be linked with the third item of the
triad [208].

We may thus reconstruct the form of the Creed that underlies
the two pseudo-Chrysostomic *expositiones symboli* CPL 915 as follows:

> *Credo in deum patrem omnipotentem*
> *et in unicum filium eius, dominum nostrum Iesum Christum*
> *natus de spiritu sancto et uirgine Maria*
> ...
> *descendit ad infernum (?)*
> ...
> *sedet ad dexteram patris*
> *inde uenturus est iudicare uiuos et mortuos*
> *credo in spiritum sanctum*
> *[sanctam ecclesiam]*

from any form of the Creed than on the text: see Caspari 1869, 243-244n99.
Kattenbusch (1894, 208) and Morin (1894, 398) write in similar veins.

[207] Otherwise Caspari 1869, 243n98.

[208] This was already noted by Kattenbusch: see Kattenbusch 1894, 208. Caspari (1869, 242-243n98) thinks that the author must at least have been acquainted with a form of the Creed that ended in *Per sanctam ecclesiam*.

*carnis resurrectionem (?)*
*uitam aeternam (?).*

Caspari, the person who drew renewed attention to the two *expositiones*, also studied the problem of their date and place of origin. He mentions a number of places where our anonymous author is dependent on Augustine, and he stamps the sermons as "freie Reden über das Symbol". In his opinion, the author was preaching at a time when Arians and Gentiles were still a force to be reckoned with. Moreover, he states that additions like *Creatorem caeli et terrae, Conceptus, Passus* and *Mortuus, Catholicam,* and *Sanctorum communionem* are all absent from the underlying form of the Creed. For these reasons, Caspari dates the two sermons to the period 450-550 [209]. Although he abstains from saying anything more definite about the place where the sermons were written, he dwells for some time on the fact that the credal formulations *Et uirgine Maria, Tertia die a mortuis resurrexit,* and *Per sanctam ecclesiam* only have parallels in African forms of the Creed [210].

In the first volume of his monograph on the Creed, Kattenbusch largely agrees with Caspari's analysis, but considers an Italian origin more probable than an African one [211]. He seems to be followed in this respect by Hahn, who ranks the underlying credal variant among his "Symbolformeln unbekannten, aber vermuthlich italischen, Ursprungs" [212].

In the meantime, Morin discovered that the two *expositiones symboli* belong to a more extensive sermon collection, for which a number of manuscript witnesses exist and which comprises at least 27 pieces [213]. Morin subscribes to Caspari's and Kattenbusch's views but thinks that something more can be said. Certain liturgical pecu-

---

[209] Caspari 1869, 234-235+nn88-89.

[210] Caspari 1869, 235-236 and 243n98.

[211] Kattenbusch 1894, 207-209.

[212] Hahn 1897, 50+n82.

[213] Morin 1894, 385-391; on p. 386, Morin speaks misleadingly about "vingt-six discours". A year later, Morin identified four more pseudo-Chrysostomic texts that belong to the same collection: see Morin 1895, 290. This would bring the total number to 31 sermons, but, as a matter of fact, Morin's third and fourth additional texts constitute only one sermon: see Bouhot 1970, 139 and 141-142. Later on, Morin speaks about a "recueil de XXX homélies": see Morin 1913, 37 and 1923, 243. Nevertheless, both Dekkers and Frede continue to give 31 sermons in their overviews: see Dekkers 1995, 301 and Frede 1995, 570-571.

liarities that can be seen in the anonymous collection recur in two manuscripts of British origin that testify to Neapolitan liturgical usage. On the basis of this fact and the circumstance that the anonymous sermon collection was ascribed to **John** Chrysostom, Morin tentatively identifies the author with Johannes Mediocris, bishop of Naples from about 533 to 553 [214].

Kattenbusch seems to be following Morin's train of thought when he proposes another possible author - Hadrian, abbot of Nisidanum (probably situated on modern Nísida, an Italian island off the coast of Naples), who lived in the second half of the seventh century, and was presumably the person who introduced Neapolitan rites to Britain [215]. Kattenbusch presents the following arguments for his identification: (1) according to Bede, Hadrian was an African by birth, which would account for the African peculiarities in his form of the Creed; (2) the anonymous author seems to be acquainted with Benedict of Nurcia's *regula* (c. 535; CPL 1852); (3) the mention of Gentiles would fit a British context better than a South Italian one. Kattenbusch dismisses Caspari's arguments for dating the *expositiones* earlier than 550 [216]. Finally he states that the form of the Creed is essentially Neapolitan, though the *expositiones* were probably preached for a British audience [217].

Morin first declares himself not convinced by Kattenbusch's suggestion [218], but later abandons his initial point of view and states that the author was probably a disciple of Augustine, like Quodvultdeus driven out of Africa by the Vandals, though he does not say what has made him change his mind [219]. As a matter of fact, the question of the origin of the pseudo-Chrysostomic sermon collection seemed to have come to a dead end. No opinion can be said to have prevailed, though the choice of birthplace seems to be limited to Italy and Africa [220].

---

[214] Morin 1894, 398-402.

[215] See for more details about Hadrian of Nisidanum Gougaud 1912 and Aubert 1988.

[216] Kattenbusch 1900, 456-457n39.

[217] Kattenbusch 1900, 953n154.

[218] See Morin 1905b, 333n1.

[219] Morin 1913, 37; similarly Morin 1923, 243.

[220] See Bouhot 1970, 139-144 with footnotes for fuller details. Bouhot himself opts for Africa: see Bouhot 1970, 144-146. Not much new light is thrown on the question by De Vogüé 1979 and 1980. Rather astonishingly, Frede (1995, 570-

Let us see, then, whether a closer study of the underlying form of the Creed can yield any conclusions that may be helpful in assessing the date and place of origin of the pseudo-Chrysostomic sermon collection CPL 915. Before we start with an analysis of 'unique', 'other', and 'general features', however, we should make the preliminary remark that we have not been able to use any South Italian texts for our credal typology. This implies that we simply do not possess the tools to check whether the Creed form under discussion may or may not stem from Naples or another South Italian place. This implies again that, whatever the outcome of our investigation, the possibility remains that the pseudo-Chrysostomic sermon collection originated somewhere in Southern Italy.

We can point out one formulation that we have classified as a 'unique feature', viz. the wording *Tertia die a mortuis resurrexit*, a wording that is apparently not found outside Africa. Further, our reconstruction of the anonymous author's form of the Creed yields a number of formulations that cannot be found elsewhere in our overview. These are the formulation of the second article as *Et in unicum filium eius, dominum nostrum Iesum Christum*, the formulation of the third article with *Natus* in the nominative but without *Qui* or *Est*, and the Descent to Hell in the form *Descendit ad infernum*. The last of these, however, does figure in the pseudo-Augustinian *expositio super symbolum* CPL 365, a text that we have assigned to Gaul [221]. As far as the wording of the second article is concerned, this comes closest to what we find in EUSh10 (*Credo et in filium eius unicum dominum nostrum Iesum Christum*), PRIS (*Et (in?) unum dominum Iesum Christum*), and RUF (*Et in Iesum Christum, unicum filium eius, dominum nostrum*). A formulation of the third article with *Natus est* but without *Qui* is only certainly yielded by the pseudo-Fulgentian *sermo de symbolo* CPL 846, an African text [222], and possibly by APS.

On the basis of a search for 'unique features', therefore, Africa seems to present itself as the most obvious birthplace for the form of the Creed under discussion because of the formulation of the fifth

---

571) ascribes the collection to Johannes Mediocris. Dekkers (1995, 301) is a little bit more cautious.

[221] See above, chapter 4.4, pp. 305-307.

[222] See above, chapter 4.6.

article, which is not only 'unique' for, but also 'general' in Africa. The formulation of the third article can be taken to support this suggestion. One should remember, however, that the formulation of the fifth article as *Tertia die a mortuis resurrexit* was presumably caused by the fact that the two words *A mortuis* constitute an addition to the original form of the article, which we have reconstructed as *Tertia die resurrexit*[223]. This phenomenon was not limited to Africa, but has left its traces in Gaul, Spain, and Italy as well. Therefore, the wording of the fifth article in the credal variant under discussion by no means implies that this variant can only stem from Africa.

This conclusion seems to be supported when the 'other features' are also taken into account. The wording of the first and seventh articles as well as the addition of Eternal Life may be found in any region. The word order *Virgine Maria* in the third article may be seen in Africa ('general') and in Northern Italy (AU-M). The wording of the eighth (with *Est*) occurs in Africa ('general') and Gaul (EUSh9), that of the ninth (*Credo in spiritum sanctum*) in Africa ('general'), Gaul (FAU-R), and Spain (MART, EB). It should be noted, however, that the similar formulation *Credo in sanctum spiritum* occurs in Northern Italy (PC) and in the Latin Balkans (APS). As far as the absence of the eleventh article is concerned, this only has parallels in two Gallican forms of the Creed (CAE-B and CAE-C).

When these data are combined with a study of the 'general features', however, the picture starts to change. First of all, a most important African 'general feature' is missing, viz. the position of the tenth article at the end of the Creed. Since we have seen that this feature was probably general in Africa from the third century onwards, this is a fact that cannot be lightly dismissed. One could try to circumvent the problem by dating the two *expositiones* as early as possible, but that would not accord with the (probable) presence of the Descent to Hell. This addition is not attested any earlier than the end of the fourth century, and can probably only be found in Africa from the fifth century onwards[224].

[223] See above, chapter 3.7, pp. 239-240.
[224] See our discussion of the date of the pseudo-Fulgentian *sermo de symbolo* CPL 846 in chapter 4.6, pp. 326-328.

Secondly, the absence of *Conceptus* in the third article seems to make a Gallican origin impossible. This is a strong argument, especially in combination with the presence of the Descent to Hell, which is not attested in Gaul before the fifth or even sixth century. As we have seen that the Creed probably entered Ireland by way of Gaul, the absence of *Conceptus* also makes it difficult to assume an Irish origin for the credal variant under discussion.

With regard to Spain, no 'general features' can be said to be lacking in the credal variant under discussion, but its form of the second article (*Et in unicum filium eius, dominum nostrum Iesum Christum*) would be rather difficult to fit into the picture if our variant were of Spanish origin. The second article probably entered Spain in its full form (*Et in Iesum Christum, filium eius unicum dominum nostrum*), which would make it difficult to imagine that the formulation that is found in the pseudo-Chrysostomic *expositiones* is Spanish. In that case, one would have to assume that the second article entered Spain in a shorter form, which would not have left any traces in the later Spanish formulations of the Creed. Along these lines, one would have to date the credal variant under discussion fairly early, which would again conflict with the presence of the Descent to Hell. A similar argument also pleads against a North Italian origin of our anonymous author's credal variant.

Actually, the Latin Balkans remain as the most probable home for the form of the Creed that is yielded by the two pseudo-Chrysostomic *sermones*. The only 'general feature' lacking is the use of *Viuus* in the fifth article, but we have already had reason to presume that this addition need not have played a role everywhere in the Balkans, and that different formulations of the fifth article may have been in use there from the start [225]. As a matter of fact, the formulation that is found in our two *expositiones* fits such a situation fairly well. On the other hand, as long as no single positive indication points East of the Adriatic, it would be rather presumptive to assign the two pseudo-Chrysostomic *expositiones* to the Latin Balkans only because no other region really fits their underlying form of the Creed.

---

[225] See above, chapter 4.2, p. 290.

In these circumstances, Morin's hypothesis of a South Italian origin for the pseudo-Chrysostomic sermon collection receives at least indirect support from our credal typology. But perhaps something more can be said as well. First of all, in the case of a South Italian origin of the collection, the two African features in the credal variant of our two sermons (the word order *Virgine Maria* and the formulation *Tertia die a mortuis resurrexit*) could either be explained as caused by Morin's theory that an African bishop had fled to Southern Italy during the Vandal conquest of Africa and therefore used an Italian form of the Creed in which he had unconsciously inserted one or two peculiarities of his native variant [226], or by the vicinity of Southern Italy to Northern Africa. In the second place, it is natural to assume that Southern Italy, because of its closeness to Rome, was one of the first regions to adopt the Apostles' Creed. In such a case some rather conservative form of the Creed would probably enter the region first, so that one would expect certain conservative traits in later credal variant from Southern Italy as well. Now, we have seen that the formulation of the second and fifth articles in the credal variant under discussion indeed testify to a process of addition of later elements after the Creed had already begun to spread, and the absence of the eleventh article is a very conservative feature. On the other hand, the presence of additions like *Vnicum*, *Dominum nostrum*, *Descendit ad infernum*, *A mortuis*, and *Credo* prohibit too early a date for this form of the Creed.

Our first conclusion, then, is that the credal variant of the two pseudo-Chrysostomic *expositiones symboli* CPL 915 does not fit in very well with our credal typology. This may perhaps be taken to support Morin's initial hypothesis that this credal variant belongs to Southern Italy. Although we know nothing about the form of the Creed in that region whatsoever, we can make some reasonable guesses about its features there. As precisely such features happen to be presented by the two pseudo-Chrysostomic texts, the conclusion seems justified that a South Italian origin would form at least a good working hypothesis for further investigation.

---

[226] Compare the case of the word order *Virgine Maria* in AU-M: see above, chapter 3.7, p. 233.

## 4.8 The Pseudo-Augustinian *sermo 244* or *excarpsum de fide catholica* (CPL 368, 244), Ascribed to Caesarius of Arles (CPL 1008, 10)

The *excarpsum de fide catholica* has been handed down in the manuscript tradition as a sermon by Augustine. The Maurini, however, editing the text as *sermo 244* in their appendix to the Augustinian sermons, already decided that it was spurious and strongly surmised that Caesarius was its real author: "Caesarium revera sapit, non Augustinum" [227]. The text has been edited by Morin as a genuine Caesarian sermon, although among those "ex aliis ... fontibus ita haustos, ut Caesarii tamen dicendi genus et ingenium in portione haud temnenda certo deprehendatur" and reprinted as such by *Corpus Christianorum* [228].

The pseudo-Augustinian *excarpsum* briefly comments upon the Apostles' Creed in the following way: *Credite ergo, carissimi, in deum patrem omnipotentem, credite et in Iesum Christum filium eius unicum dominum nostrum. Credite eum conceptum esse de spiritu sancto et natum ex Maria uirgine, quae uirgo ante partum et uirgo post partum semper fuit et absque contagione uel macula peccati perdurauit. Credite eum pro nostris peccatis passum sub Pontio Pilato, credite crucifixum, credite mortuum et sepultum. Credite eum ad inferna descendisse, diabolum obligasse et animas sanctorum quae sub custodia detinebantur liberasse secumque ad caelestem patriam perduxisse. Credite eum tertia die a mortuis resurrexisse et nobis exemplum resurrectionis ostendisse. Credite eum in caelis cum carne quam de nostro assumpsit ascendisse. Credite quod in dextera sedet patris. Credite quod uenturus sit iudicare uiuos et mortuos. Credite in spiritum sanctum, credite sanctam ecclesiam catholicam, credite sanctorum communionem, credite carnis resurrectionem, credite remissionem peccatorum, credite et uitam aeternam* [229].

---

[227] Text and note were reprinted by Migne: PL 39, 2194-2196 and 2194nb.

[228] Morin 1937, CXV and 50-53; CCSL 103, CXXII and 50-53. The same text also in SChr 175, 376-382. Morin does not enter into the question of how much non-Caesarian material has found a place in the *excarpsum* and where it comes from. This is quite surprising when one realizes that Morin does so in the prolegomena and notes to all of the more than 50 other sermons of this category.

[229] *Excarpsum de fide catholica* 1; CCSL 103, 51-52.

A number of general observations may be made here. First of all, although the author does not explicitly refer to the Creed, his seventeen-fold use of *credite*, in combination with the contents of his exhortation, clearly indicates as much. He may use *credite* more than once within one article (*Credite eum pro nostris peccatis passum sub Pontio Pilato, credite crucifixum, credite mortuum et sepultum ...*), but never in his commenting phrases. This provides us with a fairly safe instrument to separate the parts where the author refers to the wording of the Creed and where he comments upon it. This feature makes the presence of *Conceptus* in the third article and that of *Passus* and *Mortuus* in the fourth certain. Secondly, the author does not expound each and every article, as appears from the beginning and the end of the section: *Credite ergo, carissimi, in deum patrem omnipotentem, credite et in Iesum Christum filium eius unicum dominum nostrum. Credite eum conceptum esse ... Credite in spiritum sanctum, credite sanctam ecclesiam catholicam, credite sanctorum communionem, credite carnis resurrectionem, credite remissionem peccatorum, credite et uitam aeternam.* This procedure can be taken as a safe guarantee that the author intends to mention all elements of the Creed. For this reason, we may confidently assume that the underlying form of the Creed did not contain any additions such as *Creatorem caeli et terrae* in the first article or *Dei ... omnipotentis* in the seventh. Finally, it is obvious that the third to eighth articles are not quoted but rather freely referred to. This is due to the repeated use of *credite*, which is followed by various constructions. The very fact that the author does not even refer to his material in a consistent way (*Credite **eum** ... **ascendisse**, Credite **quod** in dextera patris **sedet**, Credite **quod** uenturus **sit** ...*) seems to rule out any reconstruction of these articles [230]. On the other hand, no changes other than the

---

[230] Thus also Kattenbusch 1894, 164 and 1900, 741. Nevertheless, Kattenbusch goes out of his way to show that the formula *Credite eum in caelis cum carne quam de nostro assumpsit ascendisse* refers to a form of the sixth article which may well have run *In caelis cum carne ascendit*: see Kattenbusch 1894, 401-402 (but slightly differently 1900, 741). His explanation that the author uses two types of commentary, one pointing out the importance of parts of the Creed for our salvation, the other clarifying in a more general way, and that the words *quam de nostro assumpsit* belong to the second type, does not seem very convincing. The entire phrase *cum carne ... assumpsit* is equally well explained as a short commentary of Kattenbusch's first type. Hahn (1897, 73n168) seems to take the references to articles three to eight as more or less literal quotations.

insertion of *credite* (occasionally ousting *Credo*: see below) seem to have been made in the first two and final four articles, so that these may be reconstructed with a fair amount of confidence [231]. Only the formula *credite et in Iesum Christum ...* may equally well refer to a form of the second article beginning with *Credo et in ...* as to one with just *Et in ...*

A few final points should be observed before we present our partial reconstruction. The ninth article may safely be reconstructed as *Credo in spiritum sanctum.* If the introduction *Et* or *Credo et* was used in the author's form of this article, we would expect to read *Credite et in spiritum sanctum* because of *credite et in Iesum Christum ...* and *credite et uitam aeternam* [232]. Further, we should bear in mind the possibility that the words *credite sanctam ecclesiam catholicam* represent a tenth article of the form *Credo sanctam ecclesiam catholicam.* Next, there seems to be no reason to doubt the word order *Carnis resurrectionem, remissionem peccatorum* in the credal variant under discussion [233].

We may thus reconstruct the underlying credal variant of the pseudo-Augustinian *excarpsum de fide catholica* as follows:

*Credo in deum patrem omnipotentem*
*(credo?) et in Iesum Christum, filium eius unicum dominum nostrum*
*[... conceptum esse de spiritu sancto et natum ex Maria uirgine ...*
*... passum sub Pontio Pilato ... crucifixum ... mortuum et sepultum*
*...*
*... ad inferna descendisse ...*
*... tertia die resurrexisse ...*
*... in caelis ... ascendisse*
*... in dextera sedet patris*

[231] Similarly Lejay 1906, 45-46. Burn offers a complete reconstruction of the author's credal variant which deviates in a number of points from the wording of the *excarpsum.*

[232] Otherwise Kattenbusch 1894, 164: "... über die Konstruktion dieses Symbols [ist] überhaupt nichts auszumachen."

[233] Kattenbusch (1894, 165) is more cautious. Burn (1899, 226), without any explanation, reconstructs *Remissionem peccatorum, carnis resurrectionem.* Lejay's remark on this point ("On pourrait se demander peut-être si l'insertion de la cummunion des saints n'est pas la cause indirecte de cette inversion"; Lejay 1906, 46) is gratuitous and does not explain anything.

*... uenturus sit iudicare uiuos et mortuos]*
*credo in spiritum sanctum*
*(credo?) sanctam ecclesiam catholicam*
*sanctorum communionem*
*carnis resurrectionem*
*remissionem peccatorum*
*et uitam aeternam.*

Discussion of the *excarpsum* has mainly centred around two questions, viz. that of its authorship and that of its relationship with the *expositio de fide catholica* CPL 505 [234] and with the anonymous *expositio symboli* CPL 1763 [235]. We shall pay due attention to the question of the relationship between these three texts later, and shall concentrate now on the probable date and place of origin of the credal variant in order to say something more about the first question.

As far as the authorship of the *excarpsum* is concerned, the first person to contribute to the discussion after the Maurini seems to have been Kattenbusch who, after an analysis of Caesarius's style, came to the conclusion that the *excarpsum* can only belong to that author [236]. Later on, he became somewhat less certain because Burn had in the meantime pointed out the existence of a variant of the *excarpsum* in which the section on the Apostles' Creed has been left out [237]. Since all the Caesarian features that he had found occur in precisely the remaining part of the text, Kattenbusch now considered the possibility that the shorter variant found by Burn may have stemmed from Caesarius himself, and that the pseudo-Augustinian *excarpsum* may have been conflated by some later author [238].

Paul Lejay has now also started investigating the literary legacy of Caesarius of Arles, among which he also numbers our *excarp-*

---

[234] See above, chapter 4.5.

[235] See below, chapter 4.16.

[236] Kattenbusch 1894, 164-170. Kattenbusch is followed by Burn (1896, lxxxii, 1899, 151 and 224, and 1909, 2), Hahn (1897, 72n167), and Krüger (Schanz 1920, 562).

[237] See Burn 1899, 224.

[238] Kattenbusch 1900, 745-746. Morin (1911, 184n3) also mentions this text but, as far as I can tell, never comments upon Burn's theory. Nor has he used Burn's manuscript for his edition of the *excarpsum*.

sum [239]. Morin first declared himself convinced that the *excarpsum* cannot have blossomed from Caesarius's pen [240], but he nevertheless included it in his edition of Caesarius of Arles [241].

Nevertheless, the circumstance that the credal variant that is yielded by the *excarpsum* is identical with neither of the two Creed forms in the Caesarian *sermo 9* [242] already justifies a fresh investigation into the place and date of origin of the former. Moreover, both Kattenbusch and Morin have indicated that Caesarius may well be the author of only parts of the *excarpsum* [243]. It will thus be advisable to take a closer look at the form of the Creed to which the pseudo-Augustinian *excarpsum de fide catholica* (*sermo 244*) testifies.

As in the case of the pseudo-Augustinian *sermo super symbolum* CPL 365, the combined presence of *Conceptus*, *Passus*, and *Mortuus* constitutes a very strong argument in favour of a Gallican origin of the credal variant under discussion [244]. This impression is supported by the presence of three Gallican 'general features' - the word order *Iesum Christum* in the second article, the use of *Credo* in the ninth article, and the presence of *Catholicam* in the tenth article. One feature of our reconstructed credal variant deserves special attention,

[239] Lejay 1895, 393-394. For the same opinion, see Lejay 1906, 44-46.

[240] Morin 1911, 182-187. On pp. 182-185+nn, Morin gives a more detailed overview of the history of scholarship on this point.

[241] See above, p. 343 with footnote 228. Although he does not explicitly say so, Morin's change of mind was probably caused by his discovery that Caesarius knew and used the Athanasian Creed, a text which is also quoted in the *excarpsum*: see Morin 1911, 182 on the one hand and 1932, 207-215 on the other. Since Morin's edition, no one has apparently doubted the Caesarian origin of the *excarpsum*: see PLS 4, 246, Dekkers 1995, 137, and Frede 1995, 273 and 338.

[242] Differences with CAE-A include the absence of *Creatorem caeli et terrae*, the formulation of the second article with *Vnicum dominum nostrum* instead of *Vnigenitum sempiternum*, the absence of the addition *Dei ... omnipotentis* in the seventh article, the word order *Spiritum sanctum* instead of *Sanctum spiritum*, the position of the eleventh article after *Carnis resurrectionem*, and the presence of *Et* before *Vitam aeternam*. Of these, the formulation of the second article with *Vnicum dominum nostrum*, of the seventh article with *Patris* only, of the ninth with *Spiritum sanctum*, and of the twelfth with *Et uitam aeternam* also constitute differences with CAE-B; additional differences with CAE-B are the presence of the Descent to Hell and of *Remissionem peccatorum*. Morin chooses to ignore this: see Morin 1934a, 184-186 and especially 185n5.

[243] See above, footnotes 228 and 238.

[244] See above, chapter 4.4, p. 305.

viz. the placement of *Remissionem peccatorum* after *Carnis resurrectionem*. We have so far not met with other variants that exhibit this feature, and the questions under which circumstances could it occur, and in which region may such circumstances be expected to have prevailed for a shorter or longer period naturally arise.

As a matter of fact, the formulation *Carnis resurrectionem, remissionem peccatorum et uitam aeternam* fits in very well with our theory that the eleventh article did not belong to proto-*R*, the original form of the Apostles' Creed, and that it was still absent in at least some of the forms that found their way from Rome to other parts of the Latin church. We have seen that some formulations without the eleventh article have indeed come down to us, whereas a number of others still show traces of the repair of something which was evidently felt to be a defect later [245]. Along these lines, the wording of the credal variant of the *excarpsum* can be perfectly explained by assuming that at some date a certain church, which had until then used a form of the Creed without *Remissionem peccatorum* or a similar phrase, became aware that in most if not all other churches more complete variants could be heard, and accordingly decided to add *Remissionem peccatorum* to its local variant but, either intentionally or by accident, inserted it in the wrong place [246]. Explained thus, the wording *Carnis resurrectionem, remissionem peccatorum* again points to Gaul as no other region shows any trace of credal variants lacking the eleventh article [247].

Since all of the more marked features of the credal variant of the pseudo-Augustinian *excarpsum* point to Gaul, no Gallican 'general features' seem to be absent, and other regions are improbable as a place of origin precisely because of the absence of at least one 'gen-

[245] See above, chapter 3.7, p. 253.

[246] The variety in word order in the different formulations of the second article is a good parallel (see above, chapter 3.7, p. 229). One could think of a number of reasons for adding *Remissionem peccatorum* after *Carnis resurrectionem*. For one thing, people may have been reluctant to interrupt a familiar sequence and therefore decided to put the new addition at the end of the Creed (which would imply that Eternal Life was added even later). Or, if Remission of Sins was understood to refer to the Last Judgement, a position after *Carnis resurrectionem* would just be the most natural one.

[247] But compare the case of the pseudo-Chrysostomic *expositiones symboli*, discussed in the previous section, p. 335.

eral feature' [248], the conclusion seems safe that this form of the Creed stems from Gaul.

The next questions, of course, are to which period should our credal variant be assigned, and does it or does it not represent the form of Caesarius's bishopric Arles, as is implied by the general ascription of the *excarpsum* to that author [249]. In order to tackle this problem, it seems best first to investigate the indications about its date that are provided by the form of the Creed itself, and then to compare this form with those yielded by Caesarius's *sermo 9*.

Points that seem significant for the dating of the credal variant of the *excarpsum de fide catholica* are the following: the absence of *Creatorem caeli et terrae* or a similar addition to the first article, the complete form of the second article, the presence of *Mortuus* in the fourth article, the addition of the Descent to Hell, the addition of *Catholicam* and *Sanctorum communionem* to the tenth article, the position of *Remissionem peccatorum*, and the addition of *Et uitam aeternam* at the end of the Creed. Most of these yield *termini post quem*. Thus a form of the second article with both *Vnicum* and *Dominum nostrum* is not found in Gaul before the end of the fifth century (FAU-R), whereas we have to wait till the seventh to find a wording possibly identical to the one that is testified to by the *excarpsum* (MGV, Bobbio C). Similarly, the Descent to Hell is not found in Gaul before the sixth century (CAE-A), though it may have been imported from Northern Italy somewhat earlier. *Mortuus, Catholicam, Sanctorum communionem,* and *Et uitam aeternam* are probably all earlier additions, so that these do not alter the impression that we have here a credal variant from the sixth century or later. On the other hand, the use of a short form of the first article is not found any more in Gallican variants of the Creed later than the sixth century, and the position of the eleventh article after *Carnis resurrectionem* is a decidedly conservative trait. The use of *Patris*

---

[248] For Spain, we would expect a fourth article with *Passus* but without *Mortuus*; for Africa, the formula *Per sanctam ecclesiam* at the end of the Creed; for Italy, the absence of the Communion of Saints. In all these regions as well as in the Latin Balkans, the position of the eleventh article before *Carnis resurrectionem* may also be considered as a 'general feature'.

[249] See above, footnotes 236 and 241. Kattenbusch mentions the possibility that Caesarius is referring here to the credal variant of his birthplace Châlons (ancient Calibonum): see Kattenbusch 1894, 402-403.

only in the seventh article is even more distinctive - it is not found in any of our Gallican witnesses later than the fifth century. All this suggests a date not too far from 500, and certainly no later than 600.

Our first conclusion, therefore, must be that the credal variant of the *excarpsum de fide catholica* may well be contemporary with Caesarius's occupation of the see of Arles (503-542). It might, therefore, indeed be the form of the Creed that was used by Caesarius himself, in which case there is little reason to deny him the authorship of the complete sermon. Matters, however, are complicated by the circumstances that we have another *expositio symboli*, undoubtedly preached by Caesarius, and yielding no less than two credal variants, either of which may also constitute Caesarius's form of the Creed: CAE-A and CAE-B [250]. The credal variant of the *excarpsum* is closer to CAE-B than to CAE-A. It lacks the addition *Creatorem caeli et terrae* (present in CAE-A, absent from CAE-B), and its way of mentioning the Remission of Sins is reminiscent of the variants without that addition such as CAE-B. Moreover, it is more conservative than either CAE-A or CAE-B in not having the addition *Dei ... omnipotentis*. On the other hand, it shares with CAE-A the Descent to Hell, which is absent from CAE-B [251]. In the light of these considerations, it seems most probable that CAE-B represents the form of the Creed that was used by Caesarius of Arles himself and CAE-A is the form of one of the compilers of the *Missale Gallicanum Vetus* [252]. The *excarpsum*, finally, which may well contain elements by other writers that were taken over by Caesarius [253], probably offers a Gallican Creed form from some other city that is roughly contemporary with Caesarius. Precisely the fact that the text does not intend to quote the Creed in too exact a way would make it possible for the bishop of Arles to retain the wording of this 'foreign' credal variant.

[250] See above, chapter 3.2, footnote 83.

[251] See above, footnote 242 for a more complete overview of differences between the credal variant of the *excarpsum* on the one hand and CAE-A and CAE-B on the other.

[252] See also above, chapter 3.2, pp. 125-126 with footnote 83.

[253] See above, footnotes 228 and 238.

4.9 The Pseudo-Athanasian *enarratio in symbolum apostolorum* CPL 1744a

This text, like the anonymous *expositio symboli* CPL 229a, was discovered in the eighteenth century by an Italian humanist. Josephus Blanchinus's [254] critical edition has remained the only one thus far. Since the original edition is hard to obtain and the reprint in Migne ignores many of Blanchinus's corrections of the manuscript reading, we have included a new edition in the appendix.

The pseudo-Athanasian *enarratio* yields its form of the Creed in a clear and unambiguous way. The author starts each section of his commentary either with a literal quotation of an article or with part of one. For the first article, we find no less than nine, mostly partial, quotations; the other articles are, as far as one can see, quoted only once [255]. Although the structure of the sermon makes it crystal clear that the author is making literal quotations, we also find a number of explicit references to the Creed: *Initium sacramenti confessione credulitatis imbuitur* ... [256], *Confessio quae patrem signat statim confitetur et filium* ... *Catholicae fidei claram confessionem* ... *ordo uerborum* ... *hoc confessionis exordio* ... [257], *Sequitur uirginis partum in confessione nostra* ... *insinuat nobis descendisse ad inferna confessio* ... *resurrectionis celeritatem fatemur* ... [258], *sedere ad dexteram patris filium confitemur* ... [259], *Quod post tantorum mysteriorum confessionem nunc in fidei nostrae sacramento sanctum spiritum confitemur* ... [260], and *Subiungitur denique* ... [261].

---

[254] The Italian form Giuseppe Bianchini may also be found.

[255] See for example pseudo-Athanasius, *enarratio in symbolum apostolorum* 3-6: *Credo in deum. Initium sacramenti* ... *Credo in deum. Hic est* ... *Credo in deum patrem. Dei nomini* ... (see below, pp. 460-461) and 13-14: *Ex Maria uirgine. Honor materni* ... *Qui sub Pontio Pilato crucifixus est et sepultus. Sequitur uirginis partum* ... (see below, p. 462). Only the third article was probably also quoted in two parts or more; we have no information for the second article because of a lacuna (see below).

[256] Pseudo-Athanasius, *enarratio in symbolum apostolorum* 3; see below, p. 460.

[257] Pseudo-Athanasius, *enarratio in symbolum apostolorum* 7-10; see below, p. 461.

[258] Pseudo-Athanasius, *enarratio in symbolum apostolorum* 14-16; see below, p. 462.

[259] Pseudo-Athanasius, *enarratio in symbolum apostolorum* 19; see below, p. 463.

[260] Pseudo-Athanasius, *enarratio in symbolum apostolorum* 21; see below, p. 463.

[261] Pseudo-Athanasius, *enarratio in symbolum apostolorum* 24; see below, p. 464.

Nevertheless, two major difficulties are connected with the reconstruction of a credal variant from the *enarratio*. First, there is a lacuna of two pages, which covers the closing part of the section on the first article, the complete discussion of the second, and the beginning of that of the third. This means that we cannot be sure whether the first article simply ran *Credo in deum patrem omnipotentem* or whether an addition of some kind was linked to it. The latter is perfectly possible, since the author has given only partial quotations up to the point where he is (presumably) going to discuss the word *Omnipotentem* [262], though nothing precludes the possibility of a short first article either [263]. Similarly, we are completely ignorant about the form of the second article in the author's credal variant. However, we are able to say something more about the third article. After the lacuna, the text continues: ... *ret. Sed quamuis peccato esse libera, non tamen alia habeatur quam quae possit esse peccatrix. Ex Maria uirgine. Honor materni sexus ...* [264]. The next paragraph expounds the fourth article and it is certain, therefore, that the third article ended ... *ex Maria uirgine*. The author seems to have been concerned with quoting syntactic units [265], so that it seems safe to assume that not *Et* nor *Natus* nor *Natum* was the immediately preceding word. In fact, this leaves only a formulation not too unlike *Natus de spiritu sancto ex Maria uirgine* as a possible reconstruction for the author's form of the third article [266].

The second difficulty is connected with the end of the author's credal variant. The last quotation in the *enarratio*, following the

[262] After quoting *Credo in deum* three and *Credo in deum patrem* five times (pseudo-Athanasius, *enarratio in symbolum apostolorum* 3-10; see below, pp. 460-461). The lacuna begins shortly after the next quotation: *Credo in deum patrem omnipotentem. Quae enim alia natura ...* (*ibid.*, 11; see below, p. 462).

[263] Thus also Kattenbusch (1894, 145), who points out that no conclusions may be drawn from the size of the lacuna.

[264] Pseudo-Athanasius, *enarratio in symbolum apostolorum* 12-13; see below, p. 462.

[265] This is revealed by his treatment of the first article. He never quotes *Patrem* or *Omnipotentem* only but always *Credo in deum patrem* or *Credo in deum patrem omnipotentem* (see above, footnote 262).

[266] The use of *Qui* in the fourth article (see above, footnote 255) strongly suggests the wording *Qui natus est de spiritu sancto ex Maria uirgine*, but this cannot be taken for certain. Blanchinus reconstructs *Qui natus de spiritu sancto ex Maria uirgine* (Blanchinus 1732, 46; taken over in Hahn 1897, 57-58n103).

exposition of the ninth article, runs thus: *Subiungitur denique: In sanctam matrem ecclesiam*, after which a short commentary closes the text [267]. This poses a number of problems. On the one hand, the author seems concerned with offering the text of the Creed in a complete and literal way. The meticulousness with which most parts of the Creed have hitherto been quoted almost compels one to assume that the author's form of the Creed was indeed concluded by the phrase *In sanctam matrem ecclesiam*, and did not contain any mention of the Remission of Sins or the Resurrection of the Flesh. On the other hand, however, the circumstance that at least the latter element was part and parcel of the Apostles' Creed from the very beginning makes such a conclusion extremely difficult to accept. In this light, the best solution is probably to assume that there is not only a lacuna in the first part of the *enarratio*, but that its end is incomplete as well [268]. In that case, there seem to be two possibilities. The first one is that the underlying form of the Creed really closed with the words *In sanctam matrem ecclesiam*. This would have a parallel in a number of African credal variants, which all express the thought that Remission of Sins, Resurrection of the Flesh, and Eternal Life are only to be gained by or in the Church [269]. One would have to assume, then, that the section of the *enarratio* treating those parts of the Creed has been lost [270]. The commentary on the tenth article, however, only stresses that the Church is *sancta* and *mater* and that it has been instituted by the doctrine of the Lord [271] and says nothing whatsoever about its

---

[267] Pseudo-Athanasius, *enarratio in symbolum apostolorum* 24: *Subiungitur denique: In sanctam matrem ecclesiam, ut illa una ecclesia et sancta apud nos habeatur et mater, quam in apostolis domini doctrina constituit. Amen* (see below, p. 464).

[268] Thus also Kattenbusch 1894, 146. Hahn (1897, 58n106) seems to assume that we have the complete text and therefore also the complete credal variant here. That at some point in the transmission of the text, sections ran the risk of being skipped or left out is at least suggested by pseudo-Athanasius, *enarratio in symbolum apostolorum* 6-10. In § 7, the word *Patrem* is said to imply belief in the Son, but both in § 6 and in §§ 8-10, the discussion centres around the relationship between the terms *Deum* and *Patrem*. The impression is inescapable that § 7 belongs either before § 6 or after § 10.

[269] See above, chapter 3.7, p. 249. It would be preferable to read *In sancta matre ecclesia* for such an interpretation.

[270] Compare Kattenbusch 1894, 145-146.

[271] See above, footnote 267.

function for gaining salvation. Therefore, the other possibility seems to be more probable, viz. that the article on the Church followed that on the Holy Spirit, and that we are missing the final part of the *enarratio*. The words *Subiungitur denique* seem to speak against such a theory but, as has been pointed out by Kattenbusch, *denique* may also serve to introduce the part of the *enarratio* in which the final three articles were to be discussed. In particular, the author's concern for a correct understanding of the doctrines of Trinity and Christology fits in well with such a hypothesis [272]. If we accept this as the most likely explanation for the state of affairs in the *enarratio*, we should not forget that we cannot know for sure whether the words *In sanctam matrem ecclesiam* constituted the complete tenth article of the author's form of the Creed, or *Catholicam* or a similar addition also had a place in it [273].

We may thus reconstruct the underlying credal variant of the pseudo-Athanasian *enarratio in symbolum apostolorum* CPL 1744a as follows:

> *Credo in deum patrem omnipotentem (...?)*
> ...
> *(qui natus est de spiritu sancto?) ex Maria uirgine*
> *qui sub Pontio Pilato crucifixus est et sepultus*
> *descendit ad inferna*
> *die tertio resurrexit a mortuis*
> *ascendit in caelos*
> *sedet ad dexteram patris*
> *inde uenturus iudicaturus de uiuis et mortuis*
> *credo in spiritum sanctum*

---

[272] See Kattenbusch 1894, 146. Later on, Kattenbusch (1900, 452n34) thinks that the words *In sanctam matrem ecclesiam* do not constitute a credal quotation, but the use of *Subiungitur* and the syntactic break both before and after these words render such a solution very improbable. Blanchinus also envisages the possibility that the author does not offer the complete end of the Creed. He mentions two possible explanations - either the *enarratio* has come down to us without its final part, or the author intended to discuss the closing articles of the Creed in another sermon: see Blanchinus 1732, 22-23. Nevertheless, on the basis of African parallels in particular, he concludes that the *enarratio* testifies to a form of the Creed that did not contain any mention of the eleventh and twelfth articles: see Blanchinus 1732, 26-29.

[273] Differently Blanchinus 1732, 27.

*in sanctam matrem ecclesiam (...?)*

...

Blanchinus's edition is accompanied by an extensive introduction and a number of notes ('adnotationes'). In the introduction, he investigates the origin of the *enarratio*, whereas the notes are mainly concerned with parallels in other credal texts. As far as the origin of the text is concerned, Blanchinus makes a number of observations. First of all, he finds that the Greek Father Athanasius, under whose name the text has come down to us, cannot be the author of the *enarratio*, because there are no traces of translation from the Greek, and several expressions are clearly originally Latin [274]. Blanchinus seriously considers the possibility that the *enarratio* is part of another Latin pseudo-Athanasian work, the twelve books *de trinitate* CPL 105 which have been ascribed to several authors and the real origin of which is still uncertain [275]. Blanchinus, who thought that this work was written by the African bishop Vigilius of Thapsus (end of the fifth century), therefore investigates more closely the relationship between the *enarratio* and Vigilius's works [276]. He does indeed find a number of points of resemblance, but also of difference, mainly concerning biblical quotations. The latter in particular lead him to the conclusion that the *enarratio* was not written by Vigilius [277]. Blanchinus does not propose any other author but believes that the *enarratio* was probably written before the Pelagian or at least semi-Pelagian controversy [278], and that it is an African text [279].

Since Blanchinus's edition, not much attention has been paid to the pseudo-Athanasian *enarratio*. Apart from some notes in the

[274] Blanchinus 1732, 2-9. This conclusion has been adopted by Kattenbusch (1894, 145) and Hahn (1897, 57n102).

[275] See Dekkers 1995, 34 and Frede 1995, 791-792.

[276] Apart from the pseudo-Athanasian *de trinitate*, he also used genuine works like *aduersus Eutycheten* (CPL 806) and *contra Arrianos, Sabellianos, Photinianos dialogus* (CPL 807).

[277] Blanchinus 1732, 15-19; the supposed shortness of the credal variant also plays a role in his argument: see above, footnote 272.

[278] Mainly because of pseudo-Athanasius, *enarratio in symbolum apostolorum* 2: ... *quoniam quamuis uelle nostrum sit, perficere tamen sine illo non inuenimus*: see Blanchinus 1732, 19-22. Later on, Blanchinus (1732, 29) combines the supposed brevity of the underlying form of the Creed with this argument.

[279] Blanchinus 1732, 58.

works of earlier credal scholars [280], Kattenbusch was the first to discuss the text more extensively again. After ample discussion of the
question of whether the *enarratio* may or may not testify to a form
of the Creed which contained the typical African phrases *Vniuer-*
*sorum creatorem, regem saeculorum, immortalem et inuisibilem* (in the
first article) and *Per sanctam ecclesiam* (at the end of the Creed), he
concludes that nothing can be proved or disproved here, and that
the *enarratio* may therefore stem from anywhere [281]. Later, he
declares that the underlying form of the Creed most probably
belongs to his 'Western European type', so that it should stem from
Gaul, Spain, or the British Isles [282].

Hahn disagrees with Kattenbusch and thinks that the *enarratio*
offers the complete end of its credal variant and ranks it among
his African forms of the Creed [283]. Kattenbusch returns to the question of the origin of the *enarratio* in the second volume of his monograph. He claims the presence of the Descent to Hell in the
underlying credal variant as a point in favour of his theory of a
Western European origin. Moreover, he thinks that the formulation
of the eighth article (*Inde uenturus iudicaturus de uiuis et mortuis*)
might well indicate Gaul as the original home of the *enarratio*
because of parallels with a number of Gallican texts. Since Hilary
of Arles (*c.* 409-440) seems to have written an *expositio symboli* that
has not yet been found, Kattenbusch suggests him as the possible
author of the *enarratio in symbolum apostolorum* CPL 1744a [284]. At
any rate, certain dogmatic traits lead Kattenbusch to the conclusion that the text was probably written in the fifth century [285].

---

[280] See Kattenbusch 1894, 145n1 and Hahn 1897, 57n102.

[281] Kattenbusch 1894, 145-146. Kattenbusch continues with a study of the
possibility of Vigilius's authorship, which he believes to be Blanchinus's opinion.
He denies the text to Vigilus because of a difference in the wording of Matt. 28,
19 as found in the *enarratio* and in Vigilius's genuine works: see Kattenbusch
1894, 146-149.

[282] Kattenbusch 1894, 202n1.

[283] Hahn 1897, 57-58+n106.

[284] Kattenbusch 1900, 451n34 and 453n35. Kattenbusch (1900, 889n31) does
not regard the absence of *Passus* and *Mortuus* in the fourth article as an insur-
mountable difficulty for his theory.

[285] Kattenbusch 1900, 451-452+n34 and 898.

Since then, not much has been said about the pseudo-Athanasian *enarratio*. Hamman seems to accept Kattenbusch's dating [286]; Dekkers and Frede are prepared to consider the text as even older, but do not say why [287]. Dekkers, moreover, seems to adopt Blanchinus's opinion that the *enarratio* is connected with the twelve pseudo-Athanasian books *de trinitate* [288].

All in all, the question of the date and place of origin of the pseudo-Athanasian *enarratio* still seems to be an open one. It will therefore be all the more interesting to see whether our credal typology may help to say something more definite. Can the text be assigned to one distinct region, and if so, what is its most probable age?

Proceeding in our usual way, then, and looking for 'unique features' first, we find one such formulation, to wit the fourth article in the form *Qui sub Pontio Pilato crucifixus est et sepultus*. As far as we can see, this wording is confined to the region of Northern Italy, though it should be noted that a very similar formulation occurs in the pseudo-Ambrosian *exhortatio ad neophytos de symbolo* CPL 178 (*Qui sub Pontio Pilato crucifixus et sepultus*), which we have assigned to the Latin Balkans [289].

Next, our attention is drawn to three articles that are formulated in a way that we have not previously found in the source texts for our typology. These are the fifth article with its use of *Die tertio*, the eighth article running *Inde uenturus iudicaturus de uiuis et mortuis*, and the tenth article that is formulated *In sanctam matrem ecclesiam*. The question is, of course, where do these formulations fit best when considered in the light of the history of the form of the Creed as we have reconstructed it. For the fifth article in the form *Die tertio resurrexit a mortuis*, it seems impossible to say much that is definite. We have only one parallel for the masculine form *Tertio*. This occurs in the credal variant of the pseudo-Fulgentian *sermo de symbolo* CPL 846, which we have assigned to Africa [290].

---

[286] He offers the text among the "auctores saeculi quinti ineuntis": see PLS 1, 786-787.

[287] Dekkers 1995, 569 and Frede 1995, 197.

[288] See above, p. 355 and Dekkers 1995, 569. Possibly, the unpublished work of Samuel Cavallin has played a role here: see PLS 1, 787.

[289] See above, chapter 4.2, pp. 287-291.

[290] See above, chapter 4.6, pp. 324-326.

There seem to be no parallels for the inverted word order which puts *Die* before its numeral. The occurrence of *Tertio* instead of *Tertia* in one African form of the Creed seems to be too isolated an indication to draw any conclusions from it. Moreover, the phrase *Die tertio* has the appearance of a rather unimportant change in wording that does not have anything to do with the process of enlargement of the article which we have postulated for some regions. This means that the wording of the fifth article does not take us any further.

The wording *Inde uenturus iudicaturus de uiuis et mortuis* for the eighth article is unique because of its special combination of two features that occur in other credal variants as well. The use of the participle *Iudicaturus* instead of the infinitive *Iudicare* has parallels in Gaul (CY-T: *Inde uenturus iudicaturus uiuos ac mortuos*), Spain (MM: *Inde uenturus iudicaturus uiuos et mortuos*; PRIS: *Inde uenturus et iudicaturus de uiuis et mortuis* [?]), and Northern Italy (AU-M: *Inde uenturus iudicaturus uiuos et mortuos*). The use of *De* instead of an accusative has only one probable parallel in the Spanish form of the Creed to which PRIS testifies (see above). Again, the fact that both features only affect the wording of the article seems to rule out any rigid conclusions[291], but the use of the participle *Iudicaturus* in particular, which occurs several times in Gaul, Spain, and Northern Italy, but never in Africa and the Latin Balkans, seems to make an African or Balkan origin for the pseudo-Athanasian *enarratio* less likely. It is tempting to contemplate the possibility of a Spanish origin on the basis of the combined presence of *Iudicaturus* and *De*, but that would probably be asking too much of the evidence.

The formulation *In sanctam matrem ecclesiam* contains two theologically relevant changes in the tenth article. First, the use of the preposition *In* seems to be connected with the controversy about the status of belief in the Holy Church in the Creed. We have seen that different changes were made to distinguish the Church from the three divine persons in a number of regions[292]. In the credal variant under discussion, the alternative opinion seems to have gained the upper hand as *In* puts the Church on the same level as

---

[291] Compare chapter 3.7, p. 245 above.
[292] See above, chapter 3.7, pp. 249-250.

the Father, the Son, and the Holy Spirit. We have found traces of
this discussion in Gaul, the Latin Balkans, Ireland, and possibly
Africa as well. In this light, the credal variant under discussion
could belong to any of these regions. But the possibility of a Spanish or North Italian provenance cannot be excluded either. The circumstance that we have not found any traces of the discussion
there need not mean that no discussion concerning the relationship
between belief in the three divine persons and belief in the Holy
Church ever took place in Spain and Northern Italy. In fact, changing nothing in the Creed at this point could equally well be a
deliberate decision, meant to put belief in God and belief in the
Church on the same level. In that case, the presence of *In* in our
pseudo-Athanasian form of the Creed would point to Spain or
Northern Italy and not to one of the other regions. Second, there
is the addition of *Matrem*. Rather unfortunately, this is a unique
addition which could probably have been made in any region [293].
All in all, then, the form of the tenth article does not exclude any
region as a possible home for the credal variant under discussion,
with the exception of Africa, where the position of the article on
the Church at the end of the Creed seems to have been general
since the fourth century or an even earlier date.

As this leaves the question of the origin of our pseudo-Athanasian *enarratio* still open to all intents and purposes, it will be advisable to investigate the 'general features' for the several regions as
well. In other words, are there any features lacking which should be
present in order to make it possible to ascribe the credal variant to
a certain region? We have already seen that an African origin is
extremely unlikely because the article on the Church is placed after
the ninth article and not after the twelfth in the credal variant
under discussion [294]. But what is the situation for other regions?

With regard to Gaul, we miss the 'general features' of *Conceptus*,
*Passus*, and *Catholicam*. The absence of *Conceptus* in the third article is not completely certain but at least very probable. Since the
use of *Conceptus* played a role in Gallican forms of the Creed from
a very early stage, its probable absence in our credal variant makes

---

[293] Compare Kattenbusch 1894, 202n1: "Wenn jemand "communionem sanctorum" hier einzuschalten ein Interesse finden konnte, so ein anderer "matrem"."

[294] We also miss the 'general' African word order *Virgine Maria* in the third
article.

a Gallican origin of this variant rather unlikely. The same holds true for the probable absence of *Catholicam* in the tenth article. This addition may have been imported from Northern Italy or the Latin Balkans as early as the end of the fourth century and found its way into all extant Gallican variants. Again, the use of *Passus* in the fourth article made its entrance into Gallican Creed forms at around the same date and gained roughly equal acceptance [295]. Moreover, the use of *Qui ... est* in the fourth article had to all probability already been dropped by the time the Creed first entered Gaul. It is perhaps possible that the credal variant of the pseudo-Athanasian *enarratio* stems from Gaul, but if it did, it would probably be a specimen that testified to the Gallican form of the Creed in the first half of the fourth century.

For Spain, where *Passus* may well have played a role before it did in Gaul and *Qui ... est* is never found in the fourth article either, the same conclusion may be drawn as for Gaul. No 'general features' are absent for a possible North Italian origin. For the Latin Balkans, one can point to three missing 'general features': *Passus* in the fourth article, *Viuus* in the fifth and *Catholicam* in the tenth. As in the case of Gaul, these features played a role in Balkan forms of the Creed from the fourth century onwards, so that our credal variant, if it stems from the Latin Balkans, can hardly be younger than the fourth century [296].

Thus, the study of 'general features' yields four possibilites - either the credal variant of the pseudo-Athanasian *enarratio* is an early, possibly fourth-century, Gallican, Spanish, or Balkan form of the Creed, or else it is a North Italian form. In fact, only the fourth possibility remains when we take 'other features' into account as well. Here, one major addition in particular that occurs in the credal variant under discussion is important: *Descendit ad inferna*. This addition is probably of Italian origin and entered other regions rather late. We do not find it in Gaul and Spain before the sixth century, and it seems entirely absent from the Latin Balkans. The presence of the Descent to Hell, therefore, is difficult to combine

[295] Only in the anonymous *expositio de fide catholica* CPL 505 do we encounter an apparently Gallican credal variant which lacks *Passus*: see above, chapter 4.5, p. 315.

[296] Compare the case of the pseudo-Ambrosian *exhortatio de symbolo ad neophytos* CPL 178: see above, chapter 4.2, pp. 290-291.

with the theory of an early Gallican, Spanish, or Balkan origin. We conclude, then, that the form of the Creed of the pseudo-Athanasian *enarratio in symbolum apostolorum* CPL 1744a probably stems from Northern Italy [297].

It seems impossible to say much about the date. The form of the Creed fits a fourth-century North Italian origin, but a fifth or even sixth-century date cannot be excluded either. If Kattenbusch's observation of certain dogmatic traits is correct [298], a fifth-century origin seems to be the most likely conclusion.

## 4.10 The Anonymous *tractatus symboli* CPL 1751

This text, which is part of a complete liturgy for the *traditio symboli*, was first edited by Caspari, who found it in a Florentine manuscript of the twelfth century [299]. Later, Morin discovered a second manuscript of the same rite in Oxford [300]. Although it was of major importance both for the constitution of the text of the *tractatus* and for our knowledge of its underlying credal variant, Morin's find hardly received any attention [301]. The *tractatus* was reprinted with one or two errors in the Supplement Series to Migne's *Patrologia Latina* [302] from Caspari's edition alone, and neither Dekkers nor Frede seem to be aware of the existence of a second manuscript [303]. For that reason, a new edition of the anonymous *tractatus symboli* seems to be appropriate. This new edition can be found in the appendix to our study.

As indicated above, the discovery of the Oxford manuscript is of considerable interest for our study of the form of the Apostles' Creed. In the Florentine manuscript, the Creed is expounded in the traditional way - one or two articles are first indicated and then commented upon. Some of these indications are explicit quotations

---

[297] The fact that the formulations *Descendit ad inferna* and *Credo in spiritum sanctum* do not occur in our North Italian source texts is no objection to this conclusion because we can see there the closely resembling *Descendit in inferna* and *Credo in sanctum spiritum*.

[298] See above, footnote 285.

[299] Caspari 1879, 290-304.

[300] Morin 1905a, 505-507.

[301] The only exception I know of is De Ghellinck 1949, 95n3.

[302] PLS 4, 2145-2148.

[303] Dekkers 1995, 572 and Frede 1995, 474.

but others are not, so that a fair amount of critical judgement is required to distil the form of the Creed as it was probably used by the author. This, indeed, is exactly what Caspari, Kattenbusch, and Hahn have done in their studies [304]. In the Oxford manuscript, however, the Creed is quoted in full before the exposition of the several articles begins. Since the quotations and indications in the expository part of the *tractatus* hardly differ from this complete form of the Creed, the conclusion seems safe that the *tractatus symboli* refers to only one form of the Creed, and not to two like Caesarius of Arles' *sermo 9* and the *traditio symboli* in the Bobbio Missal [305]. Nevertheless, there are one or two places which deserve some more detailed discussion.

First of all, one can point to the fact that the complete quotation of the Creed offers the third article in the form *Qui natus est de spiritu sancto et Maria uirgine* [306], whereas the commentary has *Natum, inquit, de spiritu sancto et Maria uirgine. Crede ergo ...* [307]. Although we know of forms of the Creed in which the third article is indeed formulated in such a way, it seems best to interpret this phrase as an indirect or embedded quotation ("It says that he was born ...") so that there is no discrepancy with the first quotation.

Next, the section on the fourth article is introduced in both manuscripts in the following way: *Sicut audistis, fratres, secundum traditionem apostolorumque (B: apostolorum) doctrinam sequitur in symbolo (BL: symbolum) : Inquit sub Pontio Pilato crucifixus est et sepultus (B: sepultus est)* [308], but quoted earlier in the form *Qui sub*

---

[304] Caspari 1879, 302-304n76, Kattenbusch 1894, 133-134 and 1900, 946n141, and Hahn 1897, 46-47+n71. Hahn's reconstruction is taken over by Denzinger 1991, 28.

[305] See above, chapter 3.2, pp. 124-125 and 140-141.

[306] *Tractatus symboli* 7; see below, p. 470.

[307] *Tractatus symboli* 10; see below, p. 471. This is the beginning of the section on the third article. The fact that the first article is introduced by means of the words *Audistis, fratres, in symbolo quia dictum est: Credis in deum patrem omnipotentem?* (*tractatus symboli* 8; see below, p. 470), whereas the complete variant begins *Credo in deum patrem omnipotentem* (*ibid.*, 7), is not a real difference, since declaratory and interrogatory forms of the same formula were equally designated as *symbolum*: see above, chapter 1.13. Caspari's proposal to change *Credis* into *Credo* (Caspari 1879, 308) is therefore unnecessary.

[308] *Tractatus symboli* 11; see below, p. 471.

*Pontio Pilato crucifixus est et sepultus* [309]. The text in the commentary cannot be correct as it stands because *inquit* has to follow the first word, or words, of a quotation. For that reason, Caspari ventured the conjecture *Passus est, inquit ...* [310]. In fact, however, the form *inquit*, a superfluous repetition of *sequitur in symbolo*, is in itself already suspect. Therefore, it is paleographically as well as intrinsically more attractive to read *Qui* for *Inquit* [311], which makes the commentary tally with the preceding quotation of the entire Creed.

In the third place, there are some difficulties connected with the closing articles of the Creed. In the complete quotation we read: *Sanctam ecclesiam catholicam, in remissionem peccatorum, carnis resurrectionem, et uitam aeternam. Amen* [312]. In the corresponding part of the commentary, however, we find: *Sequitur: In sanctam ecclesiam, in remissionem peccatorum. Sancta ecclesia una et uera est, in qua sanctorum communio in remissionem peccatorum, in qua huius carnis nostrae resurrectio praedicatur. Credite ergo ex fide, et omnia uobis peccata remittuntur, ut credentes habeatis uitam aeternam, ut immaculati possitis peruenire ad regna caelorum ...* [313]. Here, several questions raise their heads. First of all, does the text of the commentary imply that *Sanctorum communionem* was part of its underlying form of the Creed or not? Caspari thought it did [314], Kattenbusch and Hahn that it did not [315]. The latter is probably the correct interpretation as the anonymous author mentions the Communion of Saints here only as one of the things that are preached in the Holy Church. In fact, only the words *In sanctam ecclesiam, in remissionem peccatorum* are explicitly said to inform us about the contents of the Creed; the rest of the sermon is couched in too general terms to admit of any conclusions about the underlying credal variant.

---

[309] *Tractatus symboli* 7; see below, p. 470.

[310] Caspari 1879, 298n57. Nevertheless, Caspari (1879, 302-303n76) reconstructs the fourth article as *Sub Pontio Pilato crucifixus est et sepultus*.

[311] Compare Kattenbusch's proposal to read *Qui, inquit ...*: see Kattenbusch 1894, 133-134.

[312] *Tractatus symboli* 7; see below, p. 470.

[313] *Tractatus symboli* 16-17; see below, p. 472.

[314] Caspari 1879, 303-304n76.

[315] Kattenbusch 1894, 134 (but compare Kattenbusch 1900, 946n141) and Hahn 1897, 46n71.

There is also the difference between the complete quotation, which adds *Catholicam* to *Ecclesiam*, and the quotation of the tenth article in the commentary, where this addition is absent. Since *Catholicam* also occurs in *T*, the form of the Creed with which most scribes from the eighth century onwards were best acquainted, the possibility suggests itself that *Catholicam* should be deleted here. On the other hand, we know that in credal commentaries in particular quotations tend to be abbreviated. The question is, therefore, which possibility is the more probable one in the case of the *tractatus symboli*. When we take the preceding articles into consideration, it can be observed that the author is concerned with giving complete quotations of each article, even where he does not feel obliged to comment upon every individual element of them. Thus he quotes *Et in Iesum Christum, filium eius unicum dominum nostrum ... Qui sub Pontio Pilato crucifixus est et sepultus ... Tertia die resurrexit a mortuis ... Inde uenturus est iudicare uiuos et mortuos* [316] but does not comment upon the words *Dominum nostrum, Sub Pontio Pilato, Sepultus, Tertia die*, or *Viuos et mortuos*. In the light of this, it is difficult to imagine that he would have used a tenth article with *Catholicam* but have omitted this word from his quotation of that article. The conclusion seems inevitable, therefore, that the presence of *Catholicam* in the complete quotation is due to a scribal error under the influence of *T*.

Finally, one may ask whether the preposition *In* did or did not figure in this part of the Creed form under discussion. The circumstance that both the complete quotation and the commentary yield *In remissionem peccatorum* makes it practically certain that *In* was indeed prefixed to the eleventh article. A form of the Creed running *... Et in spiritum sanctum, sanctam ecclesiam, in remissionem peccatorum ...*, however, is difficult to imagine, so that it is very attractive to assume that the scribe of *B* (the manuscript which preserves the complete quotation of the Creed) or one of its ancestors did indeed write down the tenth article in the form which he knew by heart (*Sanctam ecclesiam catholicam*) instead of the form that must have been used by the anonymous author (*In sanctam ecclesiam*).

All in all, we may reconstruct the credal variant of the anonymous *tractatus symboli* CPL 1751 as follows:

---

[316] *Tractatus symboli* 9, 11, 12, and 14; see below, pp. 470-471.

*Credo in deum patrem omnipotentem*
*et in Iesum Christum, filium eius unicum dominum nostrum*
*qui natus est de spiritu sancto et Maria uirgine*
*qui sub Pontio Pilato crucifixus est et sepultus*
*tertia die resurrexit a mortuis*
*ascendit in caelis*
*sedet ad dexteram patris*
*inde uenturus est iudicare uiuos et mortuos*
*et in spiritum sanctum*
*in sanctam ecclesiam*
*in remissionem peccatorum*
*carnis resurrectionem*
*et uitam aeternam.*

Like many other anonymous and pseudonymous credal texts, the *tractatus symboli* has received only a limited amount of scholarly interest. Only its editor Caspari devoted more than two pages of text to it. In particular, he discusses the underlying form of the Creed [317] and the date of the *tractatus*. Caspari states that the *tractatus* may well be older than the rite in which it occurs, which he considers to stem from eighth or ninth-century Italy [318]. In his opinion, the conservative form of the Creed as well as certain dogmatic and liturgical peculiarities all point to a date well before the eighth century [319]. On the other hand, the *tractatus* contains many echoes of earlier patristic writers, of which Caspari considers Nicetas of Aquileia (that is, Nicetas of Remesiana) to be the youngest [320]. This leads him to take the end of the fifth century as a *terminus a quo*. In fact, Caspari thinks that the *tractatus* resembles a compilation rather than an original text and therefore assigns it to the seventh or possibly even eighth century [321]. As far as its place of origin is concerned, Caspari assumes that the text stems from Florence, the same town where the missal in which it is preserved was used [322].

---

[317] See above, footnote 304.

[318] Caspari 1879, 305-306.

[319] Caspari 1879, 307.

[320] Caspari finds echoes of 'Nicetas of Aquileia' (second half of the fifth century), Rufinus, Ambrose, and Peter Chrysologus: see Caspari 1879, 294-302nn28-75.

[321] Caspari 1879, 307-308.

[322] Caspari 1879, 308.

Kattenbusch is, as usual, very cautious. He does not agree with Caspari that the *tractatus* must stem from Florence or even from Italy (although he discusses the text in his chapter on "Italische Symbole"), and states that, apart from the dependence on other authors, he can find no clues as to the date of the text[323]. For the rest, most scholars content themselves with repeating Caspari's conclusions[324].

It will be interesting to see, therefore, whether Caspari's conclusions are supported by a fresh analysis of the form of the Creed that is presented by his anonymous *tractatus symboli*. First of all, one may point out one 'unique feature', viz. the formulation of the fourth article as *Qui sub Pontio Pilato crucifixus est et sepultus*. This formulation can only be seen in our North Italian sources for the form of the Creed, though it should be borne in mind that a very similar one (*Qui sub Pontio Pilato crucifixus et sepultus*) is offered by the pseudo-Ambrosian *exhortatio de symbolo ad neophytos* CPL 178, a text that we have connected with the Latin Balkans[325]. Moreover, the tenth and eleventh articles are presented by the *tractatus symboli* in a way that lacks any parallels with the credal variants that we have used for our typology: *In sanctam ecclesiam, in remissionem peccatorum*. There is a parallel for the use of *In* in the tenth article, however, in the pseudo-Athanasian *enarratio in symbolum apostolorum* CPL 1744a. In our discussion of that text and its credal variant, we have seen that the use of *In* here probably reflects a theological discussion that has left its traces in most regions, but we also saw reason to assume that the *enarratio* is a North Italian text[326]. Thus, our study of 'unique features' seems to point to Northern Italy rather than to any of our other regions.

---

[323] Kattenbusch 1894, 133. Later, Kattenbusch (1900, 801n65a) seems convinced again that the *tractatus* is a Florentine or at least Italian text. See for Kattenbusch's discussion of the underlying form of the Creed above, footnote 304.

[324] Thus Hahn 1897, 46n71, Denzinger 1991, 28, Dekkers 1995, 572, and Frede 1995, 474. Morin (1905a, 506), presenting his discovery of a second manuscript of the text, does not say anything about the *tractatus* except the fact that it was edited by Caspari.

[325] See above, chapter 4.2, pp. 287-291.

[326] See above, chapter 4.9, pp. 359-361.

In these circumstances, it will be a good idea to investigate which region is the most probable home for the credal variant under discussion on the basis of the presence and absence of 'general features'. First, a Gallican provenance becomes rather unlikely because of the absence of no less than six 'general features' - the use of *Conceptus* in the third article, the loss of *Qui* in the fourth article, the presence of *Passus* in the same, the use of *Credo* in the ninth article, that of *Catholicam* in the tenth, and the addition of Eternal Life at the end of the Creed. Of these, the absence of *Conceptus*, *Passus*, *Catholicam*, and Eternal Life can be explained by assuming a quite early (fourth-century) Gallican origin, but that would not tally with the echoes of Peter Chrysologus in the *tractatus* [327]. Moreover, the loss of *Qui* in the fourth article and the use of *Credo* in the ninth were probably already among the features of the first Gallican forms of the Creed. All in all, therefore, a Gallican origin is hardly likely for the credal variant of the anonymous *tractatus symboli*. A similar argument holds true for Spain, which would require the absence of *Qui* in the fourth article, the use of *Passus* in the same, and the presence of *Credo* in the ninth article again. Here, as in the case of Gaul, *Passus* constitutes one of the earliest additions to the form of the Creed in Spain, whereas a fourth article without *Qui* and a ninth with *Credo* belong to the Spanish features of the Creed from the beginning. Next, we miss the word order *Virgine Maria* in the third article, the construction of the fourth article with a participle in the accusative case, the word order *A mortuis resurrexit* in the fifth article, the use of *Credo* in the ninth, and the position of the tenth article at the end of the Creed for an African origin of the credal variant under discussion. Although not all of these are equally binding as 'general features' (the pseudo-Fulgentian *sermo de symbolo* CPL 846 has a fourth article beginning with *Crucifixus* ... [328]), their combined absence seems to be sufficient reason to deny our anonymous *tractatus symboli* an African origin. If the Latin Balkans were the home of the credal variant under discussion, we should expect *Passus* again, *Viuus* in the fifth article (although both features are also lacking in the Creed form of the

---

[327] See above, footnote 320
[328] See above, chapter 4.6, pp. 325-326.

pseudo-Ambrosian *exhortatio* [329]), the plural *Caelos* in the sixth article, and the addition of *Catholicam* in the tenth. In the absence of these features, an early Balkan origin of the credal variant of the *tractatus symboli* could be envisaged but such a theory would again ill accord with the fact that the text cannot be older than the second half of the fifth century because of the Chrysologan borrowings (see above).

For Northern Italy, on the other hand, only one 'general feature' is missing, viz. the formulation of the tenth article as *Sanctam ecclesiam*. This, however, is due to the formulation *In sanctam ecclesiam*, which would be new to any region, so that it may not be used as an argument against a North Italian origin.

On the basis of our credal typology, therefore, the credal variant of the anonymous *tractatus symboli* CPL 1751 should unequivocally be assigned to Northern Italy. But can we say anything in addition about the possibility that it stems from Florence, as is indicated by the manuscript tradition and assumed by most credal scholars? Here, of course, our credal typology is not of much use, as Florence, being situated south of the Apennines, cannot be said to belong to Northern Italy without any problems. Of course, the forms of the Creed that were in use throughout Italy may be expected to resemble each other more than those of other regions, so that it would not be surprising for a Florentine form of the Creed to resemble our North Italian type. Thus, our typology may be said to offer indirect evidence for the possibility of a Florentine origin of the text and its Creed form. But there is a second consideration which makes the possibility of a Central or South Italian origin for the credal variant under discussion no less probable. This is connected with the form of the eleventh article: *In remissionem peccatorum*. This form is perhaps best explained as due to perseveration, as it is difficult to think of a theological reason for prefixing *In* to *Remissionem peccatorum* and not to *Carnis resurrectionem*. It could be maintained, however, that such a case of perseveration would be more prone to occur if there was an element of doubt about the correct form of the eleventh article. Now, we know that the eleventh article did not play a role in each and every local form of the Creed from the start, but rather that it was added later to a number of

---

[329] See above, chapter 4.2, p. 290.

credal variants in Rome and Gaul. If the two pseudo-Chrysostomic *expositiones symboli* CPL 915 indeed originated in some Italian church south of the Apennines, Southern Italy may be added to the places where this peculiarity has left its traces [330]. In that case, the formulation *In remissionem peccatorum* would possibly point to Southern Italy [331].

This seems to be the farthest we can go. The form of the Creed of the anonymous *tractatus symboli* CPL 1751 is certainly Italian, and may very well stem from Florence. The credal variant itself does not offer any clues to its date, but the literary influences that have been noted by Caspari point to the second half of the fifth century as the earliest possible time of origin. The close resemblance with R (*Et uitam aeternam* is the only substantial addition when the testimony of the *tractatus* is compared with that form of the Creed) seems to favour a date not too much later than this *terminus a quo*, but to say anything more definite would amount to sheer guess-work.

## 4.11 The Anonymous *symbolum apostolorum* CPL 1758

This anonymous text was discovered and first edited by Burn [332]. A reprint of this edition has been included in the Supplement Series to Migne's *Patrologia Latina* [333]. Burn knew of only one manuscript of the *symbolum apostolorum* but there are at least two more. A new edition based on the three known manuscripts is offered in the appendix to our study.

It is not difficult to elicit a form of the Creed from this anonymous text. In the oldest manuscript (*G*), the commentary is presented in the form of marginal notes to a complete credal variant that has been written out in full. In the other two (*MN*), the credal quotations are interspersed with the commentary and do not constitute a complete form of the Creed, but there are two reasons for considering the testimony of *G* as the most original. First, the scrib-

---

[330] See above, chapter 4.7, p. 342.

[331] In Rome, the eleventh article was added in the form *Remissionem peccatorum*, as is borne out by the testimony of *R* and most local Creed forms, whereas Gaul has already been discarded above as a possible home for our anonymous *tractatus*.

[332] Burn 1898, 184-186.

[333] PLS 4, 1521-1522.

al errors in the wording of the final articles of the Creed in *MN* suggest that the text in this manuscript was copied from an original in which the commentary had the form of marginal notes as in *G* [334], and second, the quotations in *M* and *N* are clearly abbreviated quotations which hardly deviate from the credal variant in *G* [335].

Therefore, the anonymous *symbolum apostolorum* CPL 1758 can be taken to offer the following credal variant:

> *Credo in deum patrem omnipotentem, creatorem caeli et terrae*
> *et in Iesum Christum, filium eius unicum dominum nostrum*
> *qui conceptus est de spiritu sancto, natus ex Maria uirgine*
> *passus sub Pontio Pilato, crucifixus, mortuus et sepultus*
> *descendit ad inferna*
> *tertia die resurrexit a mortuis*
> *ascendit ad caelos*
> *sedet ad dexteram dei patris omnipotentis*
> *inde uenturus iudicare uiuos et mortuos*
> *credo in spiritum sanctum*
> *sanctam ecclesiam catholicam*
> *sanctorum communionem*
> *remissionem peccatorum*
> *carnis resurrectionem*
> *uitam aeternam.*

The anonymous *symbolum apostolorum* has hardly received any scholarly attention. Even Burn, its first editor, only points out some parallels with other credal texts (including Nicetas of Remesiana's *libellus* V) but does not say anything about its possible origin [336]. Kattenbusch only states that the credal variant is identical with *T* [337]. Hamman tentatively dates the text to the sixth century but does not give any reasons for his opinion [338]. Frede assigns the text to Gaul [339], and Dekkers does not go beyond Burn's remarks [340].

---

[334] See the preface to our edition (below, pp. 474-475) for more details.
[335] See the preface again, below, p. 475.
[336] Burn 1898, 184.
[337] Kattenbusch 1900, 748.
[338] PLS 4, 1497-1498.
[339] Frede 1995, 473.
[340] Dekkers 1995, 573.

The study of the underlying form of the Creed need not detain us very long, as the anonymous *symbolum apostolorum* indeed offers a familiar form of the Creed. This form is, however, not that of *T* as was claimed by Kattenbusch [341], but that of PIRM, albeit it with the difference that PIRM has the verb form *Surrexit* instead of *Resurrexit* in the fifth article [342]. The conclusion seems safe, therefore, that the *symbolum apostolorum* is a Gallican text from the seventh century or later. There is even the possibility that it belongs to the period following Charlemagne's endeavour towards a uniform wording of the Creed, in which case it might stem from anywhere in the Latin church except Spain or Africa [343].

## 4.12 The Anonymous *sermo de symbolo* CPL 1759

Like the text that was discussed in the previous section, this anonymous sermon was discovered and first edited by Burn [344]. His edition was reprinted with one serious error in the Supplement Series to Migne's *Patrologia Latina* [345]. At any rate, this edition, which makes use of only one manuscript, should now be considered outdated as more manuscripts of the text have become available. Therefore, a fresh edition on the basis of three witnesses is offered in our appendix.

It is not difficult to reconstruct the author's form of the Creed from the anonymous *sermo de symbolo*. Each article is first quoted and then explained. The author seems to be concerned with saying something about each article or even each individual element of the Creed. Thus he comments upon the following parts of the Creed: *Credo in deum, Patrem, Omnipotentem, Et in Iesum Christum filium eius, Vnicum, Dominum nostrum, Natum de spiritu sancto, Et Maria uirgine, Passus sub Pontio Pilato, Crucifixus et sepultus, Descendit ad inferos, Tertia die resurrexit a mortuis, Ascendit ad caelos, Sedet ad*

---

[341] See above, footnote 337. Kattenbusch notices as a difference with *T* that our anonymous author connects *Vnicum* with *Dominum*, but is silent about the absence of *Est* in the eighth article and the presence of *Et* before *Vitam aeternam*, more substantial differences with the form of *T* he offers himself (see Kattenbusch 1900, 761). Compare chapter 1.1, footnote 7.

[342] See above, chapter 3.2, pp. 136-137 with footnotes 123 and 119.

[343] See above, chapter 1.1, p. 21 and footnote 4.

[344] Burn 1898, 186-190.

[345] PLS 4, 2156-2159. For this error, see next footnote.

*dexteram dei patris, Inde uenturus iudicare, Viuos et mortuos, Credo in spiritum sanctum, Sanctam ecclesiam catholicam, Remissionem peccatorum, Carnis resurrectionem.* Some articles or parts of articles are quoted more than once in the same form, and syntactic breaks as well as tags like *id est, quia, quomodo* serve to distinguish the quotations from the commentary. Here are just a few examples: *Omnipotentem. Id est ... Et in Iesum Christum, filium eius. Quomodo dicit ... Vnicum dominum nostrum. Id est, quomodo dicit unicum dominum? Quia legimus ... Vnicum dominum nostrum, id est ... Natum de spiritu sancto et Maria uirgine. Quomodo dicit? ... Et Maria uirgine. Id est ...* [346]. Sometimes the author also explicitly refers to the Creed, as in the following cases: *Credo in deum. Hoc curiose inquiri solet quis istum uersum de sanctis apostolis primus cantasset* and *Credo in spiritum sanctum. Quando superius nominauit patrem et filium, cur nunc dixit spiritum sanctum? Sed mos est scripturae ex ordine narrare* [347].

The few exceptions to the rule that our anonymous text yields its credal quotations in a clear and unambiguous way include the following. First, the word *Patrem* is not given in a quotation but only in an indication: *Nos credimus in deum patrem. Et haeretici ...* [348]. The fact that we have the literal quotations *Credo in deum* and *Omnipotentem* [349], together with a long discussion of precisely the word *pater* as a designation of God, prove that the first article of the author's form of the Creed ran *Credo in deum patrem omnipotentem.* Next, the seventh article is quoted twice. First, we read: *Ascendit ad caelos, sedet ad dexteram dei patris*, then further on: *Sedet ad dexteram patris. Id est ...* [350]. It seems best to follow the initial quotation here for our reconstruction, and to consider the second one as a slightly shortened reference to the first. The alternative solution, that the author referred to the seventh article with a slightly extended quotation first, would contrast with the procedure he follows elsewhere. Again, the eighth article is discussed thus: *Inde uenturus iudicare uiuos ac mortuos. Inde uenturus est: de*

---

[346] *Sermo de symbolo* 8-13; see below, pp. 489-490. In the last quotation but one, Hamman erroneously reads *De Maria uirgine.*

[347] *Sermo de symbolo* 4 and 20; see below, pp. 489 and 491.

[348] *Sermo de symbolo* 5; see below, p. 489.

[349] See above, footnotes 49 and 48.

[350] *Sermo de symbolo* 18; see below, p. 491.

*prosperitate uitae aeternae uenturus est. Iudicare uiuos ac mortuos. Viuos: tunc qui corporaliter uiuunt, et mortuos: qui ab initio mortui sunt. Aliter, uiuos: qui uiuunt in anima deo, et mortuos: qui mortui sunt peccato, sicut dixit propheta: Post biduum uisitabo uos et in die tertio resuscitabo uos* [351]. There are two differences between the initial quotation and two later introductions to parts of the article - the former has *Venturus* and *Ac*, whereas in the latter we read *Venturus est* and *Et*. In the light of the author's practice in the rest of the sermon, it seems best to consider the initial quotation as the literal one, and the slightly deviating phrases further below as free references to it. Finally, the first part of the commentary on the tenth article needs attention. Here we read: *Sanctam ecclesiam catholicam, remissionem peccatorum. Non dixit: In sanctam ecclesiam catholicam, sed: Credo sanctam ecclesiam catholicam. Id est uniuersalis ecclesia in toto mundo diffusa. Dum dicit: Catholica est ecclesia, non catholicae haereticorum ecclesiae sunt, quia illae non sunt uniuersales, sed extremis partibus uel locis pertinentes* [352]. Here, the words *Non dixit ... sed ... catholicam* probably do not constitute a literal quotation but only serve to make clear that, in the author's opinion, the accusative *Sanctam ecclesiam catholicam* does not depend on the preposition *In* but rather directly on the verb form *Credo* in the ninth article. This motive can be met with in several other *expositiones symboli* [353].

We may thus reconstruct the following credal variant from the anonymous *sermo de symbolo* CPL 1759:

*Credo in deum patrem omnipotentem*
*et in Iesum Christum, filium eius unicum dominum nostrum*
*natum de spiritu sancto et Maria uirgine*

---

[351] *Sermo de symbolo* 19; see below, p. 491.

[352] *Sermo de symbolo* 22; see below, p. 492.

[353] See for example Rufinus, *expositio symboli* 34: *Sequitur namque post hunc sermonem: Sanctam ecclesiam, remissionem peccatorum, huius carnis resurrectionem. Non dixit: In sanctam ecclesiam, nec: In remissionem peccatorum, nec: In carnis resurrectionem. Si enim addidisset 'in' praepositionem, una cum superioribus eademque uis fuerat* (CCSL 20, 169-170). Matters are complicated by the fact that our author then explains the word *Catholicam* (*Id est uniuersalis ... pertinentes*), and returns to the theme of the difference between God and the Church with the words *Per similitudinem potest intellegere ...* (*sermo de symbolo* 23; see below, p. 492). This procedure fits in well with the occasional lack of coherence of his text.

*passus sub Pontio Pilato, crucifixus et sepultus*
*descendit ad inferos*
*tertia die resurrexit a mortuis*
*ascendit ad caelos*
*sedet ad dexteram dei patris*
*inde uenturus iudicare uiuos ac mortuos*
*credo in spiritum sanctum*
*sanctam ecclesiam catholicam*
*remissionem peccatorum*
*carnis resurrectionem.*

Because of a curious coincidence, the anonymous *sermo de symbolo* CPL 1759 as well as its underlying form of the Creed have received a fair amount of scholarly attention. The fact is that, some years before Burn's edition of our anonymous sermon, Eduard Bratke published an isolated credal variant from a Bern manuscript which he considered to stem either from Gaul or from the British Isles, and certainly to reflect the form of the Creed as it was in use in fifth-century Gaul [354]. This credal variant closely resembles the form that is yielded by Burn's *sermo de symbolo*. Apart from points of spelling and grammatical barbarisms, the only two substantial differences are that Bratke's variant lacks *Dei* in the seventh article and adds *In uitam aeternam* at the end of the Creed [355]. For this reason, the two credal variants were to all intents and purposes identified with each other by Kattenbusch and subsequent scholars. This resulted in a discussion of their origin in which data from Bratke's manuscript as well as observations on Bratke's credal variant that had been made by others were used for conclusions on Burn's *sermo*, and vice versa. In this way, the two credal variants and the anonymous *sermo de symbolo* CPL 1759 have been connected with Gaul, the British Isles, and Southern Germany [356].

---

[354] Bratke 1895, 158-167. Hahn reprints the Creed form and assigns it to Germany: see Hahn 1897, 95+n237. A facsimile of the form can be seen in Burn 1909, plate IV.

[355] The formulation *Pass**us** sub Pontio Pilato, crucifix**um** et sepult**um*** in Bratke's variant may possibly be taken to imply that *Passus* did not belong to the original credal variant but that it was added by the scribe: see Bratke 1895, 159+n2, Burn 1899, 242, and Burn 1909, 4.

[356] See Hahn 1897, 95n237, Burn 1899, 241-242, Kattenbusch 1900, 592n185a, 748-750 and 881n14, and Burn 1909, 3-4.

Nevertheless, the fact remains that there are two real differences between Bratke's form of the Creed and our anonymous author's, so that such a procedure is not in fact justified. Since no other methods have been tried to assess date and place of origin of the anonymous *sermo de symbolo* CPL 1759, this means that the question of its origin is essentially still as open as when Burn discovered it a hundred years ago [357]. Therefore, a fresh investigation of its underlying form of the Creed on the basis of our typology seems to be in place here.

Starting with the 'unique features' we can point to the formulation of the sixth article with *Ad* and the presence of *Dei* in the seventh article without *Omnipotentis*, both of which are only found in Gallican sources for our typology. Moreover, the use of *Inferos* only has a parallel in BAN, one of our two Irish texts.

Our anonymous text also contains one credal formulation which seems to be entirely without parallel - the wording of the third article as *Natum de spiritu sancto et Maria uirgine*. Of course, there are several other cases where the third article is formulated with a participle in the accusative and the same holds true for the conservative wording *de spiritu sancto et Maria uirgine*, but their combination here is new. This peculiar formulation may have originated in any region except Northern Italy, where forms of the Creed consistently seem to retain *Qui* in the third article.

Next, it might be significant that our anonymous author's form of the Creed combines the use of the accusative in the third article with that of the nominative in the fourth. This has a parallel only in one Spanish source (MM), whereas the Irish witness BAN has the third article and the first part of the fourth in the accusative, and the second part of the fourth in the nominative (*Conceptum ... natum ... passum ... qui crucifixus et sepultus*; the reverse can be seen in Bobbio B: *Qui conceptus ... Passum ...*). Again, the use of *Ac* in the eighth article seems to be confined to Gaul and Ireland.

Our first impression, therefore, is that the credal variant under discussion might well stem from Gaul or Spain, whereas some peculiarities also point to Ireland. That the other regions can indeed not be its most likely home is confirmed by the study of 'general fea-

---

[357] Dekkers (1995, 573) and Frede (1995, 473) are completely silent about this question.

tures'[358]. So what is the case with the possibilities for Gaul and Spain? Although most indications seemed hitherto to favour a Gallican origin of the credal variant of our anonymous *sermo*, two important Gallican 'general features' are lacking - the use of a form of *Conceptus* in the third article and the addition of Eternal Life at the end of the Creed. A Spanish origin was suggested by a smaller number of indications but is only contradicted by the use of *Ad* instead of *In* in the sixth article. On the basis of our credal typology, then, two possibilities suggest themselves - either we have a Gallican credal variant, with some Spanish features and lacking two 'general' Gallican ones, or it is Spanish, but with several Gallican formulations, and lacking one 'general' Spanish feature. It seems best to investigate first which possibility is the more probable, and then to pay some attention to the formulations that pointed to Ireland.

For a Gallican form of the Creed, then, the absence of *Conceptus* and of Eternal Life are rather difficult to explain. The absence of *Mortuus*, though not a 'general feature' in the strict sense of the word, may be added to these. We have seen that there probably was a time when all these formulations were absent from Gallican forms of the Creed, but this can hardly have outlasted the fourth century. So, in theory, we could have a conservative, and therefore probably early, Gallican form of the Creed in the anonymous *sermo de symbolo*. This, however, would hardly combine with the presence of the Descent to Hell, which does not occur before the sixth century in our Gallican source material. In the case of Spain, the situation is somewhat different as both the absent 'general features' and the 'unique' Gallican ones only affect details of wording and are therefore easier to account for. Thus the formulation of the sixth article with *Ad caelos* instead of *In caelos* may be without any

---

[358] For Africa, we miss the word order *Virgine Maria* in the third article, the use of an accusative construction in the fourth article, the addition of Eternal Life, and the mention of the Holy Church at the end of the Creed (to mention only the most important); for Northern Italy, we miss the use of *Qui* in the third article, that of *In* in the sixth, the absence of additions to the seventh article, and a tenth article without *Catholicam* (but compare the case of the anonymous *expositio symboli* CPL 229a: see above, chapter 4.3, p. 296); for the Latin Balkans, we should expect a credal variant without the Descent to Hell, with *In* in the sixth article, and without any additions to the seventh.

Spanish parallel but its occurrence hardly seems to justify the denial of a Spanish origin to a form of the Creed that contains it, especially when it has achieved some success in a neighbouring region such as Gaul. Similarly, as we already possess Spanish forms of the seventh article with *Patris* and with *Dei patris omnipotentis*, the formulation *Dei patris* can hardly cause surprise. Again, the use of *Ac* instead of *Et* in the eighth article may be due to Gallican influence in Spain. On the other hand, all the formulations that were difficult to combine with the theory of a Gallican origin of the credal variant under discussion fit in perfectly with our reconstruction of the history of the Creed in Spain. Thus the absence of *Conceptus* and *Mortuus* are general in Spain, and Eternal Life is only found from the sixth century onwards, though it was probably already introduced in the fourth or fifth century. The addition of *Dei ... patris* can be followed up to the fourth century, but a form without it can still be found in the sixth. The Descent to Hell may have been introduced in the fifth century, and its presence therefore does not pose any problems here. The only conspicuously absent Spanish innovation is the phrase *Deum et dominum nostrum* in the second article, which may have originated in the late fourth or early fifth century, but appears to be general from the sixth century onwards, but this fits in rather well with the absence of Eternal Life, which probably made its entrance in Spanish forms of the Creed around the same date. The same holds true for the formulation of the fifth article without *Viuus*, which probably had a place in Spanish forms of the Creed from the start but seems to disappear after the fifth century.

Therefore, our credal typology decidedly favours a Spanish origin of the credal variant of the anonymous *sermo de symbolo* CPL 1759. In that case, it should probably be dated to the fifth century. The absence of Eternal Life, *Viuus*, and *Deum et dominum nostrum*, which have become general in Spain by the sixth century, seems to rule out a later dating, whereas the presence of *Passus, Descendit ad inferos, Dei*, and *Catholicam*, the entrance of which in Spain can be dated to the fourth and fifth centuries, indicates the beginning of the fifth century as a *terminus post quem*. As far as the possibility of an Irish origin is concerned, this can be neither proved nor disproved because of the scarcity of Irish witnesses for the form of the Creed. The only direct support for this possibility is the formu-

lation of the Descent to Hell with *Inferos* instead of *Inferna*. The
other apparently Irish features (*Passus* without *Mortuus*, change
from the accusative to the nominative in the fourth article, use of
*Ac*) all have parallels in either Spain or Gaul. As we have already
seen that the form of the Creed in Ireland was probably influenced
by Gallican and/or Spanish formulations, this observation does not
take us any further. All in all, it seems safest to stick to a fifth-
century Spanish origin for our credal variant, but to bear in mind
that it could be Irish as well.

## 4.13 The Anonymous *expositio super symbolum* CPL 1760

The first edition of this anonymous sermon on the Creed was
published by Burn in 1900 [359]. Burn made use of three manuscripts
which, unfortunately, belong to a subgroup that is some steps
removed from the archetype of the eight or nine manuscripts that
are known nowadays. Moreover, Burn could only inspect one manuscript in person and had to rely for the other two on collations that
were made for him by others. Therefore, his edition does not seem
to be quite as accurate as his work on the texts of similar sermons.
A new edition, based on more and 'better' manuscripts, can be
found in the appendix to our study.

It is fairly easy to distil a credal variant from the anonymous
*expositio super symbolum*. Each article or part of an article is first
quoted and then explained. The quotations are not explicitly indicated as such, but the consistent way in which each individual article is treated seems to vouch sufficiently for the reliability of the
quotations. Since the commentary does not refer to each and every
element of a quotation [360], it seems safe to assume that the author is

---

[359] Burn 1900, 128-132. Earlier, Morin (1897, 485-486) had already given a
description of the sermon according to one manuscript (quoting, as a matter of
fact, the wrong *explicit*; compare Kattenbusch 1900, 874). Caspari (1879,
280n182; copied by Kattenbusch 1900, 17n14) had already edited the introduction from another manuscript. Burn's edition was reprinted by Hamman in PLS
4, 2160-2162 (with an erroneous *indicii* in *expositio symboli* 16 [see below, p. 508]
tacitly emended to *iudicii*).

[360] See for example the sections on the first article and that on the seventh,
*expositio super symbolum* 2: *Credo in deum patrem omnipotentem, creatorem caeli et
terrae. Omnipotens deus dicitur quia ipse creauit omnia bona sua potentia. Malum
et mendacium uel malitia non sunt a deo creata sed a diabolo et malis hominibus*

concerned with offering complete quotations. There are a few places where not all manuscripts agree in their wording of the Creed but these are usually cases where some witnesses have adapted a quotation to the form of *T*. Thus, for the wording of the sixth article (*Ascendit uictor ad caelos*) we find a variant without *Victor* in many of the younger manuscripts [361]. Similarly, in the quotation of the ninth article (*Credo et in spiritum sanctum*), *Et* is omitted by the majority [362]. Also, the Descent to Hell has been prefixed to the quotation of the fifth article in three manuscripts [363].

We may thus reconstruct the anonymous author's form of the Creed as presented by the *expositio super symbolum* CPL 1760 as follows:

> *Credo in deum patrem omnipotentem, creatorem caeli et terrae*
> *et in Iesum Christum, filium eius unicum dominum nostrum*
> *qui conceptus est de spiritu sancto, natus ex Maria uirgine*
> *passus sub Pontio Pilato, crucifixus, mortuus et sepultus*
> *tertia die resurrexit a mortuis*
> *ascendit uictor ad caelos*
> *sedet ad dexteram dei patris omnipotentis*
> *inde uenturus iudicare uiuos et mortuos*
> *credo et in spiritum sanctum*
> *sanctam ecclesiam catholicam*
> *sanctorum communionem*
> *remissionem peccatorum*
> *carnis resurrectionem*
> *uitam aeternam.*

Not much has been written about either the *expositio super symbolum* or its credal variant. Caspari, who was acquainted with the text of the sermon before it was edited, maintained that it should be dated to the early Middle Ages [364]. Morin reports the credal vari-

---

*sunt inuenta* and 10: *Sedet ad dexteram dei patris omnipotentis. Dextera dei non est corporea, quod nefas est de deo sentire, quia diuina maiestas non secundum humanam speciem designatur. Deus totus dexter est, quia totus bonus est* (see below, p. 506).

[361] *Expositio super symbolum* 9; see below, p. 506 with *app.*
[362] *Expositio super symbolum* 12; see below, p. 507 with *app.*
[363] *Expositio super symbolum* 8; see below, p. 506 with *app.*
[364] Caspari 1879, 280n182.

ant of one manuscript and describes the text as of "assez haute
antiquité" [365]. Burn is silent about the date and origin of the text
but states that its form of the Creed "ist im wesentlichen der textus
receptus" [366]. Even Kattenbusch, who devotes at least some pages
to our anonymous text, limits himself to reproducing the credal variant that is offered by Burn's edition and repeating Caspari's
dating [367]. Kelly ignores Burn's edition and directly quotes one of
the manuscripts (S of our edition), in which, according to him, the
credal variant is identical with T [368]. Finally, Dekkers and Frede
tentatively date the text to the seventh century [369].

Since nothing seems as yet to have been said about the place of
origin of the *expositio super symbolum* and only little about its date,
it will be worthwhile investigating its underlying credal variant
from the perspective of our credal typology. First of all, one may
point to two formulations that we have classified as 'unique features' for Gaul - the formulation of the fourth article with *Passus*
and *Mortuus* added, and that of the sixth with the addition *Victor*
and the preposition *Ad* instead of *In*. The possibility of a Gallican
provenance is also suggested by the addition *Creatorem caeli et terrae*
to the first article (only found in Gaul and the Latin Balkans, the
use of *Conceptus*, and the formulation of the ninth article as *Credo et
in spiritum sanctum* (both only found in Gaul and Ireland).

In fact, nothing suggests any other home than Gaul for the credal
variant under discussion. No Gallican 'general features' are lacking,
and a Gallican parallel can be found for the wording of each article.
Since all the other regions would require 'general features' that are
absent from this variant [370], the Gallican origin of the form of the

[365] Morin 1897, 485-486.

[366] Burn 1900, 128.

[367] Kattenbusch 1900, 872-874. Later, Kattenbusch (*ibidem*, 974n21) follows
Burn in stating that the credal variant under discussion is essentially identical
with *T*.

[368] Kelly 1976, 429.

[369] Dekkers 1995, 574 and Frede 1995, 473.

[370] For a Spanish origin, we would expect a fourth article with *Passus* but
without *Mortuus* and a ninth article with *Credo in*; for an African origin, to mention only the most salient features, the word order *Virgine Maria* in the third
article, the word order *A mortuis resurrexit* in the fifth article, the formulation
of the ninth article with *Credo in* again, and the position of the tenth article at
the end of the Creed; for a North Italian origin, the formulation of the third

Creed of the anonymous *expositio super symbolum* CPL 1760 may be taken for certain.

With regard to its date, the underlying credal variant also offers some clues. The presence not only of early Gallican innovations like *Conceptus* and *Dei ... omnipotentis*, but also of *Passus* and *Mortuus*, *Sanctorum communionem*, and *Vitam aeternam* yield the fifth century as the earliest possible date. Since, however, all these fifth-century changes took some time to establish themselves in the Gallican forms of the Creed, their combined presence in the credal variant of the *expositio super symbolum* makes a sixth-century origin more probable than a fifth-century one. A sixth rather than a fifth-century origin is also suggested by the presence of the addition *Creatorem caeli et terrae* and by the formulation of the sixth article (*Ascendit uictor ad caelos*). The addition to the first article, the use of *Victor*, and the use of *Ad* are all, as far as one can tell, probably only found in Gallican witnesses from the sixth century onwards. The only addition that is conspicuously absent from the credal variant under discussion is the Descent to Hell. Since, however, we have at least one seventh-century Gallican source in which this phrase is not found either, its absence here does not take us much further. We may conclude, then, that the underlying form of the Creed of the anonymous *expositio super symbolum* CPL 1760 suggests a sixth or seventh-century Gallican origin for the text.

## 4.14 The Anonymous *expositio symboli* CPL 1761

Like the previous one, this anonymous sermon on the Creed was first edited by Burn [371]. His edition of the text has remained the only one, as Hamman, identifying it with pseudo-Alcuin's *de diuinis officiis* 41 (*de symbolo*), refrained from reprinting Burn's text [372]. Pseudo-Alcuin, however, offers a quite different text, which resembles our *expositio* only in the introduction [373]. Since Burn's edition is

---

article with *Qui* and the absence of the Communion of Saints; for a Balkan origin, the use of *Viuus* in the fifth article, the use of *In* in the sixth article, and the absence of *Omnipotentis* from the seventh article (but compare for the first of these 'general features' the case of the pseudo-Ambrosian *exhortatio de symbolo ad neophytos* CPL 178; see above, chapter 4.2, p. 290). Moreover, all these regions would require the absence of *Conceptus* in the third article.

[371] Burn 1900, 135-137.

[372] See PLS 4, 2143. This error is reproduced in Dekkers 1995, 574.

not very accessible and, moreover, contains a number of errors, a
fresh edition has been included in the appendix to our study.

As far as the underlying form of the Creed of the anonymous
*expositio symboli* CPL 1761 is concerned, some of its articles are
quoted in a clear and unambiguous way. This applies to articles
two to four (partially) and five to eight. Here, syntactic breaks
and the occasional occurrence of the author, after a credal quotation, referring directly to the commentary on the preceding article
as if no quotation of a fresh article had intervened, serve to distinguish the credal quotations from the commenting parts. The relevant passages are the following: *Vnicum dominum nostrum.*
*Vnicum uel singularem ... Qui conceptus est de spiritus sancto. Non*
*ex uirili coitu ... conceptus est ... Descendit ad inferna. Tantummodo*
*anima ... Tertia die resurrexit a mortuis. Tertio quoque die ... Sedet ad*
*dexteram dei patris omnipotentis. Quod uero dicitur ... Inde uenturus*
*iudicare uiuos et mortuos. De qua sede* (referring to God's Right
Hand) ... [374]. This seems to justify the assumption that both the
opening statements about the second half of the third article and
those about the sixth and ninth, where no syntactic break occurs,
constitute literal quotations: *Natus ex Maria uirgine, non uiolato*
*uirginis utero, Ascendit in caelum, ubi numquam defuit secundum*
*humanitatem,* and *Credo in spiritum sanctum, qui a patre filioque pro-*
*cessit ...* [375].

On the other hand, the sections on the first article, on the beginning of the second, and on the final three articles are more ambiguous. It will be worthwhile quoting the exposition of the first article
and the beginning of the second in full: *Credo in deum. Id est, fir-*
*mitatem fidei meae profiteor. Deus a timore dicitur, eo quod cunctis*
*colentibus sit timori. Credo deum esse sine principio et sine fine, inui-*
*sibilem et incomprehensibilem. Et quando dico: Patrem, credo quod*
*coaeternum et coaequalem sibi per omnia genuit filium, ut Iohannes*
*ait: In principio erat uerbum, et psalmista dicit: Ante luciferum genui*
*te. Cur omnipotens deus? Eo quod omnia possit et omnia contineat*
*potestate. Et credo in eum qui creauit caelum et terram ex nihilo. Et*
*credo in Iesum Christum, filium eius. Iesus in Hebraeo eloquio, Latine*

---

[373] See PLS 101, 1271-1273.
[374] *Expositio symboli* 4-5, 8-9, and 11-12; see below, pp. 516-517.
[375] *Expositio symboli* 6, 10, and 13; see below, pp. 516-517.

*salutaris siue saluator interpretatur. Christus Graece a chrismate nomen accepit, Latine unctus dicitur, de quo in Psalmo dicitur: Propterea unxit te, deus, deus tuus, et reliqua. Non terreno oleo ut reges et sacerdotes solent perungui, sed unctio ista incorporea et inuisibilis fuit. Filium eius dicit eo quod habeat patrem, patrem uero eo quod habeat filium, genitum namque ante omnia tempora, ut Iohannes ait: Omnia per ipsum facta sunt et sine ipso factum est nihil* [376]. Beyond the fact that the words *Credo in deum* are an obvious quotation, not much else seems to be immediately clear. Nevertheless, the section on the first article in particular allows a fairly certain reconstruction of the wording of the Creed. First of all, the word *Patrem* is certainly part of the article because of the words *Et quando dico: Patrem, credo quod* .... Next, it may be observed that the author has couched his commentary partly in the first person singular: *Credo in deum. Id est, firmitatem fidei meae profiteor ... Credo deum esse ... et quando dico ... Et credo in eum qui creauit caelum et terram ex nihilo*. The phrase *Et credo ...* in particular seems to indicate that the commentary is shifting to a new part of the Creed [377]. Therefore, the presence of the phrase *Creatorem caeli et terrae* in the author's credal variant is practically certain. Moreover, the presence of *Omnipotentem* in the first article seems to be guaranteed by the phrase *Cur omnipotens deus? Eo quod ...*, which would be rather enigmatic if *Omnipotentem* was absent from the form of the Creed the text is referring to. Therefore, it seems safe to reconstruct the author's form of the first article as *Credo in deum patrem omnipotentem, creatorem caeli et terrae*.

For the introduction of the second article, the author uses his formula with *Et credo* again. This means that one cannot know exactly how this article was connected with the preceding one in the author's declaratory form of the Creed. On the other hand, the words *Iesum Christum, filium eius* seem to be vouched for by the commentary: *Iesum in Hebraeo eloquio ... Christus Graece ... Filium eius dicit eo quod ...* Moreover, in the light of the elaborate way in which the author circumvents the use of that preposition in the final three articles, the use of *In* in the introduction to the second article seems to guarantee its presence in the article itself as well.

---

[376] *Expositio symboli* 2-3; see below, p. 516.

[377] See in particular the final part of the text, which will be discussed immediately below.

The formulation of the fourth article also poses some problems. The relevant section runs thus: *Passusque sub Pontio Pilato. Passionem uero crucis sustinens ex parte humanitatis sub Pilato Romano principe qui ortus fuit in Pontio, ut dictum est cruci affixus ante portas Hierusalem in Caluario monte, in hoc quoque patibulo mortuus humanitate ac sepultus est in monumento. Descendit ad inferna* ... [378]. Here, the sequence *Passionem uero crucis sustinens ... sub Pontio Romano principe ... cruci affixus ... in hoc quoque patibulo mortuus humanitate ac sepultus* ... seems to confirm that not only *Passus* and *Sub Pontio Pilato*, but also the words *Crucifixus, Mortuus* and *Sepultus* had a place in the fourth article of the credal variant under discussion. The most probable wording is of course *Crucifixus, mortuus et sepultus*, but it will be well to bear in mind that the exact formulation of this part of the Creed may have been slightly different in the author's form of the Creed. With regard to the words *Passusque sub Pontio Pilato*, these seem best to be taken as a literal quotation, despite the unprecedented use of *-que*[379]. The author's usually meticulous way of quoting the middle articles hardly allows of any other conclusion. Moreover, *-que* cannot refer to the immediately preceding part of the commentary as Christ is not the subject there[380], and would therefore be pointless as a deliberate addition by the author[381].

When turning to the final three articles of the Creed, the use of the formula *Et credo* can be observed again: *Et credo sanctam ecclesiam catholicam, diffusam per uniuersum orbem, id est congregationem fidelium electorum siue uniuersalem ... Et credo sanctorum communionem habere, id est ... Et remissionem peccatorum firmiter spero me habere ... Carnis resurrectionem. Et credo carnem ... Et uitam aeternam credo me habere* ... [382]. Here, apart from the twelfth article, which is quoted directly, each article or part of it seems to be introduced by

---

[378] *Expositio symboli* 7-8; see below, p. 517.

[379] Kattenbusch (1900, 973n18) thinks that the words *Passusque ... Pilato* only serve to indicate the fourth article. But his remark that "Die Art der Einführung der einzelnen Artikel ist eine laxe" does not do justice to the facts.

[380] *Expositio symboli* 6: ... *sed: Virgo ante partum, uirgo in partu, uirgoque post partum.*

[381] Unless one takes the complete commentary on the second half of the third article as a kind of interjection. But it is clearly the author's main intention to explain the Creed, not to present its wording.

[382] *Expositio symboli* 14-18; see below, pp. 517-518.

means of the words *Et credo*. This implies that the presence of the Communion of Saints and Eternal Life in the credal variant under discussion is practically certain. The presence of the addition *Catholicam* is less certain, but at least strongly suggested by the commentary: *Et credo sanctam ecclesiam catholicam, diffusam per uniuersum orbem, id est congregationem fidelium electorum siue uniuersalem*. The alternative is that either *catholicam* belongs to the commentary, which would yield a rather awkward syntax, or the words *diffusam per uniuersum orbem* are part of the quotation, which would be absolutely unprecedented. In the last case, moreover, the commentary would hardly fit the quotation. It seems more probable that the author has combined several familiar thoughts on the tenth article, and that the commentary starts as a gloss with the words *diffusam per ...*, followed by another explanation that is introduced with *id est*.

We may thus reconstruct the underlying form of the Creed of the anonymous *expositio symboli* CPL 1761 as follows:

*Credo in deum patrem omnipotentem, creatorem caeli et terrae*
*... in Iesum Christum, filium eius unicum dominum nostrum*
*qui conceptus est de spiritu sancto, natus ex Maria uirgine*
*passusque sub Pontio Pilato, crucifixus, mortuus et sepultus (?)*
*descendit ad inferna*
*tertia die resurrexit a mortuis*
*ascendit in caelum*
*sedet ad dexteram dei patris omnipotentis*
*inde uenturus iudicare uiuos et mortuos*
*credo in spiritum sanctum*
*sanctam ecclesiam catholicam*
*sanctorum communionem*
*remissionem peccatorum,*
*carnis resurrectionem*
*uitam aeternam.*

Although the anonymous *expositio symboli* CPL 1761 was discovered more than a century ago, no one seems hitherto to have ventured any suggestions about its date and place of origin [383].

---

[383] Burn (see above, footnote 371) does not go beyond offering an edition, whereas Kattenbusch (1900, 973-974) limits himself to a reproduction of the

Therefore, a study of the underlying form of the Creed in relation to
our credal typology seems to be in order. The close resemblance of
this form of the Creed with that found in the *symbolum apostolorum*
CPL 1758 and the *expositio super symbolum* CPL 1760 can hardly
escape attention. The only differences with the credal variant of
the former, which is practically identical with that of PIRM [384],
comprise the formulation with *Passusque* in the fourth article and
the formulation of the sixth with *In caelum*. The same differences
apply when the credal variant under discussion is compared with
the second. In addition, one may point to the presence of the Descent to Hell, which is absent from the *expositio super symbolum*
CPL 1760, and to the formulation of the ninth article with *Credo
in*, where the other variant has *Credo et in* [385]. As the two other credal variants can be assigned to Gaul, the same origin seems to be
strongly suggested for the variant under discussion as well. In fact,
many of the features that point to a Gallican origin for the *expositio
super symbolum* (use of *Passus* and *Mortuus* in the fourth article,
addition of *Creatorem caeli et terrae* to the first, use of *Conceptus* in
the third) are also presented by our anonymous text. Nor does it
lack any 'general Gallican features', and the absence of practically
the same 'general features' in other regions seems to rule out any
other provenance than a Gallican one [386]. The wording of the fourth
and sixth articles (with *Passusque* and *In caelum*) does not pose any
problems either, since there is a Gallican parallel for the latter, and
the former would be new to any region.

   Since the credal variant of the anonymous *expositio symboli* CPL
1761 deviates from that of PIRM in details of wording only, and
both variants present exactly the same additions to the original
form of the Creed, it seems safe to presume that the two formulations are about equally old. This implies that our anonymous *expositio* is probably a Gallican text that may be dated to the seventh
century.

---

credal quotations and the presentation of some parallels. Dekkers (1995, 574)
and Frede (1995, 474) do not add anything.

   [384] See above, chapter 4.11, p. 371.

   [385] See above, chapter 4.11, p. 370, and 4.13, p. 379.

   [386] See above, chapter 4.13, pp. 380-381 with footnote 370. The even stronger
resemblance with *T* points directly to Gaul as the home for the credal variant of
our anonymous *expositio*.

4.15 The Anonymous *de fide trinitatis quomodo exponitur* CPL 1762

This text was first edited by Burn. Burn used two *Vaticani* and, for the middle part of the text, the manuscript *Sessorianus* 52, which, among other credal texts, also contains the anonymous *sermo super symbolum* CPL 1760 [387]. Apart from some mistakes in Burn's text, two reasons seem to justify a new edition of the anonymous treatise. The first is our conclusion that of the two Vatican manuscripts, the one that was deemed older by Burn is actually younger and probably dependent on the other, so that his text should be altered in a number of places. The second is the existence of two more sources for the text of the middle part [388]. A new edition can therefore be found in the appendix to our study.

The anonymous treatise *de fide trinitatis quomodo exponitur* yields its credal variant without any problems as the author makes each of the twelve apostles quote one phrase of the Creed: *Ideo apostoli symbolum composuerunt. Primus Simon Petrus dixit: Credo in deum patrem omnipotentem. Andreas frater eius: Et in Iesum Christum ... Mathias: Carnis resurrectionem et uitam futuri saeculi. Amen* [389]. In this way, we gain the following form of the Creed [390]:

> *Credo in deum patrem omnipotentem*
> *et in Iesum Christum, filium eius unicum*
> *qui natus est de spiritu sancto et Maria semper uirgine*
> *qui sub Pontio Pilato crucifixus et sepultus est*
> *resurrexit tertia die a mortuis*
> *ascendit uictor ad caelos*
> *sedet ad dexteram patris*
> *inde uenturus est iudicare uiuos et mortuos*
> *et in spiritum sanctum*
> *sanctam ecclesiam*
> *remissionem peccatorum*
> *carnis resurrectionem*
> *et uitam futuri saeculi.*

---

[387] Burn 1900, 133-135. This edition was reprinted in PLS 4, 2163-2164.

[388] See below, pp. 519-520.

[389] *De fide trinitatis quomodo exponitur* 2; see below, pp. 522-523.

[390] This portion of the text is also quoted in Kattenbusch 1900, 971-972. Kattenbusch's remark that *Semper* in the credal quotation is written above the line is erroneous.

Like similar texts that were discovered by Burn, the anonymous
*de fide trinitatis quomodo exponitur* CPL 1762 has hardly received
any scholarly attention. Burn and Kattenbusch pointed out the
compilatory character of the text and mentioned a number of parallels with other credal texts [391]. Further, both authors state that
the underlying credal variant is practically identical with *R* [392]. Kattenbusch ventures the hypothesis that the complete sermon constitutes "eine Partie des Gelasianums ... zum Teil verkürzt, zum Teil
interpoliert ..." [393]. Finally, Kelly (on the basis of manuscript *S*; see
the preface to our edition) observes that the text contains a credal
variant that closely resembles *R* [394]. Nothing has been added to
these remarks by later authors [395].

Thus, the date and place of origin of the anonymous sermon *de
fide trinitatis quomodo exponitur* are still obscure, so that it will be
all the more interesting to investigate its credal variant on the basis
of our typology. First of all, one may point to two 'unique features'
- the formulation of the sixth article as *Ascendit uictor ad caelos*,
which is typical for Gaul, and the use of *Qui* in the fourth article,
which according to our typology is limited to Northern Italy (but
compare the case of the pseudo-Ambrosian *exhortatio de symbolo ad
neophytos* CPL 178) [396]. There are also a number of formulations
without any parallels in the sources for our credal typology. The
first of these is the second article, formulated as *Et in Iesum Christum, filium eius unicum*. This formulation comes close to our reconstruction of the second article in proto-*R*, *Et in Christum Iesum,
filium eius*. The inversion of the two names of Christ is practically
standard in later forms of the Creed, and for the rest only *Vnicum*
has been added. This reminds one of Gallican formulations like
*Credo (et) in Iesum Christum, filium eius unigenitum sempiternum*
(CAE-A, CAE-B, CAE-C, Bobbio A), which also lack *Dominum nos-*

---

[391] Burn 1900, 133-134 and Kattenbusch 1900, 972-973.

[392] Burn 1900, 133 and Kattenbusch 1900, 972. Thus already Burn 1899, 237,
where Burn signals the form of the Creed and mentions its deviations from *R*
(overlooking, however, the absence of *Dominum nostrum*); compare Kattenbusch
1900, 752 and 972n16.

[393] Kattenbusch 1900, 973.

[394] Kelly 1976, 429.

[395] See Dekkers 1995, 574 and Frede 1995, 474.

[396] See above, chapter 4.2, p. 288.

*trum*. Nevertheless, the presence of the formulation under discussion is possible in any region in which the original form of the second article has left its traces. This implies that, on the basis of the available evidence, this form of the second article suggests a Gallican, African, Balkan, or possibly North Italian origin for our anonymous text. Next, the use of *Semper* in the third article (*Qui natus est de spiritu sancto et Maria semper uirgine*) lacks any parallel in the variants that we have examined so far. This means that the formulation of the third article does not help us any further here. In the third place, the formulation of the fourth article (*Qui sub Pontio Pilato crucifixus et sepultus est*) is new to our typology [397]. Although no direct parallels for this formulation exist, it reminds one of the variety in the wording of the fourth article that is offered by our North Italian witnesses (RUF: *Crucifixus sub Pontio Pilato et sepultus*; AU-M: *Sub Pontio Pilato crucifixus et sepultus*; PC: *Qui sub Pontio Pilato crucifixus est et sepultus*). Again, the word order *Resurrexit tertia die* in the fifth article is unprecedented. Perhaps this inversion is due to the addition of *A mortuis* to the article, a change that has left its traces in all regions except Africa. Finally, the closing phrase of the credal variant under discussion also seems to be new: *Et in uitam futuri saeculi*. This wording, which was probably borrowed from the Nicaeno-Constantinopolitan Creed [398], bears some similarity with the Irish formulation *Credo uitam post mortem* (DIM and BAN). All in all, then, our search for 'unique features' has yielded a wide variety of suggestions. Those of a Gallican, North Italian, or Balkan origin, however, seem to have slightly stronger claims than those of an Irish or African one.

In the second place, it will be advisable to investigate which 'general features' for the several regions are absent from the form of the Creed of the anonymous treatise. To start with Gaul, it may be observed that the following 'general' Gallican features are missing - the use of *Conceptus* in the third article, that of *Passus* in the fourth, that of *Credo* in the ninth, and the addition of *Catholicam* to the tenth article. For Spain, the use of *Passus* again, the use of *In* in the sixth article, and the introduction of the ninth article by

---

[397] Kattenbusch (1900, 762n16) considered this feature and the next one as due to scribal errors.

[398] See Kattenbusch 1900, 972n17.

means of *Credo in* are absent. We also miss the following 'general' African features - the word order *Virgine Maria* in the third article, the construction of the fourth article with a participle in the accusative, the word order *A mortuis resurrexit* in the fifth article, the use of *Credo in* again, and the position of the tenth article, formulated with *Per*, at the end of the Creed. Next, for Northern Italy, the addition of *Dominum nostrum* to the second article and the use of *In* in the sixth article are lacking. For the Latin Balkans, finally, one misses the use of *Passus* in the fourth article once again, the use of *Viuus* in the fifth article (but compare the case of the pseudo-Ambrosian *exhortatio*), the use of *In* in the sixth article, and the addition of *Catholicam* to the tenth.

The first conclusion that may be drawn from this material is that Gaul, though rather strongly suggested by the 'unique features', is not the most likely home for our anonymous text. It is true that the formulation *Ascendit uictor ad caelos* in the sixth article of its credal variant has hitherto been found in Gallican sources only, but then, any 'unique' Gallican feature may in reality have known acceptance outside Gaul as well. Such a thing would in any case be more likely than the occurrence of a Gallican form of the Creed without *Conceptus, Passus, Credo* (in the ninth article), and *Catholicam*, all additions which we saw reason to date early and which, as far as we can tell, are found in all extant Gallican variants. Next, a Spanish or African origin of the credal variant of our anoymous sermon is not likely either, in the first place because of the absence of any positive indications, and in the second in view of the absence of important 'general features' like *Passus* (Spain) and *Per sanctam ecclesiam* (Africa). The two possibilities that remain, therefore, are that of a North Italian and that of a Balkan origin. We shall therefore have to discuss these two possibilites in more detail [399].

The difficulties that one has to explain when trying to assign the form of the Creed that is found in the anonymous *de fide trinitatis*

---

[399] It is difficult to say anything concrete about the form of the Creed in Ireland. Nevertheless, certain Gallican or Spanish features (*Conceptus, Passus, Catholicam*) which are absent in the form of the Creed under discussion could be expected in an Irish credal variant. Moreover, the parallel with DIM and BAN that was noted above does not say much, as our credal variant has taken over the formulation of *C*, with which churches in any region may be assumed to have been acquainted.

to Northern Italy are twofold. First of all, one has to assume that the formulation *Ascendit uictor ad caelos* was not limited to Gaul. We have already seen, however, that it is indeed perfectly possible that a formulation that is classified as 'unique' for one region in our typology may in reality have known a wider diffusion. In the second place, a form of the second article without *Dominum nostrum* does not have any parallels in other North Italian credal variants. There is, however, reason to assume that such a short form of the second article was nevertheless in North Italian use. In that light, the wording of our anonymous text could be explained as a remnant of an older formulation that was replaced in most but not all North Italian forms of the Creed.

When we turn to the other possibility, viz. that the credal variant under discussion stems from the Latin Balkans, the formulation of the sixth article appears as the first obstacle again. Just as the use of *Victor* and *Ad* can be imagined for Northern Italy, nothing prohibits their travelling to the Balkans either. More serious is the absence of *Catholicam*. We have seen that this addition was probably brought from Africa to the Balkans in the fourth century, and it is present in every Balkan form of the Creed we have encountered so far. Therefore, the conclusion seems safest that the Creed form of our anonymous text is a North Italian one.

We now come to the question of the date of the credal variant under discussion. A certain *terminus post quem* is the year 381 because of the borrowing from the Nicaeno-Constantinopolitan Creed. Moreover, if the phrase *Ascendit uictor ad caelos* was really imported from Gaul to Northern Italy and not the other way round - this is at least strongly suggested by the fact that *Victor* and *Ad* figure in a number of Gallican witnesses, whereas their presence in Northern Italy is unprecedented - the credal variant under discussion can hardly be older than the fifth century [400]. On the other hand, the archaic wording of the second article favours an earlier date rather than a later one. Thus, the fifth century appears as the

---

[400] In the sources for our typology, *Victor* is only found in the seventh-century MGV. In our anonymous texts, we found it in the anonymous *expositio de fide catholica* CPL 505 and the anonymous *expositio super symbolum* CPL 1760. The first of these can probably be dated to the fifth century: see above, chapter 4.5, pp. 316-318. The same addition also occurs in the anonymous *expositio fidei* CPL 1763: see below, chapter 4.16.

most probable date, though a later one can of course not be
excluded. We conclude, therefore, that on the basis of our credal
typology, the anonymous sermon *de fide trinitatis quomodo exponitur*
CPL 1762 probably stems from fifth-century, and possibly from
sixth or even seventh-century Northern Italy.

## 4.16 The Anonymous *expositio fidei* CPL 1763

The anonymous *expositio fidei* CPL 1763 was first edited by
G.D.W. Ommanney in 1880 in the appendix to his work *Early History of the Athanasian Creed* [401]. This edition omits the exhortatory
part except for the final paragraph (*Si haec quae* ...). Three years
later, Caspari, who did not know of Ommanney's work, edited the
complete text [402]. As Ommanney's edition is hard to obtain and
both his and Caspari's exhibit a good number of errors, a fresh edition of the *expositio fidei* is offered in the appendix to our study.

A peculiarity of this anonymous *expositio* is that its first part, the
section on the Apostles' Creed, closely resembles the *expositio de fide
catholica* CPL 505 [403]. In fact, the first part of our text and the *expositio de fide catholica* may be considered two versions of the same
text. As they differ (with one exception) only with respect to the
expository parts and exhibit an identical structure, the same princi-
ples may be applied to distil a credal variant from both of them.
This is a legitimate and useful procedure because the *expositio fidei*
CPL 1763 is as a whole a different text from the other *expositio*.
This implies that, in all probability, it goes back to a different
author (or redactor), who also knew and used a different form of
the Creed [404].

---

[401] Ommanney 1880, 393-396. The only reference to this edition seems to be
found in Kattenbusch 1900, 454n37 (it should be noted that Kattenbusch consistently spells the name Ommaney). Other scholars give Caspari's edition (see next
footnote) as the first one. In addition, Ommanney (1880, 396-397) offers the expository part of the pseudo-Augustinian *excarpsum* (see above, chapter 4.8), but
he does not say from which source.

[402] Caspari 1883, 283-289. This text was reprinted in PLS 4, 2165-2167.

[403] See below and the preface to our edition of the *expositio fidei* CPL 1763,
p. 526.

[404] Kattenbusch (1900, 746-747) seems to recognize this point but is sceptical
about the possibility of reconstructing a form of the Creed from either text.

Therefore, we may reconstruct the underlying credal variant of the anonymous *expositio fidei* CPL 1763 as follows:

*Credo in deum patrem omnipotentem, inuisibilem uisibilium et inuisibilium omnium rerum conditorem*
*(credo?) et in Iesum Christum, filium eius unicum dominum nostrum*
 *conceptum de spiritu sancto, natum ex Maria uirgine*
 *crucifixum sub Pontio Pilato (praeside?) et sepultum*
 *tertia die resurrexit ex mortuis*
 *uictor ascendit ad caelos*
 *sedet in dexteram dei patris*
 *inde uenturus (est?) iudicare uiuos ac mortuos*
 *(credo?) et in spiritum sanctum*
 *... ecclesiam catholicam*
 remissionem peccatorum (?)
 ... [405].

Apart from remarks concerning its credal variant, scholarly discussion of the anonymous *expositio fidei* has mainly centred around the question of its origin and its relationship with the pseudo-Augustinian *excarpsum de fide catholica* and, after the publication of that text in 1898, the anonymous *expositio de fide catholica* CPL 505. First of all, Ommanney makes some short remarks concerning the credal variant [406]. Next, Caspari offers in the notes to his edition some linguistic remarks as well as numerous parallels with other texts [407]. It is interesting to observe that Caspari, though of course unacquainted with the *expositio de fide catholica*, already states that the *expositio fidei* consists of two parts, either of which could derive from a distinct source, and identifies the second of these with the pseudo-Augustinian *excarpsum* (which he considers a sermon of Caesarius of Arles) [408]. Moreover, Caspari thinks that the *expositio* must

---

[405] In his reconstruction of the same variant, Hahn (1897, 73-74) starts the second article with *Et*, retains *Resurgentem* in the fifth, reconstructs the eighth article without *Est*, and offers the following wording for the final four articles: *Et in spiritum sanctum unam habentem substantiam cum patre et filio, ecclesiam catholicam, remissionem peccatorum, communem omnium corporum resurrectionem post mortem, et uitam aeternam.*

[406] Ommanney 1880, 396.

[407] Caspari 1883a, 283-289nn.

[408] Caspari 1883a, XV-XVI.

be later than Caesarius for certain theological and literary reasons, and tentatively dates it to seventh or possibly sixth-century Gaul [409].

A few additional parallels are mentioned by Kattenbusch in the first volume of his monograph on the Creed [410]. Caspari's dating is contradicted by Hahn, who finds in the formulation of the first and fourth articles as well as in the absence of the Descent to Hell and the Communion of Saints some arguments for "eine frühe Zeit". Hahn agrees with Caspari that the form of the Creed of the *expositio* must be Gallican on the basis of the formulation of the third article with *Conceptus* [411].

After the publication of the *expositio de fide catholica* CPL 505, the question of its relationship with our text came to the fore. Burn, the editor of the other *expositio*, claims to have found in it the model for the first part of the *expositio fidei* [412]. Kattenbusch agrees with Burn in this respect and states that Burn's *expositio* and the pseudo-Augustinian *excarpsum* are the two sources for the *expositio fidei* [413]. The last person to make a detailed study of our *expositio* seems to be Lejay, who ascribes it, together with its two then known related texts and the Athanasian Creed, to Caesarius of Arles [414].

After Lejay, we only find some isolated remarks on the anonymous *expositio*. Thus Morin states that the *expositio* has been conflated from the *excarpsum* and the *dicta Pirminii* [415]. Again, Hamman holds that the *expositio* depends on pseudo-Augustine *sermo 250* and Pirminius's *scarapsus* [416]. Frede, on the other hand, returns to Burn's and Kattenbusch's opinion that the *expositio* goes back to the *expositio de fide catholica* CPL 505 and the *excarpsum* [417]. Dekkers, finally, is silent about any literary dependencies, but repeats Caspari's dating [418].

---

[409] Caspari 1883a, XVI-XVII+n1.
[410] Kattenbusch 1894, 191n4.
[411] Hahn 1897, 73-74n170.
[412] Burn 1898, 180.
[413] Kattenbusch 1900, 745-748.
[414] See above, chapter 4.5, p. 313 with footnote 125.
[415] Morin 1937, 934; reprinted in CCSL 104, 985.
[416] See PLS 4, 2144.
[417] Frede 1995, 125.
[418] Dekkers 1995, 574.

It appears from a closer study of the textual differences between the anonymous *expositio fidei* CPL 1763 on the one hand and the *expositio de fide catholica* and the *excarpsum* on the other, that Burn and Kattenbusch were probably right, and that our *expositio* is indeed dependent on those two texts [419]. This conclusion is supported by the underlying credal variant of our *expositio*, which only differs from that of the other *expositio* in two points. First, where the *expositio de fide catholica* yields *Credo in deum patrem omnipotentem, inuisibilem uisibilium et inuisibilium conditorem*, the *expositio fidei* adds *Omnium rerum* before *Conditorem*. The amplification of an existing formulation indeed suggests that the credal variant of the redactor of the *expositio fidei* is slightly younger than that of the author of the other *expositio*. Second, our anonymous *expositio fidei* testifies to a form of the seventh article which makes use of the preposition *In*, whereas the *expositio de fide catholica* has *Ad*, which is what we find in all the other extant witnesses as well. As the two variants are for the rest practically identical (that is, as far as one can tell from the sometimes rather vague indications in both texts), the conclusion seems justified that Caspari was right in situating the *expositio* in Gaul, the region to which we have ascribed the credal variant of the *expositio de fide catholica* [420]. Caspari's dating, however, seems to be decidedly too late. We have seen that the *expositio de fide catholica* could be dated between 400 and 500 on the basis of its underlying credal variant, which implies that our *expositio* cannot be much younger [421]. This accords well with our dating of the *excarpsum* to the first half of the sixth century [422]. We conclude, therefore, that the anonymous *expositio fidei* CPL 1763 is a Gallican text that was probably composed around or after the middle of the sixth century.

## 4.17 A Newly Discovered Anonymous *expositio symboli*

During a study visit to a number of Italian libraries in 1995, I naturally checked the manuscript catalogues for entries like *symbolum* and *expositio symboli*. In most cases, this did not yield any new

[419] See the preface to our edition of the text below, pp. 528-530.
[420] See above, chapter 4.5, pp. 314-316.
[421] See above, chapter 4.5, pp. 316-318.
[422] See above, chapter 4.8, pp. 349-350.

material for our study; sometimes I could add a witness to one of the texts that have been discussed in this chapter, and once I found an *expositio symboli* that appeared new to me and clearly antedated the replacement of local credal forms by *T*. Since the CD-ROMs of both Migne and CETEDOC strengthened my surmise that I had hit upon an unedited text, I decided to include it in the present study. An edition of the text is therefore presented in the appendix.

The anonymous *expositio symboli*, after a short introduction, starts by following the wording of the Creed closely, exhibiting a clear distinction between quotations (or indications) of articles (or parts of them) and commentary, and apparently concerned with commenting upon every individual element of the Creed. Thus, the first article is yielded in an unproblematic way: *Credo in deum, id est ... Credo deum: subauditur esse; credo deo: subauditur dictis eius. Patrem. Pater dicitur ... Omnipotens dicitur quia ... Creatorem, id est factorem, caeli et terrae, id est caelestium et terrestrium rerum* [423]. Similarly, the wording of the third, seventh, eighth, and tenth articles is easily gained: *Qui conceptus dicitur de spiritu sancto, et non est filius spiritus sancti. Sic et homines ... Natus ex Maria dicitur, id est ex substantia matris* [424] and *Sedet ad dexteram patris, id est in dignitate paterna. Inde uenturus, id est de caelis, iudicare uiuos et mortuos, id est siue ... Sanctam ecclesiam catholicam, subauditur credo esse. Ecclesia dicitur conuocatio, catholicam uniuersalis* [425]. It may be observed that any mention of *Virgine* is lacking in the section on the third article. However, both the possibility of a lacuna in the only known manuscript and that of an unintentional skip on the part of the author are more probable than the assumption that this word was really absent from his form of the Creed.

We then meet a somewhat less formal way of introduction, which we have already encountered within the section on the first article (*Omnipotens dicitur ...*). Nevertheless, the circumstance that the author definitely seems determined not to forget any element of the Creed makes a reconstruction of the articles in question often practically certain. Thus, we reconstruct the second article as ... *Iesum Christum, filium ... unicum* from *expositio symboli* 3: *Iesus*

---

[423] *Expositio symboli* 2; see below, p. 537.
[424] *Expositio symboli* 4; see below, p. 537.
[425] *Expositio symboli* 7-8; see below, p. 538.

*Hebraice ... Christus Graece ... Filius dicitur a felicitate parentum ... Vnicus, quia ille solus est natura, nos adoptiui filii* [426] and the fourth as *Passus sub Pontio Pilato, crucifixus, mortuus et sepultus* from *expositio symboli* 5-6: *Passus etiam dicitur tempore quo Pilatus praefuit tributis Hierosolymis. Pontius uero a loco dicitur. Crucifigi uoluit quia totum mundum redimere uenerat. Nam quattuor cornua crucis ... Mortuus est ut nos uiuificaret, siue ut et nos mundo moriamur. Sepultus est Christus, sed in sola carne* [427], though the syntax of neither article can exactly be determined.

Next, a number of phrases clearly indicate the contents of the Descent to Hell and of the fifth and sixth articles: *Descendit Christus ad inferna, sed in anima sola, ut inde nos liberaret. Et quia tribus gradibus uenimus ad mortem, id est suggestione, delectatione et consensu, ipse tertia die resurgendo nos reuocauit ad uitam. Ascendit ad caelos, ut pararet nobis locum* [428]. Here, the use of *Christus* and *ipse* seem to be best explained as deliberate insertions on the part of the author to stress the opposition with the numerous instances of *nos* in the commentary (similarly above: *Sepultus est Christus* ...). Thus, the reconstruction *Descendit ad inferna ... Ascendit ad caelos* seems reasonably safe again. With regard to the fifth article, the use of *Tertia die* and of *Resurrexit* are strongly suggested by the commentary. Perhaps the words *nos reuocauit **ad uitam*** have been deliberately chosen to correspond to *A mortuis*, but this is no more than a guess.

Finally, the concluding part of the Creed poses a number of specific problems. Our *expositio* closes in the following way: *In spiritum uero sanctum credimus, quia deus est sicut pater et filius ... Credo communionem sanctorum, id est et hic per fidem et post in regno, et remissionem, subauditur credo, peccatorum, per baptismum. Credo etiam quod in eadem carne qua uiuimus sumus resurrecturi, ut recipiat unusquisque prouti est ... Credo et uitam aeternam. Aeternam adicimus ad distinctionem temporalis uitae* [429]. Here, the wording of the ninth article seems to be beyond our reach. But what should be said about the Communion of Saints? On the one hand, the form *Credo* looks rather novel as part of the Creed here. On the other hand, the

---

[426] See below, p. 537.
[427] See below, p. 537.
[428] *Expositio symboli* 6-7; see below, pp. 537-538.
[429] *Expositio symboli* 8-10; see below, p. 538.

subsequent use of *id est* strongly suggests that it belongs to a literal quotation. Moreover, the singular *Credo* would be illogical as part of the commentary, as the author consistently uses the first person plural to formulate the correct interpretation of the Creed [430]. Thus, the Communion of Saints appears to have been formulated in the author's variant of the Creed as *Credo communionem sanctorum*. Similarly, the eleventh article seems to be best reconstructed as *Et remissionem peccatorum*. That *per baptismum* is part of the commentary seems certain, as otherwise, this would be the only instance of a quotation without commentary in the whole *expositio*. More difficult is the case of the twelfth article. *Credo etiam quod in eadem carne qua uiuimus sumus resurrecturi* hardly presents itself as a literal quotation, but on the other hand, it seems clear that with *ut recipiat* ... we are in the commentary. It is perhaps best to interpret the phrase *Credo ... resurrecturi* as a free rendition of the twelfth article (with an explanation of *Carnis* or some similar term already included), and to abstain from reconstructing its wording. Finally, the phrase *Credo et uitam aeternam* is probably a direct quotaton again, as otherwise, the author could easily have avoided the repetition of *Aeternam*.

We may reconstruct a form of the Creed from our newly discovered *expositio symboli* thus:

*Credo in deum patrem omnipotentem, creatorem caeli et terrae*
*... Iesum Christum, filium eius unicum*
*qui conceptus de spiritu sancto, natus ex Maria (...?) (?)*
*passus sub Pontio Pilato, crucifixus, mortuus et sepultus (?)*
*descendit ad inferna*
*tertia die resurrexit (a mortuis?)*
*ascendit ad caelos*
*sedet ad dexteram patris*
*inde uenturus iudicare uiuos et mortuos*

---

[430] The twofold use of the singular *credo* in the commentary on the first article has a different function, viz. to illustrate several different constructions of the verb *credo*, and thus to clarify its meaning in the context of the Creed. This is a fairly common procedure in later expositions of the Creed. See for example the anonymous *liber Quare, additio 35* b: *Credo in deum. Aliud est credo deo, aliud est credo deum, et aliud est credo in deum. Credo deo: deum esse; credo deum: uera dicere; credo in deum: credendo illum diligo* (CCCM 60, 185-186).

[in spiritum sanctum credimus]
sanctam ecclesiam catholicam
credo communionem sanctorum
et remissionem peccatorum
[credo etiam quod in eadem carne qua uiuimus sumus resurrecturi]
credo et uitam aeternam.

As scholarly attention for the anonymous *expositio symboli* under discussion has yet to start, the question of its origin is still a completely open one. What, then, does our credal typology suggest as its date and its birthplace?

If we look for 'unique features' first, we can point to the presence of *Mortuus* in the fourth article and the use of *Ad* in the sixth, both typical for the form of the Creed in Gaul. The formulation *credo etiam quod in eadem carne qua uiuimus sumus resurrecturi* possibly hides a twelfth article not too dissimilar to *Credo me resurgere* (DIM) or *Vitam habere post mortem, in gloriam Christi resurgere* (Bobbio C). Two other features that are without any parallel in our sources are the wording of the Communion of Saints as *Credo communionem sanctorum* and the use of *Et* in the eleventh article. In fact, the impression arises that the Communion of Saints and the Remission of Sins were introduced to the form of the Creed under discussion together with *Credo in communionem sanctorum et remissionem peccatorum*. This, again, would only be possible in Gaul (or perhaps Ireland), as the other regions seem to have known the Remission of Sins ever since their first acquaintance with the Creed. Thus, a Gallican origin is suggested by two Gallican 'unique features', whereas two features that lack any direct parallels might perhaps be taken to support this suggestion. This fits in with the presence of the addition *Creatorem caeli et terrae* in the first article, which only occurs in the Latin Balkans and Gaul.

As no 'unique features' that point to other regions occur, no Gallican 'general features' are absent, and other possible regions are discarded on the basis of the absence of one or more 'general features' [431], the conclusion seems safe that the anonymous *expositio symboli* comments upon a Gallican form of the Creed.

---

[431] For Spain, we would require the presence of *Dominum nostrum* and the formulation of the fourth article with *Passus* but without *Mortuus*; for Africa, among other things, the word order *Virgine Maria*, the absence of the Commun-

Finally, when trying to fix the credal variant under discussion in time, the combination of certain conservative elements with a number of innovations strikes one as significant. To begin with the former, we have a second article without *Dominum nostrum*. We have seen that these words are indeed a later addition to the article, but one that is already present in *R* and has found a place in practically all extant credal variants. Nevertheless, a number of Gallican witnesses stand out which still lack this addition: SAL and EUSh9 (probably), and CAE-A, CAE-B, and CAE-C (certainly). This implies that Gallican variants of the Creed without *Dominum nostrum* could be found as late as the seventh century, which rather diminishes their value for determining a *terminus ad quem*. In addition, it should be observed that the credal variant of the anonymous *expositio symboli* has retained the original wording of the seventh article without *Dei* or *Omnipotentis*. The only other Gallican witness that exhibits this trait is the sixth-century CY-T, whereas all other sources add either *Dei* or *Omnipotentis*, but usually both. Thus, a date not too far removed from the sixth century suggests itself as more probable than a later one. Finally, if our idea that the Communion of Saints and the Remission of Sins entered the credal variant under discussion together is somehow near the truth, it is logical to date this combined addition as early as possible, that is to say, not too long after the fifth century, when the Communion of Saints began to make its appearance in the Creed.

On the other hand, our credal variant contains all major additions that are found in later Gallican variants: *Creatorem caeli et terrae*, the Descent to Hell, the Communion of Saints, and Eternal Life. The last two of these are attested from the fifth century onwards, the first two from the sixth. Although *Creatorem caeli et terrae* and the Descent to Hell both have an earlier history, the fact that they are still far from general in sixth-century Gaul seems to make a fifth-century origin too early for a form of the Creed in which they are present together. A possible additional argument against too early a date could be the peculiar formulation of the closing part of the Creed, with at least a twofold *Credo* and perhaps

ion of Saints, and the closing of the Creed with *Per sanctam ecclesiam*; for Northern Italy, the presence of *Dominum nostrum* as well as the absence of *Catholicam* and of the Communion of Saints; for the Latin Balkans, the absence of the Descent to Hell and of the Communion of Saints again.

the use of a verb in the twelfth article, features that rather remind one of formulations like those of Bobbio C, BAN, and DIM.

Thus, the conclusion that our anonymous *expositio symboli* represents a sixth-century Gallican form of the Creed is hard to avoid. An earlier date would make the *expositio* the earliest witness to the additions of *Creatorem caeli et terrae* and of the Descent to Hell in Gaul, whereas a later date would be incompatible with the conservative wording of the seventh article, and possibly with the peculiar combination of the Communion of Saints with the Remission of Sins as well. Therefore, as long as no other arguments are adduced, it seems best to connect this newly discovered commentary on the Apostles' Creed with sixth-century Gaul.

# CONCLUSION

At the end of our investigations, which have ranged from the study of secondary literature via polemics down to close reading and textual criticism, it seems appropriate to repeat the most important conclusions. As is indicated by this methodical variety, the questions that we have tried to answer in this book do not always follow directly from each other. Consequently, not all our answers and all our findings have the same or even the same kind of relevance for the study of the Apostles' Creed. Nevertheless, a single goal can be said to have inspired the entire enterprise - that of gaining a fuller understanding of the **development** of the Apostles' Creed as a **formula**. Thus, questions that we have tried to answer in the course of this study comprise those of time, place, and circumstances of the birth of the Creed, its original manifestation, the factors that influenced its growth, the various forms in which it presents itself over the course of time, the sources for our knowledge of these forms, and the way they can be classified. Clustering around these and similar questions, the main results may be summarized as follows.

First of all, it can be maintained that the time-honoured theory of Usher and Vossius, according to which the earliest extant formulation of the Apostles' Creed should be connected with fourth-century Rome, has proved itself as still best for explaining the available data. This is the result of a fresh examination in the light of the criticism that this theory has evoked from Kinzig and Vinzent. In this process, not only has the new alternative been refuted in our opinion, but an important feature of the older theory has come more visibly to the fore, viz. that it depends on a combination of indirect sources. Thus, the existence of an Old Roman Creed and its outline are vouched for by Rufinus (and to a lesser extent by Ambrose and Augustine), its wording is preserved in a number of anonymous manuscripts, and it is only provided with a firm fourth-century date by Marcellus of Ancyra. As is shown in particular by Vinzent's study, this combination of indirect evidence is vulnerable to attack. Although we have found that the traditional explanation is still stronger than any modern reconstruction, the conclusion that it is time for a fresh and comprehensive investigation of the evidence for *R* is inescapable, something which has not been done since the days of Heurtley and Caspari.

In the same context of the dispute with Vinzent and Kinzig, the latter's study of early and medieval baptismal questions forced us to rethink the relationship between the Apostles' Creed, generally conceived of as a declaratory text, and its interrogatory equivalents. To that purpose, we have studied a number of sources expressly with an eye to understanding that relationship better, something which has apparently not been attempted before. Although here again it appears that the traditional opinion, viz. that declaratory forms of the Creed and similarly formulated baptismal questions are interchangeable manifestations of the same formula, is also the most probable one, it is to Kinzig's credit that he has called attention to the problem of the origin of the many, sometimes astonishingly diverse baptismal questions that seem to be unrelated to the Apostles' Creed.

Next, a number of criticisms of Kelly's account of the relationship between *R* and *H* indicated that some rethinking was also required with respect to the pre-fourth-century history of the Creed. Thus, we were led to reflect upon the nature of the, necessarily hypothetical, original wording of the Apostles' Creed. As a result, we arrived at the reconstruction of what we have called proto-*R*, a formula that may be considered to represent the ultimate ancestor of all extant credal variants. The relatively unknown contribution of Smulders turned out to be a fundamental guide here. Thus, if our reconstruction is convincing, his name is entitled to equal honours with Kelly's in the future historiography of the study of the Apostles' Creed.

Although much is by necessity unclear in this field, we have, in addition, been able to connect our interpretation of the earliest sources for *R* as well as our subsequent reconstruction to what is known about the oldest summaries of Christian faith. Thus, the basic intention of the Creed, professing one's *fides qua*, as well as that of its counterpart the *regula fidei*, defining one's *fides quae*, could be traced back to nuclear formulations that might well hark back to the first century. Again, a comprehensive study of such and similar formulations seems long overdue, and again, following some of the suggestions by Smulders might well prove profitable here.

Turning from the protohistory and prehistory of the Creed to its subsequent development down to *c.* 800, we conducted a number of investigations that pertain to credal change and variety. The existence of both had been noted long ago but has received little or no scholarly attention so that our efforts in this respect often moved in areas that were practically or completely untouched. First of all, we could determine three different reactions to changes in the form of the Creed for the period under discussion - violent disapproval, defence as a necessary updating with a view to heresies, and silence. The latter, perhaps best explained as entailing that even the more conspicuous additions were not envisaged as real changes but more as glosses, is by far the most common reaction. Our evaluation of this silence would constitute an interesting hypothesis for a possible future study of patristic and early medieval interpretations of the Apostles' Creed.

Secondly, a number of concrete changes in the formulation of the Creed could be isolated and studied at relatively close quarters. As possible causes of change this yielded dogmatic or pastoral updating on the one hand, and personal Latin usage and style on the other. The latter are strongly favoured as changing factors by the nature of the Creed as a liturgical text that was used only a few times a year and, at least for a considerable period, one that people were discouraged from writing down.

Both results appear to be compatible with a further more or less traditional theory, viz. that the Apostles' Creed, when spreading from Rome over the Western Church, developed a number of regional types. If that theory is somewhere near the truth, one should expect the following two tendencies to present themselves in the total number of credal variants: 1) that relatively minor changes of wording will be confined to one or two regions only, and 2) that more substantial changes of content will travel relatively easily from one region to another.

In the subsequent survey of some thirty different credal formulations, it appears that this double hypothesis is confirmed, and that the theory of the existence of regional types of the Apostles' Creed is essentially correct. Nevertheless, there is one important respect in which changes in the form of the Creed do not behave in the way we expected them to. In fact, changes of Roman origin, even comparatively insignificant ones, were found to have left their traces in practically all of the Western Church. For the rest, however, changes of wording indeed tend to remain confined to one or two regions (nine out of thirteen) and changes of content tend to spread themselves over more than two (seven out of twelve), as appears from a detailed reconstruction of the history of the Creed, presented both in a systematic (article by article) way and in a geographic (region by region) one. Here, an unforeseen but interesting phenomenon corroborating our theory was that some changes of content indeed spread over several regions but, in the process, gave rise to new variants of wording that remained limited to one region only. All in all, it proved possible to describe the concrete features of five distinct regional types of the Creed. Our description of these types is the first on this scale and renders it unnecessary to have to use the inaccurate and incomplete accounts by Kelly and Glorie any longer.

To arrive at this point, it proved necessary to undertake a detailed analysis of all hitherto adduced sources for the form of the Apostles' Creed in the period under discussion. Although this analysis has required a considerable amount of space, it yields, we hope, two additional consequences that might well be fruitful for future credal research. First, it claims to replace the overview of sources by Hahn (that is to say, for the **Latin** sources of the **Apostles'** Creed). As this has been a desideratum for some considerable time, the results of our analysis have been listed separately in a separate appendix to our study. Second, this analysis develops a number of tools for assessing the value of possible credal quotations that can be used for the study of other sources, both of the Apostles' Creed and of other creeds.

Part of the overview of sources in this book is only presented after our reconstruction of five regional types of the Creed. Some sixteen texts are granted a separate treatment as they are either generally considered to be anonymous or have, in our opinion, recently but falsely been ascribed to a certain author (pseudo-Peter Chrysologus, *sermo 62bis* and pseudo-Caesarius of Arles, *sermo 10*). In either case, such texts could not help to test our hypothesis because of the uncertainty of their origin. Conversely, however, our account of the regional development of the form of the Creed does help to assess more precisely their date and place of birth. Thus, we could date and locate the following anonymous texts (indicated by CPL number only) in the following way:

CPL 178: Latin Balkans, fourth century or later
CPL 229a: Northern Italy, fifth century or later
CPL 365: Gaul, 550-600
CPL 505: Gaul, fifth century (?)
CPL 846: Africa, fifth or sixth century
CPL 915, 26 and 28: no direct assessment possible
CPL 1008, 10: Gaul, sixth century
CPL 1744a: Northern Italy, fourth century or later
CPL 1751: Northern Italy, 450-550
CPL 1758: Gaul, seventh century or later
CPL 1759: Spain (Irish??), fifth century
CPL 1760: Gaul, sixth or seventh century
CPL 1761: Gaul, seventh century or later
CPL 1762: Northern Italy, fifth century or later
CPL 1763: Gaul, 550-600
new text: Gaul, sixth century

Incidentally, the proportion of the various regions of provenance within this group of newly studied texts is quite similar to the one in the group on which our credal typology was based. Thus, we found eight probably Gallican texts (against fifteen), one Spanish one (against seven), four North Italian ones (against five), one African one (against four), and one from the Latin Balkans (against three). Nevertheless, much work still remains to be done in this field. Not only do we still await the edition of a number of anonymous sources for the form of the Creed, but a renewed search of medieval manuscript catalogues may well also yield fresh material for analysis. It is my hope that the present study has developed both a theory and some tools to assess such material in a scientific way, and thus may contribute in the future to a better understanding of both the history and the meaning of the Apostles' Creed.

*Maior autem horum est caritas.*

# APPENDIX I

## Source Texts for the Anonymous Forms of the Creed

In this appendix, all the texts that have been discussed in chapters 4.2-4.17 are presented in full. As has been indicated in more detail for each individual case above, a completely new critical edition of a text was often necessary. Thus, the discovery of fresh manuscript material has considerably increased our knowledge of the anonymous texts with CPL numbers 178, 505, 1751, and 1758-1762. Moreover, one text was not yet available in a printed edition. In addition, the editions of the texts with CPL numbers 229a, 365, 846, 1744a, and 1763 sometimes stood badly in need of revision, whereas some were also difficult to obtain. Finally, a forthcoming text edition has been included for CPL 915, 26 and 28.

Nevertheless, it should be borne in mind that the new editions that are presented here can by no means be considered to constitute **the** new texts for the relevant pieces. In the prefaces, sufficient material has, I trust, been adduced to justify our choices for the constitution of the text, but nothing more. Similarly, data from earlier printed editions have only sparingly been included in the critical apparatus of most texts. In the future, these defects are planned to be emended in a 'real' edition for *Corpus Christianorum*. For the present, however, this first step towards that goal may suffice for readers who want to follow the discussions and check the decisions that are set out in chapter four.

The textual transmission of the  *exhortatio de symbolo ad neophytos de symbolo* CPL 178

Six manuscripts of the pseudo-Ambrosian *exhortatio de symbolo ad neophytos* are available to us. One of them, the thirteenth-century (?) Uppsalensis (Universitetsbibliotek C 194, f. 34R-34V; *U*) does not contain the complete text but only a very free paraphrase of it, and has therefore been omitted from our apparatus [1]. The other five are a tenth-century Augiensis (*A*), an eleventh-century Remensis (*R*), a thirteenth-century Parisiensis (*P*), and two fourteenth-century Vindobonienses (*V* and *W*, the latter from the fifteenth century according to Caspari [2]).

Some obvious scribal errors prove that none of *A* or *P* or *R* can have been the ancestor of any other extant manuscript. The errors are the following.

Typical errors in *A*:

> *recitaturus sim* for *recitaturus sum* (thus *RPVW*) in *exhortatio* 2
> *et* for *ut* (thus *PVW*; *R* has *cum*) in 2
> *eodem* for *eidem* (thus *RPVW*) in 13
> *ipse* for *ipsi* (thus *RPVW*) in 21
> *legatus* for *legato* (thus *RPVW*) in 24

Typical errors in *P*:

> *saeculum* for *saeculum saeculi* (thus *ARVW*) in *exhortatio* 1
> *confuso* for *confusor* (thus *ARVW*) in 6
> *de deo* for *deum de deo* (thus *AR*; *VW* have *deum deus de deo* in 14
> *caelo* for *caelos* (thus *ARVW*) in 19
> *figuraret* for *fugaret* (thus *ARVW*) in 27

Typical errors in *R*:

> *uersutum* for *uersuto* (thus *APVW*) in *exhortatio* 4
> *interimant* for *intereant* (thus *APVW*) in 11
> *noueris quae* for *noueris* (thus *APVW*) in 18
> *consciens* for *consentiens* (thus *APVW*) in 20

---

[1] *R* and *U* share one quite conspicuous mistake, which makes it practically certain that *U* has either been copied from *R* or is very closely akin to it: both read *filium dei ex deo et filium hominis ex **patre*** (instead of *matre*; thus *APVW*) in *exhortatio* 23.

[2] Caspari 1879, 186

*inspiratum* for *insperatum* (thus *APVW*) in 22
*memorie* for *memoria* (thus *APVW*) in 27

According to Caspari, *W* may well have been copied from *V* [3]. This indeed seems to be the case. The two manuscripts have rather a lot of mistakes in common, such as *maiestatem* for *maiestatem suam* (thus *ARP*) in *exhortatio* 9 and *successoribus* for *successionibus* (thus *ARP*) in 16. Moreover, there are no cases where *W* obviously has a correct, and *V* obviously an incorrect reading. There is only one exception to this, where *V* reads *sed* and *W si* (*exhortatio* 14). The mistake in *V*, however, is quite obvious, so that *W* may well have corrected it. There are two possibilities, therefore, either *W* is copied from *V*, adopting all of its errors except one and adding a few of its own, or *V* and *W* have a common ancestor. In the latter case, however, it is difficult to explain why *W* has so many false readings of its own and *V* so few. Therefore, it is more probable that *W* is a copy of *V*. We shall therefore usually designate the two manuscripts together as *v*.

The three manuscripts *VWP* share a number of errors as well. Among the most obvious are the following.

Errors common to *P* and *v*:

omission of *ut coccinum* in *exhortatio* 1
*ut impletur* for *impletur* (thus *AR*) in 4
*insuper fide* for *in superficie* (thus *AR*) in 4
*ueridicum* for *ueridico* (thus *R*, *A* has *ueredico*) in 13

The four manuscripts *VWPA* also have quite a few errors in common. The following can be reckoned undisputable mistakes.

Errors common to *A*, *P*, and *v*:

*uitae ueritatis* for *uitae et ueritatis* (thus *R*) in *exhortatio* 9
*audies* for *audias* (thus *R*) in 18
*eius* for *eius quae* (thus *R*) in 19
*misso* for *missum* (thus *R*) in 21
*dominum* for *deum* (thus *R*) in 23

These two groups of common errors give rise to the hypothesis that *APv* all descend from one ancestor (*p*), responsible for the

---

[3] Caspari 1869, 131

errors they have in common. This ancestor *p* must have been copied independently by *A* and another lost manuscript, *q*. This latter hypothetical manuscript is responsible for the false readings that *P* and *v* have in common, with both *P* and *V* copied from it. Manuscript *R* must be independent of this group.

This hypothesis is corroborated by the fact that none of *A* or *P* or *V* ever offers a correct reading where all other manuscripts are obviously wrong. Moreover, there are no instances where *R*, together with one or more, but not all, members of the descendants of *q*, offers a false reading, with the exception of one instance, where both *A* and *R* lack the words *tunc enim* (*exhortatio* 24), preserved in *Pv*. The two places where *R* together with *v* offers the correct reading (*patris nomen* instead of *patris nomen patris* [thus *AP*] in 15 and *omnis* in stead of *omnia* [thus *AP*] in 19) can be explained by the fact that the error, which *q* must still have contained, was obvious enough to be corrected by *V* (*A* was corrected as well).

Therefore we propose the following stemma.

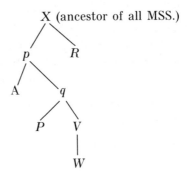

With this stemma in hand, the following rule for evaluating the several textual variants can be deduced. Where consensus between *R* and *Pv* or *R* and *A* (*Av*) occurs, such a reading generally will have to be preferred. Where *R* and *APv* differ, however, the best reading has to be chosen using other criteria.

Naturally, instances will remain where no single manuscript offers a satisfactory reading. These fall into two groups - those where our archetype must already have contained an error, and those where *p* and *R* both must have been mistaken. Examples of the first group are the following.

Errors in *X*:

uincuntur (thus *codd.*) in *exhortatio* 5 (corrected to *conuincuntur* by Caspari)

non possit (thus *codd.*) in 7 (*non* deleted by Caspari)

nostri Iesu Christi (thus *codd.*) in 12 (recognized as hiding a form of *nomen* by Caspari)

ualetudinis ignorans (thus *codd.*) in 22 (inverted by Caspari)

Two instances where both *R* and *p* seem to have made a different mistake are *exhortatio* 4, where *R* has *caecorum duces duces et caei* and *APv caecorum duces caeci* (for the probable *caecorum duces et caeci*) and *exhortatio* 27, where *R* reads *per gratiam* and *p* presumably read *et a gratia* (thus *Pv*, *A* has *et ad gratiam*; the most probable correction is *et per gratiam*).

codices:

A     Karlsruhe, Badische Landesbibliothek, Augiensis 18, ff. 30V-32R, saec. X

R     Remensis, Bibliothèque Municipale 295, ff. 18V-21V, saec. XI

P     Parisiensis, Bibliothèque Mazarine 627, ff. 29V-31R, saec. XIII

V     Vindobonensis, Nationalbibliothek 1471, ff. 223V-226R, saec. XIV

W     Vindobonensis, Nationalbibliothek 4602, ff. 335V-337R, saec. XIV/XV

v     consensus codicum VW

editiones:

Ca1   CASPARI, C.P., *Ungedruckte, unbeachtete und wenig beachtete Quellen zur Geschichte des Taufsymbols und der Glaubensregel ... II*, Christiania, 1869, 132-140

Ca2   CASPARI, C.P., *Alte und neue Quellen zur Geschichte des Taufsymbols und der Glaubensregel*, Christiania, 1879, 187-195

Ca3   PLS 1, 606-611

Ca    consensus harum trium editionum

exhortatio ad neophytos de symbolo CPL 178

1. Gratia uobis et pax a deo patre et filio et spiritu sancto assistat et abundet (cf. Rom. 1, 7. I Cor. 1, 3. II Cor. 1, 2. Gal. 1, 3. Eph. 1, 2. I Petr. 1, 2. II Petr. 1, 2. Iudae 2) benedicti a domino (cf. Gen. 24, 31), *qui uocat uos in suum regnum et gloriam* (I Thess. 2, 12. cf. II Thess. 2, 13. I Petr. 5, 10), quoniam apud ipsum et ipse fons uitae est, in cuius lumine spiritali uidebimus lumen aeternum (cf. Ps. 36, 10). Dicam itaque uobis in uoce Psalmi: *Accedite ad eum et illuminamini, et uultus uestri non erubescent* (Ps. 34, 6), dicam in oratione prophetica: *Lauamini, mundi estote, et si fuerint peccata uestra ut coccinum, ut niuem dealbabo* (Is. 1, 16. 18). *Lex* enim, inquit, *domini irreprehensibilis, conuertens animas, praeceptum domini lucidum, illuminans oculos, timor domini castus, permanet in saeculum saeculi* (Ps. 19, 8-10). *Venite* itaque *filii, audite me, timorem domini docebo uos* (Ps. 34, 12), timorem domini hunc qui castus et sanctus est. 2. Fons huius timoris est fides. Ad cuius confessionem

ediscendam hodie conuenistis. Symbolum enim, quod uobis perci-
piendo baptisma praeordinatis recitaturus sum sermone praesenti,
salutiferae signaculum fidei nostrae et confessionis est titulus. Sic
enim salus nostra perficitur, ut uerbum euangelicae praedicationis
quod corde concipimus ore promamus, quia neque iustitiam facere
possumus si dubio corde credamus, neque salutem acquirimus si eru-
bescamus id quod credimus confiteri (cf. Rom. 10, 10). Ideo ipse
dominus in Euangelio dicit: *Quia qui me uel meos sermones confessus
fuerit coram hominibus, et ego confitebor eum coram patre meo qui in
caelis est. Si autem negauerit me coram hominibus, et ego illum negabo
coram angelis patris mei* (Matth. 10, 32-33. Luc. 12, 8-9).

3. Credimus itaque in deum patrem omnipotentem saeculorum
omnium et creaturarum regem et conditorem, et in Iesum Christum
filium eius unicum dominum nostrum, qui natus est de spiritu
sancto et ex Maria uirgine, qui sub Pontio Pilato crucifixus et sepultus, tertia die resurrexit a mortuis, ascendit in caelos, sedet ad dexteram dei patris, inde uenturus est iudicare uiuos et mortuos, et in
spiritum sanctum, et sanctam ecclesiam catholicam, remissionem
peccatorum, carnis resurrectionem.

4. Huius symboli forma multis etiam haereticis in specie confessionis uidetur esse communis, sed impletur sermo qui scriptus est (cf.
Ioh. 15, 25): *Ore suo benedicebant et corde suo maledicebant* (Ps. 62,
5). Nam eos qui in superficie uerborum symboli adumbratam speciem ueritatis ore mentiri uidentur et impium corde uersuto tenere
mendacium, detegit peruersa doctrina et eorum a quibus audiuntur
euidens et aperta subuersio, ut simul in ministris et discipulis praedicationis sermo euangelicae ueritatis eluceat, quia caecorum duces
et caeci pariter in foueam tenebrarum cadunt (cf. Matth. 15, 14.
Luc. 6, 30), quos uno gurgite communis error inuoluit et inferni
puteo mors una demergit (cf. Ps. 55, 24). 5. Nam omnipotentem
patrem non credere conuincuntur qui filium a substantia patris conantur abducere, se potius a corpore ipsius uitae, *qui ueritatem dei in
mendacio detinent* (Rom. 1, 18), abscidentes, et deum uerum, hoc est
patrem et filium, deum unum, quem labiis mendacibus credere se
confitentur factis negare impiis aguntur (cf. Tit. 1, 16). 6. Quomodo
enim aut Arrius omnipotentem deum uere dicit, quem negare conuincitur impietate doctrinae, qua eum aequalem ex sua substantia
filium non genuisse confirmat, aut Sabellius per similitudinem sacri-
legii, qui dissimilitudine quidem erroris ab Arrio separatur, sed

propter qualitatem blasphemiae errore diuerso in eundem mortis lacum (cf. Ps. 88, 7) confluens, tam hic impius confusor quam ille diuisor? 7. Qui eundem et patrem et filium et spiritum sanctum audet asserere, tantis stultitiae tenebris ex impia uoluntate caecatus ut incommutabili deo, quod est trinitas, mutabilem designet naturam et, diabolicae nequitiae similem uarietatem, uti ipse sit idem pater et filius et spiritus sanctus, non personaliter in trinitate distincta subsistens, sed solitarie singularis et triformiter in singularitate mutabilis, ut quando uult pater esse filius possit, et quando personam filii suscipit deponat patris, et rursum deposito patris et filii nomine spiritus sancti nomen assumat. 8. Atque ita et ipsi, de uia ueritatis auersi, in deuiis uagantur erroribus, quia sic astruunt unitatem ut abnegent trinitatem, sicut Arriani, ex impari daemoniorum doctrina (cf. I Tim. 4, 1) pares homicidae (cf. Ioh. 8, 44), tam impie separant ut nefarie diuidant unitatem. 9. Verum utrosque ipse fons uitae et ueritatis una sententia simul arguit et confundit et destruit, quia maiestatem suam magistra humilitate declarans ait: *Ego et pater unum sumus* (Ioh. 10, 33). 'Vnum' enim dicendo confudit Arrianum impie separantem, 'sumus' adiciens destruxit Sabellium nefarie confundentem. 10. Nos itaque, propitio ipso domino qui illuxit nobis et sedentes in tenebris et umbra mortis (cf. Is. 9, 1. Luc. 1, 78) eduxit nos, non solum ore sed et corde depromimus catholicam confessionem, quia uere credimus in deum patrem omnipotentem, qui eum non adulatorie sed uere et proprie ut est omnipotentem dicimus. Et ideo non dubitamus per eam omnipotentiam qua cuncta rerum fecit ex nihilo, et filium de se ipso genuisse aequalem sibi et per omnia parem, hoc est uoluntate, substantia et similitudine maiestatis et aequalitate uirtutis et societate unitatis et infinitate aeternitatis. 11. Neque enim sibi praestare non potuit, quod creaturis suis mortalibus et corruptibilibus praestare dignatur, ut secundum genus suum ipse generaret hanc gloriam, et ipse tantum, quod illorum profano ore sic dictum est, dissimilem sibi filium gignere, ut maiestatis suae detrimentum operaretur in sua plebe, cum etiam hominis confessione potuerit filios Abrahae de lapidibus generare (cf. Matth. 3, 9). Ipsi potius, stirpe uitali per intellectum mortiferum mente peruersa degenerantes, intereant cum patre mortis suae diabolo, cuius progeniem se ipsi fecerunt, doctrinam eius praeferendo doctrinae et regulae ueritatis.

12. Credimus itaque et in Iesum Christum filium dei omnipotentem aequalem deo, quoniam et nomine et forma et potentia diuinitatis aequalem patri scripturarum caelestium praemissa uerissima auctoritate cognouimus. De ipso enim dicit Iohannes: *In principio erat uerbum, et uerbum erat apud deum, et deus erat uerbum* (Ioh. 1, 1). Hunc et propheta Dauid filium patris et dei et domini nomini indiscrete copulans, ait: *Propterea unxit te, deus, deus tuus oleo laetitiae* (Ps. 45, 8), et: *Dixit dominus domino meo: Sede a dextris meis* (Ps. 110, 1). Consubstantialem ergo patri indicat euangelista, cum ait: *Verbum erat apud deum, et deus erat uerbum* (Ioh. 1, 1), sed et Dauid propheta similiter, qui personas diuidens uno tamen nomine et unctum et unguentem 'deus' appellat (cf. Ps. 45, 8). 13. Et dominum omnipotentem, uere coopificem patri filium in omnibus creaturis idem auctor ostendit, de filio utique uerbo dicens: *Omnia per ipsum facta sunt, et sine ipso factum est nihil* (Ioh. 1, 3). Conformem uero eidem patri aeque ueridico alterius apostoli sermone conspicimus: *Qui cum esset,* inquit, *in forma dei non rapinam arbitratus est esse se aequalem deo patri* (Phil. 2, 6).

14. Credite ergo et confitemini deum patrem omnipotentem et filium coomnipotentem, coopificem, coaeternum patri filium, non creatum, sed natum, deum de deo, lumen de lumine. Absit omnis error et mentis et uerbi. Si enim uerbum non factura, si filius non seruus, si genitus ex natura non adoptatus ex gratia. 15. Hoc uerbum, deus, dei filius, ante saecula ineffabili generatione genitus ab ingenito, per omnia aequalis et similis et uniformis patri, excepto filii nomine, quo patris nomen ostenditur, quia in patre et filio naturaliter una substantia, personaliter distincta nominibus, de patre filium et patrem reuelat in filio. Per haec nomina contexitur ordo pietatis et naturae unitas indicatur, quia nec pater sine filio nec filius sine patre dici potest. 16. Nec tamen non solum in creatore sed uel in creatura ulla potest patris et filii natura discerni. Si enim ex ipso uerbo secundum genus omnia creari iussa perpetuis successionibus legem praecepti caelestis obseruant, quanto magis ipse omnium dominus et creator secundum genus suum genuit talem qualis ipse est et tantum quantus ipse est. Et ideo omnia per ipsum et sine ipso nihil fecit (cf. Ioh. 1, 3. Col. 1, 16). 17. Et quis audet homo de generatione ipsius disputare, cum propheta in spiritu sancto sine fine principium, omnium rerum initium et finem genitum uidens ait: *Generationem eius quis enarrabit* (Is. 53, 8)? Sed

neque caelestes creaturae, archangeli, principatus, dominationes, throni (cf. Col. 1, 16) possunt sibi diuinae eius natiuitatis conscientiam uindicare. Quae enim uidere potuit ortum filii dei ex deo, cum *omnia per ipsum facta sunt, et sine ipso factum est nihil* (Ioh. 1, 3)? *Verbo* enim, inquit, *domini caeli firmati sunt et spiritu oris eius omnis uirtus eorum* (Ps. 33, 6). 18. Quid ergo tu, homo haeretice, qui terra es et in terram ibis (cf. Gen. 3, 19. Ps. 145, 4. Eccle. 3, 20 et 12, 7. I Mach. 2, 63), quia terram sapis audes praesumere tibi scientiam de natura dei, quam per cogitationum tuarum figmenta corrumpis (cf. Rom. 9, 20)? Cum propheticum testimonium audias, uerbo domini, id est filio dei, quem tu aequalem patri denegas, firmamenta caelorum esse perfecta, et spiritu oris eius, id est spiritu sancto, omnem caelestium elementorum uirtutem esse solidatam (cf. Ps. 33, 6), si caeli non possunt scire generationem filii dei, quia creatore ipso senior creatura esse non potuit, quomodo tu tibi, terra, praesumis ut noueris? 19. Tot creaturae operum eius quae supra te sunt - et caelum et ornamenta caeli et omnis militia siderum, solis et lunae luminaria magna (Gen. 1, 16) et caeli caelorum et aquae quae super caelos sunt (Gen. 1, 7) (cf. Deut. 4, 19 et alibi) et innumerae legiones angelorum et exercitus principatuum et ministeria dominationum et thronorum (cf. Col. 1, 16) - et tamen altiorem sibi altissimum scire nequeunt. Adorando potestates non scrutando perquirunt, sed suspiciendo tremunt, seruiendo uenerantur, laudando benedicunt, peruigilando celebrant.

20. Hoc *uerbum caro factum est et habitauit in nobis* (Ioh. 1, 14), hoc est, homo factus uoluntate misericordiae et oboedientia pietatis, pro salute nostra consentiens patri ut opus commune seruaret ineffabili sacramento et salutari mysterio, per omnipotentiae uirtutem, cooperante patre et spiritu sancto, conceptus a uirgine et natus ex uirgine. 21. Huius quidem natiuitatis arcanum cui umquam creaturae in terris aut in caelis reuelatum, nisi hominibus per unum prophetam qui ante saecula operis huius praedixerat sacramentum: *Ecce uirgo accipiet in utero et pariet filium* (Is. 7, 14), et deinde ipsi beatae Mariae per unum archangelum ex ore diuino ad eam missum, ut ei conceptionem partumque diuini pignoris nuntiaret (Luc. 1, 26-31)? 22. Scilicet ne tanti ignara mysterii ad insperatum corporis inuiolati tumorem puella expauesceret, et causam insolitae conceptionis ignorans ualetudinis propriae crederet esse prodigium, si nesciret opus esse diuinum, hominem sine homine secundo esse conceptum et in

utero de carnis suae materia sine carnis semine fabricandum, ut ineffabili generationis sacramento ipse esset in uirgine creator sui, qui se per spiritum sanctum operabatur creandum. 23. Itaque hunc filium dei et filium hominis credite et confitemini, sed filium dei ex deo et filium hominis ex matre, ita ut sine matre filius dei et sine patre sit filius hominis, quia nec corporis sexus deo nec uiri coitus in uirgine. Hunc *dominum maiestatis* (I Cor. 2, 8) ut perfectum deum secundum naturam et formam dei patris credimus, ita et perfectum hominem ex matre uirgine. 24. De humano corpore uestimentum carnis assumpsit, iuxta symboli ordinem crucifixum sub Pontio Pilato, per illud tempus Iudaeae prouinciae legato, id est Romanis fascibus imperante. Tunc enim praenuntiatam a prophetis suis pas-sionem et mortem pro nobis suscepit. 25. Sepultus tertia die resur-rexit a mortuis, et cum surrexisset per quadraginta dies, sicut Actis Apostolorum docemur, conuersatus cum hominibus electis atque dilectis sibi (Act. 1, 3), coram ipsis et quingentis uiris testibus post resurrectionem uisus (I Cor. 15, 6) in corpore quo crucifixus fuerat et sepultus. 26. Ascendit in caelos, sedet ad dexteram dei patris, inde uenturus iudicare uiuos et mortuos.

27. Hunc ordinem, quem memoria continendum, ore reddendum accipitis, recti fide credite, retinete, intellegenter considerate, sem-per attendite, ut et timor et amor domini confirmetur in uobis. Quia per caritatem pro nobis mortuus est, ut resurrectionem nostram in corpore suo, id est habitu nostrae fragilitatis, ostenderet nobis et metum mortis fugaret a nobis, nosque per metum iudicii sui a pec-catis * * * et per gratiam baptismatis expiatos coheredes sibi ad regni caelestis gloriam praepararet, cui gloria in saecula saeculorum. Amen.

apparatus criticus apud *exhortationem de symboli ad neophytos* CPL 178

1. et filio *codd.*] *om.* Ca2-3        benedicti a R] benedicti Pv, benedicti *e* benedic-tio A        in ARPV] ad W        ipse RPv] ipse *ex* in ipso A        spiritali A] spi-ritali *e* spiritalitali P, spirituali Rv        uoce APv] uocem R        mundi ARP] et mundi *v*        ut coccinum AR] *om.* Pv        saeculum saeculi ARv] saeculum P
2. ediscendam ARPV] ediscenda ?W        baptisma praeordinatis *scripsi*] bap-tisma praeordinatum A, baptisma praedicandum R, baptismo praedestinatum Pv        sum RPv] sim A        salutiferae RPv] saluti fere A        nostrae AR P *(ut uide-tur)*] uestrae *v*        ut Pv] et A, cum R        concipimus ARP Ca1] percipimus *v*, concepimus Ca2-3        corde credamus RPv Ca1] credamus corde A Ca2-3

3. et ex *APv Ca1*] et *R Ca2-3* sepultus *ARPV*] sepultus est *W* in caelos *ARPV*] ad caelos *W* sedet *RPv*] sedit *A* uenturus est *ARv Ca1*] uenturus *P Ca2-3*

4. forma *RPv*] forma *e* formam *A* specie *RPv*] specie *e* speciem *A* impletur *AR*] ut impletur *Pv* in superficie uerborum *AR Ca2-3*] insuper fide uerborum *Pv*, in supra recitata fide uerborum *coni. Ca1* impium *ARP*] impii *v* uersuto *APv*] uersutum *R* ministris *ARPv*] magistris *Ca* euangelicae *AR*] et euangelicae *Pv* caecorum duces et *conieci*] caecorum duces duces et *R*, caecorum duces *APv* inferni puteo *AR*] in infernum puteum *Pv*

5. conuincuntur *coni. Ca*] uincuntur *ARPv* hoc *ARP*] hic *v* arguuntur *Ca*] a$^r$g$^u$untur *A*, aguntur *RPv*

6. conuincitur *ARv*] conuincitur *e* conuincuntur *P* confluens *APv*] defluens *R* tam hic *R*] tam *Pv*, tam *e* tamquam *A* confusor *ARv*] confuso *P*

7. designet *ARP*] designat *W, incertum quid V* naturam *ARv*] natura *P* uti *ARP*] ut *v* spiritus sanctus *ARv*] spiritus *P* et *RPv*] om. *A* possit *coni. Ca2-3*] non possit *ARPv Ca1*, omnino possit *coni. Ca1* suscipit *Pv*] suscepit *R*, suscipit *e* suscepit *A*

8. in deuiis *RP*] inde deuiis *A* inde tuis *V* inde uiis *W* separant *ARPV*] separat *W*

9. uitae et *R*] uitae *APv* confundit *ARv*] confudit *P* quia *APv*] qui *R* maiestatem suam *ARP*] maiestatem *v* magistra *ARv*] magista *P* unum enim *codd. Ca1*] unum *Ca2-3* confudit *RPv Ca1*] confu$^n$dit *A*, confundit *coni. Ca1, Ca2-3* destruxit *R*] destruit *APv*

10. sed et *AR*] sed *Pv* depromimus *R*] depromemus *A*, depromamus *PV* uere *RPv*] uere *e* uero *A* deum patrem *APv*] patrem *R* adulatorie *R*] adolatoria *P*, adolatoria *v*, adolatoria *ex* adolatorie *A* de se ipso *Pv*] de ipso *AR*

11. non potuit *R*] potuit *APv* corruptibilibus *ARv*] corruptilibus *P* et *scripsi*] ut *codd.* sibi filium *conieci*] sibi *codd.* gignere ut *conieci*] gigneret et *codd.* sua *ARPW*] su a *V* in lapidibus *conieci*] hominibus *codd.* se posse *conieci*] confessione *ARPV*, confessio ne *W* dixerit *conieci*] dederit *codd.* generare *conieci*] degeneres *codd.* stirpe *codd. Ca1*] a stirpe *coni. Ca2-3* intereant *APv*] interimant *R* mortis *ARPV*] motis *W*

12. itaque et *R*] itaque *APv* omnipotentem *codd. Ca1*] omnipotentis *Ca2-3* quoniam *A*] qm *RPv*: quoniam *an* quem *incertum* praemissa *RPv*] promissa *A Ca* dicit *RPv*] dixit *A* patris *codd. Ca1*] patri *coni. Ca2-3* nomini *scripsi*] nomine *coni. Ca2-3*, nostri Iesu Christi *codd. Ca1* et *RPv*] et dixit *A* ergo patri *codd. Ca1*] ergo *Ca2-3* euangelista *ARv*] et euangelista *P* Dauid propheta *ARPv Ca1*] Dauid *Ca2-3* personas *RPv*] personas *e* personans *A* uno tamen *ARP*] ullo tamen *v* unguentem *RPv*] ung$^u$entem *A* deus appellat *scripsi*] dominum appellat *APV*, dominus appellat *R, om. W*

13. omnipotentem *R*] coomnipotentem *APV, om. W* auctor *ARPV*] auctorem *?W* ipso *codd. Ca1*] eo *Ca2-3* eidem *RPv*] eodem *A* ueridico *R*] ueredico *A*, ueridicum *Pv* apostoli *R*] apostolis *Pv*, apostoli *ex* apostolus *A* inquit *ARv*] om. *P* esse se *AR*] esse *Pv* patri *ARP*] patri ... *?V*, patri etc *W*

14. deum *R Ca*] dominum *APv*      natum *ARPW*] genitum natum *V*
deum de deo *AR*] deum deus de deo *v*, de deo *P*      et mentis *ARPV*] mentis
*W*      si *ARPW*] sed *V*      ex *ARP*] et *v*
15. genitus *AR*] genitus est *Pv*      patris nomen *Rv*] patris nomen patris
*A P*      nominibus de *RP*] nominis de *A*, pro nominibus de (?in ) *V*, pro nominibus in *W*      nomina *Pv*] nomina *e* nomine *A*, omnia *R*      unitas *ARP*]
unita *v*
16. nec tamen non *APv*] non tamen non *R*      non solum in creatore sed uel in
creatura ulla *R*] non solum in creatore sed uel in creatura illa ulla *A*, non solum
in cretore sed uel in creatura ulla *P*, non solum in creatura ulla *v Ca1*, non solum
in creatura sed uel in creatore ulla *coni. Ca2-3*      ipso uerbo *ARv*] illo uerbo *P*
successionibus *ARP*] successoribus *v*      praecepti *RPv*] praecepti *e* percepti
*A*      talem qualis ipse est et tantum quantus *A Ca2-3 (A:* quantus *e* quantum*; Ca2:* et *pro* est *)*] talem qualis ipse est et tantum quantum *R*, talem quantus *PV Ca1*, talem quantum *W*
17. natiuitatis *ARP*] natiuitates *v*      uindicare *APv*] uindicare *e* uindicare
potuit *P*
18. quia *AR*] qui *Pv*      terram *AR*] terrena *Pv*      cum *AR*] cum per *P*, cum
enim per *v*      audias *R*] audies *APv*      firmamenta *ARPV*] firmamentum *W*
omnem *AP*] omnium *Rv*      uirtutem *RPv*] uirtutem *e* uirtutum *A*      creatore
*ARPV*] creatorem *W*      noueris *APv*] noueris quae *R*
19. eius quae *R*] eius *APv*      omnis *Rv*] omnis *ex* omnia *A*, omnia *P*      caelos *ARv*] caelo *P*      ministeria *ARP*] misteria *v*      ante *sed* aut *post* potestates
*lacunam suspicitur Ca1-2; forsitan* et *pro* sed *legendum*      suspiciendo *AR*] sus-
cipiendo *Pv*      tremunt *ARP Ca2-3*] tremt =? tremunt *v*, circueunt *coni. Ca1*
20. habitauit *ARPV*] habitabit *W*      consentiens *APv*] consciens *R*      et
salutari *AR*] et saluti *PV*, ut saluti *W*      omnipotentiae uirtutem *RPv*] omnipotentiae uirtutum *A*      et natus ex uirgine *ARPV*] *om. W*
21. cui umquam *AR*] cui nulli umquam *Pv*      reuelatum *APv*] reuelatum est
*R*      accipiet *ARPV*] concipiet *W*      ipsi *RPv*] ipse *A*      per unum archangelum *ARPV*] archangelum *W*      missum *R Ca*] misso *APv*      diuini
*RPV*] diuini *e* diuine *A*, diuino *W*
22. tanti *RPv*] tanti *e* tanti ne tanti *A*      ignara *RPv*] ignora *A*      insperatum *Pv*] in speratum *A* inspiratum *R*      ignorans ualetudinis *Ca*] ualetudinis
ignorans *codd.*      secundo esse *scripsi*] secundum deum esse *R*, sed cum deo
esse *AP Ca2-3*, et cum deo esse *v Ca1*      et in utero de *Pv*] et in utero sine
de *A*, in utero de *R*      sacramento *coni. Ca2-3*] argumento *codd. Ca1*
23. et filium hominis *coni. Ca*] homines *codd.*      matre *APv*] patre *R*      ut
perfectum deum *R*] ut perfectum dominum *A*, et perfectum dominum *Pv*
ita et *R*] ita ut *APv Ca1*, et *Ca2-3*
24. symboli *ARv*] syboli *P*      Iudaeae *ARv*] ?uidete ?iudece *P*      legato
*RPv*] legatus *A*      tunc enim *Pv*] *om. AR*      praenuntiatam *R Ca2-3*] pro-
nuntiatam *APv Ca1*
25. surrexisset *AR*] resurrexisset *Pv Ca1*, surrexit *Ca2-3*      actis *APv*] actibus
*R*      quingentis uiris *APv*] quingentis uiris *R*      uisus *ARP*] ?uisus uisus
?uisus iustis *V*, uisus iustis *W*
26. patris *ARP*] patris omnipotentis *v*      uenturus *ARP*] uenturus est *v*

27. memoria *APv*] memorie *R*     recti fide *AR*] recta fide *PV*, rectam fide
*(?*fidem *) W*     retinete *AR*] et retinete *Pv*     ut et *ARPV*] et ut *W*
domini *codd.* Ca1] dei *Ca2-3*     uobis *W*] u$^n$obis *A*, nobis *RV ?P*     quia
*APv*] qui *R*     ut *AR*] ut et *?P v*     habitu *R*] habitum *A*, in habitu
*Pv*     fugaret *Rv*] fugaret *e* fugeret *A*, figuraret *P*     iudicii sui a *ARP*] iudicii una *v*     *post* peccatis *lacunam suspicor unius uerbi*     et per gratiam
*scripsi*] per gratiam *R coni. Ca2-3*, et ad gratia *ex* et ad gratiam *A*, et a gratia
*Pv Ca1*     ad regni caelestis gloriam *scripsi*] in regni caelestis gloria *ARPv Ca*
cui *ARP*] cum *v*

The textual transmission of the anonymous *expositio symboli* (CPL 229a)

The anonymous *expositio symboli* CPL 229a has come down to us in one fourteenth-century manuscript: Cividale del Friuli, Biblioteca del Museo Archeologico Nazionale, cod. 77 (*C*). It was first edited by De Rubeis in 1754. The first edition would remain the only one for more than two centuries. Olivar had the manuscript consulted by J.C. Menis [1] and offered a new edition in 1962. De Rubeis's text has been reprinted twice (once by himself in 1762 and once by Olivar in 1961), and Olivar's once (in CCSL 24, published in 1975). No two of these five editions, however, offer an identical text. De Rubeis made a number of mistakes, as do most editors who present an *editio princeps*, and added one further in 1762. Olivar, naturally, copied these mistakes in his reprint of De Rubeis's 1754 edition, but made a considerable number of his own as well. Not all of the old errors were corrected in Olivar's 1962 edition. On the contrary, some new ones were added. Corruption continued in his final 1975 edition, so that the latest edition of the anonymous *expositio symboli* thus far is also the worst.

A new edition, based on an autopsy of the manuscript in Cividale, is therefore presented below. With one possible exception, we have retained the text of the manuscript, which is intelligible throughout and nowhere more barbarous than is usual in late patristic sources.

[1] See Olivar 1962, 371 for this particular point.

codex:

C    Cividale del Friuli, Biblioteca del Museo Archeologico Nazionale, cod. 77, 26V-28R, saec. XIV

editiones:

*Ru1*    DE RUBEIS, F.J.B.M., *Dissertationes duae* ..., Venetiis, 1754, 242

*Ru2*    DE RUBEIS, F.J.B.M., *Dissertationes variae eruditionis* ..., Venetiis, 1762, 19-20

*Ru3*    Olivar, A., 'San Pedro Crisólogo autor de la Expositio Symboli de Cividale', in: *Sacris Erudiri* 12, 1961, 310-312

*Ol1*    Olivar, A., *Los sermones de San Pedro Crisólogo* ..., Abadia de Montserrat, 1962, 494-495

*Ol2*    CCSL 24, 354-355

*Ru*    consensus editionum *Ru1*, *Ru2* et *Ru3*
*Ol*    consensus editionum *Ol1* et *Ol2*

expositio symboli CPL 229a

1. Credo in deum patrem omnipotentem. Si credidisti dubitare noli, noli facere de credulitate perfidiam, noli uitium sociare uirtuti. Dixisti: Credo in deum patrem. In unum deum totam confessus es trinitatem.

2. Et in Iesum Christum. Iesus saluator, Christus unctus mystice nuncupatur. Saluator dicitur quia ipse suae saluator factus est creaturae. Sicut enim reges oleo (cf. I Reg. 10, 1 et 16, 13. III Reg. 1, 34. 39. I Par. 11, 3), ita plenitudine est diuinitatis infusus.

3. Filium eius unicum dominum nostrum. Quia esse filii, esse domini, acceperunt alii per ipsius gratiam, ipse autem quod est filius, quod est dominus, suam possidet per naturam.

4. Qui natus est de spiritu sancto et Maria uirgine. Virgo et spiritus sanctus commercium uirtutis est, caeleste consortium, maiestatis insigne. Quod ergo generat uirgo diuinum est, non humanum. Mundus non capit, ratio non habet, sapit fides, non sapit saeculi inquisitor.

5. Qui sub Pontio Pilato crucifixus est et spultus. Audisti nomen iudicis ne tempus persecutionis ignores. Audisti crucifixum ut scias uitam redisse per lignum. Audisti sepultum ne mortem perfunctoriam suspiceris. Mortem fugisse timoris est, uicisse uirtutis.

6. Tertia die resurrexit uiuus a mortuis. Quia quod passus est solius est carnis, quod resurrexit totius gloria trinitatis.

7. Ascendit in caelum, nos ferens, non se referens, qui non deerat caelo.

8. Sedet ad dexteram patris, totum tenendo quod paternae potestatis est et honoris.

9. Inde uenturus est iudicare uiuos et mortuos, quos aut mittat ad gloriam aut damnet ad poenam (cf. Dan. 12, 2. Ioh. 5, 29).

10. Credo in sanctum spiritum. Sicut credimus in deum patrem, ita credimus in spiritum sanctum. Spiritus sanctus quomodo putabitur minor esse deitate? Patrem et filium et spiritum sanctum manifestatos uocabulis, non diuisos substantia sentiamus, et perfectos personis, non minoratos ordine fateamur.

11. Sanctam ecclesiam catholicam, quia ipsa est corpus Christi et ipsius caput est Christus (cf. Eph. 1, 23. Col. 1, 18). Christum ergo in sancta ecclesia confitemur.

12. Remissionem peccatorum. Qui sibi credit dari regnum caeli, quomodo sibi dimitti peccata non credit? Caelum innocentes recipit, non nocentes. Credimus enim nobis omnia remittenda esse peccata quia nisi sancti sancta non possumus possidere.

13. Carnis resurrectionem. Resurget ergo caro nostra ut quae fuit particeps aut uirtutis aut criminis, uel praemii particeps possit esse uel poenae (cf. 2 Cor. 5, 10).

14. Credimus et uitam aeternam, quia homo tunc uiuere incipit quando se nesciet mori.

apparatus criticus apud expositionem symboli CPL 229a

1. dubitare noli *C Ol*] noli dubitare *Ru*
2. nuncupatur *C Ru1-2 Ol*] nuncupantur *Ru3*     ipse suae *C Ru1,3 Ol*] ipse *Ru2*     enim *C Ol*] etiam *Ru*
3. ipsius gratiam *C Ol*] gratiam *Ru*     quod *1° Ru*] quia *Ol*; ꝗ *C, quod in fine regulae spatio deficiente pro usitato* q°d *intellegendum haudquaquam dubito*
4. et *1° C Ol*] ex *Ru*
5. qui *C*] dicitur *Ru,* dicitur qui *Ol*
6. uiuus *C Ol2*] uiuens *Ru Ol1*
8. paternae potestatis *C Ol*] potestatis *Ru*
10. sanctum spiritum *C Ol*] spiritum sanctum *Ru*     sicut ... sanctum] *om. Ol2* deitate *C*] diuinitate *edd.*     minoratos *edd.*] minorato *C*
11. catholicam] *del. Ol2* quia *C Ru*] qua *Ol2*
12. regnum caeli *C Ru1-2*] regnum *Ru3 Ol*     credit *C*] credat *edd.*
13. possit esse *C*] esse possit *edd.*
14. nesciet *C Ru1-2*] nesciat *Ru3 Ol*

The textual transmission of the *expositio super symbolum* CPL 365

The *expositio super symbolum* CPL 365 has been transmitted in a 1477 incunabulum (Hain 8395). Caspari first edited the *expositio* from a Bamberg and a Munich exemplar of this incunabulum, for which he used the designations *B* and *M*[1]. These two sources, however, are just two copies of the same printed text, which we shall indicate as *B*. The *expositio* is presented as *expositio beati Augustini episcopi super symbolum*, and can be seen on ff. 6R-7V of the incunabulum. It has not as yet been found in manuscripts, but this may be due to the fact that it shares its preface with the well-known pseudo-Augustinian *sermo 242* (CPL 368).

Caspari states that the text of the main part of the *expositio* as it has been transmitted is rather corrupt, and that that of the introduction is even more so[2]. He only prints the main part of the sermon, omitting the introduction, which can also be found in editions of pseudo-Augustine *sermo 242*. In fact, this main part does not often stand in need of real correction, although the Latin is awkward in places. As long as it can reasonably be defended that the incunabulum text may represent what the author intended to write, we have chosen to retain its readings. Thus, for example, we did not inverse the word order *recte beatitudinem* in the phrase *ad ueram nemo potest recte beatitudinem peruenire* (*expositio super symbolum* 4), nor did we change *retinetur* to the more logical *profertur* where the author states: *Sicut enim nihil profutura est fides quae ore retinetur et corde non creditur, ita nihil profutura est fides quae corde tenetur si ore non profertur* (*expositio* 5) or the slightly constrained expression *iudicii sui aduentus* (referring to the Second Coming) to the more natural *iudicis sui aduentus* (*expositio* 16). Where the text of the incunabulum is clearly corrupt, however, we only had the tool of conjectural emendation at our disposal to arrive at an intelligible text. Thus, we have followed Caspari in supplying *Creatorem omnium* in the quotation of the first article of the Creed (*B: credamus in deum patrem omnipotentem quae sunt uisibilium et inuisibi-*

---

[1] At least two more copies of the same incunabulum exist - one in Bamberg (see our edition) and one in London (see Copinger 1895, 249). The possibility that more incunabula contain the same *expositio* cannot be excluded either: see Hain 2107 and 8390-8392.

[2] Caspari 1883a, XVIII-XIX+n4.

*lium; expositio* 7) [3] and changing *essem* to *essemus* in a context which otherwise makes use of the first person plural (*expositio* 9). An instance where a more substantial amount of conjecture seemed to be necessary is *expositio super symbolum* 11, where *B* reads: *Qui non in auro, non in aurgento, hominis creaturam, qui omnia creauit ex nihilo, sed proprio sanguine suo redemit.* Here, the object *nos* has been added before the first *non*, the twofold *in* has been deleted, and *creaturam* has been emended to *creatura* to arrive at an intelligible and correct Latin phrase. For reasons concerning content, we decided to change the incunabulum reading *uitam aeternam* (*expositio* 19) into *carnis resurrectionem* [4]. Finally, the verb *saluari* is an apparent gloss in the phrase *ut de illa* (viz. the Resurrection of the Flesh) *nos nullatenus dubitemus saluari* (*ibid.*), which was therefore deleted.

The text of the introduction is indeed much worse than that of the *expositio* proper. Nevertheless, we have basically followed the same procedure for both parts of the text. Although the introduction to our *expositio* is clearly based on the introduction to pseudo-Augustine *sermo 242 de symbolo*, it differs from its original in numerous points, which cannot all be due to textual corruption in the usual sense of the word. We know that the pseudo-Augustinian *sermo 242* was very popular in the Middle Ages [5], and the introduction as it stands in our *expositio super symbolum* looks more like a distinct recension that was the result of repeated use over the course of the centuries than anything else. Therefore, we have again retained as much as possible of the incunabulum text, and where emendation was necessary, we have not automatically supplied the vulgate text of pseudo-Augustine *sermo 242*, but have tried to reconstruct what the author probably intended. Thus, to give an example, where the incunabulum reads *Hoc totum breuiter ... symbolum in se continet confitendo tenendo. Ergo, fratres carissimi ...* (*expositio super symbolum* 2-3), we have only changed *tenendo* to *tenendum*, though the pseudo-Augustinian *sermo 242* reads *Totum hoc breuiter ... symbolum in se continet confitendum. Tenendo ergo, fratres carissimi ...* [6].

---

[3] See chapter 4.4, footnote 82 for more details on this question.
[4] See chapter 4.4, footnote 90 for the details.
[5] See for example Kattenbusch 1900, 461 and 772-774+n22.
[6] Pseudo-Augustine, *sermo 242 de symbolo* 1; PL 39, 2192.

codex:

*B*    Bambergensis, Staatsbibliothek Inc. typ. Q XI 24/1b (uel Inc. typ. B V 19, uel Monacensis, Bayerische Staatsbibliothek, Latinus 23817

editio:

*Ca*    C.P. Caspari, *Kirchenhistorische Anecdota nebst neuen Ausgaben patristischer und kirchlich-mittelalterlichter Schriften ... I. Lateinische Schriften. Die Texte und die Anmerkungen*, Christiania, 1883, 290-292 (= PLS 2, 1361-1363)

expositio super symbolum CPL 365

1. Quaeso uos, fratres, ut nobis reserantibus expositionem symboli attentius audiatis, quia haec trina uirtus symboli est sacramenti doctrina, illuminatio animae, plenitudo credendi. In eo si quid docetur aut dicitur et unitas est trinitatis, distincta et trinitas personis, et opulentia creatoris, et redemptio passionis. Hic nexus infidelitatis absoluitur, hic uitae ianua panditur, hic gloria confessionis ostenditur. Symbolum, dilectissimi fratres, breue est uerbis sed magnum est sacramentis, paruum ostendens imminutione latitudinis sed totum continens compendio breuitatis. Exiguus ut memoriam non obruat sed diffusus intelligentiam supercedat, confirmans omnes perfectiones credendi, desideria confitendi, fiduciam resurgendi. 2. Digne ergo et attentiores et frequentiores et pro ratione temporis ipsius puriores ad audiendum symbolum conuenistis. Quicquid enim praefiguratum est in patriarchis, quicquid denuntiatum est in scripturis, quicquid praedicatum est in prophetis, uel de deo ingenito uel ex deo in deum nato uel de spiritu sancto, quamuis latenter ostensum sit, uel de suscipiendi hominis sacramento uel de morte domini et resurrectionis mysterio, hoc totum breuiter iuxta oraculum propheticum symbolum in se continet confitendo tenendum.

3. Ergo, fratres carissimi, consolatione fidei et gratia professionis mysterio memoriae commendato, iam ad ipsius symboli perfectionis sacramentum textumque ueniamus. Credo in deum patrem omnipotentem, et cetera. 4. Nosse debemus et nouimus, fratres carissimi, quod ad ueram nemo potest recte beatitudinem peruenire, nisi per fidem. Beatus autem nemo potest esse, nisi credendo bene uixerit, bene uiuendo fidem rectam custodierit, quoniam qui credit merito

inuocat et quaerit. 5. In corde deus respicit fidem (cf. Luc. 16, 15), ubi non se possunt homines excusare qui ore simulant ueritatis professionem et corde retentant impietatis errorem. Sicut enim nihil proficit fides quae ore retinetur et corde non creditur, ita nihil profutura est fides quae corde tenetur si ore non profertur. 6. Vnde dicit apostolus, corde credere ad iustitiam, ore autem eandem fidem confessione ad salutem proferre (Rom. 10, 10). Nam si fides sine operibus otiosa et mortua est (Iac. 2, 17. 20. 26), tamen sine fide nemo potest placere deo (Hebr. 11, 6).

7. Ideo autem credamus in deum patrem omnipotentem creatorem omnium quae sunt uisibilium et inuisibilium. Ipse est deus pater, ipse est uerus deus. Quoniam uerum eum dicimus agnoscamus eum naturaliter filium deum genuisse. In quo autem deus deum genuit, aequalem sibi sine initio per omnia genuit, non minorem, neque in ullo dissimilem. 8. Proinde, desiderantissimi, credentes in deum patrem omnipotentem omnium creatorem, credamus et in Iesum Christum filium eius unicum dominum nostrum. Ipse est enim unigenitus deus, non diuina potentia creatus, sed solus de patris substantia natus, cui una aeternitas, una diuinitas, una et coaequalis per omnia uirtus et potestas. Per ipsum nos deus pater mirabiliter creauit, per ipsum nos de morte misericorditer liberauit. 9. Qui conceptus est de spiritu sancto, natus ex Maria uirgine. Qui de deo patre natus est deus ante omnia tempora, ipse in tempore ex Maria uirgine natus est homo, ut idem unus deus uerus esset et homo. Qui cum in natura dei deus esset aequalis per omnia patri (cf. Fil. 2, 6), idem homo fieri uoluit, ut nos faceret filios dei (cf. Gal. 4, 4-5), ut quod ipse erat per naturam essemus per gratiam. 10. Passus sub Pontio Pilato, crucifixus, mortuus et sepultus. Ecce quanta pro nobis pertulit unigenitus deus, cui parum fuit ut pro salute nostra nasceretur nisi insuper pateretur in cruce. Audite, fratres, quis pro quibus tanta sustinuit. Christus, unicus dei filius, secundum carnis ueritatem quam sumpsit a nobis crucifixus ab iniquis et impiis Iudaeis, ipse *mortuus est pro peccatis nostris* (I Cor. 15, 3), ut nos ad uitam reuocaret aeternam. 11. Ipse omnipotens creator noster, ipse dignatus est fieri redemptor noster, qui nos non auro, non argento, hominis creatura (cf. I Petr. 1,18), qui omnia creauit ex nihilo (cf. II Mach. 7, 28), sed proprio sanguine suo redemit (cf. Rom. 3, 24-25. Apoc. 5, 9) et pro nobis crucis tormenta patienter sustinuit. Ipse nos ab aeterna damnatione et morte redemit, ipse

pro nobis mortuus est et sepultus. 12. Descendit ad infernum, ut nos misericordia sua eleuaret in caelum. Vere misericors et beatus, qui misericorditer uisitauit locum miseriae nostrae, ut nos perduceret ad locum beatitudinis suae.

13. Deinde tertia die resurrexit a mortuis. Ipse pro nobis pertulit mortem, ut nostram nobis redderet immortalitatem et uitam. Christus mortuus est secundum carnem, ut nos carnaliter pro ipso mori uel concupiscentiis mundi (cf. Gal. 5, 24. Col. 3, 5) non timeremus. Resurrexit Christus a mortuis, ut nos resurrectionem certissime crederemus. 14. Ascendit in caelum, sedet ad dexteram dei patris omnipotentis, ut nos crederemus, si eum ex toto corde sequeremur bona operatione, quo ipse praecessit nos eum sequeremur anima et carne, quia quo ascendit redemptor illuc ascendet redempta familia, si non deest sequendi illuc Christiani cordis affectus. 15. Christus nos sua morte reuocauit ad caelestem patriam, et nos econtra remanendo in peccatis (cf. Rom. 6, 1) amamus potius terrenae peregrinationis exilium (cf. II Cor. 5, 1-8. Hebr. 11, 13), Christus nos proprio sanguine ad aeternas diuitias comparauit, nos econtra in aeterna indigentia uolumus remanere. 16. Christus sicut ascendit in caelum, ita inde uenturus est (cf. Act. 1, 11) iudicare uiuos et mortuos. Qui uenerat cum mansuetudine, ueniet cum magno terrore. Quem iudicii sui aduentum diligunt iusti (II Tim. 4, 8), ut accipiant regnum, timent iniusti, ne in ignem mittantur aeternum (cf. Matth. 25, 34. 41). 17. Quapropter, dilectissimi, priusquam illud iudicium ueniat, unusquisque nostrum componat causam suam et corrigat uitam suam, ut non cum impiis ad poenam, sed cum iustis perueniat ad coronam.

18. Credentes itaque in deum patrem, et filium eius unicum dominum nostrum Iesum Christum, credamus et in spiritum sanctum, qui est uerus deus sicut pater et filius, quia ipse est unus patris et filii spiritus sanctus. Pater ergo et filius et spiritus sanctus, sancta trinitas, naturaliter unus uerus et bonus est deus. Haec est una fides, haec est uera fides, per quam iustificamur (cf. Rom. 3, 26. Gal. 2, 16. Eph. 4, 5), per quam ab omni peccato mundamur (cf. Tit. 2, 14. I Ioh. 1, 7). 19. Credamus ergo sanctam ecclesiam catholicam, sine qua et extra quam nemo saluatur. In qua omnis *qui crediderit et baptizatus fuerit* (Marc. 16, 16) omnium peccatorum suorum remissionem consequetur et carnis resurrectionem, quam in semet ipso nobis demonstrauit Christus, ut de illa nos nullatenus

dubitemus. 20. Quapropter, dilectissimi, bene uiuamus, ut non ad poenam sed ad aeternam uitam resurgamus (cf. Dan. 12, 2) per Christum, dominum ac redemptorem nostrum, uiuentem et regnantem per omnia saecula saeculorum.

apparatus criticus apud *expositionem super symbolum* CPL 365

1. trinitatis *conieci*] trinitas *B*        infidelitatis *conieci*] et fidelitatis *B*        exiguus ... diffusus *conieci*] exiguis ... diffusis *B*
2. tenendum *conieci*] tenendo *B*
3. commendato *conieci*] commendacio *B*
7. omnipotentem creatorem omnium *coniecit Ca*] omnipotentem *B*
9. essemus *coniecit Ca*] essem *B*
11. nos non auro non argento *conieci*] non in auro non in aurgento *B*        creatura *conieci*] creaturam *B*
14. sequeremur *2° B*] sequemur *Ca cum nota* "... man erwartet «secuturos esse»", *quod fortasse scribendum*        ascendet *conieci*] ascenderet *B*
19. carnis resurrectionem *conieci*] uitam aeternam *B*        dubitemus *conieci*] dubitemus saluari *B*

The manuscript tradition of the *expositio de fide catholica* CPL 505

Four manuscripts with the complete text of this *expositio* were available to us - one in the Bodleian Library in Oxford (*B*), one in Wolfenbüttel (*W*; both from the ninth century), one in Munich (*M*; tenth century), and one in Karlsruhe, the Augiensis 18, which we have already met in connection with the pseudo-Ambrosian *exhortatio de symbolo ad neophytos* (CPL 178) and shall meet again for a good number of other texts (also from the tenth century). Parts of the *expositio de fide catholica* CPL 505 also occur in the *expositio fidei* CPL 1763, of which two manuscripts are known to us - a ninth-century and a tenth-century *Parisiensis* (*P* and *Q*, together *p*).

Since the two manuscripts *PQ* exhibit an essentially different text from that of the other four manuscripts, it will be clear from the outset that neither of them can be the parent of any of the others[1]. As far as the relationships between the other four witnesses *ABMW* are concerned, it can be said that none of *A* or *B* or *M* can be the direct ancestor of any of the others, as these three manuscripts all contain a number of obvious errors which are not shared by the others. The following examples may suffice to illustrate this point.

Typical errors in *A*:

> *et Iesum Christum filium eius unicum dominum* for *et in Iesum Christum filium eius unicum dominum nostrum* in *expositio* 2
> omission of *quando ueniat cum cruce sua* in 4
> *et spiritum sanctum* for *et in spiritum sanctum* in 5
> *quasi non* for *et non* (*ibidem*)
> omission of *habebunt* in 11

Typical errors in *B*:

> *possidebunt* for *possidebit* in *expositio* 1
> *sanctos peccatores* for *sanctos et peccatores* in 4
> *spiritus* for *spiritus sanctus* in 6
> omission of *computatur* in 9

---

[1] In the preface to our edition of the *expositio fidei* CPL 1763, it will be argued that *Q* is a copy of *P* for that text. We shall therefore exclude it from the present analysis.

Typical errors in $M$:

*uiuos et mortuos* for *uiuos ac mortuos* in *expositio* 4 [2]
*paenitentiae* for *paenitentia* (*ibidem*)
*uniuersalis uniuerso* for *uniuersalem uniuerso mundo* in 8
*angelis* for *angelis eius* in 9
*per baptismum* for *pro baptismo* (*ibidem*)
omission of *iuuenes* in 11
*post praemia* for *praemia* (*ibidem*)
omission of *aeterno* (*ibidem*)

Next, it can be observed that $B$ not only disagrees quite often with the group $AMW$, but that it also frequently offers a correct reading in those cases. Thus, it has the correct *tanta* instead of *tantos* ($AMW$) in *expositio* 10, alone preserves the words *ex hoc saeculo* before *transierint* (11), and has *iusti uero* as opposed to the less probable *et iusti* ($AMW$; *ibidem*). Its reading *ex patre et filio* as opposed to *a patre et filio* ($AMW$; 6) may be a similar case. Since no other manuscript can lay similar claim, it seems reasonable to assume that $B$ and the group $AMW$ constitute the two main branches of the tradition [3].

Within the group $AMW$, the manuscripts $WM$ seem to stand out with a number of errors common to both. We may point to the following obvious cases.

Common errors in $W$ and $M$:

*uigiliis* for *uigilia* (thus $AB$) in *expositio* 4
*obseruauerit* for *obseruatis* (thus $P$; $A$ has *obseruabitis* and $B$ has *obseruas*) in 9
*communionem* ($M$: *communionem sanctorum*) for *communem* (thus $ABP$) in 10

Although these cases strongly suggest that $M$ is dependent on $W$, this cannot be all there is to it, since there is at least one instance where $M$ broadly agrees with the other manuscripts and $W$ has a lacuna - it omits the words *senior ... nec* in *expositio* 7 and thus produces nonsense. Nevertheless, the fact that $M$ is dependent on $W$ or at least a manuscript that resembled it very closely cannot be

---

[2] A clear case of the influence of the *textus receptus* of the Creed.
[3] Nevertheless, Künstle (1900, 87-89) argues that $BMW$ derive from $A$.

denied. In fact, practically all errors in *W* can be found in *M* as well [4]. To account for both phenomena, therefore, it seems best to assume that *M* basically derives from *W*, but that its scribe also had access to another manuscript [5].

With regard to *P*, it should be observed first that it offers a number of readings that look like more or less independent changes to the text. Thus it replaces *in caelo* (*expositio* 2) with *de patre deus ante saecula et homo de matre* and *in terra* (*ibidem*) with *in fine saeculorum*, it fills up the apparent lacuna in *expositio* 4, and adds *in trinitate personarum et unitate diuinitatis* in 8 as well as *et capillos* to *ossa* in 10. Next, it agrees in (probable) error with *A*, *M*, *MW*, and *AMW*, but only once with *B* (omission of *et* before *pulchriora* in *expositio* 11).

Common errors in *P* and one or more members of the group *AMW*:

*in uniuerso mundo* (*AP*) for *uniuerso mundo* (*BW*) in *expositio* 8
*tantos* (*AMWP*) for *tanta* (*B*) in 10
*resurrectionem* (*MP*) for *resurrectione* (ABW; *ibidem*)
*annorum* (*MWP*) for *annis* (thus *B*; *A* has *annos*) in 11
omission in *AMW* of *ex hoc saeculo* (thus *B*; *ibidem*)
*et iusti* (*AMWP*) for *iusti uero* (thus *B*; *ibidem*)

Thus, it seems justified to take *P* together with *AMW* as one of the two branches of the textual tradition of the *expositio*, and *B* as the other. For the rest, it is difficult to postulate any direct relationships between *APW*. All three manuscripts agree individually at times with *B*, usually correctly, while the other two side with each another. Thus the (probable) addition of *semper* to *uirgine* in *AMW* (*expositio* 2) is absent from *BP*. Again, *BW* read the more difficult but doubtlessly correct *diabolo* in 9 against *diaboli* in *AMP*. Similarly, *annos* in *A* (11) comes closer to *annis* in *B*, which is probably original, whereas *MPW* read *annorum*. Nothing more can be said, therefore, than that *AMP* all derive from one ancestor.

---

[4] The two exceptions are the cases where *M* shares the correct readings *conditorem* (*expositio* 1) and *patre carnali* (2) with *ABP* and *BP* respectively, whereas *W* has *conditorum* and *patri carnali*. But these could well be independent corrections.

[5] This manuscript was probably not too unlike *W*, as apart from the case of the lacuna in *W*, *M* does not offer any important deviations from the text of that manuscript.

We propose, then, the following stemma:

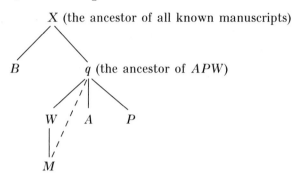

codices:

B     Oxoniensis, Bodleian Library, Iunius 25, ff. 69-71, saec. IX
W     Guelferbytanus, Herzog-Augustbibliothek 91, ff. 114R-115R,
      saec. IX
A     Karlsruhe, Badische Landesbibliothek, Augiensis 18, f. 57V,
      saec. X
M     Monacensis, Bayerische Staatsbibliothek, Latinus 14508, 70R-
      71R, saec. X
P     Parisiensis, Bibliothèque Nationale, Latinus 2123, ff. 21V-
      24V, saec. IX
Q     Parisiensis, Bibliothèque Nationale, Latinus 3848B, ff. 43R-
      46V, saec. X

p     consensus codicum P et Q

editiones:

Bu    BURN, A.E., 'Neue Texte zur Geschichte des apostolischen
      Symbols', in: Zeitschrift für Kirchengeschichte 19, 1898, 180-
      182
Kü    KÜNSTLE, K., Eine Bibliothek der Symbole und Theologischer
      Tractate zur Bekämpfung des Priscillianismus und westgothi-
      schen Arianismus aus dem VI. Jahrhundert. Ein Beitrag zur
      Geschichte der theologischen Litteratur in Spanien, Mainz, 1900
      (EHRHARD, A. - KIRSCH, J.P. [edd.], Forschungen zur
      Christlichen Litteratur und Dogmengeschichte ..., I 4), Mainz,
      1900, 173-175 (= PLS 3, 57-58)

expositio de fide catholica (CPL 505)

1. Auscultate expositionem de fide catholica quam si quis digne
non habuerit regnum dei non possidebit. Credite in deum patrem
omnipotentem inuisibilem uisibilium et inuisibilium conditorem,
hoc est quia omnia creauit simul uerbo potentiae suae. 2. Credite
et in Iesum Christum filium eius unicum dominum nostrum, conceptum de spiritu sancto natum ex Maria uirgine, hoc est sine matre in
caelo, sine patre carnali in terra. 3. Crucifixum sub Pontio Pilato
praeside et sepultum, tertia die resurgentem ex mortuis, hoc est in
uera sua carne quam accepit ex Maria semper uirgine. Per ueram
resurrectionem resurrexit, postquam diabolum ligauit et animas
sanctorum de inferno liberauit. 4. Victor * * * sedet in dexteram

dei patris. Inde credite uenturum iudicare uiuos ac mortuos, hoc est sanctos et peccatores, aut mortuos de sepulcris et uiuos quos dies iudicii inueniet uiuentes. Et tunc, in illo die, timebunt eum qui non amabant, quando ueniet cum cruce sua et parebunt in eo signa clauorum et plaga lanceae. Qui iniuste iudicatus est ab hominibus per iustitiam iudicabit omnes (cf. Ps. 9, 9 et 96, 10. 13 et 98, 9). Qua fronte uidebunt eum in illo die qui uicem passionis suae non habuerunt, aut in martyrio aut in dura paenitentia aut in ieiunio aut in uigilia et in omnibus laboribus.

5. Credite et in spiritum sanctum, deum omnipotentem, unam habentem substantiam cum patre et filio. Sed tamen intimare debemus quod pater deus est et filius deus est et spiritus sanctus deus est et non sunt tres dii sed unus est deus, sicut ignis et flamma et calor una res est. 6. Pater non est genitus, filius a patre genitus est, spiritus sanctus nec genitus nec ingenitus sed ex patre et filio procedit. 7. Pater non est senior de filio secundum diuinitatem nec filius iuuenior de patre, sed una aetas, una substantia, una uirtus, una maiestas, una diuinitas, una potentia est patris et filii et spiritus sancti.

8. Credite ecclesiam catholicam, hoc est uniuersalem uniuerso mundo ubi unus deus colitur, unum baptisma habetur, una fides seruatur (cf. Eph. 4, 5-6). Et qui non est in unitate ecclesiae, aut clericus aut laicus aut masculus aut femina aut ingenuus aut seruus (cf. Gal. 3, 28), partem in regno dei non habebit. 9. Credite remissionem peccatorum, aut per baptismum si obseruatis legem eius, hoc est abrenuntiationem diabolo et angelis eius et pompis saeculi, aut per paenitentiam ueram, id est commissa deflere et paenitenda non committere, aut per martyrium, ubi sanguis pro baptismo computatur. 10. Credite communem omnium corporum resurrectionem post mortem. Sine dubio enim erit sicut scriptum est: *Et resurgent qui in monumentis sunt* (Is. 26, 19 LXX). Quanta membra et ossa habuit homo, tanta habebit in resurrectione. 11. Non in altera carne resurgent sed in ea ipsa quam habuerunt (cf. Iob 19, 25-27) - sed tamen resurgent homines iuuenes quasi triginta annis licet senes aut infantes ex hoc saeculo transierint (cf. Is. 65, 20), et pulchriora corpora et tenuiora habebunt -, ut peccatores aeternas sustineant poenas, iusti uero et sancti praemia caelestia in eisdem corporibus possideant, praestante Christo qui cum aeterno patre et spiritu sancto uiuit et regnat in saecula saeculorum. Amen.

apparatus criticus apud  *expositionem de fide catholica*  CPL 505

1. possidebit *AMWp*] possidebunt *B*          uisibilium et inuisibilium *coni. Bu*] uisibilium et inuisilium *B*, uisibilem et inuisibilium *M*, uisibilium rerum et inuisibilium *W* *(rerum punctis deletum)*, uisibilium et inuisibilium rerum *A*, uisibilium et inuisibilium omnium rerum *p*          conditorem *ABMp*] conditorum *W*          quia omnia *BWp*] quia *A*, qui omnia *M*

2. et in *BMWp*] et *A*          dominum nostrum *BMWp*] dominum *A*          uirgine *Bp*] semper uirgine *AMW*          in caelo *ABMW*] de patre deus ante saecula et homo de matre *p*          patre carnali *BMp*] patre carnale *A*, patri carnali *W* in terra *ABMW*] in fine saeculorum *p*

3. hoc est *AMp*] hoc *BW*          sua carne *ABWp*] carne sua *M*          resurrexit *BMWp*] resurgentem resurrexit *A*

4. uictor ... sedet] *lacunam indicauit Bu;* uictor redit *A*, uictor sedit *BMW*, uictor ascendit ad caelos sedit *p; uide supra, p. 310*          in dexteram dei patris *Bp*] ad dexteram dei patris *A*, in dextera dei patris *W*, in dexteram patris *M*          ac *ABWp*] et *M*          sanctos et *AMWp*] sanctos *B*          aut *ABMW*] ac *P*, hac *Q* et tunc ... laboribus *ABMW*] *om. p*          illo *ABW*] illa *M*          quando ueniet cum cruce sua *BMW*] *om. A*, q.u.c. carne s. *Bu*          qui *ABMW*] et qui *coni. Bu* hominibus *ABW*] omnibus *M*          iudicabit *ABW*] iudicabitur *M*          illo *ABW*] illa *M*          paenitentia *ABW*] paenitentiae *M*          uigilia *AB*] uigiliis *M*, uigiliis *e* uigilia *W*          et *ABW*] aut *M*

5. et in *BMWp*] et *A*          et non *BMWp*] quasi non *A*          res *AMWp*] *punctis deletum in W ut uidetur*

6. pater ... procedit *ABMW*] *om. p*          spiritus sanctus *AMW*] spiritus *B* ex *B*] a *AMW*

7. non est *ABMW*] non *p*          senior ... nec *ABMp*] *om. W*          iuuenior *BW*] iunior est *AM*, iuuenior est *p*          de *ABMp*] *rasura W*          est patris *ABMW*] patris *p*

8. uniuersalem *ABWp*] uniuersalis *M*          uniuerso mundo *BW*] in uniuerso mundo *Ap*, uniuerso *M*          deus colitur *ABMW*] deus in trinitate personarum et unitate diuinitatis colitur *p*          masculus *ABMWP*] masculos *Q*

9. peccatorum *BMWp*] peccatorem *A*          obseruatis *p*] obseruabitis *A*, obseruas *B*, obseruauerit *MW*          abrenuntiationem *AMW*] abrenuntiatione *Bp*          diabolo *BW*] diaboli *AMp*          angelis eius *ABWp*] angelis *M*          hoc est *ABMW*] hoc *p*          pro baptismo *ABWp*] per baptismum *M*          computatur *AMWp*] *om. B*

10. communem *ABp*] commu^nio^nem *W*, communionem sanctorum *M*          ossa *ABMW*] ossa et capillos *p*          tanta *B*] tantos *AMWp*          resurrectione *ABW*] resurrectionem *Mp*

11. resurget *BMp*] resurge^n^t *W*, resurgit ?*A*          homines iuuenes *ABWp*] homines *M*          annis *B*] annos *A*, annorum *MWp*          ex hoc saeculo transierint *B*] transierunt *AW*, transierint *Mp*          et pulchriora *AMW*] pulchriora *Bp* tenuiora *p*] teneriora *AW*, tenuora *B*, tenio^ri^ra *M*          habebunt *BMWp*] *om. A*          iusti uero *B*] et iusti *AMWp*          praemia *ABWp*] post praemia *M* aeterno patre *ABWp*] patre *M*

The textual transmission of the pseudo-Fulgentian *sermo de symbolo* CPL 846

This pseudo-Fulgentian sermon was first mentioned by Morin, who found it in a homiliary that is preserved in the Österreichische Nationalbibliothek (*V*). This manuscript was probably produced in Northern Italy towards the end of the eighth or at the beginning of the ninth century [1]. The manuscript offers a basically sound text, though it tends to confuse -*um* and -*o*, -*am* and -*a*, -*em* and -*e*, -*et* and -*it*, -*es* and -*is*, and also *u* and *b*. Most of these cases are indicated by Morin in his apparatus. Morin also makes a number of other corrections that are fairly obvious. Thus, in *sermo de symbolo* 5 (*Omnibus enim baptizatis dicit apostolus ... Induetis ergo Christum bonum et inuictum, quo nullus est melior ... ut ipsum prae omnibus diligere debeatis*) he writes *omnibus, quo,* and *prae* instead of the manuscript readings *ominibus, quod,* and *pro*. In one case (*sermo de symbolo* 22), Morin makes a mistake by omitting the two words *unum est* in the phrase *Illud quod trinitas est unum est, aeternum est, uerbum est, caro est* at the end of the discussion of the relationship of the three persons of the Trinity. In *sermo de symbolo* 21, where the manuscript reading is obviously corrupt, Morin's reconstruction can be questioned - instead of *et in spiritum sanctum*, it seems better to read *in spiritum sanctum* for the manuscript's *et spiritu sanctum* [2]. For the rest, we have ventured one or two more corrections with respect to spelling and syntax - *renuntiate* for *renuntietis, et* for *est*, and *iudiciariam* for *iudicariam*.

Although no other manuscript containing the complete pseudo-Fulgentian *sermo de symbolo* has come to light so far, it should be noted that parts of it are also preserved in another Vienna manuscript, the so-called Mondsee homiliary (*M*). Parts of our pseudo-Fulgentian text have been incorporated in number 127 of this sermon collection [3]. It is difficult to assess whether this conflated sermon can be taken as a witness for the text of its pseudo-Fulgentian original or not. On the one hand, the Mondsee homiliary can be

---

[1] See Lambot 1958, 186-189 and Grégoire 1980, 281. Morin states that *V* was written in Salzburg between 790 and 810, but this seems to be based on outdated information (see Morin 1923, 233+n1 and Lambot 1958, 187+n1).

[2] See chapter 4.6, pp. 321-322, for more details.

[3] See Lemarié 1993, 569; the text of this sermon is presented on pp. 580-582.

dated between 811 and 819 [4], so that it could be contemporary with
or even earlier than V. Therefore it may well preserve correct readings that can no longer be found in V. It is indeed true that the
text of M seems at least as good as that of V in a number of places.
Examples of such possibly more original readings in M are *renuntiastis* (*renuntiatis* V) in *sermo de symbolo* 4, *diabolica* (*diaboli* V; *ibidem*), *puram* ... *caritatem* (*caritate* V; *ibidem*), and *bonae
conuersationis* (*bonam* V; 33). On the other hand, the compiler of
sermon 127 in the Mondsee homiliary handles his material quite
freely. The parts from the pseudo-Fulgentian *sermo de symbolo* are
offered in a different order from the original one, and the author
sometimes seems to rewrite portions of the text. Thus, lines 25-34
of Lemarié's edition of the conflated sermon contain four different
passages from the original text (§ 22, ll. 1-3, § 23, ll. 1-2, § 23, ll. 4-
6, and § 33, ll. 2-5 in our edition), all in a more or less adapted
form. Actually, nothing prohibits the assumption that the writer of
M had V before him when composing his compilation, in which case
M would entirely lose its critical value. Since this question cannot
be resolved on the basis of this case alone, however, it will be best
to follow V as a matter of principle and to present the deviant
readings of M in the critical apparatus [5].

---

[4] See Barré 1961, 78-79.

[5] A number of other manuscripts offer a sermon collection that is based upon
that of the Mondsee homiliary. In theory, parts of the pseudo-Fulgentian *sermo
de symbolo* could be found in these manuscripts as well. Since, however, the compiler of this new collection has used his sources very freely, we have abstained
from searching this material. See Barré 1961, 85-89.

codices:

V    Vindobonensis, Österreichische Nationalbibliothek, Latinus
     1616, ff. 70R-78V, saec. VIII exeuntis aut IX ineuntis
M    Vindobonensis, Österreichische Nationalbibliothek, Latinus
     1014, ff. 75V-76V, saec. IX ineuntis

editio

Mo   MORIN, G., 'Deux sermons africains du Ve/VIe siècle avec
     un texte inédit du symbole', in: *Revue Bénédictine* 33, 1923,
     236-242 (= PLS 3, 1370-1376)

sermo de symbolo CPL 846

1. Audite, dilectissimi, qui desideratis carere iugum seruitutis (cf.
II Par. 10, 4. Gal. 5, 1. I Tim. 6, 1), ut gaudeatis donum saluberri-
mae libertatis (cf. Ioh. 8, 36. Rom. 6, 18-22 et 8, 21. I Petr. 2, 16).
Praebete aures (cf. Is. 55, 3) non solum corporis sed etiam cordis (cf.
Deut. 10, 6. Ier. 4, 4 et 6, 10. Act. 7, 51), audite intenti sacramentorum caelestium rationem, percipite nostrae redemptionis integram
ueritatem. Quid enim confugimus ad gratiam Christi, nisi ut possimus a diaboli nequitia liberari? Si autem a serpentino ueneno liberari cupimus, uiriliter concertemus ut domus cordis nostri domino
Christo possessori legitimo praeparemus (cf. Luc. 11, 21-26. Eph. 3,
17). Ille nos potest legitime possidere, qui hominem gratuita bonitate fecit, non ille qui hominem callida malignitate decepit. Ille nos
potest legitime possidere, qui *hominem ad imaginem suam creauit*
(Gen. 1, 27), non ille qui ipsam imaginem in homine deprauauit. Ille
ergo nos possideat qui ad uitam condidit hominem, non ille qui eum
praecipitauit in mortem. 2. Quapropter, dilectissimi fratres, repellite
a uobis principem mortis et recipite in uos auctorem humanae salutis, recedite a diabolo et adhaerete Christo, diligite redemptorem
uestrum et facite uoluntatem eius et renuntiate diabolo, pompis et
angelis eius. Sic renuntiate uerbis ut renuntietis et factis, sic renuntiate sermonibus ut renuntietis et moribus. Ex eo quod in ecclesia
bene uiuitis, apparet uerum esse quod dicitis. 3. Tunc enim uobis
proderit quod nunc diabolo renuntiatis, si aduersus temptamenta
eius sollicita cordis intentione certetis. Temptamenta uero eius ipsa
sunt arma eius, quae duplicia contra nos consueuit arripere. Quae
sunt autem arma diaboli? Infidelitas et mundana cupiditas, ista
sunt arma quibus contra nos diabolus pugnat, per haec arma nobis

insidiari non cessat, hoc indesinenter agens, hoc multiplici liuoris immanitate contendens, ut quos potuerit ab ecclesia per infidelitatem separet, alios uero temporalium rerum immoderata dilectione captiuet. 4. Vos itaque, carissimi, contra haec arma diaboli *accipite arma dei* (Eph. 6, 13 et cf. 11). Quae sunt arma dei? Fides, qua in deum recte creditur, et caritas, qua deus proximusque diligitur. Infidelitas et cupiditas duo sunt mala, fides et caritas duo sunt bona. Illa ergo duo mala fugite, ista duo bona fortiter custodite. Contra infidelitatem tenete catholicae fidei ueritatem, et contra mundanam cupiditatem tenete dei et proximi caritatem. 5. Si enim armis fidei et caritatis induti diabolo repugnaritis, in omni certamine uictores eritis, nec erit unde diabolum timeatis quia ipsum Christum in sacramento baptismatis induetis. Omnibus enim baptizatis dicit apostolus Paulus: *Quotquot in Christo baptizati estis, Christum induistis* (Gal. 3, 27). Induetis ergo Christum bonum et inuictum, quo nullus est melior, nullus est fortior, qui sic est bonus, ut ipsum prae omnibus diligere debeatis, et sic est inuictus, ut in illo certissime confidatis. *Subditi ergo estote* Christo et auxiliabitur uobis, *resistite autem diabolo et fugiet a uobis* (Iac. 4, 7).

6. Renuntiantes autem diabolo, fideliter atque indubitanter credite in deum patrem omnipotentem. Deus enim pater sicut uerus deus, sic uerus credendus est pater. Est enim in illo uera diuinitas et diuina paternitas. Vera diuinitate mundum fecit, diuina paternitate de sua natura uerum filium genuit. Nam si uerus deus non esset uisibilia et inuisibilia non fecisset (cf. Col. 1, 16), si uerus pater non esset deum filium de se non genuisset, sed quoniam sicut uerus deus sic uerus est pater, digne creditur deum filium genuisse de natura sua, mundum uero de nihilo fecisse (cf. II Mach. 7, 28) omnipotentia sua. 7. Quoniam ergo uera est et diuinitas et paternitas dei patris, sicut in mundo uera apparet operatio creatoris, sic in filio uera naturaliter manet substantia genitoris. Vniuersam itaque creaturam uisibilem atque inuisibilem deus pater per uerbum suum fecit ex nihilo (cf. II Mach. 7, 28. Ioh. 1, 3. Col. 1, 16), ipsum uero uerbum genuit de semetipso. Deus ergo uerus aequalem sibi genuit deum uerum, deus aeternus aequalem sibi deum genuit coaeternum, immensus aequalem sibi deum genuit immensum, altissimus aequalem sibi deum genuit altissimum, inuisibilis aequaliter inuisibilem, incommutabilis aequaliter incommutabilem, immortalis aequaliter immortalem, omnipotens aequaliter omnipotentem, rerum omnium

creator aequaliter rerum omnium creatorem. 8. Ideo credentes in deum patrem omnipotentem uniuersorum creatorem, credite in filium eius Iesum Christum dominum nostrum. Ipse est enim unigenitus deus, non diuina potentia creatus, sed solus de patris substantia natus. Huic genito filio naturaliter una est cum patre diuinitas, una aeternitas, una bonitas, una immensitas, una potestas, unaque maiestas. Per ipsum nos deus pater mirabiliter creauit, per ipsum nos de morte misericorditer liberauit.

9. Iste unigenitus dei filius uerus naturaliter deus et cum patre unus deus, ut quos fecerat reficeret et quos creauerat recrearet, natus est de spiritu sancto ex uirgine Maria. Qui enim de patre natus est deus de deo ipse de matre natus est deus homo, et qui est aeternus sine initio deus de patre suo ipse in tempore *tamquam sponsus procedens de thalamo suo* (Ps. 19, 6). Vnus est ergo Christus dei filius de patre ante omnnia natus et de matre inter opera sua creatus. 10. Ipse natus de patre creauit nos, ipse creatus de matre saluauit nos. Natus est enim de patre creator et creatus est de matre saluator. Ipse est *qui cum in forma dei esset formam serui accepit* (Phil. 2, 6-7) et nos quos peccati seruos inuenit liberos fecit (cf. Ioh. 8, 34-36. Rom. 6, 20). Vt captiuos redimeret, suum sanguinem dedit. Ideo autem sanguinem suum fecit pretium captiuorum, ut regnum suum faceret praemium redemptorum.

11. Redemptor ergo noster Christus dei filius crucifixus est sub Pontio Pilato et sepultus. Ecce quantum se pro nobis humiliauit altissimus (cf. Phil. 2, 8), ecce quanta pro nobis pertulit unigenitus deus, cui parum fuit ut pro nobis nasceretur ex uirgine, nisi etiam pro nobis penderet in cruce. 12. Christus ergo dei filius crucifixus est et sepultus. Quis pro quibus? Quis a quibus? Audite pro quibus. Apostolus dicit: *Etenim Christus pro nobis mortuus est* (Rom. 5, 8). Audite a quibus. Ab iniquis iudicatus est iustus, et iudicio iniquo non iusto (cf. I Petr. 2, 23 Lat.). Ille immaculatus (cf. Is. 53, 8-9 LXX. I Petr. 2, 23), *in iniquis est deputatus* (Is. 53, 12. Marc. 15, 28. Luc. 22, 37), ille *qui peccatum non fecit* (Is. 53, 9. I Petr. 2, 22), a peccatoribus palmas in facie accepit (cf. Matth. 26, 67), ille per quem factus est caelum et terra (cf. Ioh. 1, 3. Gen. 1, 1), *dorsum suum posuit ad flagella* (Is. 50, 6 LXX), ille dominus qui est aeterna suauitas angelorum (cf. Prou. 8, 30-31), *faciem suam non auertit a confusione sputorum* (Is. 50, 6 LXX). A malis condemnatus est bonus, a mortuis occisus est uiuus, ab hominibus crucifixus est deus. 13. Reuera enim, fratres, unigeni-

tus deus crucifixus et sepultus est pro nobis, secundum ueritatem carnis quam sumpsit ex nobis. Verum tamen ille omnipotens creator et bonus redemptor patienter sustinuit hominum malignitatem, quibus diuinam uolebat impendere bonitatem. Leuatur in ligno (cf. Deut. 21, 23. Act. 5, 30 et 10, 39), deponitur in sepulcro (cf. Matth. 27, 60. Marc. 15, 46. Luc. 23, 53), et cum ipse debitor non esset sed uniuersos debitores generaliter inuenisset, non solum debita nobis uniuersa donauit uerum etiam omnia quae nos debebamus reddidit, ut quos liberabat de tanto cumulo debiti liberaret de dominatione peccati. 14. Christus ergo dei filius crucifixus et sepultus descendit etiam in infernum, ut nos leuaret in caelum. Ille misericors et beatus misericorditer uisitauit loca miseriae nostrae, ut nos perduceret ad locum beatitudinis suae.

15. Deinde tertio die a mortuis resurrexit. Audisti, homo, quid dei filius pertulit pro te, audi quid tibi promittat in se. Pertulit enim pro te mortem tuam, promittit tibi uitam suam. Christus mortuus timorem mortis abstulit, Christus resurgens ueram spem futurae resurrectionis ostendit. Christus mortuus est secundum carnem ut mortem carnis non timeremus et resurrexit Christus secundum carnem ut resurrectionem carnis certissime speraremus. 16. Non solum autem resurrexit, sed etiam in caelum ascendit, et in dextera patris sedet. Quo ergo praecessit caput, illuc sequantur et membra, quo ascendit redemptor, illuc ascendat redempta familia, et si non potest illuc ascendere mortalis hominis corpus, ascendat illuc Christiani cordis affectus. 17. Christus nos uocat ad caelestem domum, quare nos amamus terrenae peregrinationis exilium (cf. II Cor. 5, 1-8. Hebr. 11, 13)? Christus nobis uult aeternas diuitias dare, quare nos uolumus in aeterna indigentia remanere? Christus nobis promittit quod semper habeamus, quare nos hoc diligimus, quod uelimus nolimus celerius relinquimus? Quare non oboedit homo deo iubenti? Quare non adhaeret promittenti? An forte hoc putatur, quia Christus quos redemit non iudicabit? Audite quid in symbolo sequitur.

18. Christus qui ascendit in caelum, inde uenturus est iudicare uiuos et mortuos. Veniet iudicaturus qui uenerat iudicandus. Qui uenerat cum mansuetudine ueniet cum uigore, qui uenerat occultus ueniet manifestus, qui uenerat in carne humilis ueniet in maiestate terribilis, qui demonstrauit egregiam humilitatem exercebit iudiciariam potestatem (cf. Matth. 25, 31). 19. Illud iudicium multum diligant boni, multum timeant mali. Diligant boni quia accepturi sunt

regnum, timeant mali ne in ignem mittantur aeternum. Diligant boni quia ponentur ad dexteram, timeant mali ne deueniant ad sinistram (cf. Matth. 25, 34. 41). Tunc autem salubris erit et bonis ista dilectio et malis illa formido, si boni ista dilectione in bono proficiant et mali illa formidine a malo discedant. 20. Quapropter, dilectissimi, priusquam illud iudicium ueniat, unusquisque nostrum componat causam suam et corrigat uitam suam. Iudex enim uenturus est cuius scientiam nemo fallit, cuius oculos nemo fugit, cuius uirtuti nemo resistit, cuius potestati nemo succedit, cuius aequitatem nemo corrumpit. Hoc ergo agamus, ut iudex ille, cum uenerit, non in nobis inueniat quod damnet, sed potius inueniat quod coronet (cf. Matth. 24, 45-51. Luc. 12, 42-46).

21. Credentes itaque in deum patrem omnipotentem, et in filium eius dominum nostrum Iesum Christum, credite in spiritum sanctum. Spiritus enim sanctus deus uerus est sicut pater et filius, quia ipse est patris et filii unus spiritus et cum patre et filio naturaliter unus deus, una bonitas patris et filii, una caritas genitoris et geniti. 22. Pater ergo et filius et spiritus sanctus, id est sancta trinitas, naturaliter unus uerus et bonus est deus unius naturae uniusque substantiae. In ista trinitatis diuina substantia nihil est creatum quia nihil est inchoatum, nec aliquid ibi superius aut inferius agnoscitur quia nihil anterius aut posterius inuenitur. Illud quod trinitas est unum est, aeternum est, uerbum est, caro est.

23. Haec est una fides quia haec est uera fides (cf. Rom. 3, 26. Gal. 2, 16), et ideo haec est catholica fides, unius substantiae sanctam credere trinitatem et in dei filio carnis atque animae nostrae naturalem cognoscere ueritatem. Ista fide iustificamur, hac fide mundamur, ista fide saluamur, in hac fide nobis tribuitur remissio peccatorum. 24. Ideo enim filius dei filius hominis factus est, ut pro nobis impiis iustum sanguinem funderet et remissis peccatis deo patri nos filios adoptaret. Et hoc est primum beneficium ex aqua et spiritu renatorum (Ioh. 3, 5), quia in baptismo fit omnium remissio peccatorum (cf. Act. 2, 38).

25. Credite etiam carnis resurrectionem, quam in se ipso nobis demonstrauit Christus ut de illa nos nullatenus desperemus. Haec resurrectio carnis in Christo facta est, in nobis futura est, data est capiti, danda est corpori. Sit ergo certissima spes omnibus nobis quia uera resurrectio carnis, quae praecessit in Christo, sequitur in nobis. 26. Caro itaque omnium hominum mortuorum siue fidelium

siue infidelium resurget in fine, sed caro fidelium resurget ad gloriam, caro infidelium resurget ad poenam. Animae fideles cum suis semper corporibus laetabuntur, animae quoque infideles cum suis semper corporibus torquebuntur, ac si quidquid ibi animae cum carne sua recipient, non amittent quando nec bonis poterit auferri gaudium nec a malis umquam poterit remoueri supplicium. 27. Sicut autem Christus ipsam carnem recepit resurgens qua se exuit moriens, sic nos istam carnem in qua nunc sumus, in qua nunc uiuimus, ipsam resurrectionis tempore resumemus. Ita fiet ut caro ista nostra quae nunc moritur ipsa in die nouissimo resuscitetur (cf. Iob 19, 25-27).

28. *Quia uero Christus surgens a mortuis iam non moritur et mors ei ultra non dominabitur* (Rom. 6, 9), et quod in se ostendit hoc suis fidelibus repromisit, credite etiam uitam aeternam, quia nos quoque resurgemus semper uiuituri, numquam corde peccaturi, numquam corpore morituri. Tunc nobis uera beatitudo dabitur, quando nobis aeterna dei uisio tribuetur, tunc anima nostra nulla poterit maculari delectatione peccati, tunc corpus nostrum nec corrumpi poterit omnino nec mori. De corpore quippe bonorum fidelium dicit apostolus, quia *seminabitur in corruptione, surget in incorruptione* (I Cor. 15, 42). De ipsis item dicit: *Oportet enim corruptibile hoc induere incorruptionem, et mortale hoc induere immortalitatem* (I Cor. 15, 53).

29. Accipiemus itaque uitam aeternam per sanctam ecclesiam. Ipsa est ciuitas sancta, Hierusalem superna, Hierusalem aeterna. In ista sola ecclesia est uita aeterna quia rex eius est uita aeterna. Huius ecclesiae pars exultat et regnat in caelis, pars autem peregrinatur adhuc et laborat in terris. Ipsa est una sancta ecclesia in qua nunc iustificamur, in qua nunc ambulamus per fidem, et in qua tunc perueniemus ad speciem. 30. Ipsa est una sponsa Christi, columba Christi, uirgo Christi, mater membrorum Christi. Ipsa nos concepit, ipsa nos peperit, ipsa nos nutrit. Ipsa uos modo conceptos parturiet et pro uobis sollicite gemit, ipsa etiam uos pariet et integritatis gratiam non amittet. Est enim uera uirgo et uera mater. Est uera uirgo quia numquam corrumpitur, est uera mater quia mirabiliter fecundatur. 31. Istam ueram matrem sicut boni filii unanimiter diligamus, uberibus eius delectabiliter inhaereamus. Vnde nascimur inde pascamur. Huius ergo matris gemitus nemo despiciat, monita eius nemo contemnat, de sinu eius nemo discedat. Ipse enim ad dei

patris perueniet hereditatem, qui ecclesiae matris in fide et dilectione seruauerit unitatem.

32. In ecclesia ergo catholica permanete, diuinis eloquiis humiliter
oboedite, praecepta dei sollicite custodite (cf. I Cor. 7, 19. I Ioh. 2,
3-4 et alibi). Qui enim praecepta dei contemnunt semper ardebunt,
qui uero eius mandata custodiunt sine fine gaudebunt, et sicut con-
temptoribus erit aeterna mors et aeterna miseria, sic oboedientibus
aeterna uita dabitur et aeterna laetitia. 33. Hoc ergo uobis expedit,
ut ea quae symboli tenor continet sine dubitatione credatis et in
uera fide manentes mala opera fugiatis, bonam uitam in omnibus
habeatis, ut non ad aeterna supplicia sed ad aeterna paradisi praemia perueniatis.

apparatus criticus apud sermonem de symbolo CPL 846

1. rationem *coni. Mo*] ratione *V*      liberari *(bis) Mo*] liberari *e* liberare *V (uel
uice uersa?)*      domus *Mo*] domos *e* domus *V*      bonitate *coni. Mo*] bonitatem *V*      homine *coni. Mo*] hominem *V*

2. principem *coni. Mo*] principe *V*      auctorem *coni. Mo*] auctore *V*      uoluntatem *coni. Mo*] uoluntate *V*      renuntiate *(2° ) conieci*] renuntietis *V Mo*
uerbis *Mo*] uerbi[s] *V*

3. nunc *V*] *om. M*      renuntiatis *V*] renuntiastis *M*      certetis *V*] certatis
*M*      diaboli *V*] diabolica *M*      infidelitatem *Mo*] infidelitate *V*

4. qua *1° coni. Mo*] quam *V*      mundanam *coni. Mo*] mundana *V*      dei *V*]
puram dei *M*      caritatem *coni. Mo*] caritate *V*

5. repugnaritis *V*] repugnaueritis *M*      sacramento *coni. Mo*] sacramentum
*V*      induetis *V*] induistis *M*      omnibus *coni. Mo*] ominibus *V*      quo *coni.
Mo*] quod *V*      prae *coni. Mo*] pro *V*

6. et diuina *conieci*] est diuina *V Mo*      mundum *coni. Mo*] mundo *V*      uisibilia et *conieci*] uisibilia *V Mo*      mundum *coni. Mo*] mundo *V*

7. apparet *conieci*] paret *V Mo*      semetipso *coni. Mo*] semetipsum *V*      inuisibilis *Mo*] inuisibiles *V*

8. patris *coni. Mo*] patri *V*      ipsum *coni. Mo*] ipso *V*      ipsum *Mo*] ipso *V*

9. recrearet *Mo*] recreeret *e* recrearit *V*      patre *(1° ) coni. Mo*] patrem *V*

10. saluauit *coni. Mo*] saluabit *V*      est *coni. Mo*] es *V*      forma *coni. Mo*]
formam *V*      suum *(1° ) coni. Mo*] suo *V*

12. iniquis *coni. Mo*] iniquus *ex* iniquos *V*      deputatus *coni. Mo*] deputatus *e*
depotatus *V*      peccatum *coni. Mo*] peccato *V*      a confusione *coni. Mo*] ad
confusionem *V*

13. ueritatem *coni. Mo*] ueritate *V*      diuinam *coni. Mo*] diuina *V*      debita
*coni. Mo*] debitam *V*      cumulo debiti *coni. Mo*] cum molo debet *V*

14. caelum *coni. Mo*] caelo *V*

15. quid *2° coni. Mo*] quia *V*      promittit *coni. Mo*] promittet *V*      timorem
*coni. Mo*] timore *V*      resurrectionem *coni. Mo*] resurrectionis *V*

17. quare *(4° ) Mo*] qua^{re} V      putatur *coni. Mo*] potatur V      iudicabit *coni. Mo*] iudicauit V

18. caelum *coni. Mo*] caelo V      mansuetudine *coni. Mo*] mansuetudinem V      exercebit *coni. Mo*] exercet V      iudiciariam *conieci*] iudicariam V *Mo*

19. multum *(2° ) coni. Mo*] multi V      quia *coni. Mo*] qui V      ignem mittantur *coni. Mo*] igne mittatur V      discedant *Mo*] disceda^{n}t V

20. uirtuti *coni. Mo*] uirtute V      aequitatem *coni. Mo*] aequitate V

21. deum *coni. Mo*] deo V      in spiritum *conieci*] et spiritu V et in spiritum *coni. Mo*      patris *(2° ) coni. Mo*] patri V

22. bonus *coni. Mo*] bonos V      ibi *coni. Mo*] sibi V      unum est V] *om. Mo*      caro est V] *suspicitur Mo*      ideo V] *om.* M      ista V] ista ergo M      iustificamur V] iustificamur ab omni iniquitate M      hac *coni. Mo*] haec V ista M      mundamur V] mundamur ab omni peccato M      saluamur V] saluamur ab omni malo M      nobis tribuitur *coni. Mo*] nobis tribuit V nobis credamus tribui M      peccatorum V] omnium peccatorum M

24. adoptaret *coni. Mo*] adoptare V baptismo *coni. Mo*] baptismum V

25. Christo *coni. Mo*] Christi V      sequitur V] *fortasse* sequetur *legendum esse putat Mo*

26. resurget *(ter) coni. Mo*] resurgit V      fine *Mo*] fine *e* fide V      fideles *coni. Mo*] fidelis V      infideles *coni. Mo*] infidelis V      si V] sic *coni. Mo*      auferri *coni. Mo*] auferre V      remoueri *coni. Mo*] remori V

27. ipsam carnem *coni. Mo*] ipsa carne V      qua *coni. Mo*] quam V      istam *coni. Mo*] ista *ex* ita V      resumemus *coni. Mo*] resumimus V      quae *coni. Mo*] qui V

28. surgens V] resurgens *Mo*      resurgemus *coni. Mo*] resurgimus V      peccaturi *coni. Mo*] peccatori V      tribuetur *coni. Mo*] tribuitur V      incorruptione *coni. Mo*] corruptione V

29. aeterna *(1° ) coni. Mo*] aeternam V      perueniemus *coni. Mo*] peruenimus V      conceptos *coni. Mo*] conceptus V

30. amittet *coni. Mo*] amittit V

31. monita *coni. Mo*] monitis V      qui ecclesiae *coni. Mo*] quia ecclesia V

33. et in uera fide V] in hac ergo M      fugiatis V] fugite M      bonam V] bonae conuersationis M      habeatis V] habetote M      paradisi V] *om.* M      perueniatis V] perueniatur M

Two Pseudo-Chrysostomic *expositiones symboli* CPL 915

The following edition was prepared by M. Ntshiniti, assistant to F. Leroy. Since Ntshiniti's decease, Leroy has undertaken to finish the edition of the entire sermon collection for *Corpus Christianorum*. It is by kind permission of both Leroy and *Corpus Christianorum* that we can present a reliable text of these two relatively unknown sermons on the Creed.

The *sigla* in the critical apparatus refer to the following manuscripts and editions:

*G*   Gent, Bibl. Univ. 507 (cat. 537), saec. XI
*O*   Paris, BN Lat. 13.347, saec. IX
*B*   Breslau, B. Univ. ms. lat. I F.23, saec. XI
*A*   Angers, BM 280 (271), saec. XI
*N*   Brussels, 5463-67, saec. XI
*P*   Paris, BN Lat. 9521, saec. XI
*H*   Zagreb, Bibl. Univ. MR (Cathedral), ms. 125, saec. XII

*r*   Basel, Cratander 1525
*e*   Basel, Froben 1530
*h*   Paris, Chevallon 1536 (= Hamman, PLS 4)

*homilia 26*

*expositio symboli*

1. Vniversalis ecclesia congaudet in una regula caritatis Christi et in fide nominis Christi exsultat, maxime quando credentium lucris locupletatur. Crescente ergo populo peculiari, *dilatatur cor credentium ad iustitiam*, ore autem celebrant *confessionem in salutem*.

*Vos ergo, genus electum*, grex nouellus dei, qui competitis a rege regum et domino dominorum munus gratiae, qui baptismum salutarem speratis uobis affuturum, audite professionis uestrae uerba regularis. Ista doctrina confirmat credentes, adiuuat proficiscentes, consolatur uiatores, confortat perseuerantes, coronat peruenientes. Ergo audite hanc ut dixi regulam uestrae confessionis.

2. Credo in deum patrem omnipotentem. Videte qui, cui loquimini et quid loquimini. Dixistis: Credo. Quam breue est, quam modicum est. Si ad latitudinem litterarum redigatis, quinque litterae sunt, si ad syllabarum numerum, duae sunt syllabae. Haec credulitas, si conquadret moribus et uocibus, fructum inuenit salutis. Credulitas haec in toto mundo sparsa est: credit Christianus in ecclesia dimitti sibi peccata, credit moribus compositis deo placere, credit indulgentiam mereri, credit uitae aeternae promissionem, credit poenam promissam peccatoribus.

3. Ergo creditis deo omnipotenti, quia posse ipsius non potet inuenire non posse. Tamen, aliqua non potest, ut puta falli, fallere, mentiri, ignorare, initium et finem habere, non praeuidere, praeterita obliuisci, praesentia non attendere, futura nescire; ad ultimum, negare seipsum non potest. Ecce quanta non potest. Tamen, *ideo est omnipotens* quia superius comprehensa *non potest*. Ergo: Credo in deum patrem omnipotentem.

4. Ecce patrem deum uocatis. Ad honorem patris uiuite, mores patris custodite, eius uoluntatem implete si uultis hereditatem eius accipere. Quis est filius contemnens patrem qui mereatur eius accipere hereditatem? Ergo, si dcsideratis ea quae promittit mereri, uiuite pro uoto eius, in praeceptis eius permanete, quae iubet fieri facite et quae prohibet ne fiant, facere nolite. Ecce isti qui hoc faciunt libere dicunt: Credo in deum patrem omnipotentem.

5. Sequitur dicens: Et in unicum filium eius, dominum nostrum Iesum Christum. Iste quare unicus? Quia alter filius non est. Quare primogenitus? Quia in saeculo nemo sic natus est. Istum unicum dei

filium, de substantia patris natum et genitum confitemur et initium
de patre habere dicimus. Patri coaequalis in deitate, deus et deus,
sed tamen non duo dii, sed unus deus. In potestate, una potestas; in
esse, una essentia, in substantia, una uirtus, una maiestas. Hoc credite ne haereticorum colloquia mala corrumpant mores uestros
bonos. Dicunt enim patrem maiorem, filium minorem. Hoc anathe-
matizat ecclesia catholica. Aeque dicunt spiritum sanctum creaturam. Etiam haec abominatur talem doctrinam. Ergo iste natus est
de spiritu sancto et uirgine Maria.

6. Iste spiritus uenit ad Mariam, ingressus in eam *uerbum caro
factum est.* Creuit aluus uirginis, uirgo erat et praegnans; creuit et
uirginitatem non amisit. Iste ergo natus creuit, ad passionem peruenit, crucifixus est sub Pontio Pilato.

Eia, fratres, in hac praedicatione nullus piger inueniatur. Quis ei
rependat uicissitudinem? Crucifixus est innocens pro nocentibus,
non reus pro reis; non indigens indiguit lucra acquirere patri. Iste
Pontius Pilatus praesidatum gerebat, iussit eum crucifigi. Sepultus
est postquam mortuus, ut nobis uitam praestaret moriendo mortem
occidit; leo de tribu Iuda rugientem leonem superauit; pro peccatoribus pati uoluit ne in peccatis mundus totus moreretur. Alapis cae-
sus, flagellatus, aceto et felle potatus, in his omnibus ostendens
patientiam, non est iratus sed e contrario mansuetudinem demonstrans, clamauit patri dicens: *Ignosce illis quia nesciunt quid faciunt.*
Videtis quale exemplum nobis patientiae dimisit. Et uos, fratres
carissimi, qui suspiratis ad gratiam peruenire, qui clamatis: *Anima
nostra uelut terra sine aqua tibi,* cito exaudi nos, - imitamini caput
nostrum Christum, qui *cum malediceretur, non remaledicebat, cum
iniuriam pateretur non comminabatur; tradebat autem se iudicanti
iniuste.*

7. Ergo iste crucifixus, sepultus, tertia die a mortuis resurrexit.
Ecce quanta potentia. Et in ista potentia eius, mentiti sunt ei inimici eius ut dicerent: *Nobis dormientibus uenerunt discipuli et furati
sunt eum.* Impletum est quod dictum est: *In multitudine potentiae
tuae, mentientur tibi inimici tui.*

8. Sedet ad dexteram patris. Cum auditis: Sedet, nolite credere
sessionem humanam; genus est locutionis; sedere dicitur permanere.
Nam dicimus: ille sedit tres annos in illa ciuitate, id est mansit.
Ergo, manet ad dexteram patris. Aeque cum auditis patris dexteram, nolite putare deum corporeum esse aut membris humanis com-

positum; sed scitote quia deus ita de se uoluit dici quod possimus intelligere, non quod ipse est. Nam si dexteram habet corpoream, habet et sinistram; et si manum habet, est ubi non tangit; si oculos habet, est ubi non uidet; si aures habet, in longinquo non audit. Ergo hoc nolite credere cum auditis: Sedet ad dexteram patris. Dextera eius potentia eius, brachium eius, magnitudo eius; nam deus noster spiritus est, ubique totus; totus in caelo, totus in terra, totus in cordibus sanctis, pudicis, simplicibus, sobriis, immaculatis. Ergo: Sedet ad dexteram patris.

9. Inde uenturus est iudicare uiuos et mortuos. Hic geminum intellectum parit: uiui agnoscuntur, qui in corpore erunt in aduentu eius; mortui, qui ex hac luce migrauerunt. Aeque alio intellectu uiuos agnoscimus sanctos, mortuos peccatores.

10. Credo in spiritum sanctum. Iste spiritus ubique totus est; ubi uult spirat; ipse est qui dixit: *Separate mihi Paulum et Barnabam in opus ad quod assumpsi eos*. Iste est spiritus procedens de patre et filio, qui *diuidit* proprio dona singulis *prout uult*. Ergo iste spiritus consecrat, sanctificat, benedicit, honorificat, gubernat, protegit, consolatur, perducit ad sanctam ecclesiam. Quia uelut nauis est in mari posita, haec ecclesia portat epibatas, portat credentes in una caritate, in una modulatione, in uno remigio sanctitatis, in funibus caritatis, in uelo orationis, in arbore crucis, in pice paenitentiae, in stuppa castitatis, in tabulis pacis, in anchora fidei.

11. Ista ergo ecclesia, in una modulatione cantans, peruenit ad portum aeternitatis, ad ciuitatem pacis. Ipsa est quae dimittit peccata, exonerat omnia pondera, eliquata corda perducit ad palmam promissam supernae uocationis. Promittit carnis resurrectionem, promittit uitam aeternam, quia mortale hoc induet immortalitatem et corruptibile hoc induet incorruptionem. Credite carnis resurrectionem.

Credite quia *staturi sumus ante tribunal christi et reddituri rationem quae per corpus gessimus*, siue bonum siue malum. Credite uitam aeternam, promissam pro ista gratia data, ut gratuita gratia accepta perseueret in uobis; cum perseuerauerit, quae audistis et uidistis et didicistis a nobis, haec agite et *deus pacis* erit uobiscum. Amen.

*homilia 28*

*alia expositio symboli*

1. Super fabricam totius ecclesiae nihil aliud in fundamento ponunt sapientes architecti, qui sunt uerbi praedicatores, nisi Iesum Christum; de quo fundamento credulitas surgit. Et quia fides totum sibi uindicat, de deo uos habere conuenit hanc fidem, dei electi, qui nuper ad ueram credulitatem confessionis accedistis. Sed quia *corde creditur ad iustitiam, ore uero confessio celebratur in salutem*, fides primo uobis praedicanda est, secundo spes, tertio caritas. Nam de ipsa credulitate fit initium confessionis.

2. Quid enim dicturi estis? Audite et intellegite, quia cum audieritis et intellexeritis, laetitiam uobis acquiretis, dicente propheta: *Auditui meo dabis exsultationem et laetitiam*. Dicite ergo quod a nobis auditis: Credo in deum patrem omnipotentem. Videte, unde coepistis? Credo, dixistis. Haec credulitas conferet uobis praesentis uitae securitatem et futurae uitae aeternitatem. Ergo, ponite in fundamento cordis hanc credulitatem.

3. Sed in quo? Videte: In patrem. Quod dixistis in capite orationis: *Pater noster, qui es in caelis*, hoc dicitis et in symboli confessione: Credo in deum patrem omnipotentem; totus in caelo, totus in terra, totus in miraculis, totus in cordibus, totus in uirtutibus. Omnipotens dicitur quia posse ipsius non potest inuenire non posse, dicente propheta: *Omnia quaecumque uoluit, fecit in caelo et in terra*. Ipsa est ergo omnipotentia ut totum quod uult possit. Nam si dicimus de non posse ipsius, nihil dicimus quia tantae pietatis est ut negare se non possit, praesertim credentibus. Ecce quia de fide diximus dei patris omnipotentis, dicamus et de spe, ut fides credat, spes accipiat, caritas iungat.

4. Ergo creditis in unicum filium eius, dominum nostrum Iesum Christum. Iste unicus, qui semper fuit apud patrem, et aeternitatem habet cum patre; minor non potest esse a patre sed unam habet cum patre potestatem. Iste unicus, quem confitemur genitum sini initio de patre, qui semper fuit apud patrem et prodidit illum uerbo suo, qui fuit *apud deum; et ipse erat deus; hoc fuit in principio apud deum*. Non dicatis minorem esse filium de patre genitum, sed istum qui natus est de spiritu sancto et Maria uirgine. Non intellegatis patrem Christi secundum carnem spiritum sanctum esse, quia non omnis qui filius alicuius dicitur, de eo generatus intellegitur. Nam

dicimus filios adoptiuos regeneratos ex aqua et spiritu; numquid filii
sunt aquae? Dicimus filios regni, filios ecclesiae, sicut ait apostolus:
*Per euangelium ego uos genui*; numquid filii sumus apostoli? Nam si
uelimus de rebus indignis loqui, iniuriam facimus tanto sacramento:
dicimus filios gehennae, qui sunt *filii irae*, apostolo dicente: *Fuistis
aliquando filiii irae, sicut et ceteri*, licet talia tantae magnitudini
comparanda non sunt. Ideo diximus ista quia dictum est: Natus de
spiritu sancto. Itaque credendum est spiritum sanctum patris esse et
filii.

5. Et quia deus spiritus est uenit in Mariam, dicente angelo:
*Spiritus sanctus superueniet in te et uirtus altissimi obumbrabit tibi;
propter hoc, quod nascetur ex te sanctum, uocabitur filius dei*. Natus
de spiritu sancto. Istum spiritum sanctum dicimus patri et filio esse
coaequalem et procedentem de patre et filio. Hoc credite, ne colloquia mala corrumpant mores uestros bonos.

Sunt enim haeretici quorum sermo uelut cancer serpit, qui dicunt
filium minorem a patre, spiritum sanctum inter creaturas esse ordi-
natum. Sed cum haec audieritis a peruersis, nolite peruerti. Quod
accepistis et didicistis a nobis, hoc tenete, hoc credite. Haec credulitas confirmata sit in uobis, ut *deus pacis regnet uobiscum*. Ergo
creditis in unicum dominum nostrum Iesum Christum, natum de
spiritu sancto et uirgine Maria. 6. Sed dicturi uobis sunt gentiles,
deprauantes fidem nostram: Quomodo potuit uirgo concipere, uirgo
parere uirgoque manere? Contra naturam est. - Hoc dicturi sunt
uobis. Et uos e contrario respondete eis: Credulitas nostra, quod
uerbis explicari non potest, fide tenet. Nec enim qui ex nihilo fecit
mundum, cunctam creaturam disposuit, elementa constituit, mari
terminum posuit, impossibile illi erat introire in uisceribus humanis
et carnem fieri et possidere pudica uiscera matris. Nam homines,
nati de masculo et femina, si interrogentur, quomodo coagulati sunt
in secreto matris, quomodo ossa durata sunt, omnis compago membrorum artusque omnes ordinati sunt, in harmonia corporis disposita, quis exinde rationem reddit? Si ergo de natiuitate, quae
semper in isto fluuio saeculi uenit et transit, rationem non reddis,
de singulari natiuitate Christi rationem reddes?

7. Quid dicturi sumus? Si dicamus testimonium fidei nostrae,
forte non credunt gentiles; sed quod illis non proficit ad salutem,
uobis credentibus proficiat. Quomodo introiuit Christus ianuis clau-
sis ad discipulos suos, super mare ambulauit, imperauit uento et

tempestati et *facta est tranquillitas magna*? Quia ergo ista super nos sunt et rationem de talibus miraculis reddere non ualemus, fide tenemus. Ergo, hoc credite, deum in filii natiuitate, unici filii sui, facere quod nos cogitatione inuestigare non possumus.

8. Ergo natus de spiritu sancto et de uirgine Maria crucifixus est sub Pontio Pilato. Quare hoc passus est, innocens pro nocentibus, liber pro seruis? Vt quia nos in transgressione per Adam, primum hominem, mortui eramus, in patibulo crucifixi resuscitaremur. Fixus est cruci. Magnum sacramentum, magna altitudo crucis, magna *latitudo*, magna *profunditas*. Altitudo, ut ad patrem clamaret: *Pater, ignosce illis, quia nesciunt quid faciunt*. Latitudo, quia *maiorem caritatem nemo habet quam ut animam suam ponat pro amicis suis*. Profundum, ut ecclesia ad deum clamaret: *De profundis clamaui ad te, domine. Domine, exaudi uocem meam*; et exaudiretur pro filiis uox eius.

Iste Pontius Pilatus praesidatum gerebat apud Hierosolymitanam ciuitatem; ibi et Herodes erat, qui inimicitiam tenebat cum Pontio Pilato. Sed illa pietas Christi fecit ex inimicis in morte sua duos amicos, scilicet Pontium Pilatum et Herodem. Fecit etiam et nos amicos patri, tollens *parietem* inimicitiarum, qui erat inter nos et deum, ut reconciliaret nos patri. Nam ipse dixit: *Si feceritis ea quae mando uobis, iam non dicam uos seruos sed amicos*.

9. Ergo iste crucifixus sub Pontio Pilato sepultus est, ut in morte sua nos uiuificaret. Ipse mori uoluit, ne nos moreremur; ipse se obtulit seipsum pro nobis hostiam et oblationem *in odorem suauitatis*, ut de captiuis liberos faceret, de superbis humiles, de inimicis amicos. Descendit ad infernum, ut et ibi a miraculo non uacaret. Nam *multa corpora sanctorum resurrexerunt cum Christo*, quae postea mortua sunt, sicut Lazarus, sicut filia archisynagogi, sicut filius uiduae. Quod fecit in istis tribus, hoc fecit per propriam resurrectionem in multis sanctis. Nam *multa corpora sanctorum resurrexerunt cum Christo*, de quibus dixit apostolus: *Ex quibus plures manent usque adhuc, quidam autem dormierunt*. Tertia die a mortuis resurrexit, ne caro eius uideret corruptionem. Resurrexit iam non corruptibilis, caro non passibilis; sed talis caro resurrexit qualis hodie cum patre permanet in caelo.

10. Videte ubique sacramentum trinitatis; ecce et in spiritum sanctum credimus. Qui spiritus sanctus, procedens de patre et filio, caritate coniungitur. *Manent enim fides, spes, caritas*. Haec fides in

patre, una uirtus in filio; iste spiritus sanctus, ipse est, qui *propria dona singulis tribuit prout uult.*

Ecce uidete alia tria: in carnis resurrectione fides, in uita aeterna spes, in sancta ecclesia caritas. Credite carnis resurrectionem. Nam in Ezechiele propheta, ossa arida legimus fuisse collecta, quae fuerunt sparsa; et accepta carne, membra singula se agnouerunt; acceperunt spiritum et resurrexerunt. Nullus uos seducat inanibus uerbis dicens: Qui a feris comesti sunt, qui combusti sunt, qui in mari a piscibus deuorati sunt, unde resurgent qui tumulati non sunt, qui sepulturam non meruerunt? Ne mireris ad potentiam dei, quia non est impossibile ei restituere quod erat, qui fecit id quod non erat.

11. Credite ergo uitam aeternam, ubi mors non nominatur, corruptio, uarietas, miseria et tentatio non accidit. Erunt homines in resurrectione, in uita aeterna, sicut angeli in caelo, per sanctam ecclesiam peruenientes, quae mittit perfectos, quae dimittit peccata, quae candidatos in martyrio acquisiuit, quae castos et pudicos perfecit, quae nescientes ad perfectam scientiam perduxit. Nam uox eius est: *Imperfectum meum uiderunt oculi tui*; sed quoniam ipsos perfectos fecit, in libro tuo omnes scribentur. Quotquot ergo perfecti sumus, hoc sapiamus ut credentes, *deus pacis* sit nobiscum. Amen.

apparatus criticus apud expositiones symboli CPL 915

homilia 26

congaudet] gaudet *GBh*      celebrant *h*] celebrat $O^2$ *P*, celebrans $O^1$      in salutem] ad salutem *h*, in salute *H*      ergo *O*] autem *PGh*      et] et a *h*      salutarem] salutare *NP*      proficiscentes] proficientes *h*
2. qui] quid *P*      loquimini *(1° )*] *om. h*      loquimini *(2° )*] loquamini $O^2$ *B*      litterarum] *om. A*      redigatis] redigatur *h*      dimitti sibi] sibi dimitti *N*
3. quia] qui *OGAN*      ut puta] utpote *G*      non attendere *h*] attendere *codd.*
4. ecce ... patris] *om. N*      uiuite *OANP*] uenite *Gh*      hereditatem eius] hereditatem $N^1$      eius accipere *(1°)*] accipite *A*      eius accipere *(2°)*] accipere eius *h*      facere nolite] nolite facere *N*
5. in] *om. A*      unicum ... nostrum] unici filio domino nostro $O^1$      potestas ... uirtus] *scripsit in rasura N*      filium minorem] minorem filium *N*      haec] hoc *O*      abominatur] abominat $O^1$      natus est] natus $O^1$
6. spiritus] spiritus sanctus *N*      eam] eam et *Bh*      uirginis] uirginis et *h*      creuit *2 o h*] creauit *codd.*      acquirere patri] patri acquirere *P*      donaret *GhAP*] praestet *O*      flagellatus] flagellatus est *h*      his] iis *h*      dicens] dicens pater *P*      uidetis] *add. s. l. $O^2$*      nostrum] uestrum *h*      remaledicebat] maledicebat Bh      se iudicanti] iudicanti se *h*

7. ista] ipsa *P*      mentiti ... eius] *om. B*      sunt ei] ei sunt *h*      impletum
est] impletum *P*
8. sedet *(bis) APh*] sedit *OG*      sedit] sedet *Ah*]      ad dexteram patris]
patris ad dexteram *h*      auditis] audimus *N*      dexteram] ad dexteram
*Gh*      possimus] possemus *e*, possumus *h*      manum habet] habet manum
*G*      auditis] audistis *1556*      patris] dei patris *P*      ubique totus] ubique
totus est *P*      sedet] sedit *O*
9. hic] hoc *h*      aduentu] aduentum *O¹*      ex] in *A¹ h*      alio intellectu]
alium intellectum *O*
10. ad quod *h*] quod *codd.*      diuidit] diuidet *O¹*      dona singulis] singulis
dona *Bh*      honorificat] horificat *O¹*      sanctam ecclesiam] ecclesiam sanctam
*P*      uelut] *add. s. l. O²*
11. ipsa] ista *P*      uobis *h*] uobis ut *codd. aliqui (An corrigendum dein
agate?)*      perseuerauerit] perseuerauerint *T*      amen] *om. GANP*

homilia 28

1. uindicat] uendicat *PBrh*      uobis] nobis *Bh*
2. quia] qui *O¹ a.c.*      exsultationem] gaudium *P*      dicite] dicete *O¹ a.c.*
unde] unde unde *OG¹ A*      conferet] confert *GBrh*      futurae uitae] futurae *h*
3. uidete] uide *h*      patrem *O*] patre *GrhAPB*      orationis] lectionis *P¹*
inuenire] inueniri *N*      posse] potest *P*      ipsa est] ipsa *Grh*      dicamus et]
dicamus *GP*
4. in] *add. s. l. A, om. B*      unicum ... Christum] unico ... Christo *O¹*      et
aeternitatem] aeternitatem *Grh*      non potest esse] esse non potest *h*
istum] iste *O¹*      regeneratos] generatos *O¹*      spiritu] spiritu sancto *N*
apostolo dicente] dicente apostolo *P*      magnitudini] magnitudinis *A a.c.*
sunt *OG^{a.c.} N^{a.c.}*] sint *G² rhN² P*      itaque] ita *O¹*      spiritum sanctum] spiritum *N*
5. deus spiritus est] spiritus *h*, deus spiritus *G*      Mariam] Maria *A*      hoc *(1°
)] add. s.l. O²*      dicunt] *Grh*      patre] patre aestimant *rh*      audieritis]
audieris *O¹*      hoc ... hoc] haec ... haec *O¹*
6. creditis] credite *h*      in] *add. A s. l., om. B*      unicum] unum *h*      unicum ... Christum] unicom dominom ... Christom *O¹*      et uirgine *O² P*] ex uirgine *O¹*      uirgine Maria *O*] Maria uirgine *GrhAP*      uobis sunt] sunt uobis
*PB*      nostram] uestram *Grh*      uirgoque] uirgo *N*      dicturi sunt] dicturi
*O*      uobis *O*] nobis *NP*      e] *om. N*      respondete] respondetis *GB*, respon-
debitis *rh*      enim] enim ei *h*      uisceribus humanis] uiscera humanis *G*, uiscera hominis *rh*      coagulati] conquagolati *O¹*      reddes] reddis *O¹*
7. illis] *om. P*      uobis] nobis *OB*      super nos] supra nos *h*      in filii] in *Bh*,
in filii sui *P*      sui] sui hoc *h*
8. de uirgine] uirgine *h*      est *(1° )] add. s.l. O²*      quia nos] quos nos *O¹*
quid faciunt *codd.*] quod faciunt *h*      ponat] ponat quis *PB*      ecclesia] ecclesiam *A a.c.*      domine domine] domine *h*      filiis] filiis eius *NP*      Hieroso-
lymitanam] Hierosolimam *h*      tenebat cum Pontio Pilato] cum P.P. habebat
*P*      amicos patri] patri amicos *A*      qui *N*] quod *OGrAP*, quae *h*      et] et
inter *A*      ut] et *O¹*      dicam] dico *h*

9. crucifixus] crucifixus est *B*      in morte sua nos] nos in morte sua *N*
captiuis] captiuos *O¹*      liberos faceret] liberos *P*      amicos] amicos faceret
*P*      cum Christo] *om. P, in quo adest rasura*      quae *r*] qui *h*      quae ...
cum Christo] *om. N*      non corruptibilis] incorruptibile *A a.c.*
10. manent enim] *om. O¹ , add. i.m. O²*      in filio] *add s.l. O²*      spiritus sanc-
tus] spiritus *om. h*      resurrectione] resurrectionis *O¹*      collecta] congregata
*A*      fuerunt sparsa] sparsa fuerant *rh*      nullus] nullos *O¹*      combusti
sunt] igni combusti sunt *N,* combusti *P*      resurgent *O² GP*] resurgunt *O¹*
*h*      ne] non *h*      ei] *add. s.l. O²*
11. quae dimittit] qui dimittit *a.c. O¹*      quotquot] quodquod *O¹*      hoc
sapiamus] *om. A*      ut credentes] ut credentibus *P,* credentes ut *Bh*

The textual transmission of the pseudo-Athanasian *enarratio in sym-bolum apostolorum* CPL 1744a

The pseudo-Athanasian *enarratio in symbolum apostolorum* CPL 1744a was discovered in a sixth or seventh-century manuscript by Josephus Blanchinus [1], the Veronensis LIX (57). Thus far, no further manuscripts of the text have been found. Blanchinus edited the *enarratio* in 1732 with an introduction, critical notes, and com-mentary [2]. Blanchinus's text has been reprinted without any changes in the Supplement Series to Migne's *Patrologia Latina* by Hamman [3].

A new edition of the text seems to be desirable for several rea-sons. The most important of these is that Blanchinus's edition is rather hard to obtain nowadays. The reprint in Migne is faithful enough, but does not indicate where it departs from the manuscript because Blanchinus's notes have not been included. To make mat-ters worse, Blanchinus made quite a number of emendations, but only printed those in the text that were so obvious as to exclude all possible doubt, though one or two instances remain open to dis-cussion. His more brilliant corrections, together with his more modest proposals, only received a place in the critical notes, the sometimes clearly corrupt manuscript reading being printed in the text.

The text that is offered below is based upon a fresh investigation of the manuscript. Many of Blanchinus's emendations have been adopted, in which case they are marked as such in the critical appa-ratus. In a few places, our text departs from Blanchinus's, practi-cally always on the basis of conjecture. Until new witnesses to the text of the *enarratio* emerge, this seems to be both the least and the most one can do.

---

[1] The Italian form Giuseppe Bianchini may also be found.

[2] Blanchinus 1732, 1-65, text on pp. 30-40.

[3] PLS 1, 786-790. Hamman has announced a new edition by Samuel Cavallin as complete and forthcoming, but this edition has apparently not yet seen the light of day.

codex:

V    Veronensis, Biblioteca Capitolare LIX (57), saec. VI/VII

editio

*Bl*   BLANCHINVS, J., *Enarratio pseudo-Athanasiana in Symbolum ante hac inedita. Et Vigilii Tapsitani de Trinitate ad Theophilum liber VI. Nunc primum genuinus, atque assumentis carens; prolatus ex vetustissimo codice Amplissi Capituli Veronensis* ..., Veronae, 1732, 30-40 (= PLS 1, 786-790)

*coni. Bl*   correcturae uel coniecturae a Blanchino non in textum receptae sed solum in apparatu critico notatae

enarratio in symbolum apostolorum CPL 1744a

1. *Vna fides* (Gal. 4, 5), sed non in omnibus fidei una mensura est. Sic et in illa eremi uia, cum diuinae uirtutis indultu populus angelico cibo aleretur (cf. Ps. 78, 25), non erat omnibus manna quod manna est, sed aliis caelestem saporem incorrupta suauitate custodientibus uiles quidam pepones et tristem caeparum acrimoniam Aegyptia cruditate eructuabant (cf. Sap. 16, 20-21). Sicque in unoquoque eorum erat non gratia accepti muneris sed propriae desiderium uoluptatis (Num. 11, 4-8). 2. Securus itaque de instituti tui indole manna hoc nostrum caelestibus ferculis (cf. II Cor. 4, 7) defero, confidens in domino nostro Iesu Christo (cf. Rom. 14, 14) quod is qui coepit te cibis suis alere perseuerantis saporis perpetem gratiam tibi tribuat (cf. I Cor. 3, 2. Hebr. 5, 12-14. I Petr. 2, 2), quoniam quamuis uelle nostrum sit, perficere tamen sine illo non inuenimus (cf. Rom. 9, 16. I Cor. 3, 7).

3. Credo in deum. Initium sacramenti confessione credulitatis imbuitur, ut per hoc immensitas dei quae comprehendi humanis sensibus non potest approbetur. Fidei enim secreto recondendum est quod capacitatem existimationis excedit. 4. Credo in deum. Hic est Christiani nominis titulus, hic humani fructus officii, duo in famulatu dei quae principalia in nobis habemus offerre, cordis fidem et oris confessionem, quia *corde creditur ad iustitiam, ore autem confessio fit ad salutem* (Rom. 10, 10). 5. Credo in deum. Hoc est quod illum *gentium patrem* (Gen. 17, 4-5. Eccli. 44, 19. Rom. 4, 17-18) a ueterno uitae prioris exemit (Gen. 12, 1), hoc quod multiplicationem immensi seminis (cf. Gen. 26, 4. Hebr. 11, 11-12) fideli sponsione

firmauit (Gen. 22, 16-18), hoc quod iustitiae praemio manente usque ad nos mercedem (cf. Gen. 15, 1. Rom. 4, 4) transmisit (cf. Rom. 4, 23-24), sicut legimus: *Credidit Abraham deo et reputatum ei ad iustitiam* (Gen. 15, 6. Rom. 4, 3. 22-23. Gal. 3, 6. I Mach. 2, 52. Iac. 2, 23).

6. Credo in deum patrem. Dei nomini paternum connectitur sacramentum. Inane enim erat et uacuum deum sine paterno uocabulo credidisse. Hoc et gentes nouerunt (cf. Act. 17, 23) et daemones confitentur (cf. Matth. 8, 29. Marc. 1, 24 et 3, 11. Luc. 4, 34. Iac. 2, 19). Nobis autem quibus uita aeterna promittitur, salutare mysterium publicatur ut credamus non in deum tantum sed in deum patrem, quod et patris nomen nimium generale est sine deo et dei uirtus minus clara sine patris nomine. Ac per hoc, nomine alterutro cum utroque connexo, fundari non potest fides, nisi et paterna generatio uim deitatis teneat et maiestas deitatis sacramentum paterni nominis non omittat.

7. Credo in deum patrem. Confessio quae patrem signat statim confitetur et filium. Vacat enim sine alio aliud nomen, quia nomen patris est filius. Nemo sine generationis fide appellat auctorem, quia gignentis nuncupatio natura nascentis est. Ac sic nullum inter alterutrum gradum credas, cum utrumque in uno cognoscas.

8. Credo in deum patrem. Catholicae fidei claram confessionem. Nullum interstitium inter deum et patrem ponitur, nulla intercapedo seruatur, utriusque nominis natura coniuncta est. Vt deum credimus confitemur et patrem, connexorum uocabulorum tempora nescientes, quia paternae appellationis nuncupatio a dei confessione non distat. Si quis deum non aeternum nouit patrem aestimet non aeternum. 9. Credo in deum patrem. Hoc ipsum quod ordo uerborum, quamuis connexione coniuncta, deum nominat antequam patrem incorruptae fidei laudabile continet argumentum, ne quis prauae aestimationis errore non ad unum omnia aestimet referri debere principium. Nam cum deum dicimus primitus et patris nomen dei nomini non auellimus. Vnum quidem auctorem prodimus, sed eum qui ex auctoritate est coaeternum fatemur auctori.

10. Credo in deum patrem. Praeiudicatum tenetur hoc confessionis exordio ut filium deum credat qui deum patrem se confessus est credidisse, quia generi suo caelestis natura respondet, nec simile sibi potest esse quod suum est. Humana tantum condicio et degenerati-

onem respicit et profectum. Ceterum qui ex deo patre nascitur non potest filius esse nisi deus sit.

11. Credo in deum patrem omnipotentem. Quae enim alia natura
* * *

* * *

12. * * *ret. Sed quamuis peccato esse libera, non tamen alia habeatur quam quae possit esse peccatrix.

13. Ex Maria uirgine. Honor materni sexus incorruptae uirginitatis professione monstratur, ne diuisus esset homo et deus, quamuis habens utriusque status plenitudinem credatur. Sed quamuis homo nasceretur ex Maria, dei tamen uirtus probatur ex uirgine, ut et fides generis maneret in carne et potentia maiestatis appareret in incorruptione.

14. Qui sub Pontio Pilato crucifixus est et sepultus. Sequitur uirginis partum in confessione nostra iudicium, crux, sepultura, ne deus gestans hominem aliquem excusatae carnis excitaret errorem et euacuati hominis iniectae suspicioni ueritatem conferret, sed manente, ac solido, quod iudicari, crucifigi, sepeliri possit redimeret nos in deo uirtus sua, nostra substantia.

15. Descendit ad inferna. Ne in filio dei deo pleno dubitaretur fuisse hominis plenitudo insinuat nobis descendisse ad inferna confessio. Vacaret enim tanti mysterii gratia si caro solum inanima, id est quae animam non haberet, cruci fuisset affixa. Nam cuius praemii Christus dominus noster posset nobis imputare mercedem si nihil in illo fuisset quod aut doloris sensum haberet aut mortis cum ab utroque eorum et maiestas dominica et carnis insensibilitas se uindicaret?

16. Die tertio resurrexit a mortuis. Post creditum ad inferna descensum resurrectionis celeritatem fatemur, ne reliquisse assumptum hominem deus uel apud inferos putaretur, cum supradictam sedem ille adiisset condicione mortis, iste potestate uirtutis, suae quisque naturae partibus functus, ille legem infirmitatis complens, hic potentiam resurrectionis ostendens.

17. Ascendit in caelos, ne alium Christum in filio dei, alium in hominis filio putaremus. Quamuis distantiae fide distinctas naturas sic ubique coniungit, ut una in sensibus nostris utraque teneatur. Christus ad inferna descendit, sed deum mortis condicio non attingit. Christus ascendit in caelos, sed hominem diuina non respuunt.

18. Sedet ad dexteram patris. Non nouam putare debemus aut subitam istam in filio dei gloriam quam se et apud patrem semper et ante saecula, sicut et in Euangelio legimus, propriae uocis testimonio profitetur habuisse (cf. Ioh. 8, 25. 54. 58 et 16, 15 et 17, 10. 22. 24), sed ideo nunc filius hominis delatae sedis honore donatur quem in humanis passionibus non reliquit, ut istam clarificationem diuinae dignitatis hominibus adueheret. 19. Denique ut huiusmodi intelligentiae secretum humanos possit sensus intrare sedere ad dexteram patris filium confitemur, cum immensitatem dei nec corporalitas definiat nec localitas comprehendat.

20. Inde uenturus iudicaturus de uiuis et mortuis. Venturi quoque ad iudicandum potestas quamuis filium dei deum designet manentem, tamen in eo intelligentiam filii hominis non reliquit. Quamuis enim scriptum legamus in paterna eum claritate uenturum (cf. Ioh. 5, 21-23), tamen et illud diuinis eloquiis proditur: *Et uidebunt in quem compunxerunt* (Zach. 12, 10. Ioh. 19, 37. Apoc. 1, 7). Ipsa enim potestas de uiuis et mortuis iudicandi utramque naturam una cum claritate collectam in Christo mediatore testatur, quia uiuos iudicare et homo potest, mortuos ad iudicium exhibere nisi deus non potest.

21. Credo in spiritum sanctum. Quod post tantorum mysteriorum confessionem nunc in fidei nostrae sacramento sanctum spiritum confitemur non iniuriosa imminutio deitatis est sed catholicae fidei cauta praescriptio, ne forte si prius confessio sancti spiritus fuisset inserta personarum aliqua confusio crederetur quas sub unius deitatis maiestate discretas humana salus est credidisse, quia in sacramento aeternae spei pater et filius et spiritus sanctus ita tres personae sunt, ne tres dii sint, ita deus unus est, ne una persona sit. 22. Hoc Christus apostolis tradidit, hoc nobis apostoli tradiderunt. Haec enim sunt saluatoris ascensuri ad caelum paene ultima ad totius doctrinae conclusionem data: *Ite, baptizate gentes unguentes eas in nomine patris et filii et spiritus sancti* (Matth. 28, 19). Non dixit: in nominibus, sed: in nomine patris et filii et spiritus sancti, ut unius nominis significatio unum deum traderet, tres uero personas coniunctio adiecta disiungeret. 23. Videamus nunc an fideles discipuli accepta seruarint. Respondeat nobis pro cunctis Iohannes, qui in pectore domini nostri familiariter recubans (Ioh. 13, 23) totius doctrinae potuit arcana cognoscere, qui quod reliqui apostoli scire cupiant dominum solus interrogat (Ioh. 13, 24-25), qui comprehenso domino atrium sacerdotis non negaturus ingreditur (Ioh. 18, 15), qui

suscipienti se matri uicarius affectus a domino delegatur (Ioh. 19, 26-27), qui ad monumentum domini etiam Petrum festinus anteue-nit (Ioh. 20, 4). *Tres sunt*, inquit, *qui testimonium perhibent in caelo, pater, uerbum, et spiritus, et hi tres unum sunt* (I Ioh. 5, 7). Nonne post haec nobis huiusmodi fidem et mors est perdere et salus est custodisse?

24. Subiungitur denique: In sanctam matrem ecclesiam, ut illa una ecclesia et sancta apud nos habeatur et mater, quam in aposto-lis domini doctrina constituit. Amen.

apparatus criticus apud enarrationem in symbolum apostolorum CPL 1744a

1. populus *Bl*] populos *V*     caelestem *Bl*] caeleste *V*     cruditate *Bl*] crude-litate *V*
2. is *Bl*] his *V*
3. quae *coni. Bl*] qua *V*     existimationis *conieci*] extimationis *V*, aestimationis *Bl*
5. a ueterno *coni. Bl*] ab aeterno *V*     reputatum *V*] reputatur *Bl*     inane *Bl*] inanem *V*     nomen nimium *conieci*] nomen *V Bl*     ac *Bl*] hac *V* nomine alterutro cum utroque *conieci*] sine alt. et eo utrumque *V*, sine alt. et eo utroque *Bl*, sine alt. et eo utrimque *coni. Bl*
7. fide *Bl*] fidem *V*     alterutrum *coni. Bl*] alterum *V*
8. claram *Bl*] clara *V*     paternae *Bl*] paternam *V*
9. ipsum *V*] ipso *coni. Bl*     deum *Bl*] dei *V*
10. respondet *Bl*] respondit *V*
11. natura ... ret] *lacunam duarum paginarum indicat Bl*
12. esse ... habeatur ... possit *conieci*] esse ... haberetur ... possit *V*, esset ... haberetur ... posset *Bl*     sexus *Bl*] sexui *V*     credatur *conieci*] crederetur *V Bl*     probatur *conieci*] probaretur *V Bl*     incorruptione *Bl*] incorruptio[nem]: Nam *V*
14. partum *Bl*] partus *V*     excusatae *coni. Bl (uel* accusatae *uel* incusatae *)*] excusate *V*     hominis iniectae suspicioni ueritatem conferret *(uel* hominis iniectas suspiciones ueritate conferret *aut* confutaret *) coni. Bl*] homines iniecta suspicionis ueritate conferret *V*     sua *V*] sub *uel* sua in *coni. Bl*     nostra substantia *V Bl*] *num* in homine *addendum?*
15. posset *Bl*] possit *V*     dominica et carnis ins. se uind. *conieci*] domini et carnem ins. uind. *V*, domini et carnis ins. uind. *uel* dominum et carnem ins. uind. *uel* domini et ins. uind. carnem *coni. Bl*
16. supradictam *Bl*] supradictum *V*     uirtutis, suae *interpunxi*] *non interpungit V, post* suae *interpunxit Bl*     quisque *coni. Bl*] quique *V*     legem ... poten-tiam *Bl*] lege ... potentia *V*
17. quamuis dist. fide distinctas naturas sic ubique coniungit *conieci*] quamuis dist. fidem distincta natura. Sic ub. coniungitur *V* quamuis *(id est* omnem *)* dist. fidem distincta natura sic ub. coniungit *coni. Bl*

18. sed ideo ... quem *conieci*] sed in eo ... quem ideo *V*      humanis ... diuinae dignitatis hominibus *conieci*] omnibus humanis ... diuinam dignitatis *V*

20. quoque *Bl*] quodque *V*      eum claritate *Bl* cum claritatem *V*      collectam in *coni. Bl*] collectam *V*

21. spiritum sanctum *conieci*] spiritu^m sancto^m *V*, spiritu sancto *Bl*      fidei *Bl*] fide *V*      fuisset *Bl*] fuisse *V*      maiestate discretas *Bl*] maiestatem desr...tas ? *V*

22. ultima ad *Bl*] ultima *V*      data *V*] dicta *coni. Bl*      Non dixit ... sancti] *V in margine*

23. qui suscipienti se matri uic. aff. a dom. delegatur *conieci*] cuius suscipienti te matris uic. aff. a dom. diligatur *V* cuius suscipientis et matris uic. aff. a dom. delegatur *(uel* cuius suscipientis aff. et matris uic. a dom. delegatur , *uel* cuius aff. delegatur a dom. uic. matris suscipientis se *) coni. Bl*      hi *conieci*] hii *V*, ii *Bl*

24. ecclesia et *conieci*] ecclesiae *V*, ecclesia *Bl*

The manuscript tradition of the anonymous *tractatus symboli* CPL 1751

Two manuscripts of the anonymous *tractatus symboli* have been known since 1905: a Laurentianus (*L*) and a Bodleianus (*B*), both stemming from the twelfth century. A collation of the manuscripts shows that neither can have been the ancestor of the other, since both exhibit a number of unmistakable errors of their own. Thus we may point to the following unmistakable errors in *B*:

> *fidei* for *filii* (thus *L*) in *tractatus symboli* 2
> *symbolum* for *symbolum dicitur symbolum* (thus *L*) in 5-6
> *certum est habeat* for *certum est quod habeat* (thus *L*) in 8
> omission of *dissipationem* (present in *L*) in 9
> *nascetur* for *nasceretur* (thus *L*) in 9
> *apostolorum* for *apostolorumque* (thus *L*) in 11
> omission of the words *in remissionem peccatorum. Sancta ecclesia una et uera est, in qua sanctorum communio* (present in *L*) in 16

On the other hand, *L* is obviously wrong in the following readings:

> *carum est* for *carum* (thus *B*) in *tractatus symboli* 1
> *deo hominibus* for *deo homines* (thus *B*) in 1
> *caelestis* for *regni caelestis* (thus *B*) in 3
> *nuntia* for *nunc iam* (thus *B*) in 7
> *a filio ... a creatura* for *ad filium ... ad creaturam* (thus *B*) in 8
> *deus* for *dicitur* (thus *B*) in 9
> *stultitiam* for *stultitia est* (thus *B*) in 11
> *factum* for *factus* (thus *B*) in 12
> *creditur* for *credite* (thus *B*) in 17

*B* and *L* are therefore to be treated as independent witnesses. Although combined they go a long way towards offering a complete and sound text, they also present a considerable number of common errors. These comprise the following:

> *sepulcrum cinerem* (*L*: *cinere*) for (probably) *sepulcri cineres* in *tractatus symboli* 1
> *alibi quis* (*L*: *ab aliquis*), probably to be emended to *alibi quis-quis*, in 2
> *quod nunc* for *nunc quod* in 3
> *tegebatur* for *tegebat* in 3

*ianuam ... introitum* for *ianua ... introitus* in 3

*factum* for *pactum* (unless the anonymous author was already mistaken on this point) in 6

*alicui* for *alicuius* in 6

*hanc succedit et collaudationis doctrinae* (an obviously corrupt place, even when our solution is far from certain) in 6

*quia filius* (a similar case) in 9

omission of *homo* before *agnoscitur* in 10

*sedentis* for *sedere* in 13

*subiaceant* for *subiciat* in 13

The conclusion seems obvious that *B* and *L* derive from some common ancestor in which these errors were already present. If one wanted to draw a stemma for these two manuscripts only, it would look like this:

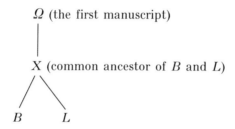

$\Omega$ (the first manuscript)

$X$ (common ancestor of *B* and *L*)

B      L

A special point of difference between *B* and *L* can be seen in the short liturgical notes that introduce the several parts of the *tractatus*. *L* mentions a *diaconus* in these notes, who calls for silence and attention and admonishes the catechumens to cross themselves when the Creed is recited, and a *presbyter* delivers the sermon. In *B*, no separate roles are indicated, but here, phrases that are abbreviated by means of *ut supra* or similar words in *L* are sometimes written out in full. The most likely explanation for this state of affairs is that X, the ancestor of our two manuscripts, exhibited both the divison of parts between two speakers and the full formulae, and that *B* and *L* (or intermediate manuscripts between them and X) simplified the text each in its own way. It seems best, therefore, to combine the evidence of the two manuscripts to gain as complete a text as possible in this respect.

There is only one earlier edition of the *tractatus symboli*. It was published by Caspari in 1879 on the basis of *L* alone in his *Alte und Neue Quellen* ... Although Caspari on the whole offers an intelligible text, his edition bears the marks of a too hasty preparation. There are quite a number of mistakes in his account of the manuscript text, and not all his corrections are noted as such. On the other hand, it should be acknowledged that many of his emendations are corroborated by *B*. Most of these were included in his text, the readings of *L* being relegated to the footnotes, but where Caspari did not feel sufficiently certain about his corrections, he followed the opposite procedure [1].

---

[1] See Caspari 1879, 291.

codices

*B*    Oxoniensis, Bodleian Library, Ms. Canonici Lit. 345, saec. XII

*L*    Florentinus, Bibliotheca Laurentiana, Plut. 16.8, saec. XII

editio

*Ca*    CASPARI, C.P., *Alte und neue Quellen zur Geschichte des Taufsymbols und der Glaubensregel*, Christiania, 1879, 290-304

*coni. Ca*    coniecturae a Caspari non in textum receptae sed solum in adnotationibus adhibitae

tractatus symboli CPL 1751

Et adnuntiat diaconus: State cum silentio, audite. Et sequitur presbyter his uerbis:

1. Primum omnium, filii carissimi, uenientes ad fidem catholicam obseruate ne quis infideliter ueniat, quia fides carum deo atque hominibus nomen est. Fides diuini muneris portio est, fides deo homines sociat, fides praesentia et futura coniungit, fides etiam quae inuisibilia sunt facit uidere (cf. Hebr. 11, 1. 3), fides omnibus post sepulcri cinerem caelum promittit (cf. Rom. 4, 16-17. II Petr. 3, 13). Quodsi haec omnia fides facit, quanto magis ex catechumeno fidelem nonnisi fides faciet? 2. Ideo ergo et nos a uobis hodie, filii, competentibus, uolentibus diuinum munus accipere, non exposcimus ut uasa aurea uel argentea deferatis in quibus susceptum dei donum portare possitis (cf. II Tim. 2, 20), sed uasa fictilia cordis uestri portate et hospitia conscientiae uestrae mundate (cf. Ps. 24, 4 et 51, 12. Matth. 5, 8. I Tim. 1, 5). Tale palatium quaerit fides, regina uirtutum, nec alibi quisquis potest diuinum seruare thesaurum, sicut et sanctus apostolus docet: *Habemus thesaurum hunc in uasis fictilibus ut sublimitas uirtutis sit dei, non ex nobis* (II Cor. 4, 7). 3. Huius ergo uobis caelestis thesauri hodie ianuam pandimus, et reuelamus uobis nunc quod ante oculos positum uelamen ignorantiae tegebat (cf. Ex. 34, 34. II Cor. 3, 13-16). Ingressus uitae aeternae et ianua salutis atque introitus regni caelestis (cf. Ps. 24, 7. 9) singularis fidei nostrae innocens et pura confessio, dicente propheta: *Intrate portas eius in confessione, atria eius in hymnis confessionum* (Ps. 100, 4).

4. Absistat omnis hinc, quaeso, alienus, absistat omnis profanus, audite mysterium fidei, non audiat infidelis.

5. Vos ergo, fratres, quos praesciuit deus et praedestinauit, quos uocauit et iustificauit (cf. Rom. 8, 29-30), audite hoc quod tradimus uobis hodie in conspectu dei, astantibus et audientibus angelis (cf. Luc. 15, 10. I Cor. 4, 9), symbolum. 6. Dicitur symbolum, uel autem pactum significat, uel magnae alicuius rei indicium salutaris. Huc accedit et collaudatio doctrinae. Sed quia ergo totius fidei breuiarium quoddam est nostrae salutis remedium ab apostolis collectum, ab iisdem symbolum nominatum est.

7. Sed nunc iam et ipsa uerba quorum rationem audistis accipite.

Iterum adnuntiat diaconus: Signate uos, audite symbolum. Et sequitur presbyter:

Credo in deum patrem omnipotentem, et in Iesum Christum filium eius unicum dominum nostrum, qui natus est de spiritu sancto et Maria uirgine, qui sub Pontio Pilato crucifixus est et sepultus, tertia die resurrexit a mortuis, ascendit in caelis, sedet ad dexteram patris, inde uenturus est iudicare uiuos et mortuos, et in spiritum sanctum, in sanctam ecclesiam, in remissionem peccatorum, carnis resurrectionem et uitam aeternam. Amen.

8. Audistis, fratres, in symbolo quia dictum est: Credis in deum patrem omnipotentem? Hoc est initium fidei, sicut apostolus dicit: *Quia accedentem ad deum credere primum oportet quia deus creator omnium est* (Hebr. 11, 6). Audistis deum, naturam ipsam et fontem diuinitatis intellegite. Audistis patrem, certum est quod habeat filium. Audistis omnipotentem, intellegite quod uniuersae creaturae teneat potentatum. Quod ergo ad filium spectat pater est, quod ad creaturam omnipotens.

9. Sequitur in symbolo: Et in Iesum Christum, filium eius unicum dominum nostrum. Iesus ergo lingua Hebraeorum saluator interpretatur, Christus autem ad unguendum regale uocabulum trahit. Vnicus ideo dicitur, ut eum intellegas non humanae progeniem sed diuinae esse uirtutis. Ex uno enim unicus nascitur, et unus splendor ex uera luce procedit. Pater ingenitus et inuisibilis et impassibilis dicitur quia fons et origo deitatis est, filius dissipationem carnis assumpsit ut nos redimeret. Sicut apostolus dicit: *Magnum est mysterium pietatis eius* (I Tim. 3, 16), ut qui manebat dei filius ex sancta uirgine Maria hominis filius nasceretur, et iterum: *Qui cum in forma dei esset, non rapinam arbitratus est se deo aequalem esse,*

*sed semetipsum exinaniuit formam serui suscipiens* (Phil. 2, 6-7), cum ipse sit uirtus et sapientia dei (cf. I Cor. 1, 24). Ipse unigenitus dei filius qui erat ante saecula cum patre et apud patrem (cf. Ioh. 1, 1. 18 et 3, 18-19 et 8, 58) in hoc mundo apparuit (cf. Ioh. 1, 9 et 12, 46 et 16, 28 et 18, 37. I Ioh. 1, 2).

10. Natum, inquit, de spiritu sancto et Maria uirgine. Crede ergo et hunc qui ex uirgine nascitur *nobiscum* esse *deum* (Is. 7, 14. Matth. 1, 23), deum ante saecula genitum de patre et hominem ex uirgine matre. Propterea ergo utrumque credendus est, deus et homo, quia sicut ex passionibus homo agnoscitur ita deus ex diuinis operationibus comprobatur.

Adnuntiat diaconus: Signate uos et audite symbolum. Et repetunt ut supra: Credo in deum. Et sequitur his uerbis:

11. Sicut audistis, fratres, secundum traditionem apostolorumque doctrinam sequitur in symbolo: Qui sub Pontio Pilato crucifixus est et sepultus. Crux enim domini *Iudaeis quidem scandalum est, gentibus autem stultitia est* (I Cor. 1, 23; cf. Gal. 5, 11), *nobis uero* (I Cor. 1, 18; cf. 24) credentibus salus est (cf. I Cor. 1, 21) et praemium uitae aeternae. Passus est dominus noster ut nos a passionibus corporalibus liberaret, mortuus est ut mortis iura dissolueret. 12. Tertia die resurrexit a mortuis, ut nobis futurae resurrectionis mysterium in suo corpore demonstraret, secundum prophetam: *Factus* est enim *inter mortuos liber* (Ps. 88, 5-6). Non enim a morte potuit teneri (cf. Rom. 6, 9), qui et mortis et uitae totam obtinet potestatem (cf. Matth. 28, 18. Ioh. 3, 13. Apoc. 1, 18).

13. Sequitur in symbolo, fratres: Ascendit in caelis, sedet ad dexteram patris. Ascendit ipse qui descenderat, quia: *Nemo ascendit in caelum nisi qui de caelo descendit* (Ioh. 3, 13). Descendisse de caelo misericordia fuit, ascendisse uirtus est, sedisse autem ad dexteram patris gloria est aeternae beatitudinis. Nam sedere in iudicium iudicantis ostendit arbitrium, et patris dextera beatitudo est sempiterna iustorum. 14. Inde uenturus est iudicare uiuos et mortuos. Iudicabit enim in illa die occulta hominum qui *reddet unicuique secundum opera sua* (Prov. 24, 12. Eccli. 35, 22 LXX. Matth. 16, 27. Rom. 2, 6. Apoc. 2, 23 et 22, 12; cf. Iob 34, 11), ut iustos constituat in uitam aeternam, impios autem aeternae poenae subiciat (cf. Dan 12, 2. Rom. 2, 7-8. II Thess. 1, 8-9).

Diaconus: Signate uos et audite symbolum. Credo in deum, et sicut supra.

15. Sequitur in symbolo: Et in spiritum sanctum. Sanctus spiritus unus est, qui de patre procedit et filio coaeternus, unitas amborum. Cum spiritu sancto indiuisa manet trinitas, * * * dominationis maiestas. 16. Sequitur: In sanctam ecclesiam, in remissionem peccatorum. Sancta ecclesia una et uera est, in qua sanctorum communio in remissionem peccatorum, in qua huius carnis nostrae resurrectio praedicatur. 17. Credite ergo ex fide, et omnia uobis peccata remittuntur, *ut credentes habeatis uitam aeternam* (Ioh. 20, 31 *u.l.*; cf. I Ioh. 5, 13), ut immaculati possitis peruenire ad regna caelorum (cf. I Cor. 1, 8. I Thess. 5, 23. II Petr. 3, 14. Iudae 24). Deus et pater domini nostri Iesu Christi uos faciat per multa spatia temporum et curricula annorum diei istius festiuitatem laetos et laetas suscipere, per dominum nostrum Iesum Christum, filium eius, qui cum eo uiuit et regnat in saecula saeculorum (cf. I Petr. 4, 11. Apoc. 1, 6). Amen.

apparatus criticus apud tractatum symboli CPL 1751

incipit tractatus symboli *B Ca*] incipit tractatum symboli *L*

1. carum *B*] carum est *L Ca*      nomen *BL*] nomini *coni. Ca*      deo homines *B*] deo hominibus *L*, deum hominibus *Ca*      uidere *BL*] uideri *Ca*      sepulcri cinerem *conieci*] sepulcrum cinerem *B*, sepulcrum cinere *L*, sepulcri cineres *Ca*, sepulcrorum cineres *coni. Ca*      faciet *conieci*] facit *BL Ca*
2. filii *L Ca*] fidei *B*      dei donum *B*] donum dei *L Ca*      sed uasa *conieci*] uasa *BL Ca*      alibi quisquis *conieci*] alibi quis *B*, ab aliquis *L*, ab aliis *Ca*      seruare *BL*] seruari *Ca*      nobis *B Ca*] uobis *L*
3. nunc quod *conieci*] quod nc *BL*, quod ante *Ca e lecto* quod ne      uelamen ignorantiae *BL*] uelamen *Ca*      tegebat *Ca*] tegebatur *BL*      ianua ... introitus *Ca*] ianuam ... introitum *BL*      regni caelestis *B*] caelestis *L*, gloriae caelestis *Ca*      nostrae *L Ca*] uestrae *B*
6. dicitur symbolum *L Ca*] *om. B*      pactum *Ca*] factum *BL*      alicuius *Ca*] alicui *BL*      salutaris *BL*] salutare *Ca*      huc accedit *conieci*] hanc succedit *BL*, hoc succedit *coni. Ca*      collaudatio *coni. Ca*] collaudationis *BL*      quoddam *B Ca*] quodam *L*
7. nunc iam *B*] nuntia *L*, adnuntia *coni. Ca*      quorum *B*] quarum *L Ca*      iterum adnuntiat diaconus *L Ca*] *om. B*      et sequitur presbyter *L Ca*] *om. B*      unicum ... amen *B*] ut supra *L Ca*      spiritum sanctum *conieci*] spiritu sancto *B*      in sanctam ecclesiam *conieci*] sanctam ecclesiam catholicam *B*
8. symbolo *B Ca*] symbolum *L*      quia *L Ca*] qui *B*      naturam ipsam *Ca*] natura ipsa *BL*      quod habeat *L*] habeat *B*      ad filium ... ad creaturam *B Ca*] a filio ... a creatura *L*      spectat *Ca*] expectat *BL*

9. in symbolo *Ca*] symbolo *B*, in symbolum *L*    trahit *BL*] trahitur *coni.*
*Ca*    dicitur *B Ca*] deus *L*    eum *coni. Ca*] uni *BL*    humanae progeniem
*conieci*] humana progenie *BL Ca*    filius *conieci*] quia filius *BL, lacunam ante*
quia *coni. Ca*    dissipationem *L*] *spatium duodecim litterarum exhibit B*, dispensationem *Ca*    uirgine Maria *Ca*] uirginis Maria *L*, uirgine *B*    nasceretur *L*
*Ca*] nascetur *B*    suscipiens *B*] accipiens *L Ca*    dei filius *B*] filius dei *L*,
filius *Ca*

10. crede *Ca*] credo *BL*    deum deum *conieci*] deum *BL Ca*    homo agnoscitur *Ca*] agnoscitur *BL*    adnuntiat diaconus *L Ca*] *om. B*    uos et *B Ca*]
et uos *L*    repetunt ut supra *L Ca*] repetent sicut supernis *(?) B*    credo in
deum *B*] *om. L Ca*    et sequitur his uerbis *B*] sequitur haec dicta *L*, sequitur
hoc dicto *Ca*

11. apostolorumque *L Ca*] apostolorum *B*    symbolo *Ca*] symbolum *BL*
qui *conieci*] inquit *BL*, passus est inquit *coni. Ca*    sepultus *L Ca*] sepultus
est *B*    stultitia est *B*] stultitiam *L*, stultitia *Ca*    passionibus corporalibus
*B*] passionibus *L Ca*

12. factus *B Ca*] factum *L*    a morte *BL*] morte *Ca*    totam *L Ca*] totum
*B*

13. symbolo *Ca*] symbolum *BL*    caelis *B*] caelum *L Ca*    de caelo descendit *B*] descendit de caelo *L Ca*    misericordia *BL*] misericordiae *Ca*    uirtus
*conieci*] uirtutis *BL*    sedere *Ca*] sedentis *BL*    dextera *B Ca*] dexteram
*L*    subiciat *Ca*] subiaceant *BL*    diaconus ut supra *L Ca*] *om. B*    et
audite symbolum *B*] *om. L Ca*    et sicut supra *conieci*] sicut ut supra *B*, *om. L*

15. symbolo *Ca*] symbolum *BL*    spiritum sanctum *conieci*] spiritu sancto *BL*
*Ca*    sanctus spiritus *B*] spiritus sanctus *L Ca*    *ante* dominationis *lacunam*
*suspicor*

16. sanctam ecclesiam *Ca*] sancta ecclesia *BL*    in remissionem ... remissionem peccatorum *L*] in remissione peccatorum *B*, in remissionem ... remissione
peccatorum *Ca*

17. credite *B Ca*] creditur *L*    festiuitatem *Ca*] festiuitate *L*, festiuitatis
*B*    per multa *B Ca*] multa *L*    nostrum ... amen *L Ca*] *om. B*

The manuscript tradition of the anonymous *symbolum apostolorum*
CPL 1758

Three manuscripts were available to us for the edition of this
brief commentary on the Creed, one from Sankt Gallen (*G*; ninth
century) and two from Munich (*M* and *N*; tenth and twelfth centuries). All three offer a fairly correct text, although *N* omits some
portions towards the end. The only obvious errors that they have
in common are the accusative *animas* where a nominative is
required in *symbolum apostolorum* 7, and the meaningless *breuiarie*
in the introduction (Burn read *breuiare*; we have ventured the
emendation *breuiarii*).

There are two major differences between *G* on the one hand, and
*M* and *N* on the other. The first of these concerns the format of the
text. Whereas *MN* present the text as a continuous unit of alter-
nating credal quotations and commenting paragraphs, *G* has the
text of the Creed written out in large characters in the middle of
the page and offers the commentary in the form of marginal notes.
One peculiarity in the text of *M* and *N* suggests strongly that the
format of *G* was probably also the format of their direct ancestor,
and that it therefore may well be the original format of the text.
The fact is that *MN* omit the mention of the Holy Church immediately after the Holy Spirit in *symbolum apostolorum* 9 (the ensuing
commentary treats both, and thus secures the wording of *G* as the
correct one) and insert it at the wrong place in 10 (as is indicated
by the commentary again)[1]. Such a mistake can hardly be
explained by assuming that the original or originals of *MN* presented the text in the usual way, but a format like that of *G* would
account for it perfectly. This conclusion is supported by the observation that in *N*, the credal phrases have been written in larger
characters right across the width of the page, with the commentary
in between. In particular, the circumstance that *N* leaves some
open space between the commentary on the Communion of Saints
and the quotation of the words *Remissionem peccatorum*, and again

---

[1] In *N*, this is where the error stops - the Communion of Saints followed by its
proper commentary is mentioned after the Holy Church. In *M*, however, the
Communion of Saints is relegated to the next paragraph, that on the Remission
of Sins, and the Remission of Sins is transferred to the paragraph on the Resurrection of the Flesh.

between these and *Carnis resurrectionem*, strongly suggests that the articles of the Creed were copied first and the commentary inserted later. All this, together with the fact that *MN* relatively frequently unite against *G*, seems to allow the conclusion that the two manuscripts *MN* descend from a common original that must have resembled *G* quite closely. That *G* is not identical with that original is borne out by the readings *intellegi* and *affectum* (*symbolum apostolorum* 8 and 11) in *G*, where *MN* have the doubtless correct *intellegere* and *M* in addition offers the equally correct *affectu*.

The second important difference between *G* and *MN* comprises the fact that *G* offers a complete variant of the Apostles' Creed, whereas *MN* do not. These omissions, however, do not bear the same character in *M* and *N*. With regard to the former, the scribe of *M* was clearly not concerned with offering complete quotations of all articles. Sometimes he only copied the first words of one, clearly supposing that the reader knew the wording of the Creed by heart. Thus, he omits *Omnipotentem creatorem caeli et terrae* in *symbolum apostolorum* 2, *Filium eius unicum dominum nostrum* in 3, *De spiritu sancto natus ex Maria uirgine* in 4, *Pilato crucifixus mortuus et sepultus* in 5, and so on. *N*, on the other hand, apparently allotted each credal quotation to a single line, and only skipped those words that would otherwise exceed it. This seems to explain the omission of *Et terrae* in *symbolum apostolorum* 2, *Et sepultus* in 5, *A mortuis* in 6, and *Et mortuos* in 8 [2]. As *N* agrees with *G* in all other places where *M* omits parts of the Creed, the possibility that *N* directly derives from *M* seems to be excluded.

We propose, therefore, the following stemma:

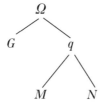

---

[2] Probably for the same reason, *N* abbreviates *patris omnipotentis* to $\overline{p}$ $\overline{o}$ in *symbolum apostolorum* 7.

There is only one earlier edition of the *symbolum apostolorum*,
which was presented by Burn in 1898 on the basis of *G* alone [3].
Although his edition is on the whole very accurate, Burn has overlooked the closing words of the commentary (from *fatemur*
onwards). At the bottom of the right margin of f. 691 of *G*, the
words *Absque ulla dubitatione* seem to close the commentary. In reality, however, the text continues at the top of the right margin of
the next page. The additional circumstances that the *Canticum
Simeonis* begins on that page, also accompanied by marginal notes,
and that in front of *fatemur* a capital *F* has been written [4] is probably the reason for Burn's misjudgement.

---

[3] Burn 1898, 184-186. A faithful reprint of Burn's text can be found in PLS 4,
1521-1522.

[4] Since, moreover, *Absque* lacks its capital in *G*, it seems safe to assume that
the rubricator had already made the same mistake as Burn here.

codices:

G   Sangallensis, Stiftsbibliothek 27, saec. IX, ff. 690-692
M   Monacensis, Bayerische Staatsbibliothek, Latinus 3729, ff. 307R-308V, saec. X
N   Monacensis, Bayerische Staatsbibliothek, Latinus 14501, ff. 204R-204V, saec. XII

editio:

Bu   BURN, A.E., 'Neue Texte zur Geschichte des apostolischen Symbols', in: *Zeitschrift für Kirchengeschichte* 19, 1898, 184-186 (= PLS 4, 1521-1522)

symbolum apostolorum CPL 1758

1. Symbolum est quod seniores nostri collationem ac pignus esse dixerunt. Inde collationem, quia sicut per Christum ex multis membris unum ecclesiae corpus effectum est (cf. Rom. 12, 5), ita et per discipulos Christi in unum breuiarii textum salutaria uerba collecta sunt.

2. Credo in deum patrem omnipotentem, creatorem caeli et terrae. Pater ergo per filium est, habens utique filium cuius sit pater. Omnipotens dicitur eo quod omnia potest. Creatorem caeli et terrae. Non enim aliquid esse potest cuius non sit creator, cum sit omnipotens.

3. Et in Iesum Christum, filius eius unicum dominum nostrum. Credens ergo in deum patrem statim te confiteberis credere et in filium eius Iesum Christum. Hic est filius dei.

4. Qui conceptus est de spiritu sancto, natus ex Maria uirgine. Natum de spiritu sancto dicit pro administratione spiritus sancti. Illo cooperante datus est filius ubi angelus ad Mariam dicit: *Spiritus sanctus superueniet in te,* et cetera (Luc. 1, 35).

5. Passus sub Pontio Pilato, crucifixus, mortuus et sepultus. Ideo Pontium Pilatum hic nominauit, ut nullus alius Christus credatur nisi ille qui sub Pontio Pilato crucifixus est. Quod autem crucifixus et mortuus legitur secundum hominem dictum est.

6. Descendit ad inferna, tertia die resurrexit a mortuis. Descendit utique non ut mortalium lege detineretur a morte (cf. Rom. 6, 9), sed ut ianuas mortis (cf. Ion. 2, 7) aperiret. Tertia die resurrexit ut nobis exemplum resurrectionis ostenderet.

7. Ascendit ad caelos, sedet ad dexteram dei patris omnipotentis. Ascendere pro parte carnis dicit, quia postquam ille ascendit animae sanctorum illic sursum ubi antea non fuerant modo ascenderunt. Dextera uita aeterna intellegitur, sinistra uita praesens.

8. Inde uenturus iudicare uiuos et mortuos. Ille iudicatus fuit a terra, ille iudicaturus est terram. Viuos dicit qui inuenti in carne fuerimus, mortuos qui iam longo tempore transierunt, uel uiuos sanctos possumus intellegere, mortuos id est peccatores.

9. Credo in spiritum sanctum, sanctam ecclesiam catholicam. In spiritum utique sanctum qui ex patre et filio procedit, qui patri et filio est coaequalis. Non dicit: Credo in sanctam ecclesiam, sed: Credo ipsam esse sanctam.

10. Sanctorum communionem. Id est cum illis sanctis qui in hac quam suscepimus fide defuncti sunt societate et spei communione teneamur.

11. Remissionem peccatorum. Oportet enim post remissionem quae nobis praestatur in baptismo ut plenae credulitatis teneamus affectum.

12. Carnis resurrectionem. Carnem quam in hac uita sub mortali condicione portamus, resurrecturam esse immortalem credamus (cf. I Cor. 15, 49 et 52-53).

13. Vitam aeternam, amen. Absque ulla dubitatione fatemur nos uitam aeternam consecuturos si haec quae exposita sunt sacramenta fideliter teneamus ac bonis operibus conseruemus.

apparatus criticus apud symbolum apostolorum CPL 1758

1. breuiarii *conieci*] breuiarie *GMN*, breuiare *Bu*     uerba collecta sunt *GM*] *om. N*

2. omnipotentem creatorem caeli et terrae *G*] omnipotentem creatorem caeli *N*, *om. M*     omnipotens *GM*] pater omnipotens *N*     dicitur *N*] *G* ds *an* dr *habeat incertum*, dicit *M*, deus *Bu*     omnia *GM*] omnium *N*     potest *MN*] potenst *G*

3. filium ... nostrum *GN*] *om. M*

4. de spiritu ... uirgine *GN*] *om. M*

5. Pilato crucifixus mortuus et sepultus *G*] Pilato crucifixus mortuus *N*, *om. M*

6. tertia die resurrexit a mortuis *G*] tertia die resurrexit *N*, *om. M*     resurrexit *GN*] resurrexit a mortuis *M*

7. sedet ... omnipotentis *GN*] *om. M*     quia *G*] qui *M*, quia *e* quam *N*     animae ... praesens] *om. N, exhibens spatium duarum linearum*     animae *conieci*] animas *GM Bu*     dextera ... sinistra *M*] dexteram ... sinistram *G Bu*

8. uenturus *GM*] uenturus est *N*      iudicare uiuos et mortuos *G*] iudicare uiuos *N*, *om. M*      a terra *GM*] a terra *ex* iterum *N*      dicit *N*] dt *G*, dixit *M*, dicitur *Bu*      fuerimus *G*] fuerint *MN*      intellegere *MN*] intellegi *G*

9. sanctam ... catholicam *G*] *om. MN*      et filio *GM*] filioque *N*      ipsam esse sanctam *GM*] in spiritum sanctum *N*

10. sanctorum communionem *G*] sanctam ecclesiam *M*, sanctam ecclesiam catholicam sanctorum communionem *N*

11. remissionem peccatorum *GN*] sanctorum communionem *M*      oportet ... affectum] *om. N, exhibens ante* resurrectionem peccatorum *spatium quattuor linearum et post trium*      affectu *M*] affectum *G*

12. carnis resurrectionem *GN*] remissionem peccatorum carnis resurrectionem *M*      uita *GN*] *om. M*

13. uitam aeternam amen *G*] uitam aeternam *M*, et uitam aeternam *N*      absque ... conseruemus] *om. N*      absque *M*] bsque *G*      fatemur ... conseruemus *M*] F fatemur ... conseruemus *G*, *om. Bu*

The manuscript tradition of the anonymous *sermo de symbolo* CPL 1759

Three manuscripts of this anonymous *sermo de symbolo* are known to us - two from the ninth century (*B* and *W*) and one from the tenth (*M*)[1]. On the basis of *M* alone, Burn offered the editio princeps in 1898[2]. Although the presence of *B* and *W* is of considerable help for the edition of the sermon, the constitution of an intelligible text is hindered by three circumstances.

First of all, the author does not everywhere seem to be concerned with offering his thoughts on the Creed in a logical way. Thus, the explanation of the mutual relationship between the three divine persons is rather enigmatic: *Per similitudinem rerum creaturarum cognoscitur creator, non ut creatura coniungatur creatori, sed sicut Paulus ait: Doceant terrena quae sunt caelestia, id est aqua, ignis, anima et sol. Sic pater et filius et spiritus sanctus: una diuinitas et una potestas est illis*[3]. Again, in the exposition of the word *Vnicum*, the author twice quotes the phrase *Vnicum **dominum** nostrum*, but explains why Jesus is called Only **Son**: *Vnicum dominum nostrum. Id est, quomodo dicit unicum dominum? Quia legimus in sacris scrip-*

---

[1] Of these, *WM* are identical with the manuscripts *W* and *M* of the *expositio de fide catholica* CPL 505.

[2] Burn 1898, 186-190. A fairly accurate reprint of this edition can be found in PLS 4, 2156-2159. After finishing his edition, Burn discovered *B* (see Burn 1909, 4) but this discovery has not been noted by later students of the text. Three other manuscripts that are mentioned by Burn in the same context (*ibid.*, n3) do not offer the anonymous *sermo de symbolo* but rather a related text. In one case, this concerns manuscript *Z* of the anonymous *expositio super symbolum* CPL 1760: see below, pp. 497-514). The other two manuscripts that are mentioned by Burn in this context are Monacensis Latinus 3909 and Sangallensis 676. In the first of these (ff. 23R-23V), we do indeed find an introduction to the Creed which makes use of the same simile as *sermo de symbolo* CPL 1759 (*Quicumque transmarinas partes transfretare uoluerint pecuniam hinc inde ad nauem congregant ...*), followed by a quotation of the several articles (*Petrus dixit: Credo ...*). No exposition ensues, however. The same introduction can also be seen in Zürich C 64, this time followed by the Creed as well as a commentary (ff. 1R-5V). An abbreviated version of this introduction, followed by the Creed but a different exposition, is offered by Sangallensis 40, ff. 322-325. Of the Creed forms, that in CLM 3909 is identical with *T*, but those in Zürich C 64 and Sangallensis 40 offer older variants. I encountered these texts too late, however, to include them in the present study.

[3] *Sermo de symbolo* 6; see below, p. 489.

*turis deum duos filios habuisse et sanctam Mariam similiter, eo quod et ipsa duos filios habuit ... Vnicum dominum nostrum, id est unicum dei patris dum et unicum sanctae Mariae, quia nec antea alium habuit nec postea ...* [4]. Similarly, we find a quotation of John 2, 19 in the exposition of the fifth article. This would be obvious enough in an explanation of the words *Tertia die*, but our anonymous author makes the quotation in support of his claim that Christ rose truly from the dead: ... *quia uera morte et uera resurrectione <resurrexit>, id est uerus deus et uerus homo, sicut in Euangelio ait: Destruite hoc templum et in tres dies suscitabo illud* [5]. Equally illogical is the quotation of Hos. 6, 3 (*Post biduum uisitabo uos et in die tertio resuscitabo uos*) in the explanation of the phrase *Viuos ac mortuos:* ... *uiuos: qui uiuunt in anima deo, et mortuos: qui mortui sunt peccato, sicut dixit propheta: Post biduum ...* [6]. Finally, when the author comes to the ninth article, he tackles the question of why the Holy Spirit is not mentioned at an earlier point in the Creed. His answer is, to say the least, rather rambling: *Credo in spiritum sanctum. Quando superius nominauit patrem et filium, cur nunc (non B; om. WM) dixit spiritum sanctum? Sed mos est scripturae ex ordine narrare, sicut et antea uoluit narrare de sua natiuitate et de sua passione, postea uero de sua ascensione. Sed ubi inuenis unam personam totas tres personas intellege. Sed merito sic erat ut spiritus sanctus iuxta ipsam creaturam positus esset, unde illa creatura illuminata est. Sic sequitur: Sanctam ecclesiam catholicam* [7]. All this leaves the impression that the author has pieced together several fragments of credal exegesis, but without caring too much about the coherence of his product [8].

---

[4] *Sermo de symbolo* 10; see below, p. 490. Unless the author means 'as both God and Mary had more than one son, *Vnicum* can only apply to *Dominum*'. But this ill accords with the closing words of our quotation.

[5] *Sermo de symbolo* 17; see below, p. 491.

[6] *Sermo de symbolo* 19; see below, p. 491. The quotation of Hosea could make sense at an earlier place in the commentary, viz. after the possible explanation *Viuos: tunc qui corporaliter uiuunt, et mortuos: qui ab initio mortui sunt.* In that case, the two verbs *uisitabo* and *resuscitabo* could be taken to refer to God's activity towards the living and the dead respectively.

[7] *Sermo de symbolo* 20; see below, p. 491.

[8] The end of the introduction (on the meaning of the word *symbolum*) is not very logical either, but this may be due to a gloss: see below, p. 485. With regard to *sermo de symbolo* 22-23, see the discussion of the underlying form of the Creed in chapter 4.12, p. 373.

Next, the anonymous author's Latin is rather different from classical standards. He consistently uses the auxiliaries *debere* (*ubi eorum pecunia multiplicare debeat, futurum est ut pseudochristi... surgere debeant* [9]) and *habere* (*omnes homines resurgere habent* [10]) to form the future, and uses the active infinitive of the present to express the passive as well (see the examples above; also *quia non potest dicere pater* and *tamen hoc ... cum cautela dicere debet* [11]). He also clearly experiences some difficulties when trying to write more elaborate periods, which results in an abundant use of *hoc, id est, sed, sic,* and *ille.* For example: *Hoc curiose inquiri solet quis ..., hoc nostrum non est ad discernendum quis ...* [12]; *Omnipotentem. Id est, omnipotens dicitur quia ..., Vnicum dominum nostrum. Id est, quomodo dicit ...* [13]; *Natum de spiritu sancto et Maria uirgine. Quomodo dicit? Dum superius diximus: Credo in deum patrem, numquid filius duos patres habuit? Sed non, absit a nobis sic credere, sed spiritu sancto cooperante et administrante, uel pro sanctificatione uteri uirginis Mariae, sic natus est filius dei* [14]; *illum portum ubi, illas animas quae ... illas dominus secum traxit* [15]). In itself, this is of course no problem at all, but in combination with the sometimes absolutely barbarous Latin of the manuscripts, it creates a serious difficulty for the constitution of the text. The fact is that *B, W,* and *M* freely interchange *u* and *o, e* and *i,* as well as the endings *-am* and *-a, -em* and *-e,* and *-um* and *o.* The resulting confusion between dative, accusative, and ablative, in combination with other errors and the author's typical style, renders interpretation of the sermon rather exacting at times.

A third difficulty is constituted by the fact that none of the three manuscripts seems to present a text that has escaped more serious mutilation. Thus, in the section on the origin of the Creed, this is styled a *collatio bonorum operum* in all three manuscripts. But the

---

[9] *Sermo de symbolo* 1 and 14; see below, pp. 488 and 490.

[10] *Sermo de symbolo* 25; see below, p. 492.

[11] *Sermo de symbolo* 5 and 8; see below, p. 489.

[12] *Sermo de symbolo* 4; see below, p. 489.

[13] *Sermo de symbolo* 8 and 10; see below, pp. 489 and 490.

[14] *Sermo de symbolo* 12; see below, p. 490. See also the quotation from § 20 above, p. 481.

[15] *Sermo de symbolo* 1 and 16; see below, pp. 488 and 491.

Creed is, of course, not 'a collection of good works' [16]. Next, in the exposition of the first article, the obviously corrupt words *sed tamen a pluris incertum est* are found in all three manuscripts [17]. Again, the phrase *spiritus sanctus ab utriusque procedens* is offered unanimously, but it is clear that it should be emended in some way or another [18]. Similarly, in the phrase *Sed nos omnipotentes non sumus*, all three manuscripts exhibit the superfluous words *mori falli* after *nos* (*nossim mori falli B*; *nos qui mori falli possumus WM*) [19]. Again, at the end of the exposition of the second article, one should probably read *noster quia de nostra natura accepit humanitatem* [20], but all three manuscripts omit the indispensable *natura*: *de nostra accepit M, de nostrum accepit W, nostra accepit B*. Finally, when the author reflects on the fate of the just and the unjust after the Resurrection of the Flesh, we read: *Modo anima gloriatur apud deum, sed post iudicium corpus* (*et corpus B*) *et anima. Similiter* (*om. B*) *modo et a* (*ad M*; *om. B*) *peccatoribus duplicatur eorum poena, quia modo anima cruciatur* (*cruciat W*) *, sed postea anima et corpus* (*et corpus et anima B*) [21]. Here, it is clear that something like *poena exigitur, sed tunc* is missing before *duplicatur*.

When we turn to the relationship between the three witnesses *B*, *W* and *M*, then, one glance at the critical apparatus already strongly suggests that *B* represents one branch of the tradition and *WM* another. First of all, *B* seems to offer a better reading in the following examples:

*negotiatores* and *natonis* (as an abbreviation for *negotiationis*) in *sermo de symbolo* 1 (*WM*: *nautones/ nautores*)
*autem unusquisque* (*ibid.*; *W*: *autem autem*, *M*: *unusquisque*)

---

[16] *Sermo de symbolo* 3; see below, p. 489. The most obvious explanation is that we should read *bonorum* ('a collection of good things'), which either intentionally or not was expanded to the more usual *bonorum operum*.

[17] *Sermo de symbolo* 4; see below, p. 489. We have emended *a pluris incertum* to *apostolus is incertus*.

[18] *Sermo de symbolo* 7; see below, p. 489. We have inserted *natura* after *utriusque*.

[19] *Sermo de symbolo* 8; see below, p. 490.

[20] *Sermo de symbolo* 11; see below, p. 490.

[21] *Sermo de symbolo* 25; see below, p. 492.

*quaditur* (for *quatitur*) in 2 (*M*: *patitur*, *W*: *portatur* [22])
*regit et gubernat* (*ibid.*; *WM*: *regit*)
*inquiri solent* in 4 (*WM*: *inquirere uolunt*) [23]
*quia* in 10 (*W*: *qui*, corrected to *quae* in *M*)
*ad inferos* in 15 (*W*: *adferos*, *M*: *ad inferna*)
*humanitas ubi animae corpus* in 16 (*W*: *et anima corpus*, *M*: *et
anima et corpus*) [24]
*ait* in 17 (omitted in *WM*)
*peccato* in 19 (*W*: *peccati*, omitted in *M*: see the critical apparatus
for more details)
*cur non* [25] in 20 (*WM*: *cur*)
*id* in 22 (*WM*: *ita*)
*pertinent* [26] (*ibid.*; omitted in *WM*)
*moriuntur boni moriuntur* in 25 (*WM*: *moriuntur*).

On the other hand, *WM* seem to be closer to the truth in the
following cases:

*habet* in *sermo de symbolo* 1 (*B*: *mittit*)
*lignum ... saluatur* in 2 (omitted in *B*)
*et haeretici ... esse* in 5 (omitted in *B*)
*creaturarum cognoscitur creator* in 6 (*B*: *creator*)
*quia omnia potens est* in 8 (*B*: *qui omnipotens est*)
*tria supradicta* (*ibid.*; *B*: *tria*)
*quia fuerunt aliae Mariae* in 13 (omitted in *B*)
*quare commemorat* in 14 (*B*: *cur commendat*)
*tempore Pilati* (*Pilato W*) (*ibid.*; *B*: *timore Pilato*)
*anima* in 16 (*B*: *omnia*)
*sedet ... caelos* in 18 (omitted in *B*)
*inde uenturus est ... tunc* in 19 (the same)
*et ipse rex uel potens* in 23 (the same).

---

[22] This looks most like an independent correction.
[23] The reading of *B* is probably to be emended into *inquiri solet*; that of *WM*
is either a further corruption or a correction.
[24] The reading of *B* is obviously corrupt, but in any case better than those of
*W* and *M*: *humanitas* seems to be indispensable, and *animae* is easily emended to
*anima et*.
[25] A probable corruption of *cur nunc*.
[26] Probably to be corrected to *pertinentes*.

Since there are no instances where either *BW* or *BM* share an unmistakable and not too common error, the conclusion seems safe that *B* and *WM* indeed constitute the two main branches of the tradition here.

As far as the relationship between *W* and *M* is concerned, it may be observed that both *W* and *M* sometimes contain a number of words or even complete phrases that are missing in the other manuscript. Some of these omissions are unmistakable errors. Among these are the following cases.

Omissions in *M*:

> *ipse sit pater ipse filius (ipse ...)* in *sermo de symbolo* 5 [27]
> *debeant contra fidem ecclesiae. Tunc ecclesia dicit quia non* in 14
> (*Inde uenturus est iudicare uiuos et mortuos.*) *Inde uenturus est: de prosperitate uitae aeternae uenturus est. Iudicare uiuos et mortuos.* (*Viuos: qui tunc ...*) in 19 [28]

Omission in *W*:

> (*... narrare,*) *sicut et antea uoluit narrare* in *sermo de symbolo* 20 [29]

There are, however, also a number of cases in which the words that are presented by only one manuscript look more like glosses or secondary additions than otherwise. The instances in question are the following. In the introduction, we read *Sed hoc inquirendum est quid (quod M) intellegitur per istam (ista B) similitudinem* [30]. Here, *W* adds *mare uel nauis et reliqua* after *intellegitur*. This is not only ungrammatical (it duplicates *per istam similitudinem*), but also superfluous, since the text immediately continues with the explanation *Per mare mundus intellegitur ... per nauem sancta ecclesia*, and so on. Similarly, the author states that it is useless to wonder which Apostle laid the foundation of the Creed by saying *Credo in deum*, since ... *toti perfecti et honorandi (honorati M) sunt apud deum* [31]. *W*

---

[27] *W* adds *spiritus* before *sit pater*. The omission in *M* is obviously caused by the anaphora of *ipse*.

[28] The care with which the author treats each single element of the Creed vouches for the originality of the phrase in *BW*, whereas its omission is easily explained by the repetition of *Viuos ac mortuos*.

[29] The twofold occurrence of *narrare* is clearly the cause of the omission.

[30] *Sermo de symbolo* 2; see below, p. 488.

[31] *Sermo de symbolo* 4; see below, p. 489.

adds *excepto Iuda proditore*, but this is illogical, as Judas was of course not among the Apostles who, according to the legend, composed the Creed. Finally, at the beginning of the commentary on the second article, the author asks: *Quomodo dicit in Iesum credere? Quia Iesus filius fuit Naue?* and goes on to state: *Absit ut in hominem purum* (*in hominem puro* B, *homine puro* W, *in homine porro* M) *debeat credere, quia dixit* ...[32]. In *M*, we find the words *magis quam in deum* added after *credere* and *ipse* before *dixit*. Not only are these words unnecessary, but the fact that *B* and *W* omit both the phrase *magis quam in deum* and the pronoun *ipse* strongly suggests that these are not original.

This brings us to the conclusion that at some point in the manuscript tradition marginal or supralinear notes were added to the text, some of which found their way into *W* and some of which into *M*. The question is how can *W* contain two later additions to the text which are absent from *M*, whereas *M* has a similar addition which is absent from *W*. This can hardly be due to the separate glossing activities of the scribes, as we know that *M* had access to *W* or at least a very similar manuscript for the anonymous *expositio de fide catholica* (CPL 505), though it used another manuscript of that text as well[33]. On the other hand, *W* itself does not betray the glosses it contains as such. Therefore, it seems most natural to assume that *M* is also a contaminated witness for the anonymous *sermo de symbolo* CPL 1759[34]. If this assumption is anywhere near the truth, *M* will have made critical use of two manuscripts for the text of our anonymous *sermo de symbolo*, both of which contained a different set of additions to, and possibly also omissions from, the original text. This again implies that its two originals, one of which was probably *W*, already contained a deliberately selected set of additions. In other words, the additions must have been recogniz-

---

[32] *Sermo de symbolo* 9; see below, p. 490.

[33] See above, pp. 433-434.

[34] The considerable number of reasonably sound corrections in *M* (*qui* into *quae* in *sermo de symbolo* 10 [the correct reading, offered by *B*, is probably *quia*, but *quae* is certainly better than the ungrammatical *qui*], *sanctificationis* into *sanctificatione* in 12, *haec* into *hoc* in 16, *dicam* into *dicat* in 16, and so on) can be taken to support this hypothesis, especially as, in the light of the many remaining barbarisms in *M*, these corrections can hardly have been the independent work of its scribe.

able as such in the archetype of these two originals, so that each could choose in every individual case whether or not to incorporate a certain addition.

This means that we may draw the following stemma:

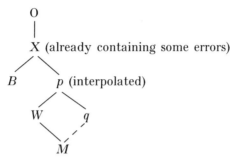

We may conclude that the consensus of $W$ with $B$ or that of $M$ with $B$ will probably yield the best reading in most cases. Where one of the three witnesses is absent, the two remaining ones should be regarded as having equal value for the constitution of the text, so that we should then decide on intrinsic grounds which may present the correct reading where they part ways. Finally, because $X$ must already have contained a good number of errors, some conjectures of our own will remain inevitable.

codices:

*B* Bibliotheca Apostolica Vaticana, Barberinianus Latinus 671, ff. 157R-160R, saec. IX

*W* Guelferbytanus, Herzog-Augustbibliothek 91, ff. 106V-111R, saec. IX

*M* Monacensis, Bayerische Staatsbibliothek, Latinus 14508, ff. 67R-70R, saec. X

editiones:

*Bu1* Burn, A.E., 'Neue Texte zur Geschichte des apostolischen Symbols', in: *Zeitschrift für Kirchengeschichte* 19, 1898, 186-190

*Bu2* PLS 4, 2156-2159

*Bu* consensus harum editionum

coniecturae:

*Pa* coniecturae ineditae a Martino Parmentier propositae

sermo de symbolo CPL 1759

1. Dum de symbolo conferre uolumus, hoc inquirendum est nobis symbolum in cuius lingua nuncupetur. Symbolum in Graeca dicitur lingua quod in Latino sonat collatio siue congregatio pecuniae. Augustinus dicit quod hoc per similitudinem intellegitur. Negotiatores quando in partibus marinis transmeare conantur nauem emunt et ibidem negotiationis constituunt tractores et gubernatorem et mittunt pecuniam. Pecunias autem unusquisque quas habet mittit, alius plus, alius minus et sic ut uelit saluam facere ille qui minus habet quantum ille qui plus. Postea pergunt ad illum portum ubi eorum pecunia multiplicare debeat. 2. Sed hoc inquirendum est quid intellegitur per istam similitudinem. Id est, per mare mundus intellegitur, per nauem sancta ecclesia, quia sicut nauis in mari fluctibus quatitur, sic ecclesia in praesenti uita tribulationes sustinet. Per negotiatores et tractores intelleguntur apostoli uel imitatores eorum, per gubernatorem Christus qui regit et gubernat ecclesiam suam. Per pecuniam collatam bonorum apostolorum intellegere possumus hos duodecim uersiculos. Per lignum nauis per quod saluatur pecunia intellegitur lignum crucis per quam saluatur ecclesia. Illi negotiatores tendunt ad illum portum ubi saluentur, ita et sancti apostoli uel imitatores apostolorum (cf. I Cor. 4, 16 et 11, 1. Phil.

3, 17. I Thess. 1, 6 et 2, 14) festinant ad portum uitae aeternae ubi eorum merces multiplicare uel crescere debeat. 3. Et aliam similitudinem dixit. Duo reges antequam iungantur ad proelium unusquisque suum signum ponit. Sic ecclesia in primordio quando coepit florere in fide, tunc semina haereticorum pullulabant. Sed cum essent sancti apostoli in unum congregati antequam in mundo dispersi essent in praedicationem sic fecerunt istam collationem bonorum et posuerunt signum inter Christianos et haereticos ut per hoc cognoscerent quis esset Christianus uel quis haereticus, ut istos uersiculos duodecim unusquisque Christianus memoriter tenere debeat.

4. Credo in deum. Hoc curiose inquiri solet quis istum uersum de sanctis apostolis primus cantasset, sed tamen apostolus is incertus est quia hoc non narrat historia. Tamen scimus quia toti perfecti et honorandi sunt apud deum. Hoc nostrum non est ad discernendum quis primus, maior merito, ut istum uersum cantasset. Sed qui dixit bene dixit: Credo in deum. 5. Nos credimus in deum patrem. Et haeretici credunt patrem esse. In hoc credunt patrem haeretici pro eo quod pater est omnium creaturarum uel quia hominem fecit. Non credunt quod habeat filium naturae sicut nos credimus, quia non potest dicere pater nisi habeat filium, nec filius nisi habeat patrem. Ipsi haeretici sic dicunt quod ipse sit pater, ipse filius, ipse et spiritus sanctus. Qui sic dixit anathematizatus est inter populum Christianum. 6. Sed nos sic credimus sicut alius auctor dixit: Deus pater, deus filius, deus et spiritus sanctus. Personis ac nominibus distinguuntur, sed una diuinitas et una potestas est illis. Per similitudinem rerum creaturarum cognoscitur creator, non ut creatura coniungatur creatori, sed, sicut Paulus ait, doceant terrena quae sunt caelestia (cf. I Cor. 15, 36-48), id est aqua, ignis, anima et sol. Sic pater et filius et spiritus sanctus: una diuinitas et una potestas est illis. 7. Sed dum ipsi haeretici sic dicunt quod ipse sit pater, ipse filius, ipse et spiritus sanctus, hoc inquirendum est si habeat pater quod non habeat filius, aut filius quod non habeat pater, aut spiritus sanctus quod nec pater nec filius habeat. Habent propria, id est nomina et personas. Pater dicitur eo quod habeat filium, filius dicitur eo quod habeat patrem, spiritus sanctus ab utriusque natura procedens, quia toti tres coaeterni et coaequales sibi sunt in regendo et gubernando et dominando et sustinendo rerum creaturarum. 8. Omnipotentem. Id est, omnipotens dicitur quia omnia potens est. Tamen hoc ad brutos et indoctos cum cautela dicere debet ne forte

dum tu dicis in bene, ille non recipiat in malum, dum tu dicis:
Omnipotens, ille dicit: Non omnipotens, quia deus tres non potest,
mori, falli uel peccare. Quare non potuit? Quia non uoluit nec
potuit. Et si ista tria supradicta potuisset omnipotens non esset.
Sed nos omnipotentes non sumus, quia ista supradicta facere possumus.

9. Et in Iesum Christum, filium eius. Quomodo dicit in Iesum
credere? Quia Iesus filius fuit Naue (cf. Ios. 1, 1 et al.)? Absit ut
in hominem purum debeat credere, quia dixit: *Maledictus homo qui
in hominem ponit spem suam* (Ier. 17, 5), et alibi: *Benedictus uir qui
confidit in domino* (Ier. 17, 7). Sed nos in Iesum Christum filium eius
credimus, uerum deum et uerum hominem et cetera. 10. Vnicum
dominum nostrum. Id est, quomodo dicit unicum dominum? Quia
legimus in sacris scripturis deum duos filios habuisse et sanctam
Mariam similiter, eo quod et ipsa duos filios habuit. Deus: ut legimus: *Adae, qui fuit dei* (Luc. 3, 38). Et sancta Maria: legimus de illo
discipulo quem Iesus amauit plurimum. Cum esset in cruce dixit:
*Mulier, ecce filius tuus, et ad illum discipulum: Ecce mater tua. Et
suscepit eam in suam* (Ioh. 19, 26-27). Vnicum dominum nostrum,
id est unicum dei patris dum et unicum sanctae Mariae, quia nec
antea alium habuit nec postea, quia uirgo ante partum et uirgo post
partum. 11. Dominus dicitur eo quod dominatur suam creaturam,
noster quia de nostra natura accepit humanitatem.

12. Natum de spiritu sancto et Maria uirgine. Quomodo dicit?
Dum superius diximus: Credo in deum patrem, numquid filius duos
patres habuit? Sed non, absit a nobis sic credere, sed spiritu sancto
cooperante et administrante, uel pro sanctificatione uteri uirginis
Mariae, sic natus est filius dei. 13. Et Maria uirgine. Id est, distinctionem facit inter Mariam et Marias, quia fuerunt aliae Mariae non
uirgines, sed ista Maria uirgo ante partum et uirgo post partum.

14. Passus sub Pontio Pilato. Quare commemorat hominem
cruentum uel tam pessimum? Propter hoc illum commemorat, quia
futurum est ut *pseudochristi et pseudoprophetae* siue apostoli *surgere
debeant* (Matth. 24, 24. Marc. 13, 22. cf. II Cor. 11, 13) contra fidem
ecclesiae. Tunc ecclesia dicit quia non credit alium Christum nisi
illum qui sub tempore Herodis est natus et sub tempore Pilati est
passus. 15. Crucifixus et sepultus, descendit ad inferos. Id est, crucifixus dominus sicut dixit propheta: *Ipse infirmitates nostras accepit
et aegrotationes nostras portauit* (Is. 53, 4). Sed dum dicit: Crucifixus,

quia legimus quod diuinitas attraxit humanitatem, non humanitas diuinitatem, sic sustinuit diuinitas passionem? Non, sed humanitas. Per similitudinem intellegitur, id est: arbor stans in platea inciditur et radius solis in scissura intrat et sol illaesus permanet. Ita et diuinitas illaesa et impassibilis permansit, quia humanitatem caedebant et diuinitati non nocebant. 16. Descendit ad inferos. Hoc inquirendum est ubi fuit diuinitas, ubi humanitas, ubi anima et corpus? Corpus in sepulcro, diuinitas in caelo, anima simul cum diuinitate triumphauit. Ad inferos, quia illas animas quae sub debito Adae erant detentae, illas dominus secum traxit, sicut dixit propheta: *O mors, ero mors tua, ero morsus tuus, o inferne* (Hos. 13, 14). Sicut sanctus Gregorius dixit: Ac si dicat: Partem momordit et partem reliquit: Partem momordit, quia nullum de electis suis ibidem reliquit, partem reliquit, id est infidelium, et fortis est captus a domino fortiore (cf. 11, 21-22), id est diabolus.

17. Tertia die resurrexit a mortuis, quia uera morte et uera resurrectione resurrexit, id est uerus deus et uerus homo, sicut in Euangelio ait: *Destruite hoc templum et in tres dies suscitabo illud. Ipse dicebat de templo corporis sui* (Ioh. 2, 19 et 21). 18. Ascendit ad caelos, sedet ad dexteram dei patris. Ascendit ad caelos. Hoc est, super sanctos angelos exaltauit humanitatem. Sedet ad dexteram patris. Id est, in prosperitate uitae aeternae. 19. Inde uenturus iudicare uiuos ac mortuos. Inde uenturus est: de prosperitate uitae aeternae uenturus est. Iudicare uiuos ac mortuos. Viuos: tunc qui corporaliter uiuunt, et mortuos: qui ab initio mortui sunt. Aliter, uiuos: qui uiuunt in anima deo, et mortuos: qui mortui sunt peccato, sicut dixit propheta: *Post biduum uisitabo uos et in die tertio resuscitabo uos* (Hos. 6, 3).

20. Credo in spiritum sanctum. Quando superius nominauit patrem et filium, cur nunc dixit spiritum sanctum? Sed mos est scripturae ex ordine narrare, sicut et antea uoluit narrare de sua natiuitate et de sua passione, postea uero de sua ascensione. Sed ubi inuenis unam personam totas tres personas intellege. Sed merito sic erat ut spiritus sanctus iuxta ipsam creaturam positus esset, unde illa creatura illuminata est. Sic sequitur: Sanctam ecclesiam catholicam. 21. Hoc inquirendum est, spiritus sanctus proprie quid sit? Hoc est caritas quae est inter patrem et filium, id est dilectio, sicut Paulus ait: *Quia caritas dei diffusa est in cordibus nostris per spiritum sanctum qui datus est nobis* (Rom. 5, 5).

22. Sanctam ecclesiam catholicam, remissionem peccatorum. Non dixit: In sanctam ecclesiam catholicam, sed: Credo sanctam ecclesiam catholicam. Id est uniuersalis ecclesia in toto mundo diffusa. Dum dicit: Catholica est ecclesia, non catholicae haereticorum ecclesiae sunt, quia illae non sunt uniuersales, sed extremis partibus uel locis pertinentes. 23. Per similitudinem potest intellegere. Homo quando mittit legatarium ad regem uel ad potentes, et ipse rex uel potens qui est exornat domum suam de auro uel de argento, sedet hic legatarius non ad illud aurum sed ad habitatorem declinat. Sic et nos non creaturam sed creatorem, non habitaculum sed habitatorem adoramus, hoc est Christum. 24. Credimus remissionem peccatorum, quia ubi est consortium sanctorum, ibi est remissio peccatorum. 25. Carnis resurrectionem. Ostendit uera prima resurrectione quia omnes homines resurgere habent cum corporibus suis. Moriuntur boni, moriuntur et mali. Accipiunt boni, accipiunt et mali. Boni accipiunt stolas (cf. Apoc. 7, 9-14 et 22, 14) et mali accipiunt poenas. Modo anima gloriatur apud deum, sed post iudicium corpus et anima. Similiter modo et a peccatoribus * * * duplicatur eorum poena, quia modo anima cruciatur, sed postea anima et corpus. Et tunc iusti gloriabuntur cum domino in saecula saeculorum (cf. Apoc. 22, 5). Amen.

apparatus criticus apud sermonem de symbolo CPL 1759

sermo de symbolo *Bu2*] incipit explanatio symboli *B, deest titulus in WM Bu1*
1. uolumus hoc *B*] uoluimus *W*, uolumus *M*      est nobis symbolum *WM*] nobis
$^{est}$ *B*      nuncupetur *WM*] nuncupatur *B*      in Graeca dicitur lingua *B*] Graecum est *WM*      Latino *M*] Latinum *BW*      dicit *BW*] dixit *M*      quod hoc
*B*] quod *WM*      intellegitur *B*] intelleguntur *WM*      negotiatores *B*] nautones *W*, nautores *M*      in partibus *WM*] partibus *B*      emunt *WM*] eme$^u$nt
*B*      negotiationis *conieci*] natonis *B*, nautones *W*, nautores *M*      gubernatorem et *conieci*] gubernatores *BWM*      pecuniam pecunias *conieci*] pecuniam
*B*, pecunias *WM*      autem unusquisque *B*] autem autem *W*, unusquisque
*M*      quas habet mittit *WM*] quantum quod habent mittunt *B*      sic ut uelit
*conieci*] sic uelit *B*, sic uellet *W*, sic uult *M*      saluam *WM*] saluum *B*
habet *WM*] mittit *B*      quantum *WM*] quamtum et *B*, et quantum *Bu*
pecunia multiplicare debeat *BW*] pecuniam multiplicare debeant *M*
2. quid *BW*] quod *M*      intellegitur *BM*] intellegitur mare uel nauis et reliqua
*W*      istam *WM*] ista *B*      id est per mare *BM*] per mare *W*      mundus
intellegitur *W*] mundus *B*, mund<u>s</u> $^{istius\ mundi}$ *M*      quia *WM*] qui *B*      mari
*conieci*] mare *BWM*      quatitur *conieci*] quaditur *B*, portatur *W*, patitur
*M*      ecclesia *WM*] sancta $^{ecclesia}$ *B*      tribulationes *WM*] tribulatione
*B*      negotiatores *conieci*] nautores *BM*, nautones *W*      et *WM*] uel *B*

intelleguntur *WM*] intellegitur *B*      Christus *WM*] Christum *B*      regit et gubernat *B*] regit *WM*      collatam *BW*] collata *M*      possumus *W*] possimus *BM*      hos ... uersiculos *W Burn*] haec ... uersiculos *B*, haec ... uersiculis *M*      quod *coni. Bu*] quo *BWM*      lignum ... saluatur] *om. B*      quam *W*] quo *M*, quod *coni. Bu*      negotiatores *conieci*] nautores *BM*, nautones *W*      merces *M*] mercis *BW*      debeat *WM*] debea<sup>n</sup>t *B*      3. et aliam *conieci*] aliam *BWM*      similitudinem dixit *WM*] dixit similitudinem *B*      suum signum *M*] suo signum *B*, sui signum *W*      sic *BW*] si *M*      pullulabant *BW*] pullulabat *M*, pullalat *Bu*      mundo *WM*] mundum *B*      istam collationem *conieci*] ista collatio *B*, ista collata *W*, istam consolatam *M*      bonorum *B*] bonorum operum *WM*      signum *WM*] signa *B*      uel quis *W*] uel qui *BM*, ut qui *Bu, lacunam indicans post* qui      istos uersiculos *WM*] istut uersiculus *B*
4. curiose *BW*] curiosius *M*      inquiri solet *conieci*] inquiri solent *B*, inquirere uolunt *WM*      primus *WM*] prius *B*      apostolus is incertus *conieci*] a pluris incertum *BWM*      quia hoc *WM*] quia *B*      honorandi *BW*] honorati *M*      deum *BM*] deum excepto Iuda proditore *W*      primus *WM*] prius *B*      istum uersum *WM*] in isto uerso *B*      cantasset *WM*] cantasset *e* casta sit *B*
5. et haeretici ... esse] *om. B*      et haeretici *conieci*] haeretici *WM*      in hoc credunt *BW*] N credimus *M*, credimus *Bu, lacunam ante* credimus *indicans*      haeretici *WM*] haeretice *B*      pater est *BW*] pater *M*      quia *B*] qui *WM*      quod *B*] ut *WM*      filium naturae *BW*] naturae *M*      habeat filium *BW*] habeas filium *M*      patrem *WM*] pater *B*      ipse sit *B*] ipse spiritus sit *W*      ipse sit ... filius] *om. M*      ipse et spiritus *WM*] ipse spiritus *B*      populum Christianum *BM*] populo Christiano *W*
6. alius *BW*] aliquis *M*      dixit *WM*] sic dixit *B*      deus et spiritus *WM*] deus spiritus *B*      personis ac *W*] personis hac *B*, personae his *M*      et una potestas est illis *B*] est illis et una potestas *WM*      creaturarum cognoscitur creator *WM*] cognoscitur *B*      creatura coniungatur creatori *Pa*] creator cognoscat creatore *B*, creatura coniungat a creatore *W*, creatura coniungat creatorem *M*      doceant *BW*] docent *M*      quae *WM*] quo *B*      caelestia *BWM*] accaelestia *Bu*      ignis *coni. Bu*] igne *BWM*      et sol *BWM*] sol *Bu*
7. ipsi *BW*] ipse *M*      ipse et *W*] ipse *BM*      hoc inquirendum ... sanctus] *om. B*      hoc *conieci*] sed hoc *W*, sed *M*      si habeat *conieci*] si non *B*, si non habet *WM*      propria *BW*] proprie *M*      nomina et *BW*] nomina *M*      utriusque natura *conieci*] utriusque *BWM*      toti *WM*] totae *B*      coaeterni *M*] coaeternae *B*, quo aeterni *W*      coaequales *W*] aequales *B*, quo aequales *M*
8. omnipotentem *B*] omnipotenti *WM*      id est *WM*] quod *B*      dicitur *BW*] deus *M*      quia omnia potens est *WM*] qui omnipotens est *B*      hoc ad brutos et indoctos *M*] abrutus et indoctus *B*, hoc ab inbrutus et indoctis *W*      dicere debet *WM*] dici debent *B*      dum *BW*] cum *M*      non recipiat *BW*] recipiat *M*      tu dicis *B*] dicis *M*, dicit *W*      Quare ... nec potuit. Et si ... esset *transposui*] Et si ... esset. Quare .. nec potuit *BWM*      tria supradicta *WM*] tria *B*      nos *conieci*] nossim mori falli *B*, nos qui possumus mori falli *WM*      omnipotentes *WM*] omnipotentis *B*      supradicta *BM*] supra *W*      possumus *BM*] possimus *W*

9. filium eius *WM*] filium *B*     Naue *BWM*] nam *Bu*     in hominem purum *conieci*] in hominem puro *B*, homine puro *W*, in homine porro *M*, in hominem porro *Bu*     credere quia *BW*] credere magis quam in deum quia ipse *M*     in hominem *(*homine *M)* ponit spem suam *WM*] spem suam ponit in homine *B*     Iesum Christum *BW*] Iesum *M*     filium eius *WM*] filium *B*     uerum hominem *WM*] uirum hominem *B*

10. id est *WM*] *om. B*, id est si *Bu*     deum *M*] deus *B*, deo *W*     habuisse et *W*] habuisset et *B*, habuisse̊et *M*     sanctam Mariam *M*] sancta Maria *BW*     eo quod *B*] quod *WM*     duos filios *BW*] duos *M*     Adae qui *WM*] qui *B*     Iesus *WM*] dominus Iesus *B*     plurimum *WM*] plurimus *B*     illum discipulum *Bu*] illo discipulo *BWM*     id est *BM*] id es *W*     unicum *W*] unicus *B*, cum *M*     dum et *WM*] dum in *B*     quia *B*] qui *W*, quae *e* qui *M*, quae *Bu*     antea alium *M*] ante alium *W*, ante nec aliim nec *B*     uirgo post *WM*] post *B*

11. dicitur *B*] dicetur *W*, deus *M*     dominatur *BW*] dominator *M*     suam creaturam *W Bu*] sua creatura *B*, suam creaturum *M*     noster *W*] nostrae *(uel* naturae *?) B*, nostrum *M*     de nostra natura *conieci*] nostra *B*, de nostrum *W*, de nostra *M*     humanitatem *BW*] humanitate *M*

12. et Maria uirgine *M Bu1*] et Maria uirginem *B*, et Mariam uirginem *W*, de Maria uirgine *Bu2*     dicit *B*] dicimus *WM*     deum patrem *B*] deo patri *WM*     duos patres *WM*] quos patris *B*     habuit sed non *conieci*] habuisset non *BW*, habuit si n *(*n *in margine) M*     a nobis *B*] nobis *WM*     cooperante *WM*] quo operante *B*     et administrante *Bu*] administrante *B*, et aministrante *W*, et abministrante *M*     sanctificatione *B Bu*] sanctificationis *W*, sanctificatione *e* sanctificationis *M*     uteri *Pa*] uteris *B*, uterum *WM*     natus est *WM*] natus sit *B*

13. et *BW*] ex *M*     uirgine *WM*] uirginem *B*     id est *BM*] idem *W*     facit *BW*] fecit *M*     Mariam *M*] Maria *B W?*     quia fuerunt aliae Mariae] *om. B*     aliae Mariae *M*] alias Marias *W*     ista Maria *WM*] ista *B*

14. quare commemorat *WM*] cur commendat *B*     cruentum *M*] cruentem *BW*     uel tam *W*] uel tem *B*, uel con *M (*con *in ras.),* ut *Bu*     pessimum *WM*] pessimo *B*     propter hoc *BW*] propter *M*     surgere *W*] surgi *B* sug^r-gerere *M* suggerere *Bu*     debeant ... quia non] *om. M*     contra *W*] cum *B*     ecclesia *B*] ecclesiae *W*     Herodis *M*] Herodi *B*, Herode *W*     tempore Pilati *M*] tempore Pilato *W*, timore Pilati *B*

15. ad inferos *B*] adferos *W*, ad inferna *M*     ipse *WM*] ipsi *B*     infirmitates *BM*] infirmitatis *W*     aegrotationes nostras portauit *WM*] aegritudinis portabit *B*     dicit *B*] dicitur *M*, dicetur *W*     quia *BW*] qui *M*     diuinitas *BM*] diuitas *W*     non *B*] et non *WM*     sic *conieci*] si *BWM*     sed *WM*] sit *B*     id est arbor *BM*] id es arbore *W*     platea *conieci*] platea et *BWM*     inciditur *BM*] incidetur *W*     radius *WM*] radiis *B*     scissura *WM*] cissura *B*     et sol illaesus *B*] sol illaesus *M*, sol illaeso *W*     illaesa et impassibilis *B*] impassibilis et illaesa *WM*     diuinitati *conieci*] diuinitatem *BM*, diuitatem *W*

16. hoc *BW Bu*] hoc *ex* haec *M*     diuinitas *WM*] diui^nitas *B*     humanitas ubi anima et corpus corpus *conieci*] humanitas ubi animae corpus *B*, et anima corpus *W*, et anima et corpus *M*     sepulcro *WM*] sepulcrum *B*     caelo

WM] caelum B      anima WM] omnia B      diuinitate M] diuinitatem B,
diuitate W      triumphauit WM] triumfuit B      quae sub debito M] qui sub
debito B, qui sub tebito W      erant B] in inferno erant WM      detentae M]
detentas BW      ero mors tua M] om. BW      ero morsus tuus BW M supra
lineam Bu      o inferne B] inferne WM      ac WM] hac B      dicat B] dicam
W Bu, dicat e dicam M      ibidem WM] ibidem non B      partem WM] et
partem B      captus BM] captus est W      a domino BWM (a dno )] ad
non Bu      diabolus BM] diabolo W
17. resurrectione resurrexit conieci] resurrectio W, resurrectione BM      deus et
BW] deus M      Euangelio ait B] Euangelio WM      destruite BM] destruere
W      in tres dies suscitabo illud ipse WM] tribus diebus resuscitabo illum ipsi
autem B      templo WM] templum B      corporis BW] corpori M
18. sedet ... caelos] om. B      sedet M] sedit W      ad dexteram Bu] ad tex-
teram W, a dexteram M      sanctos angelos WM] sanctus angelus B      sedet
M] sedit BW      id est BM] id es W      prosperitate BM] prosperitatem W
19. uenturus BM] uenturos W      ac WM] hac B      Inde uenturus est ... ac
mortuos] om. M      Inde uenturus est ... uiuos tunc] om. B      prosperitate
conieci] prosperitatem W      et mortuos B] mortuos et WM      aliter ... mortui sunt] om. B      mortui sunt peccato conieci] mortui peccati sunt W, mortui
sunt M, peccato B      in die WM] die B
20. spiritum sanctum M] spiritu sancto BW      patrem et filium M] pater et
filium B, patri et filio W      cur nunc conieci] cur non B, cur WM      spiritum
sanctum BM] spiritu sancto W      mos est BWM] situ ist M supra lineam
scripturae BW] scripturam M, scripturarum Bu      narrare WM] enarrare
B      sicut ... narrare] om. W      narrare M] enarrare B      passione WM]
passionem B      ascensione WM] ascensionem B      unam personam M] una
persona W, una per B      totas tres M] tota tres B, totas W      intellege WM]
intellegere B      spiritus M] spiritu W, ipse B      ipsam creaturam BM] ipsa
creatura W      esset BW] est et M      sic sequitur BW] sequitur M      sanctam ecclesiam catholicam M] sancta ecclesia catholica BW
21. hoc inquirendum M] inquirendum B, hoc inquendum W      quid WM] qui
(q;) B      quae est Bu] quid est W, quae est e qui est M, qui erat B      id est
dilectio WM] delectio B
22. sanctam ecclesiam catholicam M] sancta ecclesia catholica BW      remissionem ... catholicam] om. Bu      peccatorum BW] peccatorem M      sanctam
ecclesiam catholicam conieci] sancta ecclesia catholica B, sancta ecclesiam catholicam W, sancta ecclesiam M      sed credo sanctam ecclesiam catholicam con-
ieci] sed credo sancta ecclesia catholica B, sed credo in sanctam ecclesiam
catholicam M, om. W      id B] ita WM      catholicae conieci] catholica
BWM      ecclesiae sunt Pa] ecclesiis WM, ecclesia B Bu      illae Bu] illas B,
illos W, ille M      uniuersales M] uniuersalis W, uniuersales ex uniuersalis
B      uel locis pertinentes conieci] ueloces pertinent B, uel locis M, uelocis W
23. per B] et per WM      legatarium B] legadario W, legatorium e legatarium
M      et ipse rex uel potens] om. B      de argento WM] argento B      sedet
hic legatarius conieci] sedet hoc legatarius B, sedet hoc legadarius W, sed lega-
torius e sed legatarius M      illud aurum conieci] illum aurum M, illo auro
BW      habitatorem M] habitatore BW      declinat B] declinatur WM

creaturam sed creatorem *M*] creatura sed creatore *BW*        habitaculum *WM*]
habitaculo *B*        habitatorem *M*] habitatore *B*, habitatores *W*        est Christum
*M*] est Christo *W*, Christo *B*

24. remissionem *WM*] remissione *B*        quia ubi *BW*] ubi *M*        consortium
*M*] consortius *W*, in consortio *B*        ibi *BW*] ubi *M*

25. resurrectionem *M*] resurrectione *B*, resurrectionis *W*        ostendit uera prima
resurrectione *W*] ostendit ueram primam resurrectionem *M*, *om. B*        habent ...
suis *BW*] habemus ... nostris *M*        moriuntur boni moriuntur *B*] moriuntur
*WM*        accipiunt boni *BM*] accipient boni *W*        et mali *BM*] *om. W*
stolas et *BW*] stolas *M*        poenas *B*] poena *W*, poenam *M*        corpus *WM*]
et corpus *B*        similiter modo *WM*] modo *B*        a peccatoribus *W*] ad peccatoribus *M*, peccatoribus *B*        *post* peccatoribus *lacunam indicauit Pa*        cruciatur *BM*] cruciat *W*        anima et corpus *WM*] et corpus et anima *B*        in
saecula saeculorum amen *WM*] *om. B*

The manuscript tradition of the anonymous *expositio super symbolum* CPL 1760

There seem to be ten manuscripts available for the constitution of the text of the anonymous *expositio super symbolum* CPL 1760 [1]. Although the relative brevity of our text in combination with the circumstance that many of the manuscripts show the traces of secondary changes renders the task of drawing a stemma rather hazardous, it seems possible to divide the extant witnesses into two groups: *PLA* and *VEFGSMZ*. The second group, which contains most of the younger manuscripts, permits further division.

First of all, one can point to a relatively high number of omissions which occur in *GSMZ*, which suggests that these four manuscripts may well form a distinct subgroup.

Omissions common to *GSMZ*:

> (... *salutaris in Latino*) *dicitur* in *expositio super symbolum* 3
> all of *expositio super symbolum* 5 (quotation and exposition of the phrase *Natus ex Maria uirgine*)
> *Victor* in the quotation of the sixth article in 9 [2]
> *et* in the phrase *homo et deus* in 11
> *Et* in the quotation of the ninth article in 12 [3]
> *fragilitatem et* in 16
> *sicut propheta ... sempiternum* in 17

A similar case seems to be provided by the 'sixth remission' which, according to the other manuscripts, consists in the giving of alms. This is omitted in *GZ*, whereas *SM* apparently fill up the gap with a quotation of Matt. 7, 12.

---

[1] An eleventh (*B*) only offers the opening paragraph of the sermon. Two ninth or tenth-century Parisienses (Bibliothèque Nationale, Latini 1008, ff. 19V-21V and 2373, ff. 35V-36R; *Q* and *R*), and an equally old Augustobonensis (Troyes, Bibliothèque Municipale 804, ff. 53V-54R; *T*) contain texts that, although clearly based on our *expositio*, have been largely rewritten. Of these, *RT* present essentially the same, heavily abbreviated, version, whereas *Q* stands alone with a different variant of our text. In the eleventh-century Verdunensis (Bibliothèque Municipale 27, ff. 75R-86V; *U*), parts of the *expositio super symbolum* CPL 1760 have been incorporated into a longer commentary on the Creed.

[2] Together with *L*, a coincidence that is probably due to adaptation to the *textus receptus* of the Creed.

[3] This time together with *LAF*, again a clear case of adaptation to *T*.

The surmise that *GSMZ* might well descend from a common
ancestor is reinforced by a great number of cases where all four witnesses differ from the rest. The significant instances are the following.

Common deviations in *GSMZ*:

> *mala uel* (*Z*: *malum et*) *malitia et mendacium* for *malum et menda-*
> *cium uel malitia* (thus *PLVE*) in *expositio super symbolum* 2
> *dicit* (*Z*: *dixit*) for *fuit* (thus *PLAVE*) in 7
> *quia signatur* (*Z*: *quia signetur*; *SM* omit the complete phrase) for
> *quia diuina ... designatur* in 10
> *ex operibus* for *sex operibus* in 15 [4]
> *nos resurrecturi in die iudicii absque dubio* for *nos in die iudicii*
> *absque dubio resurrecturi* in 16 [5]

Similarly, the 'seventh remission', which according to the manuscripts *PLAVE* consists in preaching, lies in *doloribus multis* according to *GS*, whereas *Z* omits it altogether.

Within the group *GSMZ*, a number of common errors in *SM*
strongly suggests that these two manuscripts derive from a common
ancestor. Apart from the cases of the quotation of Matt. 7, 12 and
the omission of the corrupt phrase *quia signatur* that have been
mentioned above, one can point to the following instances.

Common errors in *SM*:

> *per quod etiam* for *per quam* (thus all other manuscripts) in *expo-*
> *sitio super symbolum* 1
> *mortuus est* for *mortuus* (all others again) in 7
> *nam propter* for *propter* (thus *PLVEFGZ*; *A* has *propterea*) in the
> same chapter
> *nasci pati crucifigi mori et sepeliri* for *ista tota suscipere* (thus
> *PAE*; *ibidem*) [6]
> *talia* for *ista tota* (thus *PAEFG*; *L* has *ista* and *VZ* have *ista*
> *omnia*) more below in 7

---

[4] This seems to be the most probable emendation; see below, footnote 19 for a
full discussion of this passage.
[5] See the critical apparatus for minor details.
[6] The other manuscripts also offer deviating readings, but *SM* clearly stand
out; see the critical apparatus.

the addition of *Descendit ad infernum* in the credal quotation in 8 [7]

*inferni* for *in inferno* (thus *LVFZ*; *PAE* have *in infernum*, *G* has *inferno*) in 8

the addition of *resurrecturos* before *in die* (*ibidem*) [8]

*iudicaturus uiuos ac mortuos* for the phrase *omnes ... iudicaturus* in 11

omission of *aequalis gloria coaeterna maiestas* in 12

omission of *hoc ... traximus* in 15

omission of *istas sex ... faciat* (*ibidem*)

*aeternam uitam* for *aeterna uita* (thus *PAVG*; *EF* have *uita*, *Z* has *et aeterna uita*) in 17

*sine* for *sine fine* (thus all other manuscripts; *ibidem*)

*mensura* for *mansura* (thus *PAVEFZ*, *G* has *mansunt*; *ibidem*)

For the rest, *G*, *SM*, and *Z* appear as three independent witnesses within the group *GSMZ*. *G*, the oldest of the four, exhibits a number of omissions which make it clear that it cannot be the ancestor of any of the others, for example *symbolum ... demonstratur* in *expositio super symbolum* 1 and *sed inuenta* in 2. That neither *M* nor *S* can be the ancestor of *Z* is implied by the omissions that are mentioned above. *Z* itself is the youngest manuscript of the four and thus excluded from being the parent of any of the others. One possibility that remains is that *S* is a copy of *M*. The two manuscripts do indeed agree to a remarkable degree and have hardly any differences. Nevertheless, a small number of instances can be found where they do part ways. These usually relate to minor differences that hardly affect the quality of the text, such as *carne - carnem* in *expositio super symbolum* 7, *facta - factam* in 8, and *ipsa - in ipsa* in 9. Nevertheless, there are two or three instances where it seems improbable or even impossible that *S* derives from *M*. Thus, in *expositio super symbolum* 10, *M* reads *deus totus dextera est*, and *S*, together with *GZ* has *deus totus dexter est*. Next, *M* has the in itself

---

[7] *L* adds *Descendit ad inferna*.

[8] *GZ* have *resurrecturi in die*. The most probable explanation is that the scribe of the ancestor of *GSMZ* inadvertently transposed *resurrecturi* which, according to the testimony of *EF*, was found after *in die iudicii* in his original, and that the scribe of the original of *SM* changed *resurrecturi* into the grammatically more correct *resurrecturos*. See also below, footnote 11.

intelligible reading *ecclesiam non tamen in eam* in 13, whereas *S* has *ecclesiam profitemur sanctam non tamen in eam*. Here, it seems more probable that the scribe of *M* overlooked the words *profitemur sanctam* than that the scribe of *S* added them [9]. Thirdly, *M* (together with *G*) omits the phrase *id est iusti* in 16, whereas it is present in *S* (*Z*: *hoc est iusti*). Therefore, we choose to reconstruct a stemma in which *S* and *M* are sister manuscripts, deriving from a parent manuscript $\mu$ that is a sister again of *G* and *Z*, with *G*, $\mu$, and *Z* deriving from a lost parent $\gamma$.

In the second place, it should be noted that the group *EFGSMZ* also seem to share a number of significant omissions. These comprise the following cases.

Common omissions in *EFGSMZ*:

> *nam* (*Iesus proprium ...*) in *expositio* 3 (present in *PLAV*)
> *et ad hoc ... passus est* in 6
> *sicut ... sinu meo* in 16

This suggests that *EF* and $\gamma$ also derive from one and the same archetype. A number of readings seem to strengthen this hypothesis.

Common deviations in the group *EFGSMZ*:

> *Graece* in *ESMZ* for *Graeca lingua* (thus *PLAVB*) in *expositio super symbolum* 1 (*FG* omit the complete introduction)
> *creatum* and *inuentum* in *ESMZ* [10] for *creata* and *inuenta* (thus *PLV*) in 2
> the omission of the second *nos* in the phrase *nos in die iudicii absque dubio resurrecturos nos esse credamus* (thus *VL*; *PA* show some minor modifications) in 8 [11]

---

[9] On the other hand, it seems certain that the scribe of the ancestor of *GSMZ* had to cope with a mutilated or corrupt text - *G* has *et ecclesiae credere non tamen in ecclesiae*, *Z* has *ecclesiam credere non tamen in ecclesiam*. *EF*, the two manuscripts that probably derive from the same original as the ancestor of *GSMZ* (see below), have *ecclesiam* and *ecclesiam esse* respectively. The scribes of *G*, *Z*, and the parent manuscript of *SM* probably all emended this or a similar reading in their own way.

[10] *G* has *creatum* but omits *inuentum*; *F* has *creatam ... inuentam*.

[11] The second *nos* is absent in the group *EFGSMZ*, and seems to have caused further changes: $\gamma$ put *resurrecturos* (or possibly *resurrecturi*) in front, resulting in

the addition of *uiuos et mortuos* after *omnes homines iustos et* (*EF*: *ac*) in *EFGZ* in 11 (*SM* replace the complete phrase)

the readings *ecclesiam* (*F*) and *ecclesiam credere* (*E*) in combination with the various readings of *GSMZ* in 13 (see above, footnote 9)

the reading *istae sunt*, a probable corruption of *istas* (approximated by *ista sunt* in *V*) in the conclusion of the section on the six *opera misericordiae* (15) in *EGZ* (*P*: *isti sunt*, *L*: *haec sunt*, *F*: *istarum*; my photocopy of *A* is illegible at this place)

A further indication is provided by the exposition of the 'fourth remission', where two scriptural quotations (Matt. 6, 12 and 14-15) are introduced by means of the formula *sicut dicimus in oratione dominica* in *L* (*PAV* have some minor variations). *EF*, however, only quote Matt. 6, 14-15, introduced by *sicut ipse dominus dicit, G* only quotes Matt. 6, 12, and *SMZ* explicitly link the two quotations by adding the words *et ipse dominus dicit* before Matt. 6, 14-15. Here, *SMZ* probably reflect the reading of the archetype of *EFGSMZ*, which was corrupted in different ways by *EF* and *G*[12]. On the basis of these observations, the assumption that *EF* and γ both descend from a common ancestor ε seems a safe one.

Within this group a number of features suggest that *EF* do not derive directly from ε, but descend by way of a common ancestor. We may point to the following cases.

Common errors and deviations in *EF*:

the addition of *quia* in *expositio super symbolum* 5
the presence of *passus* (*F*: *passusque*) after *sub Pontio Pilato* in 6
the use of *erimus* in 8 [13]
the omission of the words *dicimus ... nostris* and the use of *sicut ipse dominus ...* in 15 (see above)
the omission of the phrase *sex operibus misericordiae* (*ibidem*)
the omission of the quotation *nudus ... operuistis me* (*ibidem*)

the variant *nos resurrecturi* (*resurrecturos SM*) *in die iudicii absque dubio esse credamus*, and *EF* rewrote the end of the phrase to *resurrecturi erimus* (omitting *absque dubio*). See also above, footnote 8.

[12] The addition of the phrase *et ipse dominus dicit* was probably added by a scribe who noticed that Matt. 6, 14-15 does not, strictly speaking, belong to the Lord's Prayer.

[13] See above, footnote 11 for more details.

the omission of the form *mouemur* in 16 (thus *PVGSZ*; *A* has *moueamur*, *L* has *moriemur*, and *M* omits the complete phrase)

the omission of the phrases *in die ... dubio* and *et dominus dicit* (*ibidem*)

the use of *uita* instead of the first *aeterna uita* (thus *PAVG*; *SM* have *aeternam uitam* and *Z* has *et aeterna uita*) in 17

In the third place, a number of instances strongly suggest that all available manuscripts may be divided into two groups, viz. *VEFGSMZ* on the one hand and *PLA* on the other, as each group is characterized by a number of common omissions and more or less certain errors.

With regard to the group *VEFGSMZ*, one can point to the following instances:

the position of *omnia bona* after *sua potentia* in *VEFSMZ* (*G* omits *sua potentia*), whereas the reverse order seems to be the original one, in *expositio super symbolum* 2 [14]

the obviously secondary *omnia peccata* in *VSMZ* (*E* has *omne peccatum* and *FG* omit the phrase) for *omnium peccata* (thus *LA*, *P* has *hominum peccata*) in 13

the word order *per primum hominem Adam* in *VEGZ* (*SM* omit the phrase; *F* omits *per*) instead of *per Adam primum hominem* (thus *A*, *PL* deviate in details) in 15 [15]

the form *cooperit* in *VEF* for the probably correct *operiet* in *A* (*ibidem*) [16]

the omission of *et* by the complete group *VEFGSMZ* in the quotation of Job 19, 26 in 16 (*et* is present in *PLA*)

For the group *PLA*, the following instances can be pointed out.

---

[14] No manuscript has preserved this formulation but it is supported by *PL* (*omnia bona sua*; my photocopy of *A* is illegible here) and, moreover, explains the two elements of the word *Omnipotentem* in the most logical order. See the critical apparatus for the details of the other manuscripts.

[15] The word order *per Adam primum hominem* is not only slightly more logical (*primum hominem* is meaningful as an explanatory apposition, whereas the apposition of *Adam* would hardly add anything to the sentence), but its corruption into *per primum hominem Adam* (with *primum* attracted by *per*) also seems more probable than the reverse procedure.

[16] That *operiet* is correct is demonstrated by the variant *operit et* in *P*. *L* has *opererit*; *SMGZ* omit the entire section here.

Common errors in *PLA*:

> the omission of *potentia* in *expositio super symbolum* 2 [17]
> *sed* instead of *quod* (thus *VEFGSMZ*) in 10
> the use of a form of *reuoco* (*PA*: *reuocet*; *L*: *reuocat*) for *uocet*
> (thus *VEGSMZ*; *F* has *uocent*) in 13 [18]
> the form *operis* instead of *operibus* (thus *VGSMZ*) in 15 [19]

In the light of these instances, it seems safe to postulate the existence of a common ancestor π for the three manuscripts *PLA*.

It is difficult to say anything more concrete about the relationship between the manuscripts of this group. *P* and *A* are of about the same age and might therefore well derive directly from π. Where they have errors in common against *L*, this can practically always be explained by the circumstance that the scribe of *L* was obviously concerned with writing a sound and coherent text [20]. For the same reason, it is impossible to reach certainty in the question of whether *L* forms a subgroup with either *P* or *A*, or stands alone among the descendants of π. All one can say is that there are a number of places where *L* betrays the influence of a manuscript like *P* [21]. These include the explanation of the word *Ecclesiam*, where *L* agrees with *P* in reading *a se* instead of *ad se* (thus *AVEFGSMZ*) before *reuocat* in *expositio super symbolum* 13, the section on the 'first remission', where only *PL* use *de* instead of *per* before the name *Adam* (15), and the conclusion of the section on the *opera misericordiae* (*ibidem*), where *L* (*haec sunt opera ...*) clearly has a cor-

---

[17] See above, footnote 14.

[18] The addition of the prefix is probably due to the immediately preceding *se*.

[19] The form occurs in the introduction to the 'fifth remission', which is said to work *per ueram caritatem*. The following words should probably be read as *hoc est sex operibus misericordiae*, with *operibus* as an instrumental ablative. This ablative is preserved in *VGSMZ* (*EF* omit the phrase), but was clearly no longer understood by the scribes of *V* or of γ - *V* has prefixed *per* to *sex operibus*, and *GSMZ* read *ex* instead of *sex*. In the group *PLA*, the ablative was corrupted to a genitive (*PA*: *sex operis*), which seems to have been emended to *per sex opera* in *L*.

[20] Nevertheless, there are no unambiguous traces of contamination in *L* or, for that matter, in any of the other manuscripts.

[21] That *L* cannot derive from *P* appears from the omissions in *P* (for example, the sentence *quomodo ... sanctum* in *expositio super symbolum* 12 and the words *credere debemus quia ecclesia* in 13), where *L* contains the words that are omitted in *P*.

rection and *P* (*isti sunt operis*) stands in most obvious need of one. It is with some hesitation, therefore, that we suggest that *PL* might derive from a common ancestor within their group.

For the rest, it should be noted that a number of errors have left their traces in all of the present manuscripts, so that π and φ cannot represent two totally different branches of the tradition, but must go back to a common archetype which was already corrupted to a certain extent. This holds true not only for relatively unimportant points of grammar (for example, in *expositio super symbolum* 1, the reading *in ista duodecim uerba* is transmitted virtually without exception [22] and thus should be considered to represent the text of the archetype of all extant manuscripts), but also for points of syntax, particularly in the longer periods. Thus, we have had to resort to conjecture both in the introduction to and at the end of the section on the *sex opera misericordiae* to arrive at an intelligible text.

All in all, then, the following stemma may be drawn for the manuscripts of the *expositio super symbolum* CPL 1760:

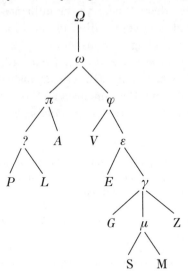

---

[22] The reading of V (*in istis duodecim uerbis*) is clearly a deliberate correction.

codices

| | |
|---|---|
| *P* | Parisiensis, Bibliothèque Nationale, Latinus 1012, ff. 55V-59R, saec. VIII/IX |
| *L* | Laudunensis, Bibliothèque Municipale 303, ff. 9R-10R, saec. XIII |
| *A* | Aurelianensis, Bibliothèque Municipale 116 (94), ff. 6V-8V, saec. IX |
| *V* | Vesulensis, Bibliothèque Municipale 73, ff. 66R-68V, saec. XI |
| *E* | Escurialensis L III 8, ff. 12R-14R, saec. X |
| *F* | Florentinus, Bibliotheca Laurentiana, Plut. 30 Sin. 4, ff. 342V-343R, saec. XI |
| *G* | Sangallensis, Stiftsbibliothek 732, ff. 156-162, saec. IX |
| *S* | Romanus, Biblioteca Nazionale Centrale, Sessorianus 52, ff. 161V-163R, saec. XII |
| *M* | Modoetiensis (Monza), Biblioteca Capitolare e 14/27, ff. 36V-38V, saec. X |
| *Z* | Lugdunensis Batavorum, Universiteitsbibliotheek, Perizonius Q 17, ff. 49V-51R, saec. XIII |
| *B* | Albigensis, Bibliothèque Municipale 38bis, f. 55R, saec. IX (*partim*) |

editiones

| | |
|---|---|
| *Bu1* | BURN, A.E., 'Neue Texte zur Geschichte des apostolischen Symbols. II, in: *Zeitschrift für Kirchengeschichte* 21, 1900, 129-132 |
| *Bu2* | PLS 4, 2160-2162 |
| *Br* | BREWER, H., *Das sogenannte Athanasianische Glaubensbekenntnis ein Werk des heiligen Ambrosius ...*, Paderborn, 1909 (EHRHARD, A. - KIRSCH, J.P. [edd.], *Forschungen zur Christlichen Litteratur- und Dogmengeschichte*, IX 2, 179-181 |

*Bu* consensus editionum *Bu1* et *Bu2*

expositio super symbolum CPL 1760

1. Symbolum Graeca lingua dicitur quod in Latino interpretatur collatio siue indicium, collatio quia duodecim apostoli duodecim uerba symboli composuerunt, indicium per quod indicatur omnis scientia ueritatis per quam possumus peruenire ad uitam aeternam.

In istis duodecim uerbis symboli tota haeresis excluditur et omnis
sapientia demonstratur.

2. Credo in deum patrem omnipotentem, creatorem caeli et terrae. Omnipotens deus dicitur quia ipse creauit omnia bona sua
potentia. Malum et mendacium uel malitia non sunt a deo creata
sed a diabolo et malis hominibus sunt inuenta.

3. Et in Iesum Christum, filium eius unicum dominum nostrum.
Iesus et Messias Hebraice dicitur, Christus et sother Graece, unctus
et saluator uel salutaris in Latino dicitur. Nam Iesus proprium
nomen est, quia sic ab angelo Gabriele priusquam conciperetur
uocatus est, sicut ipse dixit: *Ecce concipies et paries filium et uocabis
nomen eius Iesum* (Luc. 1, 31). 4. Qui conceptus est de spiritu
sancto. Id est, per administrationem spiritus sancti, sicut Gabriel
ad Mariam dixit: *Spiritus sanctus ueniet super te et uirtus altissimi
obumbrabit tibi* (Luc. 1, 35). 5. Natus ex Maria uirgine. Hoc est quod
sancta Maria semper uirgo fuit, uirgo ante partum, uirgo post partum, uirgo concepit, uirgo peperit et uirgo permansit.

6. Passus sub Pontio Pilato. Propterea dicitur sub Pontio Pilato
passus, quia ipse erat illo tempore dux in Iudaea. Et ad hoc Pilatum nomine commemorat, ut nos non in alium Christum credamus
nisi in illum qui sub illius regis tempore passus est. 7. Crucifixus,
mortuus et sepultus. Hoc secundum carnem fuit, non secundum
diuinitatem, quia diuina maiestas impassibilis est. Natus, passus,
crucifixus, mortuus et sepultus, propter nos homines dignatus est
ista tota suscipere, ut nos a peccato redimeret et de inferno liberaret
et aeternam uitam condonaret, quia nullus poterat introire in
regnum dei (cf. Marc. 10, 23) nisi ista tota sustinuisset pro nobis
filius dei.

8. Tertia die resurrexit a mortuis. Facta praeda in inferno uiuus
exiit de sepulcro. Sed sicut ipse tertia die resurrexit a mortuis, ita et
nos in die iudicii absque dubio resurrecturos nos esse credamus. 9.
Ascendit uictor ad caelos. In ipsa carne in qua natus, in qua passus,
in qua resurrexit, in ipsa ascendit ad caelos. 10. Sedet ad dexteram
dei patris omnipotentis. Dextera dei non est corporea, quod nefas
est de deo sentire, quia diuina maiestas non secundum humanam
speciem designatur. Deus totus dexter est, quia totus bonus est.

11. Inde uenturus iudicare uiuos et mortuos. Ipse homo et deus
dei filius, qui cum hominibus conuersatus est in mundo, qui numquam fuit aliquando sine patre, ipse *uenturus est in gloria* maiestatis

suae *cum angelis* et archangelis. Omnes homines, iustos et peccatores, ipse erit iudicaturus et redditurus *unicuique secundum opera sua*
(Matth. 16, 27). Viuos, proprie illi qui uiui inueniendi sunt in die
iudicii.

12. Credo et in spiritum sanctum. Quomodo credimus in patrem,
sic debemus credere in filium, ita et in spiritum sanctum, quia tres
personae in una diuinitate - aequalis gloria, coaeterna maiestas -
aequaliter absque dubio omnia possident, quia aequali cuncta uirtute fecerunt. Propterea dicitur unus deus pater et filius et spiritus
sanctus, quia una est diuinitas, aequalis gloria, coaeterna maiestas.

13. Sanctam ecclesiam catholicam. Non tamen in ecclesiam credere debemus, quia ecclesia non est deus sed domus dei est. Ecclesia
dicitur eo quod omnes ad se uocet et in unum congreget. Catholica
dicitur per uniuersum mundum diffusa, uel quia catholica, hoc est
generalis, doctrina in ea est, id est ad omnes, uel quoniam curat
omnium peccata quae per corpus et animam perficiuntur. Ibi est
ecclesia catholica ubi est congregatio fidelium qui rectam fidem credunt et tenent et in opere bono perficiunt. 14. Sanctorum communionem. Ibi est communicatio sancta per inuocationem patris et filii
et spiritus sancti, ibi omnes fideles omnibus diebus dominicis com-
municare debent.

15. Remissionem peccatorum. Septem sunt remissiones peccatorum. Prima per baptismum sicut propheta dicit: *Beati quorum
remissae sunt iniquitates* (Ps. 32, 1). Hoc est in baptismo illa sex
peccata originalia quae per Adam, primum hominem, traximus.
Secunda per paenitentiam, sicut dicit: *Et quorum tecta sunt peccata*
(Ps. 32, 1). Tertia per martyrium, ut ait: *Beatus uir cui non imputauit dominus peccatum* (Ps. 32, 2). Quarta remissio est per indulgentiam inimicorum, sicut dicimus in oratione dominica: *Dimitte nobis
debita nostra sicut et nos dimittimus debitoribus nostris. Si enim remiseritis hominibus peccata eorum, et pater uester caelestis dimittet uobis
peccata uestra. Si non remiseritis nec deus dimittet uobis* (Matth. 6, 12
et 14-15). Quinta remissio est per ueram caritatem, hoc est sex operibus misericordiae, sicut ipse dominus dicit: *Esuriui enim et dedistis
mihi manducare, sitiui et dedistis mihi bibere, hospes eram et collegistis
me, nudus et operuistis me, infirmus et uisitastis me, in carcere eram et
uenistis ad me* (Matth. 25, 35-36). Istas sex operationes misericordiae
quicumque ex fide et ex bona uoluntate ad omnes pauperes et peregrinos, ad seruos dei uel ancillas dei faciat. Sexta remissio est per

eleemosynam, sicut ipse dominus dicit: *Date eleemosynam et ecce omnia munda sunt uobis* (Luc. 11, 41). Septima remissio est per praedicationem, sicut propheta dicit: *Quodsi ergo te dicente ad impium ut impius se conuertat a uia sua mala, et ipse impius fecerit iudicium et iustitiam, uita uiuet et non morietur, dicit dominus, et tu animam tuam liberasti* (Ez. 3, 19-21). Et sanctus Iacobus ait: *Qui conuerti fecerit peccatorem ab errore uiae suae, saluabit animam eius a morte et suorum quoque operiet multitudinem peccatorum* (Iac. 5, 20).

16. Carnis resurrectionem. Sicut Iob per spiritum sanctum dicit: *Scio,* inquit, *quod redemptor meus uiuit et in nouissimo die de terra resurrecturus sum, et rursum circumdabo pellem meam et in carne mea uidebo deum, quem uisurus sum ego ipse et oculi mei conspecturi sunt et non alius. Reposita est haec spes mea in sinu meo* (Iob 19, 25-27). Et in ipsa carne in qua uiuimus, mouemur et sumus, in ipsa nos in die iudicii absque dubio resurrecturi erimus, non naturam aut sexum mutantes, sed fragilitatem et uitia deponentes. Et dominus dicit: *In resurrectione enim neque nubent neque nubentur, sed erunt sicut angeli dei in caelo* (Matth. 22, 30), hoc est iusti. 17. Vitam aeternam. Aeterna uita, hoc est sine fine mansura. Aeterna uita erit ubi mors numquam erit, sed semper perpetua felicitas, sicut propheta dicit: *Erit opus iustitiae pax, cultus iustitiae silentium et securitas usque in sempiternum* (Is. 32, 17).

apparatus criticus apud expositionem super symbolum CPL 1760

expositio super symbolum *SZ*] incipit expositio super symbolum *PV*, incipit expositio symboli *E, om. LFGM*
1. symbolum Graeca ... demonstratur] *om. GF*　　　Graeca lingua *PLAVB*] Graece *ESMZ*　　　dicitur quod *PLAVESMZ*] est *B*　　　in Latino *PAVZ*] in Latinum *LE*, in Latine *SB*, Latine *M*　　　indicium *AESB*] indicio *P*, indic^t io *V*, indictio *MZ*, iudicium *L*　　　collatio quia *PLAVESMB*] quae *Z*　　　symboli *PLSMB*] symbolum *A*, singuli *E, om. VZ*　　　composuerunt *LAVESMZB*] composuerunt et cunctis credentibus tradiderunt *P*　　　indicium *ESMZB*] indicio *P*, indictio *V*, iudicium *L*, ideo *A*　　　per quod *PLAESMZB*] ^quia per ipsum *V*　　　indicatur omnis scientia *PVESMZB*] indicatur scientia *A*, iudicatur omnis sententia *L*　　　per quam *PLAVEZB*] per quod etiam *SM*　　　possumus *PLAVESMZ*] possimus *B*　　　istis duodecim uerbis *V*] ista duodecim uerba *PLAESMZB*　　　sapientia *PLAESMZB*] sapientia ueritatis *V*
2. credo ... hominibus] *non legitur A*　　　deus dicitur *PEFSM*] dicitur deus *L*, dicitur *VZ*, deus *G*　　　quia ipse creauit omnia bona sua potentia *Pa*] quia i. cr. o. b. sua *PL*, quia sua pot. i. cr. o. b. *VSM*, quia sua pot. cr. o. b. *E*, quia in sua pot. cr. o. b. *F*, ipse cr. o. b. *G*, quia ipse sua pot. cr. o. b. *Z*　　　malum et mendacium uel malitia *PLVE*] malum et me. u. malitiam *F*, mala u. ma. et

me. *GSM*, malum et ma. et me. *Z*      sunt ... creata *L*] est ... creata *P*, est ...
creata *ex* est ... creato *V*, est ... creatum *EGSMZ*, est ... creatam *F*      sed ...
inuenta] *om. G*      et *PLAVEFSM*] et a *Z*
sunt inuenta *L*] est inuenta *PAV*, est inuentum *ESMZ*, est inuentam *F*
3. Hebraice dicitur *AVEFGSMZ*] Hebraice *PL*      Christus et ... dicitur] *om.*
*A*      Christus et sother Graece *PLESMZ*] Christus et sother Graece dicitur
*FG, om. V*      unctus et *conieci*] *om. codd.*      saluator uel salutaris *PEFSM*]
saluator salutaris *L*, saluator et salutaris *V*, saluator et saluatoris *G*, Latine
saluator uel salutaris *Z*      in Latino dicitur *PLVEF*] in Latino *GSM, om.*
*Z*      nam ... nomen est] *om. F*      nam *PLAV*] *om. EGSMZ*      Gabriele
*LAS*] Gabriel *PVEFMZ*, Gabrielo *G*      priusquam *PAVEFGSMZ*] priusquam
in utero *L*      uocatus *PLAVEFSM*] uocatum *GZ*      dixit *PLAEGSMZ*]
archangelus ad Mariam dicit *V*, ait *F*      ecce *PLAVEFSMZ*] *om. G*
4. sancto *PLAVEFSMZ*] sancto natus ex Maria uirgine *G*      per administrationem *PAGFSMZ*] per administratione *V*, pro administratione *E*, adnuntiatio-
nem *L*      Gabriel *PLAVEGSM*] ipse Gabriel *F*, Gabriel angelus *Z*      dixit
*PLAVEFZ*] dicit *GSM*      ueniet super te *PE*] superueniet in te *LAFGSMZ*,
u. s. te *e* s. te u. *V*      obumbrabit *PAEFG*] obumbrauit *LVSMZ*
5. natus ex ... permansit] *om. GSMZ*      hoc est quod *P*] hoc est quia *LA*, id
est quia *VE*, id est *F*      uirgo ante *PLVEF*] uir ante *A*      post partum
*PLAV*] et post partum quia *E*, post partum quia *F*      peperit et *PVE*] peperit
*LAF*
6. propterea *PAVEFGSMZ*] propter hoc *L*      sub Pontio Pilato passus
*PLAGSMZ*] p. sub P. P. *V*, a P. P. p. *E*, p. sub P. P. passusque *F*      quia
ipse erat *PLAVEGSM*] quia *F*      illo tempore *PAGZ*] in illo tempore *LVSM*,
illo tempore ipse erat *F, om. E*      dux *PLAVEFSMZ*] iudex *G*      et ad hoc
... passus est] *om. EFGSMZ*      ad hoc *V*] propterea *PLA*      Pilatum nomine
commemorat *conieci*] Pilato homine nominat *P*, Pilatum commemorat *LV*,
Pilato commemorat *A*      non in alium Christum credamus *conieci*] non in alio
Christo credamus *PL*, i non alio Christo credamus *A*, non in alium credamus
Christum *V*      nisi in illum qui *conieci*] nisi in illo qui *PL*, nisi in illo quae *A*,
sed illo qui *V*      regis tempore *LV*] regis temporis *P*, tempore *A*
7. mortuus *PLAVEFGZ*] mortuus est *SM*      hoc secundum ... et sepultus] *om.*
*F*      carnem *PLAVEGSZ*] carne *M*      hoc *PLVEGSMZ*] hoc est *A*      fuit
*PLAVE*] dicit *GSM*, dixit *Z*      diuina maiestas *PLAVEGSM*] diuinitas *Z*
natus ... sepultus *PLAVGS*] natus passus crucifixus *E*, natus ... sepultus hoc
secundum carnem non secundum diuinitatem *Z, om. M*      propter *PLVEFGZ*]
propterea *A*, nam propter *SM*      homines *PLAEGSM*] itaque homines *Z*,
dominus *V, om. F*      dignatus est *PLVEFGSM*] dignatus *A, om. Z*      ista
tota suscipere *PAE*] ista tota dei filius suscipere *L*, ista omnia suscipere *VG*, in
ista uita morte suscipere *F*, nasci pati crucifigi mori et sepeliri *SM*, ista omnia
sustinuit *Z*      nos *LAVEGSMZ*] nono *P, om. F*      et *PLAVEFG*] ac
*SMZ*      inferno *PLVEFGSMZ*] infernum *A*      et aeternam uitam *VEMZ*]
et aeternam uita *P*, et aeternam uitam nobis *L*, et aeterna uit *A*, atque aeternae
uitae *F*, et nobis aeternam uitam *G*, aeternam uitam *S*      condonaret
*PAVEGSMZ*] donaret *L*, condonare et *F*      nullus *PAVEFGSMZ*] nullus
homo *L*      poterat *PLVEFGSMZ*] potest *A*      regnum *PLAEFGSMZ*]

regno *V* ista tota *PAEFG*] ista *L*, ista omnia *VZ*, talia *SM* sust. p. n. f. d. *PAESMZ*] p. n. sust. f. d. *L*, sust. f. d. p. n. *G*, sust. propter nos f. d. *V*, sust. et p. n. f. d. *F*

8. tertia *PAVEFZ*] descendit ad inferna tertia *L*, descendit ad infernum tertia *SM* resurrexit a mortuis *PLAVEFGSM*] surrexit a mortuis sicut ipse dixit *Z* facta *PLA*] sicut ipse tertia die resurrexit a mortuis facta *VEGSM (M* factam *)*, sed sicut ipse dixit facta *F*, et facta est *Z* in inferno *LVFZ*] in infernum *PAE*, inferno *G*, inferni *SM* uiuus *PLAEFGSM*] et uiuus *V*, uiuusque *Z* sed sicut ... mortuis] *om. VFSM* sed sicut ipse *LZ*] sed sicut ipsa *P*, sed sicut *A*, sicut ipse *EG* resurrexit *PLAEG*] surrexit *Z* in die *LVE*] in diem *PAF*, resurrecturi in die *GZ*, resurrecturos in die *SM* absque dubio *PLAVEGSMZ*] *om. F* resurrecturos nos *PLV*] resurrectururus nos *A*, resurrecturi *EF, om. GSMZ* esse credamus *PLVGSMZ*] esse credimus *A*, erimus *EF*

9. uictor *PVE*] auctor *F, om. LGSMZ* ad caelos *PLVGSMZ*] in caelis *EF* in ipsa *PVEFGMZ*] hoc est in ipsa *L*, ipsa *S* carne ... in ipsa] *om. F* in qua passus *PVGSM*] est passus *L*, in ipsa passus *E*, passus *Z* in qua resurrexit *PLVG*] in ipsa resurrexit *E*, in qua et resurrexit *SM*, in qua surrexit *Z*

10. sedet *PLVEFSMZ*] sedit *G* dextera *LAVEFGMZ*] dexteram *PS* dei *PLAVEFGSZ*] domini *M* quod *VEFGSMZ*] sed *PLA* quia diuina ... designatur] quia signantur *G*, quia signetur *Z, om. SM* non *PLVEF*] non est *A* humanam speciem *PLVF*] humana specie *E*, humanitatem speciem *A* dexter *LAVGSZ*] dextera *PEFM* totus bonus est *PLAVEMZ*] bonus est *G*, totus est bonus *S*, totus bonus est dextera dei patris gloriae uel beatitudo aeternae dicitur *F*

11. uenturus *PLAVESMZ*] uenturus est *GF* et mortuos *LAVEFGSMZ*] ac mortuos *P* et deus *PLAVEF*] deus *GSMZ* conuersatus est *PAVEFGSMZ*] conuersatur *L* mundo *LVGSM*] mundum *PAEFZ* numquam *PAVEFGSMZ*] non *L* fuit aliquando *PLAVEF*] aliquando *GSM, om. Z* uenturus est *PAVEFGSMZ*] uenturus *L* gloria maiestatis *LAVEFSMZ*] gloriam maiestati *P*, gloriam maiestatis *G* suae *PLA VEGSMZ*] qui *F* cum *PAVEFGSMZ*] et cum *L* omnes ... iudicaturus] iudicaturus uiuos ac mortuos *SM* omnes homines *PLAEF*] et omnes homines *V*, omnesque *GZ* iustos et peccatores *PAV*] scilicet i. et p. *L*, i. *(*iustus *G)* et p. uiuos et *(*ac *EF)* mortuos *EFGZ* ipse erit *PLAEFGZ*] ipse *V* et redditurus *PLAEFGSMZ*] *om. V* uiuos proprie ... iudicii] *om. EFSM* uiuos *PLAVG*] uiuus *Z* proprie *PLVGZ*] proprii *A* illi *PAVG*] illis *Z*, illos dicit *L* uiui inueniendi *V (*uiui *supra lineam)*] inueniendi *PZ*, ueniendi *AG*, uiuendi *L* die *VGZ*] diem *PLA*

12. credo et *PE*] credo ᵉᵗ *V*, credo *LAFGSMZ* quomodo ... sanctum] *om. P* quomodo *LAVEFGZ*] sicut *M, om. S* credimus *LAVEGSMZ*] credis *F* patrem *LAVFSMZ*] patre *EG* sic *LAVEFSMZ*] si *G* debemus credere *AVEFGSMZ*] credere debemus *L* in filium *LVFSMZ*] in filio *AG*, et in filium *E* in spiritum *LVEFGSMZ*] spiritum *A* quia *PAVEFSMZ*] qui *G*, quomodo credimus quia *L* tres *PLAVEFSMZ*] in *G* personae *LVSM*] personas *PAEFGZ* una diuinitate *LAVEGSM*] unam diuinitatem

*PZ*, una deitate *F*      aequalis gloria *LAFZ*] aequalem gloriam *P*, aequali gloria *VE*, aequalis gloriae *G*, *om. SM*      coaeterna maiestas *LFG*] quaeternam maiestatem *P*, quo ...tas *A*, coaeterna maiestate *VE*, quo aeterna maiestas *Z*, *om. SM*      aequaliter *PLVEFGSMZ*] aeque et *A?*      aequali *LVG*] aequale *P*, aequaliter *EFSMZ*, elr *A?*      cuncta uirtute *PLAV*] uirtute cuncta *G*, cunctas uirtutes *Z*, cuncta *EFSM*      fecerunt *LAVEFGSMZ*] fuerunt *P* pater *PLEFGSMZ*] et pater *AV*      et filius *PLAVEFSMZ*] *om. G*      diuini- tas *PAVEFGSMZ*] diuinitatis *L*      aequalis gloria *PLAVFSMZ*] aequalis aequalis gloria *E*, aequalis gloriae *G*      coaeterna *VEFGZ*] quo aeterna *PSM*, et coaeterna *L*, quo aeternae *A*

13. sanctam ecclesiam catholicam *PLAVEGSZ*] sancta ecclesia catholicam *M*, sanctam ecclesiam *F*      non tamen in ecclesiam *A*] n. t. in ecclesia *PLV*, eccle- siam *E*, ecclesiam esse *F*, et ecclesiae credere n. t. in ecclesiae *G*, ecclesiam profi- temur sanctam n. t. in eam *S*, ecclesiam n. t. in eam *M*, ecclesiam credere n. t. in ecclesiam *Z*      credere debemus quia ecclesia] *om. P*      ecclesia *LVEFGSMZ*] ecclesiam *A*      sed ... dicitur] *om. Z*      ecclesia *PLVEGSM*] ecclesiam *AF*      omnes *PLVEFGSMZ*] omnis *A*      ad se uocet *VEGSMZ*] a se reuocet *P*, a se reuocat *L*, ad se reuocet *A*, ad se uocent *F*      in unum *PLAVEFGS*] unum *MZ*      congreget *PVEGSMZ*] congregat *LA*, congregent *F*      catholica *LVEGSMZ*] catholicam *PAF*      per *PLAEFGSMZ*] in *V*      mundum *PLAVFSMZ*] munda *E*, *om. G*      diffusa *PLAVESMZ*] dif- fusam *F*, diffusa est *G*      uel quia catholica hoc est *PLESMZ*] uel qui catho- licam hoc est *A*, uel <u>quia</u> catholica est <sup>quia</sup> *V*, hoc est *G*, uel quia e$^i$ *(ecclesia ?)* catholica dicitur eo quod *F*      d. in ea est *EFSMZ*] in ea d. est *PG*, d. est in ea *L*, n ea d. est *A*, d. est *V*      id est ... peccata] *om. F*      ad omnes uel *PLASMZ*] ad omnes homines uel *V*, omnes uel *E*, *om. G*      quoniam *PAVESMZ*] quia *L*, quia omnia peccata *G*      omnium peccata *LA*] hominum peccata *P*, omnia peccata *VSMZ*, omne peccatum *E*, *om. G*      quae *LAVGSMZ*] quia *P*, qui *E*, quod *F*      per corpus et animam perficiuntur *LSMZ*] per c. et a. perciuntur *P*, per c. et a. efficiuntur *V*, per c. et a. perficiun- tur *F*, pro corpu et anima proficuntur *E*, corpus et anima perficiunt *AG*      ibi ... ubi] id est *G*      ibi *PLAVESMZ*] ubi *F*      ecclesia catholica *PAVEFSMZ*] catholica ecclesia *L*      ubi est *LAVESM]* ubi *P*, ibi est *F*, ibi est corporis *Z*      qui *PLVEFSMZ*] quia *G*      rectam fidem *VESMZ*] recta fide *PF*, per rectam fidem *L*, recte fide *G*      credunt et tenent *EGSMZ*] cre- damus et tenent *P*, tenent et credunt *V*, credent et tenent *F*, credunt *L*      in opere bono *PVEGSM*] in opera bona *F*, in bono opere *Z*, omnia bona *L*

14. sanctorum communionem *PLAVEFGSM*] *om. Z*      ibi *PLVGZ*] id *EFSM*      communicatio sanctorum *PVEGSMZ*] communio sanctorum *L*, communicationem *F*      per inuocationem *PLEGSMZ*] *om. VF*      ibi *PEGSM*] ubi *LVZ*, quia *F*      fideles *PVEFGMZ*] fides *S*, fideles et Christiani *L*      omnibus diebus dominicis *PLVFGSM*] ... dominicis *A*, omnes dominicas *E*, omnibus dominicis *Z*      debent *PLVFGMZ*] debet *E*, se debent *S*

15. remissiones peccatorum *PLVESMZ*] remissiones peccatores *G*, *om. F* per *PLAFSMZ*] *om. VEG*      sicut *VSM*] secunda per paenitentiam tertia per martyrium sicut *PLAF*, secunda paenitentia tertia per martyrium sicut *E*, secunda paenitentia per martyrium sicut *G*, secunda per paenitentiam et per

martyrium sicut *Z* propheta dicit *LVEFGSMZ*] per propheta dicit *P*, dicit
propheta *A* beati quorum *LAVEFGSMZ*] beaticorum *P* iniquitates
*PAVEGSMZ*] iniquitates et quorum tecta sunt peccata *L*, *om. F* hoc est
... traximus] *om. SM* baptismo *EFGZ*] baptismum *PLAV* illa sex
*PAEFZ*] illa *L*, ex *V*, illa rex *G* peccata originalia *VEFZ*] peccata *P*, originalia peccata *A*, peccatum originalia *G*, originalia deleantur peccata *L* quae
*PLAVEGZ*] qui *F* per Adam primum hominem *A*] de Adam primum hominem *P*, de Adam primo homine *L*, per primum hominem Adam *VEGZ*, primum
hominem Adam *F* traximus *PLAVEGZ*] transacti sumus *F* secunda ...
peccatum] *om. LG* per paenitentiam *PVFSM*] per paenitentia *AE*, paenitentia est *Z* dicit *VESMZ*] dixit *PA*, dicitur *F* et quorum *PVEF*]
quorum *SMZ*, arrum *A?* tertium per martyrium *PAVESMZ*] *om. F*
martyrium *AVESMZ*] martyrum *P* imputauit *PAVESMZ*] imputabit
*F* quarta remissio est *LAVFGSM*] quarta remissionem *P*, quartam remissionem *E*, quarta est *Z* per indulgentiam *PLAEFGSMZ*] indulgentia *V*
dicimus ... nostris] *om. EF* dicimus *PVGSMZ*] dicitur *L*, dixit *A* oratione dominica *LAVGSMZ*] orationem dominicam *P* dimitte *PAVGSMZ*]
et dimitte *L* si enim ... deus dimittet uobis] si enim non remiseritis hominibus peccata eorum nec pater uester caelestis dimittet uobis *L*, *om. G* si enim
*PLAV*] et *(om. EF)* ipse dominus dicit si enim *EFSMZ* hominibus
*AVEFSZ*] omnibus *P*, hominis *M* et pater uester caelestis dimittet uobis
*PAEFSZ*] dimittet uo. p. ue. c. *V*, et p. ue. c. dimittit uo. *M* si non ...
uobis] *om. AF* si *PESMZ*] si autem *V* dimittet *VESZ*] dimittit
*PM* quinta remissio est *LAVEF*] quinta remissionem *P*, quinta *SMZ*, sexta
*G* hoc est *PLAVGSM*] *om. EFZ* sex operibus m. *conieci*] sex operis m.
*PA*, per sex opera m. *L*, per sex operibus m. *V*, ex operibus m. *GSMZ*, *om. EF*
ipse dominus dicit *PVEFGSM*] ipse dicit *L*, ipse dominus *A*, dominus dicit
*Z* enim et *PAVEFGSM*] et *LZ* dedistis *PLAVEFGSM*] dedisti *Z*
mihi *PLAEFGSMZ*] *om. V* manducare *PLVEFGSMZ*] mandure *A*
sitiui *LAVEFGSZ*] sitibi *P* dedistis *PLAVEGSM*] dedisti *FZ* bibere
*PLAVEFGSM*] potum *Z* eram *PLVEFGSMZ*] eram eram *A* collegistis
*PLAVEFGSZ*] collegisti *M* me *PLVGSMZ (bis) EF (semel)*] *om. A*
*(bis)* nudus ... op. me] *om. EF* operuistis *PAVGSMZ*] cooperuistis
*L* infirmus ... uis. me] *om. PGM, post* in carcere ... ad me *transp. FS*
infirmus *AVEZ*] infirmus eram *LF* carcere *LVEFSZ*] carcerem *PM*, carce
*A*, cacere *G* uenistis *PLAVEFGSM*] uisitastis me et uenistis *Z* istas sex
... faciat] *om. SM* istas *conieci*] isti sunt *P*, haec sunt *L*, ista sunt *V*, istae
sunt *EGZ*, istarum *F* operationes *EGZ*] operis *PA*, opera *LV*, operationis
*F* misericordiae *PLAVEFZ*] nostrae *G* ex fide et ex *EG*] ex fade et *P*,
illa ex fide et *L*, ex fide et *A*, ex fide est et *V*, ex bona fide et ex *F*, et ex *Z*
bona uoluntate *PLAEFGZ*] bonam uoluntatem *V* ad omnes ... faciat] *om.*
*G* pauperes *PAVEFZ*] peccatores *L* peregrinos *PVEFZ*] peregrin *A*, ad
omnes peregrinos *L* ad *PLAZ*] et ad *V*, et *EF* dei *PAVEZ*] domini *F*,
*om. L* uel *PLAV*] et *EF*, uel ad *Z* dei *PLAVEZ*] domini *F* faciat
*conieci*] faciant *P*, faciant *an* faciunt *habeat A incertum*, facit *V*, faciunt *EFZ*,
faciunt habebit partem cum deo *L* sexta ... uobis] sexta ut est *(om. M)* illud
quaecumque uultis ut faciant uobis homines ita et uos facite illis *SM*, *om.*

*GZ*    remissio est *LAEF*] remissionem *P*, remissio *V*    per *PLVEF*] pro
*A*    dicit *PLAVF*] dixit *E*    date ... propheta dicit] *om. F*    omnia
*PLVE*] omnia *A*    septima ... peccatorum] septima in *(om. G)* doloribus mul-
tis ut dictum *(*datum *G)* est per infirmitatem corporis uirtus et *(om. SM)* ani-
mae perficitur *GSM, om. Z*    remissio est *LAE*] remissionem *P*, remissio
*V*    propheta *PLAV*] ipse dominus *E*    dicit *PLVE*] dixit *A*    quodsi
*PLAV*] quod *EF*    ergo *PLAEF*] ego *V*    te dicente ad impium *LAV*] te
dicentem ad impium *P*, te dicente ad impio *E*, ad impium te dicente *F*    ut
*PLAEF*] ipse *V*    se conuertat *conieci*] se conuertatur *LAV*, si conuertatur
*PE*, sic conuertatur *F*    mala et *PVEF*] mala *L, om. A*    ipse *PLVEF*]
ipsi *A*    iud. et iust. *PLAE*] iust. et iud. *F*, iud. *V*    uita *LAVEF*] uitam
*P*    uiuet *LVEF*] uiuit *PA*    dicit dominus *PLAV*] *om. EF*    et sanctus
Iacobus ait *PAVE*] *om. L*    conuerti fecerit *V (e* conerterecerit *) LEF*] con-
uerterit fecerit *P*, conconuertit fecerit *A*    peccatorem *PLVE*] peccatore
*A*    a morte *PLVEF*] *om. A*    operiet multitudinem *A*] operit et m. *P*,
opererit m. *L*, cooperit m. *V*, m. cooperit *EF*
16. resurrectionem *LVEFSMZ*] resurrectionis *PG*, resurrectionem carnis resurrectio non est *A*    sicut ... sinu meo] *om. EFGSMZ*    sicut *PAV*] sanctus
*L*    scio inquit *PLA*] scio *V*    resurrecturus sum *A*] resurrecturus sim *PV*,
surrecturus sum *L*    rursum *PAV*] rursus *L*    circumdabo pellem meam
*AV*] circumdabor pelle mea *L*    pellem ... uidebo] *om. P*    ego ipse *PAV*]
ipse *L*    alius *LAV*] alios *P*    reposita est *PAV*] reposita *L*    et in ipsa
*PLA*] in ipsa *VESMZ*, ipsa *GF*    carne *PLAVEFSM*] carnem uel anima *G*,
carne uel anima *Z*    qua *PLAVEGSMZ*] quo *F*    mouemur et sumus
*PVGSZ*] moueamur et s. *A*. moriemur et s. *L*, et s. *EF, om. M*    nos *PLEF*]
no *A*, nos resurrecturi *SMZ*, et nos resurrecturi *G, om. V*    in die ... dubio]
*om. EF*    die *LVZ*] diem *PAGSM*    absque dubio *PLVGZ*] absque dubium
*A, om. SM*    resurrecturi erimus *PLAEF*] resurrecturi *V*, erimus *GSMZ*
naturam aut sexum *PVFSM*] naturas aut sexus *L*, natura ut secum *A*, natura
aut sexu *E*, natum autem sexum *G*, naturam sexum *Z*    mutantes
*LAVEFGMZ*] immutantes *PS*    sed fragilitatem et *PAVEF*] sed fragilitatem
aut *L*, sed *GSM*, aut *Z*    uitia deponentes *PLAVGSZ*] uitio ponentes *E*, uitia
depotentes *M*, uitam deponentes *F*    et dominus dicit *PLAVGSMZ*] *om.*
*EF*    resurrectione enim *PL*] resurrectionem enim *A*, resurrectione *VEFSM*,
resurrectionem *G*, resurrectione mortuorum *Z*    erunt *PLAESZM*] sunt
*VFG*    angeli dei *PAVEFGSMZ*] angeli *L*    hoc est iusti *AVEZ*] hoc sunt
iusti *P*, hoc est iustis *F*, id est iusti *S, om. LGM*
17. uitam a. *PLVEFGS*] in uitam a. *AZ, om. M*    aeterna ... aeterna] *om.*
*L*    aeterna uita *PAVG*] uita *EF*, aeternam uitam *SM*, et aeterna uita
*Z*    sine fine *PAVEFGZ*] sine *SM*    mansura *PAVEFZ*] mansunt *G*, men-
sura *SM*    uita erit ubi *PLAVEGSMZ*] cuncta erit ibi *F*    semper perpe-
tua *PLAVESMZ*] perpetua *F*, semper *G*    felicitas *PASMZ*] felicitas erit
*LVE*, erit felicitas *F*    sicut propheta ... sempiternum] amen *SMZ, om.*
*G*    sicut propheta dicit] *om. LEF*    sicut *PVSZ*] cut *A*    erit opus
*PAVE*] opus erit *L*, opus *F*    iustitiae pax *PLAE*] iustiae pax *V*, iustitiam
*F*    cultus iustitiae *PLV*] cultus iustitia *A*, et cultus *E*, et occultus *F*
sempiternum *PV*] sempiternum amen *LEF*, sempiternum. Finit. Et ideo, fratres

carissimi, dicamus: Gloria deo patri qui misit in mundum proprium filium suum ut nos redimeret. Gloria deo filio qui per primum *(leg.* proprium*)* sanguine<m> a diaboli seruitio nos liberauit. Gloria sancto spiritui qui illuminat per sua ... corda credentium. Gloria et laus et honor et pax et gratiarum actio et uirtus et fortitudo sancta<e> et benedicta<e> trinitas *(leg.* trinitati*)* uni deo omnipotenti qui uult omnes homines saluos fieri et neminem uult perire. Ipsi soli gloria in omnes aeternita<te>s saeculi saeculorum. Amen *A*

The manuscript tradition of the anonymous *expositio symboli* CPL 1761

The complete text of the anonymous *expositio symboli* CPL 1761 seems to be contained in the eleventh-century Ambrosianus M 79 sup. (*A*) only. Its first paragraph is also found in the Parisiensis BN lat. 2170 (*P*), dating from the twelfth century. Burn, the first editor of the *expositio*, only knew *A*. In fact, two circumstances suggest that *P* may derive from *A*. The first of these is that both manuscripts use the abbreviation *fidī* for *fidei* in the phrase *fidei integritas* in *expositio symboli* 1. The second is connected with the immediately preceding words *quia eo indicatur*. Here, *A* seems at first sight to read *quia id indicatur*. However, *id* can hardly be what the scribe meant because in the rest of the text he consistently writes non-initial *d* with an upright shaft, whereas this *d* is almost circular. For this reason, the interpretation *quia eo indicatur*, which makes excellent sense, is indicated [1]. The reading of *P* (*quia per id indicatur*) may well be explained as a correction of *quia id indicatur*, which is what *A* yields at first sight and Burn printed in his edition.

It seems best, therefore, to prefer the readings of *A* where it differs from *P*. Nevertheless, we shall include the deviant reading of *P* in the critical apparatus as its dependence on *A* can, of course, by no means be taken for certain on such a narrow basis.

---

[1] The *e* of *eo* looks more like a *c* than an *e*. However, this is also the case in other instances of the combination *eo* in *A*. See for example the bottom lines of the left-hand column of f. 28V: *Non terreno ol**eo** ... **eo** quod ... **eo** quod* ... (*expositio symboli* 3).

codices:

A    Bibliotheca Ambrosiana, M 79 sup., ff. 28V-29R, saec. XI
P    Parisiensis, Bibliothèque Nationale, Latinus 2710, f. 60R, saec. XII

editio:

Bu   BURN, A.E., 'Neue Texte zur Geschichte des apostolischen Symbols. II, in: *Zeitschrift für Kirchengeschichte* 21, 1900, 135-137

expositio symboli CPL 1761

1. Symbolum Graece, Latine indicium uel signum siue collatio dicitur. Indicium, quia eo indicatur fidei integritas. Signum, quod eo bene retento et intellecto fideles ab infidelibus discernuntur. Collatio, quia in eo apostoli omnem fidei integritatem contulerunt.

2. Credo in deum. Id est, firmitatem fidei meae profiteor. Deus a timore dicitur, eo quod cunctis colentibus sit timori. Credo deum esse sine principio et sine fine, inuisibilem et incomprehensibilem. Et quando dico: Patrem, credo quod coaeternum et coaequalem sibi per omnia genuit filium, ut Iohannes ait: *In principio erat uerbum* (Ioh. 1, 1), et psalmista dicit: *Ante luciferum genui te* (Ps. 110, 3). Cur omnipotens deus? Eo quod omnia possit et omnia contineat potestate. Et credo in eum *qui creauit caelum et terram ex nihilo* (Gen. 1, 1. Ps. 124, 8. II Mach. 7, 28).

3. Et credo in Iesum Christum, filium eius. Iesus in Hebraeo eloquio, Latine salutaris siue saluator interpretatur. Christus Graece a chrismate nomen accepit, Latine unctus dicitur, de quo in Psalmo dicitur: *Propterea unxit te, deus, deus tuus*, et reliqua (Ps. 45, 8). Non terreno oleo ut reges et sacerdotes solent perungui (cf. Ex. 29, 7-9 et 40, 13. Num. 3, 3. I Reg. 10, 1 et 16, 13. III Reg. 1, 34 et 39. I Par. 11, 3), sed unctio ista incorporea et inuisibilis fuit. Filium eius dicit eo quod habeat patrem, patrem uero eo quod habeat filium, genitum namque ante omnia tempora, ut Iohannes ait: *Omnia per ipsum facta sunt et sine ipso factum est nihil* (Ioh. 1, 3). 4. Vnicum dominum nostrum. Vnicum uel singularem dominum qui cuncta gubernat et dominat quod condidit.

5. Qui conceptus est de spiritu sancto. Non ex uirili coitu uel semine sed ex uirtute spiritus sancti conceptus est. 6. Natus ex Maria uirgine, non uiolato uirginis utero, sed: uirgo ante partum,

uirgo in partu, uirgoque post partum. 7. Passusque sub Pontio Pilato. Passionem uero crucis sustinens ex parte humanitatis sub Pilato Romano principe qui ortus fuit in Pontio, ut dictum est cruci affixus ante portas Hierusalem in Caluario monte, in hoc quoque patibulo mortuus humanitate ac sepultus est in monumento. 8. Descendit ad inferna. Tantummodo anima, sicut psalmista dicit: *Vita mea in inferno appropinquabit et factus sum sicut homo inter mortuos liber* (Ps. 88, 4-6). Descendit enim in infernum, non iniuriam pertulit, sed ut noxii soluerentur qui propter originale peccatum illic detinebantur. Partem abstulit, partem reliquit.

9. Tertia die resurrexit a mortuis. Tertio quoque die uirtute propria suscitatus a sepulcro surrexit. 10. Ascendit in caelum, ubi numquam defuit secundum diuinitatem. 11. Sedet ad dexteram dei patris omnipotentis. Quod uero dicitur deus sedere et ascendere, hoc ad carnis mysterium pertinet. Et psalmista dicit: *Parata sedes tua, deus* (Ps. 93, 2). Illucque non est sinistra pars, sed ubi sessio dei est et iustorum dextera pars congrue accipitur, quia nihil est in regno dei sinistrum. 12. Inde uenturus iudicare uiuos et mortuos. De qua sede ueniet iudicare uiuos et mortuos. Viuos dicit qui praedestinati sunt ad uitam, mortuos uero qui ad damnationem sunt praedestinati.

13. Credo in spiritum sanctum, qui a patre filioque processit quia consubstantialis est patri et filio et coaeternus. 14. Et credo sanctam ecclesiam catholicam, diffusam per uniuersum orbem, id est congregationem fidelium electorum siue uniuersalem. 15. Et credo sanctorum communionem me habere, id est societatem sanctorum, si adimpleuero quae profiteor.

16. Et remissionem peccatorum firmiter spero me habere per dei misericordiam (cf. Luc. 1, 77-78). Primo per baptismum, secundo per martyrium, tertio per eleemosyna, sicut scriptum est: *Peccata mea eleemosynis redime in misericordiis pauperum* (Dan. 4, 24). Quarto, si remittit quis peccanti in se peccata sua, iuxta illud: *Dimittite et dimittetur uobis* (Luc. 6, 37). Quinto, si per praedicationem suam aliquis et per bonorum operum exercitium alios ab errore suo conuertat, ut apostolus ait: *Quoniam qui conuerti fecerit peccatorem ab errore uiae suae* (Iac. 5, 20). Sexto per caritatem, ut dicit: *Caritas dei cooperit multitudinem peccatorum* (I Petr. 4, 8). Septimo per paenitentiam, sicut Dauid ait: *Conuersus sum in aerumna mea dum configitur spina* (Ps. 32, 4).

17. Carnis resurrectionem. Et credo carnem in qua nunc sumus resuscitandam in ultimo die cum omni integritate corporis in triginta annorum aetate. 18. Et uitam aeternam credo me habere, si deus omnipotens mihi concesserit perseuerare in operibus bonis, ut psalmista dicit: *Credo uidere bona domini in terra uiuentium* (Ps. 27, 13). 19. Amen. Quod dicitur fideliter siue firmiter.

apparatus criticus apud expositionem symboli CPL 1761

item alia expositio symboli *A Bu*] om. *P*
1. Graece *A Bu*] om. *P*　　siue *A Bu*] uel *P*　　dicitur *A Bu*] interpretatur *P* eo *A*] per id *P,* id *Bu*
2. eo *A*] deus eo *Bu*　　timori *conieci*] timor *A Bu*　　inuisibilem *conieci*] uisibilem inuisibilem *A Bu*　　contineat *conieci*] continet *A Bu*
4. quod *A*] quae *Bu*　　deus *(1°  ) Bu*] deo *A*　　congrue *conieci*] id est conuenienter *(*conuenientur *Bu)* congrue *A Bu*
14. siue *A*] suae *Bu*
15. communionem me *conieci*] communionem *A Bu*
16. primo *conieci*] primum *A Bu*　　exercitium *A*] exercitum *Bu*　　dum *A*] dii *Bu*
17. carnem *conieci*] resurrectionem carnis *A Bu*　　resuscitandam *A*] resuscitandum *Bu*
19. quod *A*] quo *Bu*

The manuscript tradition of the anonymous *de fide trinitatis quo-modo exponitur* [1] CPL 1762

This text was first edited by Burn, who designated it as "eine merkwürdige Kompilation" [2]. Burn's judgement is supported by the manuscript tradition. The introduction, the presentation of the Creed, and some general remarks on Christology and the function of the Creed [3] are apparently only preserved by two Vatican manuscripts (Vaticani Palatini Latini 212 and 220, *P* and *Q*), of which the second is dated to the ninth century and the first to the ninth or the tenth century [4]. The next section (*Haec summa ... qui uiuit et regnat*) [5] also occurs in the *Sacramentarium Gelasianum Vetus* (CPL 1899) [6] and two other manuscripts, Modoetiensis e 14/27 (*M*) and Romanus Sessorianus 52 (*S*) [7]. The rest of the text, mainly concerned with a correct understanding of the doctrines of the Trinity and God's unity [8], is again only offered by *PQ*.

In the middle part, therefore, we have to tackle the problem of the relationship between no less than five manuscripts, whereas for the opening and closing portions of the text we only have to assess the relationship between *P* and *Q*. To start with the simpler problem, it has already been observed that *P* and *Q* have practically

---

[1] For the title, which is not completely legible in *Q* and is yielded as *de fide trinitatis quo* $\overline{om}$ *exponitur*, we rely on Stevenson 1886, 42 and 47.

[2] Burn 1900, 132-135.

[3] *De fide trinitatis quomodo exponitur* 1-4.

[4] Stevenson 1886, 41 and 46. Below, it will be claimed that *Q* is a copy of *P*. In that case, both manuscripts must apparently stem from the ninth century.

[5] *De fide trinitatis quomodo exponitur* 5-6.

[6] In fact, our anonymous treatise only contains two parts of a text that forms a short sermon on the Creed in *Sacramentarium Gelasianum Vetus* 315 and 317 (Mohlberg 1968, 50-51), the latter in a slightly different form.

[7] See Burn 1900, 132 and Brewer 1909, 181-182. *S* is very closely related to *M* but does not seem to derive from it: see above, *expositio super symbolum* CPL 1760, pp. 498-500. In both manuscripts, the text *Haec summa ...* is appended to the anonymous *expositio super symbolum* CPL 1760, a fact that was overlooked by Morin in his study of *S*: see Morin 1897, 485 and Kattenbusch 1900, 971n15. *MS*, however, only contain the first section and beginning of the second section of the short sermon in the Gelasian Sacramentary (*Sacramentarium Gelasianum Vetus* 315-316; *ibid.*), the latter in a somewhat deviating recension.

[8] *De fide trinitatis quomodo exponitur* 7-11.

identical contents [9]. In addition, their texts of the anonymous sermon *de fide trinitatis* CPL 1762 only differ in details of wording, so
that the conclusion that *P* and *Q* must be very closely related
imposes itself. This conclusion is supported by a number of common
abbreviations like *apos* for *apostoli*, *ompm* for *omnipotentem* and $q\ \overline{qq}$
for (probably) *quod quiqui* in *de fide trinitatis quomodo exponitur* 2
and 4. The next question is, of course, whether *P* and *Q* should be
considered sister manuscripts, deriving from a common parent, or
whether one of them may be taken as the original of the other. In
practically all instances where *P* and *Q* differ, the reading of *P* is
better or at least not any worse than that of *Q*. The only exception
occurs in the phrase *simili exemplo comparatur* in *de fide trinitatis* 8,
where *P* has *simile*. The (incorrect) form *simile* is not original in *P*,
however, as the *-e* of *simile* has clearly been made out of an *-i* [10].
This implies that the scribe of *Q* may well still have read the (correct) form *simili* in *P*, or, if otherwise, he may have corrected *simile*
to *simili* himself [11]. The obvious conclusion is, therefore, that *Q* is a
copy of *P* [12].

For the middle part of the text, the relationship between *PQ* on
the one hand and *MS* and the *Sacramentarium Gelasianum Vetus* (*V*)
on the other needs to be investigated. It has already been noted that
not all of the five witnesses present identical versions of this part - *V*

---

[9] See Stevenson 1886, 41-43 and 46-47.

[10] The reason for this change must remain obscure. Maybe the scribe or a later
reader understood *simile exemplo* as a nominative?

[11] There are two possible exceptions in the middle part as well - the cases of
*nemo non idoneus, nemo non aptus* and *utamini* (*de fide trinitatis quomodo exponitur* 5 and 6). There, however, *P* is difficult to read or even illegible, whereas *Q*
agrees with or comes close to *V*, the main manuscript of the Gelasian Sacramentary. The possibility should be envisaged that the scribe of *Q* knew the Gelasian
Sacramentary and relied on it where he could not make sense of his original.

[12] Both manuscripts also agree in the peculiarity that they have the title of
the next piece (*praedicatio carere tormenta*) only after its first phrase (which Burn
[1900, 135] therefore included in his edition of our anonymous text; similarly
Stevenson 1886, 42): *Quicumque inuocauerit nomen domini saluus erit*. That this
indeed belongs to the next piece is borne out by the words that follow the title
in both manuscripts: ... *peccatoribus autem et impiis, homocidiis* (*sic*) *fornicatoribus
et sceleratis, mendacibus, rapacibus, parricidis, raptoribus, doloris neglegentibus,
transgressoribus dei mandata* (*sic*), *et aliis, quibusque non facientibus iustitiam,
alius praeparatur locus* ... Burn's and Stevenson's mistake was almost inevitable
because *PQ* write *peccatoribus* with a capital.

stands alone with a relatively long text, whereas *MS* on the one hand and *PQ* on the other offer shorter variants [13]. The question of which version is original and which ones are later cannot be answered here, but it is seems certain that *V*, *PQ*, and *MS* offer three distinct recensions [14]. For that reason, it is best to stick to the testimony of *PQ*, unless both manuscripts are clearly corrupt and one of the other two recensions offers a sound text. This seems to be the case with the phrase *uerae diuinitatis ratione disposita* (thus *MS*; *V* has *uera diuinitus ratione disposita*), where *PQ* have *uere diuitibus ratione disposita*. Similarly, the combination *nemo non idoneus, nemo non aptus* (thus *VMS*) has been corrupted to *nisi idoneus nemo aptus* in *P* (*Q* has *non idoneus nemo non aptus*; it could be that *P* has an erased *non* between *nemo* and *aptus*).

All in all, we shall rely on *P* for most of our edition of the anonymous *de fide trinitatis quomodo exponitur* CPL 1762. For the middle section, *V* and *MS* occasionally offer a better reading. The deviant readings of *Q* will all be incorporated in the critical apparatus.

---

[13] See above, footnotes 6 and 7.
[14] See for one possible standpoint Kattenbusch 1900, 973.

codices:

P    Bibliotheca Apostolica Vaticana, Palatinus Latinus 212, ff.
13V-15R, saec. IX

Q    Bibliotheca Apostolica Vaticana, Palatinus Latinus 220, ff.
23V-26R, saec. IX

partim:

V    Bibliotheca Apostolica Vaticana, Reginensis 316, saec. VIII,
(iuxta MOHLBERG, L.C., *Liber Sacramentorum Romanae
Aeclesiae Ordinis Anni Circuli (Cod. Vat. Reg. lat. 316/Paris
Bibl. Nat. 7193, 41/56) (Sacramentarium Gelasianum)* ...,
Roma, 1968 [= MOHLBERG, L.C. (ed.), *Rerum Ecclesiastica-
rum Documenta ... Series Maior. Fontes*, 4], 50-51)

M    Modoetiensis (Monza), Biblioteca Capitolare e 14/27, ff. 38V-
39R, saec. X

S    Romanus, Biblioteca Nazionale Centrale, Sessorianus 52, f.
163R, saec. XII

editiones

Bu   BURN, A.E., 'Neue Texte zur Geschichte des apostolischen
Symbols. II, in: *Zeitschrift für Kirchengeschichte* 21, 1900,
135-137

partim:

Br   BREWER, H., *Das sogenannte Athanasianische Glaubensbe-
kenntnis ein Werk des heiligen Ambrosius* ..., Paderborn, 1909
(EHRHARD, A. - KIRSCH, J.P. [edd.], *Forschungen zur
Christlichen Litteratur- und Dogmengeschichte*, IX 2, 181

de fide trinitatis quomodo exponitur CPL 1762

1. Quicumque uult esse saluus ante omnia opus est ut teneat
catholicam fidem, quam nisi quisque integram inuiolatamque
seruauerit absque dubio in aeternum peribit.

2. Ideo apostoli symbolum constituerunt. Primus Simon Petrus
dixit: Credo in deum patrem omnipotentem. Andreas frater eius:
Et in Iesum Christum, filium eius unicum. Iacobus Zebedaei: Qui
natus est de spiritu sancto et Maria semper uirgine. Iohannes frater
eius: Qui sub Pontio Pilato crucifixus et sepultus est. Philippus:

Resurrexit tertia die a mortuis. Bartholomaeus: Ascendit uictor ad caelos. Thomas: Sedet ad dexteram patris. Mathaeus: Inde uenturus est iudicare uiuos et mortuos. Iacobus Alphaei: Et in spiritum sanctum. Thaddaeus ipse Iudas Iacobi: Sanctam ecclesiam. Simon Cananaeus qui et Zelotes: Remissionem peccatorum. Mathias: Carnis resurrectionem et uitam futuri saeculi. Amen.

3. Sancta trinitas et uera unitas, id est filium natum ex patre et ante omnia saecula, lumen de lumine, deum uerum de deo uero, atque eundem dominum nostrum et deum Iesum Christum, consubstantialem deo patri secundum deitatem, aequalis gloriae et honoris, eandemque in tribus personis essentiam, naturam, uirtutem, potentiam, regnum, imperium, uoluntatem, operationem, incomprehensibilem, inmutabilem, summum bonum.

4. Idcirco igitur istud iudicium posuere unianimitatis et fidei suae apostoli symbolum, id est signum per quod agnoscitur deus - sicut mos est saecularibus ut in bellis symbola discreta sint, ut si forte occurrat quis de quo dubitatur, interroget et symbolum prodat ut sciat si sit hostis an socius -, quod quiqui proinde credentes accipiant ut nouerint qualiter contra diabolum fidei certamina praeparent. In quo quidem pauca sunt uerba sed omnia continent sancta sacramenta, ut qui etiam haec in corde retinent sibi sufficienter salutem animarum habent.

5. Haec summa fidei nostrae, dilectissimi nobis, haec uerba sunt symboli non sapientiae humanae sermone fuscata sed uerae diuinitatis ratione disposita, quibus comprehendendis atque seruandis nemo non idoneus, nemo non aptus est. 6. Hic dei patris et filii una et aequalis pronuntiatur potestas. Hic unigenitus dei filius de Maria uirgine et spiritu sancto secundum carnem natus ostenditur. Hic eiusdem crucifixio et sepultura ac die tertio resurrectio praedicatur. Hic ascensio ipsius super caelos et consessio in dextera paternae maiestatis agnoscitur uenturusque ad iudicandos uiuos et mortuos declaratur. Hic spiritus sanctus in eadem qua pater et filius deitate indiscretus accipitur. Hic postremo ecclesiae uocatio peccatorum remissio et carnis resurrectio perdocetur. 7. Quae breuissima plenitudo ita debet uestris cordibus inhaerere ut omni tempore praesidio huius confessionis utamini. Inuicta est enim talium armorum potestas et uobis contra omnes insidias diaboli tamquam bonis Christi militibus profutura. Diabolus, qui hominem temptare non desinit, munitos uos hoc symbolo semper inueniat, ut deiecto ad-

uersario cui renuntiastis gratiam domini incorruptam et immaculatam usque in finem, ipso quem confitemini protegente, seruetis, Iesu Christo domino nostro, qui uiuit et regnat.

8. Pater ut fons, filius ut flumen, spiritus uero sanctus ut riuus a flumine, siue pater sicut radix, filius sicut arbor, spiritus autem sanctus sicut flos. Simili exemplo comparatur pater quasi sol, filius quasi radius, spiritus enim sanctus quasi apex. Iterum pater uelut ignis, filius uelut calor, spiritus sanctus uelut candor. 9. Dabo enim exemplum aliud uobis adhuc quomodo trinitas sancta uera unitas sit certum. Vna est sapientia in homine et de una sapientia procedit intellectus, memoria, ingenium. Si ergo tu homo habere potes tria ista in una sapientia, quanto magis deus in una deitate tres quidem personas habere credendus est sed unam substantiam. 10. Nam et caput quinque sensibus constat. Habes enim in uno capite uisum, auditum, odoratum et gustum et tactum, quomodo et in uinea tres sunt, lignum, folium, fructus. Si ergo corruptibilia et terrena ita unum sunt ut uere tria sint et ita tria ut uere unum sint * * * 11. Primum ergo fructum habetis si bene creditis secundum * * * baptizabimini. Qui perseuerauerit usque in finem, hic saluus erit baptizatus (cf. Marc. 16, 16). *Corde creditur ad iustitiam, ore autem confessio fit ad salutem* (Rom. 10, 10).

apparatus criticus apud de fide trinitatis CPL 1762

de fide trinitatis quomodo exponitur] de fide trinitatis quo  m exponitur *P*, de fide trinitatis quo expon *Q*, *om. Bu, sed uide Steuenson 1886, 42 et 47*
2. dixit *conieci*] dicit *PQ*      Philippus resurrexit *P*] Philippus dixit *Q*      Thomas *P*] Thomas dicit *Q*
3. Christum consubstantialem *P*] Christi consubstantilem *Q*      eandemque *conieci*] eundemque *P, unam* eundemque *Q*      potentiam *P*] potentia *Q*
4. quod *P*] quem *Q*      sint *conieci*] sit *PQ*      occurrat *conieci*] occurreret *PQ*      interroget et *conieci*] interrogat *PQ*      prodat *conieci*] prodeat *PQ* sciat si *conieci*] si *PQ*      quiqui *conieci*] $\overline{qq}$ *PQ*, quiquam *Bu*      accipiant ut *conieci*] accipiunt *PQ*      nouerint *P*] nouerunt *Q*      praeparent *conieci*] praepararent *PQ*
5. summa *PQ*] summa est *VMS*      symboli *PVMS*] simili *Q*      humanae *MS*] humano *PQV*      fuscata *P*] fucata *Q, facta VMS*      uerae diuinitatis *S*] uera diuinitas *M,* uera diuinitus *V,* uera diuitibus *PQ*      ratione *PQVS*] narratione *M*      comprehendendis *PQVS*] comprehendentis *M*      seruandis *PQVS*] seruandi *M*      nemo non ... nemo non *VMS*] nisi ... nemo *P,* non ... nemo non *Q*      aptus est *PQ*] aptus *VMS*
6. una et *PQMS*] una *V*      dei filius *PQ*] dei *VMS*      spiritu *PQVM*] spiritus *S*      crucifixio *PQS*] crucifixo *V,* crucifixi *M*      et *PQV*] ac *MS*      ac

*PQV*] et *MS*        die tertio *PQ*] die tertia *VS*, die *M*        consessio *PQ*] confessio *VMS*        uenturusque *PQVMS*] uenturus usque *Bu*        iudicandos *PQV*]
iudicandus *M*, iudicandum *S*        eadem q. p. e. f. deitate *PQV*] eadem deitate
q. p. e. f. *MS*        qua *PQVS*] quia *M*        postremo *PVMS*] postremeo *Q*
perdocetur *PQMS*] perducitur *V*

7. quae breuissima plenitudo *PQ*] et ideo hanc breuissimam plenitudinem *V*
debet *PQ*] debetis *V*        utamini *QV*] *P non legitur (*munimini *??)*        enim
*PQ*] enim semper *V*        et uobis contra *conieci*] et contra uobis *PQ*, contra
*V*        diaboli *PQ*] inimici *V*        tamquam ... militibus *PQ*] ad bonam Christi
militiam *V*        profutura *PQ*] profuturis *V*        uos *V*] nos *PQ*        inueniat *V*]
inueniet *PQ*        renuntiastis *PQ*] renuntiatis *V*        incorruptam *PV*] incorrupta
*Q*        quem *PQ*] *om. V*

8. simili *Q*] simile *e* simili *P*        quasi sol *P*] quas sol *Q*

9. certum *conieci*] certo *e* certa *P*, certa *Q*

10. memoria *conieci*] et memoria *PQ*        credendus *P*] credendum *Q*        et tactum quomodo et in *conieci*] et tactumqu ᵏin *P (?)*, tactumque in *Q*, et tactum
quia in *Bu*        sint ... sint *P*] sunt ... sunt *Q*        *lacunam post* unum sint *indi-*
*caui*

11. creditis *P*] credetis *Q*        *lacunam post* secundum *indicaui*] secundum est
*PQ*        creditur *conieci*] credit *PQ*        *post* salutem *Bu:* quicumque inuocauerit
nomen domini saluus erit, *quod autem initium sequentis sermonis esse uidetur*

The manuscript tradition of the *expositio fidei* CPL 1763

The complete text of the anonymous *expositio fidei* CPL 1763 is only offered by two Parisienses: (*P* and *Q*, ninth and tenth century respectively). Parts of the text, however, can also be seen in the anonymous *expositio de fide catholica* CPL 505, in the pseudo-Augustinian *excarpsum de fide catholica* or *sermo 244* [1], and in a hitherto unedited text in a third, eleventh-century, Parisiensis (*R*) [2]. The first of these is practically identical with the dogmatic part of our text, *expositio fidei* 2-13. The pseudo-Augustinian *excarpsum* and our *expositio* have the introduction and the moralist part in common (*expositio fidei* 1 and 14-21; *excarpsum* ll. 2-4, §§ 2-3). In the third Parisiensis we find only the exhortatory part of our *expositio* [3]. Since all four texts bear the signs of some deliberate redaction,

---

[1] See for these two texts above, chapters 4.5 and 4.8.

[2] Bibliothèque Nationale, Latinus 2628, ff. 121V-123R.

[3] This part is preceded by the following words in *R*: *Rogo et admoneo uos, fratres, ut quicumque Christianus post baptismum criminalem culpam fecit, puram confessionem ad sacerdotem donet, paenitentiam agat et post actam paenitentiam tempore quo sacerdos ei constituerit oblationem suam ad sacerdotem offerat et corpus et sanguinem Christi suscipiat. Nullus Christianus a corpore et sanguine Christi se abstrahere uel prolongare debet, quia dominus in Euangelio ait: Ego sum panis uitae qui de caelo descendi. Si quis manducauerit ex hoc pane uiuit in aeternum. Et: Panis quem ego dabo caro mea est pro mundi uita. Et iterum: Qui manducat meam carnem et meum sanguinem bibit in me manet et ego in illo. Et iterum: Nisi manducaueritis carnem filii hominis et biberitis eius sanguinem, non habebitis uitam in uobis. Igitur, fratres carissimi, consideremus quod scriptum est: Contraria contrariis sanantur. Et dominus per prophetam ait: Quiescite agere peruerse, discite bene facere. Et iterum: Declina a malo et fac bona. Et apostolus: Noli uinci a malo, sed uince in bono malum. Et iterum: Nox praecessit, dies autem appropinquauit. Deponamus itaque opera tenebrarum et induamur arma lucis. Sicut in die honeste ambulemus. Et ecce quomodo nos pius dominus admonet ut de malo ad bona nos conuertat. Obsecro itaque uos ut quicumque talia quae supra diximus et his similia contra praeceptum domini fecit de dei misericordia (?) numquam desperet, quia per prophetam dominus ait: Nolo mortem peccatoris sed ut conuertatur et uiuat. Sed unusquisque cum fide recta confessionem puram donet et ueram paenitentiam agat, et quod male fecit perfecte defleat et per iustas eleemosynas et bonis operibus se emendet et caueat ut amplius non peccet, quia scriptum est: Lauamini, mundi estote. Et: Qui abscondit scelera sua non dirigetur, qui autem confessus fuerit et reliquerit ea ueniam merebitur. Et illud: Cum conuersus fueris et ingemueris, tunc saluus eris. Et in Euangelio: Paenitentiam agite, appropinquauit enim regnum caelorum. Et apostolus: Confitemini peccata uestra alterutrum. Et dominus nos admonet ut cessemus ab omni opere malo et conuertamus nos ad omne opus bonum. Quare tam tardi sumus ad conuertendum et emendandum nos, dum domino auxiliante in nostra sunt potes-*

each of them can only be of indirect use for the constitution of the text of one of the others. For the anonymous *expositio fidei*, this means that we should first and foremost try to gain an intelligible text from the two manuscripts *PQ*. Only then will a comparison of the four related pieces be possible.

The anonymous *expositio fidei* CPL 1763 was partly published on the basis of the two manuscripts *PQ* by Ommanney in 1880. From certain peculiarities, Ommanney drew the conclusion that *Q* must derive from *P*[4]. This hypothesis is supported by a careful examination of the manuscripts themselves. When one examines all the instances where the two manuscripts differ (other than in spelling and abbreviations), they can be divided into two classes.

First, there are several simple and obvious errors in *Q* where *P* offers a sound reading: *mortuis* for *mortuos* (twice in *expositio fidei* 4), *uidimus* for *uidemus* (5), *scriptum* for *scriptum est* (6), the omission of four words which apparently triggered the 'correction' of *ad* to *ac* (*ibidem*)[5], *fraudare* for *fraudari*, *credderitis* for *credideritis* (both in 9), *masculos* for *masculus* (11), *ita* for *ita et* (19), and *osculate* for *exosculate* (*ibidem*). All of these cases, except the hypercorrection, can easily be explained as errors made by a scribe who was working with *P*. An at first sight not so obvious case, where *Q* reads *affixus* and *P* *appensus* (*expositio fidei* 15) can also be seen to be an error in *Q* when the manuscripts themselves are consulted. In *P*, the word *appensus* (spelled *adpensus*) has been written exactly one line beneath the word *confixus*, which perfectly explains *affixus* (spelled *adfixus*) as a case of *lapsus oculi*.

Then there are obvious errors in *P* which have been corrected by *Q*: *conseruit* for *conseruet* (*expositio fidei* 1), *bibet* for *bibit* (17), *emendit* for *emendet* (20), *donit* for *donet* (20), *diuitas* for *diuinitas* (9), *resurrectionem* for *resurrectione* (13). In all these instances, it is so

---

*tate remedia quia pius dominus indulgentiam futuro tempore et gloriae ueniam promittit? Nolite tardare conuerti ad dominum et ne differatis de die in diem. Nescitis quid faciat superuenturus dies, a mane usque ad uesperum mutabitur tempus. Et alibi: Hodie si uocem eius audieritis nolite obdurare corda uestra. Et iterum: Vigilate et orate, quia nescitis diem neque horam. Igitur, fratres ...* See for some more details on this text CCSL 104, 985.

[4] Ommanney 1880, 393-396.

[5] See Ommanney 1880, 394n4.

obvious that the readings in *P* are errors that those in *Q* can without difficulty be regarded as deliberate corrections.

The only case which seems more difficult is the reading *ignem ardentem* in *Q* instead of the simple *ignem* in *P* in the phrase ... *sicut aqua extinguit ignem (ardentem), ita et eleemosyna extinguit peccatum* (*expositio fidei* 19). This is a reference to Jesus Sirach 3, 33 (Vulgate): *Ignem ardentem extinguit aqua, et eleemosyna resistit peccatis.* Since this is a reference and not a quotation, however, it is perfectly possible that *ardentem* does not belong to the original phrase but was inserted by a scribe who wanted to supply a word which he thought to be missing.

There are no instances, therefore, where *Q* supposes any other source than *P*, so that at least nothing contradicts the hypothesis that *Q* is directly dependent on *P*. One positive indication has already been mentioned - the erroneous *affixus* for *appensus* in *Q*, where the conditions for this scribal error were seen to be optimal in *P*. Another positive indication is the occurrence of the abbreviation *ds* in *P* for *deos* in *expositio fidei* 7. The context (*non tres deos sed unum*) makes it absolutely clear that *ds* cannot stand for *deus*, as it usually does, but that *deos* is what is meant. *Q* exhibits the same unusual abbreviation here, but with a small *o* above the line (*d$^{o}$s*). The obvious explanation is that the scribe of *Q* read *ds* in *P*, recognized that this abbreviation must stand for *deos* there, and added an *o* to exclude any misunderstanding. Our conclusion is, therefore, that *Q* is a direct copy of *P* [6].

Although it is only of secondary importance for our study of the anonymous *expositio fidei* CPL 1763, at least something should be said about the relationship between our text and the *expositio de fide catholica* CPL 505, the pseudo-Augustinian *excarpsum*, and the unedited sermon in *R*. First of all, it should be emphasized that each of these four texts is a text on its own, and that we cannot replace parts of one with parts of another. Nevertheless, the resemblances that exist between the four texts are so striking that it seems certain that some or more direct dependencies exist between them. The question is, of course, whether we can say something more about the direction of those dependencies.

---

[6] An additional argument is provided by the fact that the *expositio* occurs in both manuscripts in exactly the same context: see Caspari 1883a, XVin1.

First of all it has already been observed that the text of *expositio fidei* 2-13 derives from a manuscript that represents a later stage of one branch of the textual tradition of the *expositio de fide catholica* [7]. This implies that the *expositio fidei* is dependent on the *expositio de fide catholica* and not the other way round.

Next, the anonymous *expositio fidei* CPL 1763 has some portions of text in common with the pseudo-Augustinian *excarpsum* and the sermon in *R*. Here, some details of wording strongly suggest that the *expositio* is dependent on the *excarpsum*. These comprise the following cases. In the *excarpsum*, we read ... *calicem passionis quem ipse bibit biberunt*. The *expositio* has ... *calicem passionis quem bibit ipsi biberunt* [8]. Here, the use of *ipse* seems to be more meaningful with *bibit* than with *biberunt*, since following Christ is the important item here, not the followers of Christ, and, moreover, *bibit* would otherwise lack a subject. Similarly, the combination *uoracitatem et crapulam uini* (thus the *excarpsum*) seems to be more original because it contains two distinct but related items. The *expositio*, on the other hand, reads *ebrietatem et crapulam* [9], a formulation in which the two elements have become simply synonyms. The *excarpsum* is again clearly offering a more satisfactory text some lines below: *Hospites in domos uestra colligite, et pedes eorum lauate, linteo extergite ...*, where the *expositio* reads: ... *hospites in domibus uestris colligite, pedes lauate, linteum tergite ...* [10]. The last phrase in the *expositio* is particularly suspect. The phrase *linteum tergite* can be translated as "clean <their> clothes," but the wording of the *excarpsum* is much more logical: "rub <their feet> dry with a towel." The conclusion seems safe, therefore, that the anonymous *expositio fidei* is dependent on the *excarpsum*.

When we turn to the text in *R* at last, it leaps to the eye that whereas the *excarpsum* and the *expositio* both contain a fairly long exhortatory part, the anonymous sermon in *R* only has the second half of this piece. This opens up two possibilities - either the shorter text is original, and both longer ones secondary, or the longer texts are original, and the shorter one is a deliberate abbreviation. That the latter must be the case is borne out by the reading *ebrietatem et*

---

[7] See above, *expositio de fide catholica* CPL 505, pp. 433-434.
[8] Pseudo-Augustine, *excarpsum de fide catholica* 2; *expositio fidei* 17.
[9] Pseudo-Augustine, *excarpsum de fide catholica* 3; *expositio fidei* 19.
[10] Pseudo-Augustine, *excarpsum de fide catholica* 3; *expositio fidei* 19.

*crapulam uini* in *R*, where it agrees with the secondary *expositio* as opposed to the more original *excarpsum* in reading *ebrietatem*, not *uoracitatem* [11]. An indirect argument is provided by the other instance that has been discussed above, where the *excarpsum* and the *expositio* read *linteo extergite* and *linteum tergite* respectively. The sermon in *R* omits the phrase. Although this can of course be explained as a simple scribal error caused by homoioteleuton, a deliberate omission of a difficult phrase is more probable in view of the fact that the redactor of the sermon has adapted the wording of his original in more than one place [12].

Our conclusion, therefore, is that the *expositio de fide catholica* CPL 505 and the pseudo-Augustinian *excarpsum* are the oldest texts, that the redactor of the *expositio fidei* CPL 1763 made use of both, and that the redactor of the sermon in *R* made use of the *expositio fidei* CPL 1763 again.

[11] Pseudo-Augustine, *excarpsum de fide catholica* 3; *expositio fidei* 19.

[12] For example: *qui aliquando ad ecclesiam tarde ueniebat* (thus *excarpsum* 3 and *expositio* 18) has been changed into *qui tarde in ecclesiam ueniebat* in *R*; *decimas per annos singulos de omni fructu quod colligitis inter ecclesias et pauperibus erogate* (thus *excarpsum* 3; in *expositio* 19 we read *decimas de omni fructu quod colligitis inter ecclesias et pauperes erogate*) has been changed into *decimas uestras annis singulis de omni fructu quem colligitis ad ecclesias reddite*; *honoret patrem et matrem* (*excarpsum* 3 and *expositio* 20) has become *filius honoret patrem et matrem*. In all these cases, the readings of *R* bear the signs of providing a smoother or more complete text.

codices:

P    Parisiensis, Bibliothèque Nationale, Latinus 3848B, ff. 43R-
     46V, saec. IX
Q    Parisiensis, Bibliothèque Nationale, Latinus 2123, ff. 21V-
     24V, saec. X
R    Parisiensis, Bibliothèque Nationale, Latinus 2628, ff. 122V-
     123R, saec. XI (§§ 14-21 tantum)

editiones:

Om   OMMANNEY, G.D.W., *Early History of the Athanasian
     Creed. The Results of Some Original Research upon the Subject*
     ..., London - Oxford - Cambridge, 1880, 393-396 (§§ 1-13, 21
     tantum)
Ca   CASPARI, C.P., *Kirchenhistorische Anecdota nebst neuen Aus-
     gaben patristischer und kirchlich-mittelalterlichter Schriften ... I.
     Lateinische Schriften. Die Texte und die Anmerkungen*, Chris-
     tiania, 1883, 283-289 (= PLS 4, 2165-2167)

*coni. Om, coni. Ca* correcturae uel coniecturae ab editoribus non in
     textum receptae sed solum in apparatu critico notatae

expositio fidei CPL 1763

1. Rogo uos et admoneo, fratres carissimi (cf. Rom. 16, 17. I Cor.
4, 16), quicumque uult saluus esse fidem rectam catholicam firmiter
teneat inuiolatamque conseruet. Quam si quis digne non habuerit
regnum dei non possidebit.

2. Credite in deum patrem omnipotentem, inuisibilem uisibilium
et inuisibilium omnium rerum conditorem, hoc est, quia omnia
creauit simul uerbo potentiae suae. 3. Credite et in Iesum Christum,
filium eius unicum dominum nostrum, conceptum de spiritu sancto,
natum ex Maria uirgine, hoc est sine matre de patre deus ante saecula et homo de matre sine patre carnali in fine saeculorum, crucifixum   sub   Pontio   Pilato   praeside   et   sepultum,   tertia   die
resurgentem ex mortuis, hoc est, in uera sua carne quam accepit
ex Maria semper uirgine. 4. Per ueram resurrectionem resurrexit
postquam diabolum ligauit et animas sanctorum de inferno liberauit. Victor ascendit ad caelos, sedet in dexteram dei patris. Inde
credite uenturum iudicare uiuos ac mortuos, hoc est sanctos et peccatores, aut mortuos de sepulchris et uiuos quos dies iudicii inueniet
uiuentes.

5. Credite et in spiritum sanctum, deum omnipotentem, unam habentem substantiam cum patre et filio. Sed tamen intimare debemus quod pater deus est et filius deus est et spiritus sanctus deus est, et non sunt tres dii sed unus est deus, sicut ignis et flamma et calor una res est. Ecce uidemus cereum accensum, in quo conspicimus tria inseparabilia esse, ignem, lucem et motum. 6. Ignis persona intellegi poterit patris, sicut scriptum est: *Deus uester ignis consumens est* (Deut. 4, 24. Hebr. 9, 29). Lucem filius est, sicut ipse ait in Euangelio: *Ego sum lux mundi huius* (Ioh. 8, 12 et 9, 5). Motum uero spiritum sanctum, qui corda prophetarum ad uaticinium mouebat. Sicut ergo splendor de igne manat, sic filius de patre, et dum semper in patre fuerit sicut lux in igne, ita filius manens in aequalitate patris cum ad mortalium mentes prodire uoluit genitus appellatus est, quoniam non splendor ignem sed ignis splendorem generat. 7. Ita ergo patrem et filium et spiritum sanctum unum deum esse confitemur, non tres deos sed unum ut dixi, unius inquam omnipotentiae, unius diuinitatis, unius potestatis. Et tamen pater non est filius et filius non est pater nec spiritus sanctus aut pater aut filius, sed patris et filii et spiritus sancti una aeternitas, una substantia, una potestas inseparabilis. 8. Ecce duo uocabula dixi, ignem et lumen, unam tamen substantiam dico. Dum unum postulo tria accipio, nec fraudor ab alio cum unius uocabulum dixero. Verbi causa si dixero: Affer inde lumen, non statim amisi calorem ignis, aut si ignem petiero lucis fraudari possum aduentu. 9. Ita et in diuinitatem credite. Dum credideritis in patrem sine dubio et filium habebitis, si confessi fueritis filium in illo inuenietis et patrem, dum credideritis in spiritum sanctum omnem plenitudinem diuinitatis atque trinitatis inconcusse tenebitis. 10. Pater non senior de filio secundum diuinitatem nec filius iuuenior est de patre, sed una aetas, una substantia, una uirtus, una maiestas, una diuinitas, una potentia patris et filii et spiritus sancti.

11. Credite ecclesiam catholicam, hoc est uniuersalem in uniuerso mundo, ubi unus deus in trinitate personarum et in unitate diuinitatis colitur, unum baptisma habetur, una fides seruatur (cf. Eph. 4, 5-6). Et qui non est in unitate ecclesiae, aut clericus aut laicus aut masculus aut femina aut ingenuus aut seruus (cf. Gal. 3, 28), partem in regno dei non habebit. 12. Credite remissionem peccatorum, aut per baptismum, si obseruatis legem eius, hoc est abrenuntiatione diaboli et angelis eius et pompis saeculi, aut per paenitentiam

ueram, id est commissa deflere et paenitenda non committere, aut
per martyrium, ubi sanguis pro baptismo computatur. 13. Credite
communem omnium corporum resurrectionem post mortem. Sine
dubio enim erit sicut scriptum est: *Et resurgent qui in monumentis
sunt* (Is. 26, 19 LXX). Quanta membra et ossa et capillos habuit
homo tantos habebit in resurrectione. Non in altera carne resurgent
sed in ea ipsa quam habuerunt (cf. Iob 19, 25-27) - sed tamen resurgent homines iuuenes quasi triginta annorum licet senes aut infantes
transierint (cf. Is. 65, 20), et pulchriora corpora et tenuiora habebunt -, ut peccatores aeternas sustineant poenas, et iusti et sancti
praemia caelestia in iisdem corporibus possideant.

14. Igitur si quis uult discipulus Christi esse mandata sua custodiat et humilitatem discat, ut ipse ait: *Discite a me quia mitis sum et
humilis corde* (Matth. 11, 29). Ideo in corde rogat (cf. Ps. 139, 23.
Act. 15, 8. Rom. 8, 27. I Cor. 4, 5) quia multi sunt qui a foris uidentur humiles, intus autem pleni sunt tumore superbiae (cf. Luc. 18,
9-14). 15. Christus humiliauit se pro nobis *formam serui accipiens,
oboediens patri usque ad mortem, mortem autem crucis* (Phil. 2, 7-8),
pro nobis traditus ut peccata nostra deleret. Carnem humanam
accepit natus ex Maria uirgine, positus in praesepio, pannis inuolu-
tus (cf. Luc. 2, 7), a Iudaeis reprobatus, ab ipsis persecutus, compre-
hensus et flagellatus, sputis sordidatus (cf. Matth. 26, 67 et al.),
spinis coronatus (cf. Matth. 27, 29 et al.), clauis confixus, lancea
perforatus (cf. Ioh. 19, 34), cruci appensus, aceto cum felle potatus
(cf. Matth. 27, 34 et 48 et al.) et *inter iniquos reputatus* (Marc. 15,
28 et al.). Haec omnia totum sustinuit ut nos de faucibus inferni
liberaret. 16. Ergo, fratres carissimi, cum tanta et talia dominus
pro nobis sustinuit, si ad eum uolumus peruenire uestigia illius debemus sequi et exempla sanctorum imitare. Dominus ipse in Euangelio dicit: *Si quis uult post me uenire, abneget semet ipsum, tollat
crucem suam et sequatur me* (Luc. 9, 23). Et alibi dicit: *Vade, uende
omnia quae habes, da pauperibus et ueni, sequere me* (Matth. 19, 21).
17. Sancti martyres, fratres carissimi, Christi sunt uestigia secuti, et
calicem passionis quem bibit ipsi biberunt (cf. Matth. 20, 22-23.
Marc. 10, 38-39). Petrus apostolus pro nomine Christi crucifixus
est, Paulus decollatus est, Stephanus lapidatus (cf. Act. 7, 57-59),
et reliqui complures pro nomine ipsius sic passi sunt.

18. Ergo, fratres carissimi, crucifigite (cf. Gal. 5, 24) et *mortificate
membra uestra quae sunt super terram* (Col. 3, 5), ut possitis placere

illi qui uos creauit. Qui fuit superbus sit humilis, qui fuit incredulus sit fidelis, qui fuit luxuriosus sit castus, qui fuit latro sit idoneus, qui fuit ebriosus sit sobrius, qui fuit somnolentus sit uigilis, qui fuit auarus sit largus, qui fuit bilinguis sit beneloquens, qui fuit detractor aut inuidiosus sit purus et benignus, qui aliquando ad ecclesiam tarde ueniebat modo frequentius ad eam recurrat. 19. Eleemosynarum copia unusquisque se redimat, quia sicut *aqua extinguit ignem ita et eleemosyna extinguit peccatum* (Eccli. 3, 33). Decimas de omni fructu quod colligitis (cf. Lev. 27, 30 et al.) inter ecclesias et pauperes erogate, ieiunium amate, ebrietatem et crapulam deuitate, esurientes pascite, sitientes potate, nudos uestite et qui positi sunt in carcere requirite, infirmos uisitate, hospites in domibus uestris colligite (cf. Matth. 25, 34-45), pedes lauate, linteum tergite, ore exosculate et lecta ipsorum praeparate (cf. Luc. 7, 38. Ioh. 13, 5). 20. Nullus *furtum faciat,* non homicidium, non adulterium, non periurium, *non falsum testimonium* dicat, *honoret patrem et matrem ut sit longaeuus super terram* (cf. Ex. 20, 12-16. Deut. 5, 16-20), *diligat deum* plus quam se (cf. Deut. 6,5), amet *proximum sicut se ipsum* (cf. Lev. 19, 18. Matth. 23, 37 et 39. Marc. 10, 30-31. Luc. 10, 27). Et quicumque de his supradictis commisit cito emendet, confessionem purissimam donet, ueram paenitentiam agat, et remittuntur ei peccata sua.

21. Si haec quae suggessimus, fratres mei, implere uolueritis remissionem peccatorum promerebitis et uitam aeternam consequeritis, auxiliante domino nostro Iesu Christo, qui uiuit et regnat in saecula.

apparatus criticus apud expositionem fidei CPL 1763

1. conseruet *Q*] conseruit *P*
2. hoc est quia *PQ*] hoc est qui *coni. Ca*
4. sedet *conieci*] sedit *PQ*      aut mortuos *coni. Ca*] ac mortuos *P,* hac mortuis *Q*
5. habentem *PQ*] habenter *Om*      flamma et calor *PQ*] calor et flamma *Ca* mortuos *P*] mortuis *Q*      uidemus *P*] uidimus *Q*      conspicimus *PQ*] aspicimus *Ca*
6. scriptum est *P*] scriptum *Q Om*      uester *PQ*] noster *Ca*      ad uaticinium mouebat sicut ergo *P*] ac *ex* ad *Q*      uaticinium ... ergo] *om. Q*      dum semper *PQ*] deum semper *Om*
7. tres deos *Om Ca*] tres ds *P,* tres d°s *Q*
8. lumen *PQ*] lucem *Om*      dum unum *PQ*] deum unum *Om Ca*      uocabulum *Q*] uocabulum *e* uocabulo *P,* uocabula *Om*      fraudari *P*] fraudare *Q*

9. credideritis *(1º ) conieci*] creditis *PQ Om Ca*      credideritis *(2º ) P*] crederi-
tis *Q*
10. iuuenior *PQ*] iunior *Ca*      aetas *PQ*] aeternitas *coni. Om*      diuinitas *Q*
*Ca coni. Om*] diuitas *P Om*
11. masculus *P*] masculos *Q*
12. baptismum *PQ*] baptisma *Om*      abrenuntiatione *PQ*] abrenuntiationem
*coni. Ca*      id est *PQ*] id *Om*
13. resurrectione *Q*] resurrectionem *P*      carne resurgent *PQ*] carne surgent *Om*
14. custodiat et *conieci*] custodiat *PQ*      rogat *PQ*] roget *coni. Ca*
15. traditus *conieci*] traditur *PQ*      appensus *P*] affixus *Q*
16. da *P*] et da *Q*
17. carissimi Christi *PQ*] carissimi *Ca*      uestigia *PQ*] uestigia illius *coni. Ca*
bibit *Q*] bibet *P*      complures *conieci*] quam plures *PQ*
18. ergo *PQ*] igitur *R*      terram *QR*] terra *P?*      qui f. s. s. uigilis *PQ*] *om. R*
aliquando *PQ*] *om. R*      ad ecclesiam tarde *PQ*] tarde in ecclesiam *R*
recurrat *PQ*] currat *R*
19. copia *R*] copiam *PQ*      ignem *PR*] ignem ardentem *Q*      ita et *P*] ita
*QR*      decimas *PQ*] decimas uestras annis singulis *R*      quod *PQ*] quem
*R*      inter ecclesias et pauperes erogate *PQ*] ad ecclesias reddite *R*      crapulam *PQ*] crapulam uini *R*      deuitate *PQR*] euitate *Ca*      domibus uestris
*PQ*] domos uestras *R*      pedes *PQ*] pedes eorum *R*      linteum ... exosculate]
*om. R*      exosculate *P*] osculate *Q*      ipsorum *PQ*] eorum *R*
20. honoret *PQ*] filius honoret *R*      se *PQ*] semet ipsum *R*      amet proximum *PQ*] proximum *R*      se *PQ*] semet *R*      ipsum et *PQ*] ipsum *R*      de
his *PQ*] de *R*      emendet *QR*] emendit *P*      confessionem purissimam *PQ*]
confessionem *R*      donet *QR*] donit *P*
21. mei *PQ*] carissimi *Ca*      si haec ... consequeritis] *om. R*      qui *PQ*] qui
cum patre et spiritu sancto *R*      saecula *PQ*] saecula saeculorum *R*

The Manuscript Tradition of a Newly Discovered Anonymous *expositio symboli*

Thus far, only one manuscript of this text seems to be available, a twelfth-century Florentinus (*R*) [1]. Our text appears there in the context of several expository pieces on faith, the Creed, the Lord's Prayer, and certain rites. Thus, on f. 128R we find an *expositio catholicae fidei* (*Quomodo definitur fides secundum intellectum? Fides est credulitas illarum rerum quae non uidentur ... ut destrueret errorem haereticorum sed maximum* (sic) *propter Arium*), on f. 128V a commentary on the so-called Athanasian Creed (*Quicumque uult saluus esse ante omnia opus est ut teneat catholica* (sic) *fidem. Quicumque, id est unusquisque. Quicumque dicit quia non est deus personarum acceptor ... id est absque ambiguitate firmiterque crediderit saluus esse non poterit*), on f. 132R an *expositio symboli* (*Quo nomine uocatur haec doctrina fidei? Symbolum. Symbolum autem Graeca lingua dicitur, in Latina Graeca Latina* (sic) *uero dicitur collatio, hoc est collectio. Quare haec fidei doctrina dicitur collatio? Quia post ascensionem ... Amen uero uerbum est Hebraicum quod Latine dicitur uere fideliter siue fiat*), on f. 135R an *expostiio catecuminorum* (*Quare nomina eorum qui cathecizandi sunt ab acolito describuntur? Vt scilicet impleatur et in eis ... unde ipse huius regis perfectione* (sic) *demonstrans ait: Qui manducat carnem meam et bibit sanguinem meum in me manet et ego in eum*), on f. 136V an *expositio sindonis* (*Sindon Graece, Latine dicitur lineus pannus. Quare in syndone consecratur corpus domini? Ideo quia corpus domini ... ad candorem immortalitatis*), our *expositio symboli*, and on f. 137V an *expositio dominicae orationis* (*Quomodo uocatur haec oratio? Dominica. Quare dicitur dominica? Quia dominus noster ...*).

On the whole, the manuscript offers a sound and intelligible text which hardly needs any drastic corrections. A number of unambiguous errors have been emended, but for the rest we may offer this hitherto unknown *expositio symboli* as it is presented in the manuscript.

---

[1] See *Inventario e stima della Libreria Ricardi: Manoscritti e edizioni del s. XV* (Florence, 1810), p. 10: "Concilium Aquisgranense. Diui Augustini, et aliorum opuscula. Varia. Cod. membran. in fol. saec. XII mancus et imperfectus, sed plurimi faciendus".

codex:

R    Florentinus, Bibliotheca Riccardiana 256 (olim K. III. XXVII), ff. 136V-137V, saec. XII

expositio symboli

1. Quid est symbolum? Symbolum dicitur Graece, Latine interpretatur collatio siue indicium. Collatio, quia sancti apostoli post aduentum sancti spiritus hoc symbolum ediderunt ut uno modo per uniuersum mundum praedicarent. Indicium, quia his uerbis uera indicatur fides.

2. Credo in deum, id est totam spem meam in illo colloco. Credo deum, subauditur esse. Credo deo, subauditur dictis eius. Patrem. Pater dicitur a patrando siue eo quod habeat filium. Omnipotens dicitur quia nihil est ei impossibile. Creatorem, id est factorem, caeli et terrae, id est caelestium et terrestrium rerum.

3. Iesus Hebraice, Latine saluator, Christus Graece, Latine unctus dicitur. Filius dicitur a felicitate parentum, siue eo quod habeat patrem. Vnicus, quia ille solus est natura, nos adoptiui filii. 4. Qui conceptus dicitur de spiritu sancto, et non est filius spiritus sancti. Sic et homines quamuis nascantur per aquam baptismatis non dicuntur filii aquae. Natus ex Maria dicitur, id est ex substantia matris.

5. Passus etiam dicitur tempore quo Pilatus praefuit tributis Hierosolymis. Pontius uero a loco dicitur. Crucifigi uoluit quia totum mundum redimere uenerat. Nam quattuor cornua crucis quattuor partes mundi demonstrant, ut illud: *Dicant qui redempti sunt*, et paulo post, *a solis ortu et occasu, ab aquilone et mari* (Ps. 107, 2-3). Nam erecta crux ostendit esse pacificata caelestia et terrestria per sanguinem Christi. Et apostolus de ministerio crucis ita loquitur: *Quae sit longitudo, latitudo, sublimitas et profundum* (Ef. 3, 18). Longitudo crucis est perseuerantia, ut illud: *Qui perseuerauerit* et cetera (Matth. 10, 22), latitudo caritas, ut illud: *Latum mandatum tuum nimis* (Ps. 119, 96), sublimitas est spes - *Spe enim salui facti sumus* (Rom. 8, 24) -, profundum occultatio iudiciorum dei, ut illud: *Quam incomprehensibilia sunt iudicia dei* (Rom. 11, 33).

6. Mortuus est ut nos uiuificaret, siue ut et nos mundo moriamur (cf. Gal. 6, 14). Sepultus est Christus, sed in sola carne. Descendit Christus ad inferna, sed in anima sola, ut inde nos liberaret. Et quia tribus gradibus uenimus ad mortem, id est suggestione, delectatione

et consensu (cf. Gen. 3, 1-6), ipse tertia die resurgendo nos reuocauit ad uitam.

7. Ascendit ad caelos, ut pararet nobis locum. Sedet ad dexteram patris, id est in dignitate paterna. Inde uenturus, id est de caelis, iudicare uiuos et mortuos, id est siue qui ante obierint et qui tunc uiui reperiuntur, siue iustos et peccatores.

8. In spiritum uero sanctum credimus, quia deus est sicut pater et filius. Sanctam ecclesiam catholicam, subauditur credo esse. Ecclesia dicitur conuocatio, catholicam uniuersalis. 9. Credo communionem sanctorum, id est et hic per fidem et post in regno, et remissionem, subauditur credo, peccatorum, per baptismum. 10. Credo etiam quod in eadem carne qua uiuimus sumus resurrecturi, ut recipiat unusquisque prouti est, siue bonum siue malum. Credo et uitam aeternam. Aeternam adicimus ad distinctionem temporalis uitae.

apparatus criticus apud expositionem symboli

2. deo] deo *e* deum *R*       subauditur *conieci*] subaudicta *R*
3. adoptiui *conieci*] adtui *R*
5. passus *conieci*] pulsus *R*       profundum *(2°) conieci*] profundo *R*
7. pararet *conieci*] pareret *R*       in dignitate] in dignitate *ex* indignotate *R*
et *conieci*] siue *R*       uiui reperiuntur *conieci*] uiuere periuntur *R*
9. fidem *conieci*] fide *R*
10. qua *conieci*] quia *R*       est *conieci*] esit *R*

# APPENDIX II

## Overview of Variants of the Apostles' Creed

In order to facilitate quick reference to and comparison of the several forms of the Apostles' Creed that have been discussed in the present book, all these forms have been brought together in a separate appendix. This has been done as economically as possible in an already rather lengthy study. Nevertheless, a device is necessary for readers who want to consult the book to find out, for example, how many credal variants there are that testify to the Descent to Hell, and where, and when. Of course, looking up this piece of the Creed in chapter 3.7 will already yield much material, but at least three things would still remain obscure - the testimony of the anonymous credal variants (discussed in chapters 4.2-4.17) as well as that of *R*, proto-*R*, *H*, and *T* (discussed in chapter 1), the forms of the Creed that are silent on this particular point, and the combination of this phrase with, for example, the use of *Passus* and *Mortuus* in the fourth article. Thus, the simple enumeration of all our complete reconstructions seemed to be the most efficient way of making our credal material accessible. And of course, much space that is lost here is won again in the indexes.

Users should be aware that the Creed forms that are enumerated here are sometimes the result of much discussion and reconstruction, the details of which may be studied in the places referred to. In the case of the forms that have been copied from chapters one and four, a brief indication of date and place of provenance has been added, the arguments for which may be consulted in the main body of the book. Only in the case of the Creed forms from chapter three did such an indication seem to be superfluous, as all data are presented there in a fairly uniform way at the beginning of each section.

proto-*R*                                            chapter 1.16

Rome, 200-250??

*Credo in deum patrem omnipotentem*
*et in Christum Iesum, filium eius*
*qui natus est de spiritu sancto et Maria uirgine*
*qui sub Pontio Pilato crucifixus est et sepultus*
*tertia die resurrexit*
*ascendit in caelos*
*sedet ad dexteram patris*
*unde uenturus est iudicare uiuos et mortuos*
*et in spiritum sanctum*
*sanctam ecclesiam*
*carnis resurrectionem.*

*R*                                                  chapter 1.3

Rome, fourth century

*Credo in deum patrem omnipotentem*
*et in Christum Iesum, filium eius unicum dominum nostrum*
*qui natus est de spiritu sancto et Maria uirgine*
*qui sub Pontio Pilato crucifixus est et sepultus*
*tertia die resurrexit a mortuis*
*ascendit in caelos*
*sedet ad dexteram patris*
*unde uenturus est iudicare uiuos et mortuos*
*et in spiritum sanctum*
*sanctam ecclesiam*
*remissionem peccatorum*
*carnis resurrectionem.*

*H* ('Hippolytus, *traditio apostolica*')             chapter 1.12

Italy, *c.* 400?

...

*Credis in Christum Iesum, filium dei*
*qui natus est de spiritu sancto ex Maria uirgine*
*et crucifixus sub Pontio Pilato et mortuus est et sepultus*
*et resurrexit die tertia uiuus a mortuis*
*et ascendit in caelis*

*et sedet ad dexteram patris*
*uenturus iudicare uiuos et mortuos?*
*Credis in spiritum sanctum*
*et sanctam ecclesiam*
*et carnis resurrectionem?*

**T** (*textus receptus*)                                    chapter 1.1

Gaul, seventh century

*Credo in deum patrem omnipotentem, creatorem caeli et terrae*
*et in Iesum Christum, filium eius unicum dominum nostrum*
*qui conceptus est de spiritu sancto, natus ex Maria uirgine*
*passus sub Pontio Pilato, crucifixus, mortuus et sepultus*
~~*descendit ad inferna*~~
*tertia die resurrexit a mortuis*
*ascendit ad caelos*
*sedet ad dexteram dei patris omnipotentis*
*inde uenturus est iudicare uiuos et mortuos*
*credo in spiritum sanctum*
*sanctam ecclesiam catholicam*
*sanctorum communionem*
*remissionem peccatorum*
*carnis resurrectionem*
*et uitam aeternam.*

Gallican forms

SAL                                              chapter 3.2, p. 115

*Credo in deum patrem omnipotentem*
*et in Iesum Christum, filium eius (...?)*

...

...

FAU-R                                        chapter 3.2, pp. 115-118

*Credo in deum patrem omnipotentem (...?)*
*credo et in filium dei Iesum Christum, unicum dominum nostrum*
*qui conceptus est de spiritu sancto, natus ex Maria uirgine*

...

...

*credo et in spiritum sanctum*
*credo sanctam ecclesiam catholicam*
*[sanctorum communionem*
*abremissa peccatorum*
*carnis resurrectionem*
*uitam aeternam].*

FAU                                      chapter 3.2, pp. 119-121

*Credo in deum ...*
*credo et in filium eius Iesum Christum, dominum nostrum*
*conceptus de spiritu sancto, natus ex Maria uirgine*
*...*
*tertia die resurrexit (...?)*
*ascendit in caelum*
*sedet ad dexteram dei (?)*
*inde uenturus iudicare uiuos et mortuos*
*credo in spiritum sanctum*
*sanctam ecclesiam catholicam*
*[sanctorum communionem*
*abremissio peccatorum]*
*carnis resurrectionem*
*uitam aeternam.*

CAE-A                                    chapter 3.2, pp. 121-123

*Credo in deum patrem omnipotentem, creatorem caeli et terrae*
*credo et in Iesum Christum, filium eius unigenitum sempiternum*
*qui conceptus est de spiritu sancto, natus est de Maria uirgine*
*passus est sub Pontio Pilato, crucifixus, mortuus et sepultus*
*descendit ad inferna*
*tertia die resurrexit a mortuis*
*ascendit ad caelos*
*sedet ad dexteram dei patris omnipotentis*
*inde uenturus iudicare uiuos et mortuos*
*credo in sanctum spiritum*
*sanctam ecclesiam catholicam*
*sanctorum communionem*
*remissionem peccatorum*
*carnis resurrectionem*

*uitam aeternam.*

CAE-B                                       chapter 3.2, pp. 123-127

*Credo in deum patrem omnipotentem*
*credo et in Iesum Christum, filium eius unigenitum sempiternum*
*conceptus de spiritu sancto, natus de Maria uirgine*
*passus sub Pontio Pilato, crucifixus, mortuus et sepultus*
*tertia die resurrexit*
*ascendit ad caelos*
*sedet ad dexteram dei patris omnipotentis*
*inde uenturus iudicare uiuos et mortuos*
*credo in sanctum spiritum*
*credo sanctam ecclesiam catholicam*
*sanctorum communionem*
*carnis resurrectionem*
*uitam aeternam.*

CAE-C                                       chapter 3.2, pp. 127-128

*Credo in deum patrem omnipotentem, creatorem caeli et terrae*
*credo et (?) in Iesum Christum, filium eius unigenitum sempiternum*
*conceptus de spiritu sancto, natus de Maria uirgine*
*passus sub Pontio Pilato, crucifixus, mortuus et sepultus*
*tertia die resurrexit*
*ascendit ad caelum*
*sedet ad dexteram dei patris omnipotentis*
*inde uenturus iudicare uiuos ac mortuos*
*credo in spiritum sanctum*
*credo sanctam ecclesiam catholicam*
*sanctorum communionem*
*carnis resurrectionem*
*in uitam aeternam.*

CY-T                                        chapter 3.2, pp. 128-129

*Credo in deum patrem omnipotentem*
*credo et in Iesum Christum, filium eius unigenitum, dominum nostrum*
*qui conceptus de spiritu sancto, natus ex Maria uirgine*
*passus sub Pontio Pilato, crucifixus et sepultus,*
*tertia die resurrexit a mortuis*

*ascendit in caelos*
*sedet ad dexteram patris*
*inde uenturus iudicaturus uiuos ac mortuos*
...
...

PS-AU                                        chapter 3.2, pp. 129-130

...

*credo in filium eius Iesum Christum, dominum nostrum*
*qui conceptus de spiritu sancto, natus ex Maria uirgine*
*passus sub Pontio Pilato, crucifixus et sepultus*
...
...

EUSh9                                        chapter 3.2, pp. 130-134

*Credo in deum patrem omnipotentem*
*et in filium eius (...?) Iesum Christum (...?)*
*[qui conceptus est de spiritu sancto,] natus ex Maria uirgine*
...
...
*ascendit ad caelos*
*sedet ad dexteram dei patris omnipotentis*
*inde uenturus est iudicare uiuos et mortuos (?)*
*credo in sanctum spiritum*
*credo sanctam ecclesiam catholicam*
...
...

EUSh10                                       chapter 3.2, pp. 134-136

*Credo in deum ...*
*credo et in filium eius unicum dominum nostrum, Iesum Christum*
*qui conceptus est de spiritu sancto, natus ex Maria uirgine*
*[crucifixus et sepultus]*
*tertia die resurrexit*
*ascendit ad caelos*
*sedet ad dexteram dei patris omnipotentis*
*inde uenturus iudicare uiuos et mortuos*
*credo in spiritum sanctum*

*sanctam ecclesiam catholicam*
*sanctorum communionem*
*abremissa peccatorum*
*carnis resurrectionem*
*uitam aeternam.*

PIRM                                      chapter 3.2, pp. 136-137

*Credo in deum patrem omnipotentem, creatorem caeli et terrae*
*et in Iesum Christum, filium eius unicum dominum nostrum*
*qui conceptus est de spiritu sancto, natus ex Maria uirgine*
*passus sub Pontio Pilato, crucifixus, mortuus et sepultus*
*descendit ad inferna*
*tertia die surrexit a mortuis*
*ascendit ad caelos*
*sedet ad dexteram dei patris omnipotentis*
*inde uenturus iudicare uiuos et mortuos*
*credo in spiritum sanctum*
*sanctam ecclesiam catholicam*
*sanctorum communionem*
*remissionem peccatorum*
*carnis resurrectionem*
*uitam aeternam.*

MGV                                       chapter 3.2, pp. 137-138

*Credo in deum patrem omnipotentem, creatorem caeli et terrae*
*et in Iesum Christum, filium eius unicum dominum nostrum*
*qui conceptus est de spiritu sancto, natus ex Maria uirgine*
*passus sub Pontio Pilato, crucifixus, mortuus et sepultus*
*tertia die resurrexit a mortuis*
*ascendit uictor ad caelos*
*sedet ad dexteram dei patris omnipotentis*
*inde uenturus iudicare uiuos et mortuos*
*credo in sanctum spiritum*
*sanctam ecclesiam catholicam*
*sanctorum communionem*
*abremissionem peccatorum*
*carnis resurrectionem*
*uitam aeternam.*

Bobbio A                                    chapter 3.2, pp. 138-139

*Credo in deum patrem omnipotentem, creatorem caeli et terrae*
*credo in Iesum Christum, filium eius unigenitum sempiternum*
*conceptum de spiritu sancto, natum ex Maria uirgine*
*passum sub Pontio Pilato, crucifixum, mortuum et sepultum*
*descendit ad inferna*
*tertia die resurrexit a mortuis*
*ascendit ad caelos*
*sedet ad dexteram dei patris omnipotentis*
*inde uenturus iudicare uiuos et mortuos*
*credo in sanctum spiritum*
*sanctam ecclesiam catholicam*
*sanctorum communionem*
*remissionem peccatorum*
*carnis resurrectionem*
*uitam aeternam.*

Bobbio B                                    chapter 3.2, pp. 139-141

*Credo in deum ... omnipotentem (...?)*
*et in Iesum Christum, [filium eius] unicum dominum nostrum*
*qui conceptus est de spiritu sancto, natus ex Maria uirgine*
*passum sub Pontio Pilato, crucifixum, mortuum et sepultum*
*descendit ad inferna*
*tertia die resurrexit a mortuis*
*ascendit in caelis*
*sedet ad dexteram patris omnipotentis*
*inde uenturus iudicare uiuos et mortuos*
*credo in spiritum sanctum*
*sanctam ecclesiam catholicam*
*remissionem peccatorum*
*carnis resurrectionem*
*uitam aeternam.*

Bobbio C                                    chapter 3.2, pp. 141-142

*Credo in deum patrem omnipotentem, creatorem caeli et terrae*
*(credo?) et in Iesum Christum, filium eius unicum dominum nostrum*
*conceptum de spiritu sancto, natum ex Maria uirgine*
*passum sub Pontio Pilato, crucifixum et sepultum*

*descendit ad inferna*
*tertia die resurrexit a mortuis*
*ascendit in caelis*
*sedet ad dexteram dei patris omnipotentis*
*inde uenturus iudicare uiuos ac mortuos*
*(credo? et?) in sanctum spiritum*
*sanctam ecclesiam catholicam*
*sanctorum communionem*
*remissionem peccatorum*
*carnis resurrectionem*
*uitam habere post mortem, in gloriam Christi resurgere.*


Spanish forms

PRIS                                        chapter 3.3, pp. 145-146

*Credo (in?) unum deum patrem omnipotentem*
*et (in?) unum dominum Iesum Christum*
*natum (?) ex Maria uirgine ex spiritu sancto*
*passum (?) sub Pontio Pilato, crucifixum (?) et sepultum (?)*
*tertia die resurrexit*
*ascendit in caelos*
*sedet ad dexteram dei patris omnipotentis*
*inde uenturus (?) et iudicaturus (?) de uiuis et mortuis*
*credo in sanctam ecclesiam*
*sanctum spiritum*
*baptismum salutare*
*remissionem peccatorum*
*resurrectionem carnis.*

MART                                        chapter 3.3, pp. 146-148

*Credo in deum patrem omnipotentem*
*et in Iesum Christum, filium eius unicum, deum et dominum nostrum*
*qui natus est de spiritu sancto ex Maria uirgine*
*passus sub Pontio Pilato, crucifixus et sepultus*
*tertia die resurrexit uiuus a mortuis*
*ascendit in caelos*
*sedet ad dexteram patris*
*inde uenturus iudicare uiuos et mortuos*

*credo in spiritum sanctum*
*sanctam ecclesiam catholicam*
*remissionem omnium peccatorum*
*carnis resurrectionem*
*et uitam aeternam.*

MM                                   chapter 3.3, pp. 148-149

*Credo in deum patrem omnipotentem*
*et in Iesum Christum, filium eius unicum dominum nostrum*
*natum de spiritu sancto ex utero Mariae uirginis*
*passus sub Pontio Pilato, crucifixus et sepultus*
*tertia die resurrexit uiuus a mortuis*
*ascendit in caelum*
*sedet ad dexteram dei patris omnipotentis*
*inde uenturus iudicaturus uiuos et mortuos*
*credo in sanctum spiritum*
*sanctam ecclesiam catholicam*
*sanctorum communionem*
*remissionem omnium peccatorum*
*carnis huius resurrectionem*
*et uitam aeternam.*

LO                                      chapter 3.3, p. 149

*Credo in deum patrem omnipotentem*
*et in Iesum Christum, filium eius unicum, deum et dominum nostrum*
*qui natus est de spiritu sancto et Maria uirgine*
*passus sub Pontio Pilato, crucifixus et sepultus*
*descendit ad inferna*
*tertia die resurrexit uiuus a mortuis*
*ascendit in caelos*
*sedet ad dexteram dei patris omnipotentis*
*inde uenturus iudicare uiuos et mortuos*
*credo in sanctum spiritum*
*sanctam ecclesiam catholicam*
*remissionem omnium peccatorum*
*carnis huius resurrectionem*
*et uitam aeternam.*

ILD                                        chapter 3.3, pp. 150-152

*Credo in deum patrem omnipotentem*
*(credo?) et in Iesum Christum, filium dei unicum, deum et dominum*
*nostrum (?)*
*qui natus est de spiritu sancto et Maria uirgine*
*...*
*descendit ad inferna*
*tertia die resurrexit uiuus a mortuis*
*ascendit in caelum*
*sedet ad dexteram dei patris omnipotentis*
*inde uenturus iudicare uiuos et mortuos*
*credo in sanctum spiritum*
*sanctam ecclesiam catholicam*
*remissionem peccatorum*
*carnis resurrectionem*
*et uitam aeternam.*

EB                                         chapter 3.3, pp. 152-154

*Credo in deum patrem omnipotentem*
*et in Iesum Christum, filium eius unicum, deum et dominum nostrum*
*qui natus est de spiritu sancto et Maria uirgine*
*passus sub Pontio Pilato, crucifixus et sepultus*
*descendit ad inferna*
*tertia die resurrexit uiuus a mortuis*
*ascendit in caelos*
*sedet ad dexteram dei patris omnipotentis*
*inde uenturus iudicare uiuos et mortuos*
*credo in spiritum sanctum*
*sanctam ecclesiam catholicam*
*remissionem omnium peccatorum*
*carnis resurrectionem*
*et uitam aeternam.*

TOL                                        chapter 3.3, p. 154

*...*
*...*
*(...?) sub Pontio PILATO CRVcifixus (crucifixum?) ...*
*descendit AD INFERNa*

*(...?) resVRREXIT (surrexit?) Viuus (...?)*
*... caeLOS*
*SEDET AD ...*
*... IVDICARE (...?)*
*... sanCTVM ...*
*...*

*...*

*(...?) carnIS RESVRREctionem (...?).*


African forms

CY-C                                      chapter 3.4, pp. 160-163

*...*

*...*

*remissionem peccatorum*

*...*

*(...?) uitam aeternam*
*per sanctam ecclesiam.*


AU-H                                      chapter 3.4, pp. 163-168

*Credo in deum patrem omnipotentem, uniuersorum creatorem, regem*
*saeculorum, immortalem et inuisibilem*
*(credo?) et in filium eius Iesum Christum, dominum nostrum*
*natum de spiritu sancto et uirgine Maria*
*crucifixum sub Pontio Pilato et sepultum*
*tertia die a mortuis resurrexit*
*ascendit in caelum*
*sedet ad dexteram patris*
*inde uenturus est iudicare uiuos et mortuos*
*(credo?) (et?) in spiritum sanctum*
*[remissionem peccatorum*
*resurrectionem carnis]*
*in uitam aeternam*
*per sanctam ecclesiam.*


QU                                        chapter 3.4, pp. 168-178

*Credo in deum patrem omnipotentem*

*(credo?) (et?) in filium eius Iesum Christum*
*natum de spiritu sancto ex uirgine Maria*
*crucifixum sub Pontio Pilato et sepultum*
*tertia die a mortuis resurrexit*
*assumptus in caelos*
*ad dexteram patris sedet*
*inde uenturus est (?) iudicare uiuos et mortuos*
*credo in spiritum sanctum*
*remissionem peccatorum*
*carnis resurrectionem*
*(et?) (in?) uitam aeternam*
*(per?) sanctam ecclesiam.*

FU                                  chapter 3.4, pp. 178-181

*Credo in deum patrem omnipotentem, uniuersorum creatorem, regem*
*saeculorum, immortalem et inuisibilem*
*credo in Iesum Christum, filium eius unicum dominum nostrum*
*qui natus est de spiritu sancto ex uirgine Maria*
*[crucifixum quoque dicimus et sepultum*
*die tertia resurrexit*
*fatemur Christum ascendisse in caelum*
*...*
*et inde uenturum iudicare uiuos et mortuos]*
*credo in spiritum sanctum (?)*
*[remissio peccatorum*
*carnis resurrectio*
*et uita aeterna*
*sancta ecclesia].*

North Italian forms

AM                                  chapter 3.5, pp. 185-189

*Credo ...*
*et in ... filium eius unicum dominum nostrum*
*qui natus ... spiritu sancto ex Maria uirgine*
*sub ... et sepultus*
*tertia die ... a mortuis*
*ascendit ...*

*sedet ad dexteram patris*
*unde ... et mortuos*
*et in spiritum sanctum*
*... ecclesiam (...?)*
*remissionem [peccatorum*
*carnis] resurrectionem.*

## AU-M                              chapter 3.5, pp. 189-196

*Credo in deum patrem omnipotentem*
*et in Iesum Christum, filium eius unicum dominum nostrum*
*qui natus est de spiritu sancto et uirgine Maria*
*sub Pontio Pilato crucifixus et sepultus*
*tertia die resurrexit a mortuis*
*ascendit in caelum*
*sedet ad dexteram patris*
*inde uenturus iudicaturus uiuos et mortuos*
*et in spiritum sanctum*
*sanctam ecclesiam*
*remissionem peccatorum*
*carnis resurrectionem.*

## RUF                               chapter 3.5, pp. 196-199

*Credo in deum patrem omnipotentem, inuisibilem et impassibilem*
*et in Iesum Christum, unicum filium eius, dominum nostrum*
*qui natus est de spiritu sancto ex Maria uirgine*
*crucifixus sub Pontio Pilato et sepultus*
*descendit in inferna*
*tertia die resurrexit*
*ascendit in caelos*
*sedet ad dexteram patris*
*inde uenturus iudicare uiuos et mortuos*
*et in spiritum sanctum*
*sanctam ecclesiam*
*remissionem peccatorum*
*huius carnis resurrectionem.*

## PC                                chapter 3.5, pp. 199-206

*Credo in deum patrem omnipotentem*

*et in Christum Iesum, filium eius unicum dominum nostrum*
*qui natus est de spiritu sancto et Maria uirgine*
*qui sub Pontio Pilato crucifixus est et sepultus*
*tertia die surrexit (?)*
*ascendit in caelos*
*sedet ad dexteram patris*
*inde uenturus iudicare uiuos et mortuos*
*credo in sanctum spiritum*
*sanctam ecclesiam*
*remissionem peccatorum*
*carnis resurrectionem*
*uitam aeternam.*

CHRO                                    chapter 3.5, pp. 206-207

...

...

*huius carnis resurrectionem*
*in uitam aeternam.*

Other forms

LEO                                     chapter 3.6, pp. 210-211

*Credo in deum patrem omnipotentem*
*et in Christum Iesum, filium eius unicum dominum nostrum*
*qui natus est de spiritu sancto et Maria uirgine*
...

...

ARN                                     chapter 3.6, p. 211

...

... Christum Iesum, filium eius unicum dominum nostrum
*qui natus est de spiritu sancto et Maria uirgine*
...

...

NIC                                     chapter 3.6, pp. 212-216

*Credo in deum patrem omnipotentem*

*et in filium eius Iesum Christum, dominum nostrum*
*natus (natum?) ex spiritu sancto et ex Maria uirgine*
...
*tertia die resurrexit uiuus a mortuis*
*ascendit in caelos (in caelum ascendit?)*
*sedet ad dexteram (dei?) patris*
*inde uenturus (est?) iudicare uiuos et mortuos*
*et in spiritum sanctum*
*sanctam ecclesiam catholicam*
*remissionem peccatorum (?)*
*carnis resurrectionem*
*et uitam aeternam (?).*

ARR                                      chapter 3.6, pp. 216-217

*Credo in deum patrem omnipotentem, creatorem caeli et terrae*
*(credo?) et in Christum Iesum filium eius (...?)*
...
...

APS                                      chapter 3.6, pp. 217-219

...
*... domiNUM NOStrum (...?)*
*qui (?) nATVS ESt ... SPIRITV SANCTO Et (Ex?) mariA VIR-*
*GINe*
*(...?) passuS SVB POntio pilATO Crucifixus ...*
*... A MORtuis (...?)*
*asCENDIT In ...*
*sEDET Ad dexteRAM PATris*
*INDE VENTurus (est?) DIIVDICARE VIuos ...*
*CREDO IN SANCTUM SPIRITVM*
*ET SANCTAM ECclesiam CATHOLICAM*
*ReMISSIONEM PEccatoRVM*
*CAR...*

BAN                              chapter 3.6, pp. 219-220

*Credo in deum patrem omnipotentem, inuisibilem, omnium creatura-*
*rum uisibilium et inuisibilium conditorem*

*1st change*

*credo et in Iesum Christum, filium eius unicum dominum nostrum,*
*deum omnipotentem*
*conceptum de spiritu sancto, natum de Maria uirgine*
*passum sub Pontio Pilato, qui crucifixus et sepultus*
*descendit ad inferos,*
*tertia die resurrexit a mortuis*
*ascendit in caelis*
*sedetque ad dexteram dei patris omnipotentis*
*exinde uenturus iudicare uiuos ac mortuos*
*credo et in spiritum sanctum, deum omnipotentem, unam habentem*
*substantiam cum patre et filio*
*sanctam esse ecclesiam catholicam*
*abremissa peccatorum*
*sanctorum communionem*
*carnis resurrectionem*
*credo uitam post mortem et uitam aeternam in gloria Christi.*

DIM                                    chapter 3.6, p. 221

*Credo in deum patrem omnipotentem (...?)*
*credo et in Iesum Christum filium eius (...?)*
...

...

*credo et in spiritum sanctum*
...

...

*credo uitam post mortem*
*credo me resurgere.*


Anonymous forms

pseudo-Ambrose, *exhortatio de symbolo ad neophytos* CPL 178
                                    chapter 4.2

Balkans, 300-400 or later

*Credo in deum patrem omnipotentem, saeculorum omnium et creatura-*
*rum regem et conditorem*
*et in Iesum Christum, filium eius unicum dominum nostrum*
*qui natus est de spiritu sancto et ex Maria uirgine*

*qui sub Pontio Pilato crucifixus et sepultus*
*tertia die resurrexit a mortuis*
*ascendit in caelos*
*sedet ad dexteram dei patris*
*inde uenturus est (?) iudicare uiuos et mortuos*
*et in spiritum sanctum*
*et sanctam ecclesiam catholicam*
*remissionem peccatorum*
*carnis resurrectionem.*

Anonymus, *expositio symboli* CPL 229a                    chapter 4.3

North Italy, 400-700

*Credo in deum patrem omnipotentem*
*et in Iesum Christum, filium eius unicum dominum nostrum*
*qui natus est de spiritu sancto et Maria uirgine*
*qui sub Pontio Pilato crucifixus est et sepultus*
*tertia die resurrexit uiuus a mortuis*
*ascendit in caelum*
*sedet ad dexteram patris*
*inde uenturus est iudicare uiuos et mortuos*
*credo in sanctum spiritum*
*sanctam ecclesiam catholicam*
*remissionem peccatorum*
*carnis resurrectionem*
*[credimus et uitam aeternam].*

pseudo-Augustine, *expositio super symbolum* CPL 365     chapter 4.4

Gaul, c. 550-600

*Credo in deum patrem omnipotentem, creatorem omnium quae sunt*
*uisibilium et inuisibilium (Credo in deum patrem omnipotentem?)*
*credo (?) et in Iesum Christum, filium eius unicum dominum nostrum*
*qui conceptus est de spiritu sancto, natus ex Maria uirgine*
*passus sub Pontio Pilato, crucifixus, mortuus et sepultus*
*descendit ad infernum*
*tertia die resurrexit a mortuis*
*ascendit in caelum*
*sedet ad dexteram dei patris omnipotentis*

*inde uenturus est iudicare uiuos et mortuos*
*credo (?) et in spiritum sanctum*
*credo sanctam ecclesiam catholicam (?)*
*[... omnium peccatorum suorum remissionem consequetur*
*et <carnis resurrectionem> ...]*
*[ad aeternam uitam].*

Anonymus, *expositio de fide catholica* CPL 505        chapter 4.5

Gaul, 400-500

*Credo in deum patrem omnipotentem, inuisibilem uisibilium et inuisi-*
*bilium conditorem*
*(credo?) et in Iesum Christum, filium eius unicum dominum nostrum*
*conceptum de spiritu sancto, natum ex Maria uirgine*
*crucifixum sub Pontio Pilato (praeside?) et sepultum*
*tertia die resurrexit ex mortuis*
*uictor ...*
*sedet in dexteram dei patris*
*inde uenturus (est?) iudicare uiuos ac mortuos*
*(credo?) et in spiritum sanctum*
*... ecclesiam catholicam*
*remissionem peccatorum (?)*
*...*

pseudo-Fulgentius, *sermo de symbolo* CPL 846        chapter 4.6

Africa, 400-500 or later

*Credo in deum patrem omnipotentem*
*credo in filium eius Iesum Christum, dominum nostrum*
*natus est de spiritu sancto ex uirgine Maria*
*crucifixus sub Pontio Pilato et sepultus*
*descendit etiam in infernum*
*(deinde?) tertio die a mortuis resurrexit*
*in caelum ascendit*
*et in dextera patris sedet*
*inde uenturus est iudicare uiuos et mortuos*
*credo (et?) in spiritum sanctum*
*remissionem peccatorum*
*carnis resurrectionem*

*uitam aeternam*
*per sanctam ecclesiam.*

Chrysostomus Latinus C, *sermones* 26 and 28 CPL 915    chapter 4.7

unknown (Southern Italy??)

*Credo in deum patrem omnipotentem*
*et in unicum filium eius, dominum nostrum Iesum Christum*
*natus de spiritu sancto et uirgine Maria*
*...*
*descendit ad infernum (?)*
*...*
*sedet ad dexteram patris*
*inde uenturus est iudicare uiuos et mortuos*
*credo in spiritum sanctum*
*[sanctam ecclesiam]*
*carnis resurrectionem (?)*
*uitam aeternam (?).*

pseudo-Caesarius, *sermo 10* CPL 1008 (pseudo-Augustine, *sermo 244*
CPL 368)                                                        chapter 4.8

Gaul, 500-600

*Credo in deum patrem omnipotentem*
*(credo?) et in Iesum Christum, filium eius unicum dominum nostrum*
*[... conceptum esse de spiritu sancto et natum ex Maria uirgine ...*
*... passum sub Pontio Pilato ... crucifixum ... mortuum et sepultum ...*
*... ad inferna descendisse ...*
*... tertia die resurrexisse ...*
*... in caelis ... ascendisse*
*... in dextera sedet patris*
*... uenturus sit iudicare uiuos et mortuos]*
*credo in spiritum sanctum*
*(credo?) sanctam ecclesiam catholicam*
*sanctorum communionem*
*carnis resurrectionem*
*remissionem peccatorum*
*et uitam aeternam.*

pseudo-Athanasius, *enarratio in symbolum* CPL 1744a     chapter 4.9

Northern Italy, 300-600

*Credo in deum patrem omnipotentem (...?)*
*...*
*(qui natus est de spiritu sancto?) ex Maria uirgine*
*qui sub Pontio Pilato crucifixus est et sepultus*
*descendit ad inferna*
*die tertio resurrexit a mortuis*
*ascendit in caelos*
*sedet ad dexteram patris*
*inde uenturus iudicaturus de uiuis et mortuis*
*credo in spiritum sanctum*
*in sanctam matrem ecclesiam (...?)*
*...*

Anonymus, *tractatus symboli* CPL 1751          chapter 4.10

Italy or Northern Italy, *c.* 450 or later

*Credo in deum patrem omnipotentem*
*et in Iesum Christum, filium eius unicum dominum nostrum*
*qui natus est de spiritu sancto et Maria uirgine*
*qui sub Pontio Pilato crucifixus est et sepultus*
*tertia die resurrexit a mortuis*
*ascendit in caelis*
*sedet ad dexteram patris*
*inde uenturus est iudicare uiuos et mortuos*
*et in spiritum sanctum*
*in sanctam ecclesiam*
*in remissionem peccatorum*
*carnis resurrectionem*
*et uitam aeternam.*

Anonymus, *symbolum apostolorum* CPL 1758          chapter 4.11

Gaul, 600-700 or later

*Credo in deum patrem omnipotentem, creatorem caeli et terrae*
*et in Iesum Christum, filium eius unicum dominum nostrum*
*qui conceptus est de spiritu sancto, natus ex Maria uirgine*

*passus sub Pontio Pilato, crucifixus, mortuus et sepultus*
*descendit ad inferna*
*tertia die resurrexit a mortuis*
*ascendit ad caelos*
*sedet ad dexteram dei patris omnipotentis*
*inde uenturus iudicare uiuos et mortuos*
*credo in spiritum sanctum*
*sanctam ecclesiam catholicam*
*sanctorum communionem*
*remissionem peccatorum*
*carnis resurrectionem*
*uitam aeternam.*

Anonymus, *sermo de symbolo* CPL 1759                    chapter 4.12

Spain (Ireland??), 400-500

*Credo in deum patrem omnipotentem*
*et in Iesum Christum, filium eius unicum dominum nostrum*
*natum de spiritu sancto et Maria uirgine*
*passus sub Pontio Pilato, crucifixus et sepultus*
*descendit ad inferos*
*tertia die resurrexit a mortuis*
*ascendit ad caelos*
*sedet ad dexteram dei patris*
*inde uenturus iudicare uiuos ac mortuos*
*credo in spiritum sanctum*
*sanctam ecclesiam catholicam*
*remissionem peccatorum*
*carnis resurrectionem.*

Anonymus, *expositio super symbolum* CPL 1760         chapter 4.13

Gaul, 500-700

*Credo in deum patrem omnipotentem, creatorem caeli et terrae*
*et in Iesum Christum, filium eius unicum dominum nostrum*
*qui conceptus est de spiritu sancto, natus ex Maria uirgine*
*passus sub Pontio Pilato, crucifixus, mortuus et sepultus*
*tertia die resurrexit a mortuis*
*ascendit uictor ad caelos*

*sedet ad dexteram dei patris omnipotentis*
*inde uenturus iudicare uiuos et mortuos*
*credo et in spiritum sanctum*
*sanctam ecclesiam catholicam*
*sanctorum communionem*
*remissionem peccatorum*
*carnis resurrectionem*
*uitam aeternam.*

Anonymus, *expositio symboli* CPL 1761                    chapter 4.14

Gaul, 600-700

*Credo in deum patrem omnipotentem, creatorem caeli et terrae*
*... in Iesum Christum, filium eius unicum dominum nostrum*
*qui conceptus est de spiritu sancto, natus ex Maria uirgine*
*passusque sub Pontio Pilato, crucifixus, mortuus et sepultus (?)*
*descendit ad inferna*
*tertia die resurrexit a mortuis*
*ascendit in caelum*
*sedet ad dexteram dei patris omnipotentis*
*inde uenturus iudicare uiuos et mortuos*
*credo in spiritum sanctum*
*sanctam ecclesiam catholicam*
*sanctorum communionem*
*remissionem peccatorum*
*carnis resurrectionem*
*uitam aeternam.*

Anonymus, *de fide trinitatis quomodo exponitur* CPL 1762
                                                  chapter 4.15

Northern Italy, 400-500 or later

*Credo in deum patrem omnipotentem*
*et in Iesum Christum, filium eius unicum*
*qui natus est de spiritu sancto et Maria semper uirgine*
*qui sub Pontio Pilato crucifixus et sepultus est*
*resurrexit tertia die a mortuis*
*ascendit uictor ad caelos*
*sedet ad dexteram patris*
*inde uenturus est iudicare uiuos et mortuos*

*et in spiritum sanctum*
*sanctam ecclesiam*
*remissionem peccatorum*
*carnis resurrectionem*
*et uitam futuri saeculi.*

Anonymus, *expositio fidei* CPL 1763                   chapter 4.16

Gaul, *c.* 550 or later

*Credo in deum patrem omnipotentem, inuisibilem uisibilium et inuisi-*
*bilium omnium rerum conditorem*
*(credo?) et in Iesum Christum, filium eius unicum dominum nostrum*
*conceptum de spiritu sancto, natum ex Maria uirgine*
*crucifixum sub Pontio Pilato (praeside?) et sepultum*
*tertia die resurrexit ex mortuis*
*uictor ascendit ad caelos*
*sedet in dexteram dei patris*
*inde uenturus (est?) iudicare uiuos ac mortuos*
*(credo?) et in spiritum sanctum*
*... ecclesiam catholicam*
*remissionem peccatorum (?)*
*...*

Anonymus, *expositio symboli*                   chapter 4.17

Gaul, 500-600

*Credo in deum patrem omnipotentem, creatorem caeli et terrae*
*... Iesum Christum, filium eius unicum*
*qui conceptus de spiritu sancto, natus ex Maria (...?) (?)*
*passus sub Pontio Pilato, crucifixus, mortuus et sepultus (?)*
*descendit ad inferna*
*tertia die resurrexit (a mortuis?)*
*ascendit ad caelos*
*sedet ad dexteram patris*
*inde uenturus iudicare uiuos et mortuos*
*[in spiritum sanctum credimus]*
*sanctam ecclesiam catholicam*
*credo communionem sanctorum*
*et remissionem peccatorum*
*[credo etiam quod in eadem carne qua uiuimus sumus resurrecturi]*
*credo et uitam aeternam.*

# Appendix III

## Concordance with Hahn's *Bibliothek*

This appendix lists source texts in Hahn's *Bibliothek der Symbole* (Hahn 1897) that are discussed in the present work. In the left-hand columns are the relevant numbers in the headings of Hahn's work (up to § 121); in the right-hand ones are the places in our study where these texts are treated.

| Hahn (§) | Westra (ch.) | Hahn (§) | Westra (ch.) |
|---|---|---|---|
| 3 | 1.17, n. 185 | 44 | 3.4, nn. 186-187 |
| 5 | 1.11, n. 119 | 45 | 4.2 |
| 7 | 3.4, nn. 186-187 + | 46 | 4.9 |
|  | 1.11, n. 114 | 47 | 3.4, AU-H |
| 12 | 3.4, CY-C | 48 | 3.4, QU |
| 13 | 3.6, n. 414 | 49 | 3.4, FU |
| 17 | 1.8 | 49n125 | 3.4, n. 195 |
| 18-20 | 1.4 | 50 | 3.4, n. 198 |
| 21 | 3.6, LEO | 51 | 3.4 with nn. 190-194 |
| 22 | 3.5, n. 301 |  | + 2.3, n. 43 |
| 23 | 1.4 | 52 | 3.2, n. 31 |
| 25 | 1.1, n. 7 | 53 | 3.3, PRIS |
| 31a-c | 1.11, n. 118 + 3.6 n. 419 | 54 | 3.3, MART |
| 31e | 1.10 | 55 | 3.3, ILD |
| 32 | 3.5, AM | 56 | 3.3, EB |
| 32n40 | 4.1, n. 6 | 57 | 3.3, n. 149 |
| 33 | 3.5, AU-M | 58 | 3.3, MM |
| 34 | 3.5, n. 303 | 59 | 3.2, n. 30 |
| 35 | 3.5, PC | 60 | 3.2, n. 27 |
| 36 | 3.5, RUF | 61 | 3.2, EUS-G |
| 37 | 4.3 | 61n154 | 3.2, FAU-R + FAU |
| 38 | 3.5, n. 302 | 62 | 4.8 |
| 39 | 4.10 | 63 | 3.2, n. 29 |
| 40 | 3.6, NIC | 64 | 4.16 |
| 41 | 4.7 | 65 | 4.4 |
| 42 | 3.2, n. 45 | 66, 'erste Formel' |  |
| 43 | 3.5, n. 310 |  | 3.2, Bobbio A |

| Hahn (§) | Westra (ch.) | Hahn (§) | Westra (ch.) |
|---|---|---|---|
| 66nn173-179 | | 71n197 | 3.2, n.s 43, 32, |
| | 3.2, Bobbio B | | and 37 |
| 66, 'zweite Formel' | | 74 | 3.2, n. 38 |
| | 3.2, Bobbio C | 75 | 3.2 n. 40 |
| 66, 'dritte Formel' | | 76 | 3.6, BAN |
| | 3.2, n. 141 + 4.1, n. 1 | 77 | 3.6, n. 419 |
| 67 | 3.2, CAE-A | 78-89 | 3.6, n. 420 |
| 67 'B' | 3.2, MGV | 90 | 4.12, n.s 354-356 |
| 67, 'Erkl.' | CAE-B | 91 | 3.6, n. 413 + 4.1, n. 1 |
| 68 | 3.2, n. 33 | 92 | 3.2, PIRM |
| 69 | 3.2, n. 36 | 93-95 | 3.6, n. 413 |
| 70 | 3.2, n. 35 | 96 | 3.2, n. 44 |
| 71-73 | 3.2, n. 42 | 97-106 | 3.6, n. 413 |

# BIBLIOGRAPHY

Aguirre 1980 AGUIRRE, P., 'San Agustín y el Concilio XI de Toledo', in: *Augustinus* 25, 1980, 117-121

Aland 1989 ALAND, K. - ALAND, B., *Der Text des Neuen Testaments. Einführung in die wissenschaftlichen Ausgaben sowie in Theorie und Praxis der modernen Textkritik* ..., Stuttgart, 1989

De Aldama 1934 DE ALDAMA, J.A., *El Símbolo Toledano I. Su textu, su origen, su posición en la historia de los símbolos*, Romae, 1934 (*Analecta Gregoriana*, 7)

Andresen 1993 ANDRESEN, C. - RITTER, A.M., *Geschichte des Christentums I/1. Altertum*, Stuttgart - Berlin - Köln, 1993 (*Theologische Wissenschaft. Sammelwerk für Studium und Beruf*, 6,1)

Angenendt 1972 ANGENENDT, A., *Monachi Peregrini. Studien zu Pirmin und den monastischen Vorstellungen des frühen Mittelalters*, München, 1972 (*Münstersche Mittelalter-Schriften*, 6)

Aragoneses 1957 ARAGONESES, M.J., 'El primer credo epigráfico visigodo y otros restos coetaneos, descubiertos en Toledo', in: *Archivo Español de Arte* 119, 1957, 295-323

Aubert 1988 AUBERT, R., 'Hadrien', in: AUBERT, R. et al. (edd.), *Dictionnaire d'histoire et de géographie ecclésiastiques ... Tome vingt-deuxième. Grégoire - Haeglsperger*, Paris, 1988, 1492

Badcock 1930 BADCOCK, F.J., *The History of the Creeds* ..., London - New York - Toronto, 1930

Badcock 1933a BADCOCK, F.J., 'Le Credo primitif d'Afrique', in: *Revue Bénédictine* 43, 1933, 3-9

Badcock 1933b BADCOCK, F.J., 'The «Catholic» Baptismal Creed of the Fourth Century', in: *Revue Bénédictine* 43, 1933, 292-311

Badcock 1938 BADCOCK, F.J., *The History of the Creeds ... Second Edition*, London - New York, 1938

Barbet 1965 BARBET, J. - LAMBOT, C., 'Nouvelle tradition du symbole de rit gallican', in: *Revue Bénédictine* 75, 1965, 335-345

Barbian 1964 BARBIAN, K.-J., *Die altdeutschen Symbola. Beiträge zur Quellenfrage*, Steyl, 1964 (*Veröffentlichungen des Missionspriesterseminars St. Augustin, Siegburg*, 14)

Bardenhewer 1912 BARDENHEWER, O., *Geschichte der altkirchlichen Literatur. Dritter Band. Das vierte Jahrhundert mit Ausschluss der Schriftsteller syrischer Zunge*, Freiburg im Breisgau, 1912

Barlow 1950 BARLOW, C.W., *Martini Episcopi Bracarensis Opera Omnia* ..., New Haven - London - Oxford, 1950 (*Papers and Monographs of the American Academy in Rome*, 12)

Barré 1961 BARRÉ, H., 'L'homéliaire carolingien de Mondsee', in: *Revue Bénédictine* 71, 1961, 71-107

Barth 1978 BARTH, H.-M., 'Apostolisches Glaubensbekenntnis. II. Reformations- und Neuzeit', in: *TRE* 3, 1978, 554-566

Benndorf 1880 BENNDORF, O., 'Ausgrabungen in Ossero', in: *Archaeologisch-epigraphische Mittheilungen aus Oesterreich* ... 4, 1880, 73-82

Benvin 1989 BENVIN, A., 'Due frammenti del Simbolo Apostolico di Ossero (*Symbolum psarense*)', in: *Chromatius episcopus, 388-1988* (*Antichità Altoadriatiche*, 34), Udine, 1989, 185-207

Bergmann 1898 BERGMANN, W., *Studien zu einer kritischen Sichtung der südgallischen Predigtliteratur des fünften und sechsten Jahrhunderts. Teil I, Der handschriftlich bezeugte Nachlass des Faustus von Reji*, Leipzig, 1898 (BONWETSCH, N. - SEEBERG, R. [edd.], *Studien zur Geschichte der Theologie und Kirche* ..., I 4)

Bieler 1948 BIELER, L., 'The «Creeds» of St. Victorinus and St. Patrick', in: *Theological Studies* 9, 1948, 121-124

Bieler 1950 BIELER, L., 'Libri Epistolarum Sancti Patricii Episcopi. Introduction, Text and Commentary', in: *Classica et Mediaevalia* 11, 1950, 1-150

Blanchinus 1732 BLANCHINUS, J., *Enarratio pseudo-Athanasiana in Symbolum ante hac inedita. Et Vigilii Tapsitani de Trinitate ad Theophilum liber VI. Nunc primum genuinus, atque assumentis carens; prolatus ex vetustissimo codice Amplissi Capituli Veronensis* ..., Veronae, 1732

Botte 1963 BOTTE, B., *La Tradition Apostolique de saint Hippolyte. Essai de reconstitution*, Münster, 1963 (*Liturgiewissenschaftliche Quellen und Forschungen*, 39)

Bouhot 1970 BOUHOT, J.-P., 'La collection homilétique pseudo-chrysostomienne découverte par Dom Morin', in: *Revue des Études Augustiniennes* 16, 1970, 139-146

Bradshaw 1989 BRADSHAW, P.F., 'Kirchenordnungen. I. Altkirchliche', in: *TRE* 18, 1989, 662-670

Braegelmann 1942 BRAEGELMANN, A., *The Life and Writings of Saint Ildefonsus of Toledo* ..., Washington, D.C., 1942 (*Studies in Mediaeval History. N.S.*, 4)

Bratke 1895 BRATKE, E., 'Das Glaubensbekenntnis in einer Bern'er Handschrift aus dem 7.-8. Jahrhundert', in: *Theologische Studien und Kritiken* 1, 1895, 153-167

Bremmer 1998 BREMMER, J.N., 'Aspects of the *Acts of Peter*: Women, Magic, Place and Date', in: BREMMER, J.N. (ed.), *The Apocryphal Acts of Peter. Magic, Miracles and Gnosticism*, Leuven, 1998, 1-20

Brent 1995 BRENT, A., *Hippolytus and the Roman Church in the Third Century. Communities in Tension before the Emergence of a Monarch-Bishop*, Leiden - New York - Köln, 1995 (*Supplements to Vigiliae Christianae. Formerly Philosophia Patrum. Texts and Studies of Early Christian Life and Language*, 31)

Brewer 1909 BREWER, H., *Das sogenannte Athanasianische Glaubensbekenntnis ein Werk des heiligen Ambrosius* ..., Paderborn, 1909 (EHRHARD, A. - KIRSCH, J.P. [edd.], *Forschungen zur Christlichen Litteratur- und Dogmengeschichte*, IX 2

De Bruyne 1913 DE BRUYNE, D., 'De l'origine de quelques textes liturgiques mozarabes', in: *Revue Bénédictine* 30, 1913, 421-436

Van Buchem 1967 VAN BUCHEM, L.A., *L'homélie pseudo-eusébienne de Pentecôte. L'origine de la confirmatio en Gaule Méridionale et l'interprétation de ce rite par Fauste de Riez* ..., Nijmegen, 1967

Burn 1896 BURN, A.E., *The Athanasian Creed and Its Early Commentaries*, Cambridge, 1896 (*Texts and Studies. Contributions to Biblical and Patristic Literature*, IV 1)

Burn 1898 BURN, A.E., 'Neue Texte zur Geschichte des apostolischen Symbols', in: *Zeitschrift für Kirchengeschichte* 19, 1898, 179-190

Burn 1899 BURN, A.E., *An Introduction to the Creeds and to the Te Deum*, London, 1899

Burn 1900 BURN, A.E., 'Neue Texte zur Geschichte des apostolischen Symbols. II, in: *Zeitschrift für Kirchengeschichte* 21, 1900, 128-137

Burn 1905 BURN, A.E., *Niceta of Remesiana. His Life and Works*, Cambridge, 1905

Burn 1909 BURN, A.E., *Facsimiles of the Creeds from Early Manuscripts. With Palaegraphical Notes by the Late Dr. Ludwig Traube*, London, 1909 (*Henry Bradshaw Society*, 36)

Burrus 1995 BURRUS, V., *The Making of a Heretic. Gender, Authority, and the Priscillianist Controversy*, Berkeley - Los Angeles - London, 1995 (*The Transformation of the Classical Heritage*, 24)

Butterworth 1977 BUTTERWORTH, R., *Hippolytus of Rome. Contra Noetum* ..., London, 1977 (*Heythrop Monographs*, 2)

Camón Aznar 1975 CAMÓN AZNAR, J. et alii, *Beati in Apocalypsin Libri Duodecim. Codex Gerundensis. Commentaries on the Opus of Beato de Liébana* ..., Madrid, 1975

Von Campenhausen 1971 VON CAMPENHAUSEN, H., 'Taufen auf den Namen Jesu?', in: *Vigiliae Christianae* 25, 1971, 1-16

Von Campenhausen 1972 VON CAMPENHAUSEN, H., 'Das Bekenntnis im Urchristentum', in: *Zeitschrift für die neutestamentische Wissenschaft und die Kunde der älteren Kirche* 63, 1972, 210-253

Campos Ruiz 1971 BLANCO GARCIA, V. - CAMPOS RUIZ, J., *San Ildefonso de Toledo. La virginidad perpetua de Santa María. Historia de su tradición manuscrita, texto y comentario gramatical y estilístico ... El conocimiento del bautismo. El camino del desierto. Versión, introducción y notas ...*, Madrid, 1971 (*Biblioteca de Autores Cristianos. Santos Padres Españoles*, 1)

Caspari 1866 CASPARI, C.P., *Ungedruckte, unbeachtete und wenig beachtete Quellen zur Geschichte des Taufsymbols und der Glaubensregel ... I*, Christiania, 1866

Caspari 1869 CASPARI, C.P., *Ungedruckte, unbeachtete und wenig beachtete Quellen zur Geschichte des Taufsymbols und der Glaubensregel ... II*, Christiania, 1869

Caspari 1875 CASPARI, C.P., *Ungedruckte, unbeachtete und wenig beachtete Quellen zur Geschichte des Taufsymbols und der Glaubensregel ... III*, Christiania, 1875

Caspari 1879 CASPARI, C.P., *Alte und neue Quellen zur Geschichte des Taufsymbols und der Glaubensregel*, Christiania, 1879

Caspari 1883a CASPARI, C.P., *Kirchenhistorische Anecdota nebst neuen Ausgaben patristischer und kirchlich-mittelalterlichter Schriften ... I. Lateinische Schriften. Die Texte und die Anmerkungen*, Christiania, 1883

Caspari 1883b CASPARI, C.P., *Martin von Bracara's Schrift De correctione rusticorum ...*, Christiania, 1883

Chadwick 1976 CHADWICK, H., *Priscillian of Avila. The Occult and the Charismatic in the Early Church*, Oxford, 1976

Clarke 1989 CLARKE, G.W., *The Letters of St. Cyprian of Carthage. Translated and Annotated ... Volume IV. Letters 67-82*, New York - Mahwah, 1989 (BURGHARDT, W.J. - LAWLER, T.C. [edd.], *Ancient Christian Writers. The Works of the Fathers in Translation ...*, 47)

Clols 1981 CLOLS, R.J., *Martín de Braga. Sermón contra las supersticiones rurales. Texto revisado y traducción ...*, Barcelona, 1981

Colker 1991 COLKER, M.L., *Trinity College Library Dublin. Descriptive Catalogue of the Mediaeval and Renaissance Latin Manuscripts ... Volume I*, Aldershot, 1991

Connolly 1916 CONNOLLY, R.H., *The so-called Egyptian Church Order and Derived Documents* ..., Cambridge, 1916 (*Texts and Studies. Contributions to Biblical and Patristic Literature*, 8,4)

Connolly 1946 CONNOLLY, R.H., *The explanatio symboli ad initiandos. A Work of Saint Ambrose* ..., Cambridge, 1952 (*Texts and Studies. Contributions to Biblical and Patristic Literature*, 10)

Copinger 1895 COPINGER, W.A., *Supplement to Hain's Repertorium Bibliographicum. Or Collections towards a New Edition of that Work ... Part I*, London, 1895 (repr. 1992)

Countryman 1982 COUNTRYMAN, L.W., 'Tertullian and the Regula Fidei', in: *The Second Century* 2, 1982, 208-227.

Dekkers 1961 DEKKERS, E., *Clauis Patrum Latinorum qua in nouum Corpus Christianorum edendum optimas quasque scriptorum recensiones a Tertulliano ad Bedam commode recludit ... Editio altera aucta et emendata*, Steenbrugis, 1961 (*Sacris Eruditi* 3, 1961)

Dekkers 1995 DEKKERS, E., *Clauis Patrum Latinorum qua in Corpus Christianorum edendum optimas quasque scriptorum recensiones a Tertulliano ad Bedam commode recludit ... Editio tertia aucta et emendata*, Steenbrugis, 1995 (*Corpus Christianorum. Series Latina*)

Denzinger 1991 DENZINGER, H., - HÜNERMANN, P., *Enchiridion symbolorum definitionum et declarationum de rebus fidei et morum / Kompendium der Glaubensbekenntnisse und kirchlichen Lehrentscheidungen* ..., Friburgi Brisgoviae - Basileae - Romae - Vindobonae / Freiburg im Breisgau - Basel - Rom - Wien, 1991

Dix 1937 DIX, G., Ἀποστολικὴ Παράδοσις. *The Treatise on the Apostolic Tradition of St Hippolytus of Rome, Bishop and Martyr ... Volume I. Historical Introduction, Textual Materials and Translation, with* Apparatus Criticus *and some Critical Notes*, London - New York, 1937

Ehrman 1993 EHRMAN, B.D., *The Orthodox Corruption of Scripture. The Effect of Early Christological Controversies on the Text of the New Testament*, New York - Oxford, 1993

Eichenseer 1960 EICHENSEER, C., *Das Symbolum Apostolicum beim heiligen Augustinus mit Berücksichtigung des dogmengeschichtlichen Zusammenhangs*, St. Ottilien, 1960 (*Kirchgeschichtliche Quellen und Studien* ..., 4)

Elcock 1975 ELCOCK, W.D., *The Romance Languages. Revised with a New Introduction* ..., London, 1975

Ellis 1994 ELLIS, P.B. - ELLSWORTH, R., *The Book of Deer*, London, 1994 (*Library of Celtic Illuminated Manuscripts*, 1)

Étaix 1987 ÉTAIX, R., 'Trois nouveaux sermons à restituer à la collection du pseudo-Maxime', in: *Revue Bénédictine* 97, 1987, 28-41

Van den Eynde 1933 VAN DEN EYNDE, D., *Les normes de l'enseignement chrétien dans la littérature patristique des trois premiers siècles*, Gembloux - Paris, 1933 (*Universitas Catholica Lovaniensis. Dissertationes ad gradum magistri in Facultate Theologica consequendum conscriptae*, II, 25)

Férotin 1904 FÉROTIN, M., *Le Liber Ordinum en usage dans l'église wisigothique et mozarabe d'Espagne du cinquième au onzième siècle*, Paris, 1904 (*Monumenta Ecclesiae Liturgica*, 5)

Férotin 1912 FÉROTIN, M., *Le Liber Mozarabicus Sacramentorum et les manuscrits mozarabes*, Paris, 1912 (*Monumenta Ecclesiae Liturgica*, 6)

Ferrua 1942 FERRUA, A., *Epigrammata Damasiana*, Città del Vaticano, 1992 (*Sussidio allo studio delle antichità cristiane*, 2)

Franses 1920 FRANSES, D., *Die Werke des hl. Quodvultdeus Bischofs von Karthago gestorben um 453 ...*, München, 1920

Frede 1981 FREDE, H.J., *Kirchenschriftsteller. Verzeichnis und Sigel. 3e., neubearbeitete und erweiterte Auflage des «Verzeichnis der Sigel für Kirchenschriftsteller» von Bonifatius Fischer*, Freiburg, 1981 (= *Vetus Latina. Die Reste der altlateinischen Bibel. Nach Petrus Sabatier neu gesammelt und herausgegeben von der Erzabtei Beuron*, 1/1)

Frede 1995 FREDE, H.J., *Kirchenschriftsteller. Verzeichnis und Sigel. Repertorium scriptorum ecclesiasticorum latinorum saeculo nono antiquiorum ... 4e., aktualisierte Auflage*, Freiburg, 1995 (= *Vetus Latina. Die Reste der altlateinischen Bibel. Nach Petrus Sabatier neu gesammelt und in Verbindung mit der Heidelberger Akademie der Wissenschaften herausgegeben von der Erzabtei Beuron*, 1/1)

Frede 1999 FREDE, H.J. - GRYSON, R., *Kirchenschriftsteller. Verzeichnis und Sigel. Aktualisierungsheft 1999. Compléments 1999 ...*, Freiburg, 1999 (= *Vetus Latina. Die Reste der altlateinischen Bibel. Nach Petrus Sabatier neu gesammelt und herausgegeben von der Erzabtei Beuron ...*, 1/1C)

Gamber 1958 GAMBER, K., *Sakramentartypen. Versuch einer Gruppierung der Handschriften und Fragmente bis zur Jahrtausendwende*, Beuron/Hohenzollern, 1958 (*Texte und Arbeiten Herausgegeben durch die Erzabtei Beuron. I. Abteilung. Beiträge zur Ergründung des älteren lateinischen christlichen Schrifttums und Gottesdienstes*, 49/50

Gamber 1960 GAMBER, K., 'Die sechs Bücher «Ad competentes» des Niceta von Remesiana. Frühchristliche Taufkatechesen aus dem römischen Dacien', in: *Ostkirchliche Studien* 9, 1960, 123-173

Gamber 1964 GAMBER, K., *Niceta von Remesiana. Instructio ad competentes. Frühchristliche Katechesen aus Dacien*, Regensburg, 1964
(*Textus Patristici et Liturgici ...*, 1)

Gamber 1967 GAMBER, K., 'Geht die sog. Explanatio symboli ad initiandos tatsächlich auf Ambrosius zurück?', in: *Byzantinische Forschungen* 2 (= WIRTH, P. [ed.], *Polychordia. Festschrift Franz
Dölger zum 75. Geburtstag*, Amsterdam, 1967), 184-203

Geerard 1983 GEERARD, M., *Clauis Patrum Graecorum qua optimae
quaeque scriptorum patrum Graecorum recensiones a primaeuis saeculis usque ad octauum commode recluduntur. Volumen I. Patres
Antenicaeni ...*, Turnhout, 1983 (*Corpus Christianorum*)

De Ghellinck 1949 DE GHELLINCK, J., *Patristique et Moyen Age.
Études d'histoire littéraire et doctrinale. Tome I. Les recherches sur
les origines du symbole des Apôtres ...*, Bruxelles - Paris, 1949
(*Museum Lessianum. Section Historique*, 6)

Goodspeed 1914 GOODSPEED, E.J., *Die ältesten Apologeten. Texte mit
kurzen Einleitungen*, Göttingen, 1914

Gougaud 1912 GOUGAUD, L., '11. Adrien', in: BAUDRILLART, A. et
al, (edd.), *Dictionnaire d'histoire et de géographie ecclésiastiques ...
Tome premier. Aachs - Albus*, Paris, 1912, 612

Grégoire 1980 GRÉGOIRE, R., *Homéliaires liturgiques médiévaux. Ana-
lyse de manuscrits*, Spoleto, 1980 (*Biblioteca degli «Studi Medievali»*,
12)

Griffe 1973 GRIFFE, E., 'Nouveau plaidoyer pour Fauste de Riez', in:
*Bulletin de Littérature Ecclésiastique* 74, 1973, 187-192

Hadot 1971 HADOT, P., *Marius Victorinus. Recherches sur sa vie et ses
oeuvres*, Paris, 1971

Hahn 1897 HAHN, A. - HAHN, G.L., *Bibliothek der Symbole und Glaubensregeln der alten Kirche ...*, Breslau, 1897

Hahn 1980 HAHN, F. 'Bekenntnisformeln im Neuen Testament', in:
MEINHOLD, P. (ed.), *Studien zur Bekenntnisbildung. Vortragsreihe
aus den Jahren 1979-1980*, Wiesbaden, 1980, 1-15 (*Veröffentlichungen des Instituts für europäische Geschichte Mainz*, 103)

Hanson 1962 HANSON, R.P.C., *Tradition in the Early Church*, London,
1962

Hanson 1975 HANSON, R.P.C., 'Dogma and Formula in the Fathers',
in: *Studia Patristica* 13, 1975, 169-184

Hanson 1976 HANSON, R.P.C., 'The Rule of Faith of Victorinus and
of Patrick', in: O'MEARA, J.J. - NAUMAN, B., (edd.), *Latin
Script and Letters A.D. 400-900. Festschrift Presented to Ludwig Bieler on the Occasion of his 70th Birthday*, Leiden, 1976, 25-36

Hanson 1992 HANSON, R.P.C., 'Creeds and Confessions of Faith', in: *Encyclopedia of the Early Church* 1, Cambridge, 1992, 206-208

Harmless 1995 HARMLESS, W., *Augustine and the Catechumenate*, Collegeville, Minnesota, 1995

Harnack 1896 HARNACK, A., 'Apostolisches Symbolum', in: *Realencyklopädie für protestantische Theologie und Kirche* 1, 741-755, Leipzig, 1896

Haußleiter 1898 HAUSZLEITER, J., 'Das apostolische Symbol in dem Bericht des Erzbischofs Amalarius von Trier (c. 812)', in: *Neue kirchliche Zeitschrift* 9, 1898, 341-351

Hen 1995 HEN, Y., *Culture and Religion in Merovingian Gaul A.D. 481-751*, Leiden - New York - Köln, 1995 (*Cultures, Beliefs and Traditions. Medieval and Early Modern Peoples*, 1)

Heurtley 1858 Heurtley, C.A., *Harmonia Symbolica. A Collection of Creeds belonging to the Ancient Western Church, and to the Medieval English Church, Arranged in Chronological Order, and after the Manner of a Harmony*, Oxford, 1858

Hill 1993 HILL, E., *The Works of Saint Augustine. A Translation for the 21st Century. Sermons. III/6 (184-229Z) on the Liturgical Seasons. Translation and Notes*, New Rochelle, 1993 (ROTELLE, J.E. (ed.), *The Works of Saint Augustine. A Translation for the 21st Century. Part III - Sermons*, 6)

Van den Hoek 1996 VAN DEN HOEK, A., 'Techniques of Quotation in Clement of Alexandria. A View of Ancient Literary Working Methods', in: *Vigiliae Christianae* 50, 1996, 223-243

Holl 1928 HOLL, K., *Gesammelte Aufsätze zur Kirchengeschichte. II. Der Osten*, Tübingen, 1928

Holland 1965 HOLLAND, D.L., 'The Earliest Text of the Old Roman Symbol: A Debate with Hans Lietzmann and J.N.D. Kelly', in: *Church History* 34, 1965, 262-281

Holland 1970 HOLLAND, D.L., '«Credis in spiritum sanctum et sanctam ecclesiam et resurrectionem carnis?»: Ein Beitrag zur Geschichte des Apostolikums', in: *Zeitschrift für die neutestamentliche Wissenschaft und die Kunde der älteren Kirche* 61, 1970, 126-144

Janini 1980 JANINI, J., *Liber Misticus de Cuaresima y Pascua (Cod. Toledo, Bibl. Capit. 35.5). Edición ...*, Toledo, 1980 (*Instituto de Estudios Visigótico-Mozárabes de Toledo. Serie Liturgica. Fuentes*, 2)

Janini 1983 JANINI, J., *Liber Missarum de Toledo y Libros Místicos. Tomo II, Introducción. Libros Místicos*, Toledo, 1983 (*Instituto de Estudios Visigótico-Mozárabes de Toledo. Serie Liturgica. Fuentes*, 4-7)

Janini 1991 JANINI, J., *Liber Ordinum Episcopal (Cod. Silos, Arch. Monástico, 4). Edición ...*, Abadia de Silos, 1991 (*Studia Silensia*, 15)

Jecker 1927 JECKER, G., *Die Heimat des hl. Pirmin des Apostels der Alamannen*, Münster in Westfalen, 1927 (*Beiträge zur Geschichte des alten Mönchtums und des Benediktinerordens*, 13)

Joannou 1963 JOANNOU, P.-P., '*Fonti. Fascicolo IX. Discipline générale antique (IVe - IXe s.). Tome II. Les canons des Pères Grecs (Lettres Canoniques). Édition critique du texte grec et traduction française* ..., Grottaferrata (Roma), 1963

Kappelmacher 1931 KAPPELMACHER, A., 'Echte und unechte Predigten Augustins', in: *Wiener Studien* 49, 1931, 89-102

Kasper 1991 KASPER, C.M., *Theologie und Askese. Die Spiritualität des Inselmönchtums von Lérins im 5. Jahrhundert*, Münster, 1991 (*Beiträge zur Geschichte des alten Mönchtums und des Benediktinertums*, 40)

Kattenbusch 1894 KATTENBUSCH, F., *Das apostolische Symbol. Seine Entstehung, sein geschichtlicher Sinn, seine ursprüngliche Stellung im Kultus und in der Theologie der Kirche. Ein Beitrag zur Symbolik und Dogmengeschichte ... Erster Band. Die Grundgestalt des Taufsymbols*, Leipzig, 1894

Kattenbusch 1900 KATTENBUSCH, F., *Das apostolische Symbol. Seine Entstehung, sein geschichtlicher Sinn, seine ursprüngliche Stellung im Kultus und in der Theologie der Kirche. Ein Beitrag zur Symbolik und Dogmengeschichte ... Zweiter Band. Verbreitung und Bedeutung des Taufsymbols*, Leipzig, 1900

Kelly 1955 KELLY, J.N.D., *Rufinus. A Commentary on the Apostles' Creed* ..., Westminster, Maryland - London, 1955 (*Ancient Christian Writers*, 20)

Kelly 1976 KELLY, J.N.D., *Early Christian Creeds*, New York, 1976

Kinzig 1999a KINZIG, W., '«...natum et passum etc.» Zur Geschichte der Tauffragen in der lateinischen Kirche bis zu Luther', in: KINZIG, W. - MARKSCHIES, C. - VINZENT, M., *Tauffragen und Bekenntnis. Studien zur sogenannten «Traditio Apostolica» zu den «Interrogationes de fide» und zum «Römischen Glaubensbekenntnis»*, Berlin - New York, 1999 (*Arbeiten zur Kirchengeschichte*, 74), 75-183

Kinzig 1999b KINZIG, W. - VINZENT, M., - 'Recent Research on the Origin of the Creed', in *Journal of Theological Studies. New Series*, 50, 1999, 535-559

Kleinheyer 1989 KLEINHEYER, B., *Sakramentliche Feiern I. Die Feiern der Eingliederung in die Kirche*, Regensburg, 1989 (MEYER, H. B. et al. [edd.], *Gottesdienst der Kirche. Handbuch der Liturgiewissenschaft* 7,1)

Kottje 1995 KOTTJE, R., 'Haimo v. Halberstadt', in: KASPER, W. et al. (edd.), *Lexikon für Theologie und Kirche. Vierter Band. Franca bis Hermenegild*, Freiburg - Basel - Rom - Wien, 1995, 1151

Kraft 1980 KRAFT, H., 'Das apostolicum. Das apostolische Symbol', in: MEINHOLD, P., (ed.), *Studien zur Bekenntnisbildung. Vortragsreihe aus den Jahren 1979-1980*, Wiesbaden, 1980, 16-29 (*Veröffentlichungen des Instituts für europäische Geschichte Mainz*, 103)

Krüger 1886 KRÜGER, G., *Lucifer Bischof von Calaris und das Schisma der Luciferianer*, Leipzig, 1886

Krüger 1902 KRÜGER, G., 'Lucifer von Calaris', in: HAUCK, A. (ed.), *Realencyklopädie für protestantische Theologie und Kirche... Elfter Band. Konstantinische Schenkung - Luther*, Leipzig, 1902, 666-668

Kruse 1976 KRUSE, N., *Die Kölner volkssprachige Überlieferung des 9. Jahrhunderts ...*, Bonn, 1976 (*Rheinisches Archiv. Veröffentlichungen des Instituts für geschichtliche Landeskunde der Rheinlande an der Universität Bonn*, 95)

Künstle 1900 KÜNSTLE, K., *Eine Bibliothek der Symbole und Theologischer Tractate zur Bekämpfung des Priscillianismus und westgothischen Arianismus aus dem VI. Jahrhundert. Ein Beitrag zur Geschichte der theologischen Litteratur in Spanien*, Mainz, 1900 (EHRHARD, A. - KIRSCH, J.P. [edd.], *Forschungen zur Christlichen Litteratur und Dogmengeschichte ...*, I 4)

Künstle 1905 KÜNSTLE, K., *Antipriscilliana. Dogmengeschichtliche Untersuchungen und Texte aus dem Streite gegen Priscillians Irrlehre*, Freiburg im Breisgau, 1905

Labbeus 1671 LABBEUS, P. - COSSARTIUS, G., *Sacrosancta concilia ad regiam editionem exacta ... Tomus octavus. Ab anno DCCCXLVII. ad annum DCCCLXXI.*, Lutetiae Parisiorum, 1671

Lambot 1931 LAMBOT, C., *North Italian Services of the Eleventh Century. Recueil d'Ordines du XIe siècle provenant de la haute-Italie. (Milan, Bibl. Ambros. T. 27. Sup.)*, London, 1931 (*Henry Bradshaw Society*, 67)

Lambot 1939 LAMBOT, C., 'Sermons complétés. Fragments de sermons perdus. Allocution inédite de saint Augustin', in: *Revue Bénédictine* 51, 1939, 3-30

Lambot 1958 LAMBOT, C., 'Sermon inédit de saint Augustin pour une fête de martyrs dans un homiliaire de type ancien', in: *Revue Bénédictine* 68, 1958, 187-199

Leclercq 1953 LECLERCQ, H., 'Symbole', in: *Dictionnaire d'archéologie chrétienne et de liturgie* 15,2, Paris, 1953, 1756-1778

Lejay 1895 LEJAY, P., 'Les sermons de Césaire d'Arles', in: *Revue Biblique International* 4, 1895, 593-610

Lejay 1906 LEJAY, P., *Le rôle théologique de Césaire d'Arles. Etude sur l'histoire du dogme chrétien en occident au temps des royaumes barbares*, Paris, 1906

Lemarié 1993 LEMARIÉ, J., 'L'homéliaire carolingien de Mondsee, témoin de sermons d'un Pseudo-Fulgence', in: GRYSON, R., *Philologia Sacra. Biblische und patristische Studien für Hermann J. Frede und Walther Thiele zu ihrem siebzigsten Geburtstag. Band II. Apokryphen, Kirchenväter, Verschiedenes*, (= FREDE, H.J., *Vetus Latina. Die Reste der altlateinischen Bibel. Nach Petrus Sabbatier neu gesammelt und in Verbindung mit der Heidelberger Akademie der Wissenschaften herausgegeben von der Erzabtei Beuron. Aus der Geschichte der lateinischen Bibel* ..., 24/2) Freiburg, 1993, 568-582

Lietzmann 1904 LIETZMANN, H., *Apollinaris von Laodicea und seine Schule. Texte und Untersuchungen* ... *I*, Tübingen, 1904

Lietzmann 1962 LIETZMANN, H., *Kleine Schriften. III. Studien zur Liturgie- und Symbolgeschichte. Zur Wissenschaftsgeschichte* ..., Berlin, 1962 (*Texte und Untersuchungen zur Geschichte der altchristlichen Literatur* ..., 74)

Lippold 1963 LIPPOLD, A., 'Quodvultdeus. 1)', in: *RE* 47, 1396-1398

Lipsius 1891 LIPSIUS, R.A. - BONNET, M., *Acta Apostolorum Apocrypha* ... *Pars prior. Acta Petri. Acta Pauli. Acta Petri et Pauli. Acta Pauli et Theclae. Acta Thaddaei* ..., Leipzig 1891 (repr. Hildesheim, 1959)

Lowe 1920 LOWE, E.A., *The Bobbio Missal. A Gallican Mass-Book (Ms. Paris. Lat. 13246). Text*, London, 1920 (*Henry Bradshaw Society*, 58)

Lowe 1935 LOWE, E.A., *Codices Latini Antiquiores. A Palaeographical Guide to Latin Manuscripts Prior to the Ninth Century* ... *Part II. Great Britain and Ireland*, Oxford, 1935

Machielsen 1990 MACHIELSEN, I., *Clavis patristica pseudepigraphorum medii aevi. Volumen I. Opera homiletica. Pars A. (Praefatio) (Ambrosius - Augustinus)*, Turnhout, 1990 (*Corpus Christianorum. Series Latina*)

Madoz 1938a MADOZ, J., *Le symbole du XI$^e$ concile de Tolède. Ses sources, sa date, sa valeur*, Louvain, 1938 (*Spicilegium Sacrum Lovaniense. Études et Documents*, 19)

Madoz 1938b MADOZ, J., 'Le symbole du IV$^e$ concile de Tolède', in: *Revue d'Histoire Ecclésiastique* 34, 1938, 5-20

Madoz 1938c MADOZ, J., 'El símbolo del VI Concilio de Toledo (a. 638) en su centenario XIIIo', in: *Gregorianum* 19, 1938, 161-193

Madoz 1939 MADOZ J., 'Eugène de Tolède († 657), une nouvelle source du Symbole de Tolède de 675', in: *Revue d'Histoire Ecclésiastique* 35, 1939, 530-533

Madoz 1940 MADOZ, J., 'Una nueva redacción del «Libellus de fide» de Baquiario', in: *Revista Española de Teologia* 1, 1940, 457-488

Madoz 1946 MADOZ, J., *El símbolo del concilio XVI de Toledo. Su texto, sus fuentes, su valor teológico*, Madrid, 1946

Mai 1828 MAI, A., *Scriptorum veterum nova collectio e Vaticanis codicibus edita ... Tomus III*, Romae, 1828

Mandouze 1982 MANDOUZE, A., *Prosopographie de l'Afrique chrétienne (303-533) ...*, Paris, 1982 (*Prosopographie chrétienne du Bas-Empire*, 1)

Mansi 1764 MANSI, J.D., *Sacrorum conciliorum nova, et amplissima collectio ... Tomus decimus. Ab anno DXC. usque ad annum DCLIII. inclusive*, Florentiae, 1764

Marcovich 1986 MARCOVICH, M., 'Hippolyt von Rom', in: *TRE* 15, 1986, 381-387

Markschies 1995 MARKSCHIES, C., *Ambrosius von Mailand und die Trinitätstheologie. Kirchen- und theologiegeschichtliche Studien zu Antiarianismus und Neunizänismus bei Ambrosius und im lateinischen Westen (364-381 n. Chr.)*, Tübingen, 1995 (WALLMANN, J. [ed.], *Beiträge zur historischen Theologie*, 90)

Markschies 1998 MARKSCHIES, C., 'Ambrosius von Mailand', in: DÖPP, S. - GEERLINGS, W. (edd.), *Lexikon der antiken christlichen Literatur*, Freiburg - Basel - Wien, 1998, 13-22

Markschies 1999 MARKSCHIES, C., 'Wer schrieb die sogenannte *Traditio Apostolica*? Neue Beobachtungen und Hypothesen zu einer kaum lösbaren Frage aus der altkirchlichen Literaturgeschichte', in: KINZIG, W. - MARKSCHIES, C. - VINZENT, M., *Tauffragen und Bekenntnis. Studien zur sogenannten «Traditio Apostolica» zu den «Interrogationes de fide» und zum «Römischen Glaubensbekenntnis»*, Berlin - New York, 1999 (*Arbeiten zur Kirchengeschichte*, 74), 1-74

Martínez Díez 1992 MARTÍNEZ DÍEZ, G. - RODRÍGUEZ, F., *La Colección Canónica Hispana. V. Concilios Hispanos: segunda parte ...*, Madrid, 1992 (*Monumenta Hispaniae Sacra. Serie Canónica*, 5)

Meslin 1967 MESLIN, M., *Les Ariens d'Occident 335-430*, Paris, 1967

Metzger 1988 METZGER, M., 'Nouvelles perspectives pour la prétendue *Tradition apostolique*', in: *Ecclesia Orans* 5, 1988, 241-259

Metzger 1991 METZGER, M., 'A propos d'une réédition de la prétendue
*Tradition apostolique*, avec traduction allemande', in: *Archiv für
Liturgiewissenschaft* 33, 1991, 290-294

Metzger 1992 METZGER, M., 'Enquêtes autour de la prétendue *«Tradition apostolique»*, in: *Ecclesia Orans* 9, 1992, 7-36

Michel 1941 MICHEL, A., 'Symboles', in: *Dictionnaire de théologie catho-
lique* 14,2, Paris, 1941, 2925-2939

Mohlberg 1958 MOHLBERG, L.C., *Missale Gallicanum Vetus (Cod.
Vat. Palat. lat. 493)* ..., Roma, 1958 (= MOHLBERG, L.C., [ed.],
*Rerum Ecclesiasticarum Documenta ... Series Maior. Fontes*, 3)

Mohlberg 1966 MOHLBERG, L.C., *Sacramentarium Veronense (Cod.
Bibl. Capit. Veron. LXXXV[80])* ..., Roma, 1966 (= MOHL-
BERG, L.C., [ed.], *Rerum Ecclesiasticarum Documenta ... Series
Maior. Fontes*, 1)

Mohlberg 1968 MOHLBERG, L.C., *Liber Sacramentorum Romanae
Aeclesiae Ordinis Anni Circuli (Cod. Vat. Reg. lat. 316/Paris Bibl.
Nat. 7193, 41/56) (Sacramentarium Gelasianum ...)*, Roma, 1968 (=
MOHLBERG, L.C. [ed.], *Rerum Ecclesiasticarum Documenta ... Se-
ries Maior. Fontes*, 4)

Morin 1893 MORIN, G., 'Pastor et Syagrius. Deux écrivains perdus du
cinquième siècle', in: *Revue Bénédictine* 10, 1893, 385-394

Morin 1894 MORIN, G., 'Étude sur une série de discours d'un évêque
[de Naples?] du VI$^e$ siècle', in: *Revue Bénédictine* 11, 1894, 385-402

Morin 1895 MORIN, G., 'Un essai d'autocritique', in: *Revue Bénédictine*
12, 1895, 385-396

Morin 1896 MORIN, G., 'Note sur une lettre attribuée faussement à
Amalaire de Trèves dans le manuscrit lat. 21568 de Munich', in:
*Revue Bénédictine* 13, 1896, 289-294

Morin 1897 MORIN, G., 'Notice sur un manuscrit important pour l'histoire du symbole. Cod. Sessorian. 52.', in: *Revue Bénédictine* 14,
1897, 481-488

Morin 1902 MORIN, G., 'Autour des *«Tractatus Origenis»*', in: *Revue
Bénédictine* 19, 1902, 225-245

Morin 1904 MORIN, G., 'Un symbole inédit attribué à Saint Jérôme',
in: *Revue Bénédictine* 21, 1904, 1-9

Morin 1905a MORIN, G., 'Textes inédits relatifs au symbole et à la vie
chrétienne', in: *Revue Bénédictine* 22, 1905, 505-524

Morin 1905b MORIN, G., 'De la besogne pour les jeunes. Sujets de travaux sur la littérature latine du moyen âge. Conférence donnée au Séminaire historique de l'Université de Louvain le jeudi 16 février 1905', in: *Revue d'histoire ecclésiastique* 6, 1905, 327-345

Morin 1911 MORIN, G., 'L'origine du symbole d'Athanase', in: *Journal of Theological Studies* 12, 1911, 160-190 and 337-359

Morin 1913 MORIN, G., *Études, textes, découvertes. Contributions à la littérature et à l'historie des douze premiers siècles. Tome premier,* Abbaye de Maredsous - Paris, 1913 (*Anecdota Maredsolana. Seconde Série*)

Morin 1923 MORIN, G., 'Deux sermons africains du Ve/VIe siècle avec un texte inédit du symbole', in: *Revue Bénédictine* 33, 1923, 233-245

Morin 1927 MORIN, G., 'Un *Ordo scrutiniorum* de type inconnu jusqu'ici d'après le Ms. Ambros. T 27 Sup.', in: *Revue Bénédictine* 39, 1927, 56-80

Morin 1930 MORIN, G., *Sancti Augustini sermones post Maurinos reperti,* Roma, 1930 (*Miscellanea Agostiniana,* 1)

Morin 1932 MORIN, G., 'L'origine du symbole d'Athanase: témoignage inédit de s. Césaire d'Arles', in: *Revue Bénédictine* 44, 1932, 207-219

Morin 1934a MORIN, G., 'Le symbole de s. Césaire d'Arles', in: *Revue Bénédictine* 46, 1934, 178-189

Morin 1934b MORIN, G., 'Sur la date et la provenance de l'*Ordo scrutiniorum* du cod. ambros. T 27 sup.', in: *Revue Bénédictine* 46, 1934, 216-223

Morin 1937 MORIN, G., *Sancti Caesarii Arelatensis sermones ... Pars prima continens praefationem, sermones de diversis et de scriptura veteris testamenti ...,* Maretioli, 1937

Müller 1956 MÜLLER, L.G., *The De haeresibus of Saint Augustine. A Translation with an Introduction and Commentary ...,* Washington, D.C., 1956 (*Patristic Studies,* 90)

Mulders 1956 MULDERS, J., 'Victricius van Rouaan. Leven en leer', in: *Bijdragen. Tijdschrift voor Filosofie en Theologie* 17, 1956, 1-25

Mulders 1957 MULDERS, J., 'Victricius van Rouaan. Leven en leer', in: *Bijdragen. Tijdschrift voor Filosofie en Theologie* 18, 1957, 19-40 and 270-289 (sequel to Mulders 1956)

Mutzenbecher 1961 MUTZENBECHER, A., 'Bestimmung der echten Sermones des Maximus Taurinensis', in: *Sacris Erudiri* 13, 1961, 197-293

Naldini 1991 NALDINI, M., *Martino di Braga. Contro le superstizioni. Catechesi al popolo.* De correctione rusticorum, Firenze, 1991

Nerney 1952 NERNEY, D.S., 'The Bangor Symbol', in: *Irish Theological Quarterly* 19, 1952, 369-385

Nerney 1953a NERNEY, D.S., 'The Bangor Symbol. II', in: *Irish Theological Quarterly* 20, 1953, 273-286

Nerney 1953b NERNEY, D.S., 'The Bangor Symbol. III', in: *Irish Theological Quarterly* 20, 1953, 389-401

O'Callaghan 1992 O'CALLAGHAN, P., 'The Bangor Antiphonary Creed: Origins and Theology', in: *Annales Theologici* 6, 1992, 255-287

Olivar 1961 OLIVAR, A., 'San Predo Crisólogo autor de la Expositio Symboli de Cividale', in: *Sacris Erudiri* 12, 1961, 294-312

Olivar 1962 OLIVAR, A., *Los sermones de San Pedro Crisólogo. Estudio critico*, Abadia de Montserrat, 1962 (*Scripta et Documenta*, 13)

Ommanney 1880 OMMANNEY, G.D.W., *Early History of the Athanasian Creed. The Results of Some Original Research upon the Subject* ..., London - Oxford - Cambridge, 1880

Oulton 1938 OULTON, J.E.N., 'The Apostles' Creed and Belief Concerning the Church', in: *Journal of Theological Studies* 39, 1938, 239-243

Oulton 1940 OULTON, J.E.N., *The Credal Statements of St. Patrick as Contained in the Fourth Chapter of his* Confession. *A Study of their Sources*, Dublin - London, 1940

Parmentier 1991 PARMENTIER, M.F.G., 'Trying to Unravel Jacobi's Unknown Creed (CPL 1752)', in: *Bijdragen. Tijdschrift voor Filosofie en Theologie* 52, 1991, 354-378

Pitra 1888 PITRA, J.B., *Analecta sacra et classica spicilegio Solesmensi parata I*, Parisiis - Romae, 1888

Poupon 1998 POUPON, G.H., 'L'Origine africaine des *Actus Vercellenses*', in: BREMMER, J.N. (ed.), *The Apocryphal Acts of Peter. Magic, Miracles and Gnosticism*, Leuven, 1998, 192-199

Powell 1979 POWELL, D., 'Arkandisziplin', in: *TRE* 4, 1979, 1-8

Restrepo-Jaramillo 1934 RESTREPO-JARAMILLO, J.M., 'Tertuliano y la doble fórmula en el símbolo apostólico', in: *Gregorianum* 15, 1934, 3-58

Ritter 1993 RITTER, A.M., 'Creeds', in: HAZLETT, I. (ed.), *Early Christianity. Origins and Evolution to AD 600. In honour of W H C Frend*, London, 1993, ch. 8, 92-100

Rodomonti 1995 RODOMONTI, A., 'Note al «Sermo de symbolo ad catechumenos» di S. Agostino', in: *Orpheus. Rivista di Umanità Classica e Cristiana* 16, 1995, 127-139

Rordorf 1995 RORDORF, W., 'Bedeutung und Grenze der altkirchlichen ökumenischen Glaubensbekenntnisse (Apostolikum und Nicaeno-Constaninopolitanum)', in: *Theologische Zeitschrift* 51, 1995, 50-64

De Rubeis 1754 DE RUBEIS, J.F.B.M., *Dissertationes duae: Prima de Turranio, seu Tyrannio Rufino Monacho, et Presbytero: Altera de vetustis Liturgicis aliisque sacris Ritibus, qui vigebant olim in aliquibus Forojuliensis Provinciae Ecclesiis*, Venetiis, 1754

De Rubeis 1762 DE RUBEIS, J.F.B.M., *Dissertationes variae eruditionis*, Venetiis, 1762

Rubenbauer 1977 RUBENBAUER, H. - HOFMANN, J.B. - HEINE, R., *Lateinische Grammatik*, Bamberg - München, 1977

Sanders 1930 SANDERS, H.A., *Beati in Apocalipsin libri duodecim*, Rome, 1930 (*Papers and Monographs of the American Academy in Rome*, 7; = CAMÓN AZNAR, J. et alii, *Beati in Apocalypsin Libri Duodecim. Codex Gerundensis. Commentaries on the Opus of Beato de Liébana* ..., Madrid, 1975, 239-903)

Schanz 1914 SCHANZ, M., *Geschichte der römischen Litteratur bis zum Gesetzgebungswerk des Kaisers Justinian ... Vierter Teil: Die römische Litteratur von Constantin bis zum Gesetzgebungswerk Justinians. Erste Hälfte: Die Litteratur des vierten Jahrhunderts*, München, 1914 (VON MÜLLER, I. [ed.], *Handbuch der klassischen Altertums-Wissenschaft...*, VIII 4.1)

Schanz 1920 SCHANZ, M. - HOSIUS, C. - KRÜGER, G., *Geschichte der römischen Litteratur bis zum Gesetzgebungswerk des Kaisers Justinian ... Vierter Teil: Die römische Litteratur von Constantin bis zum Gesetzgebungswerk Justinians. Zweite Hälfte: Die Litteratur des fünften und sechsten Jahrhunderts*, München, 1920 (VON MÜLLER, I., [ed.], *Handbuch der klassischen Altertums-Wissenschaft* ..., VIII 4.2)

Schepss 1886 SCHEPSS, G., *Priscillian, ein neuaufgefundener lat. Schriftsteller des 4. Jahrhunderts* ..., Würzburg, 1886

Schröer 1978 SCHRÖER, H., 'Apostolisches Glaubensbekenntnis. III. Praktisch-theologisch', in: *TRE* 3, 1978, 566-571

Schwartz 1910 SCHWARTZ, E., *Über die pseudoapostolischen Kirchenordnungen*, Strassburg, 1910 (*Schriften der wissenschaftlichen Gesellschaft in Strassburg*, 6)

Schwartz 1925 SCHWARTZ, E., *Concilium Vniversale Ephesenum ... Volumen alterum. Collectio Veronensis*, Berolini - Lipsiae, 1925-1926, (SCHWARTZ, E., *Acta Conciliorum Oecumenicorum* ..., I 2)

Schwartz 1932a SCHWARTZ, E., *Concilium Vniversale Chalcedonense ... Volumen alterum. Versiones particulares. Pars prior. Collectio*

*Novariensis de re Eutychis*, Berolini - Lipsiae, 1932, (SCHWARTZ, E., *Acta Conciliorum Oecumenicorum* ..., II 2,1)

Schwartz 1932b SCHWARTZ, E., *Concilium Vniversale Chalcedonense ... Volumen quartum. Leonis papae I epistularum collectiones*, Berolini - Lipsiae, 1932, (SCHWARTZ, E., *Acta Conciliorum Oecumenicorum* ..., II 4)

Seibt 1994 SEIBT, K., *Die Theologie des Markell von Ankyra*, Berlin - New York, 1994 (*Arbeiten zur Kirchengeschichte*, 59)

Silva-Tarouca 1934 SILVA-TAROUCA, C., *S. Leonis Magni epistulae contra Eutychis haeresim. Pars prima. Epistulae quae Chalcedonensi concilio praemittuntur (aa. 449-451)* ..., Romae, 1934 (*Textus et Documenta in usum exercitationum et praelectionum academicarum. Series Theologica*, 15)

Silva-Tarouca 1959 SILVA-TAROUCA, C., *S. Leonis Magni tomus ad Flavianum episc. Constantinopolitanum (epistula XXVIII)* ..., Romae, 1959 (= 1932) (*Textus et Documenta in usum exercitationum et praelectionum academicarum. Series Theologica*, 9)

Simonetti 1958 SIMONETTI, M., 'Sulla tradizione manoscritta delle opere originali di Rufino. II', in: *Sacris Erudiri* 10, 1958, 5-42

Simonetti 1960 SIMONETTI, M., 'Alcune osservazioni a proposito di una professione di fede attribuita a Gregorio di Elvira', in: *Rivista di Cultura Classica e Medioevale* 2, 1960, 307-325

Simonetti 1975 SIMONETTI, M., *Gregorio di Elvira La fede. Introduzione, testo critico, traduzione, commento, glossario e indici ... / Gregorii Hispaniensis De fide. Prolegomena, textum criticum, italicam interpretationem, commentarium, glossarium, indices* ..., Torino / Augustae Taurinorum, 1975 (*Corona Patrum* ..., 3)

Simonetti 1978 SIMONETTI, M., 'Qualche riflessione su Quodvultdeus di Cartagine', in: *Rivista di Storia e Letteratura Religiosa* 14, 1978, 201-207

Simonetti 1996 SIMONETTI, M., 'Una nuova proposta su Ippolito', in: *Augustinianum* 36, 1996, 13-46

Smulders 1970 SMULDERS, P., 'Some Riddles in the Apostles' Creed', in: *Bijdragen. Tijdschrift voor Filosofie en Theologie* 31, 1970, 234-260

Smulders 1971 SMULDERS, P., 'Some Riddles in the Apostles' Creed. II. Creeds and Rules of Faith', in: *Bijdragen. Tijdschrift voor Filosofie en Theologie* 32, 1971, 350-366

Smulders 1975 SMULDERS, P., 'The *Sitz im Leben* of the Old Roman Creed. New Conclusions from Neglected Data', in: *Studia Patristica* 13, 1975, 409-421

Smulders 1980 SMULDERS, P., «God Father All-Sovereign». New Testament Use, the Creeds and the Liturgy: An Acclamation? Some Riddles in the Apostles' Creed III', in: *Bijdragen. Tijdschrift voor Filosofie en Theologie* 41, 1980, 3-15

Sobrero 1992 SOBRERO, G., *Anonimo Veronese. Omelie mistagogiche e catechetiche. Edizione critica e studio*, Roma, 1992 (*Bibliotheca «Ephemerides Liturgicae». «Subsidia». Monumenta Italiae Liturgica*, 1)

Von Soden 1909 VON SODEN, H., 'Sententiae LXXXVII episcoporum. Das Protokoll der Synode von Karthago am 1. Semtpember 256, textkritisch hergestellt und überlieferungsgeschichtlich untersucht', in: *Nachrichten von der Königlichen Gesellschaft der Wissenschaften zu Göttingen. Philologisch-historische Klasse* 1909, 247-307

Stead 1987 STEAD, G.C., 'The Apostles' Creed', in: RODD, C.S. (ed.), *Foundation Documents of the Faith*, Edinburgh, 1987, 1-11

Stenzel 1958 STENZEL, A., *Die Taufe. Eine genetische Erklärung der Taufliturgie*, Innsbruck, 1958 (RAHNER, H., - JUNGMANN, J.A., [edd.], *Forschungen zur Geschichte der Theologie und des innerkirchlichen Lebens* ..., 7/8)

Stevenson 1886 STEVENSON Iunior, H., *Codices Palatini Latini Bibliothecae Vaticanae ... Tomus I*, Romae, 1886

Sticotti 1914 STICOTTI, P., 'Documenti epigrafici dell'Istria medievale', in: *Atti e memorie della Società Istriana di Archeologia e Storia Patria* 30, 1914, 137-153

Tetz 1984 TETZ, M., 'Zum altrömischen Bekenntnis. Ein Beitrag des Marcellus von Ancyra', in: *Zeitschrift für die neutestamentische Wissenschaft und die Kunde der älteren Kirche* 75, 1984, 107-127

Väänänen 1981 VÄÄNÄNEN, V., *Introduction au latin vulgaire*, Paris, 1981 (*Bibliothèque française et romane ... Série A: Manuels et études linguistiques*, 6)

Valkenberg 1990 VALKENBERG, W.G.B.M., «*Did Not Our Heart Burn?*» *Place and Function of Holy Scripture in the Theology of St. Thomas Aquinas* ..., Utrecht, 1990 (*Publications of the «Thomas Instituut te Utrecht»*, 3

Verbraken 1958 VERBRAKEN, P., 'Les sermons CCXV et LVI de saint Augustin *de symbolo* et *de oratione dominica*', in: *Revue Bénédictine* 68, 1958, 5-40

Verbraken 1962 VERBRAKEN, P., 'Le sermon CCXIV de saint Augustin pour la tradition du symbole', in: *Revue Bénédictine* 72, 1962, 7-21

Verbraken 1976 VERBRAKEN, P.-P., *Études critiques sur les sermons authentiques de saint Augustin*, Steenbrugis - Hagae Comitis, 1976 (*Instrumenta Patristica*, 12)

Verbraken 1981 VERBRAKEN, P.-P., 'Le sermon LI de saint Augustin sur les généalogies du Christ selon Matthieu et selon Luc', in: *Revue Bénédictine* 91, 1981, 20-45

Vinzent 1995 VINZENT, M., *Pseudo-Athanasius, Contra Arianos IV. Eine Schrift gegen Eusebianer und Markellianer. Habilitationsschrift ...*, Heidelberg, 1995

Vinzent 1999 VINZENT, M., 'Die Entstehung des «Römischen Glaubensbekenntnisses», in: KINZIG, W. - MARKSCHIES, C. - VINZENT, M., *Tauffragen und Bekenntnis. Studien zur sogenannten «Traditio Apostolica» zu den «Interrogationes de fide» und zum «Römischen Glaubensbekenntnis»*, Berlin - New York, 1999 (*Arbeiten zur Kirchengeschichte*, 74), 185-409

Vogel 1986 VOGEL, C., *Medieval Liturgy. An Introduction to the Sources ...*, Washington D.C., 1986

De Vogüé 1979 DE VOGÜÉ, A., 'Une citation de Cyprien dans le Chrysostome latin et chez le Maître', in: *Revue Bénédictine* 89, 1979, 176-178

De Vogüé 1980 DE VOGÜÉ, A., 'Un écho de Césaire d'Arles dans le Règle du Maître, le Chrysostome latin et la «passio Iuliani»', in: *Revue Bénédictine* 90, 1980, 288-290

Vokes 1978 VOKES, F.E., 'Apostolisches Glaubensbekenntnis. I. Alte Kirche und Mittelalter', in: *TRE* 3, 1978, 528-554

De Waal 1896 DE WAAL, A., *Il Simbolo Apostolico illustrato dalle iscrizioni dei primi secoli*, Roma, 1896

Warren 1881 WARREN, F.E., *The Liturgy and Ritual of the Celtic Church*, Oxford, 1881 (repr. Woodbridge - Wolfeboro, New Hampshire, 1987, *Studies in Celtic History*, 9)

Warren 1893 WARREN, F.E., *The Antiphonary of Bangor. An Early Irish Manuscript in the Ambrosian Library at Milan. Part I. A Complete Facsimile ...*, London, 1893 (*Henry Bradshaw Society*, 4)

Warren 1895 WARREN, F.E., *The Antiphonary of Bangor. An Early Irish Manuscript in the Ambrosian Library at Milan. Part II*, London, 1895 (*Henry Bradshaw Society*, 10)

Wawra 1903 WAWRA, C., 'Ein Brief des Bischofs Cyprian von Toulon an den Bischof Maximus von Genf', in: *Theologische Quartalschrift* 85, 1903, 576-594

Westra 1995 WESTRA, L.H., 'A Never Tested Hypothesis: Regional Variants of the Apostles' Creed', in: *Bijdragen. Tijdschrift voor Filosofie en Theologie* 56, 1995, 369-386

Westra 1996a WESTRA, L.H., 'A Never Tested Hypothesis: Regional Variants of the Apostles' Creed. II', in: *Bijdragen. Tijdschrift voor Filosofie en Theologie* 57, 1996, 62-82

Westra 1996b WESTRA, L.H., 'The Authorship of an Anonymous *expositio symboli* (CPL 229A)', in: *Augustinianum* 36, 1996, 525-542

Westra 1997 WESTRA, L.H., 'Enigma Variations in Latin Patristics: Fourteen Anonymous Sermons *de symbolo* and the Original Form of the Apostles' Creed', in: *Studia Patristica* 29, 1997, 414-420

Westra 1998 WESTRA, L.H., '*Regulae fidei* and Other Credal Formulations in the *Acts of Peter*', in: BREMMER, J.N. (ed.), *The Apocryphal Acts of Peter. Magic, Miracles and Gnosticism*, Leuven, 1998, 134-147

Whittaker 1989 WHITTAKER, J., 'The Value of Indirect Tradition in the Establishment of Greek Philosophical Texts or the Art of Misquotation, in: GRANT, J.N. (ed.), *Editing Greek and Latin Texts. Papers given at the Twenty-third Annual Conference on Editorial Problems. University of Toronto, 6-7 November 1987*, New York, 1989, 63-95

Wickenden 1993 WICKENDEN, N., *G.J. Vossius and the Humanist Concept of History*, Assen, 1993 (*Respublica Literaria Neerlandica*, 8)

Wilmart 1906 WILMART, A., 'Les «Tractatus» sur le Cantique attribués à Grégoire d'Elvire', in: *Bulletin de Littérature Ecclésiastique* 7, 1906, 233-299

Wilmart 1924 WILMART, A. - LOWE, A.E., - WILSON, H.A., *The Bobbio Missal (Ms. Paris. Lat. 13246). Notes and Studies*, London, 1924 (Henry Bradshaw Society, 61)

Young 1991 YOUNG, F.M., *The Making of the Creeds*, London - Philadelphia, 1991

Ysebaert 1962 YSEBAERT, J., *Greek Baptismal Terminology. Its Origins and Early Development*, Nijmegen, 1962

# INDEX RERUM ET NOMINUM

# INDEX AUCTORUM

# INDEX LOCORUM

CONTENTS